LAOIS

History & Society

Interdisciplinary Essays
on the History of an Irish County

Editors:
PÁDRAIG G. LANE
WILLIAM NOLAN

Series Editor:
WILLIAM NOLAN

 GEOGRAPHY PUBLICATIONS

Published in Ireland by
Geography Publications,
Kennington Road,
Templeogue, Dublin 6W

© The authors 1999

ISBN 0 906602 46 7

Design and typesetting by Phototype-Set, Lee Road, Dublin Industrial Estate, Dublin 11.
Printed by The Leinster Leader, Naas

armas chomhairle chontae Laoíse

l bpáirt leis an bpobal

COAT OF ARMS

The chevronels or inverted V's, rising towards the top of the shield represent the Slieve Bloom Mountains and the Rock of Dunamaise and are charged with seven ermine spots representing the seven leading families or 'tribes' of Laois. The heraldic fountains of white and blue represent the source and beginning of the rivers Nore and Barrow. The fountains are also a mark of the county, showing its colours of white and blue. The lion rampant in base is that of Ó Mordha, Kings of Laois. The background is gold, the colour of the Ó Mordha lion and stars.

Contents

List of Figures

List of Plates

BLOCK A
Plates between pages 250 and 251

BLOCK B
Plates between pages 506 and 507

McCarthy's Ironworks, Mountrath (Redmond)

Errill, sheet 27, O.S. 1841

Errill (Redmond)

Bogland edges near Portlaoise (Redmond)

Goose Green, Timahoe (Redmond)

Newtown, sheet 31, O.S. 1841

Fleming's Fireclay, The Swan (Redmond)

Durrow district, sheet 29, O.S. 1841

Durrow (Redmond)

Castletown, sheet 16, O.S. 1841

Castletown (Eason, NLI)

Cottages at Stradbally (Redmond)

St Michael's Church, Portarlington with cabins adjacent (Lawrence, NLI)

Donaghmore and River Nore (Lawrence, NLI)

Forest track in Slieve Blooms (Redmond)

Morrissey's, Abbeyleix (Redmond)

ERRATA

Page x, Line 11 should read:
Plates between pages 252 and 253

Page xi, line 2 should read:
Plates between pages 524 and 525

Contributors and Editors

David Beaumont
Former R.B. McDowell Research Fellow, Trinity College Dublin.

John Bradley
Department of History, National University of Ireland, Maynooth.

Vincent Carey
Department of History, Platsburgh State University, New York.

John W.H. Carter
Former Headmaster, Bandon Grammar School, Co. Cork.

Ivan Cosby
Clergyman and University Lecturer, Cornwall.

Michael Deigan
Former Laois County Manager.

David Edwards
Department of History, National University of Ireland, Cork.

John Feehan
Department of Environmental Resource Management, National University of Ireland, Dublin.

Teddy Fennelly
Editor of the *Leinster Express*, Portlaoise.

Michael Gallagher
Department of Political Science, Trinity College Dublin.

Laurence Geary
Department of History, National University of Ireland, Cork.

Stephen R. Gibbons
Department of History, University of Southampton.

David J. Griffin
Irish Architectural Archive, Dublin.

Raymond P. Hylton
Department of History, Virginia Union University, U.S.A.

Elva Johnston
Department of Early Irish History, National University of Ireland, Dublin.

Valerie Keeley
Consultant Archaeologist, Athy, Co. Kildare.

Eamonn P. Kelly
National Museum of Ireland, Dublin.

Padraig G. Lane
Historian, Capuchin College, Cork.

Rolf Loeber
Settlement Historian, Pittsburgh, U.S.A.

John Maas
Postgraduate Student, National University of Ireland, Maynooth.

Donal McCartney
Former Professor of Modern Irish History, National University of Ireland, Dublin.

Michael Mills
Former Ombudsman, Dublin.

William Nolan
Department of Geography, National University of Ireland, Dublin.

Michael O'Brien
Historian, Portlaoise.

Cormac Ó Cléirigh
Postgraduate Student, Trinity College Dublin.

Kieran O'Conor
Director, Medieval Rural Settlement Project, The Discovery Programme, Dublin.

Diarmuid Ó Murchadha
Crosshaven, Co. Cork.

Sr Mary O'Riordan
Brigidine Sister, Dublin.

John M. Regan
Research Fellow, Wolfson College, Oxford.

Roger Stalley
Department of the History of Art, Trinity College Dublin.

Acknowledgements

When this volume was mooted some years ago, it received immediate encouragement from Geography Publications. The task then of bringing together a team of contributors, expert in their several fields, became indeed, a pleasurable challenge. Thereafter, the gracious correspondence at all times of those who found time within already busy schedules to lend their scholarship to this volume must be here emphasised and acknowledged. When the additional burdens of providing illustrative material and proof reading were imposed on those same contributors, that sangfroid remained.

The inestimable courtesy and help of the staffs of the National Library of Ireland; the National Archives; the National Museum; the Library of Trinity College Dublin; the Public Record Office of Northern Ireland; the library of the Royal Irish Academy and not least of the Laois County Librarian, Edwin Phelan and staff members, must be recorded. Photographs in the volume are reproduced courtesy of: Brian and Teresa Redmond of Redmond Photographers formerly of Portlaoise and now of Roscrea; Irish Architectural Archives, Merrion Square, Dublin; Trustees of the National Library of Ireland; Mr Teddy Fennelly the editor of the *Leinster Express*, Portlaoise and Mr Patrick F. Meehan for photographs of Laois politicians from P.J. Meehan *The T.D.'s and Senators for Laois and Offaly (1921-1986)*, and Laois County Council.

Michael Mills, now in busy retirement, responded positively to our request for a foreword and Teddy Fennelly kindly wrote an epilogue. Both editors and publisher gratefully acknowledge financial subventions towards publication costs from Laois County Council; The Heritage Council; the National University of Ireland and University College Dublin. The staff of the Audio-Visual Centre at University College Dublin photographed Laois maps and we wish to thank them for their attention to detail. Stephen Hannon, Geography Department, University College Dublin provided cartographic skills and we are grateful to Professor Anne Buttimer for allowing access to the Geography Department's map collection. Laois County Council through the County Manager, Michael Malone, and County Secretary, Louis Brennan were always supportive of the volume. Deasún FitzGerald compiled an index and Kieran Rankin, David Gorry and Jonathan Cherry read proofs. Ríonach Uí Ógáin and Noel Kavanagh assisted in sourcing material.

To the editor there fortunately falls the special favour of being able to appreciate the willingness of colleagues in Capuchin College, Rochestown, to listen without quailing when I spoke at length about the volume or requisitioned their assistance. Furthermore, lest all decency be forgotten, I had better pay due obeisance to my own family's forbearance.

Select list of Abbreviations

A.Cam.	*Annales Cambriae (1860).*
Administration	*Administration,* Institute of Public Administration, Dublin.
A.F.M.	*Annala rioghachta Eireann: Annals of the kingdom of Ireland by the Four Masters from the earliest period to the year 1616,* ed. John O'Donovan, 7 vols (Dublin, 1848-51).
A. I.	*The Annals of Inisfallen (MS Rawlinson B 503),* ed. and trans. Seán Mac Airt (Dublin, 1951).
Anal. Hib.	*Analecta Hibernica,* including the reports of the Irish Manuscripts Commission.
A.L.C.	*The Annals of Loch Cé: a chronicle of Irish affairs, 1014-1690,* ed. W.M. Hennessy (2 vols, London, 1871; reflex facsimile, Irish Manuscripts Commission, Dublin, 1939).
Anal. Hib.	*Analecta Hibernica, including the reports of the Irish Manuscripts Commission* (Dublin, 1930 -).
Ann. Clon.	*The Annals of Clonmacnoise, being annals of Ireland from the earliest period to AD 1408, translated into English , AD 1627, by Conell Mageoghagan,* ed. Denis Murphy (Dublin, 1896).
Ann. Conn.	*Annála Conacht ... (AD 1224-1544),* ed. A. Martin Freeman (Dublin, 1944).
Ann. Tig.	'The Annals of Tigernach' ed. W. Stokes in *Revue Celtique,* xvi-xviii (1895-7).
Arch. Ire.	*Archaeology Ireland*
Arch. Jn.	*Archaeological Journal* (London, 1844-).
Archiv. Hib.	*Archivium Hibernicum: or Irish historical records* (Maynooth, 1912-).
Ardagh and Clonmacnoise Antiq. Soc. Jn.	Journal of Ardagh and Clonmacnoise Antiquarian Society (Dublin, 1926 -).
A.U.	Annála Uladh, *The Annals of Ulster (to*

	AD 1131), Part 1, ed. S. Mac Airt and G. Mac Niocaill (Dublin, 1983).
B.A.R.	*British Archaeological Reports.*
Béaloideas	*The Journal of the Folklore of Ireland Society* (Dublin, 1927-).
Bk. Leinster	*The Book of Leinster, formerly Lebar na Núachongbála*, ed. R.I. Best, Osborn Bergin and M.A. O'Brien, 5 vols (Dublin, 1954-67).
Bk. Rights	*Lebor na Cert; The Book of Rights*, ed. Myles Dillon (Irish Texts Society, Dublin, 1962).
Bks survey & dist.	Books of survey and distribution: being abstracts of various surveys and instruments of title, MS, NLI.
B.L.	British Library.
B.M.	British Museum.
B.M., Add. MSS	British Museum, Additional MSS.
Cal. Carew MSS	*Calendar of Carew manuscripts preserved in the archiepiscopal library at Lambeth.* 1515-74 (etc.) 6 vols (London, 1867-73).
Cal. doc. Ire. (etc.)	*Calendar of documents relating to Ireland 1171-1251 (etc.)* (5 vols, London, 1875-86).
Cal. justic. rolls Ire.,	*Calendar of the justiciary rolls, or proceedings in the court of the justiciar of Ireland*, (1259-1303) (etc.), ed. J. Mills, 2 vols (Dublin, 1905, 1914).
Cal. pat. rolls Ire.	*Calendar of patent rolls, 1232-47 (etc.)*
1232-47 (etc.)	(London, 1906-).
Cal. pat. rolls Ire., Hen. VII-Eliz.	*Calendar of patent and close rolls of chancery in Ireland, Henry VII to 18th Elizabeth*, ed. James Morrin (Dublin, 1861).
Cal. pat. rolls Ire., Jas 1	*Irish patent rolls of James 1: facsimile of the Irish record commissioners' calendar prepared prior to 1830*, with foreword by M.C. Griffith (Dublin, 1966).
Cal. pat. rolls Ire., Chas. 1	*Calendar of patent and close rolls of chancery in Ireland, Charles 1*, ed. James Morrin (Dublin, 1864).

Cal. S.P. dom. 1547-80 (etc.)	*Calendar of state papers, domestic series, 1547-80 (etc.)* (London, 1856-).
Cal. S.P. for., 1547-53 (etc.)	*Calendar of state papers, foreign series, 1547-53* (London, 1861-).
Cal. S.P. Ire.,	*Calendar of the state papers relating to Ireland 1509-73* (etc.) 24 vols London, 1860-1911).
Carloviana	*Carloviana: the journal of the Old Carlow Society* (Carlow, 1947 -).
C.B.E.	*Cnuasach Bhéaloideas Éireann,* Roinn Bhéaloideas Éireann, Coláiste na hOllscoile, Baile Átha Cliath.
Celtica	*Celtica* (Dublin, 1950-).
Census Ire., 1659	*A census of Ireland circa 1659, with supplementary material from the poll money ordinances (1600-1661)* ed. S.Pender (Dublin, 1939).
Census Ire., 1841	*Report of the commissioners appointed to take the census of Ireland for the year 1841[504],* H.C. 1843.
Census Ire.,1851,I,I [etc.]	*The census of Ireland for the year 1851: part I showing the area, population and number of houses by townlands and electoral divisions,* vol.i, province of Leinster, H.C. 1852-3,xci [etc].
C.G.G.	*Cogadh Gaedhel re Gallaibh. The War of the Gaedhil with the Gaill* ed. J.H. Todd (Dublin, 1867).
Civil Survey	*The Civil Survey, A.D. 1654-56,* ed. R.C.Simington (10 vols, Dublin 1931-61).
Clogher Rec.	*Clogher Record* (Monaghan, 1953-).
Coote, *Statistical Survey*	*General view of the agriculture and manufactures of the Queen's County with observations on the means of their improvement drawn up in the year 1801. For the consideration, and under the direction of the Dublin Society* (Dublin, 1801).
Collect Hib.	*Collectanea Hibernica: sources of Irish history* (Dublin, 1958-).
Commons' jn. Ire.	*Journal of the house of commons of the kingdom of Ireland* (1613-1791, 28 vols, Dublin 1753-91; reprinted and

	continued, 1613-1800, 19 vols, Dublin 1796-1800).
Cork Arch. Hist. Soc. Jn.	*Journal of the Cork Archaeological and Historical Society* (Cork. 1892 -).
Corpus Gen. Hib.	*Corpus Genealogiarum Hiberniae, 1,* ed. M.A. O'Brien (Dublin, 1962).
C.S.	*Chronicum Scotorum* ed. W.M. Hennessy (Dublin, 1866).
C.T.S.	Catholic Truth Society.
D.D.A.	Dublin Diocesan Archives.
D.N.B.	*Dictionary of national biography,* ed. Sir Leslie Stephens and Sir Sidney Lee (66 vols, London, 1885-1901; reprinted with corrections, 22 vols, London, 1908-9).
Dáil Éireann proc. 1919-21	*Dáil Éireann, miontuarisc an chead dala 1919-1921; minutes of the proceedings of the first parliament of the republic of Ireland, 1919-1921* (Dublin Stationery Office).
Dublin Hist. Rec.	*Dublin Historical Record* (Dublin, 1938-).
Econ. Hist. Rev.	*Economic History Review* (London, 1927-).
E.H.R.	*English Historical Review.*
Éigse	*Éigse: A journal of Irish studies* (Dublin, 1939-).
Ériu	*Ériu:* founded as the *Journal of the School of Irish learning* (Dublin, 1904-).
Fél. Oeng	*Félire Oengusso* (2nd ed., London, 1905).
Fiants Ire., Hen. VIII (etc.)	'Calendar to fiants of the reign of Henry VIII' in P.R.I. rep D.K. 7-22 (Dublin 1875-90).
F.J.	*Freeman's Journal.*
G.A.A.	Gaelic Athletic Association
Galway Arch. and Hist. Soc. Jn.	*Journal of the Galway Archaeological and Historical Society* (Galway, 1900-).
Giraldus, *Expugnatio*	*Expugnatio Hibernica the conquest of Ireland by Giraldus Cambrensis* ed. by A.B. Scott and F.X. Martin (Dublin, 1978).
Gwynn and Hadcock, Med. Relig. houses Ire.	A. Gwynn and R. Hadcock, *Medieval religious houses in Ireland with an appendix to early sites* (London, 1970).

H.C.	House of commons.
H.L.	House of lords.
H.M.C.	Historical Manuscripts Commission.
Hermathena	*Hermathena: a series of papers ... by members of Trinity College Dublin* (Dublin, 1874-).
I.E.R.	*Irish Ecclesiastical Record* (Dublin, 1865-).
I.F.C.	Irish Folklore Commission.
I.H.S.	*Irish Historical Studies: the joint journal of the Irish Historical Society and the Ulster Society for Irish Historical Studies* (Dublin 1938-).
I.M.C.	Irish Manuscripts Commission.
Inq. Cancell. Hib. repert.	*Inquisitionum in officio rotulorum cancellariae hiberniae ... repertorium* (2 vols, Dublin, 1826-9).
Ir. Ancestor	*The Irish Ancestor* (Dublin, 1969-86).
Ir. Econ. Soc. Hist	*Journal of the Irish Economic and Social History Society.*
Ir. Geneal.	*The Irish Genealogist: official organ of the Irish Genealogical Research Society* (London, 1937-).
Ir. Geog.	*Irish Geography (Bulletin of the Geographical Society of Ireland)* (vols i-iv, Dublin, 1944-63); continued as *The Geographical Society of Ireland, Irish Geography* (vol v -, Dublin, 1964-).
Ir. Georgian Soc. Bull.	*Quarterly Bulletin of the Irish Georgian Society* (Dublin, 1966-).
Ir. Railway Rec. Soc. Jn.	*Journal of the Irish Railway Records Society* (Dublin, 1947-).
Ir. Sword	*Irish Sword: the journal of the Military History Society of Ireland* (Dublin, 1949-).
I.T.S.	Irish Texts Society.
Kildare Arch. Soc. Jn.	*Journal of the County Kildare Archaeological Society* (Dublin, 1891-).
L. & P. Hen. VIII, 1509-13	*Letters and papers, foreign and domestic, Henry VIII* (21 vols, London, 1862-1932).
Lodge, *Peerage Ire.*	John Lodge, *The peerage of Ireland* (4 vols. Dublin, 1754; revised by Mervyn Archdall, 7 vols, Dublin 1789).

Louth Arch. Soc. Jn.	Journal of the County Louth Archaeological Society (Dundalk, 1904-).
M.P.	Member of Parliament.
MS; MSS	manuscript; manuscripts.
N.A.I.	National Archives Ireland.
N.A. R.P.	National Archives, Rebellion papers.
N.A. S.O.C.	National Archives, State of the Country Papers.
N.H.I.	A New History of Ireland, under the auspices of the Royal Irish Academy (Dublin,1968-)
N.L.I; L.N.	National Library of Ireland, Leabharlann Náisiunta na hÉireann.
N.M.I.	National Museum of Ireland.
N. Munster Antiq. Jn.	North Munster Antiquarian Journal (Limerick, 1936-).
no.; nos	number; numbers.
N.P.	not published.
O'Hanlon and O'Leary,	Queen's County, i and ii, John Canon O'Hanlon and Rev. Edward O'Leary, Queen's County, i, history of the territory from the earliest times till it was made Queen's County by Act of Parliament in 1556 (Dublin, 1907); ii (Rev. Mathew Lalor is now a third author) History of the territory from 1556 to 1900 (Dublin, 1914).
O.P.W.	Office of Public Works.
Orpen, Normans	G.H. Orpen, Ireland under the Normans, 1169-1333, 4 vols (Oxford, 1911-20).
O.S.	Ordnance Survey of Ireland.
Ormond deeds, 1172-1350 (etc.)	Calendar of Ormond deeds 1172-1350 (etc) ed. Edmund Curtis (6 vols, Dublin, 1932-43).
Ormonde MSS	Calendar of the manuscripts of the marquess of Ormonde, preserved at Kilkenny Castle (Historical Manuscripts Commission, 11 vols, London, 1895-1920).
Otway-Ruthven, Med. Ire.	A.J. Otway-Ruthven, A history of medieval Ireland (London, 1968).
pers. comm.	personal communication.

P.H.S.L.	*Proceedings of the Hugeunot Society of London.*
Plummer, *Bethada náem nÉrenn*	Charles Plummer (ed.), *Bethada náem nÉrenn; Lives of Irish saints* (2 vols, Oxford, 1922).
Plummer, *Vitae SS Hib.*	C. Plummer (ed.), *Vitae sanctorum Hiberniae, partim hactenus ineditae* (2 vols, Oxford, 1910).
Private coll.	private collection.
P.R.O.,H.O.	Public Record Office, Home Office.
P.R.O.N.I.	Public Record Office of Northern Ireland.
Rawl. B.502	*Rawlinson B 502: a collection of pieces in prose and verse in the Irish language ... from original manuscript in the Bodleian,* with introduction by Kuno Meyer (facsimile, Oxford, 1909).
R.C.B. Library	Representative Church Body Library, Dublin.
R.D.	Registry of Deeds, Dublin.
R.D.S. Scient. Proc.	*Royal Dublin Society Scientific Proceedings.*
revd. edition	revised edition.
Revue Celt.	*Revue Celtique.*
R.I.A.; A.R.E.	Royal Irish Academy; Acadámh Ríoga na hÉireann.
R.I.A. Proc.	*Proceedings of the Royal Irish Academy.*
R.I.A. Trans.	*Transactions of the Royal Irish Academy.*
R.S.A.I. Jn.	*Journal of the Royal Society of Antiquaries of Ireland.*
Red Bk. Ormond	*The Red Book of Ormond,* ed. N.B. White (Dublin, 1932).
Reportorium Novum	*Reportorium Novum: Dublin Diocesan Historical Record* (Dublin, 1955-).
Riocht na Midhe	*Riocht na Midhe: records of the Meath Archaeological and Historical Society* (Drogheda, 1955-).
Rot. pat. Hib.	*Rotulorum patentium et clausorum cancellariae Hiberniae calendarium* (Dublin, 1828).
Seanchas Ardmhacha	*Seanchas Ardmhacha: journal of the Armagh Diocesan Historical Society* (Armagh, 1954-).

S.P. Henry VIII	*State Papers, Henry VIII* (11 vols, London, 1830-52).
Stat. Ire. Hen.VII & VIII	'The bills and statutes of the Irish parliaments of Henry VII and Henry VIII', ed. D.B. Quinn in *Analecta Hibernica,* no. 10 (Irish Manuscripts Commission, Dublin, 1941).
Studia Hib.	*Studia Hibernica* (Dublin, 1961-).
Studies	*Studies: an Irish quarterly review* (Dublin, 1912-).
T.C.D.	Trinity College Dublin.
Teathba	*Journal of the Longford Historical and Archaeological Society.*
T.H.S. Jn.	*Journal of the Tipperary Historical Society* (Thurles, 1989-).
Trip. Life	*The tripartite life of Patrick, with other documents,* ed. W. Stokes (London, 1887).
U.C.C.	University College Cork.
U.C.D.	University College Dublin.
U.C.G.	University College Galway.
U.J.A.	*Ulster Journal of Archaeology.*
vol.; vols	volume; volumes.
Wexford Hist. Soc. Jn.	*Journal of the Wexford Historical Society.*

Foreword

MICHAEL MILLS

'Laois is the only county in Ireland that doesn't touch a county that touches the sea'. It was a meaningless boast, but since we had little else to boast about, we chanted it out defiantly. We had not won an All-Ireland since 1915 and we were surrounded by 'worthless' bogland. Farming offered poor returns, industrial development was in its infancy, the rate of emigration was extremely high and generally, there was an air of pessimism about the place. Laois in the 1930s and 1940s was not a place to stay.

Mountmellick, where I was born, was once known as the Manchester of the Midlands because of the various industries flourishing there. My mother said it was also known as; 'little Belfast' because of its considerable Protestant population. I was intrigued by this description. All I ever saw of processions was distinctly Catholic. The Blessed Sacrament was carried through the streets to the Square under a canopy borne by six local and trustworthy Catholics. My father was one of them and I can still remember his neatly-pressed white gloves which all the canopy bearers had to wear.

The Square was also the setting for political gatherings. It was only ten years after the civil war and bitterness was still running high. I watched from an upstairs window as a torchlight parade of Fianna Fail supporters carried an effigy of W.T. Cosgrave through the streets and to the cheers of their followers, hurtled the effigy into a bonfire. Later, I found that the object of their hatred was a modest, deeply-committed politician who had given much to the newly formed State.

Hurling and football were our two main sports, with cricket forming a poor third. The town had a cricket team, who played on the same pitch across the river as the hurlers and footballers. Nobody saw anything incongruous about it.

The town of Durrow, where we lived subsequently, had a very different tradition as we discovered when we brought our cricket stumps to the village green and set up pitch. No sooner had the game started when a group of men, who had been standing on the corner, approached, picked up the stumps and smashed them across their knees. Our protests were in vain and Durrow was deprived of an opportunity to learn the gentlemanly game of cricket.

Durrow also had its disparate groups of political supporters and it was not a good time for a young fellow to be identified by his school mates as the son of a 'blueshirt'. Very nasty fights took place at political meetings on the Green, with supporters producing bicycle pumps from their overcoat sleeves to belt an opponent across the head. Usually, the Guards broke up the melee before anybody got seriously injured.

In Timahoe, where we later moved, the politicians from the different parties came together on the same platform to ask all able-bodied men in the community to join the local branch of the FCA, the Local Defence Force, to defend their country against possible invasion by the Germans or the British. The news of the British declaration of war on Germany had been greeted several months earlier with complete disinterest by the men playing pitch and toss at Kerr's corner on the edge of the Green. Roused by the rhetoric of the politicians, however, and the display of apparent national unity, many of the pitch and toss players signed up for service. The immediate benefits included a strong pair of boots which gave many years of useful service on the bogs and a great heavy overcoat which as a bed cover, protected many a family from the cold of winter.

About this time, the bogs which we had regarded as one of the most obvious causes of our poverty and deprivation began to attract attention. Without fuel from abroad, turf became a precious commodity. Suddenly, the bogs became sources of employment with a new respect for the previously despised sod of turf. But we never thought we would see the day scientists would start arriving from all over the world to study our boglands, which became another tourist attraction.

It was bizarre when the American environmentalists started booking in, but when the Russians commenced to arrive those of us who remembered the bogs as a main cause of our poverty and despondency could only conclude that somebody had carried out a massive and very successful scam.

Today, Laois is a thriving and vibrant county, with villages and towns taking on new and colourful life. Places like Portlaoise, Mountrath, Portarlington and Mountmellick which struggled for years for survival have assumed a new and confident appearance. Travellers who for years used Portlaoise as a passing-through point on the way to the south, now stop for a second look, to shop in the impressive, pedestrianised main street or to visit the magnificent new Dunamase Arts Centre. Laois may not be on its way to winning a second All-Ireland, but it has certainly had a Second Coming.

And, of course, we can now boast of our almost unique boglands.

Introduction

As road and rail traffic wends its way southwards, even the most blasé of travellers possesses a sense of the pivotal position of County Laois on that route. Moreover, as that traveller peers out from a train window and acknowledges Portarlington, Portlaoise and Ballybrophy *en passant*, or hastens the car through the Heath by-pass towards Cullahill or Borris-in-Ossory, a sensation of a quieter landscape develops, that softness upon which the hush of history lies and which John Betjeman in his poem 'Ireland with Emily' described as

> Spreading Leix the hill protected
> (Earl of Birkenhead, compiler, *John Betjeman's collected poems* (London, 1970), p.121.)

Indeed, that matrix of geography and human settlement that was the territory of the Laígis, with their seven septs, bound, as it were, by the Rivers Barrow and Nore, enveloped by the Slieve Bloom Mountains, the Dysert Hills and the coal country of the Castlecomer Plateau, generously endowed with bogs and woodlands, long acted as a fastness barring advance from Dublin towards Munster and Ossory. Other routes, drawing the traveller away towards Portumna, Athlone and Mullingar, across and by the Slieve Blooms, bespeak of those historical and geographical ties that the O'More county had with the West and the North Midlands. In fact, a view from the Slieve Blooms highest point, Arderin, on that meteorological phenomenon, a fine day, can encompass the spread of Laois and its neighbours- Offaly, Kildare, Carlow, Kilkenny, Tipperary, that at one time or another formed the parameters of its history.

Yet, if the evocatively-titled air Mairseáil Rí Laoíse (first published in John Playford, *The English dancing master* (London, 1651) as 'Washington's march') summons up atavistic images of the power that O'Mores and Fitzpatricks, O'Dunnes and O'Dempseys, once wielded in the cauldron of internecine Gaelic, and later, Gaelic-Viking, Gaelic-Norman and Anglo-Gaelic warfare, well documented in the chapters of this volume, another image, one of focal settled places attends upon such sites within the county as Clonenagh and Aghaboe, Timahoe and Killeshin, showing that the fastness was receptive to broader influences. In fact, as many of the chapters in this volume demonstrate, Laois over the centuries became such a melting pot of influences, Iron Age and Viking, Norman and English, Huguenot and Quaker, Agricultural and Industrial Revolution, to today's European Union, that the county was both bequeathed a rich legacy of archaeological and architectural features and a range of economic activity that shaped its landscape.

Archetypal images of a county randomly reflect the pride and consciousness of its people and in Laois's case such totems range from the Round Tower at Timahoe to Gandon's Coolbanagher Church and Luyten's Gardens at Ballinakill; from Bord na Móna's peat enterprises to Portlaoise's prison and an O'More Park still redolent with memories of the Delaneys and Tommy Murphy; from the Rock of Dunamase and the Pass of the Plumes to Robert Ballagh's more recent monument to the Laois men of 1916; and from the resonance of such placenames as Fossy Hill, Luggacurren, Wolfhill, the Swan and Clonad, to the writings of Jonah Barrington, John Keegan – of 'Poor Pinch and Caoch O'Leary' fame – and James Fintan Lalor. If, moreover, the cooling tower at Portarlington is no longer a familiar landmark, steadfast features remain in the ruinous buildings that housed the industries of the eighteenth and nineteenth centuries in towns such as Mountmellick, once termed the Manchester of Ireland; in the Georgian streetscapes of Durrow, Abbeyleix, Castletown; in Portarlington's Huguenot legacy and in the many estate towns and villages which mark out the county's geography.

Indeed, *Laois: History and Society's* multi-disciplinary approach to the county's evolution, the thirteenth in Geography Publication's Irish County History series, that draws upon the work of a range of individual scholars from at home and abroad to deepen understanding of the regional dimension, is most effectively illustrated in John Feehan's opening survey. Drawing upon his intimate knowledge of Laois above and below ground Feehan traces the county's topography and land use from its geological base and identifies three foundation blocks; the Silurian Slieve Blooms to the north; the limestone lowlands in the centre; and the limestone hills and Upper Carboniferous scarp in the south. In the process, he explains the changing nature of farming settlement from Mesolithic to Gaelic times, through Medieval Norman land use to Plantation upheaval, and on to the Agricultural Revolution, pre-Famine cultivation and modern practices, a mixture of tillage, beet, barley and pasture. Conscious of changing bio-diversity and hydrology, as natural landscape gave way to a man-made one, he enrolls toponymy in his quest for origins.

There can scarcely, however, be a better instance of the present interacting upon the past than in Valerie Keeley's account of Iron Age discoveries made at Ballydavis during construction of the Portlaoise by-pass. These finds confirm the suspected existence of Pagan Iron Age settlement and economic activity within the county and also enhance our understanding of Iron Age burial customs in Ireland. In his turn, in chapter 3, Diarmuid Ó Murchadha's study of the early history and settlements of the Laígis, while underlining the complicated genealogical origins of the peoples who gave the county its name, concentrates on their control of the plain of west Laois between Kyle and Aharney, through which the Slíge Dála ran, as the key to their role as a buffer between Dublin and Munster. If control of their base at Donághmore Mag Réta was finally wrested from the O'Mores in the tenth century by the Fitzpatricks, it becomes apparent, nevertheless, that their new base at Cullenagh gave the O'Mores dominion over all the other septs within the county.

Meanwhile, in the ninth and tenth centuries, the place now designated as the county played a crucial role in regional and national struggles involving the Vikings. Eamonn Kelly and John Maas's chapter 4 – the Vikings and the Kingdom of Laois – demonstrates just how crucial in fact the Midland alliance of Laois and Offaly was in both the O'Neill-Eóghanacht North-South struggle and the O'Carroll bid for supremacy in Leinster, as well as in the defense of the region against the Viking thrust from Dunrally Fort on the Barrow. This chapter leaves us with a detailed insight into the ramifications of the Viking threat and an appreciation of how the destruction of the foreigner's fortification at Dunrally in 862 AD by the Midland alliance proved to be a significant reverse.

If, of course, there is evidence that Laois engaged in trade with the Norsemen, either with Dublin, or along the Barrow and Nore, it is still more certain that monasteries such as Sletty, Killeshin and Clonenagh provided the magnet for the Vikings in the first instance. Elva Johnston's chapter 4 – Timahoe and the Loígse: monasticism – makes clear the role of the aristocratic Loígse in the creation of those proto-urban religious, professional and economic settlements since the seventh century and concludes that the monasteries reflected the shifting political allegiances of early medieval Ireland. More particularly, the chapter focuses on the provenance of both Timahoe and Mo Chua, its founder, and traces its fortunes until decline in the twelfth century with the onset of the reform movement and the coming of the Anglo-Normans.

Roger Stalley's chapter 5 – The Hiberno-Romanesque and the sculpture of Killeshin – captures the cultural contribution of such monasteries on the eve of that decline. Acknowledging the indigenous artistic traditions, wealth and political contexts that helped to create the Killeshin portal in the mid-twelfth century, Stalley's well illustrated study demonstrates, nevertheless, the role of English monks and craftsmen, and especially the Cistercians, in propagating new European architectural features within Leinster. The distinctive architectural features of Killeshin church, are painstakingly reconstructed and their parallels elsewhere both in Ireland and Europe noted.

Built in a time of war, the Killeshin portal also signalled the arrival of the Anglo-Normans and Cormac Ó Cléirigh's study of their impact on County Laois traces the three phases of occupation as; conquest to 1216; stability from 1216 to 1272; and crisis in the late thirteenth and early fourteenth centuries. Although suffering a major diminution in their power and influence with the building of Norman castles at Timahoe, Aghaboe, Oboy, Lea and Geashill, it could be argued that a retention of cohesion by the local Irish under that Norman overlordship produced a state of lawlessness from as early as 1272 and made Laois an unviable marginal location.

Where Ó Cléirigh for his part would recognise Dunamase as the centre of the Marshall hegemony during those years, and the cornerstone of Anglo-Norman urban development and economic growth, Kieran O'Conor's chapter 8 on Anglo-Norman castles in County Laois, would acknowledge at the same time the Gaelic reliance on the natural landscape for defense in the northern, north-western and Castlecomer Plateau districts, which remained outside the Norman core. O'Conor's chapter contributes a singular insight into the varied structures that the Normans built for the control of their fiefdom, concentrating on Lea as an example of the twenty-two masonry castles raised from the late to the early fourteenth century and identifying the more prevalent earthworks, both mottes and ringworks, that hitherto were often indistinguishable from the raised raths of an earlier age.

The O'Mores were probably the most obvious victims of the English crown's destruction of the old Gaelic polity and as Vincent Carey shows in chapter 9 – The end of the Gaelic political order – the O'More lordship of Laois 1536-1603 – their destruction had its roots in the failure of the Surrender and Regrant policy to take account of the realities of Gaelic dynastic politics. Assimilation led to destabilising dynastic struggles, an intensification of warfare, and an aggressive confiscation policy, as the Gaelic midlands were opened up to the vicissitudes of Dublin Castle policies, both conciliatory and hard-line. The cultural, legal and economic dismantling of the power of the ruling elite and the emergence of subordinate Gaelic families were particular features, even as the war to the death of the dispossessed lingered onto Hugh O' Neill's time, for as the lines of the ballad say,

> Our weapons were broken, and silent our lyres-
> O'More was a serf on the land of his sires
> (J. Frazer, 'Aileen O'Moore' in E. Hayes, *Ballads of Ireland*, ii
> (Dublin,1855), p.188.)

John Bradley in his analysis and description of the boroughs created within the county by the Anglo-Normans in the late twelfth and early thirteenth centuries in chapter 10 had a somewhat similiar problem of classification as faced by O'Conor in his earlier chapter not least because of their subsequent abandonment by the middle of the fourteenth century. Accepting that Castletown, Killabban and Newtown of Leys, or Dunamase all in the east, were the three primary boroughs established for economic and colonisation purposes, Bradley focuses on Dunamase, overlooking the gap in the Dysert Hills between the Barrow and the county's central lowlands. It was not until two centuries later that the fortified towns of Portlaoise, Ballinakill and Portarlington would begin to give the county a lasting urban network.

David Edward's story, never before told, of how the Mac Giolla Phádraigs, based in a border territory, hitched themselves to the star of the Tudors only to be double crossed in the end, epitomises the Machiavellian character of that entire period as dynastic politics, survival strategies and processes of establishment and destruction were engaged in. The complex sagas of the successive (Brian, Barnaby and Florence) Mac Giolla Phádraigs told in chapter 12 outlines their policy of bringing down the Geraldines by switching allegiance to the Butlers; of appearing to be agents of anglicisation even as they secured themselves as Gaelic chieftains; of engaging in studied neutrality and of astute playing of two sides; and of remaining wary of traditional foes while not wanting them to be weakened by other potential foes, be they Norman, Gaelic or English.

The role of English soldiers and settlers, and their identification, forms the subject matter for Ivan Cosby in chapter 11. His recognition of their mind set, of their family connections within Ireland and Britain, and of their military service at home and abroad, enables us to more fully comprehend the process of plantation in Laois. When taken in conjunction with their role in the administration and defense of the county during the Nine Years War, this detailed study of land ownership in Laois plots the region to a degree not done before. Furthermore, as Daniel Beaumont's exploratory study – Local office holding and the gentry of the Queen's County, c.1660-1750 – demonstrates in chapter 15 it was on the basis of that experience and those families, so identified by Cosby, that the administration of the county developed in the following seventeenth and eighteenth centuries.

By recognising the infrastructural deficiencies in the country's central and local government at that time, Beaumont creates a picture of the extent to which the social contours and gradations of the local gentry were reflected in the administration of the county. As an insight into the magistracy and minor officialdom, the chapter, moreover, casts light on the issues of non-conformity, electoral politics, litigation, the collection of revenue and the maintenance and economic promotion of towns that then concerned the ascendancy. The militia of Laois, had a more ceremonial than a military significance in the later years but it did reflect the exigencies of war that the county had endured since the plantation.

That warfare was best illustrated, moreover, in the sieges of the castles, tower houses and fortified dwellings of various provenance within the county in the seventeenth century, not least during the period of the Confederate Wars in the 1640s. Rolf Loeber's study – Warfare and architecture in County Laois through seventeenth century eyes – in chapter 13 is as much an inventory of the county's society and economy at that juncture as a record of its defenses, since the industrial and agricultural resources of those castles became in effect the spoils of war. As a survey in the first instance, however, of the nature of warfare and the standing of castles such as Ballinakilll, Ballybrittas, Dysert, Castle Cuffe and Fermoyle, Loeber's contribution to the history of Laois is unique.

It was as a spoil of war that Portarlington began when the earl of Arlington was granted the lands of Lewis O'Dempsey in 1666 and set out to establish an English colony there. It was not, however, until the Huguenot supporter of William of Orange, the Marquis de Ruvigny, Baron Portarlington, subsequently obtained the land in 1689 that grandiose plans for a commercial colony took root. It was then that the town's association with the language, culture and traditions of the Calvinist French noblesse, still a matter of local pride, began and Raymond Hylton's study of that colony, chapter 14, traces the economic, demographic, political and religious vicissitudes of those settlers, who were in the main military pensioners of William of Orange's Huguenot regiments. It becomes clear that there was a slow and haphazard growth from 1692 to 1697; that a dramatic upturn in the town's fortunes came in the years to 1702; then a period of uncertainty and transition from 1703 to 1720 due to religious difficulties and the effects of war; that the French noblesse still influenced policy within the town from the late 1720s to the late 1740s; and that there was a growing English influence thereafter.

Whereas Hylton emphasises Portarlington's reputation for gentility, education and a Huguenot penchant for religious tolerance, it was the very absence of those attributes that Fr. Daniel Delany noted in 1777 upon his return to the poverty-ridden Catholic people of his native Castletown from the more generous circumstances of Catholic France. Sr. Mary O'Riordan's survey of the later Bishop of Kildare and Leighlin's mission – Bishop Daniel Delany 1747-1814, chapter 16, – in furthering the education of his people through Sunday schools, the Brigidine nuns and Carlow College, in the teeth of bitter sectarianism, complements both Hylton and Beaumont's insights.

Stephen Gibbon's study – Captain Rock in the Queen's County, chapter 17 – shows how the agrarian crime of the Rockite and Whitefeet periods, c.1820-1845, originated in pre-Famine misery. While trouble within the county was often a spillover from contentious neighbouring counties, there were enough of the underlying grievances of religious levies and land discontent at home to nurture any such conflagration as John Keegan's descriptions from Shanahoe, in his *Tales of the Rockites*, bear out. The inchoate effort of labourers, including colliers, and smallholders, to stem the tide of economic change and redress greater political wrongs and the influence of substantial farmers like Patrick Lalor of Tinnakill in conditioning the mind set of the people in the later years should not be discounted.

Laurence Geary's – Medical charities in Queen's County, 1765-1851, chapter 18 – would certainly see a certain pragmatism, as well as charity and altruism, in the provision of infirmaries, dispensaries, fever hospitals and asylums for the sick poor of the county in the pre-Famine years, since it was believed that better health would improve productivity and industry and so remove the causes of unrest. There can be little doubt that there was a ready correlation between poverty and illness which manifestly arose from the people's dependence on the potato for subsistence. If, however, the medical charities were the only form of poor relief available outside the Workhouse, it becomes apparent that the State failed to adequately support that relief programme even as the crisis of poverty developed during the Famine years.

It was that crisis which crystallised James Fintan Lalor's thinking and in chapter 19 Michael O'Brien's view of the great Laois social, economic and political ideologue was that such crystallisation had as much to do with the Lalor family's incumbent sense of duty to the people as it had with radical ideologies *per se*. In terms of social and economic standing, the Lalors, on six to seven hundred acres, were far removed from the tenant masses around them but the role of James's father, Patrick, in supporting both the Anti-Tithe protests and O'Connell's Repeal agitation gave expression to Catholic middle-class leadership aspirations. That James Fintan Lalor should see agrarian reform rather than Repeal of the Union as the solution to Ireland's problems had much to do also with the lack of rapport that he had with his father. Needless to say the Famine greatly changed both the economy and society of rural Ireland and a feature of that change was the improvement in the living standards of the survivors.

Jack Carter, in his evaluation of the Land War of 1879-82, chapter 20, would carefully distinguish between the 15 per cent within the county who were 'habitually distressed' and the remainder of the population that were prepared to adjust to the 13 per cent downturn in prices that occurred at the end of the 1870s. Carter is of the opinion that the land war within Laois was carried on by an unrepresentative Land League that conjured up an anti-landlord campaign well after its birth in Connaught but failed to do any lasting damage to the landowners and brought little substantial benefit to either the tenants or labourers it purported to lead. Indeed, Carter's final contention would be that the League was a rather dubious movement racked by dissension and prone in later years to mythologise its achievements.

Government anxious to portray subversion as emanating from that same unrepresentative minority kept a close watch on prospective agitators in the period from the Land War to the Easter Rising of 1916 as Pádraig Lane's examination of intelligence gathering in chapter 23 makes clear. Police records identify those groups and individuals and show the degree to which the authorities were *au fait* with the reality of political discontent. Such police files have been increasingly used for historical reconstruction and in this case they help the reader to better understand the genesis within Laois of the revolutionary spirit of 1916.

By 1920, indeed, it was evident that a transformation in public opinion had already occurred as a young Sinn Féin generation took leadership upon itself. The role of Kevin O'Higgins in that process is re-evaluated by John M. Regan in chapter 24 as he reflects upon his subject's meteoric rise to power in the early Free State. Rather in the tradition of the Lalors, O'Higgins's family position almost pre-ordained him for a part on the political stage and distinguished him from the class of revolutionaries that had been active in conspiracies within the county before 1916. The administrative vitality that brought the young O'Higgins into the Collins circle and propelled him into the Free State Cabinet was accompanied by an equally vigorous intellect that rather moralistically stood for law and social order. As John M.Regan ably demonstrates, it was with that mind set that O'Higgins set out to confirm the State's supremacy over the Army in 1924 and, in so doing, to eradicate the old radical and militarist republicanism and create an inclusive party that would accommodate both nationalist and southern unionist constituencies.

As Regan avers, O'Higgins came to see the legitimacy of the Irish Revolution as being grounded in the election of 1918 and Michael Gallagher's perceptive analysis of politics in Laois-Offaly 1922-1992, chapter 25, indicates that voting patterns within that constituency have often been regarded as a barometer of national patterns and representative of both the changing style of campaigning and the narrow political elite from which candidates are selected. Gallagher regards the constituency as being traditional rural in terms of gender balance and occupational profile which is demonstrated by results in moral-issue referenda and the durability of core political families. He would accept the dominance of the two larger parties in the constituency for most of that time but would contend that neither of those larger parties competed for the same vote, even though it is apparent from the data that Fianna Fail candidates canvas more rigourously than Fine Gael candidates who collect votes at will.

Apocryphal tales abound in the political arena and have their own function in expressing a society's culture. In terms of seanchas also, folk memory is replete with legendary tales that have their own validity, whether these be of Fionn Mac Cumhaill's athleticism on the slopes above Ballyfin, the exploits of the highwayman Cahir na gCapall or the burial by monks of sacred vessels ahead of the impending arrival of Cromwellian troops across the Slieve Blooms. However, it is to Canon O'Hanlon's inestimable *History of the Queens County* that this present volume pays tribute and Donal McCartney's evaluation of that earlier historian, chapter 22, measures the methodology of the priest-scholar in its contemporary setting. Born in Stradbally and educated at Ballyroan and Carlow, O'Hanlon's early contributions to historical writing were in the form of hagiographical lives of saints. In this O'Hanlon was at one with fellow historians in the middle of the nineteenth century who saw the past as an arsenal of lessons for the present. He was also guided by the Bollandists who gave critical attention to sources, to the reconciliation of different authorities and to the sifting of medieval chronicles, annals and traditions in quest of the truth. O'Hanlon was influenced by the romanticism of the late eighteenth century which inspired his antiquarian quest to reconstruct the past from the relict features of history so generously distributed in County Laois. His main work, the *History of the Queen's County*, would appear to have been ventured upon as a labour of love for his native home.

A society's culture, moreover, is often best reflected in the architectural legacy bequeathed to succeeding generations and David Griffin's country houses of County Laois, chapter 21, provides an important check-list of how people of substance expressed their status and perception throughout the eighteenth and nineteenth centuries. As the insecurity of the seventeenth century gave way to the stability of Georgian Ireland, the ascendancy discovered both the desire and affluence to indulge in a taste for comfortable living and the architectural fashions of the day. Whether instanced in Castle Durrow,

Blandsfort, Heath House, Emo Court and Abbeyleix House, or in lesser-known residences, the corpus of elegant buildings still extant enriches and informs today's generation. That eighteenth century heritage, as David Griffin shows, was further consolidated in the nineteenth century through buildings such as Shean, Ballyfin, Capard House, Gracefield, Mount Henry and Rath House.

That a society is no artefact but an ever evolving entity, is demonstrated on the other hand by Michael Deigan's study in chapter 26 of Portlaoise's modern development as a county town along a national route. Whereas John Bradley earlier dealt with the town's development as a fortified centre, Michael Deigan's managerial and engineer's perspectives identify the physical and demographic pressures driving the town's expansion in the more recent past. Drawing upon the contours of the historic town he presents the late twentieth-century parameters within which the planning of Portlaoise continues to be structured.

It is possible to suggest that historical scholarship began in County Laois with the contribution of the monks of Clonenagh to the *Book of Leinster* initially and later, through its manuscripts, to the *Annals of the Four Masters*. Clonenagh and Coolbanagher, moreover, would appear to have had some input into that volume of saints lives, *Féilire Óengusso*.

Topographical writings and countrywide surveys of the seventeenth and eighteenth centuries laid the foundations for subsequent work undertaken by such as Sir Charles Coote (1801) and Shaw-Mason (1819) in their respective statistical and parochial surveys and the writings of both Richard Griffith and Robert Kane in the early nineteenth century on the geological structure and natural history of the county. O'Hanlon himself visited and recorded the antiquities identified through the labours of O'Donovan during the Ordnance Survey of Laois while acknowledging Carey's *Antiquities of the Queen's County*. John Feehan's inestimable works, *The landscape of Slieve Bloom* (1979), *An environmental history of Laois* (1983) and *The bogs of Ireland* (1996) underline the strides modern scholarship on the county has made.

Valerie Keeley points to the importance today of Environmental Impact Statements in creating an awareness of the past in the context of archaeology, while Sweetman, Alcock and Moran's *Archaeological inventory of Laois* (1995) ranks as an invaluable reference point for students of the county's heritage. Laois County Library, a valuable resource for local studies, holds among other collections Tony Candon's archaeological surveys of Clandonagh (1986) and Clarmallagh (1987) baronies; the unpublished (2nd) Report on areas and sites of historic interest in Co. Laois written by Maurice Craig and William Garner on behalf of An Foras Forbartha (1976) and the urban archaeological survey (Co. Laois) undertaken by John Bradley, Andrew Halpin and Heather King. *Laois: history and society* in the copious endnotes provided by its contributors bears witness to the diverse sources published and unpublished which form the raw material for the county's history.

Daniel Byrne's *History of the Queen's County, containing an account of its antiquities history of the ancient septs etc.* (Dublin,1856) marked, however, the first modern work of Laois historiography before O'Hanlon, a labour of service to the county that the Laois Heritage Society continues to foster and which has produced studies of Borris-in-Ossory, Durrow, Mountmellick, Stradbally and Ballyroan in the recent past. Of particular value in our own times has been the pioneering work of Patrick F. Meehan whose companion volumes on *The Members of Parliament for Laois and Offaly (Queens and King's Counties) 1801-1918* (Portlaoise,1972) and *The T.D's and Senators for Laois and Offaly 1921-1986* (Portlaoise,1987) set a standard for other counties to emulate. Teddy Fennelly, likewise, apart from his central role in Laois life as editor of *The Leinster Express* has maintained a keen interest in Laois heritage. His *The 100 years of Laois GAA* (Portlaoise,1984) emphasised the county's steadfast devotion to the games of football and hurling and *Laois Lifes* edited by him in 1991 proclaimed the contributions of a diverse range of people from this quiet county to life in modern Ireland. It is appropriate that Michael Mills, who as the political correspondent of a national newspaper has recorded some of the important events of the last fifty years of the twentieth century, should as a son of Laois have the first word in this volume and that Teddy Fennelly whose newspaper is a modern-day annals of Laois has the final word.

As a reference work, O'Hanlon's superbly illustrated volumes are still much valued to-day when, as in the present volume, the great task of covering the county's history is divided among so many specialists. He and his auxiliaries would, we feel sure, look with favour upon *Laois: History and Society* as a fitting accompaniment for the volumes already published, especially those for the adjacent counties of Tipperary, Kilkenny and Offaly.

Chapter 1

LAOIS: AN OVERVIEW OF THE COUNTY AS A PLACE WHERE HISTORY HAPPENED

JOHN FEEHAN

Towards the end of the last cold stage of the great Ice Age which has for the moment released its grip on the earth, the front of the ice sheet which covered most of the northern two-thirds of the country extended from Ballylanders between the Ballyhoura and Galtee Mountains, up past Cahir and Roscrea and on towards Kells.[1] During the time of glaciation, stone age communities hunted the animals of the cold grasslands further south:- the people whose artists or priests produced the astonishing masterpieces of the caves of southern Europe. When it was free of ice, herds of woolly mammoth shared the tundra which extended across the Irish Midlands with reindeer, giant deer and arctic fox, wolf and horse, brown bear, spotted hyena and many other animals long extinct. With so much of the world's water locked up in the form of ice at this time, Britain and Ireland were part of the European mainland, and it is very likely that adventurous parties of explorers travelled north from time to time to view with awe the icy frontier of their world, and then as the climate warmed, forcing the rapid northward meltback of the glacier, they moved into the fertile new hunting and fishing lands freed by the retreating ice.

On this scenario there was no sudden first influx of people into the Irish Midlands at some definite interval after the Ice Age, but a gradual colonisation by people who had always known this land as the edge of their world. It was a well-watered land of opportunity, whose glacially-derived nutrient-rich soils produced vegetation to support an abundant fauna, and within a few centuries of the last cold snap 10,500 to 10,000 years ago, when the Ice Age reached back a cold hand to grip the mountains in a final episode of local glaciation, there were small communities scattered across the open plains of the Midlands. Their touch upon the land was light and they left but the faintest of signs of their presence: except where the advancing raised bogs sealed the evidence beneath the peat as it did so dramatically and significantly on the other side of Slieve Bloom, at Boora in County Offaly.[2]

In a most fundamental way, it was the endowment of the ice that directed how the threads of settlement would weave together, and so determined the pattern of history. The retreating ice left a blanket of moraine of varying thickness and composition across the county, thickest in the valleys of Slieve Bloom and generally thinnest on higher ground. Associated with the moraines are eskers and outwash plains composed of sandier, water-washed sediments. Their characteristics, and the topographical and geological circumstances associated with each, essentially determined the ecological endowment of each particular locale, and by the same token its agricultural potential. Each locality has a unique natural endowment and the details of the story of how each has been utilised over time are different. The placenames which have crystallised out in each district are tokens of that distinctive quality. Many contain whispers telling of how much of the original forest world still survived when the Celtic language arrived (for example Lowhill:*leamh coill*, elmwood; Srahcullen: *sraith chuilinn*, the holly stretch; Ballacolla: *baile cholla*, hazel townland). Others retain elements of an earlier pre-Celtic and now lost linguistic legacy, mainly the names of defining physical features such as rivers and mountains. The tales in the Dindshenchas which make claim to explain the origins of names like the Barrow, Nore and Suir, or Slieve Bladhma, are in all probability attempts to take over the last elements of an earlier linguistic cultural delineation of the landscape. While many names yield the meaning of their particular topographical mottoes readily, many more remain mysterious, resisting interpretation, awaiting an inquisition based on a more informed acquaintance with the detail of local history and ecology.

Slieve Bloom

The patterns of history flow in ways which are profoundly influenced by the nature of landscape at *local* level, and its potential to support people. Two of the key aspects of any region from this perspective, topography and soils, are shaped by the unique geological history of an area. In the land of Laois three distinct geological blocks can be recognised. On the north the mountains of Slieve Bloom stretch from Roscrea round to Rosenallis, on the north-west straddling the boundary with County Offaly. This is the most ancient part of the landscape of Laois. The Silurian sandstones and siltstones of which its heart is made were once part of a mountain range of Himalayan proportions, slowly reduced over hundreds of millions of years to an alluvial plain across which at the end of the Devonian period of earth history a thin blanket of alluvial sands and other sediments was draped.[3] The Silurian rocks have few practical uses; in particular, the irregular way in which they broke made them unsuitable for most building purposes, so the greater part of the enduring fabric of the cultural landscape is made of the late Devonian – early Lower Carboniferous sandstones, which were quarried in the beds of the rivers and on the shoulders between the valleys where the best exposures occurred. Their main use was for the building of houses and walls, though some horizons yielded 'flags of the greatest dimensions' which were in much demand for chimney pieces and hearth stones.[4]

Before the Ice Age, Slieve Bloom was a very different wilderness: wooded all over, and with dramatic peaks and valleys. Two million years of glaciation smoothed and rounded the profile of the hills; the range was over-ridden by southward-moving glacial ice during the Ice Age, but towards the end the high ground checked its advance, and the glacier split into two lobes. One lobe moved across the low ground between Slieve Bloom and Devilsbit, while the other moved round by Mountmellick towards Portlaoise. As the ice retreated it left deep deposits of moraine in its wake, especially in the glens of Slieve Bloom, bequeathing them a legacy that was to be culturally important because it made the valleys and lower slopes more productive in agricultural terms. Today the summit plateau is an unbroken expanse of blanket bog, albeit nibbled away at all its edges by centuries of turf-cutting, and most of its slopes now host this century's new forests of spruce and pine. Turf cutters working on the summit come upon more ancient pines at the base of the peat, showing clearly that before the bog began, there were woods of pine on top of the mountains. There are indications that farming commenced in Slieve Bloom at an early date, because there have been occasional finds of Neolithic artifacts under the blanket bog near the summit plateau, contemporaneous with the open pinewoods that grew on the mountain in this period. These precious relics of the past belonged to the first farmers, who cleared and cultivated the upper slopes, above the more intractable broadleaved woods which grew on the heavy soils of the valleys. But all unknown to them, they were exposing the fragile soils which supported the pinewoods to the elements at a time of climatic deterioration, setting in train a sequence of events in the soil which eventually triggered the growth of bog that then spread to cover the entire summit and eventually crept down over the edges into the valleys, banishing farming for several millenia.

There are several important lessons here. We learn from it first that even this great wilderness of Slieve Bloom, which looks so natural and primeval, is due in part to human interference. Secondly, we are reminded again how very much longer people have made a living from the land of Laois than we often realise: it is a story that goes way back, long before the recent chapters that history records. Why places like the forest relics of Slieve Bloom are so important is that they put us in touch with a whole era of our past into which we cannot otherwise reach, because no written record gives it a voice. We are reminded that the landscape can speak for itself, that it retains the imprint of all the human past, written in a language we can learn to hear and decipher, and in which there is always something new to read. And thirdly, it serves as an object lesson on the way our activities can change the landscape when we act in ignorance of environmental processes: a theme which recurs throughout history and has had the most profound consequences for civilisations throughout the world, in our day more than ever before.

It was only in recent centuries that the tide of agricultural advance recovered the land it had lost to the bog on Slieve Bloom millennia before. In the first half of the twentieth century even deep blanket peat was reclaimed high on the shoulders of the hills, most notably the remarkable and well-documented experiment of William Steuart Trench at Baunreagh.[5] Today the fossil ridges (plate 1.1) of some of Steuart Trench's potato fields still survive in Castleconor, a last relic of the agricultural achievement of the pre-Famine years, set in a landscape now marked by erosion and neglect of the cultural landscape bequeathed by earlier centuries. Some of the beautifully-wrought pillars, gates, culverts (plate 1.2), drains and bridges proudly con-

Plate 1.1   Baunreagh – famine cultivation ridges.

Plate 1.2   Baunreagh – part of the drainage system.

structed as part of this demonstration of how modern farming at its best should be conducted in the decade of the Famine also survive. But these stone features, which gave such proud distinction to this great reclamation enterprise, are also falling to ruin in the landscape where farming sometimes remembers little of what it owes to past or future.

A small patch of surviving bog in the middle of the fields at Castleconor brings home the vast expenditure of human energy and fertiliser input that was required to reclaim this upland bog for agriculture. It is a monument that provides a window on the endeavour of the pre-Famine years: but it falls between the legs of the stool which define heritage, although it should be treasured as a relic of the human past as much as the few small corners of the landscape where the natural heritage survives, or as much as landscape features of archaeological significance.

Another special landscape relic of the period is the Famine Field (plate 1.3) in south-west Slieve Bloom; here the fossil lazy beds of the Famine years survived until very recently in a townland which was almost entirely depopulated by the Great Hunger and its aftermath, falling from nearly 70 people before the Famine to three by 1861. Gortnaglogh and the surrounding landscape is an area of exceptionally diverse cultural heritage, and the Famine Field in particular occupied a special place in local community tradition.[6] All the more surprising then – in spite of the bitter opposition of the local community – that an area

Plate 1.3   Gortnaglogh – the famine field.

so regarded could have been ploughed and overplanted with a grant-aided spruce plantation a few years ago. The fields at Castleconor might well go the same way. It is a clear example of the incompleteness of our record of landscape heritage, of the failure of the community as a whole to embrace that heritage with a sufficiently powerful sense of ownership, or to ensure its formal protection and sustainable management.

The limestone lowlands

The plain in which the county town stands has always been the heart of the Land of Laois. The central part of the county is underlain by flat-bedded or gently-dipping Carboniferous limestone which was karstified during the Tertiary period (65 – 2 million years ago). The last ice age ended little more than 10,000 years ago, but before that there were many others. During the Quaternary period this karst landscape was scoured repeatedly by glacial ice; there have been around 50 episodes of glaciation over the last two million years or so. What variation there is in the landscape of the lowlands today is due mainly to moraine and glaciofluvial deposits. The limestone seldom appears at the surface except where the last remnants of tower karst stand between the limestone plain and the edge of the plateau of Upper Carboniferous rocks.

Eskers are an important part of the landscape heritage of the limestone lowlands. They are most prominent north-west of Clonaslee, near Portlaoise, and around Timahoe. The esker that runs between Portlaoise and Mountmellick has a special place in the history of geology because it was here that the great pioneering glacial geologist W. J. Sollas (in company with R. L. Praeger in the summer of 1893) became convinced of the fluvioglacial origin of eskers.[7] Once their cover of woodland was cleared, the eskers provided prehistoric farmers with well-drained, easily worked land, and they were probably among the first lands in the county to be farmed. The abundance of archaeological features which are concentrated on them bears testimony to the antiquity of their fields. The eskers and related landforms were also of great strategic significance. They provided the Anglo-Norman invaders of the late twelfth century with ideal vantage points on which to erect their mottes. They had a profound influence on the location of towns in the county.

Eskers and end-moraine provided an abundance of ready-to-hand building material without the necessity of quarrying solid stone; it provided cobbles for streets and courtyards, sand for mortar and later for cement, and even for use as fertiliser. Sir Charles Coote (writing in his *Statistical Survey* at the beginning of the nineteenth century) was impressed by the providential arrangement whereby a superabundance of the fertiliser that was most necessary to the reclamation of bogland was available right in the middle of the bogs themselves. Today the most obvious value of the eskers lies in the sand and gravel they contain. In spite of this, parts of the eskers cling to their rich natural character, and they carry some of the most interesting and important woodland and grassland habitats in the county.

The upper courses of two great rivers run across the central plain of the county: the Barrow having risen in the heart of Slieve Bloom makes its way through a rocky glen carved by a river with memories of a more torrential period in its early postglacial development, before taking a slow and curving course past Portarlington and on towards Monastereven, where it swings round to flow south, separating the county from Kildare. In the centuries following the retreat of the ice, a network of lakes developed in the lower-lying areas along the Barrow, Nore and Erkina. Bogs would develop over many of these as water tables dropped and the processes of natural colonisation overtook them. But in these earlier times it seems certain that the shores of this prolific waterworld would have been a focal point for the mesolithic communities who lived here for more than four millennia before farming. In other parts of the country wave-washed limestone boulders are proving significant signposts on these ancient shorelines;[8] such markers very likely await discovery in Laois also.

But by the time the agricultural way of life had infiltrated ancient ways of living by fishing, hunting and gathering, sufficiently for people to call themselves farmers, much of lowland Laois had become a forested plain, with extensive bogs and woody swamps. These low-lying swampy areas were hostile and difficult of access, and in later prehistoric time crannógs were built in several of the shallow lakes. Wet low-lying Laois remained outside agriculture for several millennia; 'the woodland bogs of Monaster-Evan, Gallin and Slievemargy in the Queen's County' feature in Sir George Carew's list of Irish forests, compiled at the end of the sixteenth century.[9] Arterial drainage finally brought them into farming, and meadow displaced the wetland flora and fauna. Two centuries after Carew made his list, a contributor to *Anthologia Hibernica* recalled the area between the limestone hills and the Barrow as 'the scite [sic] of an ancient forest, long since no more, though some remains are still visible'.[10] What little evidence we have of the first farming people in Laois is confined to Slieve Bloom and the southern upland area of the county, where the lighter soils and more open pinewood proved easier to work and clear.

Turf has fuelled the hearths of the county for millennia, the one natural resource which was never in short supply. It is very likely that it provided the raw material for the charcoal of smiths as far back as the

Bronze Age, to smelt iron ore supplied by the natural ochre deposits of the bogs. These bog iron ore deposits were exploited extensively in the past. Bog fringes produced early spring grazing in prehistoric times, and later on, as population grew in the century and a half before the Famine, the reclaimed fens gave new fertile land to feed the growing communities. The timber of ancient trees buried millennia before as the growing bog spread to engulf the surrounding land, or growing during intervals of drier climate, provided precious building material in the treeless landscape of the same age. The blue clays underlying many midland bogs supplied the raw material for the bricks which were a most important material in the shaping of the cultural landscape from the seventeenth century on. In places the marl from the bogs and callows was valued as fertiliser in their reclamation.

The limestone hills

On the southern edge of the plain adjacent to the Upper Carboniferous plateau, the limestone rises to form an upland region of hills, many of them small and steep-sided (hums). Before the Ice Age this was the southern boundary of a vast Burren-like landscape that extended away northwards. Run the film of landscape evolution back through all the fifty Ice Ages, and here where you stand in the Land of Laois you will find yourself in a vast karstland, the climate warm and wonderful, inhabited by a flora and fauna as magic as that of the Burren today, far more diverse, and no people here or anywhere else: brooded over only by the expectant eye of God. No human ever saw this world. It extended south as far as the Laois-Kilkenny-Carlow border, and down here it still possible to get a faint sense, a mere flicker, of what Laois was like as the Ice Ages approached. Dunamase and the cluster of hills nested around it – the Sugarloaf hills as they called them in the nineteenth century – are the last bits of this ancient landscape of corroded tower karst, still surviving in spite of the succession of glaciations. Reflections like this make the millennium seem a very small turning point in history. The pulse of the Ice Ages is the real pendulum that marks the beat of landscape evolution over all the time there have been people on earth.

Many of the hums have vestiges of the caves that once honeycombed the limestone area closest to the shales and sandstones of the adjacent plateau, caverns hollowed out in an ancient time of warmer climate by acid streams rushing down from the plateau to the south. Although no evidence of prehistoric occupation by postglacial man or beast has so far come to light, it would be surprising if these caves were not at least explored by these earliest inhabitants. A substantial cavern in Killone Hill was still open in the eighteenth century, 'a deep fissure in the limestone rock, which admits a person to walk into it on the level, for a distance of over thirty feet. Then it sinks from about six to eight feet, and opens into a large cavern of irregular outline, and of considerable altitude'.[11] It seems to have been discovered a century or so earlier; if the description given in *Anthologia Hibernica*[12] is reliable, a remarkable sight has been lost to us in the two centuries intervening:

> This cavern at the entrance is narrow, but after a descent of some fathoms, opens near the base into a large saloon, 20 or 30 feet high, and somewhat more in diameter; on one side is a dark and dreadful precipice, not less from the sound of stones thrown down into it, than between 50 and 60 fathoms deep, having at the bottom a subterraneous lake which most probably communicates with those under the great heath. The cavern, when lighted only by a few candles or torches, appears dark and dismal, studded with projecting and pendant rocks, which threaten the spectator with instant destruction; but on being fully illuminated, these horrors vanish, and give place to the most brilliant scene ever exhibited by nature, or described in fairy tale; the sides, roof, and every pointed rock, are instantly covered with festoons and bouquets of pearls, diamonds, rubies, and every other precious stone, in full oriental splendour, caused by the drops of water issuing from the calcareous rocks; tho' there are no incrustations to be seen.

The Great Heath and its significance

The soils of the lowlands yielded to the plough during the Bronze Age and it is likely that this area was widely settled and farmed well before the Iron Age, although few of the monuments of the peoples who first claimed it for agriculture have survived. Nor indeed do we know a great deal more about the takeover of the territory by the aggressive bands of warriors who were the invading Celts, for these traumatic events are hidden by the mists that swirl about the dawn of Irish history, and the later accounts are themselves extremely fragmentary and difficult of interpretation. Riding out of the mists of legend which irrecoverably obscure their true origins in the Celtic iron age, the seven tribes of the Laígis, a mercenary people who supported the Laigin, were granted lands here on the borders of ancient Leinster with Munster and Ossory in return for their assistance to the invading Laigin, laying claim to the heart of the plain and in time bestowing their name on the county. Their lands centred on the open plain of the Magh Riada. Diarmuid Ó Murchadha (this volume) has convincingly argued that this is not the same as the Mag Rechet, as earlier historians have often presumed. The Magh Rechet (*magh roréidh Rechet*) was the plain that centred on the Great Heath of Maryborough (plate 1.4). This is described in the Dindshenchas as a gift to Rechet, Dian's daughter, her reward from Eogan of the Bruiden, grandson of Ross Failghe, whose father was Cathair Mór, 'a portion with no yoke upon it save the high king's' for fostering him as a child.

> From the day that her nursling set apart for Rechet this level plain, it belonged to no woman, without a burden respecting the plain, till came her time to sleep.

Here they had their communal place of ritual and bonding, assembling for their fairs and the special ceremonial that surrounded the burial of their great leaders. A fringe of the Magh Rechet survives in the name of Morett. Certainly the surviving Great Heath was its ritual focus, in all probability until the takeover of all these lands by the Normans in the late twelfth century.

During the thirteenth century all the land around Dunamase was openfield ploughland. The manorial capital was the New Town of Leys in its shadow, and there were more now lost villages in several other places.[13] When the O'Mores regained these lands around the middle of the fourteenth century there are indications that the Great Heath was returned to its ritual status. Alone of all the manorial lands it was withdrawn from cultivation and became again a tribal assembly place for various community activities (including sports), with the result that here – unique in the Norman ploughlands of the Midlands – the fossil cultivation ridges of medieval Laois are preserved between the cluster of surviving ring barrows, frozen beneath the short turf maintained by commonage grazing over five centuries. It seems no accident that an early Christian focus had earlier been established on the fringe of the pagan place of assembly; the only whisper of this that survives is the name of the ancient church and parish of Killenny (*Cill Aonaigh*) on the edge of the Heath. It is ironic that this unique aspect of its heritage escaped the notice of no less a detective than John O'Donovan, who spent some years during his early career at Heath House.[14]

There was, however, another factor at work in the abandonment of arable farming on the Heath. Conditions became much cooler and wetter in many parts of the world, including Ireland, as the sixteenth century advanced – the three centuries that followed the mid-sixteenth century are often referred to as the Little Ice Age. Peat formation on the Heath co-incides with the onset of this period of wetter conditions; C^{14} dates for the base of the peat on the Heath lie somewhere between 300

Plate 1.4   The Heath.

and 500 years BP.[15] The comment on the agricultural history of the Heath by the anonymous contributor to *Anthologia Hibernica* in the late eighteenth century could well stand as an accurate summary of the recent palaeoenvironmental investigations: 'The common has been for several centuries a sheep walk, and prior to that, appears to have been under agriculture, as the furrows of the plough are everywhere visible'.[16] It is of some interest also that pine is present throughout the pollen profile of the Heath, in spite of the same author's immediately preceding comment that

> there never was known any of this species in that part of the kingdom, except such bodies of them which have been discovered from time to time at the bottom of the adjacent bogs. If this species of pine was ever the produce of this district, it must have been in very ancient periods.

The initiation of peat on the Heath reminds us of something we might miss otherwise: under these conditions of deteriorating climate – whether peat was forming or not – farming would have become substantially more difficult, especially arable farming. So we hear an echo of a distress we might otherwise fail to hear as we focus on the events and personalities of early modern history. Poignantly, this is the territory which the English were so surprised to find productively enclosed and cultivated in the late sixteenth century. This is the area described by Fynes Moryson in his description of the Lord Deputy's expedition into Leix at the beginning of the seventeenth century:[17]

> Our captaines, and by their example (for it was otherwise painefull), the common souldiers did cut downe with their swordes all the rebels corne, to the value of ten thousand pound and upward, the onely meanes by which they were to live to keepe their bonaghts or hired soldiers. It seemed incredible that by so barbarous inhabitants the ground should be so manured, the fields so orderly fenced, the townes so frequently inhabited, and the high waies and paths so well beaten as the Lord Deputy here found them. The reason whereof was that the Queens forces during these warrs never till then came among them.

The Heath remains one of the most important focal points of the county's material landscape heritage. In modern times however, that heritage has suffered considerable erosion, largely as a result of insufficient awareness of its uniqueness and importance, and the failure to devise and implement a sustainable land-use strategy acceptable to all with an interest in the Heath. A recent study prepared at the

Department of Environmental Resource Management in UCD may provide the stimulus for such a strategy – before it is too late.[18]

The hills of the coal measures

Towards the southern edge of the county the limestone is overlain by the shales and sandstones of the Upper Carboniferous period (c. 330 million years ago). The change is marked in the landscape by a pronounced scarp, where the land rises to a tableland that extends on into Kilkenny and Carlow. The impervious shales make for badly drained land, especially in lower-lying areas. But this area may have had greater attraction during the Neolithic; it is surely significant that most of the possible megalithic structures recorded for Laois occur in these hills. There was little in the way of substantial settlement here until the later eighteenth century; before this the rushy lands of the plateau provided summer grazing for farmers who lived close to the scarp, along stream corridors or on the better land below. In the eighteenth and nineteenth centuries the main economic attraction was not the grazing, but the newly-discovered resources of coal and fireclay. Mining was a part-time occupation for many farmers, providing the necessary support to sustain an otherwise agricultural way of life. Economic interest in the thin coals is a thing of the recent past, though extraction of fireclay continues: but farming remains as ever a more difficult option than in any other part of the county, and substantial tracts are now given over to coniferous forest.

The landscape of early farming: a unique survival

The landscape of late medieval and early modern gaelic agriculture was re-modelled during the agricultural revolution that followed the transfer of the land to new owners in the sixteenth century, and the modern landscape of small fields bounded by straight hedgerows came into being (figs. 1.1, 1.2). There is little trace of the earlier field systems in the intensively farmed lands of the lowlands, but on the higher ground of the Stradbally Hills in and around the townlands of Ballyprior and Ballycoolan, with soils too shallow and close to the limestone bedrock for the plough, the outline of the Gaelic field system has survived later attempts to obliterate it. The Ordnance Survey six-inch sheet shows only the modern walls, made with the stone of the older fields: but the footings of these earlier walls are still there, enabling the old field system to be mapped (fig. 1.3). In recent years Ballycoolan has been ploughed and afforested. The early fields have been destroyed and the unique atmosphere of the place has been lost. The remaining area in Ballyprior is all the more precious on this account, and its conservation and sustainable management a matter of

Fig. 1.1   This shows the straight-edged newly-enclosed demesne landscape around
            Ballykilcavan near Stradbally in 1754.

urgency. Apart from its cultural significance, Ballyprior has the richest
waxcap flora – the colourful fungi that are indicative of ancient
grassland – known from the south Midlands.[19]

Owning the land of Laois

The events of late prehistory and history show the impermanence of
the individual claim to land, evidenced not only in the great changes in
land ownership and the composition of the landed gentry which
accompanied the familiar upheavals of history from the coming of the
Normans. In a popular nationalist view of history this is the beginning
of the process whereby the land was wrested by force from its 'rightful'
owners, until the land war of the last century and the legislation which
grew from it saw much of it return to the natives whose inheritance it
was 'of right'.

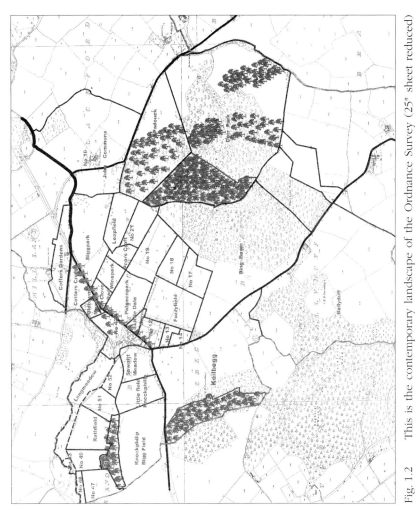

Fig. 1.2   This is the contemporary landscape of the Ordnance Survey (25" sheet reduced) with the 1754 boundaries overlain. (The original estate map is in the Walsh papers; overlay by David and Peter Walsh-Kemmis).

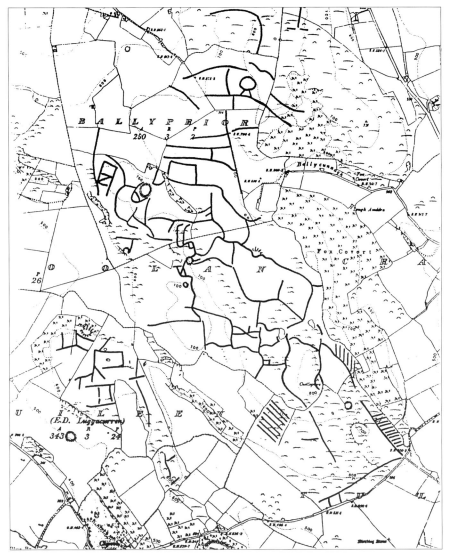

Fig. 1.3   Section of sheet 19 (1909) of the six-inch map for Laois, showing part of the limestone hill area south of Stradbally which shows Ballyprior and Ballycoolan as an open, unenclosed landscape. In fact, as is shown here, the entire area is covered by a network of dismantled old field walls which dovetail into the ringfort settlements dating to Early Christian times or the centuries following. Contrast the much more regular pattern of new eighteenth century fields in fig. 1.1.

But the establishment of the Gaelic order which dominated in the early centuries of the Christian era was itself preceded and accompanied by a long process of changing land holding patterns, where right to land was established or denied by little more than might of hand. Although the historical detail is flawed and frayed by virtue of it having been composed before our modern concept of historical truth had crystallised, the old dynastic histories of the Gaelic families are an impressive demonstration of the antiquity of the dominance of force and alliance in the claim to land, and of the impermanence and uncertainty of the possession of land in these earlier times.

The story of archaeology is certainly one of successive waves of influence breaking with greater or lesser force on existing cultures, but it is likely to have been a less aggressive pattern of cultural change before the ready availability of iron technology gave the political edge to physical force. Accordingly, there may well have been long periods during the Bronze Age and before when the pattern of settlement was less determined by aggression; but this long established rural way of Laois life was thrown into turmoil by the cascading series of upheavals that followed the arrival of successive bands of sword-wielding warriors, originating ultimately in Celtic Europe. In our own time the pattern of land ownership continues to change, but the force behind the change is now economic and social rather than political and military, and ownership is tempered and limited by an increasing recognition of the land rights of the community as a whole, and the implications of the constitutional claim that 'the land of Ireland belongs to the people of Ireland' rather than to a handful of individuals among them.

All the more poignant then, for the lost way of life they represent are the few tangible relics of these earlier times that survive in the landscape itself. The county has only a handful of eroded ritual monuments of the Bronze Age, but potentially more informative of the accompanying settlement pattern are the fulachta fiadh which record centres of domestic activity. Fulachta fiadh mark loci in the landscape where water was boiled in the open, using stones heated in an adjacent fire.[20] Although there are instances of more recent use, most of the grassed-over examples found all over the country appear to represent the activity of Bronze Age communities which did not possess much in the way of metal utensils. Although the usefulness of any pattern suggested by this distribution is limited by the probability that the techniques they mark were in use for a very long period, and we have no way at present of assigning particular monuments to a particular segment of that period, the location and distribution of the few examples recorded to date is interesting. Sometimes one marvels at the continuity in the detail of local hydrology which they often exemplify, or – equally significantly where this is the case – because of the evidence they may provide for changes in local hydrology.

Fulachta fiadh are perhaps the only class of field monuments which is substantially under-recorded in the Sites and Monuments Record, because they escaped the attention of earlier field workers in many areas (so they are absent from the documentary and cartographic record on which the SMR is substantially based), and they are not always easy to spot on aerial photographs. Although fulachta fiadh have survived in much greater numbers in places like west Cork and Clare than elsewhere, their relative paucity can now be seen as due in part at least to more intensive land use, accompanied by destruction of the monuments. All the same, increasing numbers have been revealed in most counties in recent years. There can be little doubt that careful search will discover many more in Laois, especially if this search is targeted on likely terrain, along streamsides which do not flood, and at the edge of the bogs.

A ringfort or other significant monument from the human past is important not only because it is an 'archaeological' feature. It may also be important because centuries or millennia of being left alone have allowed it to gather to itself a considerably diverse ecology, and there may well be conflict between these two in terms of their conservation. But there is a distinct third level of meaning and value, albeit enriched by the reflected light from these other two. And that is what it means for those whose home the presence of this feature enriches. It is part of the intimate landscape of our place, where nature and archaeology may be enriched with memory and experience – for people who played there as children, who picnicked there on summer days which a gilded memory illuminates with a degree of sunshine unsupported by the meteorological records, or at least has always diversified and enriched the landscape stage on which a local community in each generation uniquely enacts its short human drama. For the community, therefore, a particular feature of the landscape may be more important on this level than for more scientifically quantified reasons.

The cultures which have succeeded each other through history (and prehistory) have each patterned their productive land in different ways. Since the arrival of agriculture, fields have been the cells within the pattern. The nature and management regime of the fields have varied with culture and economy and technology, but at all times the fields have been wrested from natural land, and lost more or less of their natural diversity in the process. For a long time, however, this was the replacement of a natural land cover with a man-made one which was only a little less natural. In the case of pasture, long-term disturbance of soil was minimal and the herbaceous communities which established themselves in the fields were composed of natural grassland species. An inadequate awareness of environmental process, however, did mean that more fragile land denuded of its protective forest cover became more liable to erosion or deterioration due to podzol formation, especially at times of worsening climate. One pattern has replaced another in time, changing and ultimately dramatically reducing the occurrence of natural ecosystems, with all their biodiversity and the value it represents in human terms.

Everything about us bears testimony to the interaction between a rich natural heritage and the long succession of human communities which have found the resources to sustain their life and culture through all the millennia of this county's human story. That interaction has shaped for us a landscape where there is still a web of locations rich in wild life: relict natural places and things that have survived all the change, but more often natural places which have grown on the unattended fringes of farm, industry and settlement. But at the end of the day, this is a cultural landscape; everything about it speaks to us of the vanished communities whose work and belief shaped it. It is not only the ruined monuments which bear witness to them – from Bronze Age burial mounds to ruined churches and abandoned mills: but the memory of them is along every laneway and in the line of every hedgebank and wall. Every stone has a purpose, is part of somebody's plan at some vanished time: somebody with the same hold on life, the same confident sense of belonging and permanence, as I have. The mystique of the past is in the very fields; every single field has a story, and should never be walked or ploughed without memory and aware-ness of the spirits which people its history and still whisper. Of all the challenges which face us as the millennium ends, there are two which need to be highlighted: first of all the need to be able to hear the voices, to feel the spirits, of the vanished community, those who have handed the land on to us from generation to generation: not in any weird pseudo-mystical sense, but in the mysticism of real sensitivity to the richness of the earth, the richness of the landscape of our county. The other is the challenge to preserve with care the diversity of this land, in all its natural richness and cultural detail. Growth in knowledge fosters that sense of caring, and that is where this book comes in.

Change is the *norm* in the landscape, but over the last century the flow of change has moved predominantly in one direction: reduction of natural diversity across the county, as well as decrease in the cultural variety of the landscape palimpsest. We no longer have the excuse of the past that we don't know what's happening, or that we don't know the value of what is being lost. We need a home that has natural beauty and diversity in it every bit as much as we need the air that we breathe: and we need the whispers from the past that the relics in the landscape of vanished communities allow us to hear, helping us to find our roots, helping us to understand what, in our unique place, it means to be *at home*. One of the most positive things about our time is that we see the beginnings of awareness of what is happening to the global environment, and of the many values beyond the purely economic in the *local* environment.

The survival of nature in the historical landscape

The natural climax vegetation of the county is generally broadleaved woodland, dominated by different species of trees of which the most important are oak, elm, ash, hazel, hawthorn, yew, alder, birch, pine and a number of willows. Variation in the woodland pattern is largely a response to geology, soil and topography. It is almost certain that human settlement was widespread before the broadleaved forests spread across the county, and that the vegetational succession to climax forest after the Ice Age took place alongside the cultural and technological evolution of the human community.

With the advance of history wild Laois has been reduced to a minimum. Initially, the reduction in biodiversity in Laois consisted in a decrease in the area of forest cover. This was selective in the sense that different agricultural technologies favoured different kinds of land, and these differences were likely reflected in terms of woodland differences. Natural re-afforestation was a part of the process, at least in a limited way. By the end of the Gaelic hegemony in Laois in the sixteenth century, extensive woodland was confined to the wet lands along the floodplains of the Nore and the Barrow.[21] Most of the remainder disappeared in the seventeenth and eighteenth centuries because of the refuge they afforded the dissident Irish, because of their unsustainable exploitation for charcoal – and more fundamentally perhaps to increase the area available to agriculture. By the late eighteenth century there was virtually no forest. More progressive landowners were compelled to plant oak on land less suited to it by nature – on shallow limestone soils at Ballykilcavan for instance. Today the only areas to retain something of the county's original woodland biodiversity are remnants of those estate woods at Abbeyleix and Ballykilcavan, and small rocky woods and areas of scrub like Clopook. The area of old species-rich grassland remaining in the county is tiny – which makes the few places that are like Ballyprior and the Heath all the more important.

Drainage and reclamation, and the exploitation of the peat resource as fuel and for soil improvement, have reduced the once extensive bogs to a remnant. Only a handful of raised bogs are now considered sufficiently intact for designation as Natural Heritage Areas. The long strip of blanket bog on Slieve Bloom is the core of a blanket of peatland that once swept across the entire mountain range and extended far down the slopes. The bog fringes were lost to farming in the eighteenth and nineteenth centuries, and most of today's state plantations on Slieve Bloom are on peat or land reclaimed from peat.

On the other hand, ours is the first generation to cherish the survival of the remnants of land that retain something of their natural diversity. The more significant of these have been designated as Natural Heritage Areas and are now protected under the new Heritage Bill. Only the National Nature Reserve on Slieve Bloom is currently considered sufficiently important to merit SAC (Special Area of Conservation) status, and the protection this status provides under the EU Habitats Directive. Some thirty other areas in the county of fen, bog, grassland, woodland and marsh, most of them small, have been designated as Natural Heritage Areas (NHAs).

But outside this core of extra-special natural places there are countless others which enrich the locality in which they are located, making it a better place to be – a richer place for history to continue. A growing awareness of the importance of these places is reflected in the obligation to protect them under the REPS (Rural Environment Protection Scheme), the government's EU-supported programme for the protection and enhancement of the integrity and diversity of the rural environment, both natural and cultural. The number of participating farmers will continue to rise, and in the years to come EU agricultural policy will require *all* farmers to care for the rural landscape heritage which is the birthright of all the community.

An increasing area of the county is now under coniferous forest. This is primarily in districts of blanket bog and grass heath in upland Slieve Bloom and south Laois, and land of comparably low agricultural potential elsewhere. In the earlier part of the century, most of the planting took place in Slieve Bloom, sometimes in areas of outstanding natural beauty. The most recent phase in the spread of afforestation has enhanced the county's natural diversity in certain respects.

By 1998 a total of 23,245 hectares of the county was under forest, 13.5 per cent of the land area of Laois, the third highest county percentage in the country; nearly a third of this is private planting. The Forest Premium Scheme, introduced to increase the area of woodland across the farmed landscape as a whole, has seen a doubling in private forestry. There had been little private planting of woodland in the county before 1988, but in the ten years between then and 1999, some 3,513 hectares of woodland were planted under the Forest Premium Scheme on private land, though mostly in small plots. A growing percentage of this is broadleaved woodland; in 1998 for instance 205.69 hectares of conifers were planted, and 79.18 hectares of broadleaved trees: the beginning of an attempt to restore to Laois something that will carry forward the lost heritage of woodland which was so important in the county's past: places where the flora and fauna of woodland can continue to find refuge, and we ourselves recover the experience of woodland that recalls what it was like in the beginning.

References

1. F. Mitchell, *The Irish landscape* (London, 1976).
2. J. Feehan and G. O'Donovan, *The bogs of Ireland. An introduction to the natural, cultural and industrial heritage of Irish peatlands* (Dublin, 1996); V. Trodd, *Clonmacnois and west Offaly* (Banagher, 1998).
3. J. Feehan, 'The Old Red Sandstone rocks of the Slieve Bloom and northeastern Devilsbit Mountains' in *Journal of Earth Science*, v (1982), pp 11-30; J. Feehan, 'The Silurian rocks of Slieve Bloom, Counties Laois and Offaly' in *R.I.A. Proc.*, 82b (1982).
4. J. Feehan, *The landscape of Slieve Bloom. A study of its natural and cultural heritage* (Dublin, 1979).
5. Feehan and O'Donovan, *Bogs of Ireland*.
6. Feehan, *Slieve Bloom*.
7. W.J. Sollas, 'A map to show the distribution of Eskers in Ireland' in *Transactions of the Royal Dublin Society* (1896), pp 785-822.
8. Feehan and O'Donovan, *Bogs of Ireland*.
9. C. Litton Falkiner, 'The woods of Ireland' in *Illustrations of Irish history and topography, mainly of the seventeenth century* (London, 1904), pp 143-59.
10. Ambularius, 'Notes on the Physical Geography of Ireland' in *Anthologia Hibernica* (January, 1794), pp 3-6.
11. J. O'Hanlon, 'Notes on some undescribed, antiquities in the parishes of Killenny and Kilteale, Queen's County' in *R.I.A. Proc.*, series 2, i (1879), pp 143-54.
12. Ambularius, 'Notes'.
13. J. Feehan, *Laois: an environmental history* (Stradbally, 1983).
14. O'Hanlon, 'Parishes of Killenny and Kilteale'.
15. D. McCarthy, Palaeoenvironmental reconstructions at the Great Heath of Maryborough, Co. Laois, unpublished B.Sc. thesis, Department of Botany, NUI, Galway (1999).
16. Ambularius, 'Notes'.
17. Fynes Moryson, *Itinerary* (London, 1617), II, i, pp 76-7.
18. J. Feehan, *Fraoch Mór Máigh Rechet: the Great Heath* (Dublin 1999).
19. G. Carter, The macro-mycoflora of natural and semi-natural grasslands in Ireland, unpublished M.Sc. thesis, Department of Agriculture, UCD (1988)
20. J. Feehan, 'Fulachta fiadh in the South Midlands' in *T.H.S. Jn.* (1991), pp 202-7.
21. Feehan, *Laois*; Litton Falkiner, 'Woods of Ireland'.

Appendix 1 – 1754 Map Legend (see fig. 1.1)

Parcel No.	Description	Ac	Rd	Per
1	Robert Brostor's holding part of ditto	124	0	0
2	Abel Robert's part of ditto	90	2	35
3	John Gray part of ditto	10	2	25
4	Sergeant Jones' part of ditto	18	1	20
5	Bing Bawn as the road runs	70	1	0
6	Ballyduff as the road runs	112	0	0
7	Keilbegg	113	1	11
8	The Derr Park	113	1	11
9	The Padduck	33	3	0
10	John Commons's Holding	52	1	13
11	Blackford	88	2	20
12	The Carpenter's or Matthew Coughlin's Holding	4	1	25
13	In the tenure of Thomas Mulhall	1	2	38
14	In the possession of William Cullinan	2	0	9
15	Little Dale Grove joining Coughlin	1	2	0
16	The Fuzzy field	15	1	0
17	The field above the Fuzzy field joining Bing Bawn	6	1	30
18	The Upper field joining Bing Bawn gate	5	0	24
19	The Upper field above the Pidgeon park	12	2	24
20	The Pidgeon Park	10	2	20
21	The Clover Meadow	2	1	27
22	The Winepark	3	2	27
23	Poors Croft	3	1	0
24	The Upper field above Poors Croft	5	3	20
25	The Leap Field	18	2	9
26	The Big Park including Corcoran's Croft	21	2	20
27	Monaferrick	80	0	0
28	The unset part of Bawn and Corclone Bogg	48	0	0
29	The Revd Gipson Redmond's part of Bawn and Corclone	40	0	0
30	William Burton's part of Bawn	14	1	20
31	Lewis's part of Bawn	142	2	0
32	John McTeig other Conner's holding	6	2	26
33	The Church Meadow	5	0	27
34	A small Willow yard in the tenure of John McTeig	0	2	10
35	The Island Meadow	4	0	10
36	Rhaunaduck Bogg	20	1	30
37	Cotters Croft joining Rhaunaduck Bogg	11	1	23
38	The Great Avenue	1	2	13
39	Cotters Crofts between the Road and the Great Avenue	5	3	0
40	The Millers holding	2	0	0
41	The Oldtown Meadow	1	3	0
42	The Mansion House, Yards, Gardens, Orchards, Fishpond etc.	8	2	0
43	The Sawpitt Meadow	6	2	20
44	The Little Field of Knockphilip	8	2	0
45	The Knockphilip Big Field	21	1	35
46	The Knockphilip Wood	6	0	0
47	The Field joining Knocknacarroll between the Wood and Little Meadow	4	3	8
48	The Little Meadow	3	0	20
49	Between the Rathfield and the Little Meadow	5	2	22
50	The Rathfield being two once but the bounds ?????	8	2	22
51	The Field next the Hovill Meadow	1	3	13
52	The Hovill Meadow	3	1	30
53	An Island at the Head W??????	0	20	14

Chapter 2

IRON AGE DISCOVERIES AT BALLYDAVIS

VALERIE KEELEY

Early in the summer of 1995 in the course of archaeological monitoring on the Portlaoise By-Pass the Ballydavis site (fig. 2.1) was discovered. The site yielded evidence of an impressive complex of early Iron Age date, including four ring-ditches, furnaces and pits. The archaeological finds consist of a bronze box, fibulae, beads of coloured glass and stone and miscellaneous bronze and iron objects.

The field in which the site was located is in the townland of Ballydavis, some four kilometres north-east of Portlaoise town, on top of a low knoll (130m OD) called Neville's Hill. It is surrounded by a gently undulating landscape, somewhat flatter to the north and with a small marshy area immediately to the south. The field had been successively ploughed during recent years.

The archaeological landscape surrounding the Ballydavis site is rich in archaeological remains. Also recorded from this townland are two sub-rectilinear enclosures, an earthwork, a burial site and a ringfort. To the north-east, less than a mile away, the Great Heath retains the remains of at least nine ringbarrows, a ringfort and other earthworks. To the south-east in full view lies the imposing Rock of Dunamase.

The Ballydavis site represents the first excavation of a ring-ditch/barrow in County Laois, its discovery being a direct result of archaeological monitoring. The policy of the Department of the Environment and the National Roads Authority involves the preparation of an Environmental Impact Statement on all motorway schemes, monitoring representing the final phase in the archaeological input of such schemes.

The EC Directive 85/337/EEC which was incorporated into Irish Law by EC (Environmental Impact Assessment (Motorway)) Registration 1988, made mandatory the preparation of an Environmental Impact Statement in advance of motorway development. The EIS deals with a wide corridor within the limits of which the final route will be chosen. Along with architecture, flora, fauna and the effects of noise and pollution, an archaeological survey is conducted to determine the extent of the impact of the scheme on the archaeological record.

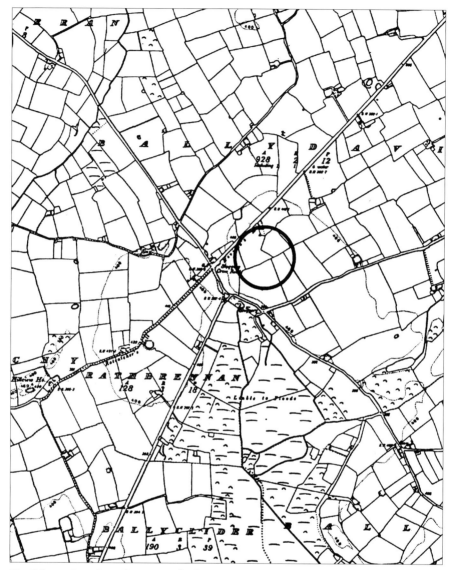

Fig. 2.1   Location of site – OS 6" Sheet 13, Co. Laois.

The Department of the Environment and the National Roads Authority have been committed to the funding of archaeological assessments, a policy which includes the early detection of archaeological sites, avoidance where possible and their investigation in advance of construction. It also allows for monitoring during the construction phase. This ongoing program favours the early identification of archaeological features which significantly minimises the impact of the motorway on the Archaeological Landscape.

When construction work begins soil-stripping is continuously monitored by an archaeologist. This is essential as some monuments which have been ploughed out leave no traces on the surface, and yet features and artifacts survive below ground level. The site at Ballydavis is an example of this. There was no record of any monument at this location and no indications had been present in the field. At the end of May 1995 the archaeologist monitoring topsoil removal noticed an arc of darker soil showing up against the yellow subsoil, the tell-tale traces of a ditch which had long been filled in. The machines were immediately stopped and a team of archaeologists began a full scale excavation. The surface of the area was cleared down with trowels, revealing a number of features. The arc which first caught the archaeologist's attention proved to be part of a circular feature, a ring-ditch. A further three ring-ditches were uncovered during the excavation, which lasted until November 1995. Though it was termed a rescue excavation, sufficient time was made available to allow for the total excavation of all the features which were uncovered.

The first ditch found proved to be the biggest of the four, measuring 16m in diameter. The ditch measured up to 1m in width at the top and was 90cm-1m in depth (fig. 2.2). The main burial was located slightly off-centre, in the interior of the ring-ditch. It consisted of a bronze-box associated with cremated bone, a bronze safety pin brooch and eighty-six beads. A second pit near the northern edge of the interior contained cremated bone and charcoal but no grave goods. A series of well defined phases of use were recorded in the stratigraphy of the ditch. Layers containing artifacts, cremated bone and charcoal, were interspersed with sterile non-activity layers and slippage. *In situ* burning, possibly of a ritual nature, was uncovered around approximately 30 per cent of the base of the ditch. This was represented by burnt clay, which was orange in colour, and carbonised wood. The wood has been identified as oak and willow. It appears that this brushwood was laid down layer by layer and then set alight. The finds from the ditch include a bronze bracelet fragment, several iron nails, an iron blade, cremated bone, charcoal, a crucible fragment and iron slag.

The second ring-ditch excavated lay to the south-east of Ring-ditch 1. It was much smaller with a diameter of 7.9m. The entrance was segmented. The ditch measured 80cm in depth and the fill contained cremated bone and charcoal. Two distinct phases of use were recorded in the fill of this ditch.

The finds include a bronze rod, four pieces of stone bracelets and iron slag. There were several small pits on the northern side of the feature and another brooch was discovered in one of these. This second ring-ditch was completely covered over by a metalled surface.

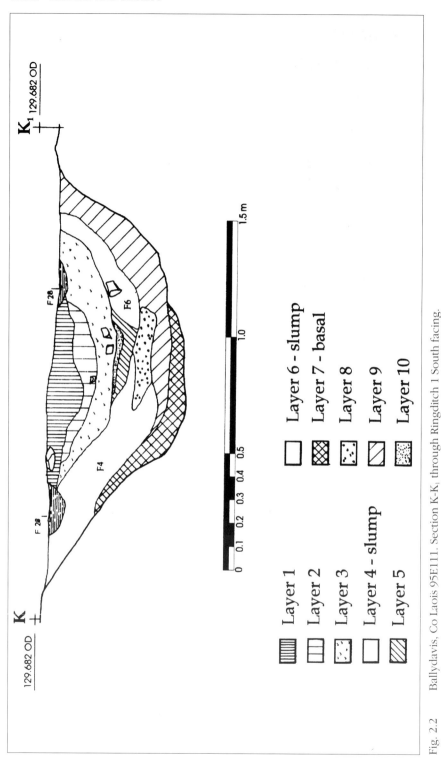

Fig. 2.2   Ballydavis, Co Laois 95E111. Section K-K₁ through Ringditch 1 South facing.

Plate 2.1   Ring-ditch 1.

This was a sterile layer containing stones and pebbles laid down as a form of cobbling. There were three postholes in line in the north-western area of the interior.

The third ring-ditch lay approximately 15m away to the east of Site 1 and 36m to the north of Site 2. It was quite small, measuring 6.55m in diameter. It was sub-circular with no apparent entrance. The feature had been disturbed by a later field boundary, which may have been quite early as it had disappeared by the time of the first Ordnance Survey six inch map in 1839. The ditch fill contained cremation deposits of bone mixed with dark charcoal rich material. Decorated beads, a possible bone sword hilt and fragments of decorated bone were recovered from the fill.

The fourth ring-ditch was the smallest measuring 5.85m in diameter. Its entrance which was quite wide, measured over 2m in width and faced west. The ditch which was 39cm in depth, contained cremated bone, charcoal and iron fragments.

A series of pits and postholes were also excavated. At least eight pits which were discovered in the vicinity of the group of ring-ditches represent the remains of furnaces. These varied in size the smallest measuring 55cm, the largest 2.30m in diameter. All were roughly circular in shape, with the exception of one which was figure-of-eight in shape. These furnaces contained layers of charcoal and burnt orange clay and iron slag, a by-product of the smelting process.

The Finds

The cylindrical bronze box, which is the first of its kind found in Ireland, is comprised of a strip of sheet bronze 38.7cm in length, 6.3cm in height and 0.8mm in thickness with the two narrow ends riveted together, to form the wall. This lies on a circular base with a slightly larger diameter of 1.36cm. The edges of this base are folded round the base of the wall and crimped to hold it in place. Opposite the riveted edge, a small flat tab with two perforations is attached to the side of the box. The riveted edge was covered by a bronze mount, 5.38cm in length, bearing three bosses decorated with concentric circles containing paste or enamel. A circular iron mount, which would have been placed in a central position on the lid of the box, was recovered from the pit. It measures 3.9cm in diameter and up to 2.8mm in thickness. It is decorated with four concentric circles of red enamel, separated by four iron ridges, surrounding a brambled central boss.

Two safety pin brooches or fibulae were found at the site. The Nauheim derivative brooch was found with the main burial deposit. It measures 3.9cm in length, the bow, with a maximum width of 6.5mm, is decorated with a series of six small tubular pieces with ribbed surfaces. The second fibula was found in a pit near Ring-ditch 2. This is a plainer type, and the pin is missing. The foot extends beyond the catch and curves back to rejoin the bow. The bow itself is narrow and

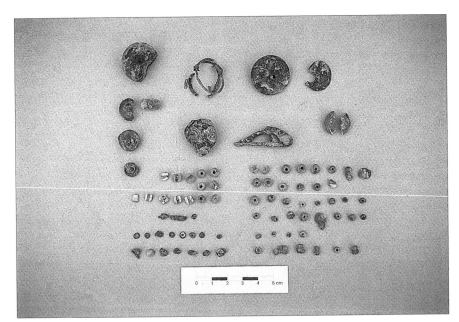

Plate 2.2   Finds associated with the box before conservation.

decorated only with a shallow U-shaped central depression. The overall surviving length is 3.6cm and the maximum width of the bow is just 3mm. A small coil of bronze wire was likewise found with the main deposit. The wire ranges from flat to round in section. Pieces of this wire were actually found retained within the perforations of several of the beads, a unique insight into how they were strung.

Other bronze objects retrieved include a fragment of a bracelet and a tiny fragment of decorated bronze which may be part of a vessel. The decoration consists of five longitudinal ribs, two of which are thinner with fine rope-work. The iron objects found at the site include several nails, two thin blades and an iron buckle (fig. 2.3).

The site yielded quite a variety of beads. They range in shape from circular to ring-shaped and cylindrical. The majority of the beads are of varying sizes of blue glass. Also present were translucent green glass and tiny yellow opaque beads. Also from the main burial was an Oldbury class bead, though in a fragmentary condition it is impressive with its deep blue colour offset by white circles. Four 'Meare Spiral' beads[1] with an inlaid decoration in yellow paste were found with cremated bone in the ditch of Ring-ditch 3.

Finds associated with metalworking include crucibles, small ceramic containers which were used to hold molten metal. Two fragments of crucibles were found, one from Ring-ditch 1, the other from one of the furnaces. The former, which includes part of the rim, measures up to

Plate 2.3   Bronze mount.

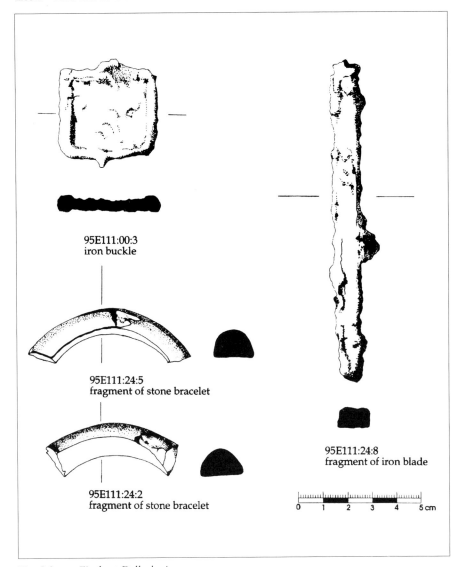

95E111:00:3
iron buckle

95E111:24:5
fragment of stone bracelet

95E111:24:2
fragment of stone bracelet

95E111:24:8
fragment of iron blade

0 1 2 3 4 5 cm

Fig. 2.3   Finds at Ballydavis.

8mm in thickness and has a white fabric and pale green glaze. The second is 16mm thick with a yellow/pink fabric and black glaze.

Additional evidence of personal adornment in the form of four sections of stone bracelets came from the fill of Ring-ditch 2. Bone artifacts were represented by several small fragments of decorated bone, and a bone hilt-guard from a small sword or dagger. The latter was found in five pieces, in Ring-ditch 3. It is boat-shaped, with flat upper and lower edges, and pointed oval ends.

Discussion

The burial record for the Iron Age in Ireland is poor. Unlike the imposing megalithic tombs of the earlier prehistoric period, monuments associated with Iron Age burials are less impressive. A combination of the nature of the monuments and the small number of excavated examples contribute to the lack of information.[2] In a sense it is the diversity of burial practices and monuments which marks this period, these being drawn together on the basis of similar associated grave goods. Both cremation and inhumation were practised, these were marked by low mounds with enclosing ditches, mounds without a ditch, or indeed deposits surrounded by a ditch. Iron Age people also interred burials in already existing monuments such as at Kiltierny, Co. Fermanagh.[3] Simple cremation pits without any associated monument are also recorded for this period.

From the excavation record it is cremation burials which appear to be specifically associated with ringbarrows. In the case of Ballydavis cremation was the exclusive burial rite. Ring-ditch 1 contained the main deposit and the interior also yielded the small cremation pit without any finds. Though no formal deposits were found in this ditch an amount of cremated bone was recovered from the main activity layers. Ring-ditch 3 contained cremation burials from the actual ditch. These were contained within a sticky, charcoal rich matrix and were associated with decorated glass beads, decorated bone fragments and the bone hilt. Though cremated bone was recorded from Ring-ditches 2 and 4 no formal deposits were present.

With regard to the ditches at Ballydavis it is likely that they represent the remains of ringbarrows. The nature of the associated mounds, which are often quite low, the barrow at Grannagh[4] measuring 61cm in height and Carrowjames Tumulus 8,[5] measuring 21cm in height, means that ploughing would have successfully levelled these structures. On the basis of size the Ballydavis structures fit well within the recorded dimensions of other excavated examples Ring-ditch 1 being just marginally larger than Carrowjames Tumulus 8[6] and Cush Tumulus III.[7]

The closest parallel for the bronze box was discovered in a chariot burial at Wetwang Slack[8] in Yorkshire. A bronze box, termed the 'bean can' was found with a chariot burial. It formed part of the grave goods with a female inhumation.

Fibulae, or safety pin brooches, have been recovered from several sites in Ireland. Three fragmentary fibulae were found at Grannagh, where cremation deposits were present in the ditch. At Loughey, Donaghadee, Co. Down,[9] a possible cremation pit, regarded as an intrusive burial, contained a fibula of the same Nauheim derivative class[10] as that from Ring-ditch 1 at Ballydavis. It also contained decorated glass beads termed 'Meare Spiral'[11] which are similar to those found in Ring-ditch 3.

The blue spiral glass bead of the Oldbury class[12] found in fragments with the central deposit at Ballydavis has a parallel at Kiltierney, Co. Fermanagh,[13] where it formed part of a secondary deposit in a probable Neolithic Mound. A fibula was also present at this site. The smaller beads have parallels at Grannagh, Oran Beg and Pollacorragune.[14]

Ballydavis represents an Early Iron Age site consisting of both burial monuments and industrial activity in the form of furnaces. As stated earlier burials reliably dated to the Pagan Iron Age are very rare in Ireland and the Ballydavis complex is unique in that it now offers a well documented site providing both well preserved monuments and rich finds.

On the basis of the finds a date in the centuries spanning the birth of Christ is put forward for the site. The presence of the Nauheim derivative brooch, a type which is exclusively associated with females, suggests that the main burial at Ballydavis was that of a woman. The importance of the Ballydavis site becomes ever more apparent as the post excavation research and analysis continues. This site is clearly one which will assist significantly in adding to our knowledge of this period of prehistory.

References

1. M. Guido, 'The Glass Beads of the Prehistoric and Roman Periods in Britain and Ireland' in *Reports of the Research Committee of the Society of Antiquaries of London* (1978), no. 35.
2. B. Raftery, 'Iron Age Burials in Ireland' in *Irish Antiquity* (1981), pp 173-204.
3. O. Davis, 'The cairn in Castle Archdale Deer-park', in *U.J.A.*, ix (1946), pp 54-7.
4. R.A.S. MacAllister, 'Excavations recently conducted in Co. Galway', *R.I.A. Proc.*, xxxiii (1916-17), p. 508.
5. J. Raftery, 'The Tumulus Cemetery of Carrowjames, Co. Mayo, Part II-Carrowjames II' in *Galway Arch. and Hist. Soc. Jn.*, xix (1940-41), p. 28.
6. Ibid.
7. S.P. Ó Riordáin, 'Excavations at Cush, Co. Limerick', *R.I.A. Proc.*, xlv (1934-35), p. 139.
8. J. Dent, 'Three Chariot burials from Wetwang, Yorkshire', *Antiquity*, lix (1985), p. 90.
9. E.M. Jope & B.C.S. Wilson, 'A burial group of the 1st Century AD from "Loughey" near Donaghadee', in *U.J.A.*, xx (1957), pp 73-94.
10. B. Raftery, 'Iron Age Burials in Ireland', p. 195.
11. M. Guido, 'Glass Beads of the Prehistoric and Roman Periods'.
12. Ibid.
13. Davis, 'The cairn in Castle Archdale Deer-park', pp 54-7.
14. F.T. Riley, 'Excavations in the townland of Pollacorragune, Tuam, Co. Galway', *Galway Arch. and Hist. Soc. Jn.*, xvii (1936), p. 48.

Chapter 3

EARLY HISTORY AND SETTLEMENTS OF THE LAÍGIS

DIARMUID Ó MURCHADHA

Introduction

The people who gave name to the present county of Laois were not in earlier times concentrated exclusively there. The Laígis,[1] together with their neighbours, the Fothairt, are generally regarded as remnants in south Leinster of a race known as the Cruithin or Cruithne, akin to Dál nAraide and Uí Echach in the north-east of Ireland, and probably to the Picts of Scotland as well.[2] The advent of the Laigin – from whom Leinster takes its name – appears to have displaced and fragmented them.

The prime source for early Laígis traditions is the tract entitled 'De Peritia et Genealogia Loíchsi' (henceforth PGL), the oldest recension of which is in the genealogical section of the Bodleian MS Rawlinson B 502,[3] compiled *c*.1132.[4] Versions of it were later incorporated in other genealogical compilations, such as those in the Book of Leinster, Book of Lecan (twice), Book of Uí Maine and Mac Fir Bhisigh's Book of Genealogies. PGL comprises several diverse elements: (a) attempts – not very credible – at explaining the origin of the name (e.g. a tale which derives it from *láech-fhes*, 'a feast fit for a warrior'); (b) a number of early – and in part rather artificial-looking – pedigrees, deriving various branches from a mythical Lugaid Laígsech, son of the equally mythical Conall Cernach; (c) a section (127 a 42 – 127 b 2) containing more credible information and more up-to-date pedigrees; and (d) the story of how the Laígis were rewarded for driving the Munstermen out of Laigin territory, together with an explanation as to why they were divided into seven parts (*na secht Laíchsi*).[5]

This last account tells how Eithne, wife of Cú Chorb (ancestral king of Laigin), advised the splitting up of the Laígis, fearing their united strength. A variant of the story ascribes the division to Medb Lethderg, then wife of Feidlimid, king of Temair, but also a former wife of Cú Chorb. Medb disposed of Lugaid Laígsech by means of a poisoned drink, and then made seven sections of the Laígis (and of the Fothairt) even before they set out.[6] This alleged removal from Temair to the territory of the Laigin was used by the genealogists to explain how free septs *(clanna sóera)* became 'outsiders' *(forslointi).*[7]

Septs of Laígis

Seven is a traditional number for such divisions, but in fact evidence from various sources indicates that more than seven branches of the Laígis once existed, in different parts of Leinster. The Tripartite Life of Patrick, compiled *c.* 900 A.D., refers to Laígis maic Fhind at Móin Choluim (now Moone, Co. Kildare).[8] Similarly, the Life of Adamnán (*c.* 960) recounts a visit to Laígis Telchae Bregmann, probably in the same area,[9] – perhaps identical with Laígis maic Fhind. The Book of Leinster glosses Laígis Raimne as Laígis Fer na Cenél[10] – the 'Fernagenal' granted by Strongbow to Maurice de Prendergast,[11] which was equivalent to the barony of Shelmaliere East, Co. Wexford. Also in that county the barony of Shelburne may have taken its name from Síl mBrain la Láechis.[12] (Adjoining it on the north is the barony of Bantry, named from the Benntraige whose genealogy is included among those of the Laígis).[13] Laígis Ua nEnechglais[14] were obviously in Uí Enechglais territory, which was mainly in the coastal area around Arklow, Co. Wicklow.[15] Loíchsi Síl nAduair i nEittiuch[16] probably settled in the parish of Ettagh in the Éile district of Co. Offaly.

Were we to include all of these as well as the others, the traditional number of seven Laígsi would be exceeded. Gilla Ísu Mac Fir Bhisigh, when compiling the Book of Lecan at the end of the fourteenth century,[17] trimmed his list to an exact seven, as follows:

> Laígis Ráeda, L. Chúili Buichle, L. Leathanfhota, L. Raimne, Dublaígis, L. Tulcha Breógain, L. Hua Cuiliúin.[18]

Two of these segments have already been referred to, and there are no further records of another three. Only the first two can with any certainty be located in the present Co. Laois. They are grouped together in a two-part genealogy in PGL – 'De genealogia Loíchsi Cúile 7 Réta'. (A scribal error led to a joining of the two names in the Lecan versions, creating a new and misleading name, 'Laígis Réta .i. Cúili Réta').[19]

The Cúl or Cúil which gave name to Laígis Chúile (Buichle) is perhaps the same as that which is found in 'Colmán Cúili .i. Colam Cúili .i. i Cluain Caín i samad Finntain'.[20] Samad Fintain ('the community of Fintan') was used *c.* 1300 as the name of a manor (Sawfyntyn) acquired by John fitz Thomas, baron of Offaly, whose tenant in 1303 was Nigellus Omorth (Niall Ó Mórdha).[21] In later centuries it became

'Siffynton', a church and ville at or close to Maryborough/Port Laoise.[22] The *samad* may have extended for some distance; Cluain Cháin may have been in the townland of Clonkeen, about two miles south-west of Port Laoise. 'Here is a field called "Church field" from containing the remains of an ancient church and graveyard'.[23] Also in this area presumably were 'Cell Cule Dumai i Laigis Chuile' and 'Dubloch i Laigis Chule',[24] scenes of conflict between rival groups of Laigin in 795 and 1024.[25] Prior to the settlement there of the Laígis it was probably part of the territory of Uí Chrimthannáin, referred to in An Dubhaltach Mac Fir Bhisigh's Book of Genealogies as 'Uí Chriomhthannáin Chúile Buichle'.[26] It later became the heart of the Laígis (Uí Mhórdha) territory, as indeed it remains the focal point of Co. Laois today.

Mag Rechet

The most prominent segment of the Laígis, the one from which the early kings, as well as the later dominant Uí Mhórdha lords, derived, was known as Laígis Réta, so-called from their tenure of Réta or Mag Réta. This plain has often been confused with Mag Rechet, and it is necessary to deal with this misnomer first. Mag Rechet is represented today by the large townland (almost 2,000 acres) called Morett, apparently the demesne of Morett castle, which in turn took its name from the surrounding Mag Rechet – just as did Caisleán Maighe Cobha in Co. Down or Caisleán Maighe Dumha in Co. Longford.

The plain included all the parish of Coolbanagher – 'Cúil Bendchuir a Muig Reicheat', where, we are told, Óengus commenced the compiling of his Martyrology[27] – as well as Ardea, a modern parish formerly part of Coolbanagher,[28] and so constituted the western half of the barony of Portnahinch. Furthermore, it extended some distance westwards into the adjoining barony of Maryborough West, at least as far as Straboe – 'Srub Bó i n-iarthar Maige Reicheat'.[29] The eastern half of Portnahinch barony consists of the parish of Lea (Léige or Léighe). In 978 the annals record the slaying of 'Congalach mac Flaind, ri Leighe 7 Rechet'.[30] Congalach probably belonged to a segment of Uí Fhailge. In the Dindshenchas poem on Mag Dumach, Rechet is listed as an Uí Fhailge territory, while the poem on Tulach Eógain (in Uí Fhailge) informs us that the plain was named after Rechet (ingen Déin) who reared Eógan.[31] In versions of *Lebor Gabála* Mag Rechet is again placed in Uí Fhailge territory.[32] A single ascription to Laígis ('a Muig Reicheat i Laígis)[33] in the fifteenth-century *Leabhar Breac* (notes to *Félire Óengusso*) is contradicted by two others in the same MS – 'i cúil bendchair in uib failge'[34] and 'Cúil Bendchuir a Muig Reicheat, hi Crich Hua Fhailge'.[35] Similarly, a genealogical compilation associated with the Book of Leinster has 'raith naí i muigh reichet i láighes',[36] where the original Book of Leinster simply says 'Ráth Núi i Laigis'.[37] The only Uí Mhórdha association with the area occurred when Niall Ó Mórdha was installed (by John fitz Thomas) as tenant of Morett in 1303.[38] Before the end of that century and for long afterwards, the castles of Morett, Tinakilly and Derrygile with their surrounding lands were held by a branch of Uí Chonchobair Fhailge whose lord was known as 'Mac Muiris Airidh'.[39] When Mag Rechet/Morett became a manor, the area as a whole was referred to as Aired/Aireadh, anglicised as Erth, Irry, etc. The 1563 map of Leix-Offaly shows the three castles in a territory named 'Eri'.[40] Like Tinnahinch (the adjoining barony to the west), Portnahinch should have been allotted to King's rather than Queen's county when their boundaries were being fixed in 1556.

Mag Réta

Confusion arose when John O'Donovan decided that Mag Réta (Magh Riada) was also equivalent to Morett. In the course of a lengthy letter on the subject, sent from Stradbally to the Ordnance Survey Office on 9 December 1838, he wrote:

> Morett is no other than the celebrated Magh Riadh or Moigh Retai of the Irish writers, as can be proved from the Irish pronunciation of the name and from the form of the name given in the English inquisitions in which it is called Moyritt, Moyrattie, and Moy Rettie (Maigh Réta) which last is as near the original Irish name as could be expected.[41]

Whatever about the (unspecified) Irish pronunciation, O'Donovan was very selective in his anglicised examples which he took from a single inquisition, dated 1612, where the name now spelt Morett is variously rendered Moyrettie, Moyrattie, Moyritty, Moritt.[42] Rarely elsewhere does a vowel ending appear in anglicised renderings of Magh Reichead, and there are dozens of examples, from as early as 1297 (Mayreyth, Mayreght, Marayeth)[43] and 1302-3 (Moyrahyd, Moyrayd, Moyrath).[44] Though the forms Morette/Morret appear as early as 1537[45] and 1540,[46] the original medial '-ch-' is noticeable in Mayrehit (1518), Morehyrt/Moyrhyrt (1540-1)[47] and Morrehitt in 1600.[48] Conall Mageoghagan's 1627 rendering is 'Moyrched'.[49]

However, after O'Donovan published his assertion in his edition of the *Annals of the Four Masters*,[50] it was accepted by place-name experts such as Hogan[51] and Joyce[52] and adopted by Celtic scholars from O'Curry[53] to Bieler.[54] The lone voice pointing out that these were two separate plains was that of Lord Walter Fitzgerald who compiled a series of well-documented articles on the history of this area for the

Journal of the Kildare Archaeological Society – though he did not go on to suggest an alternative location for Mag Réta.[55]

Both names appear in later versions of the list of plains cleared by the legendary Iriél, son of Erimón, as given in *Lebor Gabála*. There should be twelve plains but the oldest source (Book of Leinster) names only eleven (and ten in the accompanying poem).[56] Over-compensating for this, the Books of Lecan[57] and Ballymote[58] both list sixteen. Among the additions we find 'Mag Riata re Fothartaib'/'Mag Riada la Fothartaib uile'. If this is our Mag Réta, it is puzzling to find it assigned to the Fothairt. Although they were allied to the Laígis as *cliathaire Laigen* ('battlers of the Laigin'),[59] and another source tells us 'wherever in Ireland there is a Laígis there is a Fothart nearby',[60] the Fothairt are generally associated with the baronies of Forth in counties Carlow and Wexford.

At any rate, Geoffrey Keating dropped the 're Fothartaib' phrase from his *Forus Feasa*,[61] as did Míchél Ó Clérigh in his recension of *Leabhar Gabhála*,[62] as well as in his Annals. In editing the latter, John O'Donovan identified 'Magh Recheat' with Morett and described 'Magh Riatta' simply as 'a plain in Laoighis',[63] but then proceeded, as related above, to unite the two further on in the same volume.

There are evident pointers to the location of Mag Réta in the PGL story which sets out to explain the origin of the seven Laígis and the reason for the privileges extended to the king of Laigis by the king of Laigin.[64] Set in the reign of the mythical Cú Chorb, it relates how the men of Munster overran the Laigin territory 'ó Áth Lagen co Maistin'. (Maistiu (now Mullamast) was in the south of Co. Kildare, so Áth Lagen was obviously on the border between Munster and Leinster).[65] The Laigin then sent to Temair for Eochu Find and Lugaid Laígsech Cennmár, son of Conall Cernach (and alleged ancestor of the Laígis). Lugaid helped to defeat and drive out the Munstermen in three battles, the first ranging from Áth Truisten[66] to the river Barrow, the second from Áth Íi (Athy, Co. Kildare) to Corthine, and the third *i mMaig Réta ó Chorthine co Slige nDála 7 co Átha Lagen*.

Again, the last two names are clearly connected with the provincial boundaries. Slige Dála, traditionally the route from Temair to north Munster, was particularly associated with the district between Aghaboe and Roscrea. (In the Dindshenchas story, it was named after Dála, whose wife, Créa, gave her name to Roscrea).[67] According to *Acallam na Senórach*, Patrick, having passed through Mag Laíghise and Achadh Bó, traversed Slige Dála before going into what is now Co. Tipperary.[68]

Furthermore, the diocesan boundaries fixed at the Synod of Ráith Bhreasail in A.D. 1111 give the extent of Killaloe diocese (E/W) as 'ó Shlíghe Dála go Léim Chon gCulainn' (Loop Head, Co. Clare).[69]

Muirchertach Ua Briain, the chief motivator of that synod, succeeded in annexing to Killaloe diocese not only most of north Tipperary but also the Éile section of Co. Offaly plus a single parish in Co. Laois – that of Cluain Fearta Molua (now Kyle) on the Tipperary border. Slighe Dála then relates particularly to that parish; Keating, in fact, glosses it as 'Bealach Mór Osraighe',[70] a name still to be found in the townlands of Ballaghmore (Upper and Lower) in Kyle parish – between which, incidentally, the main road from Dublin to Roscrea and Limerick still runs.

Coirthine

This site, which is crucial to the location of Mag Réta, has never been satisfactorily identified.[71] The solution may lie in the Lecan version which reads 'a Muig Reta o Ath Coirthine co Sligi nDala',[72] as Áth Coirthine may have evolved into Aharney, a church site and parish straddling the Laois-Kilkenny border. In place-names *coirthe* tended more often than not to become *cairthe*,[73] so here one might expect *Áth Cairthine,[74] which with vowel-lengthening[75] would give a modern *Áth Cháirthine. The latter form could be pronounced 'Achárna', exactly what Eugene O'Curry heard in 1839 from the inhabitants 'who speak good Irish'.[76] O'Curry surmised that this was a contraction of 'Achadh Fhearna', but an inquisition (dated 1612) into the extent of 'Ossery al' upper Ossory' names part of the southern boundary as 'the brooke of Athcarny',[77] which strongly indicates that the first element was *áth*, a ford. This is confirmed by John O'Donovan's rendering, 'Athchárna, ford of the heap',[78] and by Canon Carrigan's account (1905) which gives the Irish pronunciation as 'Awcharna/Áth Chárna', popularly derived from a heap (*carn*) of bodies left at the ford after a conflict[79] – a tradition which may well retain an echo of the original battle-story.

Between Aharney and Kyle lies an extensive plain, partly in western Clarmallagh but mainly in the barony of Clandonagh. This I take to be the historic Mag Réta. It accords with the statement in PGL that the Laigin placed Lugaid Laígsech in Mag Réta because of his strength in opposing Munster ('ar méit a neirt in n-agid Muman'),[80] that, in other words, the Laígis were put in occupation of a buffer zone between Munster and the Laigin.

The Patrician Documents

Significant evidence is also provided by the early ninth-century Book of Armagh, where, in the *Notulae* (a series of notes probably compiled by Ferdomnach) we find the name 'D(omnach) M(ór) Maige Réto'.[81] The only place in Co. Laois in which there is – or ever was, as far as I can ascertain – a church/parish named Donaghmore is here in the barony of Clandonagh. It is situated in the centre of the plain referred to above, and was dedicated to St. Patrick.[82] The reason why scholars avoided this identification is that Donaghmore parish has long been part of Ossory diocese, i.e. in the territory of the Osraige. However, as I shall try to establish, the western part of Co. Laois was not originally under Osraige control, but was in the possession of Laígis (Réta) for several centuries (whereas Morett where O'Donovan located Mag Réta was certainly part of Uí Fhailge territory).

The Book of Armagh contains two late seventh-century Lives of St Patrick, compiled by Muirchú and Tírechán. The first is not concerned with Laigin territory at all, but Tírechán's Patrick did travel from the Liffey plain to Kilcullen, Co. Kildare and Sleaty, Co. Laois, then through Roigne and Belach Gabráin in Co. Kilkenny to Cashel in Munster.[83] Laígis territory was bypassed; Sléibte (Sleaty), in Uí Bairrche, is mentioned in all the Book of Armagh compilations, as is Fiacc Find, its founder, whom Muirchú describes as a young poet, apprenticed to Dubhthach maccu Lugir (the only one to stand out of respect when Patrick visited Temair).

The anonymous Tripartite Life of Patrick,[84] consisting of three homilies written *c.* 900 A.D., contains many more anecdotes than the earlier Lives. In the middle of a section devoted to Crimthann (donor of the site at Sléibte), the Uí Cheinnselaig and Fiacc Find, an episode concerning the Laígis is inserted, breaking, as Eoin MacNeill pointed out, the sequence both of narrative and topography.[85] Using 'Domnach Mór Maige Réto' from the *Notulae*, the compiler added a story taken from Muirchú's Life, one describing how Patrick heard the pagans at Collum Bouis (Druimm Bó, Co. Down) digging the fosse of a rath on a Sunday and put a curse on their work.[86] This was adapted as follows:

At Domnach Mór Maige Réta Patrick spent a Sunday. On the same day Ráith Baccáin, the royal fort of the territory, was in the course of construction. ('Both oc claidi Rátha Baccáin isin Domnach sin, rígdún inna tuaithe'). When Patrick's request to cease working was rejected, he made two prophecies: firstly, that the building would be troublesome unless offering (i.e. Mass) was made there every day, and secondly, that the fort would never be occupied until a wind (*gáeth*) came from the pits of hell![87]

This story reflects events of political significance relating to the time of writing, i.e. *c.* 900 A.D. The *gáeth* from hell was, as the writer himself informs us, Gáethíne, son of Cináed (king of Laígis Réta) who reconstructed the fort 'hi flaith Feidilmid 7 Chonchubhair hi Temair'. Since Feidilmid (son of Crimthann), king of Munster, died in 847 (*AU²/AI*) and Conchobar (son of Donnchad), king of Temair, in 833

(*AU²*), Gáethíne must have reoccupied the fort in the early ninth century. We do not know when he died, but his son, Ceinnéitig, was active as lord in 862.[88] Ceinnéitig, who was the most renowned of the early kings of Laígis, survived until 903 (*AU²*), so the story was probably written while he was still alive and the rebuilding of the fort by his father was a living memory.

Ráith Baccáin has never been identified, probably because it had undergone a name change around the time of the reconstruction. The storyteller retained the original name, but it seems as if he was attempting to provide a reason for a change – arguably to Ráith Domnaig[89] (Rathdowney), a site whose proximity fits the story, being just two miles south of Donaghmore, though in a separate parish. Preceding Domnach Mór Maige Réto in the *Notulae* list is the (unidentified) name D(omnach) Eochail(li).[90] *Eóchaill* is a name linked to Rathdowney; in *c.* 1210 Adam de Hereford was granted 'all that Thoit (*tuath*) called Mamochle in which his castle of Radoueny stands', while later in the century (1298) it is termed 'the lordship of Rathdowney and Maynochle'.[91] Mag nEóchaille was probably the royal *tuath* of Mag Réta,[92] with Domnach Eóchaille as its church.

Church and rath were apparently in close proximity, so close that after the ninth-century reconstruction of Ráith Baccáin/Domnach Eóchaille, the whole complex was renamed Ráith Domnaig, using two normally disparate elements to form a unique new name. This would also explain the unusual stipulation in the Patrick story concerning the celebration there of daily Mass.

The rath of Rathdowney was still visible at the time of John O'Donovan's visit in 1838; he described it as 'a small rath situated near the parish church'.[93] It was removed about two years later, but Canon Carrigan obtained a good description of it from the man who levelled it. It was circular, 25 to 30 yards in diameter, flat at the top and raised about eight feet over the surrounding land. It was filled with human bones (about five cart-loads of which were removed for interment elsewhere) from which Carrigan deduced that the rath was the site of an ancient churchyard. It stood at the north side of the Square in Rathdowney, in Patrick Murphy's yard and garden, 150 yards to the north-east of the present C. of I. church site.[94]

The age of saints

This whole area was notable for the number of early monastic sites in it. Many of the associated saints are listed in *Félire Óengusso*, an early calendar of Irish saints (compiled *c.* 830) and one which claimed connexions with both Clonenagh and Coolbanagher. Copies of it in later MSS, such as the fourteenth-century *Leabhar Breac,* contain detailed notes on the location of various sites. In what is now the barony of Upperwoods (known in the seventeenth century as Upper Ossory)[95] three separate monastic sites are stated to have been in Laígis territory – Men Drochait (tl. Mondrehid), Cluain Fota (tl. Clonfad) and Enach Truim (tl. Anatrim).[96]

There are several versions of the Life of Mo-Lua or Lugaid of Cluain Ferta Molua, a twelfth-century compilation which, according to Kenney, may go back to a text or texts of the ninth century.[97] The two redactions in the fourteenth-century *Codex Salmanticensis* tell us that the site at Kyle was granted to Mo-Lua by 'Berachus, filius Baccain, in finibus Lygese ... rex Lygisi'.[98] Berach, son of Baccán, would have flourished at the beginning of the seventh century, and could well have been a benefactor of the monastery, which is clearly assigned to Laígis territory.

Further south, at the southern end of what later became Upper Ossory, Manchíne Airce was so-called because his church (Dísert meicc Ciluirn) stood beside a river in Laígis called Airec.[99] This seems to be the river Erkina (flowing by Donaghmore), just south of which the parish of Erke is divided between counties Laois and Kilkenny – though Manchíne's actual church may have been the one in tl./par. Coolkerry, standing on the north bank of the Erkina.

Colmán and Senach, sons of Lugna, are two saints who were assigned a descent from Lugaid Laígse. They are placed at Tulach Mac Comgaill and at Druim Togae – which is glossed as 'isind Uachongbail'.[100] This has been identified as a site at Oughaval, in the parish and barony of Stradbally, Co. Laois, one which gave name to *Lebar na Nuachongbála*, now widely known as the Book of Leinster. The principal monastic site of the Laígis was Tech Mochua or Timahoe in the barony of Cullenagh, a study of which will be found in Dr Elva Johnston's article in this volume.[101]

Mescell and Berach

It is significant that the more dependable section of PGL (referred to above as section C) ignores completely the story of the descent from Lugaid Laígsech. The opening sentence of the introduction states instead that the 'secht Laíchsi Lagen' are all descended from one Amalgaid Réta, an ancestor who is not mentioned in any of the genealogies. This reinforces the suspicion that the earlier sections of the genealogies were fabricated. It also points to an early settlement in Mag Réta; the reference to Amalgaid continues: '.i. ó Licc Réta 7 lia ríg [is la ríg Laígsi Ráeda] a cathroe 7 a ndúnad 7 a cáin 7 a ndliged', ('i.e. from Lecc Réta, and to its king [belongs] their dwelling-places and forts, their taxes and laws'). As it happens, there is a large townland in the

Table 1
Genealogy of the kings of Laígis Réta, c. 1450-1640

(Sources: CGH pp 91 and 434; dates from annals)

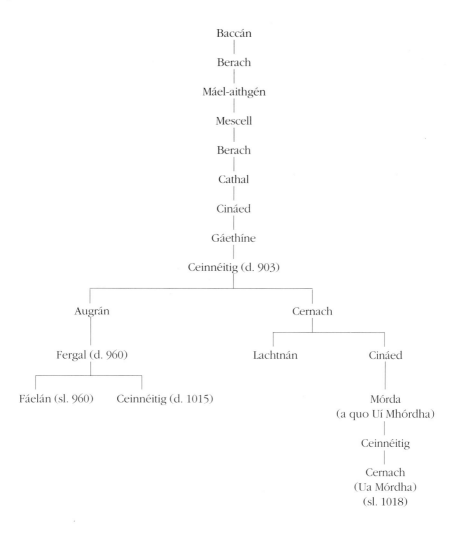

Baccán
|
Berach
|
Máel-aithgén
|
Mescell
|
Berach
|
Cathal
|
Cináed
|
Gáethíne
|
Ceinnéitig (d. 903)

Augrán

Cernach

Fergal (d. 960)

Lachtnán

Cináed

Fáelán (sl. 960)   Ceinnéitig (d. 1015)

Mórda
(a quo Uí Mhórdha)
|
Ceinnéitig
|
Cernach
(Ua Mórdha)
(sl. 1018)

parish of Rathdowney named Coolowley (*Cúil Amhalghaidh*); here too perhaps was the royal pillar-stone designated as Lecc Réta.

Another possible indication of early settlement is the name of the successor to St Ciarán of Clonmacnoise. Recorded simply as Óena in *AU²* (s.a. 570), *A. Tig.* (probably of Clonmacnoise origin) call him 'Áennu mac húi Laígse, .i. Énda mac Eógain do Laígis Ráeda'.[102]

A problem with early dating is that kings of Laígis are not mentioned in the annals until the late ninth century – with one puzzling exception. Alone among such sources, *AI* (in their sole reference to the Laígis) record the death of 'Mescell, ri Laíchse' under the year 799. Mescell happens to be one of the seminal names among the Laígis. An introductory statement in PGL tells us that from Síl mBaccáin m. Lugdach Loíchsich came Síl Mescill and Uí Dochlú (the latter not further traceable) and all of Laíches Réta.[103] But there is a major difficulty with the *AI* dating. Unless it refers to a different Mescell (of whom there is no other trace), it can hardly be correct, since as discussed earlier, Gáethíne, who, according to the genealogies was four generations later than Mescell, was active in the early ninth century and probably alive in 799. In fact, an *obit* of 699 would be much more acceptable for Mescell.[104]

Support for such a dating is provided by a tract, *Cáin Éimíne Báin*,[105] a charter of privileges granted to Éimíne's community at Monasterevin by the king of Laigin, Bran ua Fáeláin. According to the editor of the tract, Dr Erich Poppe, the historical background to the narrative suggests a setting in the late seventh century, Bran's death being recorded in *AU²* in 693.

In a subsequent article Dr Poppe has established from their placings in the genealogies that the sureties nominated to oversee this agreement do not comprise a random list of names, but rather a chronologically accurate roll of Leinster chiefs at the end of the seventh century.[106] Last in the list of sureties is 'Mescell do Loígis', who must have been a contemporary. If we accept that Mescell belonged to the late seventh century, and that his great-grandfather, Baccán, was the one who gave his name to Ráith Baccáin,[107] it further substantiates the perception that Laígis Réta were in occupation here at least as early as the late sixth century.

Mescell's son and successor, Berach, comes in for prominent mention in section C of PGL. He was entitled 'Berach na beannachtan' because Sóergus Doithnennach had bestowed blessings on his twelve sons.[108] Nine of the twelve are enumerated as follows:

> (1) Cathal, from whom descend the kings, i.e. Gáethíne and his family; (Gáethíne was grandson of Cathal); (2) Flaithnia, from whom descend Clann Beraich; (3) Duinechaid, from whom Clann Duinechda (perhaps the origin of the barony name, Clandonagh, where the parishes of Donaghmore and Rathdowney lie); (4) Cairpre, from whom Clann Chairpre; (5) Ailill, from whom Síl nAilella; (6) another Cathal, from whom Huí Fhachtna; (7) Ruaidíne, from whom Clann Ruaidíne; (8) Indrechtach, from whom Clann Indrechtaich; (9) Cathasach, from whom Clann

> Chathasaich of whom came Huí Fhínáin and Huí Ruaidíne in Cluain Eidnech (Clonenagh).

This is a straightforward account of family groups who were obviously well known in their time and shows how, in the course of a few generations, offshoots of the main line became septs and sub-septs in their own right. Bringing down the descent to Gáethíne and other great-grandsons of Berach indicates that the details were compiled in the mid-ninth century.

Osraige influence

Close neighbours of the Laígis were the Osraige, who constituted a formidable force in the marches of Muma and Laigin. From an early period they had appropriated part of what is now south Co. Laois. Because of its associations with Cainnech, one of their chief patron saints,[109] Achad Bó (Aghaboe) was the cathedral town of the Osraige in pre-Norman times. Likewise, Durrow in Co. Laois was known as Durmag Ua nDuach, the Uí Duach forming a segment of Osraige with territory mainly in the barony of Fassadinin, Co. Kilkenny. Durmach Hua nDuach and Achadh maic Airt (Aghmacart) were among the principal churches of the Osraige burned by Muirchertach Mac Lochlainn in 1156.[110]

The Osraige appear to have been one of the early group of Érainn tribes in the south of Ireland, and their territory regarded as part of Munster rather than of Leinster.[111] The connexion between Osraige and Corco Laígde has often been commented upon. Feradach Find m. Duach, king of Osraige who died in 583,[112] was described in the Bórama story in the Book of Leinster as 'de Chorco Laígde'.[113] An expanded version in the later 'Fragmentary Annals' informs us that 'seven kings of the Corco Laígde ruled Osraige and seven kings of the Osraige took the kingship of Corco Laígde'.[114]

Similarly, the Life of Ciarán of Saigir, one of the early patrons of the Osraige, emphasises the connexion by having Ciarán's father, Lugna (described as 'a nOsraighibh, .i. do Dhál mBirn'), travel to the south of Ireland where he married Liadain of the Corco Laígde, and their son, Ciarán, was born and reared on the island of Cléire in west Cork. The genealogy assigned to Ciarán also derives him from 'Óengus Osrethi', supposed ancestor of the Osraige.[115]

Accordingly, we read that when Máel Sechnaill, king of Mide, invaded Munster in 858, he took its hostages 'o Belut Gabrain co Insi Tarbnai iar nEre', i.e. from Kilmacahill (bar. Gowran, Co. Kilkenny)[116] to the Bull Rock off Dursey I., Co. Cork. When Flann, son of Máel Sechnaill, did likewise in 906, he harried Munster 'o Ghabran co Luimnech'.

The Osraige seem to have recovered their independence from the Corco Laígde by the mid-seventh century. An annalistic source tells us that in the time of Diarmait and Bláthmac, sons of Áed Sláine, Scandlán Mór expelled the Corco Laígde from Osraige,[117] – probably in the 640s.[118]

This did not, however, result in antagonism towards Munster generally, and there are few records of battles by the Osraige against their western neighbours before the late tenth century. Rather were they in contention with the Laigin to the east, and it may well be that Scandlán Mór was also responsible for expelling the Laígis from the vulnerable plain of Réta. The recovery of this territory in the late seventh century could be the basis for the PGL story of the settlement (or resettlement) of the Laígis in Mag Réta, following the defeat and expulsion of the Munstermen. If for 'Munstermen' we read 'Osraige', we can trace the events in the annals. Scandlán's successor, Tuaim Snáma, was slain by Fáelán Senchustul in 678,[119] and the genealogical account in the Book of Leinster tells us that this slaying was the culmination of seven battles in which Fáelán Senchustul of the Laigin defeated the Osraige.[120]

There could be another dating problem here, in that Fáelán Senchustul is considered to be a grandson of Crimthann (son of Énna Ceinnselach).[121] As Crimthann is supposed to have been slain in 483 (*AU²*), this would make Fáelán much too early for the era of Tuaim Snáma. It may be that he has been confused with Fáelán, son of Sílán, who was in the kingly line of Úi Cheinnselaig and who would have flourished around the late seventh century.[122] (It is noticeable that the poem in the Book of Leinster account refers simply to 'Fáelán').

At any rate, this series of battles provides a likely origin for the story regarding the Laígis, who were probably resettled in Mag Réta before the next conflict occurred between the Osraige and Laigin in 693, in which Fáelchar, king of Osraige, was slain. The Laigin then seem to have carried the war into the enemy camp, since, according to *AI*, there was in 706 a slaughter of Laigin around Gabair in Munster – presumably in the Úi Chonaill Gabra territory in west Limerick. This accords with a list of battles (in the Lecan version of PGL)[123] apparently fought after the expulsion of the Munstermen, the second of which is termed 'Cath Gabra'.

But the indications are that the Laígis did not long retain possession at this stage. The abandonment of Ráith Baccáin may have been due to the extreme pressure which the Laigin as a whole endured in the eighth century. Following an internal dispute in 719 they were visited – and devastated – five times in one year by the Úi Néill,[124] who were renewing their claim to the Bórama (tribute) from their old enemies.

Two years later, Fergal mac Maíle Dúin is credited with invading the Laigin again to impose the tribute and take hostages.[125] Then followed, in 722, the celebrated battle of Almu (Allen, Co. Kildare), a total disaster for Fergal, who was slain along with many other kings of the Uí Néill and their supporters.

The sixteen-year breathing space which this victory gave the Laigin ended when Fergal's son, Áed Alláin, inflicted a crushing vengeance on them in 738 at Áth Senaig. Not only was the king of Laigin, Áed mac Colcan, slain there, but 'men say that so many fell in this great battle that we find no comparable slaughter in a single onslaught and fierce conflict throughout all preceding ages' (AU[2]).

Seeing their weakened state, Cathal mac Finguine, king of Munster, seized the opportunity to invade the Laigin and demand their hostages, thus avenging a defeat three years earlier at Féile (735) where his ally, Cellach, king of Osraige, was slain. Cathal died in 742, but the Osraige displayed a new-found vigour when they penetrated as far as Co. Westmeath in the same year, devastating both Ceinél Fiachach and Delbna. (This may indicate that they had by then recovered control of the corridor to the north, i.e. western Co. Laois). In 750 Anmchad, son of Cú Cherca, forcibly seized the kingship of Osraige.[126] Ambitious and aggressive, he laid waste Fothairt Feá (in Co. Carlow) in 754 and defeated the Laigin in 761 at Belach Gabráin, the king of Uí Cheinnselaig being among the slain.[127] With the rise of Eóganacht Chaisil, the balance of power had altered so much that in 794 Donnchad of Mide, king of Uí Néill, made a special expedition to aid the Laigin against the Munstermen. This may have been due to the fact that Bran, king of Laigin, was married to Eithne, daughter of Domnall of Mide. However, when in the following year (795) a rival killed both Bran and Eithne (at Cell Chúile Dumai in Laígis territory) relations deteriorated rapidly. Áed, son of Niall made three attacks on the Laigin in 804, and after a fourth in 805 he divided the kingship of Laigin between two contenders.

The Viking Dimension

The situation changed dramatically in the ninth century once the Viking raids began. Leinster was particularly vulnerable to attacks radiating from Dublin, Wexford and Waterford. In 825 the *gennti* (heathens) routed the Osraige and two years later captured an encampment of the Laigin with much slaughter. From their Dublin base in 841 they despoiled both Uí Néill and Laigin as far as Sliab Bladma, Clonenagh being among the monasteries plundered.[128] In 845 Dún Masc (Dunamase) was stormed, the heathens killing Áed, abbot of Clonenagh and Terryglass, as well as Ceithernach, prior of Kildare. Cúil

Chaissíne (Coolcashin, Co. Kilkenny) in Osraige territory suffered a similar fate in 846.[129] But a new king of Osraige, Cerball, who had succeeded his father, Dúngal, in 842, now made his domain a power to be reckoned with during the Viking wars.[130] In 847, in revenge perhaps for Cúil Chaissíne, he wiped out 1,200 of the foreigners led by Agonn (or Agnonn).

A tendency to unite against a common foe manifested itself in 831 when Feidlimid mac Crimthainn, king of Munster, led a combined Munster/Laigin army to plunder Brega, while in 848 his successor, Olchobar, joined with Lorcán of the Laigin to defeat the jarl Tomrair and his *gennti* at Sciath Nechtain.

However, Cerball made use of the Vikings for his own purposes. In 857 he joined with Ímar, the Viking leader, in defeating the Ceinél Fiachach (who were assisted by 'Gall-Ghaedhil' of Leth Chuinn),[131] and two years later they were joined by another Viking, Amlaím, in leading a great army into Mide.[132] At this point (859) Máel Sechnaill, king of Temair, called a royal conference at Ráith Áeda (Rahugh, Co. Westmeath), where Cerball made obeisance to the see of Armagh, and the Osraige were alienated to Leth Chuinn – with the consent of Máel Guala, king of Munster (who was slain by Northmen the same year). Máel Sechnaill and Cerball were, according to the 'Osraige chronicle', closely connected. Cerball's sister, Lann, was – for a time – Máel Sechnaill's wife, and Máel Sechnaill's daughter was the wife of Cerball, while in or about 854 Cerball was Máel Sechnaill's emissary in Munster, demanding hostages.[133] From then on the Osraige looked on Leinster rather than Munster as their real home. So it is that *Lebor na Cert* (compiled in the eleventh century), while quoting the legendary attachment of Osraige to Munster, also puts them among the stipendaries of the king of Laigin.[134] The Osraige were also conveniently provided with a genealogy which purported to connect them with the Laigin in prehistoric times.[135]

Laígis Réta

This new orientation of the Osraige vitally affected the political fortunes of their neighbours, the Laígis. Cerball's sister, Lann, was, according to the 'Osraige chronicle', also married to Gáethíne, king of Laígis, for a time.[136] This may explain how Gáethíne is found back in Mag Réta, rebuilding the fort of Baccán in Ráith Domnaig, as related above. After his death, Cerball formed an alliance with Gáethíne's son (and his own nephew), Ceinnéitig, during whose reign (*c.*860-903) the Laígis reached the height of their power. In 862 Ceinnéitig destroyed the encampment (*longphort*) of Rothlabh, killing many of his followers.[137] In 866 a slaughter was made of the foreigners by (the people of) the north of Osraige (and) by Ceinnéitig, son of Gaéthíne, at Mindroichet (Mondrehid, par. Offerlane).[138]

In the following year Ceinnéitig, aided by Máel Ciaráin, son of Rónán (who was probably of the Osraige), marched his army to Dublin and burned the fort of Amlaím (Olaf), at Clondalkin, slaughtering a hundred of the leaders of the foreigners.[139] Ceinnéitig was now a firm adherent of Cerball, and together they invaded the territory of the Laigin after Áed, son of Niall (king of Uí Néill)[140] had overrun it in 870. They encamped at Dún Bolg, probably in Co. Wicklow.[141] The Laigin attacked the fort and 'slew Gáethíne's son' (according to AU but not the other annals; we know that Ceinnéitig survived this battle). The Laigin were driven back with some slaughter.

Again in 878[142] Ceinnéitig invaded and plundered Uí Cheinnselaig, while Cerball carried out a further slaughter there the following year.[143] But Cerball's sudden death in 888 brought this alliance to an end. Two years later Ceinnéitig's son and heir, Cináed, was slain.[144] By 900 it was the Laigin who were preying on the Osraige,[145] who seem to have had succession problems. In 902 Dúngall, son of Cerball, was fatally wounded[146] – by the Laígis, who may have been supporters of his brother, Diarmait, later a powerful king of Osraige, though not before he had subdued dissident rivals.[147] In 903 Ceinnéitig, son of Gaéthíne, king of Laígis, died.

Na Commainn

The AFM obituary describes Ceinnéitig as 'tighearna Laíghsi 7 na cComan'.[148] AFM are also the only annals[149] to chronicle an attack by the kings of the foreigners who plundered the men of the Three Plains and of the Commainn, as far as Sliabh Bladhma, during the snow on the feast of Brigid in 872.[150] In his notes on these places, John O'Donovan incorrectly located them in Co. Kilkenny.[151] The 'Trí Maighe' were probably in the east Carlow area;[152] the Commainn were certainly in Co. Laois. Their singular name, which appears to signify 'allies', indicates that they comprised a loosely-federated group of minor septs, set up perhaps in response to the menace of the Viking wars, the first mention of them being, as above, in 872. An entry dated 915/6[153] refers to 'Trí Comainn', and it looks as if the three comprised Uí Buide, Uí Chrimthannáin and Uí Fhairchelláin, whose combined territory would have stretched from the eastern boundary of Co. Laois westwards to Sliabh Bladhma.

(1) Uí Buide

In an early fourteenth-century ecclesiastical taxation list[154] the churches of Oboy were those in the parishes of Killabban, Rathaspick, Shrule and 'Kylmolydde', the first three of which are in the barony of

Slievemargy. Castletown in Killabban parish was formerly known as Baile Chaisleáin Ua mBuidhe or Castletown Omoy.[155] Sliabh Mairge was originally the name of a mountain range, not of a territory; we know that part of the south-eastern corner of the barony (and of Co. Laois) – where Sléibte was founded – lay in Uí Bairrche territory. The Uí Buide domain seems to have included also much of the present baronies of Ballyadams and Stradbally. The 'Kylmolydde' listed above, was, in fact, the earlier name of Ballyadams parish. Tullomoy (parish) in Stradbally barony comes from Tulach Ua mBuide. That the Uí Buide formed a section of Na Commainn is clear from the fact that in 969[156] the king of the group was Echthigern, son of Eitech, whose genealogy (in the Book of Lecan) places him at the head of Uí Buide.[157]

(2) Uí Chrimthannáin

Also known as Uí Chrimthainn Áin or simply Uí Chrimthainn,[158] this sept is among those named in *Lebor na Cert*, an account of, inter alia, the stipends (*tuarastal*) payable by an overking to his subject kings. From the king of Laigin the Uí Chrimthannáin were entitled to receive six horses (while the Uí Buide and the Laígis were each assigned eight).[159] A note on Damán in *Félire Óengusso* tells us that the saint was of 'Tech Damáin i n-Úib Crimthannáin'.[160] Their main stronghold was probably at Dunamase; a genealogical source refers to 'Masc a quo Dún Masc in Uíbh Crimtannáin'.[161] Ó Huidhrín's Topographical Poem preserves the memory of that ancient ownership:

> Fá Dhún Masg as míne fuinn
> Ó Duibh for Cheinél cCriombhthuinn.[162]

A reference to 'a huibh Criomhthannáin Chúile Buichle' by Mac Fir Bhisigh[163] seems to indicate that they occupied this portion of central Co. Laois before the arrival of Laígis Chúile (Buichle). Only *AFM* record their activities, the first record being in 921 (= *AU²* 923) when their lord (king), Céile, son of Anrothán, died. It is noticeable here, as with the Uí Buide, that independent lords/kings of Uí Chrimthannáin are not recorded in the annals until after the death of Augrán, son of Ceinnéitig, in 917. The Uí Anrotháin and Uí Duib were later lords of the sept. In 1069 Giolla Muire mac Duib was slain by Mac Raith Ua Mórdha at the door of the oratory of Timahoe, and two years later Lorcán, son of Flaithniadh Ua Duibh, is the last lord of Uí Chrimthannáin to be named.[164] But the name, as that of a separate territory, still existed in the thirteenth century; in 1200 Geoffrey de Costentin got a royal grant of a cantred in Connacht in exchange for the land of 'Leis and Houkreuthenan'.[165]

(3) Uí Fhairchelláin

This is the least-known of the three septs; the only indication that they may have formed one of the group is that the raid on the Commainn in 872 extended as far as Sliab Bladma. On the evidence of the parish name (Offerlane) they may have occupied the whole barony of Upperwoods, which is coterminous with the parish. At the time Ó Huidhrín compiled his poem it was, of course, in Upper Ossory; he describes Mac Giolla Phádraig as lord of Osraighe from Sliabh southwards to (somewhat anachronistically)[166] the sea. But he also names Ó Dubhshláine (O Delaney) as lord of Coill Uachtarach (Upperwoods). (At this point, one MS has an interpolated verse putting 'Ó hÚrachán' as lord over Uí Fhairchealláin;[167] perhaps there is confusion here with Uí Chrimthannáin, one of whose ruling families was Ó hAnrotháin, later Ó hAnnracháin).

The origins of Uí Fhairchelláin are as obscure as their history. Their genealogy in Rawl.B.502 is inserted at the end of the Osraige section[168] – for no apparent reason except that by the twelfth century they were part of the Osraige hegemony. The pedigree is actually that of Finnian of Clonard, abbreviated[169] to conceal the fact that Finnan's descent was traced back to Conall Cernach – which, if there was a basis for it, would make it more likely that Finnian was of the Laígis.

There were but two references to Uí Fhairchelláin in the annals, one in 904 when their lord, Furbuide, son of Cuilennán, was wounded, the second in 952 when they and the Laígis together were defeated with heavy losses by Tuathal, son of Úgaire, king of Laigin.[170]

Later developments

The Commainn had first come under Laígis domination during Gáethíne's reign in the mid-ninth century – 'as e sin cedri do Laighis do ghabh na cumainn'.[171] Ceinnéitig, as already mentioned, and his son, Augrán (Mugrón) who was slain in 917, were described as lords of Laígis and Na Commainn, while in 933 Coscrach, son of Máel Mochéirge, was titled bishop of Tech Mochua (in Laígis) and of Na Commainn.[172]

But the Viking conflict which brought fame and power to Gáethíne and to Ceinnéitig now contributed to the decline of Laígis Réta. As part of the Laigin army, Augrán, king of Laígis, shared in the great victory over the Munstermen at Belach Mugna (Ballaghmoon, Co. Kildare) in 908,[173] but in 917 the Laigin were routed by the Viking leader, Sitric, son of Ímar, at Cenn Fuait (near St Mullins, Co. Carlow), and Augrán was among the slain. Of his sons, Gáethíne had predeceased him in 911, Cináed was slain in 928, Cathal died in 933 and finally Fergal died in 960.[174] In that year also, Fergal's son, Fáelán, tánaiste of Laígis Réta, was slain,[175] in what may have been an attempted dynastic takeover. The older genealogies bring the Laígis descent no further than Fergal,[176] but two later ones name another son of Fergal, namely Ceinnéitig,[177] whose death as lord of Laígis is recorded in 1015.[178]

That there was a rival dynasty may be deduced from a reference to 'Lachtnán mac Cearnaigh, rí Dúin Nar Laoighsi', who died c. 913.[179] Lachtnán's father, Cernach, appears to have been a son of Ceinnéitig (and brother of Augrán). Cernach's other son, Cináed, had a son uniquely named Mórda, eponymous ancestor of Uí Mhórdha.[180] Lachtnán's residence, Dún Náir, has not been identified, but it may have been at Ros Náir (derived from Nár, a brother of Masc of Dún Masc),[181] which another source situates at Sliabh Bladhma.[182] Under the forms 'Ross Náir mic Edlicon' and 'Ross tíre Náir', a poem in the *Metrical Dindshenchas* also associates it with Sliab Bladma.[183] Perhaps it was in the townland of Rossadown (*Ros an Dúin) in the parish of Offerlane and in the foothills of Slieve Bloom. Three years after the death of Ceinnéitig, son of Fergal, the killing of the next lord of Laoighis is recorded.[184] He was Cearnach Ua Mórdha, probably the Cernach m. Ceinnéitig m. Mórda of the genealogies, which shows that the alternative dynasty had taken over. From then on, practically all the kings/lords of Laoighis were of the Uí Mhórdha.

Following the defeat of the Laígis and Uí Fhairchelláin in 952 Domnall Ua Néill led an army to plunder the Commainn, as far as Dún Salach, in 957,[185] further weakening the Laígis. It is no surprise to find one of the Uí Buide, Echthigern, son of Eitech, recorded as next lord of the Commainn; he died in 969.[186] In 1012 Maél Mórda, king of Laigin, on his way home from Killaloe, was entertained at Senless Abáin (presumably at Killabban) by Mac Berdai, king of Uí Buide.[187] In 1069 the death of the last independent king of the Commainn is noted – Mac Iairn, son of Dubhthach.[188]

While the Laígis were thus in decline, the Osraige were once again in the ascendant. They defeated the king of Cashel in 941, the king of Laigin in 947, plundered Clonmacnoise in 962, slew the chief vice-abbot of Clonenagh in 967, won a battle over the Uí Cheinnselaig (while losing another to the Uí Muiredaig) in 974, and so on, a spate of aggrandizement which culminated in the seizing of the kingship of all Laigin in 1037 by Donnchad, son of Gilla Pátraic,[189] described in his obituary two years later as 'airdrí Laigen 7 Osraigi'.[190] In all probability, the second half of the tenth century saw the weakened Laígis Réta again pushed out of western Co. Laois by the resurgent Osraige, this time for good, so that the area now included in the baronies of Clarmallagh, Clandonagh and Upperwoods became a fixed part of Osraige.[191] Accordingly, at the Synod of Ráith Bhreasail (1111), 'Fairche

Chille Cainnigh' (i.e. Ossory diocese) was delimited, we are told, 'ó Shliabh Bladhma go Míleadhach',[192] i.e. from Slieve Bloom southwards to Waterford harbour.[193]

The Laígis were now confined to a small section of the present county, comprising mainly the barony of Cullenagh with parts of Maryborough East and West. A poem in the twelfth-century Book of Leinster recounts the battles of Cú Chorb, one of them being 'cath Bernais', which an interlinear note locates as 'ubi Laiges Reta nunc'[194] – where Laígis Réta now are (? as against Mag Réta where they formerly were). Bernas may be the townland named Pass, in the parishes of Ballyroan and Kilcolmanbane, barony of Cullenagh.[195] In moving east-wards, Laígis Réta must have impinged on Laígis Chúile, presumably uniting with them so that the old names fell into disuse and from then on terms such as Laoighis Uí Mhórdha, or simply Uí Mhórdha, prevailed. The Uí Mhórdha claimed that they embodied the descent and patrimony of the seven Laígsi.[196] In the course of time they regained control of the Commainn; Laoighseach Ua Mórdha who died in 1149 was recorded as lord of Laoighis and of the Commainn.[197] But by then it was only a matter of decades before the Anglo-Norman occupation created a whole new power-structure to which Laoighis Uí Mhórdha had to learn to adapt.

Acknowledgements
I wish to express sincere thanks to Prof. Pádraig Ó Riain and Mr K.W. Nicholls of U.C.C. who read the first draft of this article and furnished valuable advice. They are not responsible for any of my conclusions.

References
1. The spelling of the name varies considerably – Laígis, Loígis, Laíchis, Loíchis (mod. Laoighis, Laois). Also some early sources use a nom. sg. Loíches/Laíges. The gen. sg. and nom. pl. are generally Loíchsi/Laígsi, but from an early period Laígis/Loíchis was regarded as a plural collective name.
2. See, for example, Eoin MacNeill, *Celtic Ireland* (Dublin 1921), pp 59, 93; T.F. O'Rahilly, *Early Irish history and mythology* (Dublin 1964) 34-6; Byrne, *Irish kings*, p. 39. While the main genealogical compilations merely indicate this origin by deriving the Laígis from Conall Cernach, a tract in the Book of Lecan (f. 286b, col. 2) states unequivocally: 'Do Chruithnib Erenn diu, di Dal Araidi .i. na seacht Laigsi Laigen 7 uii Sogain, 7 cach C[on]ailli fil i nErind'. (J.H. Todd, ed.), *The Irish version of the Historia Britonum of Nennius* (Dublin 1848), p. lxxiii).
3. This MS has been identified by Professor Pádraig Ó Riain (*Éigse*, xviii (1981) 161-176) with Lebor Glinne Dá Locha, the Book of Glendalough. The genealogical material in it has been published, along with variants from LL, BB, Lec. and Lec.², in M.A. O'Brien, *Corpus genealogiarum Hiberniae*, i (Dublin

1962), PGL being in pp 87-95.

4. The generally accepted date for the compilation is *c.* 1120-1130, but one of the later genealogies in the collection, that of Uí Fhailge (117 b 11-12), is headed by Donnchad (slain 1134, *AFM*), son of Cú Aifne (d. 1130, *AU²*).

5. A longer version of this story (from the Book of Lecan) has been edited by M.E. Dobbs, *Zeitschrift für Celtische Philologie*, xvi (1927), 395-405.

6. Tomás Ó Máille (ed.), 'Medb Chruachna', *ZCP*, xvii (1928), 129-146 (137).

7. O'Brien, *Corpus geneal. Hib.*, p. 138.

8. Kathleen Mulchrone (ed.), *Bethu Phátraic*, i (Dublin and London 1939), p. 114.

9. Máire Herbert, Pádraig Ó Riain, eds, *Betha Adamnáin* (ITS 1988), p. 52, and Intro., pp 8, 16-20.

10. O'Brien, *Corpus geneal. Hib.*, p. 88.

11. G.H. Orpen (ed.), T*he song of Dermot and the earl* (Oxford 1892), p. 224.

12. O'Brien, *Corpus geneal. Hib.*, p. 31; see Byrne, *Irish kings*, p. 132.

13. O'Brien, *Corpus geneal. Hib.*, p. 91.

14. Ibid., p. 256.

15. Liam Price, *The place-names of Co. Wicklow* (Dublin 1967), pp 493-4; cf 'Laighis h-Ua n-Enechlais i Cualaind' in John O'Donovan's ed. of Geinealach Chorca Laidhe in *Miscellany of the Celtic Society* (Dublin 1849), p. 8.

16. O'Brien, *Corpus geneal. Hib.*, p. 93.

17. See Tomás Ó Concheanainn, *Ériu*, 24 (1973), 76-9, and Nollaig Ó Muraíle, *The celebrated antiquary Dubhaltach Mac Fhirbisigh* (Maynooth 1996), 16-19.

18. O'Brien, *Corpus geneal. Hib.*, pp 88-9; see also *Geneal. tracts*, pp 141-2.

19. O'Brien, *Corpus geneal. Hib.*, p. 91.

20. BB 129 b 33-45; O'Brien, *Corpus geneal. Hib.*, p. 55.

21. Gearóid Mac Niocaill (ed.), *The red book of the earls of Kildare* (Dublin 1964), nos 69, 76, 82.

22. See *Inquis. in off. Rot. Canc. Hib. Rep.*, i, Leinster (1826), Queen's Co., Jac. I, no. 5 (A.D. 1616); Fiants Ire. Eliz., no. 1649 (A.D. 1570). (My thanks to Mr. K.W. Nicholls for identifying this place-name).

23. Ordnance Survey Name Books, Queen's Co., i, 17. (I wish to express my gratitude to Dr Seán Ó Cearnaigh of the Ordnance Survey for photocopies of this and other pages from the unpublished OSNB for Co. Laois).

24. R.I. Best, O.J. Bergin, M.A. O'Brien (eds), *Book of Leinster*, i (Dublin 1954), pp 182-3 (ll. 5437-8, 5480).

25. *AU²* s.a. 795, 1024.

26. U.C.D., MS Add. Ir. 14, p. 483. (For relevant transcripts of this MS I wish to thank Dr Nollaig Ó Muraíle). It should also be noted that the genealogists attached Colman Cúile to the Uí Chrimthannáin (see Ó Riain, *CGSH*, no. 242) who enjoyed a hereditary right of succession to Fintan of Cluain Eidnech.

27. Stokes, *Mart. Oengus*, p. 6 (preface from *Leabhar Breac*).

28. It does not appear in the seventeenth-century Down Survey maps, nor in Petty's *Hiberniae Delineatio* (1685). In 1430 there was one parish entitled 'Cuilbeancair alias Ardia' (*Cal. papal letters*, viii, 202).

29. Dindshenchas of Srub Bó (LL 21186).

30. *A. Tig.* s.a. 977 (= *AU²* 978); cf. also *A. Clon.* s.a. 971 and *AFM* s.a. 976.

31. Whitley Stokes, ed., *The metrical Dindshenchas*, iv (Dublin 1924), pp 260, 282.

32. Not in LL, but in the Lec./LB versions. See R.A. Macalister, ed., *Lebor Gabála*, v (ITS 1956), p. 192.

33. Whitley Stokes, *On the calendar of Oengus* (Dublin 1871), p. clvi.

34. Ibid., p. clv.

35. Stokes, *Mart. Oengus*, p. 6.
36. The end section of TCD MS 1389, which is of later date than the Book of Leinster, but was bound with it and later published in facsimile as part of it. (*Book of Leinster* (facs., Dublin 1880), 378 b 11).
37. LL 21174 (Dindshenchas, Dún Masc).
38. Mac Niocaill, *Red Book*, no. 76.
39. See Lord Walter Fitzgerald, 'The history and antiquities of the Queen's County barony of Portnahinch' in *Kildare Arch. Soc. Jn.*, iv (1905), 184-204.
40. See reproduction in this volume, p. ??.
41. O.S. Letters, Queen's Co. (Bray 1930), i, 75.
42. *Inq. Lag.* (1826), Queen's Co., Jac. I, no. 2.
43. *Cal. justic. rolls, Ire.*, i, 167, 169, 178, 193.
44. Mac Niocaill, *Red Book*, nos 35, 75, 80.
45. Cal. *Carew MSS 1515-1574*, p. 131.
46. Indenture (Lambeth Library, vol. 603, p. 105) quoted in *S.P., Henry VIII*, iii, pt iii, p. 237.
47. G. Mac Niocaill (ed.), *Crown survey of lands 1540-41* (Dublin, 1992), pp 289, 171.
48. *Cal. S.P. Ire., 1599-1600*, p. 437.
49. *A. Clon.*, p. 31.
50. 1856 ed., i, p. 496 (note y).
51. Hogan, *Onomasticon*, p. 512.
52. P.W. Joyce, *Irish names of places* (Dublin 1913), iii, p. 512.
53. Eugene O'Curry, *Lectures on the manuscript material of ancient Irish history* (Dublin 1861), p. 482.
54. Ludwig Bieler, *The Patrician texts in the Book of Armagh* (Dublin 1979), p. 257.
55. See note 39. Lord Walter was a son of the duke of Leinster and had access to the archives at Carton.
56. LL, i, pp 58-9.
57. *Book of Lecan* (facs., Dublin 1937), 287 b 32-39.
58. *Book of Ballymote* (facs., Dublin 1887), 44 b 1-10; see also Macalister, *Lebor Gabála Érenn*, v, pp 188, 190, 192.
59. O'Brien, *Corpus geneal. Hib.*, p. 26 (119a5).
60. Ó Máille, *ZCP* xvii (1928), 137.
61. P.S. Dinneen, ed., *Foras feasa ar Éirinn*, ii (ITS 1908), pp 116-8.
62. RIA MS 23 K 32, p. 84.
63. *AFM* i, 34-6 (s.a. A.M. 3520).
64. O'Brien, *Corpus geneal. Hib.*, pp 93-5.
65. *A. Clon.* Conall Mageoghagan's translation, 1627 (ed. Rev. D. Murphy (Dublin 1896), p. 56) describes 'Athlayen' as 'a foorde on the River limiting Leinster from Munster'.
66. *A. Clon.* (p. 55) refer to this place as 'a little foord neere the hill of Mullamaisden called Athantrosdan'. John O'Donovan (*AFM*, ii, 635) located it on the r. Greece, near the hill of Mullamast.
67. Gwynn, *Metr. Dind.*, iii (Dublin 1913), p. 278 (ll. 25-9).
68. Standish O'Grady ed., *Silva Gadelica* (London 1892), i, 109.
69. *Foras feasa*, iii, 304.
70. Ibid., ii, 308. *AFM* refer to it twice as 'Bealach Mór Maighe Dála' (s.a. 1580 (v, 1748), 1600 (vi, 2148)).
71. John O'Donovan (OS Letters, Queen's Co., i, 78-9) surmised that it could be tl. Carn or Curraghane, par. Coolbanagher, but, apart from onomastic difficulties,

driving the Munstermen northwards to Carn from Athy would hardly be putting them on the road home!

72. See Dobbs, *ZCP* xvi (1927), 399.

73. See Joyce, *Irish names*, i, 343.

74. In Mac Fir Bhisigh's (1645) version (Book of genealogies, pp 559-60), it is twice spelt 'Cairthine'.

75. As for example in bairnech > báirnech, and probably airne > áirne. (Although in *Contributions to a dictionary of the Irish language* the head-word is 'áirne', at least one of the examples quoted shows a short vowel (fo dubairnib : tairngib, *Metr. Dind.* iii, 62, 96)).

76. OS Letters, Co. Kilkenny (Bray 1930), p. 32.

77. *Inq. Lag.*, Queen's Co., Jac. I, no. 19.

78. OS Name Books, Cos Kilkenny and Queen's, pp 1-2. Áth Charna is now the official Irish form of the parish name as adopted by the Placenames Branch (*Liostaí logainmneacha: Cill Chainnigh* (B.Á.C. 1993), p. 1).

79. William Carrigan, *History and antiquities of the diocese of Ossory* (Dublin 1905), ii, p. 307.

80. O'Brien, *Corpus geneal. Hib.*, p. 95.

81. Bieler, *Patrician texts*, p. 182 (and intro., pp 49-52).

82. In 1491 it was referred to as the rectory of St Patrick, Dwnachmor (*Cal. papal letters,* xv, 364) and in 1577 it was '(ecc.) S. Patricii de Donaghmore' (N.B. White (ed.), *Irish monastic and episcopal deeds* (Dublin 1936), pp 216-7).

83. Bieler, op. cit., p. 162.

84. Whitley Stokes (ed.), *The Tripartite Life of Patrick* (London 1887); Kathleen Mulchrone (ed.), *Bethu Phátraic* I (Dublin and London 1939).

85. Eoin Mac Neill, 'The Vita Tripartita of St. Patrick', *Ériu,* xi (1932), pp 1-41 (33).

86. Bieler, op. cit., p. 106.

87. Mulchrone, *Bethu Phátraic*, p. 117.

88. *AFM* s.a. 860 (= *AU²* 862).

89. *AFM*'s references (s.a. 874, 909, 1069) to the lords of a place called 'Ráith Tamnaighe' probably relate to a different area, even though Mac Fir Bhisigh's transcript of *Frag. A.* substitutes Ráith Domhnaigh in one of those entries (no. 455). The name is rarely found in Irish sources, but a clear indication of the name-form in the fifteenth century may be found in the Ossory annatae (1465): '... ecclesie Draithdonhnaigh' (*Archiv. Hib.* xx (1957) p. 7). Carrigan (*Dioc. Ossory* ii, p. 339) informs us that Irish speakers in Co. Kilkenny always called it 'Raw-dhouna, i.e. Ráth Domnaigh'.

90. Bieler, op. cit., p. 182.

91. *Ormond deeds*, i (Dublin 1932), nos 36, 333.

92. The two usages of *mag* do not necessarily conflict. *Mag* originally seems to have denoted a clearing made in woodland (in this case among yew trees), but was later used as a prefix to the names of extensive non-mountainous tracts of land, e.g. Aí, Brega, Cuib, Feimen, Life, Muirtheimne – and Réta, which was probably the original name in use when Mag nEóchaille came into being.

93. O.S. Letters, Queen's Co., i, 36.

94. Carrigan, *Dioc. Ossory,* ii, pp 339-40.

95. *Census Ire. c. 1659*, p. 495.

96. Stokes, *Mart. Oengus*, pp 208, 238, 240.

97. J.F. Kenney, *The sources for the early history of Ireland: ecclesiastical* (reprint, Dublin 1993), p. 398. Richard Sharpe (*Medieval Irish saints' lives* (Oxford 1991) pp 337-9) considers its origins to be in the late eighth century. Pádraig Ó Riain

('Traces of Lug in early Irish hagiographical tradition' in *ZCP* 36 (1977) pp 138-156) believes that the name Mo-Lua and its various by-forms derive ultimately from the name of the pagan deity, Lug.

98. W.W. Heist, ed., *Vitae SS Hiberniae* (Bruxelles 1965), pp 138, 385.

99. Stokes, *Mart. Oengus*, p. 40.

100. Ó Riain, *CGSH*, no. 187 (in ibid. no. 145, and in O'Brien, *Corpus geneal. Hib.*, p. 90, they are given as sons of Comgall).

101. In *Adomnán's Life of Columba* (ed. by A.O. & M.O. Anderson, 2nd ed., Oxford 1991), p. 488, Colmán is referred to as 'sanctus Columbanus episcopus mocu-Loigse', indicating origin from the Laígis.

102. There is some doubt about the alias in *A. Tig.*; *Chron. Scot.* (also of the Clonmacnoise group of annals) has a Latin appendage: 'Óena mac Hú Laígsi ... .i. mac Eógain do Laígis, retenōs Principatum annis xxxvi quievit'. What seems to be a garbled form (?from 'retineo') here may have given the compiler of *A.Tig.* the idea that 'Réta' was the word in question. 'm. Eógain' is also doubtful; the genealogies of the saints make Óenu a son of Berach who was a grandson of Barr m. Cairthinn, an ancestral figure among the Laígis. (See Ó Riain, *CGSH*, nos 144, 662, 204).

103. O'Brien, *Corpus geneal. Hib.*, p. 88. Cf also: 'Beir mo bachall tar Berba / co síl Mescill mórergna', from a Middle Irish poem on Éimíne's bell, ed. by Erich Poppe, *Celtica,* 17 (1985) 59-72 (65).

104. The section AD 650-950 in *AI*, as pointed out by Mac Neill (R.I. Best, Eoin Mac Neill, *The annals of Inisfallen* (facs., Dublin 1933), p. 29) was produced by compilation (and obviously abbreviated) at the end of the period, and it may have occurred that a careless abridger, coming across a reference to an unaccustomed name, (St) Michel (for which see *AU²* s.a. 799), in an obscure context ('handclapping / fire from heaven'), interpreted it as an obit for Mescell.

105. Ed. by Erich Poppe, *Celtica* 18 (1987), 35-45. An earlier ed., by J.G. O'Keeffe, was published in *Anecdota from Irish MSS*, i (1907) 40-5).

106. 'The list of sureties in Cáin Éimíne' in *Celtica,* 21 (1990) 588-92.

107. There are two other possibilities: Baccán m. Brain (126b43), who was not in the regnal line, and a dubious Baccán m. Lugdach Loichsich (126b47), to whom Lec.² assigns the honour ('Baccán mac Luigdeach dia tá Ráith mBacáin i Muig Ráeda').

108. This seems to echo the story of the earlier Berach (Heist, op. cit., p. 138) of whom Mo-Lua requested a site for his church. This was gladly granted after Mo-Lua blessed some water and sprinkled it on Berach's son who was thereby cured of a near-fatal illness.

109. See Pádraig Ó Riain, 'Cainnech alias Colum Cille, patron of Ossory', in P. de Brún, S. Ó Coileáin, P. Ó Riain (eds), *Folia Gadelica* (Cork 1983).

110. *A. Tig.* s.a. 1156.

111. See O'Rahilly, *EIHM*, pp 18-19.

112. *AU²* s.a. 583 (As these are generally regarded as the most reliable source for early Irish history, it can be taken that from here on, any dated but unreferenced particulars come from these annals, the edition used being *The annals of Ulster* (to A.D. 1131) ed. by Seán Mac Airt and Gearóid Mac Niocaill (Dublin 1983)).

113. LL 38640.

114. J.N. Radner, ed., *Fragmentary annals of Ireland* (Dublin 1978), p. 2 (no. 4).

115. Charles Plummer, *Bethada náem nÉrenn* (Oxford 1968) i, 103, and Ó Riain,

CSGH, no. 288. (The Osraige managed to maintain spiritual and temporal links with Saighir, so that even today it remains an Ossory parish, 'islanded' in Killaloe diocese).

116. Cf 'i Cill meic Cathail i nHuib Bairrchi, .i. i mBelach Gabrain', Stokes, *Mart. Oengus*, p. 262 (31 Dec.), and 'Ceall Meic Cathail i mBealach Gabhráin', P. Ó Riain, *Beatha Bharra* (1994), p. 60.

117. Annals from Egerton MS 1732 (dated 1517), which Robin Flower believed to be connected with *Frag. A.* and with the lost Book of Clonenagh – see *Catalogue of Irish MSS in the British Library* (reprint, Dublin 1992), ii, 259-263. The annals were published by Standish O'Grady, *Silva Gadelica*, i, pp 390-413 (394).

118. Diarmait and Bláthmac reigned 643-665; *AFM*'s (corrected) date of 643 for the death of Scandlán may be too early; his successor for 31 years (see next note) was slain in 678, so perhaps 647 would be more accurate for Scandlán's demise.

119. *A. Tig.* s.a. 677; *Frag. A.*, no. 69; *AFM* s.a. 676. The second *AU²* reference to 'Tóim Snámha m. Flainn', king of Osraige who died in 770 (also found in *AFM*) is in error for 'Tómmíne m. Flainn', as can be seen from the list of kings of Osraige in the *Book of Leinster* (i, 189), where Tuaim Snáma is shown to have reigned for 31 years after the death of Scandlán Mór in 643 (*AFM* s.a. 640) whereas Tómmíne m. Flainn reigned after Anmchad m. Con Cerca (victor in the battle of Belach Gabráin in 761, *A. Tig.* s.a. 760). Also Tuaim Snáma's pedigree (O'Brien, *Corpus geneal. Hib.*, pp 110-1) shows that he was a contemporary (and third cousin) of Fáelchar, slain in 693.

120. O'Brien, *Corpus geneal. Hib.*, p. 347.

121. Ibid., p. 345.

122. A descendant, Cairpri m. Diarmata, six generations later, was slain in 876.

123. Dobbs, *ZCP* xvi (1927) 399. (Perhaps 'Cath Maigi', the first battle on that list, was the one in which Fáelchar was slain).

124. *A. Tig.* s.a. 718.

125. *AU²* s.a. 721; *A. Tig.* s.a. 720; Pádraig Ó Riain, in his ed. of the saga *Cath Almaine* (Dublin 1978) p. xviii, considers this entry to be an interpolation, with no basis in fact.

126. *A. Tig.* s.a. 749.

127. *AU²* s.a. 761; the battle recorded in *A. Tig.* s.a. 758, and as 'iomairecc Gabhrain' in *AFM* s.a. 754, may refer to the same event.

128. *AFM* s.a. 840.

129. *AFM* s.a. 844.

130. See *Frag. A.* There is a strong Osraige bias in this work, particularly in what the editor, Dr J.A. Radner, terms the 'Osraige chronicle' in fragments 4 and 5. According to Prof. Donnchadh Ó Corráin, *Frag. A.* 'was originally elaborated towards the middle of the eleventh century to justify the claims of the kings of Osraige to be kings of Leinster and lords of Dublin'. ('High-kings, vikings and other kings' in *IHS* xxi (1979) 283-323). Cerball or Cearbhall is the hero of this account, and his exploits fill 22 entries, some quite lengthy. He is called 'Cearbhall mac Dúnlainge' throughout, but *AU* and other annals, along with his pedigree (O'Brien, *Corpus geneal. Hib.*, pp 15, 111) make it clear that his father's name was Dúngal.

131. *AFM* s.a. 856.

132. *AFM* s.a. 857.

133. *Frag. A.*, no. 246.

134. Myles Dillon, ed., *Lebor na Cert: The Book of Rights* (ITS 1962), pp 16, 18, 134.

135. O'Brien, *Corpus geneal. Hib.*, p. 101; see Byrne, *Irish kings*, p. 163, also Kim

McCone, *Pagan past and Christian present in early Irish literature* (Maynooth 1990) pp 238-40).

136. *Frag. A.*, p. 132 (no. 366).

137. *AFM* s.a. 860. John O'Donovan has identified Rothlabh's fortress as Dunrally, in the par. of Lea, in the NE of Co. Laois, the site investigated by Eamonn Kely and John Maas in this volume. (In the *Frag. A.* account (no. 308) Ceinnéitig and Cerball together attack *longus Rodlaibh*, the fleet of Rodlabh, which had just arrived from Norway).

138. *AFM* s.a. 864; *Frag. A.*, no. 308. 'Tuaiscert Osraige' here (in two seventeenth-century compilations) reflects the usage from the twelfth century on, e.g. 'oc Dermaigh Ua nDuach (Durrow) i tuaiscert Osraighe' (W. Stokes, *The martyrology of Gorman* (London 1895) p. 200) and 'i Muig Tuathait a Tuaiscert Osraigi, .i. i n-Uib Forcellain' *Mart. Oengus* (notes) p. 198). Uí Fhairchelláin is now represented in par. Offerlane, yet the same sources give Min Droichit (Mondrehid) and Enach Truim (Annatrim) in that parish as being 'i Laíchis' (*Mart. Gorm.*, pp 178, 210; *Mart. Oengus*, pp 208, 240). The most confusing location is that given in the Latin Life of Mo-Lua, where Cluain Ferta Molua (donated by 'dux Layghse, Berachus') is placed 'inter regiones Osrayghi et Hele et Layges' (Plummer, *VSH*, ii, 216) – something possible only if the Osraige were in bar. Clandonagh and the Laígis in bar. Upperwoods (or vice-versa). The ambiguity is obviously due to successive changes of occupancy.

139. According to *AFM* (s.a. 865) and *Frag. A.* (no. 362) Ceinnéitig followed up this victory by defeating the fleet of Áth Cliath and slaying 'Odolbh Micle'.

140. Áed 'Finnliath' also (according to *Frag. A.* nos. 327, 366) had Lann, sister of Cerball, to wife for a time.

141. For identification of this site, see Liam Price, *The place-names of Co. Wicklow* (Dublin 1945), pp 162-5.

142. *AFM* s.a. 875.

143. *AFM* s.a. 876.

144. *AFM* s.a. 886 (= *AU²* 890) where Cináed is described as: *Mac rigb Ratha Bacain buain.*

145. *AFM* s.a. 895.

146. *AFM* s.a. 897.

147. *Frag. A.*, no. 443.

148. *AFM* s.a. 898.

149. Apart from *Frag. A.*, no. 407.

150. *AFM* s.a. 870.

151. *AFM* i, pp 516-7.

152. Cf 'tighearna Ua nDróna na tTrí Maighe', *AFM* s.a. 906.

153. *AFM* s.a. 915; *Chron. Scot.* s.a. 916 (= *AU²* 917).

154. *Cal. Doc. Ire., 1305-1307*, p. 249.

155. See e.g. 'Ballicaslan Omoy', Fiant Ire., Eliz., 5147; 'Castletown o'Moye', *Inq. Lag.*, Queen's Co., Jac. I, no. 22 (1622).

156. *AFM* s.a. 967.

157. O'Brien, *Corpus geneal. Hib.*, p. 29.

158. Ibid., pp 55-6.

159. Dillon, *Lebor na Cert*, p. 108.

160. Stokes, *Mart. Oengus* (1905), p. 74 (12 Feb.).

161. Section of TCD MS 1339 (see note 36), facs. 378 b 10-11.

162. James Carney (ed.), *Topographical poems by Seaán Mór Ó Dubhagáin and Giolla-na-Naomh Ó Huidhrín* (Dublin 1943), p. 38.

163. Book of Genealogies, UCD MS Add. Ir. 14, 483 a 11.
164. *AFM* s.a. 1069/1071.
165. *Cal. Doc. Ire., 1171-1251*, no. 137.
166. The Meic Ghiolla Phádraig (later Fitzpatricks) had been driven from their Kilkenny lands by the Marshals into 'Upper Ossory'. Ennobled by Henry VIII as Barons of Upper Ossory, they retained extensive lands there down to recent times. (See Nicholls, *Gaelic. Ire*, p. 169, and chapter by David Edwards in this volume.
167. Carney, *Top. poems*, ii, 1117-1132.
168. O'Brien, *Corpus geneal. Hib.*, p. 116.
169. A more complete version is given in Ó Riain, *CGSH*, no. 122. The Life of Finnian (W. Stokes, ed., *Lives of saints from the Book of Lismore* (Oxford 1890), p. 75) repeats this pedigree, though another version derives him from the Uí Loscáin of Co. Kildare (See Kenney, *Sources*, p. 375).
170. *AFM* s.a. 899, 950.
171. Séamus Pender (ed.), 'The O Clery book of genealogies' in *Anal. Hib.,* 18 (1951), p. 140.
172. *AFM* s.a. 915, 931.
173. *AU²* s.a. 908; expanded saga-type account in *Frag. A.,* no. 423.
174. *AFM* s.a. 906, 928, 933, 958.
175. *AFM* s.a. 958.
176. See O'Brien, *Corpus geneal. Hib.*, p. 91.
177. *Book of Uí Maine* (facs., Dublin 1942) 77b; Mac Fir Bhisigh, Book of Genealogies, p. 556.
178. *AFM* s.a. 1014.
179. *Frag. A.,* no. 454. Undated in MS, this entry may be later than 913.
180. Three of the main Uí Mhórdha genealogies agree on these points. They are (1) *Book of Uí Maine* (facs.) 77c; (2) one written on a previously-erased page of LL (O'Brien, *Corpus geneal*. Hib., pp 433-4); (3) Mac Fir Bhisigh, Book of Genealogies, p. 557(a). O Clery's genealogy (*Anal. Hib.* 18, p. 140) differs in that it makes Cernach son of Gáethíne and father of Mórdha.
181. O'Brien, *Corpus. geneal. Hib.*, pp 20-1.
182. TCD MS 1339, 378 b 10 (see note 36).
183. Stokes, *Metr. Dind.*, pt ii, pp 54-6.
184. *AFM* s.a. 1017.
185. *AFM* s.a. 955. 'Donsalach' was later a parish name (in the deanery of Leys). Liam Price suggested that it was tl. Doon, par. Clonenagh and Clonagheen (*J.R.S.A.I.* 91 (1961) p. 177 fn.), but K.W. Nicholls (pers. comm.) thinks that a more likely location is Tullore, a former parish name, now a townland in par. Ballyroan.
186. *AFM* s.a. 967.
187. J.H. Todd, ed., *Cogadh Gaedhel re Gallaibh* (London 1867), p. 147. (Perhaps his son was the 'Cowddy O Bearrga, who slew Aimirgen Ua Mórda in 1026, according to *A. Clon.*).
188. *AFM* s.a. 1069.
189. *AFM* s.a. 939, 945, 960, 965, 972, 1037.
190. *AU²* s.a. 1039.
191. Carrigan (*Dioc. Ossory*, i, 2) also dates the acquisition of this area by the Osraige to the tenth century.
192. Keating, op. cit., iii, 304.
193. Cf in Life of St Declan, 'fretum Miletach, quod diuidit Laginenses et Muminenses' (Plummer, *VSH* ii, 35).

194. LL 6410. (Misreading the abbreviation for 'nunc' as 'mór', Eugene O'Curry was the originator of a new name, 'Laiges Réta Mór'. (*Lectures on the MS materials of ancient Irish history* (Dublin 1861), pp 481-2)).

195. As a townland-name, 'Pass' appears to have come into use comparatively recently, judging by the absence of early forms of the name, but as a feature, the term *berna(s)* is probably much older, Pass has been identified as the 'Transitus plumarum (Bearna na gchleti)' of Philip O'Sullivan Bear (*Historiae Catholicae Iberniae Compendium*, ed. Matheus Kelly (Dublin 1850), p. 207) by, among others, Thomas O'Conor of the Ordnance Survey (OSNB, Queen's Co., par. Ballyroan, p. 22), Canon John O'Hanlon (*Proc. R.I.A.*, ser. 2, i (1879), pp 279-288) and Lord Walter Fitzgerald, 'Barnaglitty' in *Jn., R.S.A.I.*, 34 (1904), pp 199-210.

196. See poem on this subject, ed. by Anne O'Sullivan in *Celtica,* 8 (1968), pp 182-6.

197. *AFM* s.a. 1149.

Chapter 4

TIMAHOE AND THE LOÍGSE: MONASTICISM

ELVA JOHNSTON

The Loígse and early medieval Leinster

Early medieval Ireland was divided into five provinces or fifths: Munster, Ulster, Leinster, Connacht and Mide in the midlands. Furthermore, despite the fact that there were many small petty kingdoms within the provinces, only the few larger over-kingdoms were politically important. These included the provincial kingdoms of Leinster, Munster and Connacht, the Southern Uí Néill territories in Mide, the lands of the Northern Uí Néill in Ulster, the buffer states of Airgialla (Oriel) in the north and Osraige (Ossory) in the south, and the remnants of the fifth of the Ulaid in east Ulster. The Irish further imagined the island as divided into halves: the northern half of Leth Cuinn, consisting of Connacht, Mide and Ulster, and the southern half of Leth Moga, incorporating Munster and Leinster. The kingship of the entire island, largely a concept without practical significance for much of the early medieval period, was associated with the neolithic site of Tara and was the prerogative of the Uí Néill, a group of dynasties claiming descent from the eponymous Niall Nogiallach (of the nine hostages). From the end of the ninth century the office came to possess real power. The success of Brian Bóruma (Brian Boru) in winning the high-kingship for the Dál Cais, later the O'Briens, of Munster made the kingship a prize worth fighting for.[1] Eventually, by the time of the Norman invasion in the 1170s, the country was riven with the strife of the provincial kings, each trying to win the high-kingship for his own dynasty. The king of Leinster – Diarmait Mac Murchada – was one contestant. His failure in Ireland led him to turn to the Angevin king Henry II and the latter's troublesome Norman vassals. In the long term the results were momentous, and mark a turning point in the history of medieval Ireland.

The ancient territory of the Loígse, the people who gave their name to modern Laois, mainly comprised the area of the county that is part of the modern diocese of Kildare and Leighlin. During the pre-Norman period the Loígse and Fothairt were counted as *prím-forslointe*.[2] This term is used when describing a people who belong to a kingdom formally, but are not linked to the dominant dynastic group through blood. Unlike the Loígse, the Fothairt were scattered throughout Leinster. One of the most important Fothart groups was settled around Kildare. They claimed to be of the same people as Brigit, Kildare's founder-saint, and used this relationship to cement their position within the most powerful church in Leinster. Although, the Fothairt and Loígse were accounted *fortuatha*, or alien, by the genealogists, they had a favoured position within Leinster. In fact, the Loígse were easily the more important of the two.

The most powerful of the Leinster peoples were the Laigin, who gave their name to the province and claimed descent from the mythical Labraid Loingsech. Among the Laigin, the Uí Dúnlainge in the Liffey valley and the Uí Chennselaig in the south were the dominant dynasties. For much of the early medieval period the kingship of the province was controlled by the Uí Dúnlainge, exploiting the resources of the Currach Life (the Curragh) and the church of Kildare. The Uí Dúnlainge and Uí Chennselaig spheres of influence were divided by the watershed of the Liffey and Slaney known as the Gabair. The king of Uí Chennselaig was the 'rí Lagen Desgabair', the king of Leinster south of the Gabair. Logis lay within the sphere of the Uí Dúnlainge, but the decline of that dynasty in the eleventh and twelfth centuries led to its eventual incorporation into the Uí Chennselaig influenced diocese of Leighlin.

The primary reason for the relative importance of the Loígse within Leinster, despite their non-Laginian pedigree, was geographical. Their kingdom occupied the old borderlands of the province. They faced the threat of Munster, which increasingly saw Leinster as a key to wresting the high-kingship from the possession of the Uí Néill. Control of Leinster would give Munster supremacy in Leth Moga. Munster was not the only threat. The powerful buffer kingdom of Osraige was nominally, at least, under the suzerainty of the Munster kings of Cashel, until it was alienated from the province in the second half of the ninth-century. From this point Osraige played an increasingly dominant role in Leinster politics. By 1036 Donnchad mac Gilla Pátraic was king of Osraige and Leinster. The power of Osraige certainly undermined the Uí Dúnlainge. The latter's loss of the provincial kingship to the Osraige was only a prelude to the rise and eventual domination of the Uí Chennselaig.

In the earlier period, then, the Loígse on the Munster border were a bulwark against the southern enemies of Leinster. In the genealogies, important collections which were compiled from at least the early seventh century, they are described with the Fothairt, as the *clíathaire*

Lagen the defenders of Leinster.[3] This status is reflected in the *enechlann* 'compensation' assigned to the Loígse. Compensation represented the honour-price of a particular people, and honour-price in its turn marked status in early Ireland. Irish society was not egalitarian, but hierarchical,[4] with various grades of freedom and servility. For instance, freedom of movement between kingdoms was restricted to those of high status and to the learned classes. Each grade had an accompanying honour-price. The compensation of the Loígse was bronze.[5] The use of a metal, such as bronze, was an indicator of a fairly high status, if not the highest.

A hierarchical society, such as early Ireland, placed great emphasis on descent from noble ancestors. Eventually, the twelfth-century *Lebor Gabála*, the *Book of Invasions*, would trace all the important peoples in Ireland's ethnic mix back to a common ancestor Míl Espáne, and from Míl Espáne thence to Adam, linking the Irish into world history.[5] However, this idea, although it reached its completed form in the *Lebor Gabála*, was formulated over several centuries. Indeed, many of its elements were well developed in the ninth century.[7] The Loígse claimed descent from the eponymous Lugaid Loígsech, the son of the Ulster hero, and companion of Cú Chulainn, Conall Cernach.[8] Other peoples of Leth Moga, such as the Corco Óche of Limerick, claimed similar fictitious descents from the heroes of ancient Ulster. The genealogies describe how Lugaid was the foster-son of Eochaid Find Fuath nAirt, the ancestor of the Fothairt, thus linking the two *clíathaire Lagen* together.[9] Lugaid's epithet, 'Loígsech' is given two alternative explanations in the genealogies. In a truncated version of an evidently longer birth-tale, it is described how a fawn (tolg) comes past the newly-born Lugaid on the strand. The watchman calls 'leg secha', 'a fawn past him'.[10] In the longer tale Lugaid is fostered by Eochaid Find Fuath nAirt at Tara. His father Conall Cernach comes to Eochaid in old age and poverty on his way to Cruachu in Connacht, a destination which will prove ill-fated.[11] He is received and feasted by Eochaid, but leaves the next day. Lugaid, who had been away, returns after his father leaves. When he learns of his father's visit he demands to consume what his father has consumed. Eochaid gives Lugaid the same amount of food and ale as he gave Conall. Lugaid, signalling his entrance into adulthood, consumes it all, causing Eochaid to remark that he had a feast fit for a warrior, a 'láech-fhes'. Thus, Lugaid earns his adulthood and epithet.[12]

However, despite the genealogists evident concern to give the Loígse a northern pedigree and to cement their link with the Fothairt, there are signs of a different, and earlier, descent. In this scheme the Loígse are descended from Dáire, also known as Dáire Doimthech and Dáire

Sírchrechtach. Dáire was originally regarded as the ultimate ancestor, or perhaps ancestral god, of the rainn, a people once dominant throughout Ireland.[13] In the earliest extant map of Ireland that of Ptolemy, compiled in the second century AD, thought to be based on even earlier sources the Érainn, or Iverni, are shown to possess large territories, later lost to newcomers such as the Munster Eóganachta. The Corco Loígde, settled around west Cork, were among the most powerful Érainn in historical times and had clear memories of a share in the provincial kingship. There were early links between the Corco Loígde and the Osraige.[14] It is possible that the Loígse were similarly linked with the Corco Loígde, a link now only expressed in the genealogical relationship between Lugaid Loígsech and Lugaid Láigde, ancestor of the Corco Loígde, as two sons of Dáire. Indeed, the story of the newly-born Lugaid and the fawn may be related to the legend of Lugaid Láigde. In this origin legend Dáire is told that a son of his called Lugaid will be king of Ireland. As a sign of this he will catch a golden fawn. Dáire names his five sons Lugaid. The five brothers go hunting the fawn, but a magical mist descends. Lugaid Láigde, alone, catches the fawn. Following this he meets a hag and agrees to sleep with her. Upon intercourse she is transformed into a beautiful woman, and she identifies herself as the sovereignty of Ireland. Lugaid, duly, becomes king.[15] In contrast, Lugaid Loígsech's encounter with the fawn is brief, but in conjunction with the tale of Lugaid Láigde, suggests his kingship over his future people, the Loígse.

Just as there were several grades of kings in Ireland as a whole, there was a clear hierarchy within the territory of the Loígse. Loígis is described as having a seven-fold division.[16] In the genealogies the non-unitary nature of Loígis is expressed through legend. Lugaid Loígsech is imagined as driving the armies of Munster from Leinster, helping the prehistoric Leinster king Cú Chorb, and winning the land of Loígis as a reward. However, the Leinstermen fear the power of Lugaid and they take the advice of Eithne Síthbaicc, the wife of Cú Chorb, who splits the land into seven parts a divide-and-conquer policy.[17] The role of Eithne, as a symbol of sovereignty is interesting, and links her in with other legendary Irish queens who symbolise the land of Ireland.[18] An anecdote in the *Book of Leinster* assigns Eithne's role to another famous queen Medb Lethderg. Medb divides the Fothairt and the Loígse *combat lugaite a nert i n-agid ríg Lagen* 'so that their strength would be the weaker against the king of Leinster'. She also poisons Lugaid Loígse, here called the son of Loígsech Cendmár. Symbolically Lugaid is given the poisoned drink of sovereignty by the queen in her darker aspect, and his land is disunited as a result.

The actual geography of these seven divisions is uncertain.

Furthermore, the sphere of Loígse influence fluctuated. At times they seem to have dominated the branch of the widely scattered Uí Bairrche, in Sliab Mairge (Slievemargy) despite the fact that the Uí Bairrche had once exercised far more power in Leinster. The most important of the seven divisions was that of Loígis Réta. The kings of Loígis Réta controlled Mag Réta, Morrett heath around Portlaoise, from the hill-fort of Dunamase (Dún Masc), and were the overall leaders of the Loígse. Their ancestor was Berach son of Mescell, who is provided with a descent from Fachtna, the great-grandson of Lugaid Loígsech.[19] Mescell is the first king of the Loígse to be mentioned in the Annals, the chief documents for the dating of early Irish history. His death notice appears in the year 799 in the *Annals of Inisfallen*.[20] His descendants are called the *Síl Mescill*, literally the seed of Mescell.[21] The O'Mores of later medieval Laois originated from this family.

Monasticism in Loígis

Early Ireland was an aristocratic society. Irish aristocrats not only dominated lay society, but they also controlled the church, filling the high offices of the monastic community with members from their own families.[22] This was the norm in medieval Europe as a whole. Where Ireland differed, to a certain extent, was in the organisation of her church. The church was dominated by monastic federations. Each federation, called a *paruchia*, was led by a powerful church, such as Armagh, Kildare or Clonmacnoise. Monasticism seems to have been important from the introduction of christianity into Ireland in the fifth century, although the development of the paruchial system must have taken some time. Patrick, symbolically the most important, if not the only, christianiser, describes the children of Irish nobles becoming monks and virgins for Christ.[23] Whatever the true origin of this situation, abbots and lay-abbots generally controlled the monastic lands and revenues, which were extensive. Bishops did not oversee territorial dioceses, and were often attached to monastic churches. Some bishops were powerful in the secular sphere such as the ninth-century king of Munster, Feidlimid mac Crimthainn. A diocesan system was finally introduced by three great synods in the twelfth century. Modern boundaries are substantially the same as those decided at the synod of Kells-Mellifont in 1152. Until then, the abbot tended to be the most dominant figure in a complex organisation which shared the characteristics of the monastic and episcopal.[24] Moreover, monastic settlements were in many ways the proto-urban setlements of pre-Viking Ireland.[25] They were centres of trade and politics. Secular and religious life were closely intertwined.

Within Leinster the most powerful church was Kildare, and Kildare was closely linked with the ambitions of the Uí Dúnlainge kings.[26] Clonenagh (Cluain Ednech) was the most influential church in Loígis. It was situated within the territory of Loígis Réta. However, its major link was not with another church in Loígis, but with the wealthy monastery of Terryglass (Tír dá Glas). Most of the *Book of Leinster*, a famous twelfth-century Irish codex, was compiled at Terryglass.[27] The Annals record abbots of Terryglass who were also abbots of Clonenagh, and this is a clear expression of the close relationship between the churches.[28] Although Terryglass was within Munster territory its associations were with Leinster and its founder was a Leinsterman, Colum mac Crimthainn. In the various recensions of his Life, Fintan moccu Echdach (ob. AU 603), the founder of Clonenagh, is associated with Colum mac Crimthainn. Indeed, he founds Clonenagh on the advice of his mentor, Colum.[29] The Loígse are not mentioned in his *Vita*. Nevertheless, Clonenagh may have played an important role in preserving records of political events in Loígis. A chronicle based in Clonenagh seems to have been one of the sources used in the compilation of the *Annals of the Four Masters*. In addition Óengus, the author of the famous martyrology of saints which bears his name *Féilire Óengusso* had strong associations with the monastery.[20] Furthermore, the Loígse did have some influence within the monastery. The genealogies record a Cathasach among the descendants of Berach na Bennachtan (of the blessings), the son of Mescell, and ultimate ancestor of the royal dynasty. Among the families claiming descent from Cathasach are the Uí Ruaidíne 'i Cluain Eidnech'.[31] The presence of the Uí Ruaidíne in Clonenagh illustrates an important aspect of early Irish society that I have already mentioned, the domination of the clerical elite by the aristocracy.[32] Less successful branches of a noble dynasty often ended up in the church. The church provided some leeway for the upwardly mobile. Gormgal of Loígis (ob. AU 1085) died as the *comarba*, or head, of the church of Brigit in Armagh. He is called a *suí*, a sage, in learning and religion. Ecclesiastical learning could open up the closed boundaries of the early Irish kingdoms.

There were several large monastic settlements in the vicinity of Loígis. These included Aghaboe (Achad Bó Cainnig) and Clonfertmulloe (Cluain Ferta Mo Lua) in Osraige and Sletty (Sléibte) in Sliab Mairge. Clonfertmulloe at the foot of the Slieve Bloom was very much a border monastery, lying between Osraige, Éle and Loígis. It had close links with the Loígse. The Latin *Vitae* of Mo Lua, although contained in the late medieval collections of saints' Lives, bears witness to a far earlier exemplar. The political situation is very much pre-ninth-century, especially in its treatment of the equivocal position of Osraige in relationship to Munster and Leinster.[33] They describe how this monastery was founded with the help of Berach son of Balcán, king of the Loígse. This Berach appears in the genealogies as the great-grandfather of the identically-named Berach, from whom the royal dynasty of the Loígse claimed descent.[34]

Timahoe (Tech Mo Chua) was in the middle of the territory of Loígis, in what is now the parish of Fossy in the barony of Cullenagh. A round tower can still be seen at the site today. The lands of Loígis Réta lay not far to the north, and members of the dominant dynasty of the kingdom were associated with the monastery. The *Annals of the Four Masters* record the death of a Finguine[35] in 938 [AFM 936] who is described as 'secnap', or vice-abbot of Timahoe. The *secnap* was an important official often with control over monastic lands and revenue. This *secnap* was the son of a Fubthad and a member of Clann Duinechda. This lineage claimed descent from Duinechad a son of Berach na Bennachtan. Here, again is the pattern of a less politically successful lineage finding a niche in a wealthy church. And this particular wealthy monastic church remained firmly within the hands of the Loígse throughout the early medieval period.

Mo Chua the founder saint

Timahoe is named after its founder, Mo Chua. He seems to have flourished in the first half of the seventh century,[36] a century of rapid monastic expansion which saw the consolidation of the church's position within Irish society. His Life, as we have it, is a Latin *Vita* that is contained in one of the great medieval collections of saints' lives[37] It bears the hallmarks of being a late compilation of previously existing anecdotes, that circulated in both Irish and Latin. The *Vita* has no coherent structure, containing no account of the saint's early life and only a very cursory notice of his death. Rather, it recounts a series of incidents which bring Mo Chua into contact with important saints. These are Colmán Elo of Lann Elo (Lynally in Offaly), Munnu of Tech Munnu (Taghmon in Wexford), and Cianán of Dam Liacc (Duleek in Meath). While both Colmán Elo and Munnu are saints of the seventh century, Cianán belongs to the sixth. Nevertheless, the political implications, rather than the chronological accuracy, of saintly encounters is what interested the hagiographer. As such the Lives of the saints are important documents for exploring the politics of early Ireland. They are the propaganda sheets of their day. The Life of Mo Chua was certainly put together at a late stage, perhaps in the twelfth century when the jockeying of church reformers and the demarcation of diocesan boundaries were revolutionising the ecclesiastical system. Now, more than ever, the proof of a saint's power, and by extension his foundation, was important.

Mo Chua was not of the Loígse by birth. Like many Irish saints his foundation was within the territory of a different people. His genealogy makes him the son of a Lonn of the Luigne, a Connacht people (VM §1).[38] He is described as being an ex-layman, or *athláech* (VM §1), an unusual hagiographical detail, for most Irish saints are imagined as being in religious life from a very young age. This detail is also found in the Middle-Irish *scholia* that accompany manuscripts of the great martyrology of Irish saints, *Féilire Óengusso*.[39] The *Vita* elaborates the simple statement of the *scholia*, describing how Mo Chua was once a soldier of the world, but was inspired to become a soldier of Christ. Clearly, the example of Martin of Tours, recorded by Sulpicius Severus in his famous and influential fourth-century *Vita Martini* is the prime model.[40]

> *Hic in premeua etate uir erat multum bellicosus, ac de hostibus suis semper uictoriam habens. Triginta annis sic laycaliter uixit, antequam militiam Christi exerceret. Set expletis triginta illis annis, diuina inspiratione admonitus, et diuini timoris telo percussus, ad fidem Christi conuersus, et monachus factus, clericalem assumpsit habitum (VM §1)*

> In his youth he was a very warlike man and he always gained victory over his enemies. Thus, he lived as a layman for thirty years, before he drilled in the army of Christ. But, having completed thirty years, he was admonished by divine inspiration and, having been struck by the sword of heavenly fear, he was converted to the faith of Christ. He became a monk and assumed the clerical habit.

The Life tells how Mo Chua burns the estate he inherits from his uncle and, thus stripped of worldly possessions, founds Timahoe. Although this incident is more fully fleshed out than in the *Féilire* there is no mention of how Mo Chua was granted Loígse land for his monastery, although later in the Life it is his success in Loígis, which persuades Mo Chua to once again renounce the world and travel to Airgialla. There he founds the smaller church of Dairinis, where he eventually dies.

The Airgialla church, which is given some prominence (VM §§11-12), at first strikes an odd note. However, it is probably a political detail. The *Vita* describes how Mo Chua, who is credited with an unlikely number of Scottish and Irish foundations, decides to go 'ad sanctum Patritium',[41] to Saint Patrick (VM §11). Patrick lived two centuries before Mo Chua. It is likely that the life actually signifies that he decided to go to St Patrick's foundation of Armagh, which was in the kingdom of Airgialla. Nevertheless, it is interesting to note that in the twelfth-century *Acallam na Seanórach*, Mo Chua appears as a member of Patrick's retinue, so there was some confusion over chronology.[42] Thus, Mo Chua, whatever the explanation, and by extension Timahoe, is identified with Armagh interests. Yet, the Loígse were within the sphere of the Uí Dúnlainge who were linked with the church of Kildare rather than with Armagh. And indeed the *Annals of Ulster* record that Ceithernach, the *secnap* of Kildare died with Áed abbot of Terryglass and Clonenagh at Dunamase in Loígis Réta in 845, when the fortress was attacked by the Vikings. It was only later that the Loígse came under the influence of the Uí Chennselaig, as their incorporation into the diocese of Leighlin suggests. Mo Chua's visit to Patrick reflects this later situation in the eleventh and twelfth centuries. It might also echo Patrick's relationship with Sletty and its supposed founder, Fiacc. Sletty was in the territory of the neighbouring Uí Bairrche, and the grant of Sletty, by its Bishop Áed, to Armagh is recorded by the seventh-century *Additamenta* in the *Book of Armagh*.[43] Indeed, Tírechán's *Vita* of Patrick was commissioned by Bishop Áed.[44] The anecdote in Mo Chua's Life does not carry this sort of legal weight, but it points up the shifting alliances of the early medieval period.

Among the alliances of medieval Ireland, those between the various powerful, and not so powerful, monasteries were particularly significant. Such links were represented in hagiographical sources by the symbolic meetings of various church founders. These meetings, for good or ill, represented the attitude of monasteries towards their fellows. The *Vita* of Mo Chua gives the saint a privileged relationship with Colmán Elo, Munnu, and Cianán. Colmán Elo's church of Lynally was in the territory of the Uí Fhailge. The latter was an important dynasty of the Laigin, who had suffered through their border warfare with the southern Uí Néill.[45] Their lands formed the northern boundary of Loígis, and it is not surprising that Timahoe valued a good relationship with Lynally. The Life describes how Colmán Elo is struck with the loss of his learning by God as a punishment for his excessive pride (VM §2). This occurs at Killeshin (Glenn Uissen) in Sliab Mairge. An angel visits Colmán and advises him to seek his cure from Mo Chua. Colmán journeys to his fellow saint, and the dialogue which follows between the two is a classic example of the contrast drawn between the learned, and the simple, truly wise, man of God (VM §3). Mo Chua dresses in working clothes, is humble, and can understand the speech of birds, a common motif. Colmán's previous knowledge is contrasted with Mo Chua's access to divine inspiration, symbolised by the bird, and in this context it might be noted that the bird was an exceptionally common emblem for the Holy Spirit. Colmán is cured of his worldly spirit, his *spiritus immundus*, by Mo Chua, and later witnesses Mo Chua's control over nature. For, Mo Chua calls a fire-stone from heaven to warm water (VM §4). The didactic point is clear, and it cleverly plays on an aspect of Colmán's persona. This is attested in the ninth-century *Féilire Óengusso*, on which the Life might be drawing:

Colmán ó Laind Elo
la hógi alt légend,
conid hé, án núallan,
Iohain már macc nÉrenn.[46]

Colmán from Lann Elo, with perfection of high studies, so that he is, a splendid cry, the great John of Ireland's sons.

The most praiseworthy aspect of Colmán Elo is turned on its head in the anecdote from Mo Chua's *Vita*. While the anecdote shows the saints as friends it also suggests that Timahoe, although not as powerful as Lynally, is a worthy and important ally.

The episode describing the meeting of Munnu and Mo Chua (VM §5), again, glorifies the latter, but the politics involved are rather different. We are fortunate in that the incident in this *Vita* is preserved in an earlier, perhaps eighth or ninth-century, form in the recensions of the Life of Mo Lua of Clonfertmulloe[47] and in the recensions of Munnu's *Vita* (see appendix).[48] The incident is not particularly well integrated in any of the *Vitae*, and bears all the signs of an independently existing tale, that was incorporated, at some early stage, into the Lives of Munnu and Mo Lua, because of its obvious relevance to these saints. In the recensions of Mo Lua's Life it forms a *post mortem* miracle, while in the Munnu *Vitae* it is an episode in the career of that saint. In these Lives, Mo Lua dies and is received with joy by the angels in heaven. They are so delighted to see him that they neglect to visit the saints of Ireland at the usual time. Munnu complains to his angel, who replies that Mo Lua's humility and his gentle treatment of his monks have earned him this honour, in contrast to Munnu's harshness. According to the Life of Mo Lua, Munnu is struck down with leprosy by God. In the *Vita* of Munnu, the latter is so overcome with remorse that he recognises the need for punishment. God aflicts him with leprosy. It is added that Munnu only washes at Easter. The version in the Life of Mo Chua is closer to that in Munnu's *Vita*, particularly in the hagiographer's emphasis that Munnu wants to be punished. However, these are not the only versions. A very similar story is preserved in the *scholia* of *Féilire Óengusso*, again suggesting the independent existence of the tale. Here Íte, an important Munster saint, adopts the role of Munnu, although she is considerably more humble, which agrees with her general character in medieval writings. Mo Lua's holiness is celebrated in an eleventh or twelfth century poem. It resides in his kindness towards living things, rather than in his gentle monastic discipline.[49]

Moreover, the *scholia* provide another clue as to a possible source for some of the elements in the account contained in Mo Chua's Life. Here, the description of Munnu as 'trén trednach', brave, abstinent' in the ninth-century text of the martyrology, is glossed to mean that the saint is a leper.[50] Additionally, it is stated that Mo Chua, healed him of this leprosy. In return, Munnu gives a symbolic gift of a house and gift of art to Mo Chua in return.[51] These details are not found in the recensions of either Munnu's or Mo Lua's Life, and indeed it is implied or stated in all recensions that Munnu remained a leper until he died. However, the *Vita* of Mo Chua agrees with the *Scholia*. It is likely that the incident in the Life draws directly on the description from some recension in the Life of Mo Lua or Munnu and combines it with the tradition, found in the *scholia*. Thus, after seven years of suffering Munnu is cured by Mo Chua (VM §6). The description of the cure is particularly colourful in the Life. Mo Chua licks the leprous sores off Munnu's body and even extracts mucus from Munnu's nose, which miraculously turns into gold.[52] Munnu's general filth might even be a reference to the infrequent washings mentioned in that saint's *Vita*. However, the main aim of this incident is to present a sympathetic account of Mo Chua's relationship with Munnu and Taghmon. Thus, Timahoe claims links with an important south-Leinster church.

Mo Chua's encounters with Cianán serve the same general purpose. The episodes concerning Cianán and Mo Chua are linked together by a similarity of style and were undoubtedly composed together as a unit. The incidents involved contain many interesting details, legal, biblical and folkloristic. The first of these anecdotes concerns the building of Duleek, an 'ecclesia lapidea' or stone church, in the Southern Uí Néill kingdom of Brega. The Irish name literally means stone church, and reflects the fact that Duleek was regarded as the stone church *par excellence*. Indeed, Mo Chua's *Vita* claims that it was the first of its kind in Ireland. The building of this exceptional church is hampered by uncertain Irish weather. Cianán goes to all the saints of Ireland to obtain good weather. It is not enough however, and only by praying to Mo Chua and fasting against him can he gain his desire (VM §8). The fasting reflects the Irish legal idea of *troscad*.[53] This involved a person of lower status fasting against someone of higher rank, to shame him into providing legal redress. Subtly, Mo Chua is presented as being of superior status through his great

sanctity. The point is emphasised when Mo Chua subsequently conse-
crates Duleek (VM §10).

The Bible, as would be expected, permeates the *Vita*. Cianán and his
followers, cross a torrent on a cloak of Mo Chua's, a cloak which has
the same properties as that of Elijah, as the hagiographer makes explicit
(VM §9). The saint is compared to Christ resurrecting Lazarus when he
brings back to life the twelve stags that he had killed in order to feed
the crowd that had turned up to see Duleek consecrated (VM §10).
Moreover, the hagiographer makes a reference to the famous passage
in Ezekiel where the Hebrew prophet sees a valley full of dry bones,
bones that take on flesh through the power of God (Ezk 37:1).

> *Et statim ossa illa arida carnem et pellem induunt, ac spiritum
> viuificum assumunt (VM §10)*

> And immediately those dry bones put on flesh and pelt, and they
> assumed the living spirit

In a folkloristic touch, these stags are immortal and according to the
hagiographer, can still be seen in Sliab Mairge. This theme of the
semper uiuentes, the ever-living, is an international motif found in both
myth and folklore. In the *Vita* it serves to confirm the miraculous
power of Mo Chua, who as a saint can overcome death, and who, by
extension, will benefit his adherents by supporting them with his
miraculous power.

Thus, the tales collected in Mo Chua's Life, glorify the saint on the
secular and supernatural planes. On a political level, he is shown as the
companion, indeed the superior, of saints who founded important
monasteries. These monasteries are clustered in the midlands, Leinster
and Osraige, thus defining the circle of competing monasteries
surrounding Timahoe. The saint's association with a church in Airgialla,
cements Timahoe's acceptance of the primacy of Armagh, as the most
powerful of all the Irish churches. The Loígse, as patrons of Timahoe,
are thus provided with a broad set of allegiances, an important thing in
the often violent world of medieval Irish politics. On the supernatural
level, the saint, as patron of his adopted people, assures their salvation
in the next life.

Monastery and dynasty

Timahoe, of course, had to function amidst the politics of early Ireland.
As such, its abbot was an important secular figure, who combined
wealth in the form of monastic estates, with some military power. For
example, the *Annals of Ulster* record a battle between members of the
communities of Clonmacnoise and Durrow in 764 in which two

hundred men of the community of Durrow were killed. While these monasteries were considerably larger than Timahoe, the difference should be seen as one in scale rather than of kind. It has been shown that monastic communities were important centres of surplus food,[54] and as such would have been targets in times of famine. Indeed, their general wealth must have been quite a temptation, one that the Vikings were not alone in succumbing to. Furthermore, monasteries were large settlements, employing craftsmen and other professionals of various types. Obviously, they would have had to provide for their own protection, sometimes on their own, more often with the support of a dominant dynasty. The *Annals of Ulster* record the defeat of the Vikings by the Uí Chennselaig and the community of Taghmon in 828, in a successful combination of church and dynasty. Success was not always guaranteed. The destruction of Dunamase in Loígis Réta (AU 845) saw the defeat of an alliance of Kildare, Clonenagh and Terryglass. Moreover, the church's right of sanctuary and inviolability was not always respected, and the Vikings who started making incursions from the end of the eighth century added more danger to an already dangerous world. Thus, the importance of the abbot, as administrator, rather than his status as a man of God, insured that such ecclesiastical figures were commemorated in the annals. A series of entries in the *Annals of the Four Masters* record the deaths of a number of people associated with Timahoe.

The first abbot of Timahoe to be recorded is Fácarta, son of Dub Do Chell (ob. 883: AFM 880 [=883]), who unfortunately cannot be further identified. Interestingly, the *Annals of the Four Masters* record what could be an almost complete list of abbots extending from the end of the eighth century through the ninth century. These are: Diarmait son of Áed Róin (ob. 921: AFM 919 [=921]), Máel Cóemgin son of Scannlán (ob. 930: AFM 928 [=930]), Finguine ua Fiachrach (ob. 971: AFM 969 [=971]), Conaing ua Fiachrach (ob. 1002: AFM 1001 [=1002]) and Fínshnechta ua Fiachrach (ob. 1008: AFM 1007 [=1008]). Of these, Diarmait son of Áed Róin is described as an *airchinnech* rather than an abbot. An *airchinnech* administered the monastic estates, but the term often simply refers to an abbot, sometimes lay. There is also a hiatus in the list between the death of Máel Cóemgin in 930 and that of Finguine in 971. This is filled by the death notices of Coscrach son of Máel Mochóirgi, bishop of Timahoe (ob. 933: AFM 931 [=933]) and Finguine the vice-abbot (ob 938: AFM 936 [=938]). Perhaps Bishop Coscrach was the dominant figure in the monastery during much of this period, something quite possible in a church which mixed the monastic and episcopal. Of the others, the most interesting are Finguine, Conaing, and Fínshnechta, all called 'ua Fiachrach'. The Fiachra involved could well be one person, and thus all three abbots could be related. At this stage 'ua' means grandson or descendant, and is not a surname element, something it became later. The abbots could thus be the grandsons of Fiachra. Early Irish society was polygynous and the evident difference in age between Finguine and the other two, represented by his much earlier death notice, would not have been very unusual. It is even arguable that they were brothers, although it is more likely they would have been first cousins. Most importantly, such family ties and the monopolisation of the abbacy by an ecclesiastical dynasty were the norm in the Irish church. It is impossible to ascertain whether the other abbots recorded in the *Annals of the Four Masters* were closely related, but it would be unsurprising if they were.

The list of abbots at this period, perhaps, reflects on the prosperity of the monastery. The recording of the death of Gormgal the 'fer léiginn', or lector of Timahoe (ob. 953: AFM 951 [=953]) may also be an indication of this. For, the presence of a lector in a monastery at least presupposes a school, scriptorium and library. Yet, the first half of the tenth century was a period of increased Viking activity.[55] But the Viking 'threat' was soon effectively over, and the Vikings settled down to become part of the Irish polity.

However, the arrival of the raiding and trading Vikings offered a chance of expansion as well as a threat to the Irish nobility. Irish kings both fought with and against the Vikings. The most extensively recorded king of the Loígse, Cennétig son of Gáethíne (ob. AU 903),[56] flourished in the latter half of the ninth century. He is first mentioned in the *Annals of the Four Masters* in connection with his destruction of Longphort Rothlaibh (Dunrally) on the Barrow in 862 (=AFM 860) with his uncle Cerball, the king of Osraige. A *longphort* was a fortress built by the Vikings to protect their ships. From a *longphort* Viking ships could raid up the Irish rivers deep into the midlands, with their wealthy monasteries. The destruction of Dunrally occurred during a period when the Irish were putting the Vikings on the defensive, and it contrasts with the Viking attack on Dunamase almost twenty years previously. Cennétig continued his successful military activities. In these he was certainly strengthened by his alliance with the now-powerful state of Osraige. His ally and in-law Cerball was a highly influential king. In 878 (AFM 875 [=878]) Cennétig plundered Uí Chennselaig territory, an act which indicates an increase in the military capabilities of the Loígse, for the Uí Chennselaig were a major power. Significantly, it is during the successful reign of Cennétig that the death of the first abbot of Timahoe is recorded. The achievements of Cennétig's reign must have boosted the revenues of Timahoe. At his death in 903 Cennétig is styled lord of Loígis and the Comainn. The Comainn is an area a little to the south of Loígis. A similar title is accorded to Coscrach, bishop of Timahoe and the Comainn. There is a territorial sense to this title, and it certainly implies that the fortunes of Timahoe and the kings of Loígis were closely linked. In 908 the Uí Néill king Flann Sínna defeated Cormac mac Cuileannáin, the bishop-king of Munster, at Belach Mugna near Leighlinbridge. The threat of a powerful Munster, to peoples such as the Loígse, receded, but not for long.

Other kings of Loígis were not so fortunate or successful as Cennétig, although he does seem to have ensured that the kingship remained in the hands of his immediate descendants. His son Augrán[57] was killed by the Vikings (AU 917), in a campaign co-ordinated by Niall Glúndub, son of Áed, the Uí Néill high-king. Niall brought his Uí Néill armies to Munster where there had been considerable Viking activity in previous years, particularly in 915. This is usually linked in with the so-called second Viking age, beginning in 914-15 when a large fleet arrived in Waterford. Niall's incursion into Munster underlines Uí Néill ambitions for dominance over Munster. At this stage, the Eóganacht kings of the province were weak and unable to cope with either the threat of the Vikings or of Irish rivals. The failure of the Eóganacht to deal with the Vikings certainly hastened their decline. They were to succumb to the far more effective Dál Cais, ancestors of the O'Briens. At any event, Niall's campaign was unsuccessful. He was opposed by Ragnall, a Viking leader who later became king of York. Although outnumbered, Niall's forces fought well, but they failed to gain a decisive victory. He sent word to his Laigin allies, for Leinster was the equivalent of a vassal state at this stage, and asked them to attack the Vikings at Cenn Fuait, near Leixlip. However, the Laigin under their Uí Dúnlainge King, Augaire son of Ailill, were routed by the Viking Sitric. The *Annals of Ulster* record the deaths of Máel Mórda king of the East Life, Máel Máedóc a bishop and Augrán son of Cennétig, king of Loígis alongside Augaire. It is significant that Augrán's death is recorded, for it places him in the upper echelon of the Leinster nobility. No doubt, his prominence reflects the gains made by Cennétig, although this prominence was never quite as high again.

The relative importance of the Loígse was probably bolstered by the power vacuum within Leinster politics in the ninth century. During his reign Áed Oirdnide (ob. AU 818), the Uí Néill king of Tara, effectively demonstrated his supremacy over Leinster. His successor Niall Caille, actually appointed the king of Leinster in 835, and in 841 he was fighting the bishop-king of Munster, Feidlimid mac Crimthainn, for supremacy. A weak Leinster was the battleground. This weakness enabled lesser kingdoms such as Loígis, to act more independently. Indeed, Leinster fortunes continued to decline under the Uí Dúnlainge.

Like the Eóganacht in Munster they proved unable to adapt to the new conditions in post-Viking Ireland. The Leinstermen, and their Viking allies suffered a serious defeat at the hands of Brian Bóruma at Clontarf in 1014. Eventually, the Uí Chennselaig, who exploited the resources of Viking Wexford, took the provincial kingship, and the petty kingdoms lost importance. This was happening throughout the country during the eleventh century and earlier, as the ideal of a national kingship approached closer to reality.

Yet, during these unsettled times, when the various provincial kings waged long campaigns throughout the country, the kingship of the Loígse remained within the line of Cennétig. This is a remarkably stable succession, in contrast to the political manoevering between rival dynastic segments that was often the case.[58] Two sons of Augrán (ob. 917) died as kings of the Loígse: Cináed (ob. 928: AFM 926 [=928]) and Cathal (ob. 933: AFM 931 [=933]).[59] A third son, Fergal, is described as lord, to be understood as king of Loígis Réta: he and his son Fáelán, described as *tánaiste* of Loígis Réta, were slain in 960.[60] The exact significance of the term *tánaiste* is still uncertain. At one time it was believed to mean heir-apparent, and it was equated with the term *rígdomna*. Interestingly, the *tánaiste* is often the member of a rival dynastic segment, but not always. However, it does seem to imply that the holder of the title is recognised of having all the qualifications of a king, and that he or his immediate relatives may hold it at some indefinable stage in the future.[61] Indeed, Fergal's other son Cennétig (ob. 1015: AFM 1014 [=1015]) was subsequently prominent. In these fairly settled dynastic conditions, Timahoe flourished. It is hardly coincidental that Finguine, the vice-abbot of Timahoe who died in 938 was a distant relative of the ruling dynasty. Church and dynasty shared mutual interests.

During the second half of the eleventh century the Irish dynasties, as we know them from the later Middle Ages, became settled. From this period, surnames were adopted and they represent the narrowing of dynastic succession down to a specific family, something which was already happening among peoples such as the Loígse. The Uí Mhórdha, or O'Mores, descendants of the old kings, ruled in Loígis. They were descended from Mórda, the grandson of Cernach, another son of Cennétig mac Gáethíne. Cernach (ob. 1018: AFM 1017 [=1018], Mórda's grandson was the first of this line to rule.[62] The O'Mores proved tenacious and were not finally subdued until the seventeenth century. However, the Ireland of the eleventh century was an increasingly violent place, for political ambitions to rule the entire country were not only theoretical, but feasible. Dynasties such as the O'Mores, were more high-ranking vassals than kings.[63] Real power was

Plate 4.1   Round Tower and Castle Timahoe from Grose, *Antiquities*, ii, p. 11.

in the hands of the over-kings. One aspect of the increasing violence is reflected in the growing number of blindings of kings, by political rivals, recorded in the annals.[64] The Irish ideology of kingship demanded physical perfection from its rulers.[65] Blinding, which is probably a euphemism for blinding and castration destroyed this ideal perfection, as well as ensuring that the unfortunate victim could not produce any more heirs. Fáelán Ua Mórdha,[66] lord of the Loígse, suffered this fate in 1041 at the hands of Murchad son of Dúnlaing and with the connivance of Domnall son of Áed, lord of the Uí Bairrche. Murchad was the last of the truly effective Uí Dúnlainge kings.[67] He was opposed by the king of Osraige and the Uí Chennselaig king, Diarmait mac Máel na mBó. Despite Murchad's vigorous actions against opponents such as Fáelán, he was defeated and killed in 1042 at the battle of Mag Mulchet in Lóigis at the hands of Cú Chocríche Ua Mórdha, Fáelán's successor, Gilla Pátraic son of Donnchad, king of Osraige, and their allies among the Eóganacht. Donnchad son of Áed, the Uí Bairrche king was another casualty of the battle. The lines of political conflict are visible here. The Osraige had just previously tasted the kingship of Leinster, and Fáelán Ua Mórdha seems to have been their supporter. However, the Uí Bairrche, neighbours of the Loígse, supported the old ruling dynasty of the Uí Dúnlainge, represented by Murchad. Fáelán and Donnchad both fell foul of these political rivalries.

The violence of these times also involved the church. Mac Raith Ua Mórdha killed Gilla Muire, a rival, at the doorway to the oratory of Timahoe, thus violating the sanctuary of the church. Both had previously sworn on the *Caimmín*, a relic or religious object associated with Mo Chua. It was probably a crozier. Such objects were important symbols of power and religious veneration. Mac Raith's subsequent death near Aghaboe was ascribed to the revenge of the saints Fintan, Mo Chua and Colmán. Religious and secular politics were inseparable.

However, the monastic order was to undergo momentous change in the twelfth century. Muirchertach Ua Briain, the king of Munster, and for much of his reign the most powerful king in the country, sponsored church reform. This reform came from within and without the church. Clerics such as Máel Muire Ua Dúnáin,[68] Cellach abbot of Armagh and Malachy, the latter's successor, were supporters of reform. Basically, this involved a switch from a mixed monastic and episcopal system to a diocesan one, which had become the norm on the Continent. Indeed, the Gregorian reforms on the Continent probably spurred on an outward looking king such as Ua Briain. Furthermore, the older system was expensive: most monastic houses had won privileges and freedoms from the secular rulers they supported. The newer orders that the reformers supported, especially Malachy who had experienced the

Cistercian way of life at Clairvaux, would not present such acute problems. Reform presented interesting possibilities for the secular patrons of monasteries. The first reform synod at Cashel in 1101 did little to change the *status quo*. The following one in 1111 in Rath Breasail was revolutionary.[69] Old monastic churches such as Timahoe were suddenly shorn of power and influence. The clerical aristocrats, representatives of the older monastic dynasties, carried on as bishops. However, the old bases for the distinctive Irish monastic culture were destroyed, and learning tended to move outwards into lay society. Continental monastic orders, such as the Cistercians, flourished in the place of the old Irish monasteries, many of which they took over. The Friars are supposed to have lived in Timahoe until the mid-seventeenth century.[70] It is significant that there are no more references to abbots of Timahoe in the twelfth century. The great new monastic foundation was nearby Abbeyleix, and patronage flowed in its direction.

On the eve of the Norman invasion, the contest for the kingship of Ireland became even more intense. The death of Ua Briain and subsequent Munster weakness raised the stakes for rival claimants. This was the period of the kings of Ireland *co fressabra* 'with opposition'. The term described a king who had subdued most of the country, but for some important recalcitrants. Tairdelbach Ua Conchobuir, king of Connacht and king of Ireland 'with opposition', spent most of his reign on campaign. He was a very successful campaigner. During 1142 he marched through Osraige and Loígis, burning Timahoe. The lords of Loígis were no more than pawns in these wars between the great kings. In 1157 the army of Muirchertach Mac Lochlainn, king of the Northern Uí Néill and sometime ally of Diarmait Mac Murchadha, king of Leinster, caused such devastation in Loígis, Osraige and Uí Fhailge that a great number of refugees fled into Connacht. This marked one of the high points of his career. However, the next year Ruaidrí Ua Conchobuir, the son of Tairdelbach, flexed his muscles. In a demonstration of his power and his, soon to be realised, aspirations to the high-kingship, he took the hostages of Meath and north-west Leinster, including those of Mac Raith Ua Mórdha, the lord of Loígis. Eventually, Ruaidrí's success would drive Diarmait Mac Murchadha overseas in exile to Henry II. With the coming of the Normans, the political change in Ireland was irrecoverable. Timahoe sank into obscurity, as did many once prosperous monasteries, and the kings of Loígis became the O'Mores of the later Middle Ages.

Conclusion

The history of Timahoe in the early medieval period is in many ways typical of that of other monasteries. Its role was one of considerable power in the kingdom of the Loígse, and its fate was intertwined with that of its patrons. A series of powerful kings in the first half of the tenth century is mirrored by the prominence of the abbots of Timahoe in the annalistic record. Furthermore, the monastic system of Ireland was dominated by aristocrats and lay abbots. Monasteries were places of wealth and resources. Churches co-operated with the secular elite in return for various rights such as exemption from tax. In some ways, a place like Timahoe, even more so than the royal fortress of Dunamase, could claim to be a 'capital' of Loígis. The twin tragedy, from the pre-reform monastic point of view, was the reform of the church, which emasculated many of the monasteries, and the coming of the Normans. The Norman invasion helped bring an end to the delicately articulated relationship between churches and their secular patrons. Timahoe was sidelined by the new trends. Urbanisation passed it by. Thus, the medieval monastic town is now a modern village.

Appendix

This incident clearly comes from a single common source. I have used the recensions of Mo Lua's and Munnu's *Vitae* from the *Codex Salmenticensis*, because this codex tends to be the most conservative. I have italicised the sections of the text common to both and, furthermore, underlined complete verbal agreement. In general the differences are trivial. The most important is that Munnu, in his Life, more actively takes part in his punishment.

From: Heist (ed.), 'Vita Prior S. Lugidi seu Moluae' in *Sal Vitae*, pp 131-45.

§69. Ostensum est autem sancto Fintano, filio Tulchani, quod per .vii. dies post exitum Lugidi ingens letitia et epulatio in celo fuit, et pene inferni cessauerunt, et tenebre fugate sunt a facie terre, et omnis homo qui dolorem habuit in terra sanus fuit hiis .vii. diebus propter honorem Lugidi. Angelus *quoque qui* ad sanctum Fintanum semper ueniebat duobus diebus in ebdomade, *in* die dominico et *in* quinta *feria*, non *uenit* ad eum *in hiis .vii. diebus usque ad diem dominicum. Et interrogauit eum* Fintanus: '*Quare* ad me non uenisti *in quinta feria'?* Angelus respondit: 'in hiis *.vii.* diebus non uenerunt angeli ad *uisitandos* sanctos Hybernie. Hospes *mirabilis ad* celum *migrauit,* silicet Lugidus Cluana Ferta'. Fintanus *dixit: 'Nunc* apparet quod *Lugidus* solus *plus pre omnibus* mandata Dei impleuit. Vade ad *Dominum,* ut sciam pro *qua causa* carius *est* in aduentu Lugidi gaudere quam ad me uenire'. *Exiuit ergo angelus et statim* uenit ad eum, dicens: 'Quia facies hominis ante Lugidum non erubuit, et cum lenitate monachos suos corripuit; tu uero cum *asperitate* corripis monachos tuos. Verumptamen letus esto'. *Quia in quinta feria sanctus* Fintanus percussus est lepra *a capite usque ad pedes, usque ad diem mortis sue.*

From Heist (ed.), 'Vita prior S. Fintani seu Munnu' in *Sal Vitae*, pp 198-209.

§28. Angelus *Domini* ad sanctum Fintanum *salutandum* duobus in ebdomade diebus semper ueniebat, *silicet* die dominico et quinta. *Accidit autem ut quadam quinta feria* ad eum *angelus* non *ueniret, usquequo peruenit in die dominico.* Cui Fintanus *ait:* 'Dic michi meam culpam, *pro qua* ad me *die solito* non uenisti'. Angelus respondit: 'Non per necgligentiam circa te ego non ueni, *sed* in hiis diebus hospes *karrisimus intrauit in* celum, in cuius aduentu omnes *angeli* nimia exultatione et gaudio occupati *in hac ebdomoda* ad *salutandos* sanctos Hybernie non uenerunt, silicet Lugid *mac Coche* Clona Ferta'. *Cui* Fintanus *ait:* '*Lucide* apparet quod *ipse* solus mandata Dei *ueraciter* impleuit. Vade *ergo et* ad *me iterum cum responso reuertere,* ut sciam pro *qua re* carius *erat* in aduentu Lugidi *magis* gaudere quam ad me *salutandum* uenire'. Venit *ergo* ad eum angelus dicens: 'Quia facies *alicuius* hominis ante Lugidum non erubuit, et non pauciores erunt monachi ipsius in celo quam tui monachi. Tu uero monachos tuos cum *rubore* corripis'. Tunc Fintanus dixit, 'Scio quid faciem.... [part of text omitted, but it is clear from the other recensions that at this point Munnu suggests going alone on pilgrimage, but the angel objects] 'In exilium non ibis; *sed in quinte ferie* appropinquet nuncius a Deo ad te ueniet, ut non maius gaudium in celo in aduentu Lugidi quam in aduentu tuo fiat in die exitus tui'. *In nocte ergo illa,* Fintanus percussus est lepra *magni doloris, et mansit super eum .xxiiii. annis.* Et in illo tempore, ut periti, ferunt, sanctus Fintanus nec corpus suum manibus suis radebat nec balneo lauit, nisi in uno die tantum, silicet in Cena Domini.

The next text from the *scholia* of *Féilire Óengusso,* in Irish, represents another strand of the tradition. Íte takes the place of Munnu and other details are different: Íte is visited by the angel every day, and she complains to him when he visits her after a three day absense:

From Stokes (ed.), *Martyrology,* p. 182.

Is é dono in Mo Lua sin éna ro mharb n riam ⁊ nach n-anmanna eile, ⁊ ica chainidh adchonnaid Maelanfaidh in n-en occai, ⁊ is fair dorat Mthiden aingel M'Íti in test, Dia raibe M'Íte ic athcosan dó ara dermat tri trath cen biadh di; ar di nim doberthea a cuit di cecha nona, co nderbairt in t-aingel .i.

Fir nime, fir thalman,
tren rudhrach,
andar-leo ba la bratha
bás Lughdhach.

Nocho rainic, nocho ricfa,
nocho ria
nech naeb aile bad aidhbliu catu
la Dia. F

The following is taken from the Life of Mo Chua. As can be seen, this extract draws on the incident preserved in the *Vitae* of Munnu and Mo Lua. However, here the anecdote is changed to fit in with one of the major themes of the *Vita* - humility. Furthermore, these changes draw on the type of incident in the *scholia*. Like Íte, Munnu is visited every day by an angel. Also, resembling her, he complains to his angel after three days. However, the anecdote functions as an introduction to Mo Chua's miracle. Even so, it is closer to the version in Munnu's Life, although here Munnu is even more active, actually choosing to be afflicted with leprosy. I have italicised the sections which are closest to the *scholia* and used bold print to highlight those resembling the account in Munnu's Life. The incident in Mo Chua's Life is a clever reworking of these themes.

From Plummer (ed.), 'Vita Sancti Mochua abbatis de Tech Mochua' in *Vitae SS Hib.*, pp. 184-89.

§v. **Quodam alio tempore vir sanctus, Munnus nomine,** dum in cella sua *triduo moram faceret,* **angelica uisione,** *qua cotidie uisitabatur, per idem tempus frutrabatur.* Cumque **angelus Domini** *post triduum* **se uiro Dei presentaret, et ab eo, cur tantam moram faceret, sciscitaretur, respondit: 'Sancti', inquit, 'celicole communem conuentum atque consilium habuerunt, expectantes animam cuiusdam uiri sancti, nomine Molua,** qui uiam uniuerse carnis ingressus est. **Et hec causa retardationis mee fuit, ne ad te tempore solito uenirem'. Ad quem sanctus Munnu dixit: 'In quibus', inquit, 'meritis uir ille precellebat uitam mean, dum sic sim neglectus, et illius memor es'? Cui angelus respondit: 'Faciebat', inquit, 'dum uixit, quod tu non facis. Quia,**

quandiu uitam duxit in terris, nulli presenti maledixit, nec absenti unquam detraxit. Insuper et dispositionem omnis temporis secundum diuinam uoluntatem, siue in serenitate siue in tempestate, equanimiter sustiniuit et commendauit. Tu quoque superbus es, et Dominus tuus uult ut humilieris'. Cui sanctus Munnu respondit: **'Hoc libenter sufferam, si, quod ipse eligero, a Deo meo mihi concedatur'**. Cui angelus: 'Quod petis a Deo, tibi concessum est'. Tunc ait Munnu: 'Lepram mihi inter infirmitates corporales eligo'. **Per uerbum ergo angeli sanctus Munnu leprosus factus est**; et lepram illam usque ad septem annos sustinuit.

References

1. Standish Hayes O'Grady, 'The last kings of Ireland' in *E.H.R.*, 4 (1889), pp 286-303; Francis John Byrne, 'The trembling sod: Ireland in 1169' in N.H.I., ii, pp 1-42; idem, *The rise of the Uí Néill and the high-kingship of Ireland*, O'Donnell Lecture (Dublin, 1970), pp 3-27; D. Ó Corráin, *Ireland since the Normans* (Dublin, 1972), pp 131-74.

2. M. A. O'Brien (ed.), *Corpus genealogiarum Hiberniae* (Dublin, 1962), i, pp 25-6, p. 79.

3. Ibid., pp 25-6.

4. D. A. Binchy, 'Secular institutions' in Myles Dillon (ed.), *Early Irish society* (Dublin, 1954), p. 54, famously described Irish society as 'tribal, rural, hierarchical and familiar'; for much the same idea see idem, *Celtic and Anglo-Saxon kingship*, O'Donnell Lecture 1968 (Oxford, 1970).

5. O'Brien, *Corpus Geneal. Hib.*, pp 25-6.

6. R. A. S. Macalister (ed.), *Lebor Gabála Érenn: the book of the taking of Ireland* (Dublin, 1938), i; for discussion, R. M. Snowcroft 'Lebor Gabála, part I: the growth of the text' in *Ériu*, 38 (1987), pp 81-142; idem, 'Lebor Gabála, part II: the growth of the tradition' in *Ériu*, 39 (1988), pp 1-66.

7. For example in the poem 'Can a mbunadas na nGaedel'? by Máel Muire of Othain, in R. I. Best, M. A. O'Brien (ed.), *The Book of Leinster* (Dublin, 1957), iii, pp 516-23; James Carney would see the tradition as dating back to *c.* 630 and originating with Senchán Torpéist, 'Three Old Irish accentual poems' in *Ériu*, 22 (1971), pp 65-73.

8. O'Brien, *Corpus Geneal. Hib.*, pp 87, 280.

9. Ibid., pp 87, 94.

10. Ibid., p. 87.

11. Kuno Meyer (ed.), 'The cherishing of Conall Cernach and the death of Ailill and Conall Cernach' in *ZCP*, 1 (1897) pp 102-11.

12. O'Brien, *Corpus Geneal Hib.*, 87.

13. Ibid., p. 155, p. 256, although here Dáire is linked into the all Ireland scheme of genealogy, being made a descendant of Íth son of Bregon, or Íth son of Míl Espáne.

14. Byrne, *Irish kings and high kings*, pp 180-81.

15. Whitley Stokes (ed.), 'Cóir Anmann' in W. Stokes and E. Windisch (ed.), *Irische Texte*, 3 (1897), pp 316-23.

16. O'Brien, *Corpus Geneal. Hib.*, p. 94.

17. Ibid., pp 94-5.
18. R. A. Breatnach, 'The Lady and the King: a theme of Irish literature' in *Studies*, 42 (1953), pp 321-36; Proinsias MacCana, 'Aspects of the theme of king and goddess in Irish literature' in *Études Celt.*, 7 (1955-7), pp 76-104; 8 (1958), pp 59-65; Muireann Ní Bhrolcháin, 'Women in early myths and sagas' in *Crane Bag*, 14 (1980), pp 12-19; Donnchadh Ó Corráin, 'Historical need and literary narrative' in Evans et al (ed.), *Proceedings of the seventh international congress of Celtic studies* (Oxford, 1986), pp 141-58; Kim McCone, *Pagan past and christian present in early Irish literature* (Maynooth 1990), pp 107-37, esp. p. 131; Elva Johnston, 'Transforming women in Irish hagiography' in *Peritia*, 9 (1995), pp 197-220.
19. O'Brien, *Corpus Geneal. Hib.*, pp 88, 91-2.
20. A.I.
21. Erich Poppe, 'A Middle Irish poem on Émíne's bell' in *Celtica*, 17 (1985), pp 59-72 mentions Síl Mescill among other Leinster dynasties.
22. Donnchadh Ó Corráin, 'Nationality and kingship in pre-Norman Ireland' in T. W. Moody (ed.), *Nationality and the pursuit of national independence* (Belfast, 1978), pp 1-35.
23. D. R. Howlett (ed.), *The book of letters of Saint Patrick the bishop* (Dublin, 1994), p. 80.
24. Kathleen Hughes, *The church in early Irish society* (London, 1966); Donnchadh Ó Corráin, 'The early Irish church: some aspects of organisation' in Ó Corráin (ed.), *Irish antiquity* (Cork, 1981), pp 327-41; Richard Sharpe, 'Some problems concerning the organization of the church in early medieval Ireland' in *Peritia*, 3 (1984), pp 230-70; idem, 'Churches and communities in early medieval Ireland: towards a pastoral model' in John Blair and Richard Sharpe (ed.), *Pastoral care before the parish* (Leicester, 1992), pp 81-109; Thomas Charles-Edwards, 'The pastoral role of the church in early Irish laws' in *Pastoral care*, pp 63-80; Colmán Etchingham, 'The early Irish church some observations on pastoral care and dues' in *Ériu*, 42 (1991), pp 99-118; idem, 'The implications of *paruchia*' in *Ériu*, 44 (1993), pp 139-6.
25. Charles Doherty, 'The monastic town in early medieval Ireland' in H. B. Clarke and A. Simms (ed.), *The comparative history of urban origins in non-Roman Europe: Ireland, Wales, Denmark, Germany, Poland and Russia from the ninth to the thirteenth century*, BAR Int Ser 255 (Oxford, 1985), p. 55f.
26. Felim Ó Briain, 'The hagiography of Leinster' in John Ryan (ed.), *Féilsgríbhinn Eoin Mhic Néill* (Dublin, 1940), pp 454-5.
27. R. I. Best, Osborn Bergin, M. A. O'Brien, Anne O'Sullivan (ed.), *Book of Leinster* (6 vols, Dublin, 1954-83).
28. For instance, Gearóid Mac Niocaill, Seán Mac Airt (ed.), *The Annals of Ulster (to A.D. 1131)* (Dublin, 1983), [henceforth AU]; John O'Donovan (ed.), *Annála Ríoghachta Éireann: annals of the Kingdom of Ireland from the earliest times to 1616* [henceforth AFM; further dates from AFM will be adjusted in the usual manner, the original date will be placed in brackets]; AU 845 for Áed son of Dub d Crích 'abbas Tire da Glass Cluana Eidhnigh'; AFM 903 (897) and AU 903 for Máel Ciaráin.
29. Charles Plummer (ed.), *Vitae Sanctorum Hiberniae*, (2 vols, Oxford, 1910), ii, pp 96-106; W. W. Heist (ed.), *Vitae sanctorum Hiberniae ex codice olim Salmanticensi nunc Bruxellensi* (Brussels, 1965), pp 145-53.
30. Whitley Stokes (ed.), *The Martyrology of Óengus the Culdee* (London, 1905), pp 6-7.

31.   O'Brien, *Corpus Geneal. Hib.*, p. 93.

32.   Ó Corráin, 'Nationality and kingship', pp 1-35.

33.   Plummer, *Vitae SS Hib.*, ii, pp 206-25; Heist, *Sal. Vitae*, pp 132-54; pp 382-8; for a study of the collections as units and for an argument that the Life of Mo Lua dates from *c.* 750-850, Richard Sharpe, *Medieval Irish saints Lives: an introduction to the Vitae Sanctorum Hiberniae* (Oxford, 1991), esp. pp 334-37.

34.   O'Brien, *Corpus Geneal. Hib.*, pp 92, 434.

35.   AFM, perhaps significantly gives his descent for six generations: son of Fubthad, son of Donnacán, son of Fogartach, son of Duinnechaid, son of Berach, son of Mescell. Compare with O'Brien, *Corpus Geneal. Hib.*, pp 92-3.

36.   William Hennessy (ed.), *Chronicon Scotorum: A chronicle of Irish affairs from the earliest times to AD 1135, with a supplement containing events from 1141-1156* (London, 1866). The death of Mo Chua is recorded for 654, but other events under that date occur in AU 658.

37.   Plummer, *Vitae SS Hib.*, ii, pp 184-9 [henceforth VM].

38.   The Luigne also lived in the Uí Néill kingdom of Mide, and Stokes, *Martyrology*, p. 226 has him descend from Lonán of Mide; there is a metrical pedigree in the twelfth-century *Acallam*, Whitley Stokes (ed.), 'Acallam na Seanórach' in W. H. Stokes, E. R. Windisch (ed.), *Irische Texte*, 4 (Leipzig, 1900), p. 67.

39.   Stokes, *Martyrology*, p. 112 describes 'tri athlaich Erenn .i. Becán mac Cula Mo Cua mac Lonain Enna Airne', the three ex-laymen of Ireland, that is Becán mac Cula, and Mo Chua mac Lonáin and Énna of Aran; he is also an 'athláech' in *Acallam*, idem, 'Acallam', p. 67.

40.   For a study of this Life, Clare Stancliffe, *St Martin and his hagiographer: history and miracle in Sulpicius Severus* (Oxford, 1983).

41.   The form Patritius should obviously be emended to Patricius.

42.   Stokes, 'Acallam', p. 67.

43.   Ludwig Bieler (ed.), *The Patrician texts in the Book of Armagh*, Scriptores Latini Hiberniae, 10 (Dublin, 1979), p. 178; Francis John Byrne, 'A note on Trim and Sletty' in *Peritia*, 3 (1984), pp 316-19.

44.   Bieler, ibid., p. 66 (preface).

45.   Byrne, *Irish kings*, pp 138-42, 153-4.

46.   Stokes, *Martyrology*, p. 196.

47.   Plummer, *Vitae SS Hib.*, ii, pp 206-25: §53; Heist, *Sal. Vitae* pp 131-45: §69; ibid., pp 282-8: §40 (a very abbreviated account).

48.   Plummer, ibid. pp 226-38: §25; Heist, Ibid. pp 198-209: §28; ibid., pp 247-56 §24; Sharpe, *Medieval Irish Saints' Lives*, p. 329, pp 334-37, considers the longer Lives of Munnu, as well as Lua and Munnu to have have been part of a postulated collection, put together *c.* 750-850.

49.   Stokes, *Martyrology*, p. 182.

50.   Ibid., pp 217, 226.

51.   Ibid., p. 226.

52.   There is a similar detail in the Life of Féchín, Whitley Stokes (ed.), 'Life of S. Féchín of Fore' in *Revue Celt.*, 12 (1891), §38.

53.   D. A. Binchy, 'A pre-christian survival in medieval Irish hagiography' in D. Whitelock et al (ed.), *Ireland in early medieval Europe* (Cambridge, 1982), pp 165-78.

54.   A. T. Lucas, 'The plundering and burning of churches in Ireland, 7th to 16th century' in Etienne Rynne (ed.), *North Munster studies* (Limerick, 1967), pp 172-229; also Ó Corráin, *Ireland before the Normans*, pp 82-9.

55.   Ó Corráin, *Ireland before the Normans*, pp 101-02.

56. O'Brien, *Corpus Geneal. Hib.*, pp 91, 434.

57. Ibid.

58. Donnchadh Ó Corráin, 'Irish regnal succession: a reappraisal' in *Studia Hibernica*, 11 (1971), pp 7-39, for a study of the Uí Chennselaig succession.

59. The AFM forms *Oghráin* and *Odhreain* are later variants of *Augráin*.

60. AFM 958 [=960]; O'Brien, *Corpus Geneal. Hib.*, p. 91.

61. Eoin Mac Neill, *Celtic Ireland* (Dublin, 1921), pp 114-43 gives the classic argument for an orderly royal succession; James Hogan, 'The Irish law of kingship, with special reference to Ailech and Cenél Eoghain' in *RIA Proc* (C), 11 (1932), pp 186-254 has the most extreme exposition of this thesis; D. A. Binchy, 'Some Celtic legal terms' in *Celtica*, 3 (1956), pp 221-8; idem, *Celtic and Anglo-Saxon Kingship*, pp 26-30; Gearóid Mac Niocaill, 'The heir-designate in early medieval Ireland' in *Irish Jurist*, 3 (1968), pp 326-9; a revisionist view put forward by Ó Corráin, 'Regnal succession' pp 7-39.

62. O'Brien, *Corpus Geneal. Hib.*, p. 434: Cernach m. Ceinnéidig m. Mórda m. Cinnaotha m. Cernaig m. Cinnéidig.

63. In 1091 Cináed Ua Mórdha lord of Loígis and Máel Ruanaid of Éle killed each other at Ua Briain's house in Cashel. Clearly, they were there as vassals attending on a superior king.

64. The eleventh-century records the blinding of Donnchad úa Céili (AU 1009); Braen son of Máel Mórda (AU 1018); Flaithbertach úa hEochada (AU 1020); Tadc son of Gilla Pátraic (AU 1027); Donnchad son of Dúnlang (AU 1036); Ruaidrí son of Tadc (AU 1036); Flann úa Máel Sechnaill (AU 1037); Niall úa Céilecáin and Tréinfher (AU 1044); Amalgaid son of Cathal (AU 1051); Ruaidrí úa Conchobuir (AU 1092); Aed úa Canannán (AU 1093); Flaithbertach úa hAiteidh (AU 1094).

65. For a legal reflex, Thomas Charles-Edwards, Fergus Kelly (ed.), *Bechbretha* (Dublin, 1983). Congal Cáech is put out of the kingship of Tara after being blinded by a bee, §31-33; a literary example in Elizabeth A. Gray (ed.), *Cath Maige Tuired, the second battle of Mag Tuired,* (Dublin, 1982), §14.

66. O'Brien, *Corpus Geneal. Hib.*, p. 434: Fáelán m. Aimergin. m. Cinaotha m. Cernaig.

67. In 1127 a Domnall Mac Fáelán of the Uí Dúnlainge was made king of Leinster by the ambitious Tairdelbach Ua Conchobuir, but he only ruled for a short period.

68. Donnchadh Ó Corráin, 'Mael Muire Ua Dúnáin (1040-1117), reformer' in Pádraig de Brún et al (ed.), *Folia Gadelica* (Cork, 1983), pp 47-53

69. For a general study of the period, Aubrey Gwynn, *The twelfth-century reform* (Dublin, 1968).

70. Rev. M. O'Flanagan (ed.), Letters containing information relative to the antiquities of the Queen's County collected during the progress of the Ordnance Survey in 1831, i (Bray, 1933), comments by John O'Donovan, p. 91.

Chapter 5

HIBERNO-ROMANESQUE AND THE SCULPTURE OF KILLESHIN

ROGER STALLEY

Introduction

In his book on Irish churches the late Harold Leask remarked that no doorway of the Romanesque period 'is more attractive in design or epitomises so well the native features of the style than that of the ruined church of Killeshin'.[1] Hidden away in the hills above Carlow, the well preserved portal is one of the delights of Hiberno-Romanesque art (plate 5.1). From a distance the portal looks plain, the sculpture barely visible, but as one gets closer the intensity and delicacy of the carving becomes apparent. Like a page from one of the great Insular gospel books, careful scrutiny is needed to appreciate the full extent of the decoration. Although the basic structure of the doorway follows European conventions, there is no mistaking the Irish flavour of the ornamental carving. In this respect Killeshin illustrates one of the fundamental tenets of Romanesque art, a style which, though universal in Europe, was coloured by strong regional accents.

The doorway has been described on several occasions, most notably by Leask himself, but the significance of the sculpture in the context of Irish art has never been considered in any detail.[2] The fact that the portal embodies many of the typical characteristics of Hiberno-Romanesque means that its design is fundamental to arguments about the development of the style as a whole. Leask's accounts were largely descriptive and interpretations of Romanesque art have changed considerably in the forty years since he wrote. Moreover, our understanding of the historical and political contexts of the carvings have been clarified by recent research into the history of the monastery.

There are a number of important questions that need to be answered. Why was so ornate a portal constructed at a monastery which apparently lacked the prestige of more familiar sites like Clonmacnoise or Glendalough? Was the doorway part of a completely new church or was it added to an existing building? Who was responsible for the project and what does the (fragmentary) inscription

Plate 5.1   The portal at Killeshin: general view.

tell us about the status of Killeshin in the twelfth century? What was the significance of the steeply pointed gable and what was the meaning and background of the human heads which occupy such a prominent position? How does the sculpture relate to other Romanesque works in Leinster? Was the sculptor a local man and why was the carving so lightly engraved on the stone?

The history of Killeshin

It is best to begin with the status of the monastery. Generally described in the documents as Glenn Uissen, it was founded by Diarmait mac Siabairr, who is listed in early genealogies as one of the saints of the local Uí Barraiche family.[3] It is not difficult to understand why Diarmait settled at this particular site. Flowing down from the Slieve Margy hills the nearby river has cut a small gorge at Killeshin, which, a few yards from the church, opens out into a circular basin with a wide pool of water. This must always have been a mysterious, revered location. The monastery itself only comes into prominence in the tenth century, when one of its abbots, Máelmáedóc, was described as a 'distinguished scribe, anchorite, and a man of learning in Latin and Irish'.[4] His son Flann, who died in 979, was a poet of some distinction.[5] During the eleventh century the monastery was caught up in local dynastic quarrels: in 1024 a group of 'Munstermen' was killed at Killeshin by the king of Uí Barraiche and in 1041 the monastery was attacked by Diarmait mac Máel na mBó, the Uí Chennselaig pretender to the kingship of Leinster. The annals of Tigernach record: 'Killeshin was plundered by the son of Máel na mBó and its oratory was destroyed and a hundred persons were killed and seven hundred were captured'.[6] A century later, as Edel Bhreathnach has argued, the monastery may again have been embroiled in local dynastic struggles. In the year 1141 Diarmait MacMurrough killed or blinded seventeen of the nobles of Leinster, including three of the Uí Barraiche, and it is likely that he subsequently exerted direct rule over their territory, which included Killeshin. The battles and massacres of 1024 and 1041 serve to underline the extent to which the monastery was a political as well as a religious focus in the area. This is borne out by the fact that at least some of the genealogies and king lists contained in the manuscript usually known as Rawlinson B502 appear to have been compiled at Killeshin.[7] While Killeshin may not have achieved much prominence at a national level, there is no doubt that in the political context of Leinster its importance extended far beyond the religious sphere. The construction of a flamboyant portal in the twelfth century is not therefore altogether surprising. Indeed the exuberance of the sculpture suggests a community which retained a degree of wealth and vibrancy.[8] As will become evident below, the sculptors were familiar with both metalwork and manuscript illumination, a familiarity which may have been based on a study of venerated objects within the monastery itself.[9] With its tradition of learning and scholarship, the community no doubt had a substantial collection of books, some perhaps illuminated. The range of motifs found on the portal gives the impression of a monastery with well established artistic traditions of its own.

The architecture of the church

Although major Irish monasteries often contained several oratories within the monastic termon, at Killeshin the ruins of only one church survive.[10] This was rectangular in plan, with a length of approximately 27.07m (internal) and a width of 7.6m. Large sections of the north and south walls are missing, but the east wall, detached from the rest of the ruins, contains a small late Gothic window, comprising a pair of ogee-headed lights.[11] The original building was erected in the Romanesque era. When monastic life petered out after the Anglo-Norman settlement, it evidently remained in use serving the needs of the local parish.[12] The building was subsequently lengthened to the east in the later middle ages and like many a parish church it seems to have fallen into ruin during the seventeenth century. Around 1718 the ruins were adapted to form the local Protestant church, a status which they retained for about a hundred years.[13]

The one part of the building to survive relatively unscathed is the west wall, containing the famous doorway. Even this, however, shows signs of alteration. The southern corner has lost its anta and has been rebuilt with an added buttress. To judge from the character of the masonry, the top of the main gable was reconstructed at the same time. The tangent gable above the door has also been partly rebuilt and even the doorway itself has been altered. The head at the apex of the outer arch is curiously off centre, a misplacement suggesting that the stones have been re-arranged.[14] This is confirmed by the fact that the stepped pattern on the soffit of the outer order does not run evenly across all the joints. Moreover, the surfaces have worn in an uneven manner, as if some of the stones were lying on the ground for a period of time.[15] It looks as if the outer order has been reconstructed, possibly at the beginning of the eighteenth century, when the east end of the building was adapted as a Protestant church. It certainly happened long before 1877, as early photographs show the stones in the same positions as they are today.[16] Since 1880, when the ruins became a national monument, various repairs and works of conservation have been carried out by the Office of Public Works; these include the repair of the sub plinths, the insertion of square blocks to replace missing bases, and the replacement of the missing edge on the south side of the gable. Despite the various repairs and alterations, the sculpture at Killeshin is, in the context of Ireland, unusually well-preserved.

There is little doubt that the doorway was built at the same time as the rest of the church. Had the portal been a replacement for an earlier and much lower lintelled doorway, the courses of masonry in the west wall would have run evenly across the facade above a level of about 2.5 metres (i.e. above the level of a lintel). In fact the walls either side of the portal are coursed separately, with continuous courses beginning at a point just below the apex of the gable. This proves that the walls were erected *after* the stones of the doorway were set in place.[17]

Furthermore, in both the north and west walls of the church there are small gable-headed windows, the designs of which are consistent with the Romanesque doorway. There was also a Romanesque chancel arch, for in 1838 'ornamented stones' from it were visible in the walls of the Protestant church.[18] The portal was thus erected as part of a new church, a structure which evidently replaced an earlier building erected (or repaired) after the attack on Killeshin in 1041.

The inscriptions

Perhaps the most controversial aspect of the doorway are the two inscriptions, a rare occurrence on Irish portals.[19] The most extensive of the two runs horizontally along the abaci, starting on the north side (on the south face of the outer order), and continuing around the portal until the west face of the third order (plates 5.2 & 5.3). Macalister, in his study of Irish inscriptions, suggested the following reading: OR DO C... / AD.AR. / ...ILAGEN / .... / GNEIN / .AD. / ACUS DO. / ONAERCINRUBUI / ...G(DE) / BACHD (O). / ET DO / LENA / UAMEL.[20] Many of the letters, particularly those on the southern abaci are fragmentary or ambiguous and, as Macalister remarked, the restoration of the inscription as a whole seems hopeless.[21] However, along the north side, he believed the letters should read OR DA ...D.AR......I LAGEN, which he interpreted as OROIT DO DIARMAIT RI LAGEN, pray for Diarmait King of Leinster. It is difficult to know how much faith to put in Macalister's reading, for only the letters LAGEN can be identified with any confidence today (plates 5.2 & 5.17).[22] If his interpretation is correct, it provides a valuable clue to the history of the doorway. But which king of Leinster was being commemorated? Macalister, followed by Leask, assumed the Diarmait mentioned in the inscription was the ruler who died in 1117. But, as the style of the portal belongs to the middle years of the twelfth century, the inscription surely refers to a different figure. Assuming that Macalister's reading of the letters was right, the king involved must have been none other than Diarmait MacMurrough, King of Leinster from *c.* 1133 to 1171.

The second inscription, cut vertically up the north jamb, is better preserved (plate 5.9) and there is no need to question Macalister's reading: OR DO CELLACHAN, Pray for Cellachan. Unfortunately there is no way of identifying this individual. Leask and Crawford believed he may have been the sculptor responsible for the doorway, and this is certainly a possibility.[23]

Plate 5.2   The portal at Killeshin: capitals on the north jamb.

Plate 5.3   The portal at Killeshin: capitals on the south jamb.

Inscriptions on Romanesque portals are not all that common and the character of those at Killeshin follow local rather than foreign models, the formulae being similar to those found on Irish metalwork and stone crosses.[24] There is no surprise in finding the name of a king, for at much the same time the name of Turlough O Conor, king of Connacht, was inscribed on two of the high crosses at Tuam.[25] At Killeshin it seems that a practice well established in the context of shrines and crosses was now being extended to church portals. In this case the inscription appears to record Diarmait MacMurrough's role as a benefactor of the monastery. While it is possible that the abbot of Killeshin felt obliged to acknowledge the authority of the local ruler as some sort of political gesture, it is unlikely that the king's name would have been mentioned unless the monastery had received something worthwhile in return.

An elaborate doorway obviously enhanced the status of a church, and, along with it, the status of its benefactor.[26] This is illustrated by the building activities of Flathbertach Ó Brolcháin, the ambitious abbot of Derry, who, the annals of Ulster report, made a new door for his church in 1155.[27] The fact that a doorway or portal was singled out by the annalist suggests that it was something rather special. There are good reasons for thinking the Killeshin portal was also built in the 1150s, at a time when carved portals were becoming a fashion within the Irish church.[28]

The structure of the portal

With its four recessed orders, complete with bases, capitals and decorated archivolts, the portal of Killeshin is characteristic of Romanesque construction throughout Europe. Although the actual opening for the door is no more than 85 cm wide, the four concentric orders, gradually expanding in diameter, create the illusion of an enormous doorway (plate 5.1). It is the width of the outer order, not the narrow inner arch, that determines the spectator's impression of scale. Equally characteristic is the way in which the orders are recessed in depth, tending to draw the eye inwards, as if anticipating movement into the church. It is easy to take these techniques for granted and to forget that they were quite unknown in Ireland before 1130. As far as we are aware, early Irish churches were invariably entered through a simple lintelled doorway, dozens of which survived into the Romanesque era. Portals like that at Killeshin were not only extravagant replacements for what had gone before, but represented a new type of constructional expertise. In the past scholars have concentrated on the decorative motifs, overlooking the novelty of the actual technique. One of the fundamental mysteries of Hiberno-

Romanesque is to explain how and where Irish masons learnt to build portals of this type.

It was clearly not an indigenous development. During the twelfth century the portal with multiple orders became one of the standard components of European Romanesque. In the Europe of 1100 it was unusual to find an arch with more than two orders: a typical doorway might consist of a plain outer arch, enclosing an inner order with columns and capitals. Over the course of the next fifty years the number of orders tended to increase, a trend particularly obvious in northern Italy, Spain and western France. It should not be forgotton that the use of arches, supported on capitals, columns and bases, ultimately goes back to Roman practice, and as such was alien to Irish tradition. So how did these techniques reach Ireland?

The most obvious explanation is to suppose that masons trained either in England or on the continent were employed on Irish buildings. This appears to have been the case at Cashel, where many English features appear in the architecture of Cormac's Chapel (1127-34). Built on the instructions of Cormac MacCarthy, king of Munster, the chapel was evidently intended to be quite different from what had gone before. Cormac was a patron of the reform movement in the Irish church and the spectacular design of his chapel was evidently intended to proclaim a new, more international, outlook in religious affairs[29] It is unlikely that Cormac's Chapel provided the only example of foreign expertise. Indeed, many of the Romanesque features that became popular in Ireland are not found at Cashel and there must have been other models to which Irish masons could turn. If Cormac MacCarthy was prepared to employ foreign craftsmen, perhaps other kings did the same? In this context it is worth noting that the Cistercian monastery of Baltinglass, founded by Diarmait MacMurrough in 1148, was initially colonised from an English house, Louth Park (Lincolnshire).[30] If English monks were settling in Leinster before the Anglo-Norman invasion of 1169-70, it is not unlikely that English masons occasionally found their way here as well.

At this point it is worth looking in more detail at the structural components of the Killeshin portal. There are five features which deserve particular mention.

(i) Although apparently supported on columns, the engaged shafts of the three inner orders are little more than 'pseudo-columns', carved on the angle of a square jamb (plate 5.4). Compared with engaged shafts employed outside Ireland, far less of the circular column was actually defined. The shallow effects are very much in keeping with thinly carved relief systems used for the decoration of the doorway.

(ii) Where original masonry survives, the pseudo-columns are supported on bulbous bases, several of which have spurs – or remnants of spurs – on the diagonal angle (plate 5.4).

(iii) The outer order is supported on a broad pilaster, the angles of which are carved with shallow rolls. This 'pilaster' projects in front of the wall of the church by almost 30 cm, allowing it to be carved on three sides (plate 5.9).

(iv) The steeply pointed gable rests on a thin label moulding and the borders of the gable grow out of this moulding. Surprisingly, the label has no support of its own and stops abruptly on a corner of the abacus.[31] (plate 5.1)

(v) The semi-circular space at the head of the doorway is not filled with a solid tympanum, as was the case in many English portals.

The origin of the Irish 'pseudo-column' has never been explored, though as long ago as 1878 Margaret Stokes realised that it was one of the distinctive features of Hiberno-Romanesque.[32] In fact lightly incised shafts and rolls are more widespread in European Romanesque than is generally supposed. In many a French church they are found on the angles of piers or buttresses, for example.[33] What is distinctive about the Irish shafts is not the form itself, but its presence in a doorway. Presumably it appealed to Irish masons as an economical form, which involved cutting away less of the stone. There may, however, be more to it, as there is some evidence of a link with Cistercian architecture. Thin rolls were employed on the angles of the eastern chapels at Mellifont (1142-57),[34] and bolder versions can be found in the eastern parts of Baltinglass, the abbey founded by Diarmait MacMurrough in 1148 (plate 5.5). In a slightly more elaborate form they re-appeared in the transept chapels at Jerpoint.[35] It is not impossible that this type of shaft was introduced to Ireland by the Cistercians. Related forms can be found on the piers of the cloister at Fontenay,[36] one of the best representatives of Cistercian architecture in Burgundy, whence the first Cistercian mission came to Ireland.

In the case of the bulbous base, the link with the Cistercians is more definite: examples almost identical with those at Killeshin were used at Baltinglass, less than seventeen miles away (plates 5.4 & 5.5). In the Cistercian abbey two of the bases are fitted with spurs, and, as at Killeshin, they have sub bases which curve down at the angle. There can be little doubt that they were carved by the same mason (or masons). Although bulbous bases were employed in a number of Irish churches,[37] they were not an Irish invention, nor is it likely that they were introduced by the Cistercians. The form is usually associated with Anglo-Saxon architecture of the eleventh century, where it sometimes occurs in conjunction with bulbous capitals.[38] The *locus classicus* for both features are the arches illustrated in the

Plate 5.4   The portal at Killeshin: the north jamb, with beast head set at right angles on the outer jamb.

Plate 5.5   Baltinglass Abbey: bulbous base at the entrance to the chancel.

Benedictional of St Aethelwold (c. 970-80),[39] though their presence in the illuminations appears to predate their appearance in surviving buildings. Bulbous bases survived the Norman conquest and they are found sporadically in English buildings until about 1120. Their re-appearance thirty years later in Ireland is difficult to explain. Were they employed on earlier and now vanished buildings, erected long before Killeshin and Baltinglass? Some of the earlier English bases are remarkably close to those at Killeshin and Baltinglass: there are parallels for the ornate collars (as at Baltinglass) at Heckingham (Norfolk) and in a few instances the English bases are also provided with spurs, as at North Ockenden (Essex) and Milborne Port (Dorset).[40] It appears that, either the form spread from England at the beginning of the twelfth century, or that it was already established in Ireland in the context of wooden buildings. Bulbous bases are found in the Norwegian stave churches[41] and, as Stuart Rigold noted, the examples in stone may have been derived from timber prototypes. Is it possible that the bulbous bases of Killeshin and Baltinglass are relics of the wooden churches of ancient Ireland? Certainly it is difficult to believe that this very specific form was first introduced to

Plate 5.6   Roscrea: the west facade of St Cronan's Church.

the country as late as 1150, several decades after it had become obsolete in England.[42]

The tangent gable has excited far more discussion than the bulbous base. There are seven examples in Hiberno-Romanesque, the most famous and most bizarre being that at Clonfert.[43] The earliest of them appears to be that over the north portal at Cormac's Chapel (1127-34), though this was not the model for Killeshin. At Cashel the gable does not touch the extrados of the arch below and the angle of the gable is not so acute. A better comparison is with St Cronan's Roscrea, where the angle is similar (plate 5.6). However the portal at Roscrea lacks the label moulding, which at Killeshin is integrated into the edge of the gable.[44] In this respect Killeshin is unique and it is important to note that the treatment of the gable on the seven Irish examples varies quite considerably.

As Liam de Paor remarked, the form is 'fairly obviously derived from that of a porch'. At Cashel, Donaghmore and Freshford, the gables in fact mark the outer edge of stone porches and there is a hint of a porch at Roscrea. At Killeshin and Clonfert, however, the gable is little more than a decorative adjunct set against the wall of the church. As the gable became less prominent as a structural feature, it was evidently valued more highly as a field for sculpture. At Roscrea there is a much decayed full length figure (Christ? St Cronan?) and the gable at Clonfert is filled with arcades and human heads. Although the gable at Killeshin is now bare, it is possible that it too contained carvings.[45] At both Clonfert and Roscrea the area within the gable, above the arches of the door, was used to represent a heavenly setting, a pattern which can be paralleled both in England and France: at Saint-Nicholas de Brem (Vendée), for example, there is a Romanesque door with a gable containing a sculpture of Christ trampling a dragon[46] and at Lullington (Somerset) a 'tangent' gable remarkably like those found in Ireland contains a carving of Christ in Majesty (plate 5.7). Another tangent gable, this time with a niche containing a sculpture of the *agnus dei*, can be found at Patrixbourne (Kent).[47]

Although there are parallels for the tangent gable abroad, the development of the form in Ireland remains unclear. It is possible that the Irish examples survived from timber buildings; the steep angles are certainly reminiscent of the wooden stave churches of Norway, which may bear some resemblance to the early churches of Ireland.[48] But it is equally possible that the form was introduced from southern England. Shortly before 1139 a steep gable, decorated with lions, was used to decorate the cathedral at Sarum[49] and at about the same time masons from Sarum were involved in building the parish church at Lullington (Somerset), where the gable of the north portal is remarkably similar to the Irish examples.

Plate 5.7   Lullington (Somerset): the north portal.

Although the tangent gable is clearly associated with porch design, as Liam de Paor argued, it is worth noting that the form was employed long before the Romanesque period in a quite different context. In the early churches of Croatia there were stone screens with arches surmounted by such gables, as in the chapel of St Martin in the Porta Aurea at Split or the fragments at Knin (plate 5.8).[50] In most of these cases the

Plate 5.8   Knin (Croatia): stone screen with tangent gable (Strzygowski).

gable was used as a frame for a sculptured cross. The important point is that a gabled arch was being employed over the entrance to the most sacred part of the church. The examples along the Adriatic coast were probably derived from Early Christian practice in Rome, for it is known that in the fourth century the church of St John Lateran had a screen with a silver gable.[51] Was this custom known to the builders of Romanesque churches in Ireland? We can only speculate, but to explain the origin of tangent gables solely in functional terms may be to deprive the form of some of its meaning.

The broad pilaster used to support the outer order at Killeshin has an equally ambiguous background. The technique can be found on several other Irish portals, including those at Roscrea and Clonfert.[52] The pilasters stand proud of the wall of the church, helping to separate the portal from the architecture behind (plates 5.1 & 5.9). Where did Irish masons get the idea for this broad strip of masonry, supporting the outer order? In some pre-Romanesque buildings in Ireland shallow architrave bands were placed around otherwise undecorated doorways.

Plate 5.9   The portal at Killeshin: general
view of the north jambs.

A good example occurs in the round tower at Monasterboice of *c*.1100. The technique is derived from Anglo-Saxon architecture, where stripwork is commonly found around doorways and arches, a spectacular example being the continuous sculptured band at Ledsham (Yorkshire).[53] In early Irish architecture these strips were not interrupted by capitals or abaci, and in this respect they are significantly different from the pilasters used on the outer orders of later Hiberno-Romanesque portals. It is probably necessary to search elsewhere for the origin of this feature.[54]

The combination of engaged shafts and pilasters is a technique particularly associated with Romanesque art in north Italy. The three doorways on the west facade of S. Michele at Pavia, for example, are each flanked by a decorated pilaster, supporting an ornate outer order.[55] A connection with North Italy might seem far fetched, if it were not for a very specific connection between Killeshin and Verona. At Killeshin the three faces of the northern pilaster are decorated with a highly distinctive motif, consisting of a beast's head, carved in profile, with foliate scrolls spewing out of the jaws and up the surface of the pilaster (plates 5.4 and 5.9). The same motif is employed in a similar position on the west doorway at Verona cathedral.[56] It was also repeated on the Prior's Doorway at Ely Cathedral in England, a portal which has several well known connections with Italy. Another version of the motif occurs on a set of wooden door jambs from Ulvik in Norway.[57] The significance of these parallels is not just that same motif was employed in four widely separated churches but that it was employed in a similar position in each case. It is unlikely that the masons who built the portal at Killeshin had any direct knowledge of Italian Romanesque, but it seems that somehow and somewhere they had encountered features of Italian origin.[58]

The structural components of the Killeshin portal thus have a mixed and interesting background. Whereas the bulbous bases and the tangent gables have an English flavour, other features suggest France or Italy. Portals without tympana were far more standard in Poitou and the Saintonge than they were in England[59] and when considering the broad outer pilasters it is hard to ignore Italy. How Irish Romanesque masons achieved this remarkable synthesis of disparate forms remains a mystery.

The human heads

The most striking aspect of the Killeshin portal are the ten human heads which decorate the capitals, along with an eleventh on the keystone of the outer arch (plates 5.2 & 5.3). Apart from those which fill the gable at Clonfert, this is the most conspicuous use of the human head on an Irish portal. The form of the Killeshin heads falls into two categories: (a) the four which occupy the capitals of the second and third orders, and (b) the thinner heads found elsewhere. The first group are strongly modelled, with well rounded, clean shaven, faces. Large, prominent ears are flattened against the adjacent surface and an undulating wave of hair crosses the forehead. The eyelids are cut very precisely, with neat horizontal slits each side. The second group of heads have thinner faces to suit the narrower rolls on the inner and outer edges of the portal. Here the faces end with a pointed chin and each has a beard and moustache. The latter, sometimes described as a 'Chinese moustache', drops down at a sharp angle and terminates in a scroll. The head on the keystone (plate 5.10) belongs with this second type. The modelling of the cheeks and careful delineation of moustache and beard make this the finest head in the group. Despite the differences in the character of the heads, there is no doubt that they are the work of the same craftsman, a point confirmed by a comparison of the ears and eyes. The differences were deliberate and correspond with the differences in the engaged shafts. The fact that the same sculptor could produce heads of very different character provides a warning against the excessive use of connoisseurship as a means of establishing the oeuvre of individual craftsmen.

Human heads in various forms are found in the Romanesque sculpture of almost every country of Europe, something which has been ascribed to a mixture of Roman and Celtic influences.[60] The specific arrangement whereby a single head was placed on the keystone of an arch was clearly derived from Roman practice. Well preserved Roman examples can be found on the city gate at Volterra and on the mausoleum at Glanum in southern France. In the latter case there is a human head on each of the main keystones, the face of the arch being decorated with foliate scrolls (plate 5.12). The analogy with

Plate 5.10   The portal at Killeshin:
keystone on the outer
order.

Plate 5.11   The Barberini Gospels,
folio lr: canon tables
(photograph courtesy
of Biblioteca
Apostolica Vaticana).

Killeshin is quite striking, particularly the combination of a human keystone, carved in heavy relief, with flatter ornament alongside. In fact few Romanesque examples are as close to the Roman prototypes as that at Killeshin, an interesting paradox, since Ireland had no first hand experience of Roman stone carving.[61]

While isolated heads on a keystone are relatively rare in Hiberno-Romanesque, heads placed on the angle of a capital are common and there is a particular concentration of them in Leinster.[62] The heads at Killeshin are so close to those which decorate the doorway of the round tower at Timahoe that they are surely the work of the same craftsman.[63] Some heads at Kilteel (Kildare) have the same characteristic cutting of the eyelids and there has been some discussion as to whether they too are by the same hand. At Kilteel, however, the style is more developed: the hair is more elaborate and trails from the beard and moustache culminate in dense patterns of interlace. Two human heads on the chancel arch of St Saviour's church at Glendalough are distantly related to Killeshin, this time to heads in the first category. The work at Killeshin thus has links with several other churches in North Leinster (Wicklow, Kildare and Laois), and there is little doubt that the chief sculptor himself worked at Baltinglass and Timahoe. The so-called 'Killeshin Master' was evidently one of the more active and influential personalities in the area.[64]

The origin of the 'head capital' is not as clear as that of the human head on the keystone. The Romans occasionally placed small heads amidst the acanthus of Corinthian capitals, as in the well known examples from Glanum, Auxerre and Nimes.[65] But these are not really a precedent for the Romanesque heads, which take up the full height of the capital. In some respects the large human heads carved on the angles of Early Christian sarcophagi provide a more telling comparison.[66] Equally relevant, however, are the human heads used by illuminators to decorate the canon tables of gospel books.[67] By the twelfth century this had become common practice and precedents go back at least to the eighth century, as in Barberini Gospels, where the central arches of one of the canon tables are supported on a human face, taking the place of a capital.[68] The long face has a flamboyant moustache and two bird-like beasts bite the ends of the beard (plate 5.11). The proportions, as well as the two tiny beasts attacking the beard, recall the head on the keystone of the arch at Killeshin. Further human heads, this time clean shaven, are found on the St Mark initial of the Barberini Gospels, located like capitals at the top of the vertical stems.[69] Whatever the exact background of the head capital, the examples in the Barberini Gospels demonstrate that the idea was established in western art long before it was exploited by Romanesque stone carvers.

Plate 5.12   The Roman Mausoleum at Glanum (Bouches-du-Rhone).

The earliest 'head capitals' in Ireland are those on the engaged shafts inside the nave of Cormac's Chapel (1127-34). As at Killeshin the heads are placed on the angle of the capital, though they are not as fully modelled. One of the heads has a beard and moustache similar to those in the second category at Killeshin and the horizontal slit at the edge of the eye also reappears (plate 5.13). Despite the similarities, they are not by the same hand as the Killeshin 'Master'. Given the English background of much of the sculpture of Cormac's Chapel, it could be argued that the 'head capital' was imported from England, but if so, the motif found a ready audience in Ireland, where the disembodied human head had a long pedigree in metalwork and manuscript illumination. Indeed, it is the 'Irishness' of the faces that is so striking. The narrow faces, the pointed chins, and the flowing moustaches can all be traced far back into Irish art. About 1100 a face of just this type was used at the top of the 'drop' on the Clonmacnois crosier.[70]

In most contexts the head capital is employed as an independent motif, one of dozens of different designs seemingly used at random by the Romanesque sculptor. What makes Killeshin remarkable is the way in which the heads are used consistently on all the capitals (plates 5.1 & 5.2). Along with the additional head on the outer arch, they seem to be part of a well co-ordinated scheme. The faces are carved in a sober manner, without any undue distortion, and it is hard to believe that

Plate 5.13   Cormac's Chapel, Cashel, capital in the nave.

twelfth century spectators regarded them merely as 'decoration'. With their wide eyes, staring uniformly into the distance, the heads have a 'timeless' quality, a phrase frequently applied to the famous column figures in the Royal Portal at Chartres (c. 1145).[71] Unfortunately there is no means of knowing what these heads might have meant to the Romanesque viewer, nor whether the number ten was of any significance. In 1838 O'Donovan recorded the local belief that they represented ten of the apostles, with an eleventh, St Peter, being represented by the head on the keystone. There is no early evidence to support this and it is worth remembering that immediately above the heads was an inscription containing personal names. In glancing at the portal it would have been tempting to associate the sculptured faces with the patrons and benefactors recorded in the inscription.[72] However, analogies elsewhere in twelfth-century Europe would suggest that if the heads were intended to have specific connotations, they are more likely to have been interpreted as figures from the Old Testament, as on the portals of the Ile de France.

Further human faces appear on the pilasters of the outer order. There are three examples to the south, located at the bottom of each side (plate 5.14). Frontally carved, the faces have the familiar narrow chin and moustache, but in this case foliage grows out of the hair and up the pilaster. There are analogies for these faces in contemporary manuscript illumination, as in the highly decorated Corpus Missal.[73] A

Plate 5.14 The portal at Killeshin: north face of southern jamb, with human head.

Plate 5.15 The portal at Killeshin: north face of northern jamb with human head and foliage ornament

further head, this time in profile, appears on the north side of the northern pilaster (plate 5.15). The latter is so close to examples in the Book of Kells that it could have been copied directly from the famous gospel book.[74]

Animal designs

As well as its anthropomorphic decoration, the portal at Killeshin contains a wealth of animal ornament, much of it belonging to the Irish-Urnes style (plate 5.16). There are good examples at capital level, between the human heads. Most of the characteristic features of the style are present: the well developed dragon heads, the ribbon shaped bodies, the figure of eight loops and the diagonal emphasis of the patterns. Although often described as Viking, the style owes as much to traditional Irish art as it does to Scandinavia. Long before it was exploited by stone carvers, it had been used by metalworkers. Indeed some of the examples found in stone sculpture were copied quite literally from metal prototypes and this was probably the case at Killeshin.[75] There are, for example, close parallels for the Killeshin

Plate 5.16   The portal at Killeshin: northern jamb, west face: Irish Urnes ornament between the human heads on the capitals.

designs on the cross of Cong.

Less conspicuous are the tiny animals inserted into the spandrels of the chevron of the second and third order (plate 5.17). The creatures include two birds, a lion with a human face (a manticore?), a dog-like beast with something protruding from its mouth, a beast with a large beak (a griffin?), a stag and (?) a hound (fig. 5.1).[76] The way in which the animals are set in triangular panels reminded Máire de Paor of the Trewhiddle style of the late ninth century; at least one of the animals has its head bent back sharply in the manner of the Trewhiddle creatures (plate 5.18). The parallels are intriguing, not least since the triangular frames on the

Plate 5.17   The portal at Killeshin: soffit of third order, showing beaded chevron and stepped pattern on adjacent outer order. The word 'Lagen' can be seen on the abacus.

109

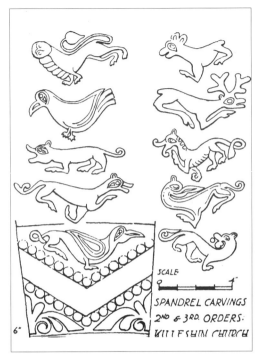

SCALE

SPANDREL CARVINGS
2ND & 3RD. ORDERS.
KILLESHIN CHURCH

Fig. 5.1   Drawings of the animals set within the chevron ornament at Killeshin (after Leask, courtesy of the Dundalgan Press).

Trewhiddle mountings consist of beaded zig-zag, a form of proto-chevron.[77] While all this might be coincidence, the analogies are difficult to ignore. In the past it has been assumed that Hiberno-Romanesque chevron was imported from England, but the versions at Killeshin suggest there may have been more to it. Is it possible that beaded zig-zags framing small animals were known to the stone sculptor through metal-work, perhaps through some venerable item owned by the monastery of Killeshin itself?

The same sculptor used similar techniques in his work at Baltinglass, where a small quadruped is set within a semi-circular frame on one of the bulbous bases (plate 5.5). This arrangement has analogies with designs in the canon tables of a Canterbury manuscript of the later eighth century,[78] and it is worth noting that animals set in semi-circular frames also appear in the canon tables of an eleventh century Anglo-Saxon Gospel Book.[79] It is difficult to believe that this is coincidence: it strengthens the impression that the 'Killeshin Master' had more than a passing familiarity with Insular manuscript illumination.

The animal designs at Killeshin can also be compared with carvings at Glendalough. In the church of St Saviour's the frame of the east window has two triangular panels formed by beaded chevron, one filled by a pair of affronted birds, the other by a lion, its head turned backwards biting its tail (plate 5.19). The curled jaws of the beast, as well as it contoured body, are repeated on some of the animals and snakes at Killeshin.

Further animals are depicted on the now badly decayed vertical face of the outer order. These include two dragons back to back, the head of a beatle-like creature seen from above, and a pair of bird heads

Plate 5.18   Anglo-Saxon silver mount from Trewhiddle (photograph courtesy of the British Museum).

(Plate 5.20). The latter are especially interesting, since their pedigree in Insular art goes back to the beginning of the eighth century. Variants of the motif survived in manuscript painting for another four hundred years. The stiff, elongated necks of the birds, together with their curved beaks, recall an initial in Rawlinson B502,[80] which as we have already seen has a Leinster origin. Other animals can be found in less conspicuous corners of the portal. A lion, for example, is carved on one of the bases on the south side and a further leonesque creature appears on a capital of the second order (south); this has extended jaws and its tail, ending in a volute, is stretched along the back.[81]

Amongst the other decorative motifs used at Killeshin, there is a variety of foliage ornament and floral patterns, as well as scroll work and spirals in the Celtic tradition (plates 5.4 & 5.9). There are also geometrical patterns reminiscent of those used in metalwork. These include a series of Greek cross motifs, found along the base of northern jambs, and a bold step pattern carved on the soffit of the outer order, a pattern which can also be

Plate 5.19   Glendalough, St. Saviour's Priory: the interior jambs of the east window.

Plate 5.20   The portal at Killeshin: vertical face of the outer order, with chevron, birds and beasts.

read as a series of linked Greek crosses (plate 5.17, top left). The latter are directly comparable with metalwork: variations of the pattern are common on book shrines and a virtually identical design appears on the shrine of St Patrick's Bell.[82] Moreover, the bands that make up the pattern at Killeshin have moulded edges, a detail which makes the comparison particularly compelling.[83]

With one exception, the chevron used on the portal follows very basic forms: in three of the orders one or two zig-zag bands, flanked by beading, run along both the face and soffits of the arch, meeting on an angle roll (plate 5.17). The chief interest of the chevron lies in the spandrel ornament, a mixture of animal, foliage and floral designs. On the face of the fourth, outer order, however, the chevron was designed in an unusual manner, through the expansion of the angle of the chevrons into circles (plate 5.20). While the circular forms are reminiscent of designs on early Irish grave slabs,[84] the whole design is astonishingly close to that on the upper knop of the Clonmacnoise crosier, as recently pointed out by Rachel Moss.[85]

The sculptors' technique
Most of the ornament at Killeshin was executed in shallow relief, as if drawn, rather than cut out of the stone, so that the designs are scarcely visible except from close range. Even the chevron ornament is gently

incised on the surface and not cut in three dimensions. While this might suggest timidity or inexperience on the part of the sculptor, it is far more likely to reflect the nature of the models. The lack of depth is compensated by surface ornament of great subtlety. As has been argued above, the sculpture of Killeshin is heavily dependent on sources in manuscript illumination and metalwork, which were for the most part two dimensional. It gives the carving a 'graphic' flavour, a quality consistently encountered in Hiberno-Romanesque.

It seems clear that the sculpture was intended from the outset to be painted and the full force of the designs must have come as much from colour, as from the sculpture itself. Although no pigment is left on the doorway, there are two reasons for concluding that paint was used. First, the stone employed is inconsistent in colour and type: it includes a light granite, a coarser yellowish granite as well as a brown sandstone.[86] No attempt was made to use the different stones in any regular pattern and, even after centuries of weathering, the masonry presents a bizarre and heterogeneous appearance (plate 5.1). Secondly, without paint the ornament would have been almost invisible. While the notion of painting such carefully wrought stone seems alien to modern taste, it is important to remember that coloured stonework would have been familiar to twelfth-century spectators. The earlier high crosses were almost certainly painted, like those in England. Moreover, without colour the intricate designs of the twelfth-century crosses would have been lost, a point very obvious at Tuam, where the relief on the market cross is even flatter than that on the portal at Killeshin.[87] What has never been established is how the paint was actually applied to the stone. Presumably some form of lime wash was used as a base. Given the quantities of pigment required, the painting of a doorway like that at Killeshin may have cost as much as the carving.

Conclusion

However much the actual structure of the portal at Killeshin owes to foreign example, the local characteristics of the ornament are very evident. The many comparisons that can be drawn with both metalwork and manuscript illumination suggest that whoever drew up the designs had ready access to work in both these media. Given the reputation of Killeshin as a centre of learning, it is not unlikely that some of the models came from within the monastery itself, from the library and from the treasury. The parallels with manuscript decoration, however, raise a more fundamental question, one which relates to Romanesque sculpture as a whole: to what extent were the stone sculptors responsible for their own designs? Is it possible that craftsmen trained in the art of illumination (or metalwork) were responsible for providing drawings from which the masons worked? It seems most unlikely that stone masons spent their spare time thumbing through manuscripts in the monastic library looking for ideas.[88] Is it possible that some of the designs seen at Killeshin were first drawn on the stone by those responsible for decorating the monastery's books?

On the basis of style, there are reasons for thinking that the church was built in the middle years of the century, perhaps about 1150-5. The head capitals are more advanced than those at Cashel, implying a date after 1134 and the same sculptor worked on the round tower at Timahoe, which was probably built sometime after the destruction of that monastery in 1142. Good parallels for both the bulbous bases and some of the animal ornament can be found at Baltinglass, the Cistercian house founded in 1148. The sculpture also has links with St Saviour's priory at Glendalough, a building which has traditionally been associated with the period when Laurence O'Toole was abbot of Glendalough (1154-62).[89] On the basis of these comparisons, the church at Killeshin must have been constructed sometime between 1145 and 1165. These dates fit comfortably within the long reign of Diarmait McMurrough as king of Leinster, one of the individuals almost certainly mentioned in the inscription. The latter definitely included the word LAGEN or Leinster and it is difficult to see why else the province would be mentioned except in connection with a king. As the portal was built during the lifetime of Diarmait McMurrough, it follows that he was the individual named. The fact that one of the Killeshin masons worked at Baltinglass, an abbey founded by Diarmait, reinforces the royal connection. It is tempting to go further and to conclude that the richly decorated portal, once vibrant with colour, was designed as some sort of acknowledgement of Diarmait McMurrough's political status at a time when his authority in Leinster was yet to be undermined.

Acknowledgements

I would like to record my thanks to the following people who either helped or gave me encouragement during the preparation of this article: Dr Marie Thérèse Flanagan, Stephen Heywood, Dr Lindy Grant, Canon George Chambers, Dr Ray Refaussé, Dr Tessa Garton, and Susan Youngs. I am particularly grateful to Rachel Moss, who read the article in typescript and made many pertinent comments.

References

1. H.G.Leask, *Irish churches and monastic Buildings* (Dundalk, 1955), i, 102.
2. In addition to Leask's description in his book on Irish churches, the major sources for the sculpture at Killeshin are Edwin Third Earl of Dunraven, *Notes on*

Irish architecture, edited by M.Stokes (London, 1877), ii, 81-5; M.Comerford, 'Killeshin and Sletty', *Ossory Archaeological Society*, ii (1882), 128-148; Lord Walter Fitzgerald, 'The Killeshin Church Ruins, Queen's County', *Journal of the Archaeological Society of the County of Kildare*, vi, no. 1 (1909), 186-205; H.S.Crawford, 'Carvings from the Doorway of Killeshin Church, near Carlow', *R.S.A.I., Jn.*, 48 (1918), 183-4; H.S.Crawford and H.G.Leask, 'Killeshin Church and its Romanesque ornament', *R.S.A.I., Jn.*, 55 (1925), 83-94; J.Brady, *The Romanesque portal at Killeshin* (unpublished BA thesis, Department of the History of Art, Trinity College, Dublin, 1989). The only published discussion of the origin of the motifs found on the doorway are the brief comments by F.Henry, *Irish art in the Romanesque period 1020-1170* (London, 1970), 177-9. One of the curious aspects of Killeshin is that it attracted very little interest from early antiquarians; drawings of the portal are rare and the church was not included in Grose's *Antiquities of Ireland* (1791-5). The only drawings I have discovered are those in the sketchbook of John Morris (1805), which are extremely crude and provide little or no useful information [NLI, MS 14122, ff 6-8] and a diagram in the *Ordnance Survey Letters, Queen's County*, ii, no. 88. In contrast Timahoe received plenty of attention, no doubt on account of the survival of its round tower.

3.   For the history of Killeshin see Edel Bhreathnach, 'Killeshin: an Irish monastery surveyed', *Cambrian Medieval Celtic Studies*, 27 (1994), 33-47. St Comgan has frequently been mentioned as the founder of the monastery, but as Edel Bhreathnach has shown, his name was a late intrusion into the affairs of the monastery.

4.   AFM, 917. Maelmaedoc was killed at the battle of Cenn Fuait in 917, Bhreathnach, 'Killeshin', 37.

5.   AFM, 979. Bhreathnach, Killeshin', 39.

6.   Bhreathnach, 'Killeshin', 41. Bhreathnach's translation of the passage differs slightly from that given by Whitley Stokes, 'The Annals of Tigernach', *Revue Celtique*, 17 (1896), 380: 'Glenn Uisin was plundered by the son of Mael na mBo and the prayer house was demolished and a hundred human beings were killed therein and seven hundred were carried off in vengence for the burning of Ferns...'.

7.   Oxford, Bodleian Library.

8.   Under the year 1147 the annals of Thady Dowling claim that Killeshin was the home of Cogganus, who wrote accounts of both St Malachy and St Bernard, *The Annals of Ireland by Friar John Clyn and Thady Dowling*, ed R.Butler (Dublin, Irish Archaeological Society, 1849), p. 8: 'Cogganus ecclesie de Killuskin aliter Killeshin in Margge Lagenie patronus floruit hisce diebus, et ut Nicholaus Magwyre testatur, scripsit gesta Malachie Armachani et Bernard Clarevallensis'. In his own life of St Malachy, Bernard records a debt to a certain Abbot Congar, 'my revered brother and sweet friend', but it has been argued that the choice of words suggests a Cistercian abbot, not the abbot of the monastery at Killeshin. Elsewhere Bernard refers to the Irish abbot as 'our Abbot Congan', Bernard of Clairvaux, *The life and death of Saint Malachy the Irishman*, translated and annotated by Robert T. Meyer (Kalamazoo, 1978), pp 132, 81, 129 n3. Nicholas Maguire, the source of the supposed link between the biographer of Malachy and Killeshin, was Bishop of Leighlin 1490-1512. It seems likely that he confused two ecclesiastics with similar names.

9.   A point first made by Francoise Henry, *Irish Art in the Romanesque period*, 178.

10.   The annals of Tigernach in 1041 refer to 'its oratory', as if there was only one

church, but it is interesting that a papal letter of 1204 refers to 'Glendussen cum ecclesiis', as if there was more than one, M.Sheehy, *Pontificia Hibernica: medieval papal chancery documents concerning Ireland 640-1261*, i (Dublin, 1962), 129, no. 61; cited by Bhreathnach, 'Killeshin', 46. A round tower remained until 1703, G.L.Barrow, *The round towers of Ireland* (Dublin, 1979), 139.

11.   The surviving ruins are described in detail in the article by Crawford and Leask 'Killeshin Church', *R.S.A.I., Jn.*, 55 (1925), 83-94.

12.   Although there appears to be no reference to Killeshin among the parishes in the diocese of Leighlin listed in the Taxation of Pope Nicholas, *Cal. doc. Ire., 1302-07*, ed. H.S.Sweetman, no. 712, the vicarage of Killeshin (variously spelt Killysne, Kellasna) is mentioned in the Papal Registers in 1465, 1502 and 1507 [*CPR*, XII, p.500, *CPR*, XVII, i, no. 982, *CPR*, XVIII, no. 746]. A vicar of Killessyn is mentioned in 1551, *Calendar of the Close Rolls*, i, p. 242, and the parish is mentioned in a 1591 visitation of the diocese of Leighlin, TCD, MS. 566, f. 110r.

13.   Comerford, 'Killeshin and Sletty', 130-1, Crawford and Leask, 'Killeshin Church', 84. The information given by these authors is based on O'Donovan's comments (1838) in the *Ordnance Survey Letters, Queen's County*, ii, pp 28-9 (RIA, typescript). O'Donovan states that about forty feet of the eastern end of the building (i.e. the medieval chancel) was converted into a 'modern little Church' and that when it was built the choir arch of the original building was pulled down, many of the ornamented stones being reused in the modern wall (the new west wall of the eighteenth-century church). This church survived until 1826, when a new building was erected, two and a half miles to the east, on the outskirts of Carlow, *The parliamentary gazetteer of Ireland* (Dublin, London and Edinburgh, 1844-5), ii, 476. This building was itself replaced in 1846 (J.B. Leslie, biographical succession list of the clergy of the diocese of Leighlin, RCB library MS. 61/2/12/2).

14.   Immediately above the head is a gap in the label moulding, which is hard to explain.

15.   Leask noted that one of the stones on the northern jambs appears to be upside down. This is the second stone from the top on the outer order, Crawford and Leask, 'Killeshin Church', 90.

16.   There is a fine photograph in the Earl of Dunraven's book, *Notes on Irish architecture*, ed. M. Stokes (London, 1877), ii, pl. CIX. This shows that the southern edge of the gable and the adjoining label moulding were missing (they have since been replaced by OPW); a beast head label stop still survived on the north side. In 1877 the bases were partially covered by the build-up of earth. In 1838 O'Donovan noted that one foot of the doorway was buried in the ground, *Ordnance Survey Letters, Queen's County*, ii, p. 30 (RIA, typescript). There is a general photograph of the church in Lord Walter FitzGerald's article, 'Killeshin church ruins', p. 184.

17   The procedures for building a Romanesque church are well illustrated at Kilmalkedar, where phases of work are indicated by bands of differently quarried stones. The patterns of masonry demonstrate that the stones of the portal were set in place *before* the adjoining walls were completed.

18.   O'Donovan, *Ordnance Survey Letters, Queen's County*, ii, p. 87 (RIA, typescript). O'Donovan's comments (p. 31) imply that the round tower, demolished in 1703, also had Romanesque decoration, pieces of which were still to be seen in neighbouring houses.

19.   There is an inscription at Freshford cut around the inner arch of the doorway (Leask, *Irish churches*, i, 156) and Dr Tadhg O'Keeffe has recently drawn

attention to the possible remains of a further inscription at Mona Incha.

20. R.A.S.Macalister, *Corpus Inscriptionum Insularum Celticarum*, ii (Dublin, 1949), 27-8, no. 574. A more cautious reading by Bhreathnach runs as follows: .......LAGEN..............N......I ACUS DO....ONAERCINNEIC....AL......O DO...LENA... UAMEL, Bhreathnach, 'Killeshin', 45.

21. The letters were already defaced in 1844, *The parliamentary gazetteer of Ireland* (Dublin, London and Edinburgh, 1844-5), ii, 475-6: 'the ruins of a church....which has a very antique and highly ornamental entrance in the Doric order of really excellent workmanship, and around which is an inscription, in very old Saxon characters, but so battered and abused as to be almost totally defaced'. Wakeman reported in 1891 that 'I was informed that many years ago a resident in the neighbourhood used to take pleasure in destroying, as far as lay in his power, the interesting capitals here represented, and that to his labours, and not to the effects of time, we may attribute the almost total obliteration of an Irish inscription which formerly extended round the abacus, and of which but few letters at present remain', W. Wakeman, *Handbook of Irish antiquities* (Dublin, 1891), 168.

22. It is worth noting that Stokes' reading was somewhat different from Macalister's: '[OR DO] ART[...RIG] LAGEN.....ACUS DO...........ON AERCINN[E]CH..........CH ....OR DO..........LENA......UAMEL.....DUACH....'; The inscription on the jambs was given as 'OR DO CELLAC AMI.....', *Christian inscriptions in the Irish language chiefly collected and drawn by George Petrie*, ed. M. Stokes (Dublin, 1878), ii, 85-7, pl. XLI. Stokes identified the word aercinnech, meaning leader or steward (presumably of the monastery) and linked Duach with the territory of Hy Duach (Idough), about a mile away from the church. Her reading was based on a rubbing of the inscription made by the Reverend James Graves in 1872.

23. Crawford and Leask, 'Killeshin Church', 92. There is nothing inherently unlikely about the suggestion. There are many examples abroad where the sculptor's name is recorded, not least in northern Italy, as at Modena (Wiligelmo), Verona (Nicolo) and Ferrara (Nicolo again), M.F. Hearn, *Romanesque sculpture* (London, 1981), 87, 158n 78. There is also of course the famous inscription at Autun in France, 'Gislebertus hoc fecit'. At Tuam the name of a craftsman, GilluChrist O'Toole, is inscribed vertically up the side of a twelfth-century cross shaft, R.A.Stalley, 'The Romanesque sculpture of Tuam', in *The vanishing past, studies of medieval art, liturgy and metrology presented to Christopher Hohler*, edited by A. Borg and A. Martindale (Oxford, B.A.R., 1981), 183.

24. The formula, consisting of a sequence of requests for prayers for various officials and benefactors, was particularly common on eleventh and twelfth century shrines, Henry, *Irish art in the Romanesque period*, chapter 4.

25. Stalley, 'Romanesque sculpture of Tuam', 182-3; P. Harbison, *The High Crosses of Ireland* (Bonn, 1992), i, 175-7.

26. As early as the seventh century the status of the church at Kildare was enhanced by a 'finely wrought' doorway, though in this case it is unclear whether it was the door itself or the frame that was embellished, S. Connolly and J. M. Picard, 'Cogitosus: Life of Saint Brigit', *R.S.A.I., Jn.*, 117 (1987), 26.

27. AU, 1155, *Annals of Ulster*, ii, ed. B. MacCarthy (Dublin, 1893), 126-9.

28. It was also a time of diocesan reorganisation, when local churches were jostling for status; was the vogue for ornate doorways in some way bound up with ecclesiastical politics?

29. As long ago as 1910 Arthur Champneys suggested that Cormac's Chapel might have represented a new departure, implying that it served as a model and

inspiration for subsequent works, *Irish ecclesiastical architecture* (London, 1910), 132. Liam de Paor subsequently demonstrated the influence of the chapel, particularly in Leinster, L. de Paor, 'Cormac's Chapel, the beginnings of Irish Romanesque' in *Munster studies*, ed E. Rynne (Limerick, 1967), 133-45.

30.   Yolande de Pontfarcy, 'A note on the two dates given for the foundation of Baltinglass', *R.S.A.I., Jn.*, 118 (1988), 163-4.

31.   The harshness of this arrangement has been exacerbated by the modern restorations on the south side of the hood mould. As Dunraven's photograph indicates, the label moulding originally terminated in animal stops, Dunraven, *Notes on Irish architecture*, ii, pl. CIX.

32.   M.Stokes, *Early Christian architecture in Ireland* (London, 1878), 114: 'The sides of the Irish doorway are but a transitional stage between the jambs of a square headed doorway and actual shafts. The angular sides of the three or four orders are rounded off and channelled into groups of bowtels, with merely slight projections at the feet scarcely to be termed bases...'. There is a brief discussion of the Irish angle colonette by Liam de Paor, *Chronological problems of Irish Romanesque*, unpublished dissertation presented for the Travelling Studentship in Archaeology in the National University of Ireland, UCD, 1956, 72-3.

33.   They are used on the exterior wall arches of the churches at Aulnay and Chadenac (Charente Maritime), for example, as well as on the exterior of the apse and on the eastern responds of the transepts at Talmont (Charente Maritime), on the piers in the cloister of St Paul de Mausole (Bouches-du-Rhone) and in countless other places.

34.   At Mellifont there is a further example, carved on a large block of stone (now in store).

35.   Stalley, *Cistercian monasteries of Ireland* (London and New Haven, 1987), pl.46. In the later years of the twelfth century, thinly cut quarter rolls became a feature of the so-called 'West Country School' in England, but, although superficially similar to the Irish pseudo-shafts, the geometry is different.

36.   On the rear of the major piers, facing into the cloister walk.

37.   Rahan, Clonmacnoise (Nuns' Church, St Finghin's and Cathedral), Boyle, Annaghdown and Ferns. There are also bulbous bases in the so-called 'chapter house' at Killeigh (Offaly), as well as at Lemanaghan (Offaly) and Inchmore (Longford). The distribution has a notably Midland emphasis. The distribution of the bulbous base and associated forms is discussed by de Paor, *Chronology of Irish Romanesque*, 77-8.
The bulbous base is currently enjoying a revival in the context of Post-Modern architecture. Splendid examples are to be seen on a recently (1995) completed office building in Tara street, Dublin.

38.   Good examples of bulbous bases can be found at Bolam (Northumberland), on the mid wall shafts of the eleventh-century tower, illustrated in E.A. Fisher, *Anglo-Saxon towers* (Newton Abbot, 1969), p. 54; at Appleton-le-Street (Yorkshire) again in a tower; Well known examples of bulbous capitals occur at Great Paxton (Huntingdonshire) and St Benet's Cambridge. For a brief comment on bulbous bases see E. Fernie, *The architecture of the Anglo-Saxons* (London, 1983), 133-4.

39.   BL, Add MS. 49598. Bulbous capitals, though not bulbous bases, are frequently depicted in Anglo-Saxon manuscripts.

40.   S. Rigold, 'Romanesque bases in and south-east of the limestone belt', *Ancient monuments and their interpretations*, ed. M.R. Apted., R. Gilyard Beer and A.D. Saunders (London and Chichester, 1977), 113. It may be of significance that

Baltinglass was founded from Louth Park (Lincolnshire), as Yolande de Pontfarcy has demonstrated, 'Foundation of Baltinglass', *R.S.A.I., Jn.*, 118 (1988), 163-4.

41. 'The ideal specimens are the great cheese-like bases to the corner posts of the earliest stave churches', as at Holtalten, Trondelay, Rigold, 'Romanesque bases', 111. Rigold cites A.Bugge, *Norwegian Stave-churches* (1953), pl. 31.

42. I am grateful to Stephen Heywood of Norwich for advice on the question of bulbous bases. The background of the Irish bases deserves more exhaustive study.

43. In addition to Cashel and Clonfert, the other examples can be found at Roscrea, Freshford, Donaghmore, and Kildare (round tower), L. de Paor, 'Cormac's Chapel, the beginnings of Irish Romanesque' in *Munster studies*, ed E. Rynne (Limerick, 1967), 136-7. See also de Paor, *Chronology of Irish Romanesque*, 51-3, where the author concludes that, despite the differences in the design of the Irish tangent gables, the distribution of the form appears to lead back to Cormac's Chapel. There are outlines of a gable in the south wall at Ballyhay (Cork), but suggestions that this is the remnant of a Romanesque tangent gable are misleading.

44. The presence of two rosettes in the gable at Roscrea provides a link with Cashel and also demonstrates a connection with the west of England, particularly with the cathedral of Old Sarum. The choir of the latter building included a steeply pitched gable (over a door?), which terminated at the apex with a pair of lions, *English Romanesque Art* (London, Arts Council, 1984), p. 64. As well as the rosettes within the gable, Rachel Moss has pointed out that there are remains of at least six further rosettes in the wall above the gable.

45. It is not clear whether the stones that fill the gable are original, and there is some suggestion that they have been replaced or reworked. If the gable did contain sculpture, one can only speculate what the subject might have been: a figure of Christ as at Roscrea perhaps, or a series of heads as at Clonfert? About half way up the gable a narrow stone projects forward from the surface, the logic of which is unclear.

46. Paul Veyriras, *Vendée Romane, Bas Poitou Romane* (Zodiaque, 1976), 51-7. The gable at Brem has almost classical proportions, being more like a pediment. It surmounts a genuine stone porch.

47. L. Musset, *L'Angleterre Romane, Le Sud de l'Angleterre* (Zodiaque, 1982), 217-9, pl. 64. Musset has also drawn attention to gables over portals in Normandy at Foulognes en Bassin and Sainte Croix at St Lo. The doorway at Sainte Croix is of particular interest in an Irish context. Although the the outline of the gable is only lightly incised in the form of a chain, there are figures at the base of the gable, in a position similar to sculptures at Freshford.

48. See the illustrations in G. Bugge, Stabkirchen, *Mittelalterliche Baukunst in Norwegen* (Regensburg 1994). Rachel Moss has pointed out that the finials on the gabled windows at Toureen Peakaun and Inchicronan could also be reminiscent of wooden structures.

49. *English Romanesque art 1066-1200* (London, Arts Council, 1984), pp 63, 176.

50. J.Strzygowski, *Early church art in Northern Europe* (London, 1928), pl. I, VIIa and p. 23. There are several examples in the Muzei Hrvatskih Arheoloskih Spornenika in Split. These include a Romanesque version with a seated Christ in the gable set between two angels. Fragments of similar gables survive at Ravenna.

51. R. Milburn, *Early Christian art and architecture* (Berkeley and Los Angeles, 1988), 88, citing *Liber Pontificalis*, ed. L. Duschesne (Paris, 1952), i, 153.

52. Similar features exist at Inchagoill (Galway), and two well preserved pilasters at Annaghdown (Galway), which are no longer *in situ,* may have had a similar

function. There are also fragments at Devenish which may belong to pilasters of this type.

53. L. Musset, *L'Angleterre Romane, Le Nord de l'Angleterre* (Zodiaque, 1988), p. 68; H.M. and J. Taylor, *Anglo-Saxon architecture*, i (Cambridge, 1980), 380-1; M.L. Faull, 'The decoration of the south doorway of Ledsham church tower', *Journal of the British Archaeological Association*, 139 (1986), 143-7.

54. An alternative hypothesis would be to see the pilasters as some sort of adaptation of the antae, which were a long established feature of Irish stone churches. On occasions these were decorated, as at St Molaise's House, Devenish. The form is not substantially different from that of pilasters flanking a portal.

55. At S. Michele the outer pilasters do not stand proud of the surface of the wall as they do in Ireland.

56. G. Zarnecki, *The early sculpture of Ely Cathedral* (London, 1958), pl. 78.

57. Ibid., 28-9, 33.

58. This may have been through intermediary buildings in England. It is worth noting that the acrobatic figure carved on the chancel jambs at Kilteel (Kildare) can also be compared with sculpture at Ely.

59. It is however important to note that many English portals were in fact constructed without tympana, the three doorways at Lincoln Cathedral being the most famous examples.

60. G. Zarnecki and F. Henry, 'Romanesque arches decorated with human and animal heads', *Journal of the British Archaeological Association*, XX-XXI (1957), 29.

61. The doorway at Freshford has an even more boldly carved head on the keystone. Other sites with heads on the keystone include Clonkeen, Kilmalkedar, Kilmore, Iniscealtra (St Caimin's), Cashel (Cormac's Chapel, north doorway), Christchurch Cathedral Dublin (door now in south transept, plus fragment from the crypt), and Ullard.

62. Kilteel, Timahoe, Duleek, Glendalough [St Saviour's, Priests' House], Clonattin and Rahan. For Clonattin see Stokes, *Early Christian architecture in Ireland*, 115. Outside Leinster head capitals appear at Inisfallen, Ardfert (Temple-na-Hoe), Inchagoill and Annaghdown, Cashel (Cormac's Chapel), Clonmacnoise (St Finghin's and the Nun's Church), Dysert O Dea, Iniscealtra, Kilmore, Roscrea etc. Tiny heads also appear on one of the capitals at Freshford (Kilkenny) and there is a beautiful fragment of what is probably a head capital at Devenish. The distribution and its significance is discussed by de Paor, *Chronology of Irish Romanesque*, 55-60.

63. Timahoe is only thirteen miles from Killeshin; the tower there probably dates from the period shortly after 1142, when 'Tech mochua' was burnt (Gwynn and Hadcock, *Med. relig. houses*, 45). The heads at Timahoe relate to the second category of those at Killeshin, with beards and moustaches.

64. Several scholars have noted the similarities between the Killeshin heads (category 2) and an unprovenanced head in the Sainsbury collection at Norwich, *English Romanesque art 1066-1200* (London, Arts Council, 1984), 163.

65. The example at Auxerre is in the Musée St Germain. For the Roman background see also the thoughtful comments of Sue McNab, 'Early Irish sculpture', *Irish Arts Review Yearbook, 1990-1*, 164-171.

66. Ibid., 170.

67. Canon tables also seem to be one of the likely sources for the so-called 'column swallowers', a popular theme in both English and French Romanesque sculpture.

68. Rome, Vatican, Biblioteca Apostolica MS Barberini Lat. 570, folio 1r, J.J.G. Alexander, *Insular manuscripts 6th to the 9th century* (London, 1978), 61-2. The provenance of the manuscript is not known, though several factors, including the colophon 'Ora pro wigbaldo', suggest an Anglo-Saxon background.

69. Folio 51r. The Barberini Gospels could not have provided the model for Irish sculptors, since they appear to have had an English background, but it is possible that lost Irish Gospels Books had similar features. The decoration of the Book of Kells of course contains numerous human heads, though none are employed in quite the 'architectural' manner seen in the Barberini Gospels.

70. It should, however, be pointed out that the heads sculptured on the vault boss of the chancel at Cormac's Chapel also belong to this stylistic category.

71. Although only heads are sculptured at Killeshin, one wonders whether it is a complete coincidence that Irish sculptors lined the inside of their portals with human forms only a few years after the idea of the column figure came into vogue in France.

72. It is highly unlikely of course that the inscription mentioned ten names.

73. Oxford, Corpus Christi College, MS 282. Both the date and provenance of this manuscript remain unclear. It contains a prayer for the king of Ireland and his son, without naming him. It has generally been assumed that the reference is to Turlough O Conor, F. Henry and G.L. Marsh-Micheli, 'A century of Irish illumination (1070-1170)', *R.I.A., Proc.*, 62 C (1962), 137-140.

74. The analogies lie in the pointed chin and the way in which a broad stem of foliage grows straight out of the forehead.

75. The links with metalwork are very obvious at Tuam, where the animal ornament on the east window of the cathedral includes bosses, apparently copied from metal rivets. The Irish Urnes style was of course equally popular with manuscript illuminators, see Henry and Marsh-Micheli, 'Century of Irish manuscript illumination', passim.

76. Drawings of them are reproduced in Leask, *Irish churches*, i, 104.

77. Máire de Paor (Máire MacDermott) drew attention to the similarities that exist with the animals found on the Kells crosier, Máire MacDermott, 'The Kells crosier', *Archaeologia*, XCVI (1955), 84-5. One of the knops on the crosier includes a stag, reminiscent of that at Killeshin, though the Romanesque version is less stylised, 'Kells crosier', 74.

78. BL, MS. Royal I.E.VI., fol. 4r, illustrated in D.M. Wilson, *Anglo-Saxon ornamental metalwork 700-1100 in the British Museum* (London, 1964), pl. V; see also Alexander, *Insular manuscripts*, no. 32, pl. 62. The semi-circular base is also found in the canon tables of the Book of Kells, though with geometric patterns rather than animals inside.

79. Trinity College, Cambridge, Ms B.10.4., fol. 13v, illustrated in Wilson, *Anglo-Saxon ornamental metalwork*, pl. VIII.

80. Reproduced in Henry and Marsh-Micheli, 'Century of Irish illumination', pl. XVI c.

81. The animal types found at Killeshin deserve more detailed study. The strange jaws were noted by Máire de Paor, 'Kells crosier', 93.

82. Well illustrated in *Treasures of early Irish art 1500B.C. to 1500 A.D.*, ed. P.Cone (New York, 1978), no. 61.

83. A more elaborate version of the design was used in the same position at Freshford (Kilkenny) and related designs can be found at Glendalough (St Saviour's, base) and Clonattin.

84. For the circular forms on grave slabs see slab number 2 at Glendalough.

85. Another unusual element is the presence of a nib or fillet on the edge of all the

angle rolls. Although usually associated with early Gothic architecture, a similar 'fillet' was used in 1158 to decorate the the portal at Aghadoe (Kerry). This important parallel was pointed out to me by Rachel Moss. For the date of Aghadoe see Henry, *Irish art in the Romanesque period*, 166. It is important to note that the fillet at Killeshin has a rounded profile, lacking the sharp edges of Gothic versions.

86. Crawford and Leask, 'Killeshin Church', 90. Both limestone and sandstone were said to be found in the parish, *Topog. dict. Ire.*, ii, 143. The weathered surfaces of the finer granite used for the portal are smooth and creamy, in appearance more like a limestone.

87. At Tuam the analogies with metalwork are particularly close: the sculptors were in effect translating a sumptuous processional cross into stone.

88. The same issue arises in regard to the famous capitals in the crypt of Canterbury Cathedral, dating from around 1100. Several of the designs were based on manuscript prototypes and it has been assumed that somehow the sculptors had access to the library. But it was the scribes and illuminators who were familiar with these sources, not the masons. The evidence is assembled by Deborah Kahn, *Canterbury Cathedral and its Romanesque sculpture* (London, 1991), chapter ii. The author, while convincingly plotting the connections between sculpture and illumination, attributes the design of the capitals to the sculptors themselves. This must be open to question.

89. The evidence linking St Saviour's Priory with St Laurence O'Toole is not conclusive. The *vita* of St Laurence states that while he was abbot of Glendalough (1154-62), the saint showed a great zeal for church building, and on this basis Francoise Henry attributed the foundation of the priory to him, Henry, *Irish art in the Romanesque period*, 44-5.

Chapter 6

THE VIKINGS AND THE KINGDOM OF LAOIS

EAMONN P. KELLY and JOHN MAAS

Introduction

The modern boundary of Co. Laois covers the whole extent of the ancient kingdom of Laois but it also incorporates portions of two other ancient territories. The barony of Upper Ossory, which now forms one third of modern Co. Laois, once belonged to the kingdom of Ossory while that portion of the modern county which now lies north of the river Glasha (or Derravarragh river), once formed part of the territory of Uí Failge.

For reasons which will emerge, it would be largely meaningless to seek to confine a study of this kind exclusively to events which occurred within the boundaries of the ancient kingdom of Laois. The impact of the Vikings was complex.[1] At times they posed a major threat to the very survival of native Irish kingdoms. More often, however, through their alliances with native kings, they became a new factor in the struggle for dominance by Irish overlords. At the end of the eighth century, when the Vikings first began to raid Ireland, the political structures and power bases of the Irish kingdoms were already undergoing a gradual evolution. A central theme in ongoing historical debate is the degree to which native political change was affected and accelerated by the Viking raids which were followed by the foundation of permanent Viking bases which possessed powerful military capability.

Donnchadh Ó Corráin's summary of the political situation in Ireland during the period is a useful starting point:

"Ireland on the eve of the Viking attacks was divided into a multiplicity of kingdoms and overkingdoms. Of these, two were outstanding: the overkingdom of the Uí Néill, which dominated the north and eastern midlands, and the overkingdom of the Eóganacht kings of Munster, who were paramount in the south of the Island".[2]

The part played by Laois in the regional and national struggles in which the Vikings also played a role, either directly or indirectly, will be the subject of this study. The study will concentrate on events in the ninth and early tenth centuries after which there was little Viking activity of any importance relating to Co. Laois.

The coming of the Vikings

Viking activity in Ireland started in the last decade of the eighth century when fleets from the Hebrides, Orkney Islands and possibly Norway itself began roving around the north and east coasts, targeting coastal monastic and population centres. Until around the year 825 the raiding was sporadic and most probably seasonal, taking place during the summer. The numbers of Viking warriors involved and the fleet sizes were probably small. From the reports in the annals it is in some cases possible to track individual fleets as they moved around the coastline.

The second phase of Viking activity in Ireland

A marked change in the intensity and scale of the raiding occurred from the mid-820s when the Vikings systematically began to target inland areas in extended raids, often covering large tracts of country. Viking military power in Ireland reached alarming levels over the next 20 years and the cumulative effect of the attacks began to threaten the existing political and social fabric in the country. Large and well-organised campaigns, which penetrated deep into the wealthy interior of the country by way of the river systems, meant that whole territories were attacked with increasing ferocity and frequency. The annals record battle after battle between local kings and the Norse marauders.[3]

The establishment of Viking bases in Ireland

It was during this period that a profound change in the nature of the Viking activity in Ireland occurred. From the mid-830s (and possibly as early as the mid-820s) it appears that the first Viking bases were founded in counties Louth and Wicklow – on the east coast – and in the north of the island as well. Perhaps seasonal at first, these bases later allowed Viking fleets to over-winter in Ireland and thus extend their campaigning season.[4] At this time the annals start to record large fleets operating off Ireland. The year 840 saw the introduction of the first definitely identifiable base at Lough Neagh which was followed by bases at Dublin and Annagassan a year later. After the foundation of Dublin, Viking bases began to proliferate and over the next five years new ones were founded in the Carlingford Lough area, the Boyne estuary, Lough Swilly and in Lough Ree.[5] The effects of this build-up of Viking power in Ireland were so great that the Annals of St. Bertin, the official Carolingian record, note under the year 847 that: 'The Irish, who had been attacked by the Northmen for a number of years, were made into regular tribute-payers. The Northmen also got control of the islands all around Ireland and stayed there without encountering resistance from anyone'.[6]

Viking attacks on the interior of Ireland

Because of its inland position, Laois escaped the effects of ever-increasing Viking raiding for the first 45 years. To the east and north the territory of Laois was protected by the Leinster kingdoms which acted as a buffer against Viking attack. From the south, Laois was protected by the kingdom of Ossory to which it was allied from the middle of the ninth century. However it was only a matter of time before the Viking forces found their way to the rich inland monasteries.[7]

Following the foundation of Dublin in 841 the main focus of Viking activity switched from the northern and eastern parts of Ireland to the hitherto largely untroubled interior of the southern half of the country. The first recorded raid into Laois occurred in 841 immediately following the foundation of the permanent bases at Dublin and Annagassan. The annals tell us that Leinster and the Southern Uí Néill were plundered as far as Slieve Bloom on the border between the territories of the Uí Néill and Laois. During the same year the Dublin garrison carried out a second major raid overland, first attacking the important monastery of Clonenagh, in the Laois heartland, before moving their attention to the important monasteries of Killeigh in Co. Offaly (one of the principal churches of the Uí Failge) and Clonard, a pre-eminent monastic centre of early Ireland, on the Co. Meath/Kildare border.[8] The following year, 842, saw the foundation of two new bases at Narrow Water, Co. Down, and on the Boyne River near Newgrange at Linn Rois. These garrisons, along with the existing ones of Dublin and Annagassan, were involved in raids into the Irish heartland.[9]

These raids were followed up in 843 by a major two-year campaign by the Vikings along the Shannon system which spread into the Southern Uí Néill kingdom of Mide[10] and also into Connaught and Munster. During this campaign the Vikings founded a base on Lough Ree and in 845, at the height of the onslaught, the ancient fortification of Dunamase in Co. Laois was attacked and plundered. Among the victims were Áed, son of Dub da Crích, abbot of the Laois monastery of Clonenagh and also Terryglass, and Ceithernach, the prior of Kildare and many others.[11]

Irish resistance

The momentum of the Viking assault on the interior of Ireland seems to have been broken in 845 by the death of their leader, Turgesius, at the hands of Máel Sechnaill, king of the Southern Uí Néill. The following year saw the beginning of a series of successful Irish counter-attacks on the Vikings. The first of these occurred in Ossory where it appears that a Viking fleet had come up the river Nore, established itself on the river Callan in Co. Kilkenny and plundered Coolcashin in the same county. Cerball king of Ossory is recorded as having besieged them for two weeks and defeated them.[12] Cerball followed up his earlier victory on the river Callan the next year with a further victory in a great battle between his forces and the Dublin Vikings at Carn Bramit in Kilkenny (identified as Bramblestown). The annals record that the Vikings lost 1,200 men and their leader Agonn (Haakon) may also have been among the casualties.[13] The following year 848 was not a good one for the Vikings in Ireland and particularly Dublin as they suffered five further heavy defeats at the hands of the Irish kings.[14] The garrison of Dublin, seriously depleted and demoralised by these defeats, had their weakness further exposed the following year in 849 when Dublin was plundered for the first time by Máel Sechnaill and Tigernach, king of South Brega.[15]

Leadership of the Viking armies

Many Viking armies throughout the ninth and tenth centuries seem to have been commanded by multiple leaders and were coalitions or amalgamations of the fleets and followers of these leaders. Thus for instance, during the height of Dublin's power in the early 860s, we know of three joint Viking kings (Olaf, Ivar and Auisle) who ruled there. Elsewhere, the great Viking armies all appear to have had multiple leaders and annalistic sources are full of incidents of individual leaders joining or hiving off their followers from such coalitions. Dublin's power in the ninth and early tenth centuries was probably largely dependent on its ability to attract such freebooting forces to its banners. Military successes by the Dublin leadership increased its attractiveness and failure and internal strife had the opposite effect. The lure of land, action and booty with the great armies in England and on the continent during the period from the death of Ivar in 873, until the return to Ireland of large Viking armies in 914, combined with the poor quality and internal problems of the Dublin leadership, was in all probability a major factor in the decline of Dublin and other Viking bases in Ireland in the latter decades of the ninth century.[16] Opportunism seems to have been a major factor motivating Viking leaders, who at times, allied themselves with opposing factions in Irish disputes. On occasions, hostility between rival Viking leaders erupted in warfare in which the Irish were mere spectators.

Civil war between the Vikings in Ireland

In 849, the troubles that the Viking garrisons of Dublin and Annagassan were having at the hands of Máel Sechnaill and other Irish kings were to pale into insignificance when compared to the internal war that erupted between them and large numbers of rival Vikings who sought to dislodge them. The trouble started in 849 when, in one form or another, most of the annals record the arrival of a fleet of 140 Viking ships at Dublin which sought to impose its authority over the existing leadership, causing great confusion.[17] Two years later the situation of the Dublin leadership dramatically worsened when a massive and well co-ordinated attack on Dublin and its sister base Annagassan was carried out by a hostile Viking fleet. The annals describe these new Vikings as Dubgentí – dark pagans – which has been interpreted by later annalistic compilations and some contemporary historians to mean Danish Vikings. The annals describe the incumbent Dublin Vikings as Finngentí – fair pagans – which has been interpreted to mean Norwegian. In the interests of simplicity we shall refer to them as Danes and Norwegians in this paper.[18] In the following year the new Viking arrivals (the Dubgentí or Danes) and the existing Finngentí or Norwegians fought it out in a huge three-day naval and land battle in Carlingford Lough. The annals record the massive scale and intensity of what must have been one of the bloodiest conflicts in Irish history up to that date.[19] The F.A. claim huge numbers were killed and they may not be so exaggerated particularly when we know that the battle lasted three days and, in an Irish context, involved unprecedented numbers of ships and Viking warriors. We know that the fleet of the Danes that arrived in 849 – and which was probably involved again in 851 in the attacks on Dublin and Annagassan – contained 140 ships and that the Norwegian fleet contained 160 ships giving a figure of 300 ships involved in the battle.[20] In 853 the situation was rescued by Olaf who assumed the leadership of the Dublin Vikings. It was however to be another three years before the Dublin garrison was strong enough to engage in major campaigning. In the meantime the internal Viking strife, and possibly the new leadership at Dublin, appears to have triggered a movement of Vikings to the south-east of the country, leading to the foundation of new Viking bases including one in Laois called *Longphort-Rothlaibh*.[21] The site has been identified as an earthwork strategically located on the west bank of the river Barrow at Dunrally, Co. Laois, at the place where it is joined by the river Glasha.[22]

Irish politics during the ninth century

Dunrally's construction was much more than just an isolated incident relating to the activities of the Vikings in Ireland. The event took place in the crucial years of the mid-ninth-century when the kingdom of Ossory was making serious attempts to become the dominant military and political force in Ireland. As a consequence Laois, Ossory's staunch ally, was also propelled onto the centre stage of Irish politics. A co-ordinated response by Cerball, king of Ossory and Cennétig, king of Laois, to the building of Dunrally was thus related to wider political matters which extended well beyond the borders of the kingdom of Laois. The drama being played out had as its prize the kingship or overlordship of Ireland and its principal players included the Uí Néill, overlords of Leth Cuinn; the kings of Cashel, overlords of Leth Moga; Cerball king of Ossory and the Viking kings of Dublin. Conflict between powerful rival Irish overlordships dominated the first half of the ninth century which is precisely the period during which the Vikings established permanent bases in Ireland and became increasingly involved as a military and political force in native power struggles. Whether they were sucked into these conflicts or entered as willing participants with a deliberate policy of exploiting them for their own ends is a matter of debate.[23] The Viking involvement in these conflicts had a profound effect as it introduced a new military dynamic into the norms of Irish warfare.

Between the 820s and 851 the rise of Uí Néill power had been successfully interrupted and partially eclipsed by the prowess of two remarkable kings of Munster: Feidlimid mac Crimthainn (820-847) and Ólchobar mac Cináeda (847-851). Such was his success that in 838 Feidlimid had even succeeded in gaining submission from the Uí Néill (according to pro-Munster sources).[24] It is perhaps no coincidence that this period of Uí Néill weakness coincides with the growth of Viking power in Leth Cuinn and the foundation there of permanent Viking bases. The concentration of Viking attacks against the north and north-east may have helped weaken the Uí Néill and in particular the Northern Uí Néill king of Ireland, Niall Caille (833-846).[25]

Between the middle of the ninth century until the emergence of Brian Boru in the late tenth century the pendulum of power swung back to the Uí Néill and they achieved a nominal dominance over the country and the notion of a kingship of Ireland began to achieve a political reality. However, the Viking intrusions and their establishment of permanent military garrisons at a number of coastal locations, particularly Dublin, became a major factor in the failure of the Uí Néill to create a centralised and permanent high-kingship. Another factor was the inherently unstable succession pattern of the Irish overlordships which in the case of the Uí Néill alternated between the northern and southern branches. Fear by each branch that the other might succeed in breaking the pattern and thus dominate the overlordship, led to internal military conflict between them. Politically and militarily, this weakened the Uí Néill branches for much of the period.[26]

From the middle of the ninth century, the willingness of the Vikings to ally themselves with Irish factions created new opportunities for the Irish kings in their power struggles.[27] Within a few years of Dublin's foundation in 841 the Vikings had become embroiled in internal Uí Néill conflicts, in most cases supporting the candidate from the rival Uí Néill branch against the incumbent holder of the overlordship. In addition, the annals provide convincing evidence that the Dublin Norse began to give military support to lesser kings under Uí Néill domination and to candidates from rival dynasties within each Uí Néill branch.[28]

As a consequence of the new circumstances, because of an ability to augment their military resources by alliances with the Vikings or the hire of Norse mercenaries, minor kingdoms could contemplate throwing off the yoke of Uí Néill domination and pursue ambitions of their own. This created a highly volatile and unstable situation which impeded the development of the high-kingship. More importantly, it opened up the tantalising possibility that the kingship of Ireland was not the sole prerogative of the Uí Néill or their Munster rivals.

The rise of Cerball, king of Ossory

One of the first Irish kings to realise and exploit the new possibilities was Cerball king of Ossory. Arguably the most dynamic Irish king of the ninth century, under his long reign between 843/4 and 888 Ossory was transformed from a relatively minor and unimportant kingdom into one of the most powerful overlordships in Ireland: and there were moments when he even threatened the Uí Néill hegemony.[29]

Central to Ossory's power was domination of the Barrow and Nore valleys which formed its borders with Leinster and Munster respectively. The close military and political alliance of Ossory with Laois assisted its rise to prominence and was a key element in the defence of her borders. In addition Cerball advanced his interests by a series of dynastic marriages with the Uí Néill.[30]

Cerball's ambitions in Leinster

The weakness of the Uí Néill in the face of aggressive kings of Cashel until 851 and the introduction of mercenary Viking armies played a significant role in the rise of Cerball whose primary ambition to the overlordship of Leinster was largely realised during his kingship. His importance and impact can perhaps be seen in the status accorded to him in non-Irish sources, particularly the Welsh annals and in the

Icelandic sagas. The Welsh annals record his death in 888 giving him equal status to the Uí Néill overlords and kings of Munster who are the only other Irish monarchs to receive this treatment.[31] Furthermore, Cerball, uniquely among the contemporary Irish Kings, is remembered in Icelandic lore as Kjarvalr Írakonungr (Kjarvall the Irish King).[32]

Relations between Ossory and the Uí Néill

It appears that Cerball's rise to prominence began in 852 when Viking ambitions in Ireland suffered a huge reversal after the civil war which broke out between various Viking factions. The net effect was total inactivity by the east coast bases for four years until 856. During this breathing space two important things happened. The Southern Uí Néill king and overlord, Máel Sechnaill, used the opportunity to begin the re-assertion of Uí Néill primacy, particularly over Munster, reversing the embarrassing interlude from 820 to 851 when the dominant overlord-ships had been those of Feidlimid and Ólchobar.

Secondly, Cerball began his campaign for a new and independent overlordship aided by Viking alliances, first with a Danish Viking leader called Horm and subsequently with Dublin. The *Fragmentary Annals* tell us that Horm, whom they identify as a leader of the victorious Danish fleet at the battle of Carlingford Lough, feared being 'overcome by the stratagems of the Norwegians'.[33] The battle at Carlingford had been essentially about the control of the Viking bases of Dublin and Annagassan. The new order in Dublin under Olaf and Ivar appears to have united the Norwegian and Danish factions under their leadership. So why Horm, a leader of the victorious Danish fleet, should seek refuge with Cerball and not take his place in the new order in Dublin remains an unsolved mystery. However the answer may lie in the bloody dynastic and family feuds that were a feature of Viking life.

Unfortunately the annals are largely silent about Cerball during the crucial period in which he rose to prominence. By 854 he had achieved sufficient status and power to be courted by Máel Sechnaill who sent him into Munster to demand hostages after the death of its king Ailgenán in 853. This was despite the fact that Munster was nominally the overlord of Ossory. Maél Sechnaill's request to Cerball may have been partially influenced by the fact that sometime between 852 and 854, Munster had requested Cerball and his Danish allies to assist it against a Norwegian army which was defeated subsequently at Crohane in Co. Tipperary.[34] The date was probably 854 because Maél Sechnaill had himself invaded Munster as far as Clonmel enforcing submission and Cerball is recorded as having escorted and presented Horm, the leader of his Viking allies, to Máel Sechnaill after his victory at Crohane.[35] Horm was killed in Wales in 856[36] and the same year saw

Máel Sechnaill back in Cashel enforcing his authority over Munster. Máel Sechnaill's successes so far, together with the loss of Horm, almost certainly threatened Cerball's ambitions. However, Máel Sechnaill's own ambitions were seriously challenged during 856 when Dublin and the east coast bases, under Olaf, now reinforced by Ivar, exploded back onto the Irish stage. Máel Sechnaill responded by entering an alliance with a Viking force of mixed origins known as the *Gall-Gaedil*.[37] As a consequence Cerball forged an alliance with the Dublin leadership. This alliance may have been sealed by the marriage of his grand-daughter to the son of the Dublin Viking king, Olaf.[38]

Hostility between Cerball and Máel Sechnaill

The first fruits of this alliance and Cerball's open hostility to Máel Sechnaill occurred in 858 when Cerball and Ivar defeated the Cenél Fiachach (a subkingdom of the Southern Uí Néill in Offaly) who were being aided by Máel Sechnaill's new allies, the *Gall-Gaedil*. The defeat occurred in north-west Tipperary and the *A.F.M.* tell us that the combined army of Cerball and Ivar numbered 6,400. Cerball followed up this victory by plundering Leinster and taking its hostages. The previous year *A.U.* record that the Viking kings of Dublin, Olaf and Ivar, routed Caitil the Fair and his *Gall-Gaedil* in Munster.[39]

Máel Sechnaill responded quickly to the situation and followed up Cerball's attacks with a major hosting into Munster and, for the first time, Ossory. He defeated Máel Guala, king of Munster, and spent a month in Munster taking hostages. He also took hostages from Cerball.[40] Máel Sechnaill's expedition availed him little as Cerball immediately responded by plundering Leinster again and taking its hostages and this, as the *Fragmentary Annals* informs us, 'despite having given hostages to Máel Sechnaill'.[41] During the same year Cerball made his most audacious move by invading Máel Sechnaill's kingdom of Mide along with Ivar and Olaf where he spent either three months or forty nights plundering it.[42]

Ossory freed from the overlordship of Munster

The intense pressure exerted by Cerball and his Viking Dublin allies forced Máel Sechnaill to seek a solution to the problem. In 859, he took the unprecedented action of convening a royal assembly which met at Rahugh on the borders of Westmeath. Present were Máel Sechnaill and the abbot of Clonard. Also present was Fethgna, abbot of Armagh, who identified with the interests of the Uí Néill. The outcome was that Cerball made complete submission to Armagh and Ossory was permanently alienated to Leth-Cuinn. Máel Guala, king of Munster, gave sureties for this alienation.[43] This notable outcome had been partially brought about by Viking force of arms in a two-year long military campaign by Cerball. The loser twice over in the process was Máel Guala, who, after being humiliated by being forced to accede to Ossory's alienation, was captured by the Vikings and stoned to death, possibly at Cerball's instigation.[44]

Cerball's alliance with Máel Sechnaill

In the following year, 860, Máel Sechnaill, along with the forces of Leinster and Connaught and his now staunch ally Cerball, led an army into the north to assert his dominance over his Northern Uí Néill cousins. The army encamped near Armagh and an inconclusive battle was fought. True to their form the Dublin Vikings under Olaf were now supporting the Northern Uí Néill king Áed against Máel Sechnaill.[45] The pressure on Máel Sechnaill from Áed and the Dublin Norse was renewed and intensified. In 861 Máel Sechnaill fought a battle against the Dublin Vikings in Offaly. During the same year Áed and Olaf invaded and plundered Mide and Máel Sechnaill was forced to call on Cerball to assist him against them.[46] The next year, during which Máel Sechnaill died on 13 November, Áed, supported by the king of Knowth (Flann son of Conaing) and the Dublin Norse, again plundered Mide. There was no support from Ossory however as Cerball had his hands full dealing with a major crisis in Laois where Vikings under the command of Rodulf had established a base at Dunrally on the river Barrow.[47]

Rodulf's career in Ireland

Sometime during the 850s and early 860s a Viking leader named Rodulf became active on the Nore and Barrow systems, attacking Ossory and Laois from a base probably located in the Waterford Harbour area. His reported activities were confined to the south-east of the country and are only noticed in the *Fragmentary Annals* and the *Annals of the Four Masters*.[48]

A total of six entries in the annals document four separate incidents of this new Viking presence in Laois and Ossory. Three of them actually name Rothlaibh or Rodulf as the leader of forces in this campaign.

The first of these in the *F.A.* concerns a raid by Rodulf and his army into Ossory. The raid, which is not dated, probably occurred in the mid-850s as it lies sequentially between entries in *F.A.* that are datable to the early and mid-850s. The Norwegian forces under Rodulf appear to have been sizeable and some at least were mounted. Although Cerball defeated Rodulf he became separated from his followers and was captured by the Vikings. Luckily, however, he was able to escape.

The battle was fought in the vicinity of a ford named Áth Muiceda which remains unidentified but is probably on the Nore.[49]

The next event reported in the *F.A.* involving a Viking attack on Cerball is the battle of Achad mic Erclaige whose likely location has been identified as Agha, alias St. John's, near the city of Kilkenny. *F.A.* report two fleets of Norwegian Vikings raiding Cerball. *A.F.M.* also carries a report of the battle and dates it to 860 and adds that the fleet involved was the fleet from Port Láirge or Waterford.[50] The account does not name Rodulf. However, in her index to the *F.A.*, Radner describes Rodulf as a Norwegian leader from Port Láirge or Waterford. Given the fact that he was active during the period on the Nore and Barrow systems it is probable that Rodulf's main base was in the estuaries of these rivers in the Waterford harbour area and that any fleet passing up these rivers would either be under his control or sanctioned by him.[51]

Waterford's foundation has traditionally been ascribed to 914 after the return of the great fleets of the grandsons of Ivar who re-established the Viking presence in Ireland after their expulsion in 902. However, a number of entries in the annals for the ninth century relate to fleets operating in the Waterford Harbour area and it is probable that the Vikings had at least one ninth century base in the area prior to the foundation of the base that grew into Waterford City.[52]

The next incident involving Rodulf is a plundering raid up the river Barrow that was initially successful but then went badly wrong for his forces when Cerball caught up with them. The raid probably occurred in 856/7 or 860/1 as its account in *F.A.* lies last in a group of entries dated to 860 and interposed between a sequence of entires dated between 856/7. The battle site at Slievemargy lies close to the river Barrow about three miles north-west of Carlow town and close to the early and important monastery of Killeshin which was the probable target of the attack. The *F.A.* tells us that, earlier on the raid, Rodulf's forces had plundered the highly important monastery of Lethglenn or Old Leighlin a little over six miles downstream from Killeshin where they killed a great number of its community and took hostages. Both monasteries are easily reached from the river. Rodulf does not appear to have been present personally as the inference is that it was his followers who were involved in the raid. Rodulf may have been safely holed up in either Waterford or Dunrally, assuming that the longphort at Dunrally was already in existence at this time. If so the raid could have started either from there or from Waterford. The Viking ships could have coasted down the river using the current (possibly at night to avoid detection) and, using the prevailing favourable winds from the south-west, could have made their way back upriver raiding as they went. Alternatively they may have been moving upriver with Dunrally as a secure end-base.[53]

The final reference to Rodulf is the destruction of his longphort in 862 which is recorded by both the *A.F.M.* and *F.A.*

> The destruction of Longphort-Rothlaibh by Cinnedidh, son of Gaithin, Lord of Laighis, on the fifth of the Ides of September; and the killing of Conal Ultach and Luirgnen with many others along with them (*A.F.M.*).

> Cerball son of Dúnlaing and Cennétig son of Gáethíne (i.e. the son of Cerball's sister) defeated Rodolb's fleet, which had come from Norway shortly before that; and Conall Ultach was killed there, and Luirgnén, and many others (*F.A.*).[54]

As can be seen there are discrepancies between both accounts. Both agree only on the deaths of many in the battle, including Conall Ultach and Luirgnén (whoever they are). There are three main differences between the accounts. The *A.F.M.* refers to the destruction of a longphort while *F.A.* refers to the defeat of a fleet. Cerball's part in the attack is omitted by *A.F.M.* and the date of the attack is omitted by *F.A.* but is given precisely in *A.F.M.* as the 9th of September.

There is no serious contradiction on the first of these points as a longphort was constructed to protect a fleet and its crews. Both entries are correct if one assumes that both the longphort and the fleet it protected were destroyed in the battle.

The inclusion of the precise date of the attack suggests that *A.F.M.* was drawing on a well informed and accurate source. The date, 9 September, fits in well with the environment of the site which is marshy. An attack after the end of summer when water levels were at their lowest would have best suited an overland assault on the site. A very similar example of the destruction of a fortified Viking camp located between a marsh and the river Dyle took place in Belgium in 891 when the Carolingian attackers also chose late summer for their assault.

The entry in *F.A.* describes the fleet and crews as having newly arrived. It may well be that Rodulf was receiving reinforcements from abroad or that a transfer of Vikings from Waterford had taken place. Such an expansion of a powerful garrison deep inland on their borders – presumably with hostile intentions towards Ossory and Laois – would have given real cause for alarm to both Cerball and Cennétig and may have spurred them into action.

This decisive military action marked a major turning point in Viking activity in Laois during the ninth century. Had the Viking base resisted successfully and survived the attack it could have threatened and dominated the kingdom of Laois and the other surrounding Leinster kingdoms. More significantly a powerful Norse base on the Barrow at this location would have left the Vikings strategically located on an important route-way along the river valley, control of which was of great military importance to competing Irish provincial kings. As noted above the strategic location of the base at Dunrally had serious implications for the aspirations of Cerball in Leinster. Located but a short distance from the royal fortress of Dunamase, the threat posed to the kingdom of Laois is also obvious. Furthermore, Dunrally, acting in concert with Dublin, would between them have been in a position to squeeze the Leinster kingdoms of Uí Failge, Uí Fáeláin and Uí Muiredaig. The situation would have been extremely serious for Leinster as the Dublin base alone had already undermined Leinster's power. As Byrne put it,

> The prestige of the Uí Dúnlainge was further weakened by the establishment in 841 of a permanent Norse settlement at Dublin which from time to time was strong enough to extend its control over a wide area and threaten the neighbouring petty kingdoms.[55]

There were implications also for the Uí Néill as Dunrally was within a short striking distance of the underbelly of Mide where Máel Sechnaill, who was Cerball's new ally from 859, was to die two months after the longphort's destruction.

A Viking base at such a strategic location as Dunrally created a situation that was intolerable to all the Irish kings concerned. It may well be that the establishment of Dunrally was a deliberate strategic move supported by, or even orchestrated by the Dublin Norse as part of their war with Máel Sechnaill. The foundation of Dunrally may have been seen as a means of putting pressure on Cerball, one of Máel Seachnaill's most powerful allies. It is interesting to note that the hostilities between Cerball and Rodulf all appear to date from the period when Cerball was in hostility to Dublin, i.e. prior to his alliance with Dublin in 857/8 and after his alliance with Máel Sechnaill against Dublin in 859. In any event the choice of Dunrally as the site for an inland fortified base appears to date to the later phase of Rodulf's activity, extending and consolidating the range of his forces in a fashion very similar to the manner of his Viking contemporaries active on the rivers Loire, Seine and elsewhere in the Carolingian realms and in Britain.

By the time of Dunrally's construction it would seem that Rodulf had been active in the general area for some considerable time and he was probably much more active than the few annalistic references we have for him would suggest. If we rely solely on the three entries in the *Fragmentary Annals* that name him, Rodulf seems to have been a singularly unlucky and unsuccessful raider because on each of these occasions he was badly mauled by Cerball. This conclusion conflicts with an undercurrent in the annals which suggests that Rodulf was a powerful and clever Viking leader who remained a thorn in Ossory's side for a number of years, earning him the wrath and hated of Cerball. It may well be that only raids involving him or his forces that were unsuccessful were chosen by the recorder and that many other successful raids were ignored in an attempt to elevate Cerball.

The *A.F.M.* credit Cennétig with the destruction of Dunrally while the *F.A.* states that the destruction was accomplished by Cerball, accompanied by Cennétig, his nephew. Cerball's omission from *A.F.M.* does not detract from the validity of the account and his inclusion in *F.A.* may be the result of conflation by the compiler of *F.A.* (who was possibly working for Donnchad Mac Gilla Pátraic, king of Ossory and eventually king of Leinster from 1036 to 1039), and who may have credited Cerball into the attack on Dunrally in order to elevate the prestige of the Ossory lineage.[56]

Rodulf's career after the destruction of Dunrally

The final mention of Rodulf in the Irish annals is the destruction of his longphort. He is not mentioned among the casualties and he may either have escaped or been elsewhere at the time.[57] Four months later, in January, 863 a Viking fleet attacked up the river Rhine and in the following year King Lothar II, in whose territory these raiders suddenly appeared, paid danegeld to a Viking named Rodulf who appears to have been the leader of the Vikings in question. The sudden appearance of the fleet suggests that it arrived from beyond the land of the Franks and the coincidence of the name and the timing of these events suggests that the Rodulf involved is the same man named in the Irish annals. The occurrence of the name Rodulf among Viking leaders is extremely rare in annalistic entries for the whole of the ninth and tenth centuries. In the Irish annals it occurs only in the entries quoted earlier and, in the Frankish annals, only in relation to the Rodulf who was active in Frisia from 863 until his death in 873. The Rodulf of the Irish annals appears to have begun his activities in the early or mid 850s. His Irish career ends with the destruction of his important base on the river Barrow in September, 862 – four months before the career of the continental Rodulf appears to have begun with the raid up the Rhine in January, 863. The coincidence of the names and timing of these activities may suggest that we are dealing with one and the same person.[58] If this is so then the Frankish annals enable us to identify Rodoulf as the son of Harold, a former king of Denmark who had settled in Frisia after being expelled from Denmark in 827. Harold appears to have died between the late 840s and early 850s, shortly before Rodulf's Irish carrer began. After his return to the continent in 863, Rodulf continued to be active in the area of Frisia until his death in 873.[59]

Archaeological evidence for Viking raiders along the rivers Barrow and Nore

Recent excavations at Dunamase have uncovered a silver Anglo-Saxon coin of Ecgberht of Wessex, dating no later than *c.* 830. It is likely that this object entered Ireland in the purse of a Viking but whether its presence in Dunamase was the result of warfare or trade cannot be stated. However, its discovery does provide evidence for an external presence of some sort in Laois around the middle of the ninth century, a fact which is supportive of the historical evidence.[60]

A Viking gold armlet which dates to the period from 850-950, found at Rathedan, near the river Barrow in Co. Carlow,[61] is unlikely to be a trade item. Possibly, it may have been a gift from a Viking leader to a native king or – more likely – booty taken by the Irish as the result of a Viking raid which went wrong. The Ballyadams, Co. Laois hoard,[62] which contains a silver ring and ingot is from the same period as the Rathedan armlet. The hoard may also relate to the activities of the Vikings along the river Barrow but whether these activities were of a trading or raiding nature is not clear. Three spearheads, apparently of Viking type, found along the river Nore are likely to relate to the activities of raiders. Two were found separately in the vicinity of Borris in Ossory and the third was found at Clashnamuck, Co. Laois.[63]

Dunrally Fort: placename evidence and the significance of the term "longphort"

'Dunrally' is not a townland name but is applied specifically to the earthwork known as Dunrally Fort.[64] A number of commentators, starting with O'Donovan, have identified Dunrally Fort as *Longphort-Rothlaibh*[65] and it is believed that Dunrally is an anglicization of *Dún Rothlaibh*, the Fort of Rodulf. the element *dún* refers to a fortification and is not normally applied to Irish ringforts (which are more often designated by the elements *rath* or *lios*).

A survey was conducted of all the extant Irish annals between the years 400-1200 AD in order to examine the meaning and context of the term *longphort*.[66] This revealed that *longphort* was first introduced into the language of the annals in 840 and 841 when it was used to describe a Viking base on Lough Neagh (840) and for the foundation of Viking bases in Dublin and Annagassan (841). Through the ninth century and the first half of the tenth century the term continued in use in contemporary annals to describe Scandinavian bases of both a temporary and permanent nature which were invariably associated with the activities of ships and fleets. During this period the term was not used to describe Irish fortified bases or marching camp which were described by the terms *dún* and *dúnadh* respectively. The term *dún* and its derivatives were, however, used by the contemporary annals to describe some notable Viking forts e.g. 'Dún Amhlaim' in *A.U.* (Olaf's fort at Clondalkin, Co. Dublin burned in 867) and the Viking fort at Cork, destroyed in 848, described in *C.S.* as 'Dún Corcaige'. Thus the dún element in the placename Dunrally is not in conflict with *A.F.M.*'s description of a longphort there or with contemporary annalistic practice. A change took place in the middle of the tenth century when the term *dúnadh,* signifying an Irish marching camp, fell into disuse and the use of the term *longphort* was extended to describe such Irish camps.

However, as *Longphort-Rothlaibh* dates to the mid ninth century it can only refer to a Viking fortification associated with the activities of a fleet.[67]

Description of Dunrally Fort

At Dunrally there is an outer rampart which encloses a D-shaped area 360 metres long and 150 metres in maximum width. It is shown on the O.S. first edition (1841) and on later editions. There is a ditch, mainly water-filled, up to 5.3 metres wide and 1.8 metres deep which joins the river Glasha with the river Barrow, thus forming a D-shaped enclosure (fig. 6.1). There is a continuous bank inside the ditch which averages 3.8 metres in width and survives to a height of 40cm above the internal ground level. There is a counterscarp bank flanking the ditch for about one third its length which may be related to re-digging in modern times for drainage purposes. It is clear that the outer ditch has been linked into the local system of drainage ditches but it is not itself primarily a drainage ditch. There is a modern entrance by means of a stone built bridge about halfway along the rampart.[68] The D-shaped enclosure was sufficiently large to ensure that the biggest of Viking fleets could have been protected on-shore and, prior to modern dredging, there was a pool on the river Barrow, immediately adjacent, where ships could have anchored.

Roughly centrally placed within the D-shaped enclosure there is an oval enclosure covering an area which measures 52 x 41 metres and

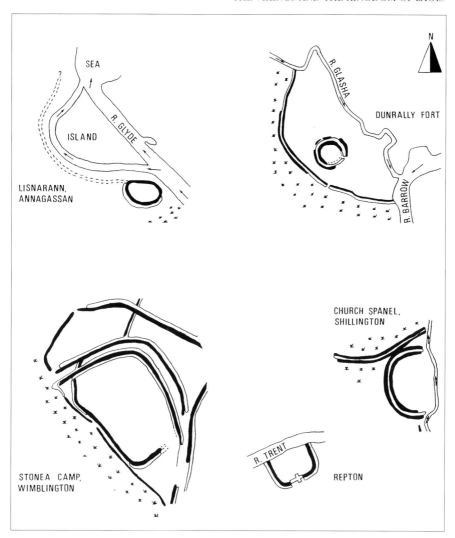

Fig. 6.1   Lisnarann, Annagassan, after Wright, 1948, with additions. Dunrally Fort
             after Kelly and Maas, 1995. Stonea Camp and Church Spanel, after Dyer,
             1972. Repton, after Biddle and Kyølbye-Biddle, 1992.

which is slightly raised. The enclosing ramparts consist of a high bank
inside a wide water-filled ditch outside of which there are the remains
of a low counterscarp bank. The inner bank is 6.2m wide; has an
interior height of 1.65m and an exterior height of 4.5m. The ditch is 7m
wide.

Location of Dunrally Fort
Dunrally Fort is located at a bend in the river Barrow where it is joined
by its tributary, the Glasha. According to O'Donovan the tributary once

formed the border between the lands of the Lóigis and the Uí Failge[69] while the river Barrow formed the border with the Uí Muiredaig. The choice of site may have aimed at taking advantage of rivalries between these kingdoms.

The Dunrally complex is sited in an inaccessible marshy area which in former times would have been reached most easily by boat. To the north of the site extended a large forest.[70] It is perhaps significant that the date of the destruction of the site is given as 9 September, 862, for at that time of year the surrounding marshy area would have been at its driest.

The construction of a *longphort* at Dunrally would have been consistent with the known practices of the Vikings elsewhere. Within the Carolingian empire, and elsewhere, the Scandinavians first consolidated estuarine areas and then extended upriver by building fortified bases on river islands[71] or inaccessible areas of river bank. The destruction of one such fortification on the river Dyle at Louvain referred to earlier is recorded in the Annals of Fulda for 891. The fort is described as having been surrounded by a ditch with a marsh on one side and the bank of the river on the other. Like *Longphort-Rothlaibh* it was destroyed in the autumn when the surrounding marshy ground was at its driest. The lengthy and very detailed description in the Carolingian annals of the attack on the Belgian site, supports the view that Dunrally may belong to a class of Viking inland forts chosen for their defensible terrain of marsh and river and hitherto unrecognised in the Irish interior.[72]

The construction of a longphort at Dunrally is neither unusual nor unique as the Irish annals are full of references to such sites. A careful scrutiny of the annals suggests that there was a much greater number of Viking bases, both permanent and temporary, than has been hitherto identified. These bases are generally associated with the activities of Viking fleets and some of them appear to have succumbed to Irish attacks or were abandoned only to be re-used decades later by other Viking fleets. Some of the bases even appear to have controlled an agricultural hinterland supporting crops, flocks and herds.[73]

The choice of location of Dunrally Fort – at the junction of two rivers is similar to that of the tenth century Irish Viking towns.[74] Another feature the fort has in common with the towns is its proximity to a crossing point on the river. Dunrally Bridge, located a short distance down-stream, now stands on what must have been a crossing place since prehistoric times as stone axes have been found in the river at the location.[75]

Another important factor in the choice of location may have been the relatively short raiding distances from Dunrally to a number of major wealthy monasteries, many of which had not been raided before because of their inland locations. Dunrally Fort would have given the

Vikings the option of raiding from either end of the river Barrow, thus increasing the element of surprise.

Comparisons between Dunrally Fort and Viking settlement sites

It would appear that all previous commentators considered Dunrally Fort to consist only of the oval enclosure. Without excavation, the age or contemporaneity of the oval and D-shaped enclosures cannot be asserted with certainty but comparison with known or probable Viking sites would appear to indicate important parallels.

The low-lying marshy location makes highly unlikely the possibility that the oval enclosure at Dunrally is an Irish ringfort.[76] However, these factors would not exclude the possibility that it is a medieval ring-work of the Norman era.[77] If that identification should prove correct then the structure was probably built to exploit the same locational factors as the D-shaped enclosure. However, the possibility that the oval enclosure is a Viking Age citadel, contemporary with the D-shaped enclosure should not be dismissed without further consideration.

Elsewhere in the Viking world the combination of a D-shaped enclosure and an oval citadel is known. The Viking towns of Hedeby in Denmark and Birka in Sweden date from around 800 AD and both have citadels – small hill forts located on high ground at the edge of (or immediately outside) D-shaped enclosures.[78] This pattern may be repeated at Annagassan, Co. Louth (fig. 6.1), where the annals record a longphort in 841. The identification of a 'Danish Fort' at Annagassan was first proposed by Wright in 1748.[79] His plan of the site – known as Lisnarann – represents it as consisting of an oval enclosure on high ground immediately overlooking a D-shaped island in the river Glyde. A continuous embankment is shown extending from the oval fort along the river bank opposite the island.[80] A similar scheme was shown by J.B. Leslie in the plan accompanying his 1909 note on the site.[81] If one includes the island as an integral part of the complex then the layout is surprisingly similar to Hedeby and Birka and comparable in its elements to Dunrally.[82]

If one considers the central enclosure at Dunrally in isolation from the other elements of the site this allows for further comparisons to be drawn. Viking oval or circular forts occur over a wide area, perhaps the best known of which are the circular forts of tenth century Denmark. Though larger than the Dunrally citadel, these compare well in other respects. Fyrkat is constructed on a ridge in a marshy valley and measures 120m internally. Trelleborg is a little bigger than Fyrkat and is also built on a ridge with marshy ground on either side. There is an annex to the site within which houses were constructed. Aggersborg, which is built overlooking a fjord, is twice as big as Fyrkat.[83] A fourth site, Nonnebakken, was the last to be discovered. It is about the same size as Fyrkat and has produced Viking antiquities dating to around 980.[84]

Circular forts of the Viking age occur in Flanders, the most extensively excavated example of which is Oost-Souburg on the island of Walcheren.[85] At Camp de Péran in Brittany there is a large oval enclosure, subdivided internally, surrounded by a 3m high bank and 4m wide ditch. Viking remains excavated within date it to the early 10th century.[86] Closer to home a series of circular/oval fortifications have been identified by James Dyer as forming a class of Viking fortifications associated with the Danelaw frontier. The sites in question are positioned on hill tops or hill slopes close to rivers and may have served as look-out posts.[87]

Dyer identifies two further types of Viking earthworks associated with the Danelaw frontier which are of relevance to the Dunrally question. One type consists of rectangular harbours which are often heavily fortified.[88] Of great relevance, however, are large D-shaped earthworks, one side butting on to water, constructed either on flat land beside navigable rivers or small islands surrounded by marsh or fenland. Dyer noted the resemblance of these sites to Birka and Hedeby but comparisons may also be drawn with the Irish Viking towns;[89] the earthwork on the River Dyle described in the Annals of Fulda;[90] and Dunrally Fort.

D   y   e   r
quotes an account from the *Anglo-Saxon Chronicle* of a Danish army which built a fortress at Tempsford in 917 in order to gain control of Bedford and the south Midlands of England. The fortress was besieged and destroyed shortly afterwards by the Saxons and its location has been a matter of controversy. Dyer proposes that a D-shaped earthwork known as Beeston Berrys is the site in question. It is five to six acres in extent with its straight side butting on the river Ivel.[91] There are a number of accounts in the *Anglo-Saxon Chronicle* which suggest that the Tempsford site was not unique. Viking armies needed to camp in defensible positions and, at first, they appear to have used natural islands such as the Isle of Sheppey and Thanet. Thereafter, fortifications were constructed and the *A.S.C.* references suggest that the Vikings preferred to make use of the sea or a river or marsh to protect them on one side. In addition to the Tempsford site constructed in 917, Viking forts were constructed in 885 at Rochester; 892 at Milton Regis and Appledore; 893 at Benfleet and Shoebury; 894 on the river Lea above London and Bridgenorth on the river Severn.[92] Sites such as these are notoriously difficult to locate and date archaeologically. However, a case has been made for the Viking construction of a D-shaped enclosure

known as Church Spanel, Shillington, which abuts a navigable stream and has a wet ditch (fig. 6.1). It measures approximately 165m x 100m and is surrounded by marshy ground.[93] A more substantial D-shaped enclosure which measures approximately 390m x 165m is located on the south-western edge of Stonea Island, Wimblington, Cambs (fig. 1). It is constructed beside Latches Fen and the Fen acts as the straight side of the enclosure.[91] A small D-shaped site abutting the river Ouse at The Hillings, Eaton Socon, Hunts, has been shown to date to pre-Norman times.[95] At the monastic site of Repton there is conclusive evidence to support the view that a D-shaped enclosure was constructed as a winter camp for the Viking army of 873-4. The river Trent forms one side and the rest of the site is surrounded by a bank and ditch into which the pre-existing monastic church is incorporated as a gatehouse (fig. 6.1). Excavations have discovered extensive Viking remains, including weapons and burials.[96] At Shoebury, Essex, a rampart enclosing a semicircular area, approximately 460m across, adjacent to the sea, may be the Viking camp of 893.[97]

It is clear therefore that fortifications which are closely comparable to Dunrally Fort occur widely throughout the Viking realms, including Ireland, and the evidence of these sites, taken in conjunction with the placename and wider historical evidence, greatly strengthens the claim of Dunrally Fort to being the *Longphort-Rothlaibh* of the annals.

Viking decline following the destruction of Dunrally Fort

Following the Dunrally attack in 862 Cerball and Cennétig are reported as acting in military unison on a number of subsequent occasions. In 863 Cerball is recorded as slaughtering Vikings and 'banishing them from the territory' at Fertagh near Johnstown, Co. Kilkenny.[98] In the same year Olaf and Ivar, now sharing the kingship of Dublin with Ausli, turned on Áed Findliath (who had become the Uí Néill overlord on Máel Sechnaill's death) and attacked and plundered his ally Flann king of Knowth. The action was in keeping with the pattern of the Dublin Vikings who almost invariably supported the enemies of the incumbent Uí Néill overlord and attacked his allies.[99] The following year Cerball was back raiding Leinster, the Leinstermen then raided Ossory in return with Viking help. During the return raid a number of the people of Ossory fled into Munster where they were killed by the Eóganacht. Cerball avenged this by hiring Norwegian mercenaries to raid Munster.[100]

In his alliance with Cerball, Cennétig was to become the main expression of Ossory's ongoing hostility with Dublin. In 866 he and the forces of north Ossory slaughtered Vikings at Monadrehid near Borris in Ossory. The same year the *F.A.* report that the Viking kings attacked Munster with huge armies but were in turn attacked and defeated at two separate locations by Cennétig and the forces of Ossory.[101] This raid from Dublin was probably the last major action by Olaf and Ivar for a number of years as they departed for Britain with substantial forces in 866 and were part of the great army that decimated much of Britain and Scotland. Ivar's forces entually captured the city of York. Thereafter, York became the centre of Viking colonisation and the seat of Viking kings in Britain.[102]

The Irish kings responded with vigour to the depleted Viking forces in Ireland. In the north the Uí Néill overlord, Áed, overran and plundered their fortresses. In the south the Déisi defeated the Viking fleet of Youghal and destroyed its fortress.[103]

However despite their weakness the Norse were far from docile. Vikings, possibly based on the Barrow, responded by sacking and destroying the monasteries of Shrule (on the east side of the Barrow north of Carlow Town); Sleaty (1 mile NNW of Killeshin) and Agha (Achad Arglais in the barony of Idrone, Co. Carlow).[104]

The next year Cennétig and a Leinster war leader called Máel Ciaráin attacked and burnt Olaf's fort at Clondalkin, slaughtering its inhabitants. Cennétig followed this up by defeating what remained of the Dublin fleet.[105]

The attacks on Viking bases continued in 868 and *A.F.M.* tell us that the lord of the Uí Bairrche Tíre (a people in the barony of Slievemargy, Co. Laois) was killed while demolishing the fortress of the foreigners. This base may have been behind the raids on the Barrow monasteries two years previously.[106]

Throughout this period Cerball (and now also Cennétig, Cerball's ally) remained staunch in his alliance with the Uí Néill which had begun with Máel Sechnaill and continued with Áed Findliath after the death of Máel Sechnaill in 862.[107] Cerball continued to act like a great overlord throughout this period plundering Leinster, Munster and even Connacht on occasion. In 871 Olaf and Ivar returned from the conquest of Britain bringing an immense booty in slaves and travelling in a fleet of 200 ships, the largest single fleet recorded in the Irish annals for the ninth century.[108] However, Olaf left Ireland for good shortly afterwards. What was to be the last major Viking attack for decades took place on 1 February, 872 when the north of Ossory and parts of Laois were plundered by Dublin.[109] In the following year, 873 Ivar – now king of the Vikings in Britain and Ireland – died.[110]

The forty years peace

From 873 until 914 Viking activity hit a low point and only sporadic raids and fratricidal murders among the Dublin Norse received notice in the annals thus confirming that the Vikings were still present in

Ireland. Yet elsewhere, during this very period – in England and in the Carolingian realms – huge Viking armies were locked in deadly campaigns extending over decades.

This period of Viking decline is, arguably, the forty years of peace referred to in *C.G.G.*.[111] Viking power in Ireland slipped to such a low ebb during this period that in 902 the king of Leinster and the king of Brega were able to attack and take Dublin and expel the Norse from it for 15 years.[112]

Death of Cerball and Cennétig

During the 40-year period of peace Cerball died in 888 and Cennétig in 903. The staunch alliance between Ossory and Laois broke down after Cerball's death. In 908 Laois and Ossory fought on opposite sides at the decisive battle of Belach Mugna which took place near Leighlinbridge astride the strategic corridor into Leinster.

The battle, fought over control of Leinster, involved an attempt by Munster to take back the overlordship of Ireland from the Uí Néill for the first time in over half a century. Ossory fought with Munster against the Uí Néill and Leinster (which was supported by Laois). Cellach, king of Ossory (Cerball's son) was among the dead. The battle was the first major internal Irish struggle for many decades in which the Vikings failed to play a major part because of their exile.[113] The break-up of the alliance between Ossory and Laois suggests that it may in the first place have been a response to the threat posed by the Vikings. With the danger apparently now passed older allegiances resurfaced once more. However, such assumptions were premature.

Despite its enforced exile in Britain the dynasty of Ivar had not given up hope of regaining its power in Ireland and in 914 made the first moves in a campaign which eventually threatened to overrun much of the country.

Return of the Viking fleets

In 914 the Irish annals report the arrival of 'a great new fleet' at Waterford and the erection of a stronghold there. It is possible to track the activities of this Viking fleet back to Brittany through the *Anglo Saxon Chronicle* and the Welsh Annals which document its activities in Wales and England before noting its departure in the autumn of 914 to Ireland. The *Anglo Saxon Chronicle* records that it was a 'great naval force' under the command of two Earls, Ohter and Hroald. Hroald was killed in Wales and Ohter eventually departed for Ireland. The *C.G.G.* also record the arrival at Waterford of an 'Earl Oiter Dubh' with a hundred ships. He was in Ireland for four years as his departure for Scotland in 918 is recorded in *A.U.*[114]

The 100 ships of Oiter were only the beginning of a five year rampage by the largest build-up of Viking power in Ireland to date. The following year Oiter's forces were augmented by 'great and frequent reinforcements of foreigners arriving in Loch-Dachaech'. The annals record that the kingdoms and churches of Munster were constantly plundered by them. Among their monastic targets were Cork, Lismore and Aghaboe. From various sources it is possible to glean that at least three more Viking fleets arrived as *C.G.G.* and *A.U.* give us the names of the Earls Gragabai, Haconn and Cossa-Nara as being commanders of this build-up.[115]

In 916 the mayhem spread deep inland into Munster and Leinster as we hear of a number of Irish kings being slain by the Vikings. It also seems that Diarmait the king of Ossory was unique among Irish kings by being in league with the Vikings. The annals record that 'Bran son of Echtighearn, Tanist of Uí-Ceinnsealaigh, was slain by the Norsemen, and by Diarmaid son of Cearbhall, lord of Osraighe'.[116]

The following year, 917, was to be the worst yet as two further large Viking fleets under the command of the grandsons of Ivar, the kings Ragnall and Sitric, arrived in the south-east. Ragnall landed at Waterford and took command while Sitric based his fleet on the Barrow close to St. Mullins. The alliance with Ossory (which although unproven is suggested by Diarmait's actions the previous year and the lack of any record of Ossory's resistance to the Vikings) would have secured one flank of Sitric's move up the Barrow and also secured Ragnall's flank, in his reported moves up the Suir and possibly the Nore.[117]

The situation was now extremely serious with at least six major Viking fleets operating together and plundering at will throughout Munster and south Leinster. In August, 917, the Uí Néill overlord, Niall Glúndub, gathered the forces of the Northern and Southern Uí Néill and marched south to Clonmel. There, after an indecisive battle against Ragnall, he remained encamped. In hostile territory, far from his supply sources and clearly not strong enough to defeat the Vikings, Niall Glúndub sought to break the stalemate and sent word to Leinster to come to his aid against the Vikings. They never arrived as the Leinster army was smashed en route by Sitric in a decisive battle at Cenn Fuait on the Barrow. Among the many royal casualties were Augaire the king of Leinster, the bishop of Leinster and Cennétig's son, Augrán king of Laois.[118] Sitric followed up his victory by sacking the rich monastery of Kildare and re-occupying Dublin while Niall Glúndub retreated.[119]

The worst was yet to come. Having achieved what was probably the main objective of the campaign in capturing Dublin, Ragnall hived off his forces in 918 and invaded Scotland with the Earls Oitir and Gragabai. The same year the annals report warfare between Niall

Glúndub and Sitric whose forces plundered Kildare again. The Vikings also plundered Old Leighlin on the Barrow.[120]

Still seeking to dislodge the Vikings from Ireland Niall Glúndub gathered his forces once more and marched on Dublin. There, in a fateful battle fought on 14 September 919, the future of the Viking presence in Ireland was secured by Sitric's overwhelming victory. The battle was the worst slaughter of Irish royalty by the Vikings in history. The casualty list included Niall Glúndub himself, the first overlord or king of Ireland to be killed by the Vikings. Among the many named dead kings were Conchobar, Máel Sechnaill's grandson and the king of the Southern Uí Néill and heir to the kinship of Ireland, the kings of Ulaid, Brega and 'many other nobles'.[121]

The victory secured the permanent Viking presence in Ireland and led to the development of the Hiberno Norse towns. During the ensuing decades the Vikings would never again threaten to overwhelm and conquer Ireland as they did in periods of the ninth century and in the five-year campaign 914. The invasion which began in largely ended Norse military activity in Laois for the rest of the Viking Age in Ireland, with the exception of two raids on the monastery of Clonenagh. The first of these in 921 was a purely Norse raid and the second, in 939, was a joint raid by the king of Munster with the Waterford Vikings who were in his service.[122]

Trading and commercial activity

Few settlement sites of the Viking Age have been excavated in Co. Laois and the resulting lack of archaeological evidence makes it difficult to assess the commercial and trading relationships which may have existed between the natives and Vikings. Fine metal-work excavated at Dunamase – two decorated copper alloy mounts of eighth-ninth century date and some pins possibly of the same period[123] – suggests that, as early as the eighth-ninth century, the Kingdom of Laois was involved in a complex system of manufacture and trade similar to that in which the nearby kingdom of Mide appears to have been engaged.[124] From the tenth century onwards, the main commercial focus of Mide was overland with Dublin.[125] This may also have been true in the case of Laois. However, it is likely that Laois was also engaged in trade which utilised the rivers Barrow and Nore. A ninth-tenth century copper alloy strap end of a type popular with both the Vikings and Irish, found in a ringfort in the Nore valley at Dunbell, Co. Kilkenny,[126] hints at such commercial activity along the rivers. Freestone Hill, Co. Kilkenny dominates an important route between the rivers Barrow and Nore. It was clearly of strategic importance from prehistoric times up to the Early Medieval period and has evidence of settlement which reflects this fact. A number of finds date to the Viking Age such as a tenth century bracelet and a ninth/tenth century harness mount.[127] The mount is of a type found in a Viking grave at Kiloran Bay on the island of Colonsay, Scotland.[128] The development of Waterford as a trading settlement during the tenth century must have benefited trade with Irish settlements upriver in the interior.[129] Hoards of tenth/eleventh century silver coins, some accompanied by ingots, found in the vicinity of the valleys of the rivers Barrow and Nore, may relate to trade with Waterford although finds from the upper Barrow in Co. Kildare and in Laois itself, may also relate to trade overland with Dublin.[130]

Conclusions

Because of its inland location Laois was largely unaffected by the Vikings during the first half century of their presence in Ireland. Around the middle of the ninth century there was a determined Viking assault on the Irish interior which the kingdom of Laois played an important role in resisting. The destruction of Dunrally Fort by the combined forces of Laois and Ossory appears to have struck a major blow against Viking ambitions at that time. There was a second major phase of Viking activity during the second decade of the tenth century which firmly established the Viking presence in Ireland and, thereafter, following the establishment of the Hiberno-Norse towns, the most important relationship between the Vikings and the Irish appears to have been in the realms of trade and commerce. Throughout most of the Viking Age, rather than being major players, the Vikings appear to have been but an additional complication in the struggles between competing Irish kings. The same might be said of the kingdom of Laois except for the period during the mid ninth century when the alliance between Laois and Ossory – coupled with the ambitions of Cerball of Ossory – thrust Laois onto the centre stage of Irish politics.

References

1. When historians discuss the Viking age they are generally agreed that it began around the year 800 but its terminus varies from place to place. For instance Viking ambitions in England largely ended in 1066 with the defeat at Stamford Bridge of Hardrada of Norway, by Harold Godwinson, and the subsequent conquest of England by William of Normandy later that year. Over the next decade William secured his hold over England despite attempts in 1069 and 1075 by the Danish king Svein Estrithson and his son Cnut to re-establish Viking power there. In Ireland the Viking age is generally considered to last longer, covering from 795 to the arrival of the Normans in 1169.
2. D. Ó Corráin, *Ireland before the Normans* (Dublin, 1972), pp 96-97.
3. By 837 the large scale of some of these individual raiding parties is indicated in *A.U.* which record: 'A naval force of the Norsemen sixty ships strong was on the Bóinn [and] another one of sixty ships was on the river Life. Those two forces

plundered the plain of Life and the plain of Brega, including churches forts and dwellings' (*A.U. 837*). The size of Viking fleets was to reach far greater levels in the following decades when the annals record fleet sizes of 160 ships in 852 (*A.U.* and *C.S. 852*; *A.F.M. 850 recte 852*) and 200 ships in 871 (*A.U.* and *C.S. 871*; *F.A. * 393*).

4. Current research by J. Maas suggests that seasonal bases may have been established as early as the mid to late 820s. One such base may have been established on the Co. Louth/Co. Meath coast. In 827 the Ciannachta in Co. Louth and north Co. Meath were invaded by the Vikings (*A.U. 827*). The following year the Vikings killed the anchorite Teimnén and mortally wounded the king of the Ciannachta (*A.U. 828*). They are also reported in *A.U.* as having carried out 'a great slaughter of porpoises' on the Ciannachta coast (*A.U. 828*). The above suggests that the Vikings returned to the Co. Louth coast in 828, possibly to a seasonal base established there in the previous year. The fact that *A.U.* reports them hunting porpoises may suggest that they were staying for extended periods in which to hunt and fish. In the following decade areas of Co. Louth and the kingdom of the Ciannachta became favourite targets of the Vikings. In 831 the Conailli Muirtheimne of north Co. Louth were plundered and their king and his brother carried off to the ships (*A.U. 831*). In 832 all the churches of the Ciannachta were plundered (*A.U.*). The following year the monastery of Dromiskin in Co. Louth was attacked and burned by the Vikings, probably from the river Boyne. In 835 the monastery of Dromin in Co. Louth was plundered by the Vikings (*A.U. 835, A.F.M. 834 recte 835*). In 836 the southern portion of the kingdom of Brega was attacked (*A.U.*) and the following year a force of sixty Viking ships is reported on the Boyne which plundered the plain of the kingdom of Brega (*A.U. 837*). The same year Saxolb, the first named Viking leader in the Irish annals, was killed by the Ciannachta. For the possibility of a Viking base in the 830s at Arklow, Co. Wicklow see C. Etchingham, 'Evidence of Scandinavian settlement in Wicklow' in K. Hannigan and W. Nolan (eds.), *Wicklow history and society* (Dublin, 1994) pp 113-38, pp 114-18. Etchingham also notes a sequence of recorded raids after 831 implying a Viking base located somewhere between the north Dublin coast and Carlingford Lough in the early 830s (*ibid.*, p. 114). A Viking fortress on Lough Neagh is referred to in *A.F.M. 839 recte 840*. The bases at Dublin and Annagassan are in *A.U.* and *C.S. 841*; *A. Clon. 838 recte 841*; *A.F.M. 840 recte 841.*

5. Carlingford Lough area at Narrow Water – "the heathens from" (*A.U. 842; A. Clon. 839 recte 842; A.F.M. 841 recte 842*). Boyne at Linn Rois and Lough Swilly (*A.U. 842; A.F.M. 841 recte 842; A. Clon. 839 recte 842*). Lough Ree (*A.U. 844 and 845; A.F.M. 842 recte 843*). In 1982 inconclusive excavations were conducted by Fanning on a fortified promontory on the shores of Lough Ree at Ballaghkeeran Little, Co. Westmeath. The excavator's belief that the site may have been a longphort – the existence of which is referred to in the annals for the mid ninth and early tenth centuries – may yet be proved correct (T. Fanning, 'Ballykeeran Little, Athlone, Co. Westmeath, medieval Britain in 1982', *Med. Arch.*, 27, 1983, 221). There is at least one other site in Co. Westmeath which might reward investigation for evidence of Viking activity. At Ballinalack, a loop in the river Inny is spanned by a rampart approximately 420m across (OS 6" sheet 6, Co. Westmeath. 42cm from W; 9cm from S. We are grateful to Tom Condit, Sites and Monuments Record, for drawing our attention to this site).

6. *AB 847*. The report in the Carolingian annals is probably a condensed account of events between the mid 830s and 845.

7. In 825 the first of the penetrating raids up the rivers Barrow and Nore and Suir occurred. This was no simple hit-and-run raid and the fleet involved appears to have been conducting a broad campaign in the south east. *A.U. 825* says the Vikings inflicted a rout on the Osraige and separately list an attack on Inisdoimle – a little Island on the river Suir estuary at Waterford or Inch, Co. Wexford (Gwynn and Hadcock, *Med. Relig. Houses*, Ireland, p. 386). Inisdoimle had already been plundered in 822 (*A.F.M. 820 recte 822; A. Clon. 819 recte 822*), but the 825 raid appears to mark the first major inland penetration in the south east. *C.G.G.* (section VII) tells us that a fleet attacked the territory of the Uí Cheinnselaig, plundering Taghmon, probably from the river Slaney estuary. The fleet then attacked the monastery of St Mullins on the Barrow, two miles above the confluence of the rivers Barrow and Nore, and then moved up the river Nore to attack the monastery of Inistioge. This was followed up with the devastation of Ossory, and, presumably, the defeat of the forces of Ossory in the process. Inroads into the country to the north east of Co. Laois were made in 827 when Vikings, presumably having sailed up the river Liffey to Kilcullen, attacked and overwhelmed an encampment of the forces of Leinster, possibly lying close to Dún Ailline (*A.U. 827* and *A.F.M. 825 recte 827*). 828 saw another raid up the river Slaney repulsed by the Uí Cheinnselaig and the community of their chief monastery, Taghmon (*A.U. 828; A.F.M. 826 recte 828; A. Clon. 825 recte 828*). In 833 the Vikings returned to the south coast attacking Lismore, Co Waterford; Innishannon on the river Bandon estuary and other monasteries (*A.U. 833; A.F.M. 831 recte 833; A. Clon. 830 recte 833; C.G.G.*, Section VII). In 835 the Vikings penetrated very deeply up the river Slaney attacking Ferns and Clonmore on the Wicklow/Carlow border. This attack was probably launched from a permanent base at Inber Dea on the Co. Wicklow coastline (*A.U. 835; A.F.M. 834 recte 835; A. Clon. 832 recte 835*). The next year the Co. Wicklow Vikings plundered Kildare from Inber Dea; burned Clonmore on Christmas night and attacked Glendalough and Durrow, Co. Offaly (*A.U. 836; A.F.M. 835 recte 836; A. Clon. 833 recte 836*). In 837 the Southern Uí Néill under Máel Ruanaid attacked the Vikings of Inber Dea but were beaten in battle (*A.U. 837; A.F.M. 836 recte 837; A. Clon. 834 recte 837*). In 839 Viking fleets returned to the south coast attacking Ferns and Cork (*A.U. 839; A.F.M. 838 recte 839; C.S. 839; A. Clon. 836 recte 839*). For the argument for a Viking base at Arklow see Etchingham, 'Scandinavian settlement in Wicklow', pp 114-18.

8. *A.F.M. 840 recte 841; A.Clon. 838 recte 841.*

9. The Annagassan garrison attacked Clonmacnoise on the Shannon (*A.F.M. 841 recte 842; C.S. 842*). Birr and Seir Kieran were plundered from either Dublin or Linn Rois (*A.U. 842; A.F.M. 841 recte 842*) and Castledermot in Co. Kildare was plundered by the Vikings of Narrow Water (*A.U. 842; A.F.M. 841 recte 842; A. Clon. 839 recte 842*).

10. The kingdom of Mide included the modern counties of Meath and Westmeath as well as parts of counties Longford and Offaly.

11. The Dunamase attack is given in *A.U. 845; A.F.M. 843 recte 845; C.S. 845; A. Clon. 842 recte 845.*

12. The plundering of Coolcashin and Cerball's siege is in *A.F.M. 844 recte 846.*

13. The battle of Carn-Brammit *A.U. 847; A.F.M. 845 recte 847; C.S. 847.*

14. Máel Sechnaill won a victory over them at Faragh near Skreen, Co. Meath; where 700 of them were slain (*A.U. 848; A.F.M. 846 recte 848; C.S. 848; A. Clon. 847 recte 848*) and his ally, Tigernach, king of South Brega, defeated them at Disert-Dachonna (unidentified) where, according to *A.U. 848* they lost 1,200. By contrast

A.F.M. 846 recte 848 and *C.S. 848* gives the figure as twelve score dead. In the south, the Eóganacht Chaisil defeated them at Dún Maíle Tuile killing 500 (*A.U. 848; A.F.M. 846 recte 848; C.S. 848*) and Ólchobar, the king of Munster, destroyed the Viking garrison of Cork demolishing their fort (*A.F.M. 846 recte 848; C.S. 848*). They suffered their worst defeat in Co. Kildare at Sciath Nechtain where the forces of Leinster and Munster killed 1,200 of them including Earl Tomrair, 'Tanist of the King of Lochlann' who was probably the leader of the Norse at Dublin (*A.U. 848; A.F.M. 846 recte 848; C.S. 848; A.I. 848*). The battle of Sciath Nechtain has been tentatively identified by Sean Mac Airt as being at Skenagun in the parish of Castledermot (*A.I.* index, p. 557). This may be related to the hoard containing Carolingian coins from Aquitaine found at Mullaghboden, Co. Kildare (near Ballymore Eustace on the upper Liffey). Dolley dated the earliest deposition of the hoard to 847: it may in fact be 848 being hidden by fleeing Vikings after the battle. For this hoard see R.H.M. Dolley and K.F. Morrison, 'Finds of Carolingian coins from Great Britain and Ireland', *Brit. Num. Jour.*, 32 (1963), pp 75-87.

15. *A.F.M. 847 recte 849; C.S. 849.*

16. For the evidence for command structures and the organisation of Viking armies see N. Brooks, 'England in the ninth century: the crucible of defeat', *Trans. Roy. Hist. Soc.*, 29 (1979), pp 1-20; N. Lund, 'Allies of God or man? The Viking expansion in a European perspective', *Viator*, 20 (1989), pp 45-59; N. Lund, 'The Danish perspective', in D. Scragg (ed.), *The battle of Maldon* (Oxford, 1991), pp 114-42. For a full discussion of the fortunes of Dublin during the latter years of the ninth century see A.P. Smyth, *Scandinavian York and Dublin* (Dublin, 1987), i, chapters 2 and 4.

17. 'A naval expedition of seven score ships (140) of the adherents of the king of the foreigners came to exact obedience from the foreigners who were in Ireland before them, and afterwards they caused confusion in the whole country' (*A.U. 849*).

18. 'The Dubhghoill arrived in Ath-cliath, and made a great slaughter of the Finnghoill, and plundered the fortress, both people and property. Another depredation by the Dubhghoill upon the Finnghoill, at Linn-Duachaill, and they made a great slaughter of them' (*A.F.M. 849 recte 851*). For a discussion of the meanings of the terms see A. Smyth, 'The black foreigners of York and the white foreigners of Dublin', *Saga-Book Vik. Soc.*, 19 (1972-76), pp 101-17.

19. 'The complement of eight score ships (160) of the fair-haired foreigners came to Snám Aignech, to do battle with the dark foreigners; they fought for three days and three nights, but the dark foreigners got the upper hand and the others abandoned their ships to them. Stain took flight, and escaped, Iercne fell beheaded' (*A.U. 852*).

20. *F.A.* * 235 says that 5,000 Norwegians and an unspecified number of Danes were killed. Viking ship sizes and crew complements can be demonstrated by a number of surviving ships from Scandinavia. The ninth century Oseberg ship had space for thirty oars. The Gokstad ship had seats for 32 oarsmen. If one assumes that in addition to the rowers there were steersmen, leaders and replacement oarsmen (the Vikings would have expected to take some casualties on raids) a factor of one and a half men to oars should give a ship's crew. Small ships of the period would have had twenty oars and larger ships like the Gokstad 30-40 oars giving average crew sizes for warships of between 30-60. If all 300 of the ships at Carlingford were of the small type there were still 9,000 men involved. Arguments in the past by some historians that the annals exaggerate fleet sizes, for example P.H. Sawyer, *The age of the Vikings* (London, 1971), pp 120-47 have

been seriously undermined by Brooks, 'England in the ninth century', pp 1-20.

21. Olaf's arrival is first noted in 849 in *F.A.* * *239* and again, in 853, in *F.A.* * *259; A.U. 853; A.F.M. 851 recte 853; C.S. 853.*

22. E.P. Kelly and J. Maas, 'Vikings on the Barrow; Dunrally Fort, a possible Viking longphort in Co. Laois', *Arch. Ire.*, 9.3 (Autumn 1995), pp 30-32.

23. To date contemporary Irish historians (e.g. Ó Corráin, *Ireland before the Normans*, p. 94) have generally explained these alliances in terms of Irish kings exploiting Viking forces in their struggles. However, it may be the case that these alliances were part of a deliberate Viking policy aimed at preventing the Uí Néill overlordship uniting the various Irish factions against them.

24. 'A great assembly of the men of Ireland in Cluain Ferta Brénainn, and Niall son of Aed, king of Temuir, submitted to Feidlimid, son of Crimthann, so that Feidlimid became full king of Ireland that day, and he occupied the abbot's chair of Cluain Ferta' (*A.I. 838*). See K. Hughes, *The church in early Irish society* (London, 1966), p. 212.

25. It is interesting to note that the annals do not record a single battle between Feidlimid and Vikings during his long reign. Instead the annals contain many references to his attacks on the Uí Néill.

26. Byrne, *Irish kings and high-kings*, p. 265, described the problem of Uí Néill succession thus: 'This paradox is symptomatic of the weakness of Uí Néill polity which was to prevent them establishing a true monarchy of Ireland. The alternation, now over a century old (in the mid-ninth century), of the kingship of Tara between the Cenél Eogain and Clann Cholmáin was a fragile convention, marked by watchful jealousy rather than friendly accord'. The apparent concentration of Viking attacks on the north and north-east, suggested by major annals (A.U.; C.S. and A.Clon.) may present a distorted picture of the facts as their main focus of interest was Leth Cuinn and the centre and east of the country in particular. However, when unique records of Viking raids contained in C.G.G. are taken into account the south of the country appears to have experienced more raiding during this period than the major annals could have us believe. See C. Etchingham, *Viking raids on Irish church settlements in the ninth century: a reconsideration of the annals* (Maynooth, 1996).

27. *Ibid.*, p. 263.

28. One of the first recorded alliances between the Vikings and an Irish King was with Cináed mac Conaing king of Knowth and all Brega in 850 when, with Viking aid, he ravaged Máel Sechnaill's and Tigernach's territories (*A.U. 850*). Cináed was to pay for this with his life the following year when Máel Sechnaill and Tigernach (king of Lagore and South Brega) had him drowned in a dirty pool in the river Nanny.

29. 'Cerball mac Dúnlainge of Osraige came now into prominence as an opportunist who defended both Munster and Leinster by skilfully playing off Norse mercenary forces one against the other. Between 870 and his death in 888 he even assumed the role of the protector of the Norse dynasty of Dublin, into which his daughters had married. His early successes in the 850s were due to his dominance of the Nore and Barrow valleys. He thus seriously unbalanced the traditional hegemonies of Leth Cuinn and Leth Moga and constituted an obstacle to the ambitions of the Uí Néill. By a judicious mixture of force and diplomacy Máel Sechnaill kept him in check and succeeded in making Osraige his stepping stone to the first real high-kingship of all Ireland'. Byrne, *Irish kings and high-kings*, pp 263-264.

30. Cerball's own marriage and those of his sister Land demonstrate this. Land had

been first married to Gáithíne king of Laois and was mother of Cerball's ally, Cennétig king of Laois. She had then married Máel Sechnaill king of the Southern Uí Néill and king of Ireland (846-862) and was mother to Flann Sinna the future king Findliath of Ireland (879-916). Following Máel Sechnaill's death she married Aéd Findlíath the Northern Uí Néill king and king of Ireland (862-879). Her daughter by Máel Sechnaill was to marry Niall Glúndub the future Northern Uí Néill king and king of Ireland (916-919). Cerball king of Ossory was married to Máel Sechnaill's sister and if we are to believe genealogical data preserved in the Icelandic sagas, hís daughters were married into the Norse dynasty of Dublin. The information is contained in a number of entries in F.A. (*246, *260, *327 & *366). Also in *Landnamabok* quoted by Todd in *C.G.G.*, appendix D, p. 297. Land is mentioned in M.C. Dobbs, 'The Ban-Shenchus', *Rev. Celt.*, 47 (1930), p. 311 & p. 335; *Rev. Celt.*, 48 (1932), p. 186 & p. 225.

31. *A. Cam. 887 recte 888; B.T. 1 887 recte 888.* For commentary and ongoing debate on the independence of the Welsh annals from Irish exemplars during the period see K. Grabowski and D. Dumville, *Chronicles and annals of medieval Ireland and Wales – the Clonmacnoise-group of texts* (Suffolk, 1984), ch. 4 and K. Hughes, 'The Welsh latin chronicles: Annales Cambriae and related texts', *Proc. Brit. Acad.*, 59 (1973), pp 3-28.

32. Byrne, *Irish kings and high-kings*, p. 162.

33. *F.A. *251.*

34. *F.A. *254.* Crohane lies two miles east of Killenaule in Co. Tipperary.

35. For Máel Sechnaill's invasion of Munster see *A.F.M. 852 recte 854* and for Horm's presentation to Máel Sechnaill see *F.A. *254.*

36. Horm's death is noticed in *A.U. 856; C.S. 856; F.A. *254.*

37. *A.U. 856* records 'great warfare between the heathens and Máel Sechnaill, supported by the Norse-Irish (Gall-Gaedil)'.

38. For Cerball's genealogy see *C.G.G.* appendix D. Todd's introduction to *C.G.G.* (p. lxxviii) correctly notes Cerball's alliance with Dublin. He also says that Cerball succeeded Ivar in 873 as King of Dublin and continued to be recognised as such until his death in 888 (p. lxxx). Todd also says that Thorstein, Olaf's son, was married to Thurida, Cerball's grand-daughter by his daughter Rafertach who had married the celebrated Eyvind Austmann, so-called because he had come to the Hebrides from Sweden. Byrne, *Irish kings and high-kings*, p. 163, does not go as far as Todd saying instead that after 873 Cerball appears to have acted as Dublin's patron or protector.

    The genealogical material on Cerball's kingship of Dublin is contained in *Landnamabok*, an Icelandic source first written down in the twelfth and thirteenth centuries – 300 years after the events. There is no evidence from the Irish annalistic sources to support Cerball's kingship of Dublin and this claim must be viewed with great scepticism particularly when it is possible to trace the succession of Norse kings of Dublin from the annals. For this see A.P. Smyth, *Scandinavian York and Dublin*, pp 27-40 & pp 60-74. It is quite possible that Cerball's daughters had married into the Norse dynasty of Dublin and it would account for the inclusion of Cerball to the exclusion of other Irish kings in the Icelandic sources. It is also possible that his grand-daughter was married to Olaf's son Thorstein who is possibly the Oistin (Eyestein) who ruled at Dublin 873-875 until his death at Albann's (Halfdan) hands in 875 (*A.U. 875*).

39. *A.F.M. 856 recte 858; C.S. 858.* Defeat of Caitil *A.U.* and *C.S. 857.*

40. 'The expedition of Máelsechnaill mac Ruanaid in 858 which made him the first high-king to obtain hostages from Munster was also directed against Cerball's

pretensions in Leinster. Although the king of Osraige eventually gave submission to the high-king, and never succeeded in gaining official recognition of his power in Leinster, he did prevent the superficially impressive succession of Uí Dúnlainge princes from exercising much effective control of the province' (Byrne, *Irish kings and high-kings*, p. 163). 'Maelsechnaill was single minded. The Eóganacht were weak, but Cerball Mac Dúnlainge with Norse help might build a power block in the South much more dangerous to the Uí Néill than they had ever been' (*Ibid.*, p. 264).

41. *F.A. * 262.*

42. For Cerball's invasion of Mide see *A.F.M. 857 recte 859. F.A. * 265* says Cerball was plundering Máel Sechnaill for three months while *F.A. * 268* says Cerball had spent the previous 40 nights (before the Rahugh conference of 859) plundering Máel Sechnaill.

43. K. Hughes, *Early Christian Ireland: introduction to the sources* (London, 1972), p. 131.

44. Radner (*F.A.*) raises the intriguing possibility that Máel Guala's death may have been at Cerball's instigation (*F.A.*, p. 200). *C.G.G.* (Section XXIII) says it was Olaf that did the killing and since Olaf was at this time Cerball's ally, and probably either present at or close to the Royal assembly with his army to guarantee the outcome, Cerball's involvement is possible.

45. *F.A. * 279.*

46. *A.U.* and *C.S. 861; A.F.M. 859 recte 861.*

47. Plundering of Mide *A.U.* and *C.S. 862; A.F.M. 860 recte 862; F.A. * 292.*

48. Although written in the seventeenth century, *A.F.M.* draws on a large range of annalistic sources including a now lost set of south-eastern annals similar to the one contained in *F.A.* (for a fuller discussion see Radner, *F.A.*, introduction pp xxii-xxxiv). F.A. seems to have been compiled from of a number of sources including a set of south-eastern annals, an Ossory Chronicle and possibly one or even two Viking sources from Limerick and Dublin.

49. *F.A. * 249.*

50. *A.F.M. 858 recte 860; F.A. * 277.*

51. Radner (*F.A.*), index, p. 226.

52. *A.F.M. 888 recte 892* record the foreigners of Waterford, Wexford and St. Mullins being overcome in battle. See also *F.A. * 278.*

53. *F.A. * 281.*

54. *A.F.M. 860 recte 862; F.A. * 308.* Radner translates Lochlann as Norway.

55. Byrne, *Irish kings and high-kings*, p. 162.

56. 'The compiler (of *F.A.*) seems to have tried to give the fullest available accounts of events. This meant, generally, that he replaced Irish World Annals entries with Chronicle narratives when the same texts were reported by both. Such cases are clear when one compares the wording of *F.A.* entries with that of entries in the other early annals ... However, the compiler did not merely shuffle and arrange the pieces of text in front of him. He rewrote many entries, and sometimes his rewriting seems to have conflated annals and chronicle accounts' (Radner, *F.A.*, p. xxvi-xxvii). Radner then lists fourteen *F.A.* entries that she believes are conflated including *F.A. * 308* which contains the *F.A.* version of the account in *A.F.M. 860 recte 862* of the destruction of Dunrally. As noted above in note 48, *A.F.M.* draws on a now lost south eastern annalistic text which is similar to the underlying annalistic text in *F.A.*

57. The new fleet which arrived at Dunrally may have been part of a larger build up of forces being directed by Rodulf from the Waterford estuary. The destruction of

THE VIKINGS AND THE KINGDOM OF LAOIS

Dunrally may have thwarted his ambitions and obliged him to look elsewhere. Other examples of such pragmatism by the Vikings can be pointed to. Following the victory of Alfred over the Danes at Edington in 878 a newly arrived Danish fleet on the Thames, on learning of the outcome of the battle, turned towards the continent where they campaigned for 13 years (J. Brøndsted, *The Vikings* (London, 1965), p. 50).

58. The death notice for Rodulf in the *Annals of Xanten* (*A.X.*, pp 368-371) provides evidence that he was active away from the Continent for much of his early career. It reports that he 'ravaged many coastal regions on the other side of the sea' which has been interpreted in the German translation to mean Britain and the British Isles (including Ireland). The reference may mean Ireland exclusively as Rodulf is not mentioned in the primary British sources but does occur in the Irish sources. As far back as 1876 the Danish scholar C.H.R. Steenstrup suggested that the two Rodulfs were the same person. Steenstrup is quoted by the German scholar Vogel who reached the same conclusion thirty years later. See W. Vogel, *Die Normannen und das frankische Reich bis zur Grundung der Normandie (799-911)*, (Heidelberg, 1906), p. 196 and p. 404.

59. A good discussion of the Continental careers of Rodulf and the rest of his dynastic family is given in I.N. Wood, 'Christians and pagans in ninth century Scandinavia' in B. Sawyer, P. Sawyer and I.N. Wood (eds.), *The Christianisation of Scandinavia* (Alingsas, Sweden, 1987), pp 36-68. It is clear from the annals that throughout his activities in Ireland Rodulf was associated with the Norwegian faction and hostile to the Danish faction. Clearly, the Rodulf of the Carolingian annals was a Dane and this fact raises a difficulty if one is to accept that they were the same person. The apparent contradiction may be explained easily by reference to the expulsion of Rodulf's father Harold from the Danish kingship which would have left him at enmity with Danish factions in Ireland allied to the Danish usurper.

60. The coin may have circulated for a number of decades before its deposition. Excavated in 1996 (details supplied by the excavator, Brian Hodkinson, in advance of publication). Earlier work on the site has been published (B. Hodkinson, 'The rock of Dunamase', *Arch. Ire.*, 9.2 (Summer 1995), pp 18-21).

61. E.C.R. Armstrong, *Guide to the collection of Irish antiquities. Catalogue of Irish gold ornaments in the Royal Irish Academy* (Dublin, 1920), no. 422.

62. E.C.R. Armstrong, 'Catalogue of the silver and ecclesiastical antiquities in the collections of the Royal Irish Academy by the late Sir William Wilde, M.D., M.R.I.A.', *R.I.A., Proc.*, 32c (1915), nos 7 & 32; J. Graham-Campbell, 'The Viking-age silver hoards of Ireland', *Proc. Seventh Vik. Con.* (Dublin, 1976), pp 39-74, p. 67 and p. 69.

63. H. Shetelig, *Viking antiquities of Great Britain and Ireland, part III, Norse antiquities in Ireland* (Oslo, 1940), pp 86-8.

64. Dunrally Fort is located in the townland of Vicarstown (Dodd), par. Moyanna, barony Stradbally, Co. Laois. OS 6" sheet 14.

65. J. O'Donovan, *Letters containing information relative to the antiquities of the queen's county collected during the process of the ordnance survey in 1838*, M. O'Flanagan, ed. (1933), p. 79. O'Hanlon and O'Leary, *Queen's county*, p. 291.

66. The results of this survey were first presented by J. Maas to the 10th Conference of Irish Medievalists, 6/7/96, in a lecture entitled 'The Significance of Longphort'. Publication is pending.

67. One of the things noted in the study, particularly as regards *A.F.M.*, was that this seventeenth century compilation, when drawing on the lost *south eastern annals*

mentioned earlier, tended to preserve the strict usage of the word longphort (noted in contemporary annals) to describe purely Scandinavian bases in the ninth and early tenth centuries. This would vindicate *A.F.M.*'s description of Dunrally as a longphort associated with the activities of a Viking fleet. When, on one occasion, the word longphort is used by *A.F.M.* to describe an Irish marching camp in 917 (*A.F.M. 915 recte 917*) the Irish camp is both described as *dunad* and *longphort* in the same passage. This may reflect a slip on the part of *A.F.M.* but, equally, may reflect the faithful transmission of a post mid-ninth century copy of annals that had already updated the language of the report, replacing *dunad* with *longphort*.

68. This was the entrance to the site in the late eighteenth century to facilitate access to a summer house. It is possible, however, that it is sited at the location of an ancient entrance. The summer house was built during the 1780s by Henry Grattan who also laid out gardens.

69. O'Donovan, *Ordnance survey letters*, pp 48-49.

70. This forest survived into the middle of the sixteenth century when it was known as 'The Great Wood'. Its extent is shown on a map made around 1563 (H.F. Hore, 'Notes on a facsimile of an ancient map of Leix, Ofaly, Irry, Clanmalier, Iregan, and Slievemargy, preserved in the British Museum', *R.S.A.I., Jn.*, 7, 1862-62, pp 345-372, map facing p. 345).

71. Adrevald of Fleury, writing in the 870s, provides a contemporary account of life in one such Viking river-base. 'The Northmen meanwhile made an anchorage for their ships and a refuge from all dangers on an island below the monastery of St. Florent, putting up huts in a sort of a village in which to keep their gangs of prisoners in irons, and to rest their bodies from their labours for a time, ready to serve on campaign' (S. Coupland, 'The Vikings in Frankia and Anglo-Saxon England to 911', *The New Cambridge Medieval History*, R. McKitterick (ed.), ii (Cambridge, 1995), p. 196. Because the Franks and Anglo-Saxons did not have suitable ships with which to attack these island bases they were virtually impregnable. An attempt by Charles the Bald to assemble a fleet to attack the Vikings on the island of Oissel, near Rouen ended in disaster (*ibid.*, p. 196).

72. *A.F. 891.*

73. See *A.U. 866* for flocks and herds.

74. For the location of Dublin; Waterford; Wexford; Limerick and Cork see P.F. Wallace, 'The archaeological identity of the Hiberno-Norse town', *R.S.A.I., Jn.*, 122 (1992), pp 35-66, fig. 1, p. 38.

75. National Museum of Ireland topographical file.

76. Ringforts are agricultural settlements with a preference for higher or sloping ground. Where they are located on lower ground they are to be found on good agricultural land. See G.T. Stout, *Archaeological survey of the barony of Ikerrin* (Roscrea, 1984), pp 29-32.

77. Ringworks are defensive earthworks which may make use of marshy ground. One such example, at Oldcastle, Co. Tipperary, is not prominently sited, but takes advantage of a natural rise in a water-logged hollow (*ibid.*, pp 114-15).

78. J. Graham-Campbell, *The Viking world* (London, 1980), p. 92 and p. 96. D-shaped enclosures are also found at other Viking settlements in Scandinavia such as Västergarn, Gotland; Aarhus, Denmark and Löddenköpinge, Sweden (R. Hodges, *Dark age economies: the origins of trade AD 600-1000* (London, 1982), fig. 13).

79. T. Wright, *Louthiana: or an introduction to the antiquities of Ireland*, i (London, 1748), pl. xx.

80. The embankment flanking the river is not included in a recent plan (V.M. Buckley and P.D. Sweetman, *Archaeological Survey of Co. Louth* (Dublin, 1991), pp 97-99, fig. 78).

81. J.B. Leslie, 'Lisnaran', *Co. Louth Arch. Jour.*, 2 1908-11), pp 140-41. P.F. Wallace proposes that the longphort of Dublin, built around the same time as Annagassan, 'was of much more Scandinavian character than the later settlement at Dublin ... It was possibly enclosed within a crescentic bank on the south bank of the river Liffey' ('Archaeology and the emergence of Dublin as the principal town of Ireland', in J. Bradley (ed.), *Settlement and society in medieval Ireland: studies presented to Francis Xavier Martin o.s.a.* (Kilkenny, 1988), pp 123-60, p. 127).

82. At Birka, Hedeby and Annagassan the citadels are placed so as to take advantage of high ground. As there is no high ground at Dunrally the location of a citadel centrally within the larger enclosure might be the next best choice in terms of security.

83. Graham-Campbell, *The Viking world*, pp 202-207; E. Roesdahl, 'The Danish geometric fortresses and their context', in R. Allen Brown (ed.), *Anglo-Norman studies: proceedings of the battle conference*, 9 (1986), pp 208-226.

84. *Ibid.*, p. 211.

85. *Ibid.*, p. 218; J.A. Trimple-Burger, 'Oost-Souburg, provence of Zeeland: a preliminary report on the excavation of the site of an ancient fortress (1969-71)', *Berichten van de R.O.B.* (1973), 355-65.

86. A coin, minted at York between 905-925, was found in a burnt layer below the collapsed rampart. Nearby a fragment of a helmet was found while elsewhere on the site a ferrule for a lance was uncovered. A large quantity of tenth century pottery was found and a series of radiocarbon dates have been obtained which cluster around 865-1045 (N.S. Price, *The Vikings in Brittany* (London, 1989), pp 55-61).

87. J. Dyer, 'Earthworks of the Danelaw frontier', in P.J. Fowler (ed.), *Archaeology and landscape: essays for L.V. Grinsell* (London, 1972), pp 222-36, pp 231-35. In relation to these sites one might here refer to Rathmooley, Co. Tipperary where there is a circular earthwork having three ramparts including a very wide and deep water-filled ditch. The site, which commands an extensive view of the surrounding countryside, does not appear to be an Irish ringfort. The possibility that it is a Viking fortification must be considered in view of the discovery there in 1925 of two Viking armrings. For an account of their discovery see D.H. Scott-O'Connell, 'Viking period silver ornaments from Rathmoley, county Tipperary', *Jour. Cork. Hist. & Arch. Soc.*, 43 (1938), pp 125-6. The armrings date to late ninth century or the first half of the tenth century. One is of a type which appears to be of Norwegian manufacture and the other is Hiberno-Norse, probably made in one of the settlements on the south coast of Ireland (J. Sheehan, 'The Rathmooley hoard and other Viking silver from Co. Tipperary', *T.H.S.* (1992), p. 214). The presence of these objects may relate to the upsurge of Viking activity in Munster recorded in the annals between 915-917 (*C.S. 914 recte 915; A. Clon. 910 recte 915; A.U. 916 & 917; A.F.M. 914 recte 916 & 915 recte 917; A.I. 916 & 917*). This followed the arrival of 'the great fleet' in Waterford in 914. Rathmooley Fort and the silver hoard found there may also have an important bearing on the major find of christian metalwork found at the monastery of Derrynaflan, a few short miles distant. The proposed date of deposition of the Derrynaflan hoard in the later 9th or 10th centuries – see M. Ryan (ed.), *The Derrynaflan hoard, I, a preliminary account* (Dublin, 1983), p. 40) – would accord well with the date of the Rathmooley hoard and with the annalistic

references to Viking activity in Munster.

88. Dyer, 'Danelaw frontier', pp 227-31 and p. 234.

89. P.F. Wallace, 'The archaeological identity of the Hiberno-Norse town', *R.S.A.I. Jn.,* 122 (1992), fig. 1.

90. *A.F. 891.*

91. Dyer, 'Danelaw frontier, pp 225-6. Dyer (p. 224) also suggests that sites of this type may have been constructed both by the Danes and Saxons. These would have been in addition to the string of important forts or burhs, constructed during the reign of Alfred to guard the frontier of Wessex, and which provides clear evidence of Saxon involvement in fort construction. *The Burghal Hidage,* a document of the early tenth century, refers to 33 burhs. It is likely that existing Roman walls formed the initial basis of this defensive system, later supplemented by new constructions. The scheme, most of the work on which should be ascribed to the years before 892, was based on permanent garrisons (N. Brooks, 'The unidentified forts of the Burghal Hidage', *Med. Arch.,* 8 (1964), pp 74-90, p. 87).

92. J.D. Richards, *Viking Age England* (London, 1991), p. 23.

93. Dyer, 'Danelaw frontier', p. 226.

94. *Ibid.,* p. 226.

95. Idem.

96. M. Biddle and B. Kjølbye-Biddle, 'Repton and the Vikings', *Ant.,* 66 (March 1992), pp 36-51; Richards, *Viking Age England,* p. 23.

97. *Ibid.,* p. 23.

98. *A.F.M. 861 recte 863; F.A. * 310.*

99. The alliance between Áed and Olaf was probably sealed by Olaf's marriage to Áed's daughter see *F.A. * 292.*

100. *F.A. * 314; A.F.M. 862 recte 864.*

101. *A.F.M. 864 recte 866; F.A. * 329; F.A. * 338.*

102. For a full discussion of the careers of the Dublin kings see A.P. Smyth, *Scandinavian York and Dublin,* i, ch. I and A.P. Smyth, *Scandinavian kings of the British Isles 850-880* (Oxford, 1977), ch. 10 to ch. 19. See also D. Ó Corráin, 'High-kings, Vikings and other kings', *I.H.S.,* 21 (1979), pp 283-323 for criticism of Smyth's thesis.

103. *A.U. 866; A.F.M. 864 recte 866; C.S. 866; A. Clon. 864 recte 866; F.A. * 327.*

104. *F.A. * 345.*

105. *A.U. 867; A.F.M. 865 recte 867; F.A. * 349; F.A. * 362.*

106. *A.F.M. 866 recte 868.* This is significant as it may indicate another Viking base on the Barrow. Uí Bairrche Tíre lay on both sides of the Barrow in the barony of Slievemargy. It is unlikely that the fort in question was Dunrally (being re-used) as there is no mention of Cerball and Cennétig in the assault. It is even possible that Dunrally was being garrisoned by Cennétig at this time because of its strategic location. It would have been an ideal launch point for attacks on the Uí Failge and other north Leinster peoples from whom Cerball was exacting tribute.

107. In 870 Cerball, Cennétig and Áed jointly plundered Leinster. Áed attacked from the north an area extending from Dublin as far as Gowran and Cerball and Cennétig attached from the opposite direction until they reached Dún Bolg (Brusselstown, Co. Wicklow, Radner *F.A.* index p. 233), *A.U. 870; A.F.M. 868 recte 870; F.A. * 387.*

108. *A.U. 871; C.S. 871; F.A. * 393.*

109. *A.F.M. 870 recte 872 & F.A. * 407.*

110. *A.U. 873; A.F.M. 871 recte 873; C.S. 873.*

111. *C.G.G.* (section XXVI).

112. *A.U. 902; A.F.M. 897 recte 902; C.S. 902.*

113. Byrne describes this battle as 'the last effective attempt by the Eóganachta to maintain their ancient status' (*Irish kings and high-kings*, p. 266). See *A.U. 908; A.F.M. 903 recte 908.*

114. For the fleet's activities in Britain see *A.S.C. 914; B.T. 2 910 recte 914; A. Cam. 913 recte 914.* For its arrival in Ireland see *A.U. 914; A.F.M. 910 recte 914* and *912 recte 914; C.S. 913 recte 914; A. Clon. 910 recte 914.* For Oiter see *A.U. 918; A.F.M. 916 recte 918* and *C.G.G.* (section XXVII and XXXV).

115. *A.U. 918, C.G.G.* (section XXVI).

116. *A.F.M. 914 recte 916.*

117. *A.U. 917; A.F.M. 915 recte 917.*

118. *A.U. 917; A.F.M. 915 recte 917; C.S. 916 recte 917.* The exact location of Cenn Fuait has been the subject of some debate. O'Donovan (*A.F.M. notes 915 recte 917*) identifies its location as being Confey, near Leixlip, Co. Kildare. However, a poem in *A.F.M.* (*915 recte 917*) says that Cenn Fuait lay in the glen over St. Mullins on the Barrow and led Smyth (*Scandinavian York and Dublin*, pp 66-68) to suggest this as the more likely location for the battle.

119. *A.U. 917; C.S. 916 recte 917; A. Clon. 917.*

120. *A.U. 918* for "warfare". *A.F.M. 916 recte 918* for Old Leighlin.

121. *A.U. 919; A.F.M. 917 recte 919; C.S. 918 recte 919; A. Clon. 915 recte 919; A.I. 919.*

122. *A.F.M. 919 recte 921. A.F.M. 937 recte 939.*

123. Brian Hodkinson, pers. comm.

124. Fine metalwork objects such as these are common on crannóg sites in Mide and are likely to have been important items of trade (E.P. Kelly, 'Observations on Irish lake dwellings', *Amer. Ear. Med. Stud.*, 1 (1991), pp 81-98, pp 86-7).

125. Kelly, 'Lake dwellings', p. 91.

126. Reg. no. NMI, RSAI. 43.

127. Both are published in B. Raftery, 'Freestone Hill, Co. Kilkenny: an Iron Age hillfort and Bronze Age cairn', *R.I.A., Proc.*, 68c, 1969, pp 1-108. The bracelet (*ibid.*, fig. 19, E61: 21 & 151) is in two fragments. Both the bracelet and the mount (*ibid.*, fig. 21) are wrongly assigned a fourth century date by Raftery (*ibid.*, pp 62-71). Thanks are due to Paul Mullarkey, National Museum of Ireland, for bringing the bracelet to our attention.

128. S. Grief, 'Viking Antiquities of Scotland' in H. Shetelig (ed.), *Viking antiquities of Great Britain and Ireland*, part 2 (Oslo), 1940, p. 57, fig. 30.

129. With reference to Viking influence in the second decade of the tenth century it has been proposed that 'The river Barrow was effectively under their control and linked Waterford to Dublin' (P. Holm, 'The slave trade of Dublin, ninth to twelfth centuries', *Peritia*, 5 (1986), pp 317-345, p. 326).

130. Tenth century finds of possible relevance are Geashill, Co. Offaly (*c.*920); Dunmore Cave, Co. Kilkenny (*c.*930); Kildare ? (*c.*935); Durrow, Co. Offaly (*c.*940); Ballitore, Co. Kildare (*c.*965); Rahan 1, Co. Offaly (*c.*970); Rahan 2, Co. Offaly (*c.*970); 'In the west of Kilkenny' (975); nr. Kildare (*c.*991); 'In the west of Kilkenny' (975). Eleventh century hoards include nr. Kilkenny (*c.*1040); Ballylinan, Co. Laois (*c.*1050) and Dunamase, Co. Laois (*c.*1095). The hoards are discussed in Graham-Campbell, 'Viking-age silver hoards', pp 39-74. Viking influence in the area of the upper Barrow is further demonstrated by a tenth century Scandinavian hog-backed tomb in the monastery of Castledermot, Co. Kildare (J.T. Lang, 'The Castledermot hogback', *R.S.A.I., Jn.*, 101 (1971), 154-58).

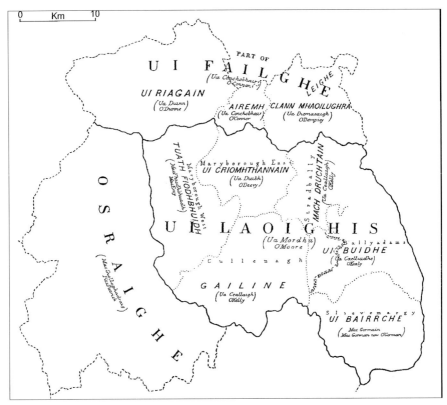

Fig. 6.2   Thirteenth-century subdivisions of Laois (from W. Fitzgerald, 'Historical notes on the O'Mores and their territory of Leix' in *Kildare Arch. Soc. Jn.*, vi (1909-11) facing p. 6).

Chapter 7

THE IMPACT OF THE ANGLO-NORMANS IN LAOIS

CORMAC Ó CLÉIRIGH

In 1169, a small group of adventurers from Pembrokeshire crossed the Irish sea with the intention of helping Diarmait MacMurchada, king of Leinster, to fulfil his dynastic ambitions. By doing so they precipitated the event now known as the Anglo-Norman invasion, thus inaugurating an era of momentous change in Ireland which had the unforeseen effect of destroying the political system in which King Diarmait had operated for the previous forty years. To a great extent, the region which now forms the county of Laois shared this experience of profound change with the rest of the island. The details of the cataclysmic event which the contemporary writer Gerald of Wales called the *Expugnatio Hibernica*, or conquest of Ireland, are both too well known and too involved to be presented in any great depth here. However, it might be useful to provide a brief outline of its more important consequences for the island in general in order to gain a better understanding of the Laois experience in particular.[1] Most obviously, the development of new links between Ireland and England permanently altered the political focus of the island. The establishment of the king of England as the lord of Ireland made the old ambitions of the Irish provincial kings to become high-king redundant. Indeed, for the rest of the middle ages, *terra Hibernie* or the land of Ireland, remained an integral part of the English crown, a state of affairs which led to the evolution of English-style institutions and to the introduction of English common law on the island. Moreover, this political revolution was underpinned by an equally significant development which occurred as a direct consequence of the adventurers' success. In the aftermath of the invasion, Ireland experienced an influx of new-comers, of varied backgrounds, who brought about a transformation of its socio-economic structures. The very landscape of the island was changed by the construction of castles at locations like Trim and Kilkenny, the foundation of towns like Kildare and New Ross, and the establishment of new religious houses such as Dunbrody in Wexford and Connell in Kildare. With the material changes came a new social organisation, namely that set of relationships and obligations which today are classified under the loose heading of feudalism. At the upper end of the social scale, the victorious adventurers were rewarded with grants of parcels of land, known variously as cantreds or *theoda*, in return for obligations of military service. This process led to the establishment of locally significant aristocratic families throughout the island, like the de Ridelisfords in south Dublin, the Carews in Carlow and the Prendergasts and Roches in Wexford. Crucially, the arrival of Anglo-Norman aristocrats was accompanied by large-scale peasant immigration from England into the relatively thinly populated island. Such individuals facilitated an agrarian revolution, by enabling the labour-intensive practice of arable farming to become more widespread than had been the case before the invasion. More importantly perhaps, their presence served to ensure that Ireland became an English colony in reality as well as in name. Overall, it could be argued that the net effect of the changes thus wrought was to introduce successfully the norms of western Christendom to Ireland.[2] The aim of this paper is to address the phenomenon and its consequences insofar as they applied to Laois during the first 150 years or so following the invasion.

As it is possible to divide the history of Anglo-Norman Laois into three distinct phases, each with its own themes and perspectives, the era's main developments will be outlined chronologically. In the first instance, a phase which could be called 'the conquest stage' will be described. This period encompassed both the invasion itself and its subsequent consolidation, and was largely complete by the death of King John in 1216. The second phase to be examined coincided roughly with the long reign of Henry III from 1216 to 1272 and appears to have been an era of stability, peace and prosperity. In fact, this period can be viewed as the apogee of Anglo-Norman lordship in the midlands. However, the final phase is of a markedly different character. The late thirteenth and early fourteenth centuries were dominated by a sense of impending crisis for the colony. In the main, this was due to the native response to the challenge posed by Anglo-Norman domination, a response which became increasingly militarised during the reign of Edward I and which is frequently cited by historians as a prime example of the phenomenon known as the Gaelic revival, or resurgence.[3] Hopefully, by providing a description of the manner of the invasion and insofar as the sources permit, the nature and scope of Anglo-Norman lordship in Laois, it will be possible to account for the success of the resurgence, which ultimately led to the collapse of the colony there. However, before describing Laois's experiences during the Anglo-Norman period, it might be useful to comment briefly upon the name of the region. For the sake of simplicity, the term 'Laois' will be used throughout this paper to describe the area which forms the modern county. Nevertheless, it should be remembered that the county was not formed until the sixteenth century and that in fact, the region did not exist as a separate entity, either before the invasion or indeed throughout the remainder of the middle ages.[4]

Before the arrival of the Anglo-Normans, Laois's most striking political feature was the fact that it was profoundly divided on several different levels. Broadly speaking, the entire region of Laois could be said to have been part of the provincial kingdom of Leinster. However, this would obscure the fact that its south-western portion, roughly comprising the modern baronies of Clarmallagh, Clandonagh and Upperwoods, lay in the important over-kingdom of Osraige or Ossory. This over-kingdom was ruled by the MacGillaPatrick dynasty, which had a semi-detached and usually hostile relationship to the rest of the province.[5] Several distinct sub-regions existed within that part of Laois which lay in the province of Leinster proper. Most obviously, the kingdom which occupied the central portion of the modern county was known as Laois and was ruled by the O'More dynasty.[6] To the south of the kingdom of Laois lay the petty state of Uí Buide and part of the territory of Uí Bairrche.[7] Lastly, in the north, the O'Dempsey and O'Dunne dynasties ruled the subkingdoms of Clann Máel Ugra and Uí Riacáin, respectively.[8] Somewhat confusingly, this northern district actually formed part of the kingdom of Uí Failge, or Offaly, an important component of Leinster which was usually ruled by the O'Connor Faly dynasty.[9] As an aside, it is worth noting that while the present county boundary is a relatively recent development, dating from 1600, the current barony boundaries seem to be older, and reflect to a large degree the pre-Norman divisions. A final example of the region's essential fragmentation comes from the activities of the individuals who were responsible for instigating a large-scale reform of the Irish church in the twelfth century. In 1152, the reforming churchmen succeeded in establishing dioceses on a territorial basis at the synod of Kells-Mellifont.[10] Not surprisingly, the new ecclesiastical boundaries were usually designed to closely reflect existing political realities, and it is significant that the region was divided amongst no less than five dioceses, namely Dublin, Ossory, Kildare, Leighlin and Killaloe.[11] The inherent fissures existing within Laois's polity were compounded by the fact that in Ireland as a whole, the century before the Anglo-Norman invasion was a period of rapid and intense political change. Admittedly, Byrne has observed that Leinster as a provincial entity was relatively stable before the coming of the Anglo-Normans, especially when compared with Meath or Munster.[12] However, Laois was not immune to the turbulence that accompanied the struggles for supremacy amongst the provincial kings. For example, an unsuccessful attempt was made by Ruaidhri Ó Conchubhair of Connacht to detach Offaly from Leinster in 1161.[13] More significantly, the innovative policies of Diarmait MacMurchada as king of Leinster had an adverse effect upon the status and security of the province's subkingdoms. Thus he replaced the ruling dynasty of Uí Buide with one of his protégés, and supported the Uí Chremthannáin of Dunamase against their overlords the O'Mores.[14] Possibly he was also responsible for the fact that on the eve of the invasion, the O'Dempseys had supplanted the O'Connor Falys as the kings of Offaly.[15] However his most serious efforts were directed against his bitter enemies the MacGillaPatricks, with whom he was frequently at war, and from whom he tried to wrest Aghaboe, to the benefit of his foster-family, the Uí Cáellaide.[16] Unquestionably, Diarmait's activities made him extremely unpopular amongst the bulk of his provincial subordinates. In fact, their rebellion against him in 1166 contributed to the sequence of events which resulted in Diarmait's expulsion from Leinster and his large-scale recruitment of Anglo-Norman adventurers, culminating in the arrival in 1170 of Richard de Clare, earl of Strigoil and Pembroke, who is better known as Strongbow.[17]

Paradoxically, the first Anglo-Normans to campaign in Laois itself were not acting for Diarmait *na nGall*, but on behalf of his arch enemy, Domhnall MacGillaPatrick of Osraige. In 1169 MacGillaPatrick invaded the kingdom of Laois with the assistance of Maurice de Prendergast, a disaffected leader of one of MacMurchada's bands of mercenaries, and ordered O'More the local king to deliver up his hostages.[18] MacMurchada responded to this threat to his overlordship by marching to the scene with his remaining mercenaries, led by Robert fitzStephen and Maurice fitzGerald, thereby securing the withdrawal of MacGillaPatrick.[19] The episode, with its marches, counter-marches and the taking of hostages was not particularly significant in itself. Nevertheless, it serves to underline the point that at this stage, notwithstanding the presence of the newcomers, kings like MacMurchada and MacGillaPatrick were still operating within the bounds of traditional Irish dynastic warfare. However, the situation changed drastically following the sudden death of Diarmait, 'the destroyer of Ireland', in May 1171.[20] While the motives behind King Henry II's intervention in December 1171 are still a subject of lively debate, its effects upon the politics of Leinster are clear. Most importantly, the kingdom itself effectively ceased to exist. Although Strongbow had become Diarmait's heir by marrying his daughter Aífe, he did not manage to secure the title of king of Leinster for himself.[21] Instead however, Henry confirmed him as the lord of Leinster, including Osraige, to be held of the king in chief as a liberty by the service of 100 knights.[22] Thus, the way was cleared for Strongbow to carry out the conversion of Leinster, and hence of Laois from a loosely bound dynastic kingdom into a tightly organised feudal lordship.

In fact, according to one of the primary texts for the invasion period, the *Song of Dermot and the Earl*, Strongbow sought to impose himself upon the region almost immediately after Henry II left Ireland. It states that the earl, in a move redolent of Irish practice raided Offaly in search of cattle and other booty, presumably to secure the submission of its king, Diarmait O'Dempsey.[23] However, the expedition was not a success, for although great booty was carried off, O'Dempsey did not submit. Furthermore, he successfully ambushed the raiders' rearguard, killing Robert de Quency, who was Strongbow's son-in-law, as well as his constable of Leinster in the process.[24] For the remainder of his life, Strongbow's efforts to transform Leinster were retarded somewhat because of his commitments elsewhere. For example, in 1173 he left Ireland in order to serve the king in France, and upon his return and appointment as *custos*, or chief governor of the fledgling colony, he was obliged to campaign in Thomond and Meath.[25] Therefore, it seems highly unlikely that extensive settlement had actually taken place in western Leinster before he died in May 1176, leaving a minor, Gilbert, as his heir.[26] Nevertheless, it is certain that Strongbow had at least begun the process. The *Song of Dermot and the Earl* notes that by 1173, he had secured the submissions and hostages of the three overlords of Laois, namely MacGillaPatrick, O'Dempsey, and O'More.[27] Moreover, as the *Song* makes clear, he had also begun the subinfeudation of Leinster by making grants of land to his followers, some of which included parts of Laois. Not surprisingly, he tended to make use of the pre-existing political boundaries when sharing out the region. Thus half of Aghaboe in Upper Ossory was given to Adam de Hereford, the territory of Uí Buide, or Oboy to Robert de Bigarz and Slievemargy to John de Clahull, the earl's marshal.[28] Offaly was granted to Robert de Bermingham and there is some evidence to suggest that the kingdom of Laois was initially assigned to Geoffrey de Costentin.[29] Finally, it seems as though Strongbow reserved the natural fortress of Dunamase for himself, to be used as a regional *caput* or base.[30]

However, there is a large difference between the dispensation of grants on paper and their implementation on the ground. Laois, with its challenging topography of forest, river and bog was neither the most desirable nor the most accessible of regions from the newcomers' perspective, and its exploitation lagged behind that which occurred elsewhere in Leinster.[31] Moreover, some of the grantees like de Hereford were also granted much better land in Kildare.[32] In any event, it appears as though settlement in the region did not begin in earnest until 1181. In that year, Meiler fitzHenry was granted the territory of Laois proper in exchange for lands which he had previously held in Kildare.[33] Interestingly, Gerald of Wales commented that as Laois was 'a hostile and difficult land', it was appropriate that it should be held by Meiler, a fellow Geraldine who was a veteran from the first wave of Anglo-Normans to arrive.[34] More importantly, Hugh de Lacy, one of the men responsible for administering the lordship of Leinster during the minority of its heir, intervened decisively to quicken the pace of settlement in the region. Specifically, he built castles at strategic points for the grantees, such as one for Meiler fitzHenry at Timahoe and another in Oboy for Roger de Bigarz.[35] From this stage onwards, it is possible to glimpse the westwards expansion of the newcomers through the surviving documentation of the newly-created administration. For example, it is known that before his death in 1203, Maurice fitzGerald, who acquired Offaly through marriage from Robert de Bermingham, had constructed a castle at Lea, which was to become a great cornerstone of Anglo-Norman lordship in the region during the following century.[36] Similarly, two years previously King John wrote to the chief governor or justicier ordering him to make provision for the adequate protection of the lands which Adam de Hereford held at Aghaboe. Significantly however, the king also commanded the justiciar to establish the exact boundaries of de Hereford's lands.[37] Since the letter was sent a quarter of a century after the original grant was made, such uncertainty raises doubts about the extent to which settlement had occurred in Upper Ossory. This impression is strengthened by the nearly contemporaneous actions of the first Anglo-Norman bishop of Ossory, Hugo de Rous who exchanged the diocese's lands at Aghaboe for a parcel beside Kilkenny.[38] At first glance, it appears as though Gerald of Wales's comments about the hostility of Laois proper might be applicable to the region as a whole, a possibility which raises the issue of the attitude of the Irish dynasties to the colonial enterprise.

In fact, insofar as the surviving evidence can tell, the introduction of new lords to the region appears to have been carried out remarkably smoothly. Admittedly, there are some references to friction between native and newcomer. For example, the *Annals of Clonmacnoise* record the treacherous capture and subsequent hanging at Dublin of two O'Dempseys in 1213.[39] However the bulk of the annalistic entries concerning the region's native dynasties refer to them as allies, or possibly servants of the Anglo-Normans. For instance, in 1196 Domhnall O'More the king of Laois was killed while attempting to prevent a raiding party of O'Connors from Connacht making off with a prey taken from the *Gaill*. Similarly, an O'Connor Faly met his end in the same year while campaigning against the Cenél nEógain of Ulster with the newcomers.[40] The pioneering historian G. H. Orpen held the view that the region was only lightly settled, which would imply that Laois's dynasts could view the new dispensation with greater equanimity than their erstwhile neighbours in the present day Kildare and Carlow.[41] Nevertheless, there is some evidence to suggest that the Irish rulers of Laois suffered a major diminution in power and influence. In the early thirteenth century, the Irish annals record a series of conflicts between families like the O'Mores and O'Dempseys and their midlands neighbours, the O'Molloys of Fercall.[42] Possibly, the hostilities were a manifestation of a power struggle amongst the midland dynasties as they attempted to maximise their control over the diminished and economically less viable territory left available to them. Within this context, the fact that both Diarmait O'Dempsey king of Offaly and the O'More king of Laois founded Cistercian monasteries at Rosglas and Abbeyleix respectively within fifteen years of the invasion is also significant.[43] It could be argued that they were simply following the precedents set by other Irish kings like MacMurchada, and thus were motivated primarily by piety. It may also be possible that they made the foundations in an effort to minimise their loss of territory through the expedient of bestowing lands to sympathetic Irish ecclesiastics. However, even if this was the case, the fact remains that organised Irish resistance to the invaders within the region appears to have ceased very rapidly after Strongbow became lord of Leinster.

Paradoxically, the greatest threat to the tranquillity of the colony in Laois during the initial phase of consolidation was caused by the settlers themselves, as a direct result of the actions of King John. Strongbow's son Gilbert died in 1185, leaving a daughter Isobel as his sole surviving heiress. In 1189, Isobel was given in marriage to William Marshal I, 'the greatest knight in Christendom', who thus became earl of Pembroke and the second lord of Leinster.[44] David Crouch, the Marshal's latest biographer has suggested that the pioneering first wave of settlers resented the way in which the Marshal intruded some of his followers like John de Erly into Leinster.[45] Undoubtedly, after King John instigated a protracted quarrel with the Marshal in 1207, he used the pioneers to undermine William's position in Ireland.[46] In particular, the king exploited the uneasy relationship between his justiciar Meiler fitzHenry, who was also the lord of Laois, and the Marshal. At some time before May 1207, John granted Meiler the Marshal's overlordship of Offaly as well as ordering him to seize the castle of Dunamase.[47] This episode had an island-wide significance, as it precipitated the first major internal conflict amongst the colonists which degenerated briefly into a condition approaching civil war.[48] More relevantly, it also provides some indication of the growing economic prosperity of the settlements in the Laois region. For example, in 1208 Marshal expressed himself to be willing to pay a fine of 300 silver marks in order to recover Offaly.[49] The fact that the earl's castle at Dunamase was confiscated on several occasions during the dispute demonstrates that it was already a centre of some importance.[50] Ultimately, the quarrel itself was resolved in the Marshal's favour, due to a combination of his exemplary loyalty and John's desperate need of his services, and both Dunamase and Offaly had been restored to him by the time he died in 1219.[51] With William's death, half a century after Strongbow's arrival, the initial phase of Anglo-Norman involvement in Laois drew to a close. The territory had been successfully subinfeudated without undue opposition from its former rulers, settlement was well underway and the Marshal family had managed to establish themselves as the lords of Leinster.

It was noted earlier that with the important exception of Dunamase, Strongbow granted most of Laois away to his followers. However, the Marshal family succeeded in recovering a large proportion of the region by various means over the ensuing four decades. For example, it was William Marshal I who acquired the lands around Aghaboe from the bishop of Ossory in the 1200s.[52] Usually however, the Marshals regained lands upon the failure of the original grantees to produce heirs. For example, the territory of Oboy returned to them in this manner.[53] Most importantly, Meiler fitzHenry, William Marshal I's old adversary died without legitimate heirs in 1220, causing the territory of Laois to revert to William Marshal II.[54] Meiler's death had the effect of placing the core of the region directly in the hands of the lord of Leinster, without the presence of an intermediate lord. Insofar as the sources can tell, this had no adverse effect upon the continuing development of the Laois settlement. On the contrary, evidence of increased prosperity in the form of urban development is forthcoming from the 1230s, when references to 'the new town of Leys' begin to appear. For example, following the death of William Marshal II in 1231, the town of Leys formed part of the widow's dower which his brother and heir Richard, offered to Eleanor, his bereaved sister-in-law.[55] Eleanor's brother happened to be King Henry III, the ultimate source of power and patronage, which suggests that earl Richard had great confidence in the town's future wealth and security. In fact, it appears as though Leys was prospering in the middle of the century, as at least seven individuals from the town were admitted into the prestigious Guild Merchant of Dublin between 1239 and 1252.[56] Apart from urban development, other indications exist that the colony in Laois was prospering under the Marshals. By the middle of the thirteenth century, the Geraldines of Offaly under the leadership of Maurice fitzGerald II had emerged as the most powerful aristocratic family to reside in the region. Significantly, during the 1240s and 1250s, they were actually expanding their property interests in Laois southwards, into the area around Fermayl in Ossory.[57] In general, it appears as though the Marshals ruled Laois as capably as they did the rest of Leinster, which undoubtedly enjoyed a period of massive economic growth under their management.[58] However, the family was struck by disaster in 1245. In that year, an extraordinary series of deaths which an English chronicler ascribed to a curse placed upon the family by the bishop of Ferns culminated with their extinction in the male line.[59] Consequently, the contemporary laws pertaining to property resulted in William Marshal I's five daughters being deemed to be the coheiresses of the vast Marshal inheritance, which included the great liberty of Leinster. This turn of events was to have profound consequences both for Leinster in general and for Laois in particular, and as such deserves to be discussed in some detail.

In 1247, Leinster was painstakingly partitioned amongst the Marshal daughters, or more accurately, as only one daughter was still living, amongst their heirs.[60] As the Marshal family had risen to the highest level of Angevin society, the division benefited most of the great baronial families of England. One important effect of this development was the introduction of absentee landholding into Leinster on a large scale. The partition itself was carried out in a manner which was designed to ensure that each set of heirs received exactly one fifth of the value of the lordship of Leinster, a sum which was assessed to be exactly £343 4s 6½d *per annum*. Basically, the fairly straightforward method of dividing Leinster into five areas, one for each group of heirs was adopted. These areas were all centred upon important pre-existing manorial centres, namely Wexford, Carlow, Kilkenny, Kildare and lastly, Dunamase, although in some cases, individual manors which were located in one region were apportioned to another, in the interests of fairness. The surviving records of this process yield the first detailed valuations to come from the settlement in Laois. Significantly, they support the impression that the colony was thriving. For example, the value of the manorial centre of Dunamase was set at £104 19s 1d *per annum.*, that of Oboy at £82 8s 5½d and that of Aghaboe at £72 6s 5d. Following the partition, the bulk of the settlements in Laois were assigned to the heirs of the Marshal's fifth daughter Eva, namely Maud, wife of Roger Mortimer of Wigmore, Eva, wife of William de Cantilupe, and Eleanor, wife of Humphrey de Bohun.[61] From henceforth, Laois, like the rest of Leinster, was largely in the hands of absentees.

On the surface, the laborious distribution of Leinster amongst the Marshals' heirs seems scrupulously fair. However, the fifth division, centred on Laois differed from the first four in one important respect. The other four regions were established as liberties, or smaller-scale models of the lordship of Leinster, each with its own administrative system based upon a liberty court and a seneschal. Laois on the other hand was not, but was divided for administrative purposes along boundaries which pre-dated the invasion.[62] Thus Dunamase and Offaly became part of the liberty of Kildare, Oboy part of the liberty of Carlow, and Aghaboe was included in the liberty of Kilkenny.[63] This division was quite predictable and logical, given that it reflected the pattern of land grants following the invasion. However, from the perspectives of the seneschals, the day-to-day administrators of the liberties, it had the effect of marginalising the settlements and manors of Laois in two ways. First, in physical terms, Laois was literally situated on the edges of the three liberties. The second problem arose from the dual nature of the seneschals' function. On the one hand, seneschals served as officers of the crown, with responsibilities for tasks like the maintenance of the defence of the liberties. On the other hand, they also acted as the stewards of the liberty-holders, with a duty to maximise their profits. Where conflicts of interest arose, the seneschals tended to favour the interests of their employers, rather than those of distant absentees. Thus in 1294, Edmund Mortimer, the lord of Dunamase, was obliged to petition the English parliament in an effort to curb the high-handed activities of Thomas Darcy, the seneschal of Kildare.[64] Although it could be said that insofar as Laois was concerned, the partition of Leinster was inherently flawed, there does not appear to have been an immediate decline in the fortunes of the settlement. One ironic by-product of the involvement of English absentees in Laois is the greater availability of surviving evidence about the colony there. For instance, Dunamase, which was the richest of the Laois manors in 1247, was re-valued in 1283 as part of an inquisition *post mortem* taken following the death of Roger Mortimer.[65] Interestingly, it seems as though the manor, or more precisely the honour, had appreciated in value since the partition of Leinster, now being worth £171 *per annum*. More importantly perhaps, the inquisition reveals something of the social structure of the manor. For example there were 127 burgesses living in the new town of Leys – quite a respectable figure, if not exactly a metropolis. Similarly, it shows a standard pattern of manorial organisation, with a demesne, farmers and free tenants, as well as healthy signs of economic activity like the presence of water-mills and breweries at Dunamase. Furthermore, the personal names mentioned suggest individuals who were of English, or at least anglicised descent.

However, the inquisition also provides evidence of a new, and unwelcome development. The description of land being now worth nothing 'because of the war of the Irish' makes an ominous appearance.[66] The period of peace and prosperity had come to an end.

Earlier, it was suggested that the Irish rulers of Laois appear to have accommodated themselves to the new order relatively easily. However, it is difficult to account for their activities, outlook and organisation with much confidence thereafter. The meagre sources available to describe the settlement in Laois seem relatively abundant when compared with the surviving evidence about the natives. The Irish annals provide absolutely no information about the inhabitants of Laois between the late 1220s and the 1280s, and the later genealogies purporting to show the descent of the leading families are extremely defective.[67] To make matters worse, the references in the Anglo-Norman sources to the Irish are almost equally unforthcoming. One important question concerns the degree to which the Irish dynasts were left to their own devices. There seems little doubt but that the population of Laois remained predominantly Irish throughout the period. However, Kenneth Nicholls has questioned the generally-held view that much of Laois was never settled, a state of affairs which would have permitted the native rulers to retain effective autonomy from the colony.[68] Specifically, he noted that in the mid-thirteenth century John fitzThomas, a Desmond Geraldine had been receiving rents from Iregan or Uí Riacáin, which was situated to the north-west of Laois.[69] Similarly, in 1306 it was stated that the manor attached to the castle of Offerlane, located in the far north of Ossory, had once been worth £26 6s 6d *per annum* to the earl of Gloucester.[70] Presumably, such a physical presence would effectively inhibit any overt displays of independence on the part of the local Irish. That said, in the 1270s, the dynasts re-emerged into the historical records having retained some degree of internal cohesion intact. For example, an administrative document dating from the mid 1270s records the gift of a horse to 'O'Dempsey', a title which implies a survival of lordship.[71] Perhaps the most likely explanation is that in those areas of Laois which did not attract large-scale settlement, the Anglo-Normans contented themselves with exercising overlordship over the pre-existing population groups in exchange for annual tribute. Certainly, a relationship of this sort existed in Longford, between the de Verduns and the O'Farrells, where a similar situation obtained.[72] In any event, it is clear that when the quality of sources referring to Laois begins to improve, the Irish of the region can be seen acting in a purposeful, organised fashion. Unfortunately for the local colonists, it also becomes apparent that the activities of the Irish were directed towards the task of destroying the settlement.

The first recorded outbreak of trouble in the region occurred in 1272, when the justiciar, Maurice fitzMaurice led an expedition into Offaly.[73] Regrettably, nothing more is known about this particular episode. However, by 1276, hostilities had spread southwards, as Thomas de Clare mounted a campaign against the 'enemies' in the Slieve Blooms, presumably the MacGillaPatricks.[74] It appears as though conditions in the region remained turbulent, as the Kilkenny annalist John Clyn recorded the killing of a MacGillaPatrick leader three years later.[75] By then, the conflict had spread into the territory of Laois proper, as before 1278 Roger Mortimer had been forced to undergo great expense in order 'to defend and preserve his lands near the king's enemies and rebels'.[76] In 1279 and again in 1280, the justiciar Robert D'Ufford felt obliged to march as far as the new town of Leys 'to conquer the Irishmen of Offaly, rebels against the king'.[77] Four years later, a Government memorandum refers in passing to the collection of carts and the levying of funds in order to pacify Offaly.[78] Thereafter, the conflict escalated sharply. In 1284 the Irish managed to burn Lea castle, the *caput* of the Geraldine lordship of Offaly.[79] A year later, an impressive alliance of Irish dynasties from the midlands, including some from Meath assembled in Offaly to defeat an invading Anglo-Norman force in pitched battle.[80] Their prisoners included the young lord of Offaly Gerald fitzMaurice III who, as Friar Clyn noted, was captured by his own Irish tenants.[81] Similarly, the hostility of the MacGillaPatricks to the colony appears to have continued, as the seneschal of Kilkenny was required to account for a fine which was owed by the Irish of Slieve Bloom in exchange for having the king's peace.[82] Further north, there was a brief hiatus in the conflict, which appears to have caused by the capture of An Calbhach O'Connor Faly, the most prominent of the Irish warlords.[83] However, An Calbhach was rapidly released in exchange for some hostages, and the war had resumed in Laois by the summer of 1288.[84] At that point the justiciar John de Sandford was forced to intervene on an unprecedented scale. In September, he mustered the feudal host of Leinster and employed it in a massive defensive system which ultimately ran from Athlone to Kilkenny, passing along the borders of Laois.[85] Notwithstanding this effort, the Irish were still at war when the traditional 40 days of service expired, so de Sandford hired several local magnates, including John fitzThomas, the new lord of Offaly to maintain the defences.[86] Despite the severe burden thus placed upon the exchequer, the war continued, and actually spread into Meath during 1289, forcing de Sandford to campaign there in April.[87] Moreover, that summer the Irish of Offaly repeated their performance of 1286 by defeating and possibly capturing John fitzThomas.[88] In fact de Sandford did not achieve peace until

October 1289, following a full-scale invasion and a 12 day campaign involving troops from Munster and Leinster, as well as some Irish from the Wicklow hills. As a result, his report somewhat optimistically concluded, 'the Irish as well of Offaly as of Laois came into the king's peace and were never hostile again'.[89]

The patchy nature of the available sources means that it is not possible to provide a definitive reason as to why the region slid, apparently precipitously, into such serious conflict. Several complementary explanations have been advanced, ranging from a famine in 1271 which, it has been argued forced the Irish living on economically marginal lands to raid for food, to the adverse effects of absentee lords milking their estates for profits while neglecting to provide for defence.[90] The fact that the trouble appears to have begun in Offaly may provide a further clue. In 1268 the lord of Offaly, Maurice fitzGerald III, drowned in the Irish sea along with a shipload of his followers, leaving the most powerful family of resident magnates to endure a minority of nearly twenty years, during which time their properties were run for the benefit of English absentees.[91] Almost certainly, the outbreak of hostilities on the part of the Irish of Offaly was at least facilitated by the resultant power vacuum. In any event, while the causes for conflict may never be explained satisfactorily, the consequences are clear enough. Despite the great and expensive labours of John de Sandford, in 1288-9 the region was again engulfed in turmoil within five years.[92] Some of the responsibility for this state of affairs has been apportioned to the local magnates in general and to John fitzThomas lord of Offaly in particular, because of their own extra-legal activities in the mid 1290s.[93] However, the administrative records confirm that the O'Connor Falys and the O'Mores, de Sandford's Irish of Offaly and Laois, respectively, went back to war on their own initiative.[94] By then, signs of the seriousness of the problem had begun to emerge. For example, in 1291 John fitzThomas retained a clerk named John de Hothum in his service. Ominously, de Hothum's indenture explicitly stated that his wages would not be drawn from fitzThomas's estates in Offaly or elsewhere in the marches.[95] From this point onwards, it is plain that the colonists were going to have to make a major effort to restore order in the region if the settlements of Laois were to survive.

To be fair to the local magnates, and indeed to the Dublin government, they appear to have recognised this need. Most notably, the ordinances of the parliament held by the justiciar John Wogan in 1297 were explicitly formulated to address the problem.[96] Sensible measures, such as obliging landowners to maintain wards on the marches, forcing absentees to contribute to the costs of defence and ensuring that the king's highways were kept clear were adopted.[97] Furthermore, Wogan was given the opportunity to reorganise the administrative structure of the region at the same time, due to the fortuitous reversion of the liberty of Kildare to the crown.[98] Significantly, he appointed a single official, or coroner to act 'in Leys and elsewhere' beyond the Barrow.[99] However, in the course of a general eyre, an administrative instrument resembling a parliament in miniature, which Wogan held at Kildare immediately afterwards in order to set the seal upon royal authority within the county, the extent of the challenge faced by the Laois settlers was revealed.[100] The eyre's records provide graphic details of the sufferings endured by the colonists over the previous seven years. For instance, it was recorded that 'Kenagh Og Omorthe, and Leyssagh fizOmorth took pledges from the faithful people of the country for victual, and extorted money, so that the country is impoverished'.[101] Acts of homicide were rife. To take a typical example a man named Nicholas Fergylyn was murdered by two Irishmen with their following outside of the new town of Leys.[102] Furthermore, the eyre revealed much evidence of fraternisation between the peasants and the rebel Irish – a development famously condemned in the 1297 parliament.[103] In the course of a punitive raid against the Irish enemies of Offaly, the company of the seneschal Nigel le Brun was ambushed by both English and Irish, at least one of whom appears to have come from the new town of Leys itself.[104] Similarly, there are references to the men of Dunamase receiving Irish felons, and of individuals making oaths 'with Irishmen against Englishmen to break the king's peace'.[105] More seriously, the records note that the Irish enemies habitually returned from their raids to areas such as Irth in Offaly, Clonboyne in Laois and Slievemargy, which were specifically stated to be outside the land of peace.[106] In other words, the Dublin government had acknowledged that there were several districts in Laois in which the king's writ simply did not run. Perhaps the clearest sign that Anglo-Norman control of the region had effectively broken down is the fact that the O'Mores and O'Connor Falys were able to use these districts as safe havens from which to raid both the settlements in Laois itself, and well beyond its borders into Kildare.[107]

Over the following decade, the local magnates made a vigorous effort to regain control of Laois with government support. John fitzThomas, the lord of Offaly was particularly active in this regard, a fact acknowledged by King Edward II when he made fitzThomas the first earl of Kildare in 1316.[108] Militarily, the magnates attempted to implement the ordinances of the 1297 parliament. Thus, garrisons were established at places like Geashill, deep in the hostile areas, a new fortress was built at Rathangan, and fitzThomas mounted several retaliatory expeditions against the Irish of Offaly.[109] He also tried to exploit the tensions inherent within Irish lordships by employing a divide-and-rule strategy. For example, in 1303 he granted the castle of Morett, which he had recently acquired from its absentee owners, to one 'Nigellus Omorthe' in exchange for his services 'against all men'.[110] More importantly, fitzThomas exploited the enmity that appears to have existed between the O'Dempseys and the other midlands dynasties. This friction had also been put to use by Robert D'Ufford during the 1270s, and may have arisen from a reassertion by the O'Connor Falys of their traditional supremacy within Offaly.[111] In any case, in 1306, fitzThomas used one Fyn O'Dempsey to fight a war by proxy against the rebels, with some success.[112] That said, the occasional enmity displayed by the other midlands dynasties towards the O'Dempseys did not guarantee their good behaviour. Around the turn of the century, their most prominent leader appears to have been Diarmait O'Dempsey, who had formed a connection with Isobel de Cadel, the daughter of one of fitzThomas's closest associates.[113] However, Diarmait had been at war against the colony in the mid 1290s, was deemed to be an enemy in 1302 and 1306, and was finally killed by the infamous Piers Gaveston in 1308.[114] Notwithstanding this, in general the O'Dempseys appear to have been the dynasty which was most amenable to the colony, possibly because of the presence of Lea castle in the midst of their territory. Most famously, according to Barbour's *The Bruce* , in 1316 they treacherously led Edward Bruce and his Scottish army into a swamp, causing great losses of horses and men, having promised to guide them safely through the midlands.[115] However, if they were motivated by a sense of loyalty to the settlements, it seems as though they were acting for a cause that was already all but lost.

The general consensus amongst historians is that the period of the Bruce invasion was one of intense trauma for the people of Ireland, who were forced to endure the combined effects of the war itself and the great European famine of 1315-7.[116] Laois was not immune to either menace. It is clear that Edward Bruce's army inflicted serious damage upon the settlements there when it passed through the region in early 1316. For example, Bruce deliberately targeted John fitzThomas's properties by destroying the castle of Lea.[117] The situation was made worse by the fact that simultaneously, the O'Mores took the opportunity to engage in the wasting of the settlements in Laois proper until they were heavily defeated at the hands of the justiciar, Edmund Butler.[118] The extent of the damage inflicted by this double blow is revealed in vivid detail by an inquisition taken in 1323 to assess the value of the manor of Dunamase. The jurors painted a picture of almost complete devastation. The Irish had laid waste to both the manor itself and to the wooden buildings of Dunamase castle, and no Englishman dared to live there for fear of them. Similarly, the new town of Leys had suffered grievously. Where there had been 127 burgesses in 1283, now only forty remained.[119] However, while the invasion was clearly harmful to the colony, it was not primarily responsible for the decline in the Anglo-Norman settlement of Laois. Instead, the available evidence strongly suggests that its future was bleak long before Bruce ever set foot on the island. Specifically, the strenuous attempts made by fitzThomas and the government to restore order in Laois were demonstrable failures. Despite their best efforts, the Irish dynasties continued to pose an almost permanent security threat. Thus, in 1307 the Irish of Offaly burned the vill of Lea and actually besieged the castle, forcing fitzThomas and Edmund Butler to mount a relieving expedition.[120] Further south, the MacGillaPatricks were behaving in a similar fashion. For example, by 1306, the administration was obliged to maintain a garrison costing £40 *per annum* at the castle of Offerlane, 'which lies in a strong march', while the lands of the manor 'lie waste on account of the war of the Irish'.[121] Against this difficult background, the government attempted to curb the problem by adopting desperate expedients. Most notoriously, in 1305 it sanctioned the murder of nearly thirty O'Connor Falys at the hands of Piers de Bermingham in his castle at Carbury in county Kildare.[122] Perhaps the most significant point to be made about this drastic effort to persuade the Irish of Laois to return to their former loyalties is that it was completely unsuccessful and, not altogether surprisingly, had in fact quite the opposite effect, of inflaming the entire region.[123] Nevertheless, it is true that the O'Mores and O'Connor Falys were occasionally forced into peace, with one of the longest periods lasting from 1308 to 1311.[124] However, the continued existence of areas which remained outside of official control meant that as far as the resumption of hostilities was concerned, the initiative usually rested with the Irish dynasties. Given a situation where the threat, if not the actuality of warfare was continuous, it was inevitable that the geographically peripheral and economically marginal region of Laois would become an unviable location for a type of lordship that was based upon the manorial system.

During the three decades following the Bruce invasion, Anglo-Norman Laois slowly disintegrated under the pressure exerted by the Irish dynasties. The contemporary annals of the Kilkenny friar John Clyn provide a vivid description of the mechanics of the so-called Irish resurgence, which basically consisted of a series of raids, burnings and killings inflicted by the Irish upon the settlers. By way of illustration, the activities of the O'Mores were typical of the general pattern. From their bases in Laois and Slievemargy, they appear to have been expanding their power southwards into Ossory and eastwards into Carlow. For example, in 1326 Clyn notes the killing of 80 men of Carlow at their hands.[125] Throughout this period, the dynasty appears to have been led by one Laoiseach Ó Mórdha. Possibly, he was the same individual as the Leyssagh fizOmorth who had been extorting food and money from the faithful people of Laois in the 1290s. In any event, it is clear that he was a formidable opponent. For instance, Clyn held Laoiseach to be responsible for the treacherous killing of Sir Raymond le Ercedekne and 13 members of his family during a parley in 1335.[126] More seriously, Laoiseach appears to have appreciated the desirability of acting in concert with the other midlands dynasties. Thus, in 1336, he led a confederation of Irish from both Leinster and northern Munster to war against the English of Ossory.[127] However, one of the most striking features of the resurgence in general was the fluid, or more accurately opportunistic nature of the alliances formed by its chief protagonists, and Laoiseach did not maintain a posture of consistent hostility towards the colonists. For example, four years before his war against the Ossory colonists, Laoiseach had been employed by the government to serve against the Irish of the Leinster mountains. The financial account for this particular campaign reveals that Laoiseach was able to supply four men-at-arms, 217 hobelars, or light horsemen and 284 footmen for the royal army. In one sense, this level of troop contribution from a small, relatively infertile region is highly impressive. As far as Laoiseach was concerned it was also quite lucrative, as he was paid £91 11s in wages in addition to £1 18s for the purchase of half a roll of cloth.[128] However, the episode has a deeper significance. In order to counter the more immediate threat posed by the Irish of the Leinster mountains, the government proved itself willing to enrich an individual like Laoiseach, despite the obvious risks involved. Arguably, this reflected an acknowledgement on the government's part that a distinct O'More lordship had emerged and was now a permanent fact of life. Interestingly, there is some evidence to suggest that Roger Mortimer, the nominal lord of Laois had come to the same conclusion. In a treatise explaining the decay of the original conquest of Ireland, the sixteenth-century writer Patrick Finglas claimed that in an effort to maximise the revenues accruing from Laois, 'he that had Donnamause in Leix retained an Irishman, one of the Moores to be his Captaine of Warr in Leix, in defence agenst Irishmen upon that Borders'.[129] However, this policy proved to be ineffective. Finglas continued by stating that early in the fourteenth century, 'the seyd Moore, that was Captain of Leix, kept that Portion as his own, and called himself O-Moore'.[130] The impression that Mortimer's lands were lost to a supposed servant is strengthened by the contemporary account provided by Friar Clyn. Laoiseach Ó Mórdha was killed in 1342, while drunk, by his own servant. His death notice in Clyn's annals reveals that, far from protecting Mortimer's interests, Laoiseach had actually destroyed eight castles, including the great castle of Dunamase, in a single day. Significantly however, Clyn said of him that by doing so, 'De servo dominus, de subjecto princeps effectus', or, from a serf he became a lord, from a subject a prince.[131]

Undoubtedly, Clyn exaggerated the precipitiousness of Laoiseach's rise. Nevertheless, the overall trend was repeated elsewhere in Laois. To the south, the MacGillaPatricks were menacing the great manor of Aghaboe by the 1340s. For example, in 1346 they wasted the manor itself and three years later, they succeeded in storming its castle.[132] Similarly, the region's principal resident magnates, the earls of Kildare, were experiencing great difficulties in maintaining their position in the north-east. For example, their castle of Lea was captured by the Irish in both 1329 and 1346.[133] The second occasion was particularly spectacular, as it arose from a co-ordinated campaign by the O'Mores, O'Connor Falys and O'Dempseys, which also led to the destruction of several other castles in the region, and which allowed the O'Mores to remain in occupation of Lea for six months.[134] Given this state of affairs, it is difficult to avoid the conclusion that Anglo-Norman Laois had effectively ceased to exist.

However, it is possible to over-emphasise the success of the Irish resurgence. Undoubtedly, the co-ordinated campaign mounted by the region's native dynasties in 1346 was highly effective. Nevertheless, it should be noted that they were exploiting a particular political crisis amongst the colonists that had resulted in the temporary incarceration of the earl of Kildare in Dublin castle.[135] Upon his release, he recaptured Lea castle almost immediately.[136] In fact, the Irish of Laois never regained complete autonomy from the colonists. Throughout the remainder of the middle ages, powerful magnates such as the fourth and eighth earls of Kildare frequently dominated Laois. However, a profound change had occurred in the region's political structures. The earls of Kildare exercised control over the Irish through a mixture of persuasion, which could involve the drawing up of personal indentures of service and the making of marriage alliances, and the application of brute force.[137] These methods were very successful, but were markedly different to the feudal lordship operating under English law originally envisaged by Strongbow and created by the Marshals. Perhaps the best way of looking at the careers of the later earls of Kildare is to regard them as living testimony to the fact that in Laois, Anglo-Irish lordship had risen from the ashes of its Anglo-Norman ancestor.

FOOTNOTES

1. For details of the invasion, see N.H.I., ii, pp 43-175; R. Frame, *Colonial Ireland, 1169-1369* (Dublin, 1981), pp 1-50 or Otway-Ruthven, *Med. Ire.* (2nd ed., 1980), pp 35-65.
2. R. Bartlett, 'Colonial aristocracies of the High Middle ages' in R. Bartlett and A. MacKay (ed.), *Medieval frontier societies* (Oxford, 1989), pp 23-47.
3. J. Lydon, *Ireland in the later Middle Ages* (Dublin, 1973), p. 62; K. Simms, *From kings to warlords* (Woodbridge, 1987), p. 19; Otway-Ruthven, *Med. Ire.*, p. 252.
4. W. Fitzgerald, 'Historical notes on the O'Mores and their territory of Leix to the end of the sixteenth century' in *Kildare Arch. Soc. Jn.* 6 (1909-11), p. 10; N.H.I., ix, p. 43.
5. N.H.I., ii, pp 23-4.
6. Ibid., p. 25.
7. Ibid., pp 24-5.
8. Ibid., p. 24.
9. Ibid., p. 24.
10. J. Watt, *The church in Medieval Ireland* (Dublin, 1972), pp 24-6.
11. N.H.I., ix, pp 26-7; B. Mitchell, *A new genealogical atlas of Ireland* (Baltimore, 1988), p. 71.
12. N.H.I., ii, pp 19, 21, 28.
13. *Ann. Tig.*, s.a. 1161.
14. N.H.I., ii, p. 27.
15. N.H.I., ii, p. 24; *A.F.M.*, s.a. 1193.
16. N.H.I., ii, p. 27.
17. *A.F.M.*, s.a. 1166; N.H.I., ii, p.75.
18. *Song of Dermot*, p. 89.
19. Ibid., pp 91-5.
20. *Ann. Tig.*, s.a. 1171; N.H.I., ii, p. 79.
21. N.H.I., ii, p. 76.
22. Ibid., p. 88; Otway-Ruthven, *Med. Ire.*, p. 49.
23. *Song of Dermot*, p. 203.
24. Ibid., pp 203-5.
25. Otway-Ruthven, *Med. Ire.*, p. 536.
26. *H.B.C.* (3rd ed., 1986), p. 477.
27. *Song of Dermot*, pp 233-5.
28. Orpen, *Normans*, i, pp 394-5; *Song of Dermot*, p. 227.
29. *Song of Dermot*, p. 227; *Cal. doc. Ire., 1171-1251*, no. 137.
30. Orpen, *Normans*, i, p. 375.
31. For maps of Laois see A.P. Smyth, *Celtic Leinster: towards a historical geography of early Irish civilisation, A.D. 500-1600* (Dublin, 1982), plates XI-XVI; Fitzgerald, 'Historical notes on the O'Mores', maps facing pp 1, 3.
32. *Ormond deeds, 1172-1350*, no. 29.
33. Giraldus, *Expugnatio*, p. 195.
34. Ibid., p. 195.
35. Ibid., p. 195.
36. *Cal. doc. Ire., 1171-1251*, no. 195.
37. *Cal. doc. Ire., 1171-1251*, no. 166.
38. H.F. Berry (ed.), 'Ancient charters in the Liber Albus Ossoriensis' in *R.I.A. Proc.* 27 C no. 3 (1908), pp 118-9.
39. *Ann. Clon.*, s.a. 1213.
40. *A.F.M.*, s.a. 1196.

41. Orpen, *Normans*, i, p. 382.
42. *Ann. Clon.* s.a. 1215, 1227.
43. Gwynn & Hadcock, *Med. relig. houses*, pp 124, 142.
44. *H.B.C.*, p. 477.
45. D. Crouch, *William Marshal* (London, 1990), pp 93-4.
46. Otway-Ruthven, *Med. Ire.*, pp 77-9.
47. T. Hardy (ed.), *Rotuli Litterarum Patentium in turri Londiensi* (London, 1835), p. 72; Orpen, *Normans*, ii, pp 217-8, citing P. Meyer (ed.), *L'Histoire de Guillaume le Maréschal, Comte de Striguil et de Pembroke* (Paris, 1891-1901), lines 14127-31.
48. Crouch, *William Marshal*, pp 101-4; Orpen, *Normans*, ii, pp 209-15.
49. *Cal. doc. Ire., 1171-1251*, no. 388.
50. Orpen, *Normans*, ii, p. 218, citing Meyer, *L'Histoire*, lines 14127-31, 14330.
51. Hardy, *Rot. Lit. Pat.*, p. 80b; *Cal. doc. Ire., 1171-1251*, nos 644, 664, 684-5.
52. Berry, 'Ancient charters', p. 118.
53. Orpen, *Normans*, i, p. 384.
54. A. J. Otway-Ruthven, 'The medieval county of Kildare' in *I.H.S.*, xi, no. 43 (1959), p. 182; Orpen, *Normans*, ii, p. 218.
55. *Cal. doc. Ire., 1171-1251*, no. 1950.
56. P. Connolly and G. Martin (ed.), *The Dublin Guild Merchant roll, c. 1190-1265* (Dublin, 1992), pp 76, 78-9, 81, 85, 88, 91.
57. *Red Bk Kildare*, nos 52-3, 55.
58. N.H.I., ii, pp 166-7
59. Ibid., pp 157-8, 166-7.
60. For details of the partition, see Orpen, *Normans*, iii, pp 79-110.
61. Ibid., p. 103.
62. Ibid., p. 107.
63. See for example, *P.R.I. rep. D.K. 42*, p. 41; *Cal. justic. rolls Ire., 1295-1303*, pp 304, 397.
64. Richardson & Sayles, *Rot. parl. hact.*, pp 36-9.
65. *Cal. doc. Ire., 1252-1284*, no. 2028; *Cal. inq. post. mort.*, ii, pp 267-8.
66. *Cal. doc. Ire., 1252-1284*, no. 2028.
67. K. Nicholls, 'The land of the Leinstermen' in *Peritia*, iii (1984), p. 542.
68. Ibid., pp 541-2.
69. Nicholls, 'The land of the Leinstermen', pp 541-2; A. J. Otway-Ruthven, 'Knight's fees in Kildare, Leix and Offaly' in *R.S.A.I. Jn.*, xci, pt. 2 (1961), p. 178; *Cal. doc. Ire., 1252-84*, no. 1912.
70. *Cal. doc. Ire., 1302-07*, no. 670.
71. *Cal. doc. Ire., 1252-84*, no. 1389, p. 258.
72. A. J. Otway-Ruthven, 'The partition of the de Verdon lands in Ireland in 1332' in *R. I. A. Proc.*, 66 C, no. 5 (1968), pp 413-4.
73. *P. R. I. rep. D. K. 36*, p. 24.
74. Ibid., p. 33; in general, for the resurgence in Upper Ossory, see C. A. Empey, 'County Kilkenny in the Anglo-Norman period' in W. Nolan and K. Whelan (ed.), *Kilkenny : History and society* (Dublin, 1990), pp 89-91.
75. Clyn, *Annals*, p. 9.
76. *Cal. doc. Ire., 1252-84*, no. 1410; *Cal. close rolls, 1272-9*, p. 435.
77. *Cal. doc. Ire., 1252-84*, no. 2291.
78. Ibid., nos. 2333-4.
79. Clyn, *Annals*, p. 9.
80. *Ann. Clon.*, s.a. 1285.

81. Clyn, *Annals*, p. 10.
82. *P. R. I. rep. D. K. 37*, p. 27.
83. Clyn, *Annals*, p. 10; *Chartul. St Mary's, Dublin*, ii, p. 319.
84. *Cal. doc. Ire., 1285-92*, no. 1018.
85. Ibid., no. 559, pp 265-7.
86. Ibid., no. 559, p. 267.
87. *Cal. doc. Ire., 1285-92*, no. 559, pp 268-70.
88. Ibid., no. 559, p. 273; *Ann. Conn.*, s.a. 1289; Clyn, *Annals*, p. 10.
89. *Cal. doc. Ire, 1285-92*, no. 559, pp 271-3.
90. N.H.I., ii, p. 264.
91. Clyn, *Annals*, p. 9; R. Flower (ed.), 'The Kilkenny chronicle' in *Anal. Hib.*, no. 2 (1931), p. 332; *Cal. close rolls, 1272-9*, p. 45; *Cal. doc. Ire., 1252-84*, nos. 866, 970.
92. *Cal. justic. rolls Ire., 1295-1303*, p. 118; *Chartul. St Mary's, Dublin*, ii, p. 323.
93. N.H.I., ii, p. 266.
94. See for example, *Cal. justic. rolls Ire., 1295-1303*, pp 168-70.
95. *Red Bk Kildare*, no. 13.
96. *Stat. Ire., John-Hen. V*, pp 195-213.
97. Ibid., pp 199, 201, 209.
98. *Stat. Ire., John-Hen. V*, p. 199.
99. *Cal. justic. rolls Ire., 1295-1303*, p. 167.
100. Ibid., pp 167-208.
101. Ibid., p. 168.
102. Ibid., pp 167, 169.
103. *Stat. Ire., John-Hen. V*, p. 211.
104. *Cal. justic. rolls Ire., 1295-1303*, p. 168.
105. Ibid., p. 193.
106. *Cal. justic. rolls Ire., 1295-1303*, pp 168-170, 183, 191.
107. Ibid., pp 176, 178, 183.
108. *Red Bk Kildare*, no. 142.
109. *Cal. justic. rolls Ire., 1295-1303*, pp 286-7, 362; *Cal. justic. rolls Ire., 1305-07*, pp 8, 85, 135, 242.
110. *Red Bk Kildare*, nos. 76, 80-2, 84.
111. *P. R. I. rep. D. K. 36*, p. 33.
112. *Cal. justic. rolls Ire., 1305-07*, pp 215, 270-1.
113. *Cal. justic. rolls Ire., 1295-1303*, p. 368.
114. Ibid., pp 169, 368; *Cal. justic. rolls Ire., 1305-07*, p. 271; *Chartul. St Mary's Dublin*, ii, p. 293.
115. R. Frame, 'The Bruces in Ireland, 1315-18' in *I.H.S.* xix, no. 73 (1974), p. 22 citing W.W. Skeat (ed.), *The Bruce* (Scot. Text. Soc., 1894), book xiv, lines 329-70.
116. N.H.I., ii, pp 294-7; Otway-Ruthven, *Med. Ire.*, pp 237-9; Orpen, *Normans*, iv, pp 205-6.
117. *Chartul. St Mary's, Dublin*, ii, p. 348.
118. Ibid., pp 348, 353.
119. P.R.O., C47/10/18, no. 17 (Chancery Miscellanea).
120. *Chartul. St Mary's, Dublin*, ii, pp 335-6.
121. *Cal. doc. Ire., 1302-07*, no. 670.
122. *A.F.M..* s.a. 1305; Clyn, *Annals*, p. 11; *Cal. justic. rolls Ire., 1305-07*, p. 82.
123. *Cal. justic. rolls Ire., 1305-07*, p. 78.
124. *Cal. justic. rolls Ire., 1308-14*, pp 226, 230.
125. Clyn, *Annals*, p. 18.

126. Clyn, *Annals*, p. 26.
127. Ibid., p. 27.
128. *P. R. I. rep. D. K. 43*, pp 54-5.
129. Patrick Finglas, 'A Breviat of the getting of Ireland, and of the decaie of the same' in Walter Harris (ed.), *Hibernica: or some antient pieces relating to Ireland* (Dublin, 1747), p. 40.
130. Finglas, 'Breviat', p. 40.
131. Clyn, *Annals*, p. 30.
132. Clyn, *Annals*, p. 32; Empey, 'Kilkenny in the Anglo-Norman period', p. 90.
133. Clyn, *Annals*, pp 21, 32.
134. Ibid., p. 32.
135. R. Frame, *English lordship in Ireland 1318-61* (Oxford, 1982), p. 281.
136. Clyn, *Annals*, p. 32
137. For examples of their methods, see *Red Bk Kildare*, nos 166-7, 169; G. MacNiocaill (ed.) *Crown surveys of lands 1540-41* (Dublin, 1992), pp 235-6, 267-9; *A.U.*, s.a. 1511.

Chapter 8

ANGLO-NORMAN CASTLES IN CO. LAOIS

KIERAN O'CONOR

Introduction

The masonry castle is clearly the most popular modern image of the Middle Ages. This is understandable as very often stone castles still dominate the skylines of many modern landscapes. Furthermore, this view has been underpinned by Hollywood, with its many films set in or around medieval castles. This all makes masonry castles interesting and exciting places to visit for both children and adults, apparently more so than other archaeological sites.

A castle was both a well-defended fortress capable of withstanding attack and a private residence, invariably of someone of status in medieval society. It was this dual function of stronghold and private lordly residence that marks a castle off from the fortresses of other periods, including our own. The main military function of a castle was to protect its owner, his family and his retainers against attack. Castles also facilitated both the conquest and retention of territory during the medieval period. Yet castles were also dwellings and this meant that they had peaceful functions as well. A castle was the centre of its owner's estate (or part of it if he were powerful). A building or room within the castle served as a court house for his tenants. This made the castle a centre of local administration and justice. Therefore, a castle had peaceful as well as military functions.[1]

The remains of at least fifty-six castles can be seen today in Co. Laois.[2] However, at least thirty-three of these standing castles are tower houses. While one or two may date to the fourteenth century, the vast majority of tower houses in Co. Laois seem to have been erected during the late fifteenth, sixteenth and seventeenth centuries by mainly Gaelic lords.[3] It might be added that eleven fortified houses of late sixteenth and seventeenth century date also occur in Laois. These are not regarded as castles in the strict sense as their original defences were not as strong as true castles.[4]

However, the objective of this paper is to examine the nature of castles built in Laois from the late twelfth century through to the early fourteenth century during the Anglo-Norman period. The present writer

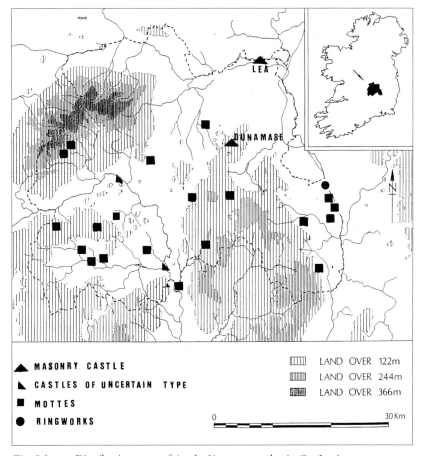

Fig. 8.1   Distribution map of Anglo-Norman castles in Co. Laois.

can identify up to twenty-five castles erected in the county during these years (fig. 8.1).

Anglo-Norman masonry castles in Co. Laois

The first phase of stone-castle building in Ireland was carried out by the Anglo-Normans from c.1180 to c.1310.[5] Laois has two standing Anglo-Norman stone castles within its boundaries.

Dunamase Castle is clearly one of the most spectacular Anglo-Norman masonry fortresses in the country, if not in the British Isles and Ireland as a whole (pl. 8.1; fig. 8.2). This is largely because it is located on a high rocky eminence, which makes the castle visible for miles around. The standing remains at this castle consist of a late twelfth

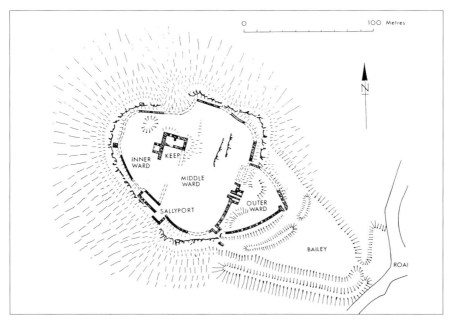

Fig. 8.2   Sketch plan of Dunamase Castle.

Plate 8.1   Dunamase Castle.

century hall-keep, two wards and one if not two barbican enclosures. It is generally held that these remains at Dunamase were built at different times between *c*.1180 and the later thirteenth century.[6] It might be added that the present writer personally believes that the standing remains visible at Dunamase Castle today were all built by late 1211, after a rapid building-campaign there by William Marshal the Elder.[7] In 1231 Dunamase was one of the most important Marshal castles in the lordship of Leinster.[8] The castle was clearly the centre of Anglo-Norman military power and administration in this part of Leinster from the late twelfth century through to the 1320s when it was finally captured by the local Irish under the command of Leysagh O'More.[9]

Much research has been carried out on Dunamase Castle over the last few years. This work has culminated in Brian Hodkinson's ongoing excavation at the site, which has produced some very interesting results. Therefore, as much has been written on Dunamase Castle since *c.* 1990, I want to concentrate on a discussion of Lea Castle, the other standing Anglo-Norman stone fortification in the county, as little systematic work has been done on this site.

It will be argued below that the first Anglo-Norman fortification at Lea consisted of a timber castle built either by Robert de Bermingham or his son-in-law Gerald fitz Maurice (ancestor of the FitzGeralds, earls of Kildare) before *c.* 1200 – a fortress which will be rather clumsily classified as a ringwork. However, the standing masonry remains at Lea Castle consist of an inner ward, within which the remains of a four-storeyed towered keep and fore-building occur, and a later outer ward which is entered by a fine three-storeyed twin-towered gatehouse (fig. 8.3, pl. 8.2). It might be added that there is a subsidiary enclosure on the site's eastern and north-eastern edges that was apparently always defended in timber.[10]

What date are the visible masonry remains at Lea Castle? This is a very difficult question to answer as it was noted above that Lea has not received the same academic attention as Dunamase. There is a general consensus amongst scholars that the twin-towered gatehouse and outer ward at Lea date, on admittedly rather flimsy historical grounds, to the late thirteenth century.[11] There is more controversy concerning the dating of the towered keep here. A towered keep was originally a rectangular structure with an attached tower at each of its four corners. It has been suggested that this keep at Lea dates to the mid-thirteenth century on the basis of the trefoil-headed windows seen on the uppermost floor of this building.[12] Alternatively it has been stated that this building was constructed by William Marshal the Elder at some stage before his death in 1219.[13]

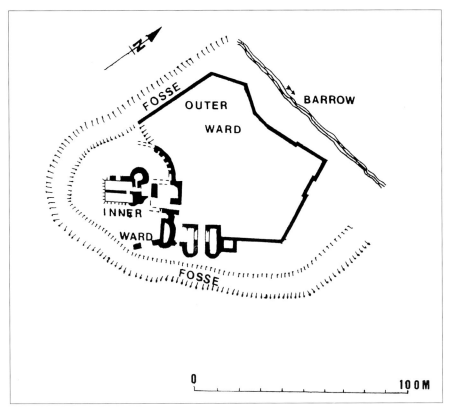

Fig. 8.3   Sketch plan of Lea Castle.

Plate 8.2   Lea Castle.

This confusion is really due to the fact that there are no specific historical references to the building of the keep at Lea. Certainly at first glance the evidence from the trefoil-headed windows on the third floor of this keep suggests a date after *c.* 1225-1230. Yet it is also noticeable upon more careful examination that the embrasures of the first and second floors of the keep have round arches over them. Alternatively the surviving embrasures in the uppermost floor of the keep have segmental arches over them. The uppermost portion of the mural stairway in the keep's north-western wall, which gives access to the third floor, is roofed by flat lintels, one on top of another as it ascends upwards. The lower two-thirds of this stairway, which corresponds in level to the first and second floors of the building, is roofed by a round arch. This change in building style between the third floor of the keep and the rest of the building must surely suggest that this uppermost storey is a later addition. Therefore, the trefoil-headed lights in the uppermost floor of the structure date to a secondary phase of building in the towered keep. The lower three storeys of the building belong to a primary phase of construction. This first period of building within the keep at Lea is associated with round-arched embrasures.

What date is this primary phase of building within the keep at Lea? The earliest towered keep in Ireland seems to be the one extant at Carlow Castle[14] which appears to have been begun by William Marshal the Elder at some stage in the period 1210-15. It seems to have been finished by the early 1220s at least.[15]

Certainly the keep at Carlow Castle has details in common with Lea. Both keeps have a first-floor entranceway in more-or-less the same position at their narrow northern ends, beside and protected by a corner tower. These attached towers at the corners of both keeps were usually provided with three plunging loops at each floor level. However, in both keeps the ground floor of the corner tower flanking the doorway was entered from above and had no loops or lights in it. This suggests that the ground floor of this tower at both keeps functioned as a prison. Furthermore, a mural stairway, entered from a small rectangular lobby beside the first floor entranceway, provides access to the upper floors and original parapets at both keeps. The first phase in both keeps is associated with round-arched embrasures. Therefore, there is good evidence to suggest that the original design of the towered keep at Lea was heavily influenced by the keep at Carlow Castle.

So when was the keep at Lea first begun and by whom was it constructed? An analysis of the surviving historical references to both the castle and manor of Lea during the early thirteenth century may provide an answer to these two questions. Lea lay within the grant of Offaly 'to the west of Offelan' given to Robert de Bermingham by Strongbow before 1176.[16] Robert was dead by the end of the twelfth century and apparently his fief was divided amongst his daughters, one of whom had married Gerald fitz Maurice.

Gerald held the lands of Lea and Geashill of the lord of Leinster, for the service of four knights, at the time of his death in 1201.[17] In 1203 the king commanded the justiciar to deliver the castles of Geashill and Lea, as well as other lands held by Gerald fitz Maurice at the time of his death, to the latter's lord William Marshal the Elder.[18] It would appear that Lea and Geashill were in Marshal's hands during the minority of Gerald's son, Maurice. The latter regained seisin of his father's holdings including Lea in 1216.[19] Lea Castle remained in Fitzgerald hands after this date. It was clearly an important Fitzgerald stronghold throughout the rest of the thirteenth century.[20] It appears that the Fitzgeralds lost control of the castle to the local Irish at some stage in the latter half of the fourteenth century. However, it was recaptured by Gearoid Mor Fitzgerald, 7th earl of Kildare, in the late fifteenth century.[21]

The main point here is that Lea Castle was a Geraldine fortress. It functioned as the *caput* of its lands in this part of Leinster for much of the medieval period. It was noted above that it is believed that the keep was constructed by William Marshal the Elder before 1219, presumably as a copy of his castle at Carlow.[22] Certainly William Marshal held Lea as lord of Leinster during the minority of Maurice fitz Gerald, his deceased vassal's son, from 1203 until 1216. Yet it is unlikely that Marshal would have wasted his resources on a castle that was only going to be in his direct keeping for a short period.

Marshal would have needed these resources elsewhere in Leinster, both for building his own seignorial castles, such as Dunamase, and for continuing the ongoing economic development of his lordship. It is far more logical to suggest that Maurice fitz Gerald built the towered keep at Lea as a direct copy of his lord's castle at Carlow, at some stage after he gained seisin of his lands in 1216, possibly around 1220. The result was a three-storeyed keep remarkably similar in design to Carlow. The fourth storey was added onto this keep at some later date.

It has been argued that the towered keep at Ferns, Co. Wexford, was probably built by William Marshal the Younger around 1224.[23] The picture emerging from both excavation and survey is that towered keeps had their genesis in early thirteenth century Leinster under Marshal aegis, seemingly in the period 1210-25.

It was recently stated that the present remains at Dysart Castle, which lies quite close to Dunamase, date to before the introduction of tower houses.[24] Yet the standing remains here seem to consist of nothing more than the corner tower of a bawn belonging to a now levelled late medieval/ early modern tower house or fortified house.

The castle of 'Offarclane' is mentioned in 1290 and 1307 as being in the hands of the de Clare earls of Gloucester.[25] The site of this castle has been identified as being located at the edge of Castletown village in Gash townland on the terrace above the Nore. However, the standing remains seem to represent part of the remains of the bawn of a late medieval tower house.[26] It is uncertain as to how this castle appeared around 1300. A castle belonging to the bishops of Ossory was located at Durrow throughout the thirteenth century.[27] Again it is not clear as to what this castle looked like during this period.

Future excavation or survey in Laois may reveal further Anglo-Norman masonry castles dating to the years *c.* 1180-1310. However Dunamase and Lea are the only two standing masonry castles in the county that definitely date to the period of Anglo-Norman control in the region.

Earthwork castles in Co. Laois

It is continually forgotten and sometimes not believed that the majority of castles throughout Western Europe in this age of chivalry during the twelfth, thirteenth, and even fourteenth centuries were constructed of earth and timber.[28] It has been argued that about five hundred and twenty five earthwork castles were constructed in Ireland during the same period.[29] This may even be a minimal figure as new earthwork castles are still being recognised by the Archaeological Survey.

What are earthwork castles? In archaeological terms earthwork castles are divided into two types. The first and most common type of earthwork castle visible in the Irish landscape is the motte. A motte can be described as a flat-topped earthen mound, whose summit would have originally carried timber buildings and defences. Sometimes a ditched and embanked enclosure known as a bailey was attached onto the base of the motte. The defences and buildings of these baileys were also built of wood or clay and wood.

The second type of earthwork castle is called the ringwork – a monument-type only recently recognised in Ireland. Most ringworks can be defined as a circular or oval area delimited by an earthen bank and girdling fosse. Again the original defences and buildings of these ringworks were made of timber or clay and wood. A variant of this type of earthwork castle is the *partial* ringwork. A partial ringwork invariably occurs on a promontory or ridge-end where there are strong natural defences. These natural defences meant that it was only necessary to throw a bank and ditch across the exposed side of the site. The natural defences on the other sides of a site like this were deemed strong enough to dispense with additional defensive structures other than perhaps a palisade or a little scarping of the natural slope.[30]

In Ireland there are problems with the identification of mottes and ringworks in the field. The next section of this paper will discuss the methods used by the present writer to identify earthwork castles in

Laois.

The field identification of mottes in Co. Laois

Little work was done on motte castles in Ireland since Goddard Orpen's seminal work on them at the beginning of this century until the mid-1970s.[31] For example, an analysis of the book *Irish castles and castellated houses* by Harold G. Leask, the OPW's Inspector of National Monuments who for many years was considered Ireland's expert on castles, shows that he believed all mottes consisted of high earthen mounds with relatively small summits and attached baileys- all easily recognisable in the Irish landscape.[32] This book is still regarded as the standard textbook on castles and many of Leask's views on mottes still permeate Irish archaeology.

However, work in England and Wales over the last half century has shown that mottes vary considerably in shape, with many mounds being low in height and having broad summits.[33] For example, the flat-topped motte at Haresfield, Gloucestershire, has a summit diameter of 55m. The top of this mound is raised a mere 1.5m-2m in height above present ground level.[34] The motte at Legsby, Lincolnshire, measures 9m by 12m across its summit. This summit is only 1.2m in height above present ground level.[35] Mottes in both England and Wales can be circular, oval, rectangular or sub-rectangular and even square in shape.[36] Furthermore, it appears that about 20 per cent of English and Welsh mottes always lacked baileys.[37]

Research carried out in Ireland over the last twenty years also shows that mottes here vary considerably in shape and size. It appears that only between 30 per cent and 34.5 per cent of mottes in Ireland had baileys associated with them during their period of usage.[38] It is also clear that many free-standing mottes (ie. without baileys) throughout Ireland tend to be relatively low in height and have broad summit diameters. This has been amply demonstrated in Ulster and to a lesser extent in Meath, Louth and Leinster.[39]

Research indicates many mottes in Ireland and Britain are low and have large summit areas in comparison to their height and lack baileys. Many mottes are very different in form to Leask's long-held idea of high castle mounds with attached baileys. It is this newly realised diversity in motte morphology that makes the field identification of this monument-type difficult at times.

Ireland has a great number of standing earthworks of all periods surviving throughout its countryside. It is clear that there is a problem in distinguishing these low, broad-topped, bailey-less mottes from raised raths, which are of ultimately Early Christian date, by fieldwork alone as both these types of site can be morphologically similar. Raised raths can be defined as heightened variants of ringforts, where habitation occurred on the summit of the mound.[40] A list has been built up by various writers of the morphological differences between these raised raths and low, broad-topped, free-standing mottes, in order to allow archaeologists to differentiate between these monument types in the field.[41]

However, even these writers would now agree that it is impossible in some cases to distinguish a motte from a raised rath by fieldwork alone, even when using this list. For example, the mound at Gransha, Co. Down, was once seen as a purpose-built Anglo-Norman motte. However, excavation has indicated that it was a raised rath of purely Early Christian date.[42] Despite setting quite rigid criteria for differentiating raised raths from mottes, McNeill still identified the mound at Deer Park Farms, Co. Antrim, as belonging to the latter class of monument.[43] Subsequent excavation has shown that it was a raised rath, constructed and inhabited in the Early Christian period.[44]

Additionally, to complicate the picture further, the present writer believes that recent work suggests that many of the morphological criteria used to distinguish raised raths from free-standing mottes are no longer valid. For example, a ramped entry up through the side of a mound to its summit is generally regarded as one of the diagnostic features of a raised rath.[45] Nevertheless, evidence for such a ramped entry was found leading to the summit at Rathmullan, Co. Down, when it was used as a motte.[46] The very definite motte at Westcourt Demesne, Callan, Co. Kilkenny, also has a ramped entry leading up from its eastern base to the summit of the mound. Something similar occurs on the south-eastern side of the motte at Middlemount, Co. Laois. Therefore, this feature is not always associated with raised raths. The existence of earthen banks around the edges of mound summits was once regarded as a feature only occurring on raised raths.[47] Earthen banks most certainly do occur around the summits of many mottes in Ireland. For example, a very definite earthen bank exists around the edge of the summit of the 7m high motte at Castletown, Co. Laois. Again it has been stated that many raised raths have very large summit diameters, much larger than mottes.[48] This statement is also no longer valid as there is a whole series of free-standing Leinster mottes with enormous summit diameters, as there are in England and Wales.[49] For example, the motte at Newcastle Middle, Co. Wicklow, has a summit diameter of c. 60m, giving the mound-top here an overall area of c. 3,000m.[50]

Seventeen mottes and three possible mottes have been located in Co. Laois (fig. 8.1). If some of the morphological criteria once used to distinguish mottes from raised raths in the field have now been invalidated, how did the present writer decide on what sites to classify

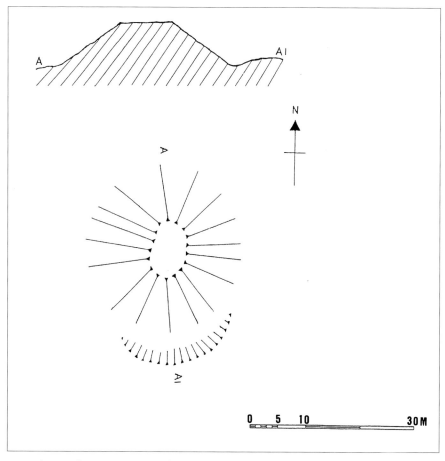

Fig. 8.4   The motte at Donaghmore, Co. Laois.

as motte castles?

Firstly, the presence of a bailey beside a flat-topped mound was taken to show the site was a motte castle. Raised raths are not associated with baileys. Nine Laois mottes have or had baileys beside them. Secondly, relatively high mounds with comparatively small summit diameters were classified as mottes simply because they are so different in shape to raised raths. Mounds that had summit diameters that were three times or less their height in size were taken to be mottes. Donaghmore, Co. Laois, is a good example of this type of free-standing high motte with a small summit diameter. Its flat-topped summit is oval in shape, having maximum dimensions of 10m north/south and 6.5m east/west. The top of this mound is raised 6m-7.5m in height above natural ground level (fig. 8.4).

Thirdly, it is clear that the surviving historical sources can be used to help identify mounds as motte castles. Laois was part of the medieval lordship of Leinster. This area (which is basically the southern half of the present province) has more surviving medieval historical sources relating to it than other regions of Ireland, apart from perhaps the eastern part of the lordship of Meath and the medieval county of Tipperary.[51] Quite detailed accounts of the conquest and subsequent subinfeudation of Leinster, including Laois, are extant.[52] The various surviving feodaries for Leinster mean that a good picture of the structure of land holding in medieval Laois can be. These sources allow the scholar to identify the *capita* (centres) of even quite minor manors in Leinster.[53] Therefore, a mound existing at the site of a historically attested manorial *caput*, borough or castle in Laois was identified as a purpose-built motte or, whatever its actual origins, to have functioned as one during the medieval period. Sixteen out of the twenty mottes and possible mottes in Laois occur at historically-attested medieval centres. In eastern Ireland it is assumed that the establishment of parishes was basically carried out under the patronage of Anglo-Norman lords from the late twelfth century onwards.[54] Here the correlation between the Anglo-Norman manor and the medieval parish has been amply demonstrated. It has been shown that manors and parishes were often territorially coincident. In the absence of detailed documentation, the medieval parish often acts as a substitute in Ireland for the geographical identification of Anglo-Norman manors carved out in the subinfeudation process. It is held that the site of a medieval parish church also marks the *caput* of an Anglo-Norman manor. This whole process is linked to a desire by the lords of these manors to have a parish church on their holdings.[55] Therefore, due to the fact that the sites of medieval parish churches are seen as marking manorial centres, the flat-topped mounds beside these places are more likely to have been mottes. This is simply because the medieval usage of these sites can again be demonstrated. Twelve Laois mottes occur beside the sites of medieval parish churches.

In theory, an earthen mound having any one of the criteria mentioned above was enough for the site to be called a motte. In practice, however, sixteen out of the twenty sites in Laois possessed two or more of these criteria.

These twenty sites identified as mottes or possible mottes in Laois show the same diversity in morphology that is apparent in this monument-type throughout the British Isles and Ireland. For example, the motte at Killdellig has no bailey and its summit has a diameter of 18m. The top of this mound is raised a mere 3m-3.5m. in height above present ground level. A wide silted-up ditch girdles the mound (fig. 8.5). This motte is located at what was the *caput* or centre of an Anglo-

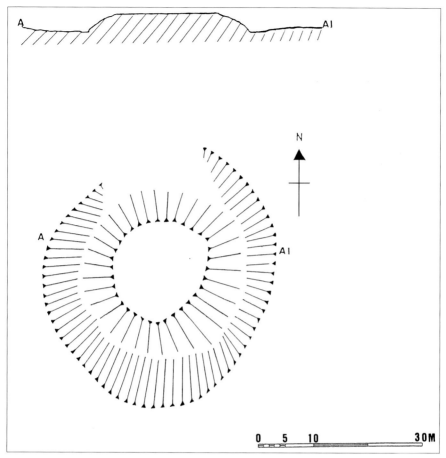

Fig. 8.5   The motte at Killdellig, Co. Laois.

Norman manor and lies beside the foundations of a medieval parish church.[56] The motte identified at Clonenagh is another low, broad-topped mound. It too has no bailey and its top has a diameter of 21m. The summit of this motte is raised a mere 2m-2.5m in height above natural ground level. A wide, silted-up ditch also girdles the site. It occurs at what was the site of an Early Christian monastery which later became an Anglo-Norman manor and borough.[57] It lies beside the remains of a medieval parish church. Both Clonenagh and Killdellig are very different in their morphology to the motte at Middlemount, which stands on a raised oval platform on top of a steep-sided esker. This motte has a summit diameter of c. 10m. Its top is raised 5.5m in height above the latter platform and 7m-7.5m in height above natural ground level on the summit of the esker. A concentric-shaped bailey occurs to the east and south-east of the motte, which is the natural line of approach to the site. A whole series of scarps, berms, banks and ditches defend the eastern and south-eastern slopes of the esker below this bailey which demonstrates that the site originally had very substantial defences.

Despite having a bailey, the motte at Raheenamanagh is very different to Middlemount. The motte at this site lies on the north-eastern edge of a large bailey, which may well be an Early Christian or even prehistoric enclosure. This motte has an oval-shaped summit which has maximum measurements of 10m north/south and 6m-7m east/west. The motte itself is raised a mere 1.5m in height above the level of the interior of the bailey and the top of the knoll the site is located upon. The oval bailey is enormous by any standard. Its maximums internal dimensions are 89m east/west and 50m north/south. It is girdled by a 12m-12.5m wide ditch, which has an earthen bank around its edges.

The sites of Clonenagh, Killdellig, Raheenamanagh and Middlemount show how mottes vary dramatically in shape and size. This is important for archaeologists to remember when faced with the identification and classification of mottes in the field throughout Ireland.

The field identification of ringworks in Laois.

It is clear that the major problem in recognising ringworks in Ireland lies in the fact that they are difficult to distinguish morphologically from many ringforts.Both can appear now as circular areas enclosed by an earthen bank and ditch.[58] The apparent defensibility of any enclosure is not sufficient grounds *on its own* to assign it to the ringwork class. Many ringforts were strongly defended with wide banks and deep ditches right from the beginning of the Early Christian period onwards.[59] However, because ringworks functioned as castles, the present writer believes that the defensibility of any given earthwork enclosure must be taken into account when assigning it to this class but only when other criteria have been fulfilled. Therefore, in purely fieldwork terms, the identification of ringworks in Ireland is a major problem.

It was noted above that two of the main criteria used by the present writer to identify mottes in Laois were either the location of the earthwork in question at an historically-attested manorial centre/castle site or beside a church. This was simply because the medieval, post-1169 usage of these sites can be demonstrated or implied. The logical extension to this argument is to state that any circular enclosures located at such sites should be classified as ringworks. McNeill, in his criticism of the methods used to identify ringworks in Ireland, strongly implies that he agrees with this opinion too.[60] Using these general methods the present writer has identified two ringworks in Laois. The earthwork at Dunbrin Lower is the first of these sites. It is located on a natural terrace just above the right bank of the Barrow. The peripheral defences on the western half of this site merely consists of an earthen bank and ditch. The eastern half of the site is really defined by the scarped sides of the natural river terrace. This gives the site a motte-like appearance on these sides but its overall morphology shows it to be a classic example of a *partial ringwork*. Milo de Stanton 'de Dunbren' granted the church here to St. Thomas's Abbey, Dublin, around the year 1200.[61] This historical evidence suggests that the site represents the *caput* of an Anglo-Norman manor *c.* 1200. Much of the site has been destroyed by quarrying over the years. Sherds of medieval pottery have also been found here.

As noted, all the masonry remains at Lea Castle seem to date to after *c.* 1216. However, the first direct mention of a castle here is in 1201.[62] What type of castle was in existence at Lea around the latter date? It has been argued that this first castle at Lea was a motte and bailey, levelled at a later date to make way for a masonry fortification.[63] There is absolutely no evidence for this statement. It seems to be based solely on the view held by scholars until relatively recently that all the earliest castles in Ireland had to be mottes.

However, by looking at Lea Castle's siting and present morphology, it is possible to suggest that the first castle here was a ringwork. Lea Castle is located in a low-lying position beside the River Barrow, which is to its north providing a formidable line of defence for the castle on this side. The site is surrounded by wet, marshy ground on its other three sides. The actual inner ward, within which the post-1216 towered keep is sited, seems to be placed on slightly higher ground to the rest of the castle and the surrounding area. It would appear that this part of the site was originally a slightly raised, dry bog-island surrounded by marshy ground and the deep wide waters of the Barrow. In corroboration of this point, an original alternative name for Lea Castle was 'Port na hinch' or the 'fort of the island'.[64] It has long been noted that the curvilinear layout of the curtain walls of certain masonry castles in Ireland point to them having ringfort or ringwork precursors.[65] In this regard the surviving remains of the curtain wall of the inner ward at Lea follows a curvilinear line. Overall it would appear that this inner ward was originally oval in shape (fig. 8.3). This all suggests that the masonry curtain wall defining the edges of the inner ward at Lea was erected on the line of an earlier earthen bank/scarp and palisade. Therefore, the original castle at Lea, in existence by *c.* 1200 at least, may have been an oval ringwork located on a natural, dry, slightly-elevated bog-island. Therefore, only two ringworks can be identified in

Laois in contrast to the seventeen, if not twenty, mottes. It is possible that the future excavation of motte castles in Laois may indicate that these sites began their existence as ringwork castles, being heightened at a later date. However, this still does not alter the fact that mottes were ultimately the preferred form of earthwork castle in medieval Laois.

It is also clear from this discussion that the overwhelming majority of these early castles in Laois are located in the southern half of the county. Apart from the motte and bailey at Srahan and the possible motte at Monelly, as well as Lea Castle, no identifiable castles of late twelfth, thirteenth or fourteenth century date can be seen across the whole northern and north-western parts of modern Laois. Even in the south of the county, the interior of that part of the Castlecomer Plateau that lies in Laois has no castles (fig. 8.1). The northern and north-western parts of the modern county, along with the Castlecomer Plateau, are precisely the areas of Laois that saw the survival of Gaelic septs during the medieval period. The MacGillapatricks were living in the Slieve Blooms by the early thirteenth century at least.[66] The O'Dempseys and O'Dunnes inhabited northern and north-western Laois, respectively, during the medieval period.[67] The O'Mores continued to live in their old lands of Laois, side by side with the new Anglo-Norman settlers.[68] Smyth puts some of this sept around the foothills of the Slieve Blooms.[69] It is also clear that the O'Mores inhabited that part of the Castlecomer Plateau which lies in Laois.[70]

Therefore, there is a negative relationship between the distribution of castles built between c. 1170 and the early fourteenth century and the regions of the county that had high Irish survival during this period. Furthermore, twenty out of the twenty-five castles identified in Laois as belonging to this period occur at the sites of historically-attested Anglo-Norman manors, boroughs and castles.[71] The motte and bailey at Raheenamanagh is one of the three castles in Laois that has no surviving historical references to them being at Anglo-Norman centres. However, it has been argued that Raheenamanagh is best explained as an Anglo-Norman fortification erected in the late thirteenth or even early fourteenth century to house a garrison who were bent on subduing the rebellious Irish of north Laois and east Offaly.[72] This leaves the motte and bailey castle at Srahan and the possible motte at Monelly. These may be Irish castles due to their location high up in the Slieve Blooms but again there is no direct evidence for this. The overall evidence suggests that Gaelic lords did not build motte, ringwork or masonry castles in Laois. The negative evidence from the historical sources also backs up this statement. There is absolutely no mention in the sources of a Gaelic castle in Laois during this period. The absence of Gaelic castles dating to these centuries is not specific only in Laois but has been noted elsewhere in Ireland. It has been·argued that Gaelic lords throughout Ireland did not use true castles during this period to protect themselves against aggression. Instead they utilised the natural landscape for defence against attack.[73]

The structures and defences associated with earthwork castles

Much of this paper has dealt with how to recognise earthwork castles in the landscape today, be they in Laois or elsewhere in Ireland. This section discusses the nature of the defences and buildings associated with these earthwork castles during the medieval period.

Harold Leask believed that the timber defences originally associated with motte castles were relatively flimsy, consisting of no more than light wooden palisades, similar to those associated with ringforts and crannogs. He also appears to have been of the opinion that only a few simple timber buildings originally existed at these sites.[74]

At first glance the evidence from the few earthwork castles excavated in Ireland backs up Leask's view that the original defences and buildings at these sites were flimsy and simple. Evidence for what were described as relatively light palisades were found around the edges of the motte summits at Lismahon,[75] Clough,[76] Dromore,[77] all in Co. Down, Doonmore, Co. Antrim,[78] and Lurgankeel, Co. Louth.[79] The first defences of the partial ringwork at Ferrycarrig, Co. Wexford, consisted of a timber palisade surmounting an earthen bank.[80] Evidence for relatively small timber towers were found on the motte tops at Doonmore[81] and Lurgankeel, Co. Louth.[82] A small, square, timber-framed house, built on earthen banks, with an attached tower, along with an adjacent free-standing workshop, was associated with the initial occupation of the motte top at Lismahon. This house was enlarged in the late thirteenth or early fourteenth century to become a regular, English-style, three-room hall building. The original tower was repaired and the palisade was seemingly rebuilt during this period as well.[83]

The existence at Clough of a hollow, 10.3m long, 4.9m wide and 90cms deep, in the centre of the motte summit was tentatively postulated as marking the basement of a primary wooden tower or hall. During the next period of occupation this hollow was deliberately filled in. A rectangular, ground floor hall, measuring 19.2m by 7.8m, was erected on the mound. The lower part of this building was constructed of masonry. However, its interior yielded evidence for burnt wood and daub. This indicates that the upper parts may have been made of timber framing infilled with wattle and daub. The Phase I palisade was still in existence at the time the hall was built, although it appears that some repairs were carried out on it. The next period, which followed shortly after the destruction of this Phase II hall, saw the erection of a small, two-storeyed rectangular masonry keep or tower on the south- western side of the motte summit. The excavator suggested that Clough was abandoned in the mid-fourteenth century. Apparently the summit of the motte was re-fortified in either the fifteenth or sixteenth century when the rectangular keep was enlarged and turned into a small tower house.[84] At Rathmullan, Co. Down, a timber-framed rectangular building, whose dimensions were 9.5m by at least 6.5m, was erected on stone footings on the summit of the motte.[85] Some sort of wattle and daub structure or building occured on the motte top at Coney Island, Co. Armagh.[86] A flimsy post-built building of irregular shape was found on the summit of Dromore motte.[87] The excavation of the bailey at Duneight, Co. Down, indicated that three, supposedly slight, timber buildings existed within it.[88] Some excavations of earthwork castles have produced no evidence for buildings or defences. The excavated motte summits at Dunsilly, Co. Antrim[89] and Castleskreen 2, Co. Down,[90] as well as the secondary motte top at Rathmullan, Co. Down,[91] apparently had no structural or defensive features associated with them despite having habitation layers. The bailey at Castleskreen 2, which appears to have been quite heavily occupied in the thirteenth century, also produced little excavated evidence for buildings within it.[92] The excavation of the ringwork at Pollardstown, Co. Kildare, found no evidence for buildings or defences at the site, despite the fact that it had been intensively occupied in the medieval period.[93]

Therefore, considering these sites were Anglo-Norman military fortresses, residences and administrative centres, much of the excavated evidence for the defences and buildings associated with earthwork castles in Ireland is disappointing at first glance. Apart from the evidence at some sites for small timber towers, the defences uncovered at many of these excavated earthwork castles appear to be no stronger than what would be expected on a well-defended Early Christian crannog or ringfort. Indeed at a number of sites there seems to be no evidence at all for buildings or defences.

Yet it must be remembered that only a few earthwork castles have been excavated in Ireland. Most were dug in the late 1950s and early 1960s, mainly in association with the Archaeological Survey of Co. Down. As yet there has been no long-term, modern research excavation of a motte or ringwork castle here. Furthermore, many of the excavations that have taken place in Ireland have been small in scale. For example, the excavation of the important motte castle at Dromore, Co. Down, consisted of nothing more than a couple of trenches across the summit of the mound [94] The excavation of baileys and off-mound habitation beside free-standing mottes is negligible.[95] It is clear that a scientific, well-ordered excavation is the goal of any archaeologist when investigating any given site. However, archaeologists often adhere too strictly to the limits of inference and this can result in a limited interpretation of the excavated material. The excavation at Rathmullan, for example, indicated that a timber-framed rectangular building, 9.5m by at least 6.5m in dimensions, was erected on stone footings on the summit of the primary motte here.[96] Nothing more was stated about how this building would have looked when it was in use. No more than the bare excavated details of the structure were given in the report. It is possible that this structure was a simple single-storeyed building. Alternatively a review of the excavated and standing medieval buildings throughout Europe suggests it could also have been a complex two or even three-storey structure.[97] It could even have been a timber keep. Basically many of the structures so far uncovered by excavation on Irish motte summits could have been a lot more complex than has been argued in the past. Furthermore, research in Britain since the 1950s suggests that the reason why certain excavated Irish mottes lacked evidence for buildings and defences within or on them is probably due to the fact that their original builders employed methods of timber construction that leave little or no archaeological trace. Recent work in England had indicated that there was a movement away from the use of earthfast posts in house or building construction during the twelfth and thirteenth centuries.[98] It must be remembered that an alternative to setting vertical posts into the ground is to use sleeper beams, into which upright timbers can be fitted to provide the basic structure of a building or palisade. Such horizontal beams can be set into bedding trenches or laid on low stone walls or earthen banks to protect the wood against damp. However, these beams can also be laid directly onto the ground surface, provided it is flat.[99] For example, it has been argued that the palisade around the bailey at Hen Domen, Powys, from the late twelfth century through to c. 1300 consisted of large thick timber beams laid directly onto the flattened top of this enclosure's girdling rampart, with upright planks set into them.[100] An excavation today would find little or no evidence for a building or palisade constructed in this way. This means that there are good reasons as to why no structures or defences were found during the excavation of various earthwork castles in Ireland. Methods of timber construction could have been used at these places that leave little archaeological trace.

This all suggests that not enough modern excavation has been carried out on earthwork castles in Ireland. The results from the few excavated sites here are at the very least ambiguous. A better picture of how these earthwork castles once looked can be gleaned from new evidence uncovered in recent excavations in Britain, surviving historical references and, to a lesser extent, fieldwork.

The motte and bailey castle at Hen Domen, Powys, was built in the 1070s and was occupied down to *c.* 1300. A research excavation, mainly concentrating on the bailey, has been carried out on this site since the early 1960s. This makes it the most intensively investigated earthwork castle in Europe. It provides clear evidence on how structurally complex and well-defended at least some earthwork castles were during the period of their usage.[101] For example, Phase X at this site, which started around 1150, emphasises this point. The bailey was full of buildings during this period, as in very other phase.

These structures included a large two-storeyed hall, a lesser hall, stables, cisterns, workshops and a possible chapel with an attached belltower. The main palisade, which had at least one mural tower along its length, seems to have been made of clay built upon a post and wattle framework during this period. This clay wall may have been up to 4m in height, with its upper portion possibly jettied out over its base. A fighting platform existed behind it. There was also an outer palisade on the edge of the inner ditch. The overall evidence from the excavation suggests that the bailey at Hen Domen was very well-defended during Phase X.[102] Pictorial evidence from contemporary manuscripts suggests that some of the palisades at earthwork castles were looped for archery.[103]

The long-term research excavation at Hen Domen suggests that the nature of the wooden buildings and defences at earthwork castles were far more complex and formidable than the view proposed by Leask. This evidence from Hen Domen is also at odds with the few, small-scale excavations carried out in Ireland on earthwork castles. Certainly the occasional surviving contemporary description from Ireland of the defences and buildings at what appear to be motte castles suggests that the Hen Domen model is the more correct one, at least in medieval Leinster, Meath and Tipperary, where demesne farming took place.

Unfortunately none of these surviving medieval descriptions are of earthwork castles located in present-day Laois. However, they do describe the buildings and defences on mottes from adjacent counties. An extent of the manor of Knocktopher, Co. Kilkenny, in 1312 lists a whole series of mostly timber buildings and defences around the castle there. This castle was apparently the motte and bailey extant at Knocktopher until *c.* 1980. Two halls, a detached kitchen, timber towers, a palisade, a cruck-built barn, a cruck-built byre and a chapel with an attached storeroom are referred to in the extent.[104] The motte at Inch, Co. Tipperary, is 6m in height and has a summit diameter of *c.*

14m. Apparently this site never had an attached bailey. An extent of the manor of *Nychaunlef* (Inch) made in 1303 describes a 'castle' (*castrum*) standing on the motte top whose edges were defended by a palisade. This *castrum* appears to have been a large wooden building, possibly a timber keep or tower. Around the motte stood a whole plethora of timber buildings. These included a hall, a chapel, a kitchen, a larder, barns, a sheepcote, a bull-pen, a byre, granaries, stables, a dovecote and a mill.[105] The motte at Westcourt Demesne, Callan, Co. Kilkenny, is sub-rectangular in shape. The summit of the motte measures 40m north-west/ south-east by 18m-22m south-west/north-east. It is raised 6m-7.5m in height above natural ground level. This appears to be the remains of the castle at Callan that went to Richard de Clare in the 1247 partition of the lordship of Leinster.[106] A 1307 extent of the manor of Callan states that a wooden hall, roofed with shingles, a small stone building, a wooden kitchen and other timber buildings lay within the castle. As this motte apparently never had a bailey, it seems probable that these wooden buildings lay on the motte summit, Furthermore, beside the castle, but not within it, lay the haggard or farmyard in which there was a barn, a byre and a stable.[107] At least some of the earthwork castles in Laois, if not all, must have had similar defences, as well as a wide array of domestic and agricultural buildings within or around them, as did these Tipperary and Kilkenny sites.

These surviving early fourteenth century references to the buildings and defences associated with motte castles in Ireland are also important for another reason. Leask clearly believed that motte castles were only temporary fortifications that dated to the earliest period of Anglo-Norman power in Ireland. He saw these sites being replaced by stone castles at some stage in the early thirteenth century.[108] It is not quite clear where Leask gained these impressions as there is absolutely no evidence for them. The historical and excavated evidence from Ireland all suggests that most earthwork castles here were still occupied in the early fourteenth century, up to one hundred and fifty years after the coming of the Anglo-Normans to Ireland. The overall evidence from Western Europe is that most earthwork castles functioned as permanent centres with a variety of peaceful and military functions.[109] Furthermore, it is clear that some motte castles continued to be built throughout the British Isles in the late thirteenth and even early fourteenth century.[110] For example, the erection of Roberton motte, Lanarkshire, took place in either the very late thirteenth or early fourteenth century during the troubled times of the early years of the Scottish War of Independence.[111] Furthermore, it has been argued that a number of mottes in Leinster, including some in Laois, were built in the same period as a response to the military pressures created by the Gaelic resurgence in the region.[112]

Fieldwork in Laois also gives some hint that the defences and buildings within motte and ringwork castles were more complex than was once thought. A very definite rectangular depression, 8m north-vest/south-east by 4m north-east/south-west, being 1m in depth, occurs on the otherwise flat summit of the motte at Middlemount, Co. Laois. Another rectangular depression occurs centrally on the motte top at Moatquarter, Co. Laois. It measures 6m by 5m and it is 50cms in depth beneath the top of this motte. What are these depressions? Rectangular or square depressions occur on the summits of other mottes in Ireland. It has been argued elsewhere that at least some of those depressions represent the silted-up and collapsed remains of cellars, cisterns and well features within these mottes, lying underneath wooden structures.[113] Such substructures also occur within English mottes. For example, the excavation of the first motte at Goltho, Lincolnshire, uncovered evidence for a basement within the mound, underneath a large timber tower. This feature functioned either as a storage cellar or as a cistern for the collection of water.[114]

Therefore, the depressions on these two motte summits in Laois may represent the remains of cisterns. Certainly a water-supply on top of any given motte would have made the mound more defensible against attack and siege. Research in Ireland has never really questioned how water was supplied to castles. It appears that wine, cider, mead and beer, rather than water, would have been the everyday drink of castle-dwellers during the whole medieval period. Yet even in peacetime water was essential for cooking and fire prevention. Livestock, stalled somewhere within the precincts of a masonry or earthwork castle, would also have needed large quantities of water each day.[115] Conversely, in times of war, an adequate supply of water was essential to a castle's ability to withstand a long siege.[116] Work in England and Wales has shown that there were a number of alternative ways to supply a castle with water. Obviously a straightforward well could be built to tap the underlying ground water or a cistern could be constructed to collect rainwater. Alternatively, water could be piped into the castle from an external source. Water could also be stored in wooden casks.[117] A depiction of Middlemount motte in the late eighteenth century indicates that a well could be seen within the bailey then.[118] This well must have supplied the everyday needs of the castle.

The large free-standing motte at Ballyroan, Co. Laois, has a berm around its base. This flat berm is 50cms-1m in width. Its outer edge is defined by a drystone wall which drops into the wet fosse girdling the mound (fig. 8.6). This feature also occurs on a number of other mottes in Ireland.[119] It has been suggested that these berms were constructed to prevent the silting of any given motte's fosse by earth washed down

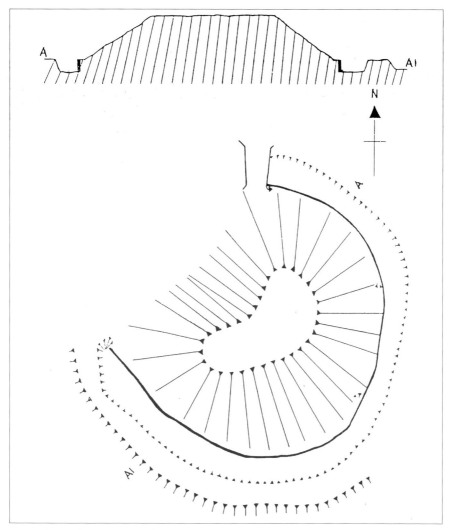

Fig. 8.6   The motte at Ballyroan, Co. Laois.

from its steep sides.[120] Another explanation could be that this berm at Ballyroan was designed to hold a palisade, constructed on horizontally-laid timber beams. This would explain why the berm here, as elsewhere, is so flat. A palisade around the base of the motte would have made the site considerably stronger from a military point of view. The other interesting feature at Ballyroan is the 8m long, 2m wide stone bridge across the motte ditch. This small bridge appears to be an original feature of the site. A castle is mentioned as being in existence at Ballyroan in 1208.[121] Therefore, it is possible that this feature was built by *c*. 1200, making it one of the earliest surviving bridges in the country.

It was noted above that the motte at Castletown, Co. Laois, has the remains of an earthen bank around its summit. This may be an indication that the original defences around the edges of this motte summit consisted of a thick clay wall with a post-and-wattle skeleton.[122] The earthen bank at Castletown could have been formed by the collapse and disintegration of an original clay wall around the edges of the motte top there.

Therefore, recent research in Britain, certain surviving historical references and fieldwork all suggest that earthwork castles in Laois and throughout Ireland were far more defensive and structurally complex than has hitherto been realised. Furthermore, the fact that many mottes and ringworks carried quite formidable timber defences also explains why these sites were described as castles by medieval clerks. The earth and timber defences at these sites were adequate protection against most attack. This is why earthwork castles were so common in medieval Ireland and played such an important role in the conquest and colonisation of many parts of the country by the Anglo-Normans.

Summary and Conclusion

Laois has two fine Anglo-Norman masonry castles within its boundaries. Dunamase Castle is one of the most magnificent ruins in the country. The first castle at Lea, near Portarlington, was probably an oval ringwork located on a small bog-island built beside the River Barrow. The historical evidence suggests that the towered keep there was built around 1220, after Maurice fitz Gerald gained seisin of his dead father's lands in 1216.

However, most Anglo-Norman castles in Laois, as elsewhere in medieval Ireland, had earth and timber defences. There are problems in identifying these earthwork castles in the Irish landscape today. The present writer outlined the methodology he used to identify mottes and ringworks in Laois. In all seventeen mottes, three possible mottes and two ringworks (if the first castle of Lea is included in this list) were identified in the county.

It appears that the timber defences and buildings at these sites were far more formidable and complex than once thought. The strong nature of the original timber defences at most mottes and ringworks explains why these sites were called castles. These earthwork castles were capable of withstanding quite serious attack. However, various historical references to buildings within or around motte castles also indicate that these sites were the centres of agricultural estates and local administration. This highlights the fact that castles were private residences and not just military fortresses.

References

1. D.J.C. King, *The castle in England and Wales* (London, 1988), pp 1-13.
2. P.D. Sweetman *et al, Archaeological inventory of County Laois* (Dublin, 1995), pp 101-3, 108-16.
3. Ibid., pp 108-16.
4. Ibid., pp 101-3, 124-6.
5. P.D. Sweetman, *Irish castles and fortified houses* (Dublin, 1995), pp 5, 8.
6. T.E. NcNeill, 'The outer gatehouse at Dunamase Castle, Co. Laois' in *Medieval Archaeology*, 37, (1993), pp 236-8; B. Hodkinson, 'The Rock of Dunamase' in *Archaeology Ireland*, 9:2 (1995), p. 10; K. O' Conor, 'Dunamase Castle, Co. Laois' in *Journal of Irish Archaeology*, 7 (1996), pp 97-108.
7. O'Conor, 'Dunamase Castle', p. 113
8. *Cal. Doc. Ire.*, 1171-1251, no. 1872.
9. *Clyn's annals*, 30.
10. O'Conor, 'Dunamase Castle', pp 111-3.
11. H.G. Leask, 'Irish Castles, 1180-1310' in Archaeological Journal, 93 (1937), p. 175; ibid., *Irish castles and castellated houses* (Dundalk, 1941), pp 50-1; Sweetman *et al, Archaeological inventory of Co. Laois*, p. 108.
12. Leask, 'Irish Castles, 1180-1310', pp 174-5; ibid., *Irish Castles*, p. 50.
13. Sweetman *et al, Archaeological inventory of Co. Laois*, pp 101-3, 108.
14. Leask, 'Irish castles, 1180-1310', pp 168-70; ibid., *Irish castles*, pp 47-9; R. Stalley, *Architecture and sculpture in Ireland* (Dublin, 1971), pp 47-50; K. O'Conor, 'Carlow Castle' in *Archaeology Ireland*, 11:3 (1997), p. 16.
15. O'Conor, 'Carlow Castle', pp 15-6.
16. G.H. Orpen (ed.), *The song of Dermot and the earl*, (Dublin 1892), Lines 3104-5; A.J. Otway-Ruthven, 'Knights' Fees in Kildare, Leix and Offaly' in *R.S.A.I. Jn.*, 91, (1961), p.178.
17. *Cal. Doc. Ire., 1171-1251*, no. 101.
18. Ibid., no.195.
19. Ibid., no. 724.
20. *Clyn's annals*, p. 8.
21. S.G. Ellis, *Tudor Ireland* (London and New York, 1985), p. 65.
22. Sweetman *et al, Archaeological inventory of Co. Laois*, p. 108.
23. P.D. Sweetman, 'Archaeological excavations at Ferns Castle, County Wexford' in *R.I.A. Proc.*, C, 79 (1979), p. 240; ibid., 'Early thirteenth century castles in Leinster' in *Chateau* (1992), p. 326; ibid., *Irish castles and fortified houses*, pp 12-3.
24. Sweetman *et al, Archaeological inventory of Co. Laois*, p. 108.
25. *Cal. Doc. Ire., 1285-1292*, no. 670; W. Carrigan, *The history and antiquities of the diocese of Ossory*, 2 (Dublin, 1905), p. 171.
26. Sweetman *et al, Archaeological inventory of Co. Laois*, pp 114-5.
27. *Cal. Doc. Ire., 1171*-1251, no. 2382.
28. R. Higham and P. Barker, *Timber castles* (London 1992).
29. K. O'Conor, 'Irish earthwork castles' in *Fortress*, 12 (1992), p. 3.
30. King, *The castle in England and Wales*, p.57.
31. G.H. Orpen, 'Motes and Norman castles in Ireland' in *R.S.A.I. Jn.*, 37 (1907), pp 123-52; ibid., 'Motes and Norman castles in Ireland' in *English Historical Review*, 22 (1907), pp 228-54, 440-67; ibid., 'Motes and Norman castles in Ossory' in *R.S.A.I. Jn...*, 39 (1909), pp 313-42; ibid., *Ireland under the Normans*, 1-4 (Oxford, 1911-20).

32. Leask, *Irish Castles*, pp 5-11.
33. King, *The castle in England and Wales*, pp 42-61; N.J.G. Pounds, *The medieval castle in England and Wales* (Cambridge, 1990), pp 3-25; Higham and Barker, *Timber castles*.
34. King, *The castle in England and Wales*, p. 47.
35. Ibid.
36. Higham and Barker, *Timber castles*, p. 199.
37. B.J. Graham, 'The mottes of the Norman Liberty of Meath' in H. Murtagh (ed.), *Irish Midland studies* (Athlone, 1980), p. 47; J. Mallory and T.E McNeill, *The archaeology of Ulster*, (Belfast, 1991), p. 262.
38. T.E. McNeill, 'Hibernia Pacata et Castellata' in *Chateau Gaillard*, 14 (1990), p. 262; T. O'Keeffe, 'The archaeology of Norman castles in Ireland. Part 1: Mottes and ringworks' in *Archaeology Ireland*, 4:3 (1990), p. 16; K. D. O'Conor, 'Earthwork castles in medieval Leinster' unpublished Ph.D Thesis (Cardiff, 1993), pp 293-4.
39. Graham, 'Mottes', pp 49-51; T.E. McNeill, *Anglo-Norman Ulster* (Edinburgh, 1980), pp 86-8; ibid., 'Hibernia Pacata', p. 264; V.M. Buckley and P.D. Sweetman, *The archaeological survey of County Louth*, (Dublin, 1992), pp 281-98; O'Conor, 'Earthwork castles in Medieval Leinster', pp 302-3.
40. T.E. McNeill, 'Ulster mottes, a checklist' in *U.J.A.*, 38 (1975), p. 49; C.J. Lynn, 'The excavation of Rathmullan, a raised rath and motte in Co. Down' in *U.J.A.*, 44-5 (1981-2), pp 149-50; T.B. Barry, *The archaeology of Medieval Ireland* (London and New York), p.45; N. Edwards, The *archaeology of Early Medieval Ireland* (London, 1990), p. 14; Mallory and McNeill, *Archaeology of Ulster*, pp 260-1.
41. McNeill, 'Ulster mottes', p. 49; Lynn, ' Rathmullan', pp 113, 150; Mallory and McNeill, *Archaeology of Ulster*, pp 186-7; B.J. Graham, 'Twelfth and thirteenth century earthwork castles in Ireland: an assessment' in *Fortress*, 9 (1991), p.25.
42. C.J. Lynn, 'Gransha' in *Excavations 1972; Summary Accounts of Archaeological Works in Ireland* (Belfast, 1972), p. 10; ibid., 'Rathmullan', pp 149, 168.
43. McNeill, 'Ulster Mottes', p. 51.
44. C.J. Lynn, 'Deer Park Farms, Glenarm, Co. Antrim' in Archaeology *Ireland*, 1:1 (1987), pp 11-15; ibid., 'Deer Park farms' in *Current Archaeology*, 113 (1989), pp 193-8.
45. McNeill, 'Ulster mottes', p. 49; Mallory and McNeill, *Archaeology of Ulster*, pp 186-7.
46. Lynn, 'Rathmullan', pp 107, 113.
47. Ibid., p. 150.
48. Graham, 'Twelfth and thirteenth century earthwork castles in Ireland', p. 25.
49. O'Conor, 'Irish earthwork castles', p. 7; ibid, 'Earthwork castles in Medieval Leinster' pp 307-15.
50. Ibid., 'Irish earthwork castles', p. 7.
51. T.B. Barry, *Medieval moated sites of south-east Ireland* (Oxford, 1977), p.11.
52. Ibid., *Archaeology of Medieval Ireland*, pp 3-12.
53. E. St.J. Brooks, *Knight's fees in Counties Wexford, Carlow and Kilkenny* (Dublin, 1950); Otway-Ruthven, 'Knight's fees', pp 163-81.
54. A.J. Otway-Ruthven, 'Parochial development in the rural deanery of Skreen' in *R.S.A.I. Jn.'* 94 (1964), pp 114-5, 117-22; ibid., *A history of Medieval Ireland* (London, 1968), pp 118-21, 126; McNeill, *Anglo-Norman Ulster*, 100; B.J. Graham, *Anglo-Norman settlement in Ireland* (Athlone, 1985), p. 11; P. Brand, 'The formation of a parish: the case of Beaulieu, Co. Louth' in J. Bradley (ed.) *Settlement and society in Medieval Ireland* (Kilkenny, 1988), p.262.

55. Otway-Ruthven, 'Parochial development', pp 114-5, 117-22; ibid., *History of Medieval Ireland*, pp 118-21, 126; McNeill, *Anglo-Norman Ulster*, 100; Graham, *Anglo-Norman settlement in Ireland*, p. 11; W. Colfer, 'Anglo-Norman Settlement in Wexford' in K.Whelan (ed.), *Wexford: history and society* (Dublin, 1987), pp 70, 73; Brand, 'Beaulieu Parish', p. 262.

56. *Ormond deeds*, 1172-1350, no. 142; H.J. Lawlor, 'Calendar of the Liber Ruber of the diocese of Ossory' in *R.I.A. Proc.*, 27 (1908), p. 78.

57. *Ormond deeds, 1172-1350*, no. 85; Brooks, *Knights fees*, pp 25, 206.

58. T.B. Barry, 'Anglo-Norman ringwork castles: some evidence' in T. Reeves-Smyth and F. Hamond (eds.), *Landscape archaeology in Ireland*, p. 299; ibid., *Archaeology of Medieval Ireland*, 45

59. S.P. O'Riordain, *Antiquities of the Irish countryside* (London, 1979), p.39; Edwards, *Archaeology of Early* Medieval *Ireland*, p.33.

60. T.E. McNeill, 'Early castles in Leinster' in *Journal of Irish Archaeology*, 5 (1989-90), p. 58; ibid., 'Hibernia Pacata', p. 262.

61. J.T. Gilbert (ed.), *Register of the Abbey of St Thomas the Martyr, Dublin* (London, 1889), p. 110.

62. *Cal. Doc. Ire., 1171-1251*, no. 101.

63. Orpen, 'Motes and Norman castles in Ireland' in *Eng. Hist. Review*, p. 253; E.S. Armitage, *Early Norman Castles of the British Isles* (London, 1912), p. 34.

64. Orpen, 'Motes and Norman Castles in Ireland' in *Eng. Hist. Review*, p. 253.

65. Leask, *Irish Castles*, p. 34; B.J. Graham, 'Timber and Earthwork Fortifications in Western Ireland' in *Medieval Archaeology*, 32 (1988), pp 124-5.

66. Carrigan, *Ossory*, i, pp 69-74; Orpen, 'Motes and Norman castles in Ossory', pp 315-6; ibid., *Ireland under the Normans*, ii, pp 133, 224-5.

67. Orpen, *Ireland under the Normans*, ii, p. 133; E. Curtis, *History of Medieval Ireland from 1110 to 1513* (London, 1927), pp 84, 123; A. Smyth, *Celtic Leinster* (Dublin, 1982), pp 104, 111-3.

68. Orpen, *Ireland Under the Normans*, ii, p. 133; Curtis, *History of Medieval Ireland*, p. 173.

69. Smyth, *Celtic Leinster*, pp 104, 111-3.

70. J. O' Hanlon and J. O'Leary, *History of the Queens County*, i (Dublin, 1907), p. 399.

71. Brooks, *Knights' fees*; Otway-Ruthven, 'Knights' fees', pp 163-81; O'Conor, 'Earthwork castles in medieval Leinster', pp 188-95.

72. K. D. O'Conor, 'The later construction and use of motte and bailey castles in Ireland: new evidence from Leinster' in *Journal Kildare Archaeological Society*, 17 (1991), p. 20.

73. O'Conor, 'Irish earthwork castles', pp 8-10; ibid., 'Earthwork castles in Medieval Leinster', pp 204-92.

74. Leask, *Irish Castles*, pp 5-11.

75. D.M.Waterman, 'Excavations at Lismahon, Co. Down' in *Medieval Archaeology*, 3 (1959), pp 146-7, 67.

76. Ibid., 'Excavations at Clough Castle, County Down' in *U.J.A.*, 17 (1954), pp 104-6.

77. Ibid., 'Excavations at Dromore Motte, County Down' in *U.J.A.*, 17 (1954), p. 166.

78. V.G. Childe, 'Doonmore, a castle mound near Fair Head, Co. Antrim' in *U.J.A.*, 1 (1938), pp 124, 128.

79. *Oibre, Offical Journal of the Office of Public Works*, 2 (1965), p. 22.

80 C. Cotter, 'Ferrycarrig, Newtown' in *Excavations, 1987:summary accounts of archaeological excavations in Ireland* (Dublin, 1987), p. 30.

81. Childe, 'Doonmore', pp 125, 128.

82. *Oibre,* p. 22.

83. Waterman, 'Lismahon', pp 148-55, 167-9.

84. Ibid., 'Clough', pp 108-22.

85. Lynn, 'Rathmullan', pp 99-116.

86. P.V. Addyman, 'Coney Island, Lough Neagh; prehistoric settlement, Anglo-Norman Castle and Elizabethan native fortress' in *U.J.A.,* 18 (1965), p. 89.

87. Waterman, 'Dromore', pp 166-7.

88. D.M. Waterman, 'Excavations at Duneight, County Down' in *U.J.A.,* 26 (1963), pp 71, 76.

89. McNeill, *Anglo-Norman Ulster,* pp 57, 84-5.

90. C. W. Dickinson and D.M. Waterman, 'Excavations of a rath with motte at Castleskreen, County Down' in *U.J.A.,* 22 (1959), pp 70, 82.

91. Lynn, 'Rathmullan', pp 116-7.

92. Dickinson and Waterman, 'Castleskreen', pp 71, 82.

93. T. Fanning. 'Excavation of a ringfort at Pollardstown, Co. Kildare' in *Journal Kildare Archaeological Society,* 15 (1973-4), pp 251-61.

94. Waterman, 'Dromore'.

95. Barry, *Archaeology of Medieval Ireland,* pp 38-9.

96. Lynn, 'Rathmullan', pp 99-116.

97. Higham and Barker, *Timber castles,* pp 114-52.

98. P. A. Barker and R.A.Higham, *Hen Domen, Montgomery; a timber castle on the English-Welsh border* (Royal Archaeological Institute, 1982) pp 41-51, 91; ibid., *Hen Domen, Montgomery: a timber castle on the English-Welsh border. Excavations 1960-1988: a summary report* (Worcester, 1988), pp 11-13; C. Dyer, 'English peasant buildings in the later Middle Ages' in *Medieval Archaeology,* 30 (1985), pp 19-45; G. Beresford, *Goltho, the development of an Early Medieval manor c. 850-1150* (London, 1987), p. 126; Higham and Barker, *Timber castles,* pp 326-47.

99. K. Greene, *Archaeology an introduction* (London, 1983), pp 85-6; O'Conor, 'Dunamase Castle', p. 113.

100. Barker and Higham, *Hen Domen, Montgomery* (1982), pp 41-51, 91; ibid., *Hen Domen, Montgomery*(1988), pp 11-13; Higham and Barker, *Timber castles,* pp 338-41.

101. Higham and Barker, *Timber castles,* p. 326.

102. Barker and Higham, '*Hen Domen, Montgomery* (1982), pp 32-40, 88-94; ibid., *Hen Domen, Montgomery* (1988), pp 8-11; Higham and Barker, *Timber castles,* pp 334-7.

103. Higham and Barker, *Timber castles,* pp 159-61; O'Conor, 'Dunamase Castle'' p. 113.

104. N.B. White (ed.), *The Red Book of Ormond,* (Dublin, 1932), pp 127-31; C.A. Empey, 'Medieval Knocktopher: a study in manorial settlement, part 1' in *Old Kilkenny Review,* 2:4 (1982), p. 332.

105. *Red Book of Ormond,* pp 52-3.

106. *Cal. Doc. Ire., 1252-84,* no. 1618.

107. *Cal. Doc. Ire., 1302-1307,* no. 659; *Cal. Inq. Post Mortem,* 4, no. 435.

108. Leask, *Irish castles,* p. 25.

109. Higham and Barker, *Timber castles,* pp 342, 349, 352.

110. King, *The castle in England and Wales,* pp 143-5; O'Conor, 'Later construction and use of motte and bailey castles in Ireland', pp 13-29.

111. G. Haggerty and C. Tabraham, 'Excavation of a motte near Roberton, Clydesdale, 1979' in *Transactions of the Dumfrieshire and Galloway Natural History and*

Antiquarian Society, 57, (1982), pp 61-2.

112. O'Conor, 'Later construction and use of motte and bailey castles in Ireland', pp 13-29; ibid., 'Earthwork castles in Medieval Leinster', pp 316-37.

113. O'Conor, 'Irish earthwork castles', p. 8; ibid., 'Earthwork castles in Medieval Leinster', pp 391-9.

114. Beresford, *Goltho, pp* 87, 100-6.

115. N.A. Ruckley, 'Water supp ly of medieval castles in the United Kingdom' in *Fortress*, 7 (1990), p. 16.

116. R.A. Brown, *English castles* (London, 1976), p.190.

117. Ruckley, 'Water supply', pp 14-15; J. Kenyon, *Medieval fortifications* (Leicester and London, 1990), p. 17.

118. G. Cunningham, *The Anglo-Norman advance into the south-west midlands of Ireland, 1185-1221* (Roscrea, 1987), p. 162.

119. O'Conor, 'Irish earthwork castles', p. 8; ibid., 'Earthwork castles in Medieval Leinster', p.338.

120. Waterman, 'Dromore', p. 167; O'Conor, 'Irish earthwork castles'' p. 8.

121. Orpen, 'Motes and Norman castles in Ossory', p. 336; Cunningham, *Anglo-Norman advance*, p. 79, n.18.

122. Higham and Barker, *Timber castles,* p.318.

Plate 8.3   Western part of Cotton map *c.* 1561 (Bh, Cotton MS Augusutus I, ii, 40).

Chapter 9

THE END OF THE GAELIC POLITICAL ORDER: THE O'MORE LORDSHIP OF LAOIS 1536-1603

VINCENT P. CAREY

It is hard today to imagine the leisurely flowing river Barrow as a line of demarcation, as the beginning of a frontier. Yet for the mid-sixteenth century traveller whose destination was the English settlement of Fort Protector this was clearly the case. Though some of the landscape to the west of the Barrow resembled that of the more settled and anglicized county Kildare, for the contemporary traveller to journey three to four miles west of the river was to enter a realm often comprised of extensive forest and bog. Nowhere is this more clearly illustrated than in the contemporary map of Laois and Offaly dating from the early 1560s (plate 8.3).[1] To cross the Barrow to the south of the Geraldine stronghold of Lea Castle or to the north of Castle-Reban was to encounter a terrain dominated by impediments like the 'the great wood' or the bog of 'Moenfanan'. Obvious too was the fact that this landscape had a contested medieval history. Further west lay the Norman-style castles of Morett and Dunamase. These were built by twelfth and thirteenth century Norman settlers, occupied by the O'Mores during the Gaelic revival of the late medieval period, and had been recently recovered by Geraldines during their late fifteenth century consolidation under the 8th and 9th earls of Kildare. Between these two castles lay the 'Frugh Mor' or the Great Heath; to cross it was to traverse one of the few extended areas of completely open ground in this region. Fort Protector itself marked the center of a landscape, which to the south beeme increasingly hilly and inhospitable, to the west and northwest boggy ('The White Bog') and elevated culminating in the Sliabh Bloom Mountains. The cartographer depicts a territory which by 1496, an exception being the area west of Athy (the unwooded section of 'Fasagh Reban'), lay outside the approximate frontier of lands subject to the royal administration.

Though as much a reflection of the harried work of the surveyor in hostile territory, the map is also a snapshot of a world in transition. The

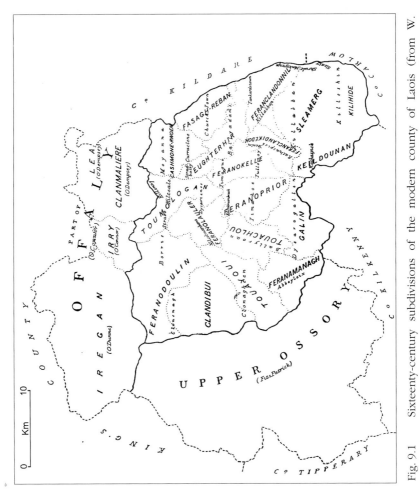

Fig. 9.1   Sixteenty-century subdivisions of the modern county of Laois (from W. Fitzgerald, 'Hitorical Notes on the O'Mores and their territory of Leix' in *Kildare Arch. Soc. Jn.*, vi (1909-11) facing p. 6).

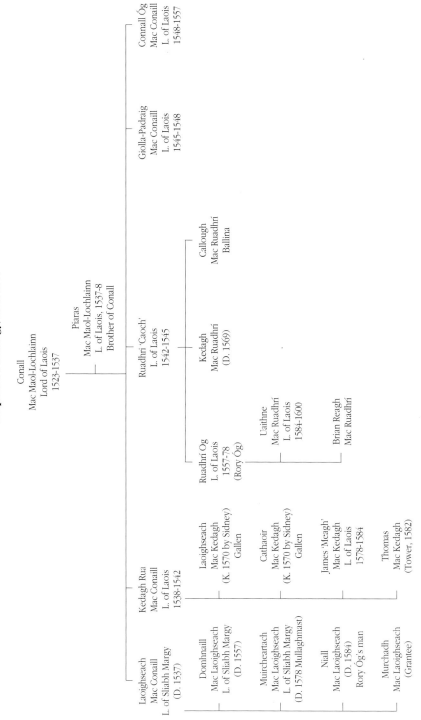

TABLE A
O'More Lords of Laois
Simplified Genealogy, 1523-1600

Conall
Mac Maol-Lochlainn
Lord of Laois
1523-1557

Piaras
Mac Maol-Lochlainn
L. of Laois, 1537-8
Brother of Conall

Giolla-Padraig
Mac Conaill
L. of Laois
1545-1548

Connall Óg
Mac Conaill
L. of Laois
1548-1557

Ruadhrí 'Caoch'
L. of Laois
1542-1545

Callough
Mac Ruadhrí
Ballina

Kedagh
Mac Ruadhrí
(D. 1569)

Ruadhrí Og
L. of Laois
1557-78
(Rory Óg)

Uaithne
Mac Ruadhrí
L. of Laois
1584-1600

Brian Reagh
Mac Ruadhrí

Kedagh Rua
Mac Conaill
L. of Laois
1538-1542

Laoighseach
Mac Conaill
L. of Sliabh Margy
(D. 1537)

Laoighseach
Mac Kedagh
(K. 1570 by Sidney)
Gallen

Cathaoir
Mac Kedagh
(K. 1570 by Sidney)
Gallen

James 'Meagh'
Mac Kedagh
L. of Laois
1578-1584

Thomas
Mac Kedagh
(Tower, 1582)

Domhnall
Mac Laoighseach
L. of Sliabh Margy
(D. 1557)

Muircheartach
Mac Laoighseach
L. of Sliabh Margy
(D. 1578 Mullaghmast)

Niall
Mac Laoighseach
(D. 1584)
Rory Óg's man

Murchadh
Mac Laoighseach
(Grantee)

215

wooded nature of the area is obvious, so also delineated is the political geography of a Gaelic world. What is represented in the winding dividing lines and raised place names ('Toumologan') are the literal and figurative traces of a once independent Gaelic political and social entity, the now struggling O'More lordship. The cartographer's evidence only hints at the fact that this social world and its Gaelic political elite, will have the dubious distinction of being the first sixteenth century victims of the English westward expansion.

This essay outlines the process by which this destruction occurred in what is usually referred to as the plantation of Laois and Offaly. As previous essays in this volume suggest, the O'More lordship of Laois was not immune to outside interference prior to the sixteenth century, nor was it incapable of interacting with and assimilating newcomers. Yet the early modern experience of conquest and settlement would radically alter Laois and its people. The plantation would shatter the Gaelic political system and decimate its ruling elite, the O'Mores. It would also usher in a new English administrative and legal system, new settlers, and a proto-urban infrastructure.

The End of the Medieval Frontier

These momentous changes had their origin in the collapse of the Kildare hegemony after the failed rebellion (1534-6) of 'Silken' Thomas Fitzgerald against Henry VIII. The late medieval earls of Kildare had controlled the Pale, policed it borders, and negotiated with the Gaelic world in what was often the mutual interest of the Geraldines and the crown of England. With the removal of the Kildare buffer zone, the Gaelic world of the Midlands was exposed to the interventions of an English born governor and administration, and to their superiors at the metropolitan court. Modern Irish historians have a much less negative view of these developments than their predecessors. Rather than viewing these early years as the first inevitable steps in the conquest of the Gaelic world, they focus on the policies of conciliation of the lord deputy Sir Anthony St. Leger, in office at intervals between 1540 and 1556. They argue that under St. Leger the English crown made a serious effort to incorporate the lords of Gaelic and Anglo-Norman Ireland into the Tudor state. At the center of this initiative was the 1541 parliamentary act 'The act for the kingly title' which recognized all of Ireland's subjects as equal before the law and their king in England. Under St. Leger the government began in 1541 to renegotiate with the Gaelic Irish the terms of their relationship with the crown. The linchpin of this approach, known to historians as surrender and regrant, was the acceptance of English law, land titles and landholding custom on the part of the Gaelic elites in return for official government recognition and security.[2]

This policy was especially favored among certain English-Irish officials in the Pale who hoped that the adoption of English law would result in the peaceful assimilation of the Gaelic Irish. They were to become subjects of the king, obedient to his laws, and eventually forsake their Irish laws, habits and customs. Surrender and regrant was to ensure above all English landholding arrangements and succession by primogeniture within the Gaelic lordships. As an approach to the realities of Gaelic dynastic politics, this policy was inherently flawed. In its simplified form, it frequently ignored the distribution of power within the lordships, a power based on a system of family or extended kin role rather than a centralized succession system. Further, it often attempted to impose an 'inflexible framework' on an 'essentially fluid' situation.[3] In fact, the government's adherence to this essentially 'gradualist policy of peaceful assimilation' often gave rise to the very de-stabilizing dynastic struggles it had hoped to solve.[4]

A good example of how the Gaelic lords found it difficult to observe the conditions attached to the recognition of English authority is provided by the example of the O'More lordship of Laois. The collapse of the Kildare hegemony brought the English government under its representative Leonard Grey into direct involvement with the internal politics of the O'More lordship by the mid-1530s. The submissions of Piaras Mac Maol-Lochlainn O'More, 'sue Nationis Principalem', and the subordinates, Kedagh 'Rua' Mac Conaill O'More and Ruaidhrí 'Caoch' Mac Conaill O'More (table A) before Grey and St. Leger in January 1538 saw the formal recognition by the crown of O'More rights to the lordship of Laois.[5] But this agreement also indicated formal recognition by the O'Mores of the replacement of the earls of Kildare with the crown in terms of over-lordship and the acceptance of a government presence in the fort at Stradbally henceforth.[6] By March 1538 the main Geraldine ally in the region, Brian O'Connor, had also submitted, and asked for the regrant of his lands from the king by letters patent. O'Connor's submission and requests anticipated the surrender and regrant form in his renunciation of Gaelic exactions and his request for the English title 'baron of Offaly'.[7] It is certain that Piaras Mac Maol-Lochlainn (Melaghlin) O'More agreed to a form of surrender and regrant for his lands.[8] These developments were important. Under lord deputy Grey the crown had begun, in the absence of the earls of Kildare, the expansion of English governmental influence beyond the medieval frontier of the Pale into the Gaelic world.[9]

The opening of the Gaelic midlands to the vicissitudes of the politics of Dublin Castle brought about a dramatic transformation in the internal affairs of the O'More lordship. By June 1538 the O'Mores had split into two factions along the lines of a wider dispute between the earl of Ormond and the lord deputy Grey. The O'More, Piaras Mac Kedagh took the side of Ormond against the lord deputy who was supported by the pro-Geraldine brothers, Kedagh Rua, Ruaidhrí 'Caoch', and Giolla-Pádraig Mac Conaill O'More.[10] Despite the imprisonment of Piers Mac Kedagh O'More, the end result of the conflict was the reconfirmation by Grey in August 1538 of Piaras Mac Kedagh, and more importantly, of the lordship status of the O'More in Laois.[11] These preliminary measures were advanced in 1540 with the appointment of Anthony St. Leger as lord deputy the main advocate of the conciliatory approach. In November of 1540, St. Leger proposed the appointment of Brian O'Connor as Baron of Offaly, and in May 1531, he advocated the recognition of the new O'More, Ruaidhrí 'Caoch' Mac Conaill O'More. Both had formally submitted to him and both awaited formal confirmation of their lands and titles from Henry VIII.[12]

The recognition of Ruaidhrí 'Caoch' as 'captain' of his name, 'by the consent and election of all the noblemen and inhabitants of the country', and the acceptance of his 'dominion' over 'Slewmargy' suggested a bright future for crown-O'More relations. Yet St. Leger's initial success with surrender and regrant in Leinster soon began to fade, as it would nationally also. For the O'Mores and O'Connors the consequences in the long term were to be dramatic.[13] The immediate background to the collapse of O'More – government relations was an internal dispute between Ruaidhrí 'Caoch' and his brother Giolla-Pádraig Mac Conaill O'More. Giolla-Pádraig, who under Gaelic custom was legitimately entitled to succeed to the title of O'More, resented his brother's increased control and allied himself with the O'Connors. This dispute coincided with a factional dispute between Ormond and St. Leger, and also one of St. Leger's periodic departures and his replacement by a more hard-line justice, lord justice Brabazon.[14]

Historians dispute the significance of what happened next on the Pale borders. For the O'Mores and the O'Connors, the period from 1547 to 1556, saw the collapse of the surrender and regrant rapprochement. This was replaced under William Brabazon (justice, 1544, 1546, and 1550), Edward Bellingham (deputy, 1548-50) and James Croft (deputy, 1551-2) with alternating phases of military incursion, fortification and confiscation of land. Some historians have seen this as representing a component in an accelerating momentum, a new departure, towards the English conquest and colonization of Ireland.[15] Ciaran Brady has recently argued against this interpretation, and has attempted to rehabilitate the reputation of the most assertive of these officials, Edward Bellingham.[16] While Brady is essentially correct when he attempts to demonstrate that the period to 1556 did not see the end of Tudor reform, the 'conciliatory' approach, nonetheless, it is hard to not see the changes that occurred in Laois and Offaly in this period as marking a dramatic and aggressive shift in government policy towards the border Gaelic lords, and especially the O'Mores and O'Connors.[17]

The degeneration in relations was occasioned by Brabazon's raid on the increasingly assertive Brian O'Connor in the summer of 1546. This incursion was followed by an O'Connor assault on the pro- Butler and pro-government Ruaidhrí 'Caoch' O'More. The end result was the death of Ruaidhrí at the hands of his brother Giolla-Pádraig. The latter, O'Connor's brother-in-law and ally, assumed the title of O'More and joined Brian in assaulting the Pale.[18] Brabazon's counter-response was swift and heavy. After a series of raids, the government captured and garrisoned O'Connor's stronghold at Daingean and the O'More castle at Ballyadams. In June 1547, the new privy council of Edward VI, under the control of the Protector Somerset, sent Sir Edward Bellingham with troops and supplies to impose a military solution on the problem of the midland frontier. Bellingham's resolution was the elaborate fortification of Daingean (renamed Fort Governor) and the establishment of a new fort in the middle of the Laois lordship, Fort Protector.[19] By the spring of 1549 Bellingham's heavy campaigning in the region had paid off. The O'Mores had been cowed and their leader Giolla-Pádraig O'More, along with Brian O'Connor, was confined in London.[20]

The Establishment of a Plantation
The implications of Bellingham's initiatives represent a significant departure for the O'More lordship. The proposal to establish urban centers encircling the forts, in particular, around Fort Protector in O'Mores country, eventually led to the establishment of the fort-town of Maryborough, the first new urban foundation of the modem era.[21] These developments also encouraged a group of prominent English followers of Bellingham to infiltrate the region, individuals who, like Francis Cosby, would have an important role to play in its future colonization.[22] Similarly, Bellingham's successful, if costly, campaign encouraged government officials to move towards the first dispossession of elements of the Gaelic Irish in the region. A minority of government officials in the late 1530s, in particular Francis Herbert and Walter Cowley, had been eager for a more aggressive approach towards the Irish, and had even suggested the settlement of Englishmen on their lands.[23] And though these views had also been endorsed in the late 1540s by Brabazon and the Lord Chancellor Alen, it was not until Bellingham's government that the first tentative leases of Irish lands to English settlers began.[24] The final significant legacy of the Bellingham era was that a new level of ferocity entered into armed

conflicts between the Gaelic Irish and crown forces in the region. According to Bellingham, the Gaelic rebels in 1548 burnt, destroyed and killed 'man, woman and child' in the Pale, while the garrison killed on one day 'more woodkerne..than the oldest man in Ireland ever saw'.[25]

Ironically, the continuation of this aggressive trend was to be in the hands of the very deputy who was identified with the conciliatory approach. Between 1550 and 1551, Sir Anthony St. Leger, Bellingham's successor, was instructed, that since 'the countries of Offalye and Lex..are now in good towardness to be wholly in our hands and possession', he should survey and plant them.[26] In November 1550 Walter Cowley, the royal surveyor, began the first systematic survey of the region.[27] By early December, the survey completed, the leasing of lands could begin. St. Leger issued 29 leases for O'More lands in Laois. Clearly these lands were granted with strategic considerations in mind: the settlers were to live on their premises, they were to be armed and ready to serve when called, and they were not to inhabit with O'Mores and O'Connors.[28] St. Leger's successor, Sir James Croft, continued the leases in the area. These land grants are significant because many of the grantees spearheaded the first early modem settlement in Laois. Indeed, some of these settlers, like the Hovendons, Lees, Bowens, Floods and Cosbys, would receive lands in later schemes, and quite a few would survive in Laois into the modern era.[29]

Though both Croft and St. Leger before him wanted to pacify the region and ease the defensive burden on the Pale by upgrading the forts into market towns and establishing English settlers on a long-term basis (fee-farm), instability on the ground made this task extremely difficult. The costly garrisons were constantly on full alert and the settlers struggled to survive against Gaelic resistance.[30] This volatile situation encouraged individuals in government circles to propose a variety of solutions in the hope of either advancing a particular political agenda, or as a means of aggrandizement, or of both.

One of the most notable of these was the first private corporate plantation proposal for Ireland. According to this scheme, a syndicate dominated by the Palesman Gerald Aylmer would take Laois in freehold from the government, settle it with English and Palesmen, dispossess the O'Mores, and maintain the forts, all in return for an annual rent of £600 Ir. Another English-Irish or Old English proposal, which also broke new ground as it attempted to outline a solution to the Laois-Offaly problem, was Edward Walshe's 'Conjectures'. Walshe advocated the use of force as a prelude to settlement in the Midlands, then drawing on Roman precedent he suggested a 'saturation' of English and English-Irish tenants on long-term leases as a means of extending English influence and law in the region.[31] These more aggressive ideas had to compete with the revival of a proposal for the reversion to the older and more conciliatory approach. Lord Chancellor Cusack proposed the shiring of Gaelic Ireland, including Laois and Offaly, and also a reinvigorated surrender and regrant approach towards the Gaelic lords. In his view, stable relations with the Irish would result if Ireland was 'made shire land, and the law may take the right course, and ill men through good persuasion brought to take their lands of the king's majesty to them and their heirs for ever'.[32]

The new Queen Mary's reappointment of St. Leger in November 1553, along with the restoration of the exiled Gerald Fitzgerald the 11th earl of Kildare, and the release of his brother-in-law Brian O'Connor, seemed to suggest that the more conciliatory policy had once again won out. Yet for the O'Mores this was to be a mixed blessing. Mac Giolla-Pádraig O'More had died in London in 1548.[33] And though Old English aristocrats were given command of the forts, Kildare was appointed to Protector and Ormond to Governor, St. Leger still proceeded with plans for the dispossession of the midland Gaelic Irish.[34]

Modern historians discern little more than a subtle shift in government policy in this period, and in fact find the midland plantation entirely consistent with 'reform' policy and even with the conciliatory approach of St. Leger. Yet even if up until 1555 crown policy represented 'no radical departure', the experience of the intervening years created an atmosphere of real mistrust on the part of the midland Gaelic Irish.[35] For some, at least, it appeared that the crown had indeed embarked on a radical course of action:

> [they] hold us in great mistrust... And also for that they knowe that some other device for their total banishment hath been set forth and that maketh them think we do but dissemble with them. And some... there be who have had their lands taken from them without cause as they alleage, and desire to have the same again.[36]

Whether or not the period 1548 and 1556 represented radical or nuanced changes in government policy towards the O'Mores and O'Connors, the appointment of Sir Thomas Radcliffe, Lord Fitzwalter (earl of Sussex from 1557) in 1556 marked a turning point in the evolution of the midland plantation. Sussex approached the government of Ireland with the goal of action on a series of pre-costed specific objectives. Sussex's programmatic approach included the expulsion of the Scots from the North, the overhaul of government finances, the suppression of the midland Gaelic Irish, and the resettlement of the area. Sussex's instructions for the territories of the O'Mores and O'Connors, were quite specific. If they co-operated with the crown they were to be given a stake in the new midlands. The area was to be shired by act of parliament, then resettled on the basis of a Gaelic section (a mere third of the region) in the west of the modern counties of Laois and Offaly. The remaining two thirds of the area was to be divided between the forts and English settlers. On the Gaelic 'reservation', as throughout the new plantation, grantees were to use English law and customs, built houses of timber or stone, and not to employ Gaelic military personnel. English grantees were to keep an English archer and not to employ those of 'Irish blood and birth'.[37]

For Sussex it was imperative to settle the problem of Laois and Offaly. Here was an example of repeated government failure in securing the Pale, and here also was a major drain on government finances. In addition, the crown had already and repeatedly committed itself to this project to be frustrated by the O'Mores and O'Connors. This resistance could not prevail if Sussex's programme for the island as a whole was to work. Yet the inclusion of a Gaelic element in this plantation scheme suggests that the Marian regime did not intend a complete dispossession of the O'Mores and their neighbours.[38] This inclusiveness implied that the earlier concept of a 'model' plantation was not abandoned. If the ideals of the assimilation of the Gaelic Irish were still the theoretical basis of this proposed colony, it has to be stated that these proposals represented a new departure in the methods to be employed.[39] Transplantation to a western zone represented one such innovation, while the systematic allotment of their former lands to English captains represented another. The core of the English settlement was to be made up of a group of English planter captains whose job it was to defend their zone and thus the Pale.[40]

Though initial discussions seemed promising, Conaill Óg Mac Conaill O'More and the O'Connors soon broke off contact and, according to Sussex, 'combined themselves together to keep out and make war against their majesties'. Sussex abruptly had the council in Dublin proclaim the O'Connors traitors on the 25 February 1557.[41] Though these proclamations did not mention Conall Óg and the O'Mores, by the end of the campaign the O'Mores were on the run, and Conall Óg, had been captured and publicly executed at Leighlin Bridge.[42]

Despite the failure to gain the co-operation of the natives, the plans for the plantation proceeded.[43] The reality of conditions in Laois and Offaly, however, are implied in the extended powers of martial law conferred on Sussex's brother Sir Henry Radcliffe, lieutenant of the forts in Laois and Offaly.[44] Regardless of the region's war footing, the deputy ploughed ahead with his midland scheme. Sussex's parliament, which met in Dublin on the first of June 1557, attempted to create a legislative basis for the future colony. The acts for 'The disposition of Leix and Offaly' and 'An act whereby the King's and Queen's majesties..be entitled to the countries', confiscated Laois and Offaly, and provided a legal basis in English eyes for the dispossession of its native inhabitants. It also gave Sussex 'full power and authority' to grant lands 'at his election or pleasure... for the more sure planting and strength of the countries with good subjects [as] shall be thought unto his wisdom and discretion meet and convenient.'[45]

Furthermore, the statute suggested that 'Leix, Slewmarge, Irry, Glinmalir, and Offaily' were to be confiscated because they were once 'their majesties former possessions'. The statute related how native occupants had rebelled, were suppressed by Sussex, and as a consequence the crown was to 'have, hold and possess' their lands 'for ever'. The two new shires were to be called the Queen's and King's counties and they were to have sheriffs, coroners, and all other officers that went to make up a county administration. Fort Protector in Laois was to be re-named Maryborough.

These acts symbolized the crossing of the Rubicon for the O'Mores and their Gaelic neighbours in Offaly. Not alone can the foundation of the modern county of Laois be traced from this date but so also can the beginning of the end of Gaelic lordship of the O'Mores. With one stroke this series of acts wiped out the legal position of all previous settlements made in the area. Not alone did this impact on the Gaelic O'Mores but it also invalidated the landholding position of all previous settlers who had attempted to plant between 1549 and 1557. The exclusive right granted to Sussex to determine who would be planted there in the future called into question the landholding position of all who had settled after 1549, and indeed the status of all who inhabited the area prior to this. Under the terms of the act it was not only the natives who stood in danger of dispossession but even the few embattled settlers in the region.

Yet these legal nuances had little impact on the bitter war being waged between the O'Mores and the English captains under Radcliffe. Martial law only held Laois and Offaly, and the fighting was serious enough to threaten the fort at Maryborough itself in June 1558. On this latter occasion the fort was saved by a furious counter-attack on the part of Radcliffe and the garrison. Francis Cosby, the head of a soon-to-be prominent English family in the region, distinguished himself in the ensuing hand -to- hand combat, and was credited with killing 30 or 40 'of the best of them'.[46]

Small skirmishes aside, the lack of progress in Laois and Offaly, and the massive cesses/impositions imposed on the Pale to maintain the forts prompted resistance form the Old English political community. This is hardly surprising when one considers that the deputy's failed efforts against the Scots in the North, against Shane O'Neill, and against the midland Gaelic dynasts entailed a massive increase in government expenditure. Cost was not the only factor. The oppression of the soldiers billeted on the Old English territory and the border areas rapidly alienated the people of the Pale. The tenor of most of the Pale objections against the Sussex regime suggested a return to surrender and regrant as a solution. Some even seemed willing to countenance a return to Kildare rule.[47] One of their spokesmen, George Dowdall, the archbishop of Armagh, proposed that the Midland O'Mores and O'Connors should be pardoned. In the spirit of the conciliatory approach of the 1540s, he suggested they be given 'some portion of their old lands as it should be thought meet, for whosoever takes the rule of Ireland in hand, he must according to the gospel, forgive unto seventy times seven'.[48]

Neither the Pale nor the Gaelic midlands were to be rid of Sussex so easily. The new Queen Elizabeth (Mary died in November 1558) re-appointed and promoted Sussex with the new title of lord lieutenant of Ireland. In every major policy area Sussex won in the debate against his Pale rivals. He returned to Ireland in June 1560 intent on making war against Shane O'Neill and finally planting Laois and Offaly. Elizabeth's instructions implicitly recognized that Sussex had done little in this area except establish a legal framework by act of parliament:

> Concerning the letting of the countries of Lexe and Offaley.., having been of late conquered and knit now to the crown by the authority of parliament and made shire ground, it seemeth very meet not to defer the order of the same any longer, but the deputy. . shall make grants and leases according to such authority as heretofore was given to him by act of parliament.[49]

It was clear to all that the plantation existed only on paper, Sussex had not issued any fiants or patents to grant lands, and in reality the army barely maintained the forts and garrisons. This is clearly indicated in the fact that Radcliffe, Cosby, and Henry Colley had their authority to rule by martial law renewed in January 1560. Elizabeth's instructions in May 1560 recognized the militarized nature of the area: 'our two countries of Less and Offaly do yet remain uninhabited, being planted only with our men of war, whereby they lie waste without peopling'.[50]

Sussex's confidence in his ability to reform Gaelic Ireland through the application of his program of action soon collapsed as he spent 1561 and 1562 in a futile quest to destroy Shane O'Neill.

Outmaneuvred at court by his factional rivals and in Ireland by the earl of Kildare, the lieutenant had little time to settle the issue of the O'Mores and their neighbors.[51] While actual bureaucratic measures were taken to advance the plantation the fact that the control of the area was left in the hands of his brother, Sir Henry Radcliffe and the English captains undermined any hope for a peaceful future for the scheme.[52]

The aggressive role of the captains was to have lasting negative consequences for future relations between the government and elements of the Gaelic Irish. The accounts of Sir Henry Sidney, vice-treasurer, for the period 1556-1563 demonstrate that almost all of the then settlers were part of the military establishment. The amounts of money due them in wages and their frequency of service suggest that not alone was the area far from peaceful but that the settlers had a vested interest in maintaining their military utility.[53] The aim of assimilating the Gaelic Irish through a planted colony was therefore weakened by the very tightly knit group on which the process depended. These figures turned the area into a military zone controlled by martial law. Though Sussex's policy was not yet realized, the personnel who would eventually carry it out were already operating there to its future detriment. Sussex's failure to organize the Laois/Offaly scheme encouraged local aggrandizement on the part of the captains who operated in these crucial years as virtual warlords. The resulting alienation of elements of the Gaelic population undermined any 'conciliatory' or reform aims the scheme might have intended. The counter-productive results of this administrative neglect are seen in a rare 1559 O'Connor proposal for bringing the area to peace. This O'Connor 'device' attributes the power of the warlords as the single most important cause for the Gaelic mistrust of Englishmen in the midlands.[54] It attributed Gaelic resistance to the arbitrary power granted to these English servitors:

> Understand the causes that moved those subjects to withdraw their heart[s] from obedience of late years, upon minor evils, without desert or order of any law, civil or marshall, all the Irish in all parts and specifically the men of great power and ability, stood in great mistrust of Englishmen and looked every hour for a conquest, since which time English captains were placed and had absolute powere and rule in Irishmen's countries and in the English borders. They found and devised such shifts and practices to slander and abuse the lords and quiet gentlemen... if it were once spoken of a soldier or captain's mother, it was a sufficient quarrell for the captain to rob, prey, and kill the person accused

and all his tenants without other authority or commission than the captain's allegation.[55]

Sussex tacitly admitted to the volatile nature of the area when he turned his attention to it in 1562. He proposed the continued rule of the English captains, the maintenance of a reinforced garrison, and the persistence of martial law.[56] Nevertheless, the lieutenant also began preparations for the thorough plantation of Laois and Offaly, the implementation of which had eluded him since 1556. In December 1561 he ordered a new survey of the area, and in September 1562 he submitted a draft of the grants to be made to the colonists.[57]

The grant as it evolved formed the conditions for Sussex's successful plantation of Laois and Offaly in 1563-4. The tenants of the colony were to hold their lands by fee-tail, and the grant was to be held by the crown as of the two principal forts by knights service (i.e. by the twentieth part of a knight's fee). The grantees were also to undertake to maintain a certain number of English horsemen, attend when called upon to serve for three days with servants and tenants armed, and give one ploughday per plough on their land to the constable of the fort. Furthermore, they were not to use the Brehon law against any subject amenable to English law, and they were to use English dress and custom. Finally they were not to maintain Irish military men who had served outside the county, and they were obliged to live on their lands. The social and cultural conditions were reinforced by two further prohibitions, that the grantee could not intermarry with the Irish living outside the area, and that they were not to accept the Gaelic military imposition of coign and livery. These social and cultural prohibitions were designed to create a model English community in the midlands. The military conditions were obviously intended to preserve this colony from internal or external threat. It is important to note that these measures did not imply the exclusion of the Gaelic Irish from the scheme. In fact this settlement was unique in that it not alone included Gaelic elements but that they were to hold their lands under similar conditions as the other grantees.[58]

Queen Elizabeth informed Sussex as early as May 1561 that though the Marian acts of parliament which authorized the confiscation and re-granting of Laois and Offaly specified that the beneficiaries be English born, it was the government's intention that Gaelic grantees be included.[59] Sussex agreed with this policy as it extended to those who had submitted to him, for the recalcitrant, the lieutenant proposed expulsion and the granting of their lands to 'mere Englishmen'.[60] Yet the lieutenant's 1563-4 scheme included no element of regional segregation as suggested in the Marian proposals. The mixing of Gaelic and English grantees, we can assume, was an attempt to draw the Irish to 'civility' by the example of their English neighbours. Special efforts were made to ensure the peaceful assimilation of the chosen Gaelic grantees. An important concession was made in the area of Gaelic succession, which was not based on primogeniture. Under the conditions of the grant a landholder was to enjoy the holding for life but the remainder was to go to 'one of the lawful begotten sons' whom the grantee could nominate during his own lifetime.[61]

The granting of lands in Laois and Offaly under these conditions began in February 1563 and was completed by May 1564. Dean Gunter White has established a profile of the total of eighty-eight grantees, fifty-five of whom received Laois lands. Most of the English grantees (12 were English by birth and 12 English-Irish), like Francis Cosby, were army men who had served in the area for quite some time, and many were proposed as grantees in the 1556 plan. The total number of horsemen due for service provide evidence for the military nature of the colony. According to White, the lieutenant of the forts could expect to raise one hundred and seventy-four horsemen from the two counties. These horsemen, combined with foot (the captain's band) and galloglass, would have been the defensive foundation on which the colony was to be built. It is assumed that these military personnel would assist their captain in the securing and developing of their holding. They also more than likely became their tenants when this work was completed. Their combined role was to defend a mainly rural settlement centered on the two forts of Maryborough and Philipstown.[62] In addition, a successful and prosperous military colony intended to induce its Gaelic neighbours to see the benefits of English 'civility'.

The excluded O'Mores, however, could not be induced to accept the fact of the renewed settlement of Laois. They had combined in December 1560 under Niall Mac Laoighseach O'More (elected O'More) and Laoighseach Mac Kedagh Ruadh O'More at a meeting at Holy Cross Abbey in county Tipperary. At the instigation of Shane O'Neill, they set about frustrating Sussex's plans.[63] For the entire year, while the administration processed the grants and the settlers attempted to establish themselves, the dispossessed O'Mores harried the area.[64] Various efforts were made to come to terms with this group. In March 1564 Sir Henry Radcliffe, along with the earls of Kildare and Ormond, met with them but to no avail. The government decided on action. Any O'Mores who did not submit before April were to be proclaimed traitors. Those who submitted were to be 'booked', hand in pledges, and to serve Radcliffe, the lieutenant of the forts. As an incentive they were to have 'apoyncted to them in the countrey, sufficient to fynde them and their men of suche lande as if not alredy bestowed, to holde the same... by patent as others in the country'.[65] Implicit in these arrangements was the clear understanding that unsatisfied Gaelic land claims, and septs or major segments excluded from the settlement, would only lead to further trouble. The proposed solution was logical-the hitherto excluded would get lands allocated to them in return for acceptance of the plantation and co-operation with the military authorities.

When Sussex departed Ireland as lord lieutenant in early 1564, to be replaced by the temporary Lord Justice Nicholas Arnold, he left behind an established if somewhat beleaguered rural military colony. Though this scheme included Gaelic elements, it also carried with it a cadre of military colonists who had long experience in the area and a history of antagonism with the native inhabitants. This was evident in the brutalities, which accompanied the unprecedented settler and government campaign against the O'Mores and O'Connors in July 1564.[66] Francis Cosby alone commanded 330 men in Laois not including the forces that were due according to the settlers' patents. Though the settlers and the army clearly subdued the natives, the end result was a further blow to Gaelic confidence in the government's ability to provide justice. Furthermore it set a new tone in the nature of Gaelic-English hostilities. The government, on the one hand, boasted of a head count of 125 dead O'Mores and O'Connors. The O'More response included massacring the settlers 'churls' or husbandmen and decapitating captured English common soldiers.[67]

This was the situation that confronted the new lord deputy Sir Henry Sidney in October 1565. Though offering the Queen a program of action for Ireland similar to Sussex's, Sidney placed greater emphasis on provincial councils and on individual colonial schemes.[68] Sidney's interest in colonization was sparked by Spanish activities in the Americas. Thus, Sidney was more than aware of the difficulties inherent in planting colonies. In addition he had observed the evolving midland's scheme, having served in Ireland there in the second half of the 1550s. This experience suggested to him that the government had a simple choice, either to pardon the 'rebel' elements or chastise and banish them for good. Sidney concluded that the former option would bring only temporary quietness but the latter would avoid future disturbances.[69] Elizabeth's instructions in October 1565, however, envisaged no such radical departure for Laois and Offaly. The lord deputy was simply to supervise the reconstruction and consolidation of the plantation. A survey was proposed to ascertain what tenants had fled the disturbances. Their estates were to be regranted to other suitable tenants.[70]

Sidney's assessment of the condition of the colony was on the whole more positive than might have been expected. In his estimation the area most in need of reform was the military establishment.[71] This had also been the conclusion of the earlier inquiry into army corruption under Justice Nicholas Arnold in 1565. The Arnold commission found Sir Henry Radcliffe, lieutenant of the forts, responsible for extensive financial mismanagement. What is interesting to note, though, is the fact that Radcliffe was accused, in addition to tampering with army accounts, of misappropriating the 'charges' of the counties to the tune of £2,341, and of usurping crown lands to the value of £8,000. These charges if true provide clear evidence of the potential profits that could accrue from involvement in the plantation.[72] Sidney's conclusions similarly suggested collusion between the military and the settlers to defraud the crown. Aside from finding many of the bands staffed with large numbers of Gaelic kerne, the deputy discovered that many of the bands employed the minor settlers as soldiers. For Sidney this resulted in a dilution of the defensive capacity of the colony:

> That divers freeholders and inhabitants within this realm, having livings of her highness at mean and reasonable prices, granted chiefly in respect that by such her Majesty's benefits they might be enabled to defend their own and assist their neighbours against the invasion of an ill-disposed strength..are nevertheless crept into the same garrison, to her majesties unnecessary charges.[73]

In fact, most of the settlers survived the war of 1564-5 intact because they were 'double-dipping' at the government's expense. As a cost-cutting measure, Sidney abolished the post of lieutenant of the forts and instead installed Francis Cosby as constable of the fort at Maryborough and seneschal of the county of Laois.[74]

Sidney's commitment to the Laois/Offaly plantation was part of his overall policy for the political and social reform of Ireland. The colony was to serve as a vehicle to extend the common law in the Gaelic midlands. The appointment of the two seneschals Cosby and Colley was to be a means to this end. These two officers were not only to command the forts but, backed by the sheriffs and judges, were to go on circuit and help introduce the proper practice of the common law. Sidney himself went on circuit with them through Laois and Offaly in April 1566.[75] With apparently quite positive results to show for this effort, Sidney reported that all the main septs of the O'Mores came into him, 'for they say they had justice'. This meeting even included the most prominent surviving son of Ruaidhrí 'Caoch' Mac Conaill O'More still living in Ireland, Ruaidhrí Óg O'More (more commonly known as

TABLE B

Division of O'More lordship based on the 1563 map of Laois/Offaly

1. TOUMOLOGAN	Tuagh Maol-Lochlainn
2. EUGHTERHIR	Eughterhir (Stradbally, Ballyadams)
3. FERANODOULIN	Fearann O'Dowling
4. GLANDIBUI/TOUAYAVI	Clan MacEvoy
5. FRRANOLAULER	Fearann O'Lalor
6. FERANOPRIOR	Fearann O'Prior
7. FERANOKELLE	Fearann O'Kelly
8. FASAGHREBAN	Fasagh Reban
9. FERANCLANDIDONILL	Fearann Clan Mac Donnell
10. FERANCLANDIKEDOH	Fearann Clan Mac Kedagh
11. TOUACHLOV	Tuagh Mac Lowe
12. FRANAMANAGH	Fearann na Manaigh
13. GALIN	Gallen
14. SLEAMERG	Sliabh Mairge
15. KILIHIDE	Killeshin
16. KEILDOUNAN	Kildounan (Rathaspick)

Rory Óg).[76] It is also apparent that the deputy realized that no peaceful transition to English law could occur if the dispossessed O'Mores were not settled with: 'beeng so hard for them that have nothing of their oune, to live withowt offending'.[77] In this regard Sidney's decision to grant lands to Laoighseach and Cathaoir Mac Kedagh O'More in July 1566 and to negotiate with the other septs is significant.[78]

By the end of the year Sidney's optimism about the future of the region is expressed in his request for the incorporation of the two plantation towns of Maryborough and Philipstown. He had spent the summer of 1566 strengthening them and hoped they would become 'rich and well peopled towns'.[79] Elizabeth acceded to the plan in August 1569 and Philipstown received its charter in March 1570 and Maryborough on 4 April 1570.[80] For Maryborough there is evidence of the existence of a real plantation town, if not the market town with bailiffs, burgesses and commoners envisaged in its charter. The unique surviving map (fig. 2) of the fort and town provides us with verification that some of the planters kept residences in the town (Francis Cosby is a good example) and that it also had a distinct population of its own.[81]

As later events would demonstrate, Sir Henry Sidney's optimism was misplaced. Even before the end of his first tour of duty in October 1567, he found himself, once again, engaged in the 'pacification' of some of the O'Mores. Yet by 1569 the government could take some satisfaction in the fact that effective English control extended beyond the Pale encompassing the former lordships of Laois and Offaly. In addition, English soldiers and settlers nervously occupied lands in both territories, and a rudimentary plantation had been effected. This marked the effective end of Gaelic lordship and the beginnings of the modern county Laois.

Gaelic Collaboration and the slow death of a lordship
The final division of Laois in 1563-4 marked an end to the successful operating of the Gaelic political system in the lordship of Laois. The extended arrival of new settlers from 1548 onwards resulted in the gradual dispossession of certain septs of the O'Mores. The subsequent demise of lordship was followed by the loss to these former-ruling clans of dues, rents and tenants. The effective dismantling of the traditional order, in legal terms at any rate, was ensured when certain Gaelic grantees (22 Laois grantees were included) acquired land to hold under English law. In theory at least, these occupiers were outside the political control of their dispossessed overlords. According to the terms of their grants, they were to be independent landowners in their own right, holding their land from the crown and giving in return rents, military services and allegiance. By setting these former dependents up as independent freeholders in their own right and thus ensuring their loyalty, the government intended to undermine the very system that gave the O'Mores and O'Connors their traditional power.

Of the three land-related groups in the hierarchy of the lordship, the third was the least affected by these changes. These were the non-landowning people who comprised the mass of the population and who as tenants and labourers worked the land for the landowners before and after plantation. The next group above these in the Gaelic hierarchy were the subordinate O'More and O'Connor septs and the subordinate clans who rendered economic and military services to the principal lords. Certain of these subordinate clans and septs were freeholders in the sense that their land belonged to them by right under Gaelic law. These owed their services and their dues to their lord, as their overlord and not as their landlord.[82] Client clans or *Uirríthe* had a similar relationship with their overlords such as the

O'Maol-Lochlainn (O'Melaghlins), MacGeoghegans or the O'Dempseys. Yet it is certain that the O'Mores also held lands in the territories of these *Uirríthe*. These lands would have supplemented the exactions that came from these sources.[83] O'More subordinate clans held lands as part of the O'More lordship while they paid their services and dues to their overlord. These clans included the O'Kellys, O'Deevys, O'Lalors, O'Dowlings, O'Dorans, and the MacEvoys.[84] There was a strong element of this social group represented in the Gaelic plantation grants, including *Uirríthe,* like the O'Dempseys and Keatings, and subordinate clans like the O'Kellys, O'Dowlings and MacEvoys. Some elements of the ruling clan, the third Gaelic grouping, received a stake in the plantation while other members were excluded. As has been seen this excluded group formed the basis of the resistance to the new order.

It would appear that within each lordship prior to plantation the dominant sept, that is the grouping within the clan that held the title of lord or O'More held most of the land.[85] The O'More lordship comprised 16 sub-divisions or sub-lordships (table B).[86] The ruling clan held quite a large proportion of these lands.[87] While the 1566 inquisition into the death of Ruaidhrí 'Caoch' O'More is ambiguous as to the exact nature of the relationship between the lord and his lordship, it is possible to arrive at certain conclusions. Ruaidhrí 'Caoch' held, by right of his 'captainship' of the O'Mores, the town of Stradbally and it was along with its benefits worth £10 per annum to him. The customs, duties and exactions that appertained to his position as lord or O'More added a further £100 to his income. The distinction is made in this inquisition between these, the benefits of his office, and his own family inheritance that included the following townlands:

> Dyrrbroke and the great wood with their appurtennces, Dyrryloghcomer, both the Collennaghes, viz Collennaghe and Collenaghemore, Dysart Eneys, Carrickeneparkye, Ballyknockane, Graignehoyn and the whole parishe of Tulloryne, which lands were unto him yerly worthe threescore and ten marks lawfull money of Ireland.[88]

He also held the temporalities of 'rymokoe alias called Farenepriorie, Moyn Rath, Killegan, Bahenegall, Dyrryn-Roye, Dromnyne, Moyane, Rathkrehyn and Garryreading', and from the 'prince' the profits of the abbeys of Stradbally and Abbeyleix.[89] Ruaidhri 'Caoch' had the possession of quite a substantial amount of the rest of the lordship of Laois but this was mortgaged. The lands and mortgages are listed in the 1566 inquisition.[90]

Other sub-clans also held some land within the lordship. These often performed special offices or tasks, for example, mercenary or galloglass families, legal or ecclesiastical families. The names of the O'More sub-territorial divisions may provide clearer evidence for how the greater lordship was once made up of client families. These sub-territories are sometimes designated as 'Feran' on the 1563 map of Laois and Offaly in reference to the Gaelic word *fearann*, a piece of reserved land or estate.[91] Fearann O'Dowling, O'Lalor, and O'Kelly suggest a concentration of these septs within these subdivisions.[92] The sub-territories of Tuath Maol-Lochlainn and Fearann Clan Mac Kedagh point to the dominance of the Maol-Lochlainn O'Mores and Clan Mac Kedagh O'Mores. Tuath Mac Lowe and Fearann Clan Mac Donnell, suggest the existence of two other distinctive families within the O'More lordship. The origins of Fearann na Manach and Fearann O'Prior are obviously church related especially since Fearann na Manach included the important abbey of Leix (Abbeyleix) and Fearann O'Prior included the ecclesiastical centers of Timahoe, Fossy and Kilcolmbrack.

These client families, O'Kelly, O'Deevy, O'Lalor, O'Dowling, O'Moran and MacEvoy, figure prominently in most of the O'More pardons issued between the years 1570 and 1600.[93] Their social status (when recorded) ranged through gentlemen, freeholders, farmers, cottiers and laborers. The description of many of them as gentlemen and freeholders suggests that some may have been independent freeholders under the O'Mores, rendering them rent and other services in return for their lands. Fearann Clan MacDonnell was obviously a galloglass-controlled area, and these probably held their land in return for their military services. Their territory was situated in the strategic area between the Castlecomer hills and the Carlow-Kildare border.

From peripheral territories such as these the lord exacted rent and other dues, usually from the client clan or sept. The lordship of Gallen, the only remaining portion of Cowley's survey of Leix, provided the ruling O'More with rent from 16 townlands The 'Captain of the country of Leix' had certain miscellaneous dues from his lordship as well as his regular rent. Cowley found that the 'captain of the country was accustomed to receive [annually] one cow of the rectory of Aghttobbrid lying in the north of Idowghe mounting to 13s.4d.'[95]

From the 1566 inquisition into the death of Ruaidhrí 'Caoch', it is clear that the ruling O'More clan held either secular or ecclesiastical portions in all the 16 O'More lordships. Many of these lordships were held partially or predominantly by sub-clients or clans and their tenure was based originally on a leasing or mortgaging of these lands with their dominant overlords, the O'Mores. Yet each ruling family within both lordships was divided into a number of branches or septs (sliocht = descendants), all of whom took their names from a common ancestor. As outlined earlier the Mac Conaill dominated the O'More clan, and these were in turn divided into three main septs, the Mac Laoighseach Mac Conaill, the Mac Kedagh Mac Conaill and the Mac Ruaidhrí Mac Conaill (table A). Each Gaelic lordship also contained some minor branches of the same family, usually descended from an eponymous ancestor different from the main branches, who held a small portion of land in the lordship.

These are clearly visible in the Ruadhrí 'Caoch' inquisition, with such groups as the Mac Ross, the Mac Niall, the Mac David, the Mac Teig and the sons of Maol-Lochlainn. We can be almost certain that their subordinate position resulted from the expansion of the more successful branches of the family. Direct involvement and co-operation with the crown in the period from 1536 to 1548 tended to consolidate the positions of these more successful families. As an example, the crown grant of the profits of monastic lands of Stradbally and Abbeyleix to Ruaidhrí 'Caoch' would have tended to strengthen further his sept's position.[95]

This process of the consolidation of particular family interests was arrested when the policy of confiscation followed the disturbances of the 1540s and 1550s. Yet, as outlined earlier, no plantation scheme envisaged the total extirpation of the Gaelic Irish from the region. It was this mindset which determined the composition of the grantees as decided in Sussex's settlement in 1563-4. As already noted 29 out of the 88 grantees were Gaelic Irish and these had the same conditions imposed on them as any of the other participants. Although it is obvious that the majority of the settlers were non-Gaelic, it is nevertheless apparent that the native element was considered integral to the settlement. In addition to their purely defensive role, the new English settlers had a cultural duty to fulfil as participants in the new plantation. The prosperity of the new English grantees was to serve as an example to their Gaelic co-grantees of the benefits of English life and law. Thus, it was hoped plantation would bring a peaceful assimilation of the native Irish.

Failure on the part of the O'More and O'Connor ruling elite to accept the new proposals was to result in banishment. When this was achieved, their lands were to be settled and their lordship effectively dismantled by giving holdings under English law to co-operative *Uirrithe* and clients. As a result of the efforts of Sussex and the earl of Kildare, the resistant O'More and O'Connor elements were removed. The members of these two clans who had submitted before February 1563 were to be included, while those who had not come in were excluded.

Virtually all the important clients and sub-septs of the O'Mores were represented in the Laois Gaelic grants. Aodh Mac Diarmada O'Dempsey, Fearganainm O'Kelly, and Murchadh (Murrough) Mac Carroll Mac Evoy, David Mac Murchadh Mac Evoy, each received a holding. Muircheartach (Murtagh) Mac Laoighseach Mac Conaill and Murris Óg O'More represented one of the three dominant O'More septs. Kedagh Mac Piaras, Domhnall Mac Giolla-Pádraig, Davy and John O'More, represented minor O'More families. The Keatings, Richard, Edmund, Walter, John and Thomas, were a kerne element planted for strategic purposes. Tadhg (Thady) Mac Donnchadh (Donogh) a surgeon, Edmund Mac Maolmórdha (Mulmory) a galloglass and Tadhg Dubh Mac Murchadh (Morgh), were clients of the O'Mores.[96] That these received a stake in the settlement and the Mac Kedagh and Mac Ruaidhrí Mac Conaill, the two dominant septs, did not, attested to the aims of the government. The administration hoped that these minor groups would, in return for the freehold of their lands, renounce their adherence to their traditional overlords. Theoretically the peaceful assimilation of these groupings would negate the O'Connor/O'More threat to the Pale, reduce the queen's costs, and provide a successful example of the benefits of English law to the rest of Gaelic Ireland.

It is evident that government policy intended to facilitate this process by the sponsoring of rising Gaelic *Uirríthe*. As it turned out the new settlement not only effectively dismantled O'More power, but it also made an *Uirrí*, Eóghan Mac Aoidh (Owen Mac Hugh) O'Dempsey, the largest grantee. Eóghan's lordship of Clanmalier was wedged between the O'Mores and O'Connors, but was chiefly subordinate to O'Connor. In order to survive the collapse of his more powerful neighbours, Eóghan Mac Aoidh O'Dempsey firmly allied himself with the government interest. In the period when the earl of Sussex was intent on crushing the O'Connor and O'More resistance, he was appointed as captain of the kerne to serve against his former over-lords. His service in this period ran from 25 May 1560 to 18 June 1565 and culminated in a massive wages bill of over £1,000.[97] This stint was generously rewarded in the plantation scheme of 1563-4, O'Dempsey receiving by far the largest grant of all the grantees, English or Irish. On 18 March 1564 he was granted English title to virtually all lands of Clanmalier, including those to which O'Connor held title, and also lands in Laois and Kildare. Eóghan's service in the suppression of the 1564 O'Connor and O'More disturbances further estranged him from his dispossessed Gaelic enemies. Regardless of the enmity of his Gaelic neighbours, he continued to seek government favor. And the crown responded in kind. In 1569 he was rewarded with title to additional lands in Offaly, Laois and Kildare. No O'More or O'Connor grant, came close to Eóghan Mac Aoidh O'Dempsey's total of 3,302 acres.[98]

Between 1560 and 1577 Eóghan successfully consolidated his political and landholding position. These years saw the successful transition of the O'Dempsey from a vassal of O'Connor to the leading Gaelic landowner in Laois and Offaly. He not only out-maneuvred his O'Connor overlords but succeeded in becoming a direct challenge to both O'More and Kildare hegemony in the midland region. This transformation could not have taken place without the direct aid and support of the government, and in particular, certain government officials. The lord deputies Sussex, Sidney and Fitzwilliam all patronized and encouraged O'Dempsey. In return Eóghan and his successor Terence supported the government throughout the sixteenth century, though this necessitated some complicated maneuvering, particularly during the Nine-Year's War.[99]

This support is best illustrated in the prominent part O'Dempsey played in the ferocious campaign against the O'Mores in the mid- to late-1570s (see below). This was a campaign characterized by treachery, massacre and pillage. His infamous participation with Francis Cosby and Robert Hartpole in the massacre of O'Mores and other Laois clansmen at Mullaghmast in 1578 was an indication of the extent of his willingness to go to any lengths to preserve his new found independence against his former overlords. As a consequence, it comes as no surprise that the O'Mores vehemently hated him. He was killed by Ruaidhrí Óg's man Niall Mac Laoighseach O'More in 1578 in the aftermath of the massacre. Yet neither Eóghan's death, nor these vicious times in Laois prevented the peaceful transfer of lands and power to Terence O'Dempsey.[100] Nor did it bring an end to the policy of co-operation with the government so carefully cultivated by Sussex, Fitzwilliam and Sidney. If one of the major objectives of plantation had been the political assimilation of the Gaelic Irish, then, to a certain extent, it succeeded in Clanmalier. Eóghan Mac Aoidh was frequently given commissions of martial law, while his heir Terence was appointed to the post of sheriff of the King's county.[101] The clan's final mark of assimilation occurred on 22 May 1599 when the earl of Essex knighted Terence O'Dempsey.[102]

The O'Dempseys were undoubtedly politically allied to the New English government, yet there is little evidence to suggest that the cause of cultural assimilation was advanced. Clanmalier, aside from its ruling elite, remained relatively undisturbed by the plantation. Though the O'Dempsey's successfully entered the English regional adminis- tration, they did not advance the aims of anglicization. O'Dempsey survival was based primarily on adapting to the political force of the New English, while at the same time maintaining their Gaelic political and cultural practices. Thus the slow deaths of the O'Connor lordship of Offaly and the O'More lordship of Laois brought about the rise of another Gaelic power, the former *Urrí* O'Dempsey, to fill the vacuum.

O'More Resistance: War to the death

As previously noted, two of the major O'More groupings, the Mac Kedagh and the Mac Ruaidhrí Mac Conaill, did not receive any stake in the plantation of 1563-4. In the case of the descendants of Ruaidhrí 'Caoch', this was a particularly glaring oversight. Ruaidhrí 'Caoch' had been ' legitimized' by the government as 'captain' of his name in the 1540s. By the standards of English law, Ruaidhrí's successor, Giolla-Pádraig and the latter's eventual successor, Conall Mac Conaill were usurpers. Thus, when the English attainted Conall, confiscated O'More land in the act of parliament of 1556-7, and re-granted the lands in 1563-4, they had in effect legalized the usurpation of Ruaidhrí 'Caoch'. As a consequence they ignored the rights of his successors under English law. Two of Ruaidhrí's younger sons, by his father's second marriage to Margaret Butler, Kedagh and Callough, would seek redress through the mechanisms of English law.[103] A third son, Ruaidhrí Óg (hereafter Rory Óg), his eldest son by his first marriage, would seek his inheritance in a more dramatic manner. Ultimately the exclusion of leading septs of the Mac Conaill O'Mores would doom the plantation of 1563-4 to years of Gaelic resistance.

Sir Henry Sidney had spent the latter part of the 1560s shoring up Sussex's plantation in the midlands. When two brothers of the Mac Kedagh sept came into him and submitted in 1566, he used the opportunity to give them a small portion of ten townlands, mostly waste, in Laois.[104] Thus only the sons of Ruaidhrí 'Caoch' were excluded entirely from the new order. The most prominent of these, Rory Óg O'More, had been in fosterage with the O'Byrnes in Wicklow and had begun to make a name for himself by 1565 as a swordsman. After service in Sir John of Desmond's country, Rory Óg began operations in Laois by 1570, more than likely encouraged by the fact that his two cousins had received lands. He was called before Sidney and the council, then meeting at Stradbally, and agreed to submit pledges and presumably await arbitration.[105]

The reasons for what happened next are rather unclear, however, in May 1570 Sidney decided against conciliation. This about face may have been connected to the mopping up operations after the Butler revolt (1569-70) in which south Laois had been repeatedly attacked with O'More assistance. Also it was clear to Sidney as early as 1566 that there were no more vacated estates in Laois and Offaly to grant to the dispossessed O'More elements. This and the participation of the Mac Kedagh O'Mores in the Butler revolt may have prompted Sidney to decide to 'sweep the house' after the revolt, and to 'bare such a hand upon the whole name of the O'Mores as I trust the Queen's county shall be a quiet county.[106]

Rory Óg O'More survived this 'sweep' because at the time he was in the service of none other than Francis Cosby the seneschal of Laois and the occupier of his father's inheritance of Stradbally! The fate of his cousins – Sidney had Laoighseach and Cathaoir Mac Kedagh killed – increased Rory's suspicions of the government's intentions. Sidney's successor, Fitzwilliam, reported that he was gathering men, refusing to meet with the government, and in the deputy's view was ready to 'go out'. It is certain that the deaths of Laoighseach and Cathaoir Mac Kedagh had a profound impact on Rory, and intelligence sources suggested that his alienation was fuelled by a desire for revenge.[107] He refused to 'come into or obey Francis Cosby' and though the latter wanted him killed there was apparently little he could do because of O'More's increasing strength. By April 1571, Rory Óg O'More was declared 'chief of his sept in Leix' and his anti-English stance was rapidly gathering support for him in the Gaelic midlands.[108]

Rory's prominence in fomenting O'Connor disturbances in Offaly in May 1572 prompted the government to act. Fitzwilliam drew up elaborate plans for a combined operation with the forces of the earls of Kildare and Ormond to crush the Gaelic 'rebel'. Fitzwilliam justified the enormous expense involved by suggesting that they, including Ormond and Cosby, had tried repeatedly to negotiate with him and failed, and that, therefore, only annihilation could end this three-year 'sore'. Rory refused pardon, safe conduct and protection. The ostensible reason for his refusal was that the war against the O'Mores under Cosby had taken a turn towards the extreme even by the standards of the already twenty-five year old struggle in the area.[109]

Rory's reasoning was made abundantly clear in a conference, which took place between him and the earls of Ormond, and Kildare at the latter's Kilkea castle in August 1572. The O'More was so distrustful of the government's intentions towards him that he at first refused to cross the Barrow to meet with the two earls. His comments to the two amounted to a Gaelic indictment of the settler's actions, and government policy towards the dispossessed inhabitants of Laois. Rory claimed that he was forced to take arms against the government as the only means to ensure his life in the volatile atmosphere of the midlands. Past experience had taught Rory that the dispossessed O'Mores could not trust the settler military officials, and even the lord deputy, leaving them no choice but to rely on their weapons:

he meaneth not to warr against the Queenes Ma[jes]tie nor yet woll he make any simple submission w[i]th owt good assurance of his lyffe and lyvinge, alledginge that his farr betters of his name submytted them selves to the late L[ord] Deputie and sarved him and that they were after taken and executed. And for the dispersing of his men, he would not by no meane for that he hath many enemyes and hath no other assurance of his lyffe but the defence of himself and his men.[110]

Rory Óg O'More's demand was consistent with the fact that his sept was ignored in the settlement of 1563-4. He simply wanted land: 'he seketh to have Galin, w[hi]ch he sought afore, which he is sure yf they meane to geve him any, they woulde be best content to part w[i]th all, for that it is wast lande'.[111] The reality of dispossession had originally forced the O'More to be 'serviceable to Cosby', however, the execution of his two cousins, Laoighseach and Cathaoir, in 1570 left him vulnerable and with no other means to pursue his claims but to harass the plantation. Yet his overall aim, as the above quote makes clear, was rather limited. He wanted lands to settle on, and since he was clearly aware that the plantation was permanent, he was willing to accept the waste and upland zone of Gallen in southwest Laois, land that had formerly been granted to his two murdered cousins.[112] Rory's willingness to accept a stake in the plantation was similar to that of his two younger brothers, Kedagh (d. 1569) and Callough O'More. But here the similarity ends, these were both protected by the earl of Ormond, were shipped to England when very young and educated at Oxford. They aimed to use the law and their influential relative to advance their claims with the government.[113] For Rory Óg, after initial rejection by the government ('w[hi]ch he sought afore'), the brutal reality of plantation Laois meant that only violence could ensure his survival and get him notice.

Despite a submission, a pardon, and the implication of some consideration of his claims, little was done to further the O'More's cause.[114] As a consequence, Rory Óg began 1573 with a new onslaught on the plantation, which had been under martial law since March 1571. Once again the settlers were thrown into disarray, and further commissions were issued.[115] The lord deputy Fitzwilliam took a fateful decision in February 1573 that would have implications for the O'Mores long after he had departed from office. A year earlier he had vainly hoped that Kildare and Ormond would 'ease the comon welthe of that disease', now in a memo of February 1573 Fitzwilliam considered the options for ridding the midlands of the problem for good.[116] After prolonged analysis and consultation with Cosby he concluded:

We fynde but 2 wayes, theone yo[u]r Ma[j]esties force w[hi]ch will breede yo[u]r excessive and continuall chardge. Th[e]-other consisteth of so manie circumstances, as it cannot be so comitted to writing, but it will admit matters disputable, whereby in sending and resending to and fro, the fit season of this yere wil[l]be mispent and the opportunitie lost not to be recovered againe. For this service must [be?] in hande at the uttermost before the begin[n]ing of June next. This waye we hope wil[l] be (respecting the weight and necessitie of the service) but an easie burden to y[ou]r Ma[jes]tie and yet such as may henceforthe keepe the O'Mores so overgrowing again [in?] that countrey.[117]

This is suggestive in the light of a massacre of a large number of O'Mores at Mullaghmast in the March of 1578. If, alternatively, the 'matters disputable' that Fitzwilliam could not commit to writing referred to a colonization scheme for Gallen, then it suggests that he was aware that his proposals were controversial. In either case what is implied is the refusal to accommodate the claims of the Mac Ruaidhrí 'Caoch' branch of the O'Mores and the intention of solving the problem of the dispossessed Gaelic inhabitants once and for all.

In April the lord deputy wrote to the chief secretary Burghley to outline a scheme to remove the O'Mores from the strategic mountainous region of Gallen. What was so controversial about Fitzwilliam's plan, a plan so sensitive he claimed he needed to speak to the Queen in person about it, was the fact that it aimed at placing Eóghan Mac Aoidh O'Dempsey in Gallen. No mention is made as to how Rory Óg and the O'Mores were to be removed. What is clear is the innovative nature of the idea. Fitzwilliam recognized that to advance a minor Gaelic lord in this region was to step on the toes of Thomas Butler, the 10th earl of Ormond, whose lands bordered on Gallen. It also bordered on the lands of Sir Barnaby Fitzpatrick the baron of Upper Ossory, Sir William O'Carroll's country of Ely and the O'Dunne territory of Iregan. The scheme even contemplated dispossessing Ormond of the Abbey of Leix (Abbeyleix) and granting it to O'Dempsey! Such was the strategic importance of this upland and wild O'More redoubt, that Fitzwilliam was able to contemplate the disturbance of Ireland's most prominent Old English lord, and a special favorite of the Queen, the earl of Ormond.[118]

The transformation of the political and social order of the former lordship of Laois was obviously complete when an English official could contemplate 'planting', along with a hundred Gaelic householders, a former vassal of the O'Connors and a subordinate of the O'Mores in the place of the O'More. Indeed the positions of the two were so reversed and the war between them so intense that Fitzwilliam could claim that 'for [the] sake of his owne, and revenge sake also, he [O'Dempsey] is the lykelyest man to be a minister of their [O'Mores] plaag.'[119] O'Dempsey was now the leading Gaelic grandee in the region, while Rory Óg survived as a mere warlord, exacting a terrible price on the settlers and Gaelic collaborators.

Such conditions could not for long go unnoticed in England. That the plantation so recently reinforced and stabilized by Sidney could now be in a state of near anarchy prompted the government in London to seek the parties responsible for the mess. The finger seemed to point to Francis Cosby the seneschal of Laois since 1566, the former ally of Rory Óg and the one responsible for its security. From the perspective of Nicholas White, one of the Old English in Ireland, it seemed that these disturbances were originally carried out with the collusion of, what he referred to as, 'low born' settlers like Cosby to the intent of advancing their own careers and holdings from the ensuing mess.[120] Yet despite the Queen's displeasure, Fitzwilliam, who was a particular friend of the Cosby family and a fellow protégé of Sussex, defended the seneschal as the only means of preserving the colony and the Pale.[121] In reality only the powerful Laois settlers like Cosby and Robert Hartpole could survive in this vicious environment. Without them, the central government in Dublin was lost. And they only survived by accommodating themselves to Gaelic practice like the hiring of kerne, and through patronizing some of the smaller dispossessed groups.[122]

Sir Henry Sidney's return to Ireland as deputy in September 1575 heralded a possible end to the trauma for the dispossessed natives and the struggling planters alike. In November 1575 Sidney surveyed the region and described the process by which the plantation was weakened. The raids of the dispossessed natives constantly hindered the colony. Warfare discouraged English farming which in turn forced the settlers to take on Gaelic tenants, thus undermining the English nature of the settlement. Although a staggering loss to the crown, the deputy was unwilling to abandon the enterprise, seeing it instead as an important example in the practical problems of colonising native lands.

> The revenue of both the countries countervayle not the xxth part of the chardge, so that the purchase of that plott is, and hath bene vearie deare, yet nowe not to be geven over in any wise; for, God willinge, it shalbe recovered and mainteined. But this may be an example, howe the like hereafter is attempted, consideringe the chardge is so great, and the honnor and proffitt so small, to wynne landes from the Irishrey so dearly, as theise twoe countries have ben to the crowne.[123]

Sidney's awareness of these fundamental problems was illustrated when he allowed Rory Óg to submit to him at St. Canice's Cathedral in Kilkenny in late November 1575. The deputy was astute enough to realize that there could be no peace until O'More had some lands granted to him, yet he was unwilling to consider the dynast's other demands. Two distinct views of the legality of the plantation emerged from this meeting. On the one hand, Rory Óg claimed title to the ancient lordship of Laois, what Sidney referred to as his' aspiringe imagination of tytle to the countrie'. The lord deputy, on the other hand, dismissed these claims as illusory and ominously threatened O'More with the loss of 'lyffe, land and all' if he was not content to accept the plantation and settle on what the crown granted him.[124]

What was also obvious to Sidney was the failure of the Laois/Offaly experiment as a model colony. In fact the colony only survived because the settlers were on garrison wages. Pessimistically, the deputy concluded in April 1575 that the debased nature of the Laois/Offaly colony called imo question the potential success of future ventures involving assimilation between settlers and natives.

> I am not yet resolved what manner of warraunt it were best to devise to encrease her majesties rent, and get her tenants. For first, to have meere Irish were verie perrillous, and of others of this countrie birthe few there be, that I knowe of wealthe, that be fermors there. And soch of that countrie birthe as are neadie, and have no wealthe, I think theim not the fittest tenaunts heere... For I will undertake for every penny she receiveth in rent for land there, shee geveth wagies xiid. to kepe that lande. Yet I will never consent that the countrie be habandoned in any sorte, for helde it shalbe. But onelye herebye to not[e] unto you by the way, what a deare purchase this is, and hath bene to the crowne, and, by the example of this you may judge of the rest that are of this nature.[125]

These discouraging conclusions did not bode well for future relations between the O'Mores and the government. Despite the fact that Rory Óg was pardoned in June 1576, Sidney hesitated to settle his claims. The discrepancy between what the O'More felt was his just portion as the O'More and former lord of Laois, and what Sidney seemed ready to countenance, followed by the delay in settling with him at all, must be credited with the eventual uprising of Rory Óg in January 1577. Another obvious contributing factor was that Sidney provocatively advanced Gaelic loyalists who had a known animosity towards Rory. In June 1576 the deputy had appointed Sir Barnaby Fitzpatrick, the baron of Upper Ossory and an old ally of Sidney's from their youth at court, to the revived post of lieutenant of the Kings and Queens counties. Fitzpatrick was given powers of martial law and immediately set about harassing the O'Mores.[126] Was Fitzpatrick to replace the O'Dempseys as the stick with which the government would finally beat the O'Mores?

Rory Óg did not wait around to find out if this was the case, his response was both daring and sensational. Attempting to transform the tangled web of local Gaelic-settler politics, O'More made a dramatic raid into the heart of the Pale on the third of March 1577 and burned a major portion of the town of Naas to the ground.[127] If the aim of O'More was to demonstrate his importance as a figure to be reckoned with in the midlands in the hope of re-opening negotiations with the government, then he was sadly mistaken. For the raid on Naas sealed his fate and the fate of the O'Mores in the eyes of Sidney. This dramatic incursion into the heart of the area of English rule exposed the vulnerability of Sidney's control just as he was under the threat of a strike against the cess within the Pale itself. Facing criticism at court, and increasing resistance to his military impositions in the Pale, Sidney was not to be humiliated by what he saw as a mere Gaelic 'Robin Hood'.[128] Sidney decided on war to the death.

Sidney issued Francis Cosby with a commission of martial law on the 18 March 1577, and from this point on it is clear that no quarter was given on either side. The deputy endorsed the actions of his sub-ordinates in the midlands. 'So muche of late hath their principall men ben bereft of them by the great dilligen[c]e, pollecye and payne takinge of my lord of Upper Osserie, Mr. Cosbye, Harpoole, and Owen Mac Huge'.[129] By August 1577, 150 O'Mores had died as a result of the campaigns of this group. In desperation Rory Óg responded by the September burning of the town of Leighlin in Carlow.[130] In reply Sidney decided upon the total extermination, either by device or stratagem, to end the 'insolencie of the rebelles'.[131] The deputy's resolve for total elimination hardened after O'More kidnapped his nephew Captain Harrington and a relative, Alexander Cosby, and burned the town of Carlow:

> I...hope, on all sides, so to hedge theim in, as somme one or other of the companye ... shall light upon theim. And although I have to deal with a flyenge foe,....yet so maney starting holes and muffets he hath to fly unto, and soch ayde and succor of somme of his neighbours, as I shall not so easilye light upon hym, but onelye by good guydinge; yet some of his best and principall followers I clayle cut of, and pare his winges by little and little as I can; for I will neither spare travell nor chardgies to make some good ende of this service...I meane, by the totall extirpacion of those rebells.[132]

The capture of his nephew made the problem of the O'Mores more acute than the damage done and the actual financial cost. It also made it intensely personal. For Rory scornfully mistreated his highly connected prisoner, 'Carying him from place to place,' in a manner described in Sidney's 'Narrative' as 'most like a slave.' Rory Óg's actions represented a serious slight to Sidney's sense of personal and family honour. O'More went on to add insult to injury when, despite entrapment in the woods, he, viciously mutilated Harrington and then, to use Sidney's term, 'miracouslye' escaped.[133]

O'More's survival was especially baffling considering the intensity and the brutality of the massive hunt for him: 'straunge that the prosecucion of hym, having bene so fervent, his escapes so beyond all opinion, the execucion so blouddye, by cutting of his company from 500 to 50...'[134] There is even evidence to suggest that the lord deputy authorized a plot to assassinate Rory.[135] Sidney could only attribute O'More's escapes, like his propagandist Derricke's invective in the *Image of Irelande* (1581), 'to either Swiftness of his footmanship, or else rather (if it be lawfull so to deme) by Sorcerie or enchauntement,' i.e. witchcraft.[136]

These extreme circumstances and this horrific campaign of attrition provide the context for the attempt by Cosby, Hartpole, and O'Dempsey to eliminate an O'More grouping at Mullaghmast in March 1578.

> A horrible and abominable act of treachery was committed by the English..upon that part of the people of Offally and Leix..It was effected thus, they were all summoned to show themselves with greatest number they could be able to bring with them, at the great rath of Mullagh-Maistean; and on their arrival at that place, they were surrounded on every side by four lines of soldiers and cavalry, who proceeded to shoot and slaughter without mercy, so that not a single individual escaped, by flight or force.[137]

It should be no surprise that official sources are silent on this event, yet that Sidney endorsed the type of activities which culminated in this particular atrocity is already apparent. Derricke provides us with sufficient evidence to suggest that the annihilation of Gaelic Irish resistance to the plantation was a goal of the Sidney administration. The level of hatred expressed against the demonized O'Mores is well expressed in Derricke's *Image*.[138]

That this was a war to the death and that Sidney endorsed it is suggested in a reference in the English state paper evidence of 1577. In a letter to the privy council in London, Sidney praises his subordinates,

Cosby and Hartpole, for the 'great diligence, pollecye and payne takinge' in the elimination of the 'principal men' of the O'Mores and O'Connors.[139] Cosby's commission of martial law issued in March 1577 specifically cleared him of responsibility for the elimination of 'Rory Óge..and all other traitors and rebels in any place where they may be found.'[140] Cosby's discretion was sweeping: 'and where he shall find the rebels have been *maintained or aided by any persons,* he may commit such to gaol *or execute them by martial law at his discretion.'*[141] Sidney endorses these sweeping powers when he declares later in November 1577 that he intends the 'totall extirpacion of those rebells'.[142] This and the earlier cited suggestions of a knowledge and approval of efforts to eliminate the recalcitrant midland Gaelic Irish, reinforce the evidence of Derricke's text, *The Image of Irelande,* which un-apologetically asserts Sidney's desire through 'sleight' and 'stratagems' to achieve the end of the O'More 'rebel' problem.[143]

Mullaghmast (Mullamast is a townland in parish of Narraghmore, Co. Kildare) is also described in another Gaelic source, the *Annals of Loch Cé*:

> Treachery was committed by Master Francis and by Macomas and the Saxons on Muirchertach O'Mordha and on his people: and the place where this treachery was committed was in the great rath of Mullagh Maistin; and Muirchertach and seventy-four men were slain there; and no uglier deed than that was ever committed in Eirinn.[144]

Both the *Loch Cé* and the *Annála Ríoghachta Éireann* accounts suggest that the victims went to the meeting under a protection, i.e. the traditional military mechanism for safe passage and parley.[145] Despite dating problems, the latter version is the more reliable of the two. It mentions a specific victim, Muirchertach O'Mordha, a supporter of Rory Óg, and a specific perpetrator, the seneschal of the Queen's County, Francis Cosby. Thady Dowling's 'Annales Hiberniae' adds further and more credible detail to the event. This local source was based on the recollections of a contemporary. Dowling, the chancellor of the diocese of Leighlin, despite a generally pro-English bias, leaves little doubt as to the treachery involved in 1577/8 and the identity of the leading colonist perpetrators, Cosby and Hartpole.

> *Moris Mc Lasy Me Conyll dominus de Merggi (ut ille asseruit) et baronis de OMergi successor, cum 40 hominibus de sua familia post confederationem suam cum Rory O'Moardha et super quadam protectione interfectus fuit apud Molaghmastyn in*

comitatu Kildarie, ad eundum locum ob id propositum per
magistrum Cosby et Robert Harpoll, sub umbra servitii accersitus
collusorie.[146]

Additional evidence that suggests that the massacre was part of a
pattern to eliminate the dispossessed O'Mores, uncharacteristically,
survives in the most unlikely of Irish written sources. A Gaelic
surgeon/scribe, Corc Óg O'Cadhla, records in the margins of a
manuscript medical treatise in March 1577/8 what he refers to as
[Gnimha nachar dhaighmaiseach] 'disgraceful deeds' which occurred
[beacan reimhe] 'a short time ago' at Mullaghmast.[147] The medical scribe
had no doubts as to who was to blame for the atrocity. According to
O'Cadhla the O'Mores were tricked into a meeting under the protection
of *'an ghiusdis. Sir Henry Sitny'* and slaughtered by, *'Harpol Saxanach*
do muinntir an ghiuisdis sin'.[148] In O'Cadhla's text Mullaghmast is seen
as part of a pattern directly linked to Sidney and the effort to
exterminate the more stubborn elements of Gaelic resistance:

> *[Agus] do tinnsenadh gnimha roghrainemla leo sin do denamh ar*
> *fud choigedh Laighen a ninphaidh sin la Saxanachaibh ..a raibhe*
> *do clannaibh Gaoideal a nasard [agus] a naimhreadh innti a*
> *mbreith fein do thabairt doibh [agus] toidhechd chum laithreach*
> *clanna Gall [agus] an ghiuisdis. [Agus] ni do badh ferr na mar do*
> *rinneadh risin fedain adubramar dogentaidhe ru uili da*
> *dtigidis.*[149]

The scribe links Mullaghmast to the effort to eliminate Rory Óg when
he reports on the unprecedented nature of this headhunt. He relates
how earlier Rory's wife was killed, 'and with her have been killed
women, and boys, and humble folk, and people young and old, who
according to all seeming, deserved not to be put to the sword'.[150]

Under these conditions it was unlikely that Rory Óg could survive for
long and at the end of June 1578 he was killed by the Gaelic kerne of
the baron of Upper Ossory, Sir Barnaby Fitzpatrick.[151] His death marked
the end to a decisive phase in O'More efforts to restore their position of
dominance in Laois and to achieve either a stake in the plantation or a
return to the old order of Gaelic lordship.[152] Rory Óg alternated
between these two obviously contradictory goals. Never again would
the O'Mores, of their own power, pose such a threat to the plantation
or the Pale.[153]

The consolidation of English control to 1603

The O'Mores were in fact so weakened in the period 1578 and 1588 that their chief, James 'Meagh' Mac Kedagh, served Captain Humphrey Mackworth in mopping up operations against the remaining Ruaidhrí Mac Conaill sept. Mackworth's rule in the midlands was brutal. Yet not uncharacteristic given Lord Deputy Grey's simultaneous and severe repression of the Baltinglass revolt and the Desmond rebellion. James 'Meagh' and the Mac Kedagh sept achieved a brief moment of prominence in Laois though co-operation with Grey (1580-82), and the ensuing administration of Sir John Perrot (1584-88).[154] Yet this came at a terrible price. They essentially turned a blind eye to Mackworth's arbitrary elimination of other prominent Laois Gaelic gentlemen. Mackworth had two of these, Maol-Lochlainn O'Kelly, and Rossa Mac Maol-Lochlainn O'More, and their followers killed in his own house in Monasterevin after a banquet in May 1582.[155] It is obvious that James 'Meagh' and the Mac Kedaghs were aware of the vicious environment in which they operated by associating with the English captains. Writing to his brother James from the Tower in London, Thomas Mac Kedagh, warns him to guard against two of his English neighbours: 'their surnames is H & M, they are accustomed to carry sugar and poison together in their mouths'. Marginal notes written by lord deputy Grey's secretary, the poet Edmund Spenser, identify these two figures as Hartpole and Mackworth.[156] In fact the clearest indication of the state of O'More power under the Mac Kedaghs was their offer in January 1584, in collaboration with Ralph Lane, the eventual commander of the failed English colony in Roanoke, to transplant themselves to Kerry. Though little came of this startling scheme, it is indicative of the alienation of the dispossessed Mac Kedaghs from their fellow O'Mores and their traditional lands in Laois.[157]

The plantation gained a breathing space between 1586 and 1596, only to be plunged into chaos again by Rory's Óg's son Uaithne (Owny) Mac Ruaidhrí. Yet his campaign was not exclusively based on O'More resources or interest. Though it started with a traditional settling of scores, an assault on the Cosby lands at Stradbally in May 1596, it was essentially carried out as an extension of the efforts of Hugh O'Neill, the earl of Tyrone. As one of O'Neill's more capable Leinster allies, Owny is noted for the damage done to the earl of Essex's forces at the 'Pass of the Plumes' in May 1599 and for the capture of 'Black Thomas' Butler the 10th earl of Ormond. Yet these actions were part of the wider conflict that was the Nine Years War (1594-1603) and, though locally important, were subordinate to the larger military actions and politics of the period.[158]

This awful war had lasting impact on all the inhabitants of Laois. For the planters it often meant flight, destruction and sometimes death. For the majority of the Gaelic population the scorched earth policy of the lord deputy Mountjoy (1600-1603) carried out in August 1600 brought famine and suffering. That same month Mountjoy's army tracked down and killed Owny Mac Rory, finally ending O'More resistance and ensuring that the planters would enter the seventeenth century secure in their holdings and dominating the local environment. This security was enhanced by the removal of the last vestiges of the Gaelic land-holding classes that had participated in the plantation. By 1603 virtually all of them had gone under as a consequence of 'rebellion' against the crown. In fact this conflict put the end to a slow attrition that had began shortly after the original granting in 1563-4. Six lost their lands by 1571 as a consequence of either settler aggrandizement or partici-pation in the Butler revolt. A further two lost their lands in the aftermath of the Rory Óg disturbances by 1578. A final ten were eliminated as a direct consequence of participation in the Nine Years War in Laois.[159]

This conclusion to Gaelic involvement in plantation was not inevitable. Though the plantation was flawed in its original exclusion of the leading O'More septs, the government had various opportunities to assimilate the dispossessed elites. Again and again, they failed to make anything of them. Repeated changes of policy, occasioned by the rotation of the senior government official, the lord deputy, did not help matters. The forced reliance on the local settler elite and the garrisons came at a high price in Gaelic-government relations. In the interest of short-term financial and military expediency, the crown was compelled to ignore the settler's record of brutal aggrandizement. From the 1550s onwards, martial law and arbitrary killings embittered relations between settlers and natives. This bitterness provided the dispossessed Gaelic elites like the Mac Conaill O'Mores with ready followers when they attempted to assert their claims by force of arms. Repeated O'More uprisings, brought repeated martial law and brutality. The crown's senior officials-lord deputies like Sussex, Fitzwilliam and Sidney-either endorsed or turned a blind eye to these actions. The ensuing cycle of violence and counter-violence culminated in the atrocity at Mullaghmast. The end result of this extended process was the virtual elimination of the entire O'More political elite. With the smashing of the Mac Conaill and Mac Kedagh septs of the O'Mores, the social and political world of the Gaelic elites collapsed. The settler community, secure in their dominance, could begin the consolidation of the political apparatus of the shire and the common law. They could also return to rebuild their castles and bawns secure in the final elimination of the last vestiges of the Gaelic lordship of Laois.[160]

References

1. 'A map of the King's and Queen's counties alias Leix and Offaly', 1563 (Trinity College, Dublin, MS 1209, 9): also a copy in the British Library, London, 'Map of the interior parts of Ireland' (Cotton MSS, Augustus I, ii, 40), and one in the National Maritime Museum, Greenwich (MS p. 49), Dartmouth Maps of Ireland, 33). For an analysis of this map/maps see J. H. Andrews and R. Loeber, 'An Elizabethan map of Leix and Offaly: cartography, topgraphy and architecture' in *Offaly: history and society,* pp 243-85.

2. The classic study of this initiative is Brendan Bradshaw's, *The Irish constitutional revolution of the sixteenth century* (Cambridge, 1979).

3. *N.H.I.,* iii, p. 49.

4. Ciaran Brady, *The chief governors: The rise and fall of reform government in Tudor Ireland, 1536-1588* (Cambridge, 1994), pp 7-29, see especially, pp 26-7: his ch. i; 'Reform as process' takes issue with Bradshaw's assessment of surrender and regrant, and with the motives of its chief practitioner, Sir Anthony St. Leger.

5. 'Concordia facta inter Petrum O'More ...', 14 Jan. 1538, *State Papers: King Henry the Eight,* 11 vols (London, 1830-52), ii, 541-2, hereafter referred to as *S.P. Hen. VIII.*

6. Ibid.

7. 'Grey to Cromwell', 11 Mar., 'Manner and form of parliament', 2 Mar., 'Forma submissionis Domini Barnardi O'Conour, nuper Domini et Capitanei de Offaley, 6 Mar. 1538, *S.P. Henry VIII,* ii, 554-556-61.

8. 'Certain articles ... by thErle of Ormond', Aug,. 1538, *S.P. Henry VIII,* iii, 77-81.

9. The implications of the ending of the medieval frontier are more broadly discussed in Steven Ellis's, *Tudor frontiers and noble power: The making of the British state* (Oxford, 1995).

10. The three Mac Conaill brothers were the sons of Conaill Mac Maol-Lochlainn O'More, who preceeded his brother Piaras as lord or captain of the O'Mores; for greater detail see, 'The council to Cromwell', 'Certaine articlis ... bi thErle of Ormunde', 'Certayne articcles ... for the parthe of O'More', 10 June 1538, *S.P. Henry VIII,* iii, 23-29; Ormond describes the Mac Conaill brothers as 'Thomas Fitz Geraldes mynons' in a letter to Robert Cowley, 20 June 1538, *S.P. Henry VIII,* iii, 33.

11. 'Identura facta inter ... Dominum Leonardum Gray ... et Petrum O'More', 24 Aug. 1538, where the O'More is recognised as having 'domina et superioritates in Lexia', *S.P. Henry VIII,* iii, 88-90.

12. 'Lord deputy [St. Leger] and council to the king', 13 Nov. 1540, *S.P. Henry VIII,* iii, 264-6, and 'Indenture', 13 May 1541, *Cal. Carew MSS, 1515-71,* 185-6.

13. Colm Lennon, *Sixteenth-century Ireland: the incomplete conquest* (Dublin, 1994), hereafter, *Sixteenth-century Ire.;* St. Leger's initiative is outlined in, ch. 6, pp 152-167.

14. Lennon, *Sixteenth-century Ire.,* pp 163-4, Giolla Pádraig married Brian O'Connor's daughter, for the dispute, see, 'Lord justice [Brabazon] and council to St. Leger', 24 Mar. 1544, *S.P. Henry VIII,* iii, 490-492, 'Brabazon to Henry VIII', 20 May 1544, *S.P. Henry VIII,* iii, 501-3, 'Rory O'More to the King', June 1544 (S.P. 60/11/49).

15. Bradshaw, *Constit. rev.,* pp 258-63; Ellis, *Tudor Ireland,* pp 228-37; and significantly, D. G. White, 'The reign of Edward VI in Ireland', *IHS,* 14 (1964-5), pp 197-211.

16. Brady, *Chief governors,* ch. 2.

17. He cites as evidence the constant re-appointment of St. Leger, and describes

Bellingham's proposals for the midlands as 'relatively modest', ibid., p. 49.

18. 'Walter Cowley to Privy Council', 1546, *S.P. Henry VIII*, iii, 578-?; Dean Gunter White, 'Tudor Plantations in Ireland to 1571' (Unpublished Ph.D. thesis, University of Dublin, 1967), 2 vols, see i, pp 181-92, hereafter, 'Tudor plantations'; and his 'Reign of Edw. VI', p. 199.

19. White estimates that the fort was established between May and June 1548, 'Tudor Plantations', i, 206.

20. D. G. White, 'The reign of Edward VI in Ireland', pp 199-204; Ellis, *Tudor Ire.*, pp 228-9; Lennon, *Sixteenth century Ire.*, pp 164-166.

21. 'Bellingham to Privy Council', Aug. 1548 (S.P. 61/1/84-5).

22. 'John Brereton, Richard Aylmer, Francis Cosby, and James Mac Gerald to Bellingham', 'Cosbie to same', 'Same to same', 'Same to same', 'Same to Travers', July 1548; 'Walter Pepparde to same', 3 Aug. 1548 (S.P. 61/1/41, 46, 47, 50, 51, 53).

23. 'Robert Cowley to Cromwell', 1537, *S.P. Henry VIII*, iii, 445-452; Francis Herbert proposed banishing the O'Connors and planting Englishmen in their stead, 'Herbert to the Duke of Norfolk', 24 Jan. 1538 (S.P. 60/6/7).

24. 'A not[e] given to ... Bellingham', Dec. 1547 (B.L., Lansdowne MS 159, no. 5), in D. G. White, 'The reign of Edward VI', pp 199-200; 'Lord Chancellor Alen to Sir William Paget', and 'Same to Protector Somerset', 21 Nov. 1548 (S.P. 61/1/129, 130), Alen proposed the banishment of O'More and O'Connor to Calais or Boulogne; for leases see, White, 'Reign', p. 104, and 'Tudor plantations', i, 222-4, especially those of Brian Jones and Giles Hovendon, 'Walter Cowley to Bellingham', 8 Mar. 1549, 'Brian Jones to same' (S.P. 61/2/24, 35); Cowley also proposed the establishment of an office of 'captainship' and a survey of the two lordships, 'Same to same', 14 Mar. 1549 (S.P. 61/2/25).

25. As above, note no. 22.

26. '[St. Leger's] remembrances', June 1550; 'King and council to St. Leger', July 1550 (S.P. 61/2/55, 57-58); 'Same', July 1550, *Cal. Carew MSS 1515-71*, 226-30; White, 'Tudor plantations', i, 239.

27. The major portion of Cowley's survey to survive is of Offaly, see Edmund Curtis, 'The survey of Offaly in 1550' in *Hermathena*, xx, no. 45 (1930), 312-52; a fragment of the Laois survey exists as 'Extent of Leix ... 1550' in *Ormond deeds*, v, 56-9.

28. The more prominent Laois beneficiaries included, Flood, Dunkerley, Apowell, John Lee, John Thomas Bowen, Giles Hovendon, Francis Cosby, Walter Peppard, Fay, King, Walkely, Herbert, March; see also, 'Walter Cowley to Earl of Wiltshire'. 21 Feb. 1551 (S.P. 61/3/2).

29. White, 'Tudor plantations', i, 252-60; 'Instructions to Sir James Croft', May 1551 (S.P. 61/3/32).

30. 'Lord deputy to Privy Council', 26 Jan. 1552 (S.P. 61/4/4); White estimates that the two forts cost 1,000 marks to run in 1550, while the £1,000 rent from the region existed only on paper; furthermore the government spent IR£43,000 in military expenses from 1550 to 1552, see 'Tudor plantations', i, 206-11.

31. 'Offer of Gerald Aylmer ...', 10 Dec. 1550 (S.P. 62/2/69}; 'Edward Walshe's 'conjectures' concerning the state of Ireland [1552]', in *I.H.S.*, v (1947), 303-33; Ellis, *Tudor Ire.*, pp 231-2.

32. 'Chancellor of Ireland to the duke of Northumberland', 6 May 1552 (B.L. Harlein MS 35, ff. 180-95, quote from F. 194a, see also, Cal. Carew MSS, 1515-1571, 235-47.

33. For more detail on the 11th earl's role, see the author's *Surviving the Tudors:*

Gerald Fitzgerald 'The Wizard Earl' and English rule in Ireland 1536-1586; Giolla-Pádraig was succeeded by his younger brother Conall Óg Mac Conaill O'More.

34. White, 'Tudor plantations', i, 339-42.

35. Ciaran Brady suggests that St. Leger endorsed limited colonization for a variety of strategic reasons but also because it served as an 'example ... of the material and cultural benefits which were to be derived from the adoption of English laws and customs'. *Chief governors,* pp 50-3.

36. 'St. Leger to privy council', 31 May 1554 (B.L. Cotton MS, Titus BXI, ff. 387-89.

37. 'Orders for Laois', 1556 (S.P. 62/1/19), 'Consignation of Laois', 1556 (S.P. 62-1/2); White, 'Tudor Plantations', chs. 5-7; for summary, see, *Sixteenth century Ire.,* pp 179-80; Ellis, *Tudor Ire.,* pp 234-5; Vincent P. Carey, 'Gaelic reaction to plantation: The case of the O'More and O'Connor lordships of Laois and Offaly (unpublished M.A. Thesis, St. Patrick's College Maynooth, 1985), hereafter, 'Gaelic reaction, ch. i; Dunlop, 'Plantation'.

38. Brady, *Chief governors,* pp 72-6, 94-6.

39. Dunlop, 'Plantation', pp 67-8.

40. 'Orders for Laois', 1556 (S.P. 62/1/19), 'Consignation of Laois', 1556 (S.P. 61/1/2).

41. 'Proc. of the deputy and council', 25 Feb. 1557, *Cal. Carew MSS, 1515-74,* pp 262-4; Dunlop, 'Plantation', *A.P.C., Ire. 1556-71,* pp 27-31.

42. 'Deputy and council to the King' [abstracts in French with notes], 'Deputy to the King [Philip] and Queen [Mary]' 4 Apr. 1557 (S.P. 61/1/28, 29); *Sixteenth century Ire.,* 181, Ellis, *Tudor Ire.,* 235, Carey, 'Gaelic reaction', p. 20.

43. 'King and Queen to deputy', 1 June, 'Secretary [John Boxoll] to deputy', 2 June, 'King and Queen to deputy', 23 June 1557 (S.P. 61/1/40, 41, 44); where the mysterious disappearance of the draft legislation for Laois/Offaly on two separate occasions is recorded.

44. 21 Oct. 1557, *A.P.C., Ire.,* pp 41-3, White, 'Tudor plantations', 396.

45. 'An act for the disposition of Leix and Offaly' 1557 (S.P. 61/1/60); see also [Statutes] *In this volume are contained all the statutes [10 Hen. VI-Eliz. I] made in Ireland* (R. Tottle, 1572).

46. *Fiants, Ire. Eliz.,* no. 31; 'Sussex to Boxoll', 8 June 1558 (S.P. 62/2/50).

47. For cesses for the forts in this period, see, *A.P.C., Ire., 1556-71,* pp 49-50, 66-7, 73-4, for Pale dissension, see Brady, *Chief governors,* 84-91.

48. 'Archbishop of Armagh's opinion touching Ireland', July 1558 (B.L. Harlein MSS, 35, no. 4), see also printed version in *County Louth Archaeological Society Journal,* ii (1909), 149-64.

49. 'Elizabeth's instructions to Sussex and council', 16 July 1559 (S.P. 63/1/61}; and *Cal. Carew MSS, 1515-71,* 279-91.

50. *Fiants Ire., Eliz.,* no. 193; 'Eliz. instr. to Sussex', May 1560 (S.P. 3/2/18).

51. Ellis, *Tudor Ire.,* pp 240-2.

52. 'Memoranda of matters ...', 25 Feb. 1561; 'Instructions for the earl of Sussex'; 24 May 15561 (S.P. 63/3/31, 78); 'Lieutenant to the queen', 23 Oct. 1561 (S.P. 63/4/61).

53. 'Vice treasurer's accounts', *H.M.C. rep. DeLisle and Dudley MSS,* i, 364-440; for table of payments, 'Gaelic reaction', p. 29.

54. 'By what meanes the countries of Ophaly and Leix ...', 1559 (S.P. 63/1/84), I am grateful to Dr. Ciaran Brady for drawing my attention to this document and for identifying Cormac O'Connor as the likely author.

55. Ibid.

56. 'Report of the earl of Sussex', 1562, *Cal. Carew MSS, 1515-71,* pp 330-44, espec. p. 338.

57. 'Sussex to Cecil', 20 Dec. 1561 (S.P. 63/4/81); 'Sussex to queen', 6 Sept. 1562 (S.P. 63/7/6, enclose iii).

58. Grant to Henry Colley, *Fiants Ire., Eliz.*, no. 474; White, 'Tudor plantations', ii, 40-44.

59. 'Instruction for the earl of Sussex', 24 May 1561 (S.P. 63/3/31).

60. 'A relation of the earl of Sussex', 1652, Cal. Carew MSS, 1515-71, pp 344-9.

61. Nor was this the only concession to Gaelic landholding practices. The grantee could not alienate or grant any part of his estate in fee simple, fee tail, or term of life, except for a third part, which they could alienate to their younger sons for term of life or lives. White, 'Tudor plantations', ii, 40-44.

62. Ibid., 44-6.

63. 'Queen of Sussex', 15 Dec. 1560, 'Same to Ormond', 16 Dec. 1560 (S.P. 63/2/50, 51); 'Examination of Domhnaill Mac Vicar', 13 or 14 Jan. 1561 (S.P. 63/3/2, and B.L., Cotton MSS, Titus BXIII, ff 29-30).

64. 'Cecil to Sussex', 3 Mar., 15 Apr. 1563 (B.L. Cotton MSS, Titus XIII, 103, 108); 'Sussex to Queen', 22 Sept. 1563 (S.P. 63/9/17); 'Cusack to Cecil', 2 Feb., 'Commissioners Wroth and Arnold to privy council', 16 Feb., 'Fitzwilliam to Cecil', 21 Feb., 'Cusack to Cecil', 17 Apr. 1564 (S.P. 63/10/12, 15, 17, 51).

65. 15 Mar. 1563, and 10 Apr. 1564, *A.P.C. Ire.,* 1556-71, 128-30, 130-32.

66. For detail on the war in the midlands between 1564-5, see White, 'Tudor plantations', ch. xiv.

67. 'Arnold and council to queen', 31 Oct. 1564 (S.P. 63/11/97); 'Fitzwilliam to Cecil', 3 Apr. 1565 (S.P. 63/13/6).

68. For Sidney's career, see *Sixteenth century Ire.,* pp 182-187, for the latest interpretation, see Brady, *Chief governors,* ch. iv, see also Nicholas Canny, *The Elizabethan conquest of Ireland: a pattern established, 1565-1576* (Hassocks, 1976).

69. 'Sir Henry Sidney's articles', 20 May 1565 (S.P. 63/13/45, 46).

70. 'Instructions for Sidney', 5 Oct. 1565 (S.P. 63/15/4).

71. He found only one estate in Laois vacant, 'Sidney and council to the privy council', 13 Apr. 1566 (S.P. 63/17/8).

72. White, 'Tudor plantations', 11, 138-42.

73. 'The Irish in Fitzwilliam's band', 1565 (S.P. 63/16/61); more detail, White, 'Tudor plantations', ii, 188-193.

74. Henry Colley was appointed for Offaly, 'Sidney to Cecil', 20 Apr. 1566 (S.P. 63/17/27).

75. Ciaran Brady, 'The Government of Ireland c. 1540-1583' (unpublished Ph.D. thesis, University of Dublin, 1980), p. 209; 'Sidney and council to the privy council', 13 Apr. 1566 (S.P. 63/17/13).

76. 'Sidney to privy council', 15 Apr. 1566 (S.P. 63/17/13).

77. 'Sidney and council to same', 13 April 1566 (S.P. 63/17/8).

78. *A.P.C.I.,* 1556-71, pp 156-7.

79. 'Sidney to Cecil', 18 Nov. 1566 (S.P. 63/19/51).

80. *Sidney State Papers 1565-70,* ed. Thomás O'Laidhin (Dublin, 1962), no. 75; *Fiants Ire., Eliz.,* nos 1500, 1510.

81. 'A plat of Maryborough', 1571 (S.P. 63/2/66), misdated as 1560 in calendar but D. G. White uses internal evidence to date no earlier than March 1571.

82. P. J. Duffy, 'The territorial organization of Gaelic landownership and its transformation in County Monaghan 1591-1641' in *Ir. Geog.,* xiv (1981), pp 1-26, see also Kenneth Nicholls, *Gaelic and Gaelicised Ireland* (Dublin, 1972), *Land, law and society in sixteenth-century Ireland* (Dublin 1976), and 'Gaelic society

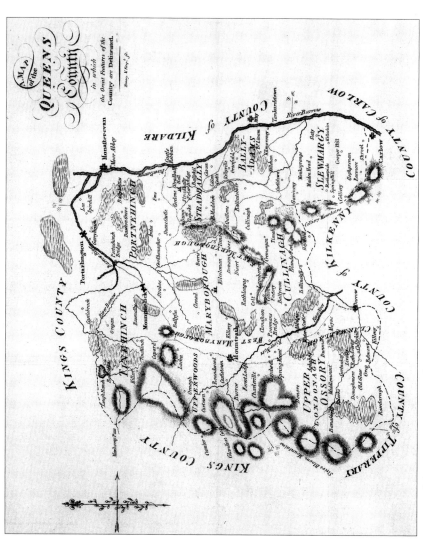

'A map of the Queen's County' from Coote, *Statistical Survey*.

Rathdowney, Sheet 28, O.S. 1841.

Rathdowney (Redmond).

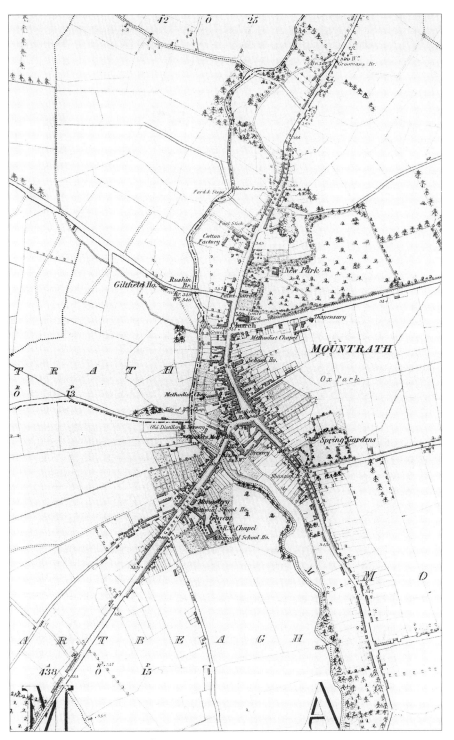

Mountrath, Sheet 17, O.S. 1841.

Mountrath (Redmond).

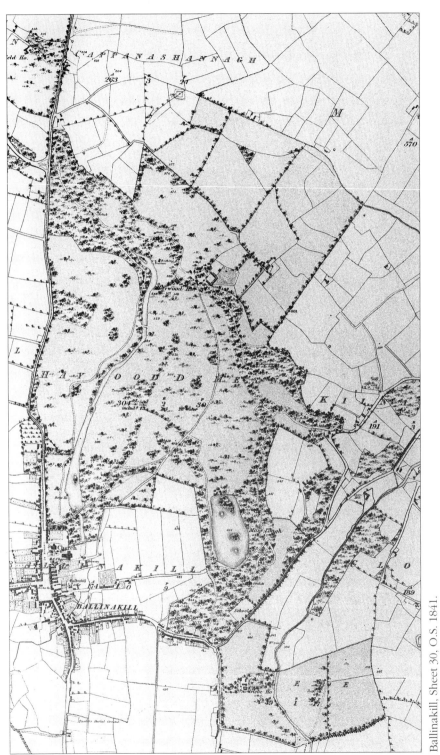

Ballinakill. Sheet 30, O.S. 1841.

Ballinakill (Redmond).

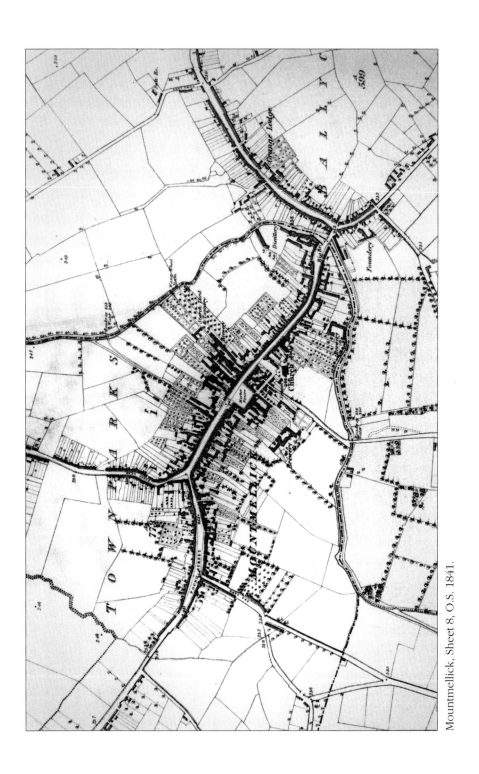

Mountmellick, Sheet 8, O.S. 1841.

Mountmellick (Redmond).

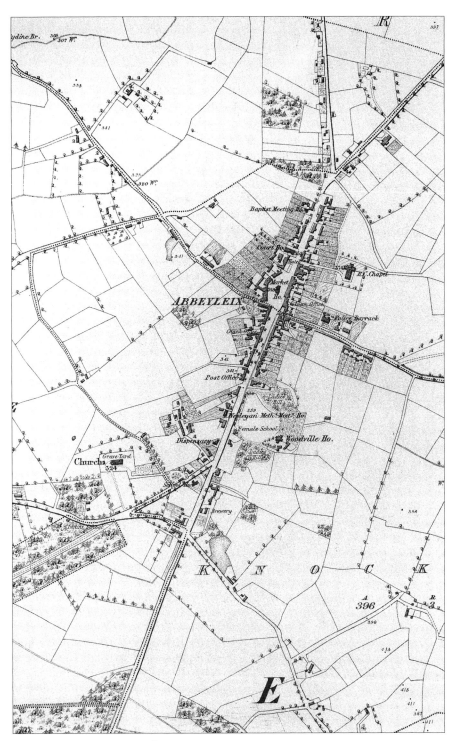

Abbeyleix, Sheet 23, O.S. 1841.

Abbeyleix (Lawrence).

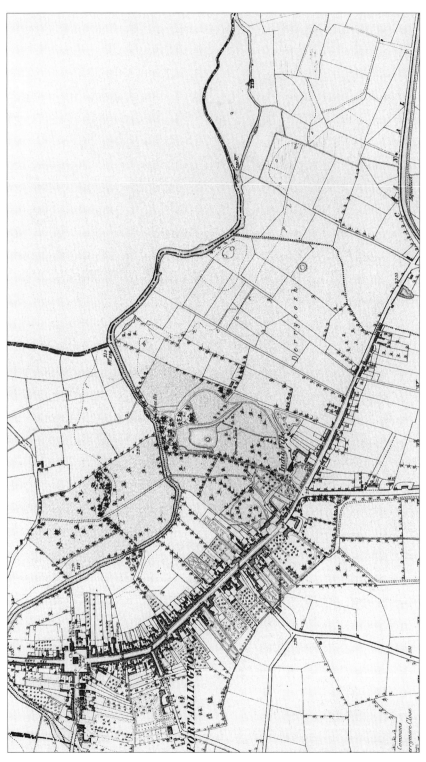

Portarlington, Sheet 5, O.S. 1841.

Portarlington (Redmond).

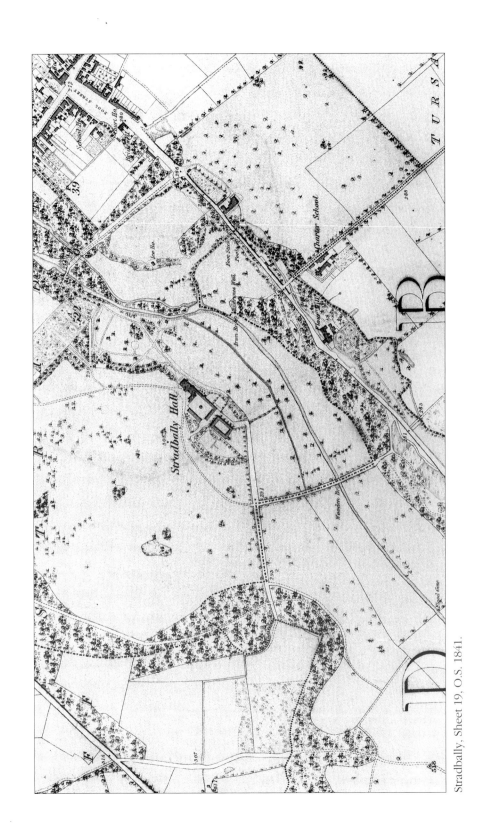

Stradbally, Sheet 19, O.S. 1841.

Stradbally (Redmond).

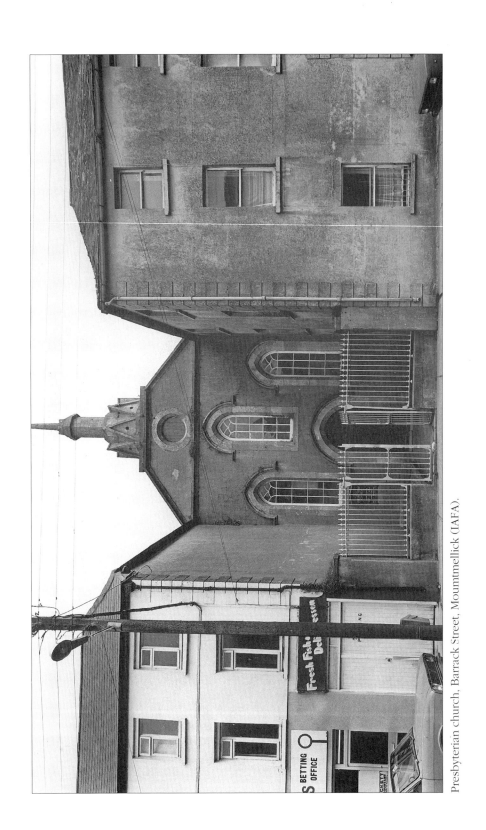

Presbyterian church, Barrack Street, Mountmellick (IAFA).

and economy in the high middle ages', in *N.H.I.*, ii, *Medieval Ireland 1169-1534*, ed. Art Cosgrove (Oxford, 1987).

83. For the O'Connor evidence, Edmund Curtis, 'Survey of Offaly', as above note, no. 27.

84. Canon John O'Hanlon and Edward O'Leary, *History of the Queen's County*, 2 vols (Dublin, 1907, 1914), hereafter, O'Hanlon, *Queen's Co.*, for client septs, see vol. ii, 443.

85. Mary O'Dowd, 'Land inheritance in early-modern Sligo', *Ir. Econ. Soc. Hist.*, x (1983), 5-18.

86. Based on B.L. Cotton MSS, Augustus I, ii, 40; and the notes of Canon O'Hanlon, *Queen's Co.*, ii, 44-6.

87. 17 June 1567, 'Queen's county chancery inquisition Eliz.', no. 1, *Inq. cancell. Hib. repert.*, i (Dublin, 1826-9); and for a more faithful transcription, see Lord Walter Fitzgerald, 'Historical notes on the O'Mores' in Kildare Arch. Soc. Jn., vi (1909-11), 1-89, transcript on 85-6.

88. Ibid.

89. Ibid.

90. 'Gaelic reaction', table 3, p. 156.

91. Katharine Simms, *From kings to warlords: The changing political structure of Gaelic Ireland in the later middle ages* (Woodbridge, 1987), p. 175.

92. Ibid., espec. ch. ix.

93. See in particular, *Fiants Ire., Eliz.*, nos. 1532, 2146, 2405, 2832, 2833, 2834, 2835, 4457, 4622, 4889, 5099 and 5367.

94. 'Extent of Leix, before Walter Cowley, 10 Dec. 1550', *Ormond deeds*, v, 56-9, for Gallen rent, see 'Gaelic reaction', p. 159.

95. 'Queen's county chancery inquis.', as above, note no. 90.

96. White, 'Tudor plantations', ii, 39-50, and for detail of lands granted, ii, appendix 2.

97. A. K. Longfield (ed.), *Fitzwilliam accounts 1560-65* (Dublin, 1960), pp 52, 53, 57, 69, 74, 78, 87, 99, 106.

98. *Fiants Ire., Eliz.*, nos. 596, 1222 and 1509, and White, 'Tudor plantations', ii, 69-70.

99. 'Gaelic reaction', ch. iv.

100. Dowling, *Annals*, p. 42; 'A livery to Sir Terance O'Dempsey', *Fiants Ire. Eliz.*, no. 3397.

101. *Fiants Ire., Eliz.*, nos. 2992, 5601.

102. 'Rough notes of manuscript history', May 1599 (S.P. 63/205/70).

103. 'Gaelic reaction', ch. iv.

104. 17 July 1566, *A.P.C. Ire., 1556-71*, p. 172.

105. 'Certificate by John Rowe', 4 Sept. 1565 (S.P. 63/15/34); *A.P.C. Ire., 1556-71*, p. 241.

106. 'Sidney to Privy Council', 13 Apr. 1566 (S.P. 63/17/8); 'Same to Sir Peter Carew', 28 May 1570 (S.P. 63/30/52).

107. 'Fitzwilliam to Cecil', 5 Feb. 1571, 'Lord chancellor to queen', 23 Mar. 1571 (S.P. 63/31/8, 33).

108. 'Fitzwilliam to queen', 7 Apr. 1571, 'Same to privy council', 12 Apr. 1572, 'Same to queen', 4 Jan. 1572 (S.P. 63/32/2, 9 and S.P. 63/35/2).

109. 'Fitzwilliam to Burghley', 5 May, 'Same to privy council', 6 May, 'Henry Colley to Burghley', 12 May, 'Fitzwilliam to privy council', 28 June 1572 (S.P. 63/36/16, 17, 19, 48); 'Same to Burghley', 5 Aug. 1572 (S.P. 63/37/25), White, 'Tudor plantations', ii, 313,

110. 'Report by earls of Ormond and Kildare of their proceedings with Rory oge', 14 Aug. 1572 (S.P. 63/37/37).
111. Ibid.
112. Evidence for the granting of Gallen to the Mac Kedagh's is in 'Fitzwilliam to Burghley', 7 Apr. 1573 (S.P. 63/40/3).
113. for their story see 'Gaelic reaction', ch. iv.
114. 'Lord deputy to the privy council', 26 Aug. 1572, 'Same to same', 26 Aug. (S.P. 63/37/41, 42); Rory and eighty nine followers received a pardon on 19 Sept. 1572, this pardon included many O'More 'gentlemen' and, in particular, some of the sons of the Gaelic grantees, see *Fiants Ire., Eliz.*, no. 2146.
115. *Fiants Ire., Eliz.*, nos 1782, 1810, 1848, 2115, 2146, 2163, 2164, 2174, 3200; Fitzwilliam to the queen', 8 Feb. 1573 (S.P. 63/39/27).
116. 'Fitzwilliam to Burghley', 5 May 1572 (S.P. 63/36/15), 'Same to the queen', 18 Feb. 1573 (S.P. 63/39/27).
117. 'Fitzwilliam to the Queen', 18 Feb. 1573 (S.P. 63/39/27).
118. 'Fitzwilliam to Burghley', 7 Apr. 1573 (S.P. 63/40/3); 'Council to Fitzwilliam', 20 Mar. 1573 (Bodleian Library, Oxford, Carte MSS, 56, f. 137); Dunlop, 'Plantations', 77-8.
119. 'Fitzwilliam to Burghley', 7 Apr.
120. 'Nicholas White to Burghley', 17 July 1573 (S.P. 63/41/80).
121. 'Fitzwilliam to the Queen', 18 Feb., 'Same to Burghley, Sussex, Leicester and Walsingham', 18 Apr. 1574 (S.P. 63/45/72).
122. For detail, see 'Gaelic reaction', chs. ii and iii, and for a brief description, *Brady, Chief governors*, pp 261-4.
123. 'Sidney to the privy council', 15 Dec. 1575 (S.P. 63/54/17); Arthur Collins, *Letters and memorials of state*, 2 vols. (London, 1746), i, 81-85, hereafter, Collins, *Letters*.
124. Ibid.
125. 'Sidney to Walsingham', 27 Apr. 1576 (S.P. 63/55/37); Collins, *Letters*, i, 110-11.
126. Pardon for Rory Óg, 4 June, *Fiants Ire., Eliz.*, no. 2833; Grant of office to Sir Barnaby Fitzpatrick, 8 June 1576, *Fiants Ire., Eliz.*, no. 2843; 'Signey to Walsingham', 23 Jan. 1577, Collins, *Letters*, 156-9; 'Fitzpatrick to same', 30 Jan. 1577 (S.P. 63/57/8); see chapter 12 in this volume, David Edwards, 'The MacGiollapadraigs (Fitzpatricks) of Upper Ossory, 1532-1641'.
127. 'Sidney to the privy council', 17 Mar. 1577 (S.P. 63/57/39); Collins, *Letters*, i, 164-8; Dunlop, 'Plantations', pp 80-1.
128. For Sidney's difficulties over the cess, see Brady, *Chief governors*, pp 146-58.
129. See below, note no. 130.
130. Comm. to Francis Cosby, 18 Mar. 1577, *Fiants, Ire., Eliz.*, no. 2997; 'Sidney to queen', Aug. 1577, Collins, *Letters*, 205-6; 'Privy council [Ire.] to queen', 12 Sept. 1577 (S.P. 63/59/6), and Collins, *Letters*, i, 216-8.
131. 'Sir Henry Sidney to council in England', February 1577/8; 'Notes for Lodovick Briskett for the court', 14 June 1578, Collins, *Letters*, i, pp. 240-4, 261-2.
132. 'Sidney to the privy council', 26 Nov. 1577 (S.P. 63/59/57) and Collins, *Letters*, 229-3.
133. 'The villanous rebel fell upon my most dear nephue, being tyed in chaynes and him, most shamefully hacked ..., to the effusion of such a quantity of blood as was incredible to be tould. He brake his arm with that blunt sword, and cut off the little finger of one of his hands, and in his head so wounded him as I myself in his dressing did see his braynes moving', Sir Henry Sidney, 'Narrative ... to Sir Francis Walsingham', 1 Mar. 1583 (S.P. 12/159/1); published as 'Memoir ... addressed to Sir Francis Walsingham, 1583', in *U.J.A.*, 1st. ser., ii (1855), pp 33-52,

85-109, 336-57; 5 (1857), pp 299-322; 8 (1866), pp 179-95.

134. 'Sidney and council to Elizabeth', 20 Apr. 1578 (S.P. 63/60/42) and *Letters*, 248-51.

135. Henry Chettle, *Englandes mourning garment* (London, 1603), C1; Ciaran Brady, *Shane O'Neill* (Dublin, 1996), no. 6, pp 51-2.

136. 'Sidney to the privy council', 20 Apr. 1578 (S.P. 63/60/42); Collins, *Letters;* 248-51: for an extended discussion of the ideological background to the massacre, and for the dating of it in March 1578, see the author's John Derricke's *Image of Irelande*, Sir Henry Sidney, and the Massacre at Mullaghmast, 1578' in *I.H.S.*, xxxi, no. 723 (May, 1999).

137. *A.F.M.*, pp 1694-6; and for commentary, pp 1694-8.

138. *Image of Irelande*, p. 213.

139. 'Same to same', 17 March 1576/7, *Letters and memorials of state*, i, p. 167.

140. 18 March 1577, *Fiants Ire., Eliz.*, no. 2997.

141. Italics added by author, *Fiants Ire., Eliz.*, no. 2997.

142. 26 Nov. 1577, Collins, *Letters*, i, pp. 229-31.

143. For 'stratagems' and 'sleights', see *Image of Irelande*, pp 202 and 205.

144. *A.L.C.*, ii, pp 396-7.

145. For a discussion of the dating issue, see the author's 'The road to Mullaghmast', as above, note no. 136.

146. 'Annales Hiberniae' in *Annals of Ireland by Friar John Clyn and Thady Dowling*, ed. Richard Butler (Dublin, 1849), p. 42.

147. 'Lilium medicinae', *R.I.A.*, MS 24 P 14; copied in T. F. O'Rahilly, *Catalogue of the Irish manuscruips in the Royal Irish Academy* (Dublin, 1928); edited by Paul Walsh, 'Scraps from an Irish scribe' in *The Catholic Bulletin and Book Review*, Feb. 1930), pp 141-55.

148. According to Ó Cadhla, Muirchertach Mac Laoighseach O'More surrendered his hostages to Sidney in return for his protection, Harpole then killed them the next day. The act preceeded the atrocity at Mullaghmast; quoted in Walsh's 'Scraps', p. 146.

149. 'And a commencement was made at that time by the English of the doing of other very horrible deeds throughout the province of Leinster, namely, all the difficult and troublesome men of the province were ordered, under threat of penalty, to present themselves before the English and the Lord Justice, And a fate not better than that which befell those we have spoken of would have overtaken them all had they so presented themselves', text and translation from Walsh, 'Scraps', pp 47-8.

150. Ibid. Ó Cadhla dating of this portion of the manuscript on the 22 Mar. 1577, and his relation of the earlier death of 'Mairghred Mhaol' O'More, Rory's wife helps us positively fix the date of the massacre in March 1578, for more detailed evidence on a 1578 dating of this event, see my forthcoming 'Massacre at Mullaghmast', as above note no. 136.

151. 'Sidney to privy council', 1 July (S.P. 63/61/29), Collins, *Letters*, 263-5; 'Sir Edward Fitton to Burghley', 1 July, 'Some to Burghley', 6 July, Sir Nicholas Malbie to same', 26 July (S.P. 63/61/31, 32, 41); 'Council [Ire.] to the queen', 12 Sept. 1578 (S.P. 63/8).

152. Dowling, 'Annales Hiberniae', p. 42.

153. Ibid. Dowling summarised the damage O'More inflicted with the list of towns he burnt: 'Naas, Athy, Caterlough, Leighlin-Pontem, Rathcoyl, Tassagard, Kilbrid, Ballymore, Killy et Rathmore in Lagenia'.

154. For a discussion of the period, Ellis, *Tudor Ire.*, pp 278-297; Lennon, *Sixteenth century Ire.*, pp 187-236.
155. 'Gaelic reaction', 120-4.
156. 'Grey to Walsingham', 29 June 1582 (S.P. 63/93/64, enclosure i).
157. James 'Meagh' died in March 1595, 'Gaelic reaction', pp 197-203; Dunlop, 'Plantations', pp 86-7.
158. Dunlop, 'Plantations', pp 87-91, O'Hanlon, *History*, ii, 470-91.
159. The sons of Richard, Edmund, Walter, John and Thomas, the Keating grantees, Cathal Mac Fearganainm O'Kelly, Muircheartach Óg and Laoighseach Mac Muircheartach O'More, Edward Mac Maolmórdha and Seán Mac Kedagh O'More all lost their lives in the rebellion, 'Gaelic reaction', table vi; pp 209-10; and appendix ii.
160. Nicholas Canny describes the prosperity of many of the Laois settlers in the first half of the seventeenth century in 'The marginal kingdom: Ireland as a problem in the first British Empire' in Bernard Bailyn and Phillip Morgan (eds), *Strangers within the realm cultural margins of the first British empire* (Chapel Hill, 1991), pp 43-8. I would like to thank Dr. Colm Lennon, Prof. P.J. Corish, Dr. Lawrence Soroka and Debra Kimok for assistance with this project.

Chapter 10

EARLY URBAN DEVELOPMENT IN COUNTY LAOIS

JOHN BRADLEY

The early urban history of Laois is localised and specific, short-lived and sporadic. It began during the late twelfth and early thirteenth centuries when urbanisation was very much a feature of the eastern part of the county, focused in particular on the boroughs of Castletown, Killabban and the Newtown of Leys. By the middle of the fourteenth century these settlements were largely abandoned and never regained their earlier importance. For the succeeding two centuries (if the market place at Aghaboe is excluded because of its unclear status) Laois was without urban spaces. When town life resumed in the sixteenth century, it was effectively confined to one place, Port Laoise or Maryborough as it was then called. Port Laoise experienced ups and downs during the seventeenth century when, with the foundation of Ballinakill and Portarlington, new urban development was a trait of the extreme north and south. It was not until the eighteenth century that a county-wide urban network emerged. One of the major reasons for this interrupted and haphazard pattern of urban development is that the modern county is neither a natural geographical entity nor is it particularly ancient. When first shired, as Queen's County, in 1556 it consisted of little more than the eastern half of the present county. It then comprised the barony of Portnahinch, ruled by the Ó Ceallaigh (O'Kellys) of Uí Failge, and ancient Laoighis, ruled by the Ó Mórdha which was roughly equivalent to that part of the county which lies within the diocese of Leighlin, i.e. the baronies of Slievemargy, Ballyadams, Stradbally, Cullenagh, and Maryborough East and West. In 1572 the barony of Tinnahinch was added and in 1602 Upper Ossory, consisting of the baronies of Clandonagh, Clarmallagh and Upperwoods, was included. The present boundaries bear no relation to territorial units earlier than the sixteenth century and thirteenth century Laois, for instance, was divided between the medieval counties of Kildare, Carlow and Kilkenny, in addition to having unshired areas under Gaelic control.

Anglo-Norman urban development

Despite the presence of important central places at locations such as Aghaboe, Timahoe, Killeshin and Dunamase, there is no evidence for urban centres in Laois prior to the coming of the Anglo-Normans. The colonization began early. Adam de Hereford was granted the half-cantred of Aghaboe in c.1172, while settlement had commenced in Ui Buidhe (Oboy), Slievemargy and Timahoe by 1176.[1] All of these inroads were a result of expansion from the successful colonization of Kildare and most of the conquered territory was to be administered as part of that county for as long as Anglo-Norman power lasted in the region.[2] It was one thing to conquer an area but it was another to hold onto it and, in order to achieve this, the Anglo-Normans had to introduce settlers on whose loyalty they could rely. The standard means of achieving this was to offer land or privileges to prospective colonists. Land could only be granted to individuals of knightly class whereas privileges could be extended to everyone. The key attraction of the boroughs and towns established by the Anglo-Normans in Ireland was the set of privileges which they bestowed upon those willing to build a house within the settlement and work at some craft or trade. These individuals, known as burgesses, had a varied set of immunities but they normally included the rights of participating in urban government, of trial before equals, of marrying without needing the permission of a lord, of setting up in business or trade, and the freedom to travel.[3] The desire to become a burgess was based as much on the social status it conferred as on the opportunities it afforded of gaining wealth. Burgesses paid an annual rent, normally 1s., to the lord of the soil and a successful borough could be an important source of income for its founder. The motivation for establishing boroughs was essentially economic and although these settlements had the legal privileges of towns, they seem to have functioned as large villages. Although the Anglo-Normans initiated no towns in Laois they founded at least three boroughs, Castletown, Killabban and the Newtown of Leys, all in the east of the county. There may have been other boroughs, at centres like Aghaboe, Killeshin and Timahoe, but the historical documentation is lacking. It is interesting to note that two of the Laois boroughs were settlements prior to the coming of the Anglo-Normans. Killabban was a church site and Dunamase a secular fortress. The fact that the Anglo-Normans chose these locations for their boroughs may indicate that some form of nucleated settlements existed in these places at the time of their arrival.

Castletown

The deserted borough of Castletown is situated in the south-east corner of county Laois just off the main road between Port Laoise and Carlow, on relatively low-lying ground overlooking the Barrow valley to the east. The site has been mistakenly identified on occasion with the modern village of Castletown in Upper Ossory but the documentary evidence makes it clear that the borough was in the medieval county of Kildare.

Orpen indicated that Castletown was the manorial centre of Uí Buidhe (Oboy), the pre-Norman territory which was granted by Strongbow to Robert de Bigarz before 1176.[4] According to Giraldus Cambrensis, Hugh de Lacy built a castle in 1182 for Robert de Bigarz at Oboy, close to Timahoe.[5] There is no general agreement on the site of this castle and it has been suggested that it was at either Tullomoy or Kilmoroney.[6] There is, however, no motte at Tullomoy but the example at Kilmoroney is strategically sited above the Barrow, 2 km south of Athy. Although the situation of Kilmoroney motte is impressive, Castletown was the manorial centre of Oboy and it is more likely to be the site of the castle built in 1182. The motte, as it now survives, is a round conical mound 10-12 m high, overgrown with bushes and shrubs. It tapers from the base, ranging in diameter from 27 to 34 m, to a flat summit, 6.5 m across, which is enclosed by a low gapped bank. It is particularly steep-sided on the west, north and east sides but the south-east section is more gradual, largely because of a series of stone steps set into the mound during the eighteenth or nineteenth century. There are slight traces of a ditch with an external bank on the north side where the modern road skirts the motte. South-east of the motte the ground is raised some 1-2 m above the level of the surrounding fields; it may be the remains of a landscaped bailey.

It is not clear how long the manor of Oboy was held by Bigarz or his descendants but by 1245 it had reverted back to the Lord of Leinster and in the partition of Leinster between William Marshall's five daughters, Castletown was granted to William de Cantilupe, husband of Eva, Marshall's youngest daughter.[7] In 1273 de Cantilupe's son, George, died and four years later the custody of the manor of Oboy was given to Milo of Down until George de Cantilupe's heirs came of age.[8] In 1283 John de Hastings, de Cantilupe's nephew, obtained possession of the manor and retained it until at least 1300 when his tenants paid a subsidy of 4 marks towards Edward I's Scottish wars.[9] Sometime between 1300 and 1318 de Hastings granted the manor of 'Castro Obewy' to William de Werrewyk because in 1318 de Werrewyk obtained royal permission to re-enfeoff de Hastings of the manor.[10]

The reference to William, bailiff of 'Castro Oboy', in 1298 may refer to the principal officer of the borough but it is equally possible that it denotes the steward of the manor or perhaps William de Werrewyk himself.[11] In that year the bailiff was acquitted of the charge of combining with one of the Ó Mórdha to steal sixty cows from the prior of Athy. In a licence of 1318 William de Werrewyk was allowed to return the manors of Killaban and 'Castro Oboy' to John de Hastings.[12] In 1348 these manors are described as Killaban and 'Castleton', indicating that the place-name Castletown began to replace Castle Oboy about this time.[13] In 1348, on the death of Laurence de Hastings, earl of Pembroke (grandson of John de Hastings), it was recorded that the burgesses of Castletown rendered 30s. yearly to the earl for their burgages and the returns from the borough court are also mentioned.[14] The same document records that the borough was given as dower to de Hastings' widow, Agnes. This is the clearest documentary reference to the borough and it suggests that the borough was functioning in 1348. While one has to be careful in equating rents with population size, it also suggests that Castletown was inhabited by thirty families or perhaps 150 people. There are no surviving standing remains of the borough but it was probably located in the area between the motte and the church. There are no early references to the parish church although it may be one of the unidentified church sites mentioned in the ecclesiastical taxation of 1302-7.[15]

After 1348, however, nothing further is heard of Castletown until the late sixteenth century, when a number of land grants are recorded in the fiants of Elizabeth.[16] This would suggest that despite the positive image of 1348, Castletown declined or collapsed after the mid-fourteenth century.

Dunmase (the Newtown of Leys)

Central Laois is dominated by the Rock of Dunamase, a natural fortress with precipitous sides on the north, west and south, and only one gradual approach route, from the east. This limestone outcrop affords commanding views across the plains of Laois towards the Devil's Bit (Co. Tipperary) on the south-west, the Slieve Bloom mountains on the west, the Hill of Allen on the north, and towards Kildare town on the north-east. The view is restricted on the east and south by the Dysert Hills, but the castle controls the gap through these hills from the Stradbally valley. This gap is important topographically because it connects the Barrow valley to the central lowlands of Laois.

The Rock of Dunamase

This was the location of an important fortress for some time before the coming of the Normans. It is first referred to in 845 when Dún Masc was plundered by the Vikings.[17] The recent archaeological excavations have uncovered evidence of pre-Norman occupation including traces of a perimeter wall, while a large hoard of Hiberno-Norse coins, deposited *c*.1095, was found on the site during the eighteenth century.[18] After the Norman invasion Dunamase became the most important Anglo-Norman fortification in Laois. It has been claimed that the site was granted to Strongbow in 1170 by Diarmait Mac Murchada as part of his daughter Aoife's dowry but the effective builder of the first castle, a keep enclosed by a curtain wall (the upper ward), appears to have been Meiler FitzHenry who held the site until 1208.[19] William Marshall gained possession in that year and extended the defences substantially to include a lower ward, and an inner and outer barbican.[20] In 1210 it was taken into royal hands by King John, but returned to Marshall in 1215.[21] The castle remained in Marshall hands until, with the death of the last male heir, the lands of Leinster were partitioned in 1247. Dunamase was inherited by Roger de Mortimer, who was married to William Marshall's grand-daughter Maud. An inquisition of de Mortimer lands in 1323 found that the castle had been burned by the Irish and by 1325, perhaps as an aspect of the struggle between Edward II and de Mortimer, Dunamase had been forfeited to the king.[22] In 1342, on the death of Laoighseah Ó Mórdha, Clyn's Annals record that during his lifetime he had destroyed the 'noble castle of Dunamase' and usurped de Mortimer's power.[23] It is likely that from the mid 1320s the manor and castle of Dunamase were under *de facto* Ó Mórdha control.[24] It has been suggested that the Mortimers recovered and refortified Dunamase after Ó Mórdha's death but there is no evidence to support this.[25] Dunamase Castle is specifically named in the 1538 submission of Piers Mac Maolsheachlainn Ó Mórdha which he made as part of the policy of surrender and regrant. In 1609 the castle was granted to Donat O'Brien, earl of Thomond.[26] In 1646 it was recaptured for the Confederates by Eoin Rua O Neill but in 1650 it was destroyed by the Cromwellian generals Hewson and Reynolds. The site was visited *c*.1790 by the antiquarian Edward Ledwich who published a useful description together with a ground plan and view.[27] Two further views, showing the castle in much the same state as it is today, were published by Grose (1791). In 1795 Sir John Parnell erected banqueting halls and other buildings on the site and planted it with trees but the buildings fell into decay in the early nineteenth century.[28]

The Newtown of Leys

It has long been suggested that the borough of Dunamase is to be identified with the Newtown of Leys, frequently mentioned in thirteenth and fourteenth century sources.[29] The identification is not certain, however. The townland of Newton immediately beside Stradbally has been proposed;[30] Borris Great and Borris Little (in the civil parish of Borris), immediately east of Port Laoise, were pointed to by the late Helen M. Roe, while Lea Castle in northern Laois has also been suggested.[31] The claims of Newton and Lea do not bear up under scrutiny, however, because the medieval documentation indicates that the Newtown of Leys was part of the manor of Dunamase. This is clear from a comparison of the documents concerning the partition of Leinster in 1247 with the extents of the inheritor's lands in 1283. In the partition of 1247, Roger de Mortimer was allocated the borough of Dunamase but in the extent made after his death in 1283 there are no burgage returns for Dunamase.[32] Instead, the extent noted that 'the burgesses of the New Town of Leys hold 127 free burgages in that vill' and it stated that the New Town of Leys was part of the manor of Dunamase.[33] From both this extent and the grant in 1284 of the castle of Dunamase and the Newtown of Leys by Maud de Mortimer to her son Edmund,[34] it is evident that Dunamase and the Newtown of Leys were closely associated. The unanswered question, however, relates to their physical proximity. How far apart were they? Was the Newtown of Leys at Dunamase itself or could it have been located at Borris, 5 km to the west? The factors favouring the location at Dunamase are the interchangeability of the names in medieval documentation, the surviving earthworks of a deserted settlement, and the expectation that the largest borough in Anglo-Norman Laois would be closely associated with the most important manor. There are problems, however. The medieval documentation refers to the existence of a church and two watermills in association with the settlement. It is difficult to identify the church site and there is no river, stream or flow of water in the immediate vicinity of the Rock of Dunamase, where the only water source consists of pools. Borris has the attraction of being on flat ground with water sources nearby, there is a documented church site,[35] and the place-name suggests the former presence of a borough or of burgage-land. The difficulties with Borris are its distance from the castle and the fact that it is unclear whether it actually formed part of the manor of Dunamase or not. Whichever location is the correct one, however, there can be little doubt but that in the thirteenth and early fourteenth centuries the borough of 'Dunamase' was synonymous with that of Newtown Leys.

The first reference to the Newtown of Leys as a borough occurs in 1232 when it was listed as part of the dower offered by Earl Richard Marshall to the countess of Pembroke.[36] By 1283, as already mentioned, it had 127 free burgages, two watermills and, perhaps, a population of about 600 people. Blacksmiths, millers, bakers, butchers, carpenters, masons and wine merchants are all documented in the late thirteenth century and there was also a church, first evidenced in 1297.[37] In the ecclesiastical taxation of 1302-6 the church was valued at 12 marks (£8).[38] In 1315, however, the Newtown of Leys was attacked by Bruce and, according to the sixteenth century Book of Howth, the church was burnt and its church bells melted.[39] The location of the church is unclear. Dunamase itself lies within the civil parish of Dysertros and its parish church is located about 2 km to the south west of the Rock.[40] The present Church of Ireland church at Dunamase appears to be of relatively recent origin and there is no visible evidence that it is located on an ancient site, although this may be the case.

The destruction caused to the borough by the Bruce Wars appears to have been extensive and in an inquisition of 1323 the manor of Dunamase is described as waste while only a few burgages remained in the Newton of Leys.[41] No further references to the borough are known suggesting that it declined soon after this date. The remains of the medieval settlement at Dunamase consist of a series of earthworks in a field on raised ground to west of the Rock.[42] The elevated situation affords views to the north, towards Monasterevan and Kildare, but elsewhere it is restricted by the enclosing high ground while the Rock itself is concealed from the borough by a low forested hill on the south. The earthworks are aligned on a north-south hollow way. There are four large rectangular enclosures or tofts on the south of the hollow-way, and at least two on the north. Three of these tofts are shown on the Ordnance Survey first edition map.

Killabban

Killaban is a deserted borough situated on the edge of the Barrow Valley in the south-east corner of county Laois, about six miles north of Carlow town. The name Cill Abbain, i.e. Abban's church, is derived from a monastic foundation thought to have been established by St Abban about the middle of the seventh century.[43] Nothing is known of the early monastic foundation but it is probable that it was still functioning during the late twelfth century when it provided the focus for Anglo-Norman settlement. There are no surface indications of the location of the early monastic site but the monastic boundary is apparent from aerial photographs (plate 10.1). A broad arc is outlined by a cropmark, in the field immediately north of the graveyard, which appears to be a continuation of the western boundary of the churchyard. This would permit the reconstruction of an oval enclosure about 135 m across. Alternatively, it may have been a larger enclosure linked into the arced depression with slight traces of an internal bank, 35 m south of the graveyard.

Killabban was an important manor in the Anglo-Norman period although no details of its history survive prior to 1318 when William de

Plate 10.1   Killabban (Cambridge University Collection of air photographs).

Werrewyk returned the manor to John de Hastings.[44] It is probable, however, that Killabban formed part of Robert de Bigarz grant of Oboy and that, like Castletown, it had passed to John de Hastings in 1283 from the de Cantilupes who had inherited it from the Marshalls in 1247. On the death of Laurence de Hastings, earl of Pembroke, in 1348 it was recorded that the burgesses of Killabban rendered 60s. yearly for their burgages.[45] In 1358 the king ordered the sheriff of Carlow to see that Maurice, earl of Kildare, was paid 60s. owed to him for defending Killabban during recent wars against the Ó Mórdha of Slemargy.[46] This is the latest direct reference to the borough as a functioning unit and its decline would appear to have set in during the later fourteenth century. The borough was sited most likely in the field connecting the church with the motte but there are no surviving surface features. The motte, which was presumably the centre of the manor, consisted of a round conical mound 6 m high; it tapered from a rounded base, measuring 18 by 16 m, to a flat summit 5 m across. There were slight traces of an enclosing fosse. The monument was levelled by a local farmer in 1986.[47] The earliest direct reference to the medieval church of Killabban occurs in the ecclesiastical taxation of 1302-6.[48] In 1335 Philip, vicar of Killabban, was a collector of the grant to the king for the Scottish wars while in 1402, another cleric, Adam Taillor is mentioned, when he was appointed to the church of Killabban.[49] He appears to have been succeeded in 1412 by Richard Leaclor and, whatever the fate of the settlement, it is likely that the church continued to function throughout the Later Middle Ages because in 1537-40 David Omor was presented to the church as perpetual vicar while in 1560 John Owenton was presented.[50]

The surviving remains are those of a nave and chancel structure built of coursed limestone rubble.[51] Two phases are apparent from the jambs of the east window. The earlier jambs are of granite and are of thirteenth century date; the later jambs are of limestone and belong to the fifteenth century. The chancel is an addition to the nave but it probably dates to the thirteenth century. The walls of the nave are now ivy clad and details may be obscured. Fragmentary remains of a stone sarcophagus, unique in this area, indicate the presence of a wealthy individual, presumably a patron of the church, in the thirteenth century.[52] There are about fifteen pieces of cut stone in the graveyard which are derived from door and window jambs. These provide added support for alterations to the fabric of the church during the fifteenth century and also indicate that further work was carried out in the sixteenth century. One piece, a mid fifteenth century door-jamb with a representation of a small male figure, is particularly fine.[53] The fact that the church was rebuilt and modified in the later middle ages indicates that, even if the borough had been abandoned, there was still a population with some resources in the neighbourhood.

Urban decline in late medieval Laois

The Anglo-Norman colony began to fail in central Laois in the mid 1320s although the beginnings of the Gaelic resurgence can be traced to the 1280s.[54] Two major reasons for this revival were, firstly, the fact that large areas were never conquered, and secondly, that within the ostensibly conquered territory large enclaves were left in native control.[55] By 1323 most of the Newtown of Leys appears to have been abandoned and, while the burgage rents of Castletown and Killabban were still being paid in 1348, the absence of any subsequent references to these sites as settlements, together with the devastating effects of the Black Death in that year and the on-going Gaelic revival, suggests that decline probably set in shortly after 1350. The continued references to clerics at Killaban may indicate the continuity of some form of settlement there but, in this instance, the change from clerical nominees with English surnames in the fifteenth century to an Ó Mórdha in 1537-40 indicates that it eventually became fully Gaelicised. The differences between the Gaelic Irish economy and the Anglo-Norman one meant that towns and boroughs were largely superfluous in Gaelic controlled areas. This did not prevent some Gaelic lords, notably the O'Reillys at Cavan, from founding towns and markets. These developments were part of a commercialisation of Gaelic society which occurred mostly during the sixteenth century. Merchants from Bristol are known to have travelled extensively in Gaelic Ulster trading exotic commodities in exchange for salmon, hides, tallow and yarn.[56] Annual fairs were a traditional feature of Gaelic society but native rulers also discovered that more frequent fairs could be a source of income and prestige. By 1542 a fortnightly market was being held on Thursdays at Aghaboe under the patronage of Brian Mac Giolla Pádraig (Barnaby Fitzpatrick), lord of Upper Ossory, and it was sufficiently successful for the corporation of Kilkenny to pass a regulation barring any of its townspeople from buying or selling there on pain of a fine of 40s.[57] It is unfortunate that this fair is not better documented and it is unclear whether or not any permanent settlement was associated with it. The earthworks of a probable deserted village, consisting of the remains of six flat rectangular areas or tofts, survive between the motte and parish church at Aghaboe.[58] The surface indications suggest that some of the tofts pre-date the Dominican friary, founded in 1382.[59] In the absence of excavation, however, it is unclear whether all formed part of the Anglo-Norman settlement (*villa*) burnt by Diarmaid Mac Giolla Padraig in 1346 or if any may have been connected with a later Gaelic establishment.[60]

The first Plantation towns

From the 1530s onwards there was a rebirth of English government interest in the Irish midlands, directed initially at curbing the traditional power of the great Anglo-Irish lords, the earls of Kildare, Desmond and Ormond. The revolt of Silken Thomas in 1534 afforded the opportunity of tackling the Kildares head-on and it was ruthlessly suppressed. The Ó Mórdha and Ó Conchobhar Failge were allies of the Kildares and they used the occasion to attack the borders of the Pale. Successive lord deputies endeavoured to contain them but it was only after a long campaign of ravaging Laois/Offaly in 1548, and the construction of a fort at Port Laoise (known as Fort Protector or the Fort of Leys), that the Gaelic lords submitted and were shipped to London for confinement in the Tower.[61] The initial plan seems to have been to restore the Gaelic leaders to their lands along the lines of the Surrender and Regrant policy but in 1550 the idea of a plantation, financed by private enterprise, was floated by members of the Dublin government.[62] In 1551 speculative leases were granted to some of the Pale gentry and to soldiers who had helped to suppress the revolt but the scheme was not immediately successful. A second attempt in 1556 also failed and in the following year Laois and Offaly were confiscated and shired, and responsibility for colonization was placed in the hands of the lord deputy.[63] It was one thing to pass an act of parliament in Dublin but quite another to colonise the shired ground successfully. The government forces were often inadequate and the settlers ill-equipped to cope with frontier conditions. The Gaelic leaders reacted aggressively and during the 1570s, under Rory Óg Ó Mórdha, they campaigned in Carlow and Kildare, burning Leighlinbridge and capturing Naas in 1576.[64] It was not until the late 1580s and 1590s that the plantation actually began to take root and, even then, there was instability.[65] Maryborough was burned in 1597 and attacked again in the following year. Throughout the second half of the sixteenth century there was only one town, Port Laoise (Maryborough), in the county but after the conclusion of the Nine Years War, when more settled conditions permitted two new urban centres were established, Ballinakill and Portarlington.

Port Laoise (Maryborough)

Centrally located within the county, Port Laoise is the principal town of Laois. It is situated on relatively flat, low-lying ground beside the river Triogue, a tributary of the Barrow. It sits at an important junction of routeways linking Cork and Limerick with Dublin. The name Port Laoise is a revival of the Irish name for the sixteenth century fort to which the town owes its existence, but until the second quarter of the twentieth century it was known as Maryborough.

The town originated as a fort erected as part of the Dublin government's attempts to subdue the territories of the Ó Mórdha (O'Mores) and the Ó Conchobhar Failge (O'Connor Faly) during the reign of Edward VI.[66] In 1548, according to the *Annals of the Four Masters*, Sir Francis Bryan, lord justice and marshall of Ireland built two forts, one at Port Laoise, the other at Daingean in Offaly. In 1556, the fort at Port Laoise, known as 'Fort Protector' or 'the Fort of Leix', was re-named Maryborough in honour of Queen Mary.[67] The fort attracted settlers and a map of about 1560 shows a small walled town around the fort at that date (plate 10.2). Maryborough was granted a market in 1567, it attained borough status in 1569, and was incorporated by Elizabeth I in 1570.[68] Many settlers moved into the town at this time and the fiants record a high number of property grants between 1569 and 1571.[69] Both town and colony were exposed, however. In 1580 it was plundered by John, son of the earl of Desmond; in 1597 it was burned by Onie MacRory Ó Mórdha and it appears to have been burned again the following year.[70]

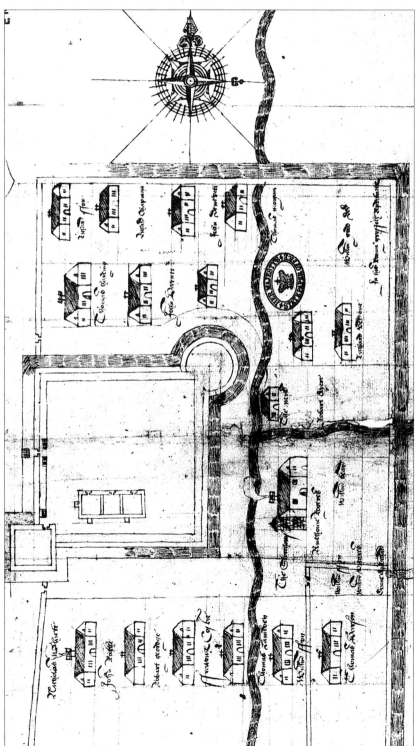

Plate 10.2   Map of Maryborough *c.* 1560 (P.R.O. London, MPF 277).

Street pattern, market place, domestic houses and industrial features

It is difficult to reconstruct the sixteenth century street pattern because it is not clearly shown on the map of *c*.1560 (plate 2). The position of the fort and the course of the stream can be identified without difficulty but the alignment of the houses bears no relation to the present layout of property boundaries. This apparent lack of consistency is due in part to the schematic nature of the map but it may also have been caused by the burnings of Port Laoise in the later sixteenth century. The map shows only one definite street, that entering from the west immediately south of the fort's rectangular tower and exiting through the east wall. This can be tentatively identified with Bridge Street and the eastern section of Main Street. The map also shows a break in the west wall immediately north of the fort. This also appears to signify a street which curved southwards around the fort's circular tower. Today, this can be identified with the eastern portion of Church Street and perhaps with the southern part of Church Avenue. The present junction of Church Avenue and Church Street is likely to be original because it is too far east of the line of the stream (culverted in this area) but it can be seen on the north and south sides of the town. The street plan displays no regularity, a surprising feature which is difficult to explain in a plantation town of this period. The original market place was probably in Main Street in the area between the south side of the street and the fort, if one is to judge from the map of 1721.[71] Farm produce was still exposed for sale here on market day at the beginning of the twentieth century.[72] The present Market Square is of eighteenth century date[73] but it is clear from the location of the seventeenth century church outside the fort that the town began to expand westwards in the seventeenth century. Railway Street and the western parts of Main and Church Streets probably belong to that time also.

The map of *c*.1560 shows fourteen houses (plate 10.2). These are portrayed as gabled, single-floored structures with a loft on the first floor and all have a central hearth. Nothing remains of these houses today although some of the narrow lanes opening southwards from Main Street have tall narrow houses built over them, parts of which may be of seventeenth century date. The map also provides evidence for the presence of a mill, east of the stream from the fort's circular tower, on the site now occupied by Ranks Mills. The broken remains of the mill-race channel were uncovered during archaeological excavations in 1996.[74]

The Fort

The 'court' or 'mansion' (*cúirt*) at the Campa built in 1548 marks the first construction of a fort at Port Laoise but precise details of its constructional history are not known.[75] Henry Wyse was described as captain of the Fort of Leix in 1552 while in 1565-6 when Francis Cosbie was made constable of the fort, its garrison consisted of 'one porter, one drummer, one ensign, one surgeon and thirty-nine arquebusiers.[76] It was captured and burned in 1597 by Tirrell and Onie MacRory Ó Mórdha and substantially demolished by the Cromwellians under Hewson and Reynolds in 1650.[77]

The fort was sited on rising ground south-west of the Triogue river. Its ground-plan is preserved in the plan of c.1560 and in another of late sixteenth century date, now in Trinity College Dublin. These show a rectangular enclosure, described as measuring 1120 by 1110 yards, with a projecting circular tower at the north-east corner and a rectangular tower, described as 17 by 14 yards, at the south-west corner. The only entrance was in the west wall, and a two-storied range of buildings, described as 132 yards long, appears in the south of the enclosure. An external ditch, partly filled with water, is shown on the plan of c.1560. This was subsequently back-filled and the owners of properties on Main Street acquired the extra piece of ground adjoining the wall of the fort. The line of the ditch is preserved in the kink which a number of these allotments have near the fort. A separate ground rent was paid for this stretch of land.[78]

The remains consist of the north, south and east walls, a circular tower at the north-east angle, and a portion of the west wall. Sections are now concealed by later buildings and are inaccessible. The entrance was in the west wall in the portion which is now missing and the fort was protected by two towers, a rectangular example at the south-west angle and a circular one on the north-east. The rectangular tower is missing. The north-west corner forms the boundary wall of the Technical School. The gapped lower section of the wall survives to a height of 2.5 m and has an external batter. The north-west corner is rounded and from here the wall continues eastwards along Church Street where it forms the garden wall of two houses. The remainder of the Church Street section is between 5 and 6 m high but it is punctuated by entrances. The circular tower at the north-east angle has an internal diameter of 8.2 m and walls 1.5 m thick. Internally, two floor ledges are present indicating that the tower was a three-floored structure. Both tower and the eastern section of the wall adjoining it are incorporated into the modern flour mill. The southern end of the east wall borders Church Avenue where it has an external height of 3 m but the interior is built up by landscaped school grounds. The south wall also borders the school grounds and survives to a height of 3.8 m. The remaining short sections are present behind the outbuildings and backyards of the houses fronting onto Main Street. Within the fort was a rectangular building demolished about 1835.[79] The fort was the focus of little antiquarian attention but Grose illustrated part of the remains, probably the rectangular tower, as it was in his day.[80]

Town defences

The map of c.1560 shows that the settlement around the fort was enclosed by a wall delimiting a rectangular area. No mural towers are indicated but two openings in the west wall, immediately north and south of the fort, and a probable opening in the east wall, are shown. A lease of 1569-71 mentions the 'east gate' of Maryborough.[81] The town's charter of 1570 empowered the corporation to 'fortify the borough with ditches and stone walls' which may indicate that the defences shown in the map of c.1560 were considered inadequate by then. There is no definite evidence, however, for the construction of fortifications at Maryborough after 1570.There are no surviving remains of the defences and it is difficult to gauge their exact route. The east side of the town was bounded by a natural gravel ridge. There is no obvious boundary on the north where the ground tends to become swampy in the vicinity of the railway line. The eastern boundary of the town is probably preserved in the modern course of the Triogue but it is possible that it may have extended to the western side of Ridge Road. The southern wall was probably close to the townland boundary, while the western edge is most likely preserved in the line of Railway Street and Lyster Lane. The sixteenth century map shows two openings in the west wall, which may represent gatehouses. These lay immediately north and south of the fort controlling entry to Main Street and Church Street. There is a similar opening in the east wall in Bridge Street. An unusual feature depicted on the map of c.1560 is the presence of an intra-mural walled enclosure in the south-east angle. Its function is unknown.

Parish Church

In 1556 it was ordered that a church should be built in every town within three years.[82] The church at Maryborough may date to this time but the earliest definite evidence for its existence is a reference to David Good, vicar of Maryborough, in 1598.[83] The building is situated within its own churchyard, west of the fort, and outside the sixteenth century defences. Its remains consist of the west tower and the north wall of the nave.[84]

Ballinakill

Ballinakill is situated in the extreme south centre of County Laois, three miles south-west of Abbeyleix. The placename has been explained as an Anglicisation of Baile na Cille, 'town of the church', but the absence of an early church in the immediate vicinity favours the alternative derivation from Baile na Coille, 'town of the wood'.[85] The latter form is also supported by seventeenth century accounts which describe the area as forested.

Earliest documentary references to Ballinakill occur in the late sixteenth century. In 1570 the lands of 'Ballenekyll' were granted to Alexander Cosby and his wife Dorcas Sydney, a grant which was renewed in 1593.[86] The urban history of Ballinakill, however, begins in 1606 when Sir Thomas Coatch was granted the right to hold a market and fair there.[87] An English colony was established soon after by Sir Thomas Ridgeway and in 1613 the town was incorporated by a charter of James I.[88] The borough owed its development primarily to the proximity of the ironworks at Kilrush 1.3 km south-east of Ballinakill itself.[89] On his death in 1631 Ridgeway, then earl of Londonderry, was described as holding the manor of Gallenridgeway alias Balinekill, containing a large mansion or castle, one hundred messuages, a dovecot, two watermills, a fulling-mill, an iron-mill, courts leet and baron, three fairs and two markets in the town.[90] In 1642 it was described as:

> seated among woods in a place soe watered with springs as
> afforded the Earle convenience to make many fish ponds neare
> the Castle hee built there; which hee likewise fortified with a
> strong wall, and that with turrets and flankers; besides that the
> towne since it had been planted was well inhabited, the iron mill
> there kept many lustie men at work [91]

The town suffered during the wars of the Confederation but in 1659 it was still the third most populous town within Laois, with a population of 204, one-quarter of whom were English.[92] In the eighteenth century Ballinakill was one of the most important fair towns within county Laois and much of its present layout belongs to that period. In 1801 it was also a major tanning centre with a brewery and several small woollen businesses.[93] The corporation and borough of Ballinakill were dissolved at the Act of Union in 1800.

Street pattern and burgage plots
The present settlement at Ballinakill is arranged around a rectangular square, on which three streets converge. Church Street lies to the north, Bride Street to the west and Stanhope Street to the south. The present configuration of streets, however, is largely the result of eighteenth century activity. The seventeenth century borough was laid out along

the long axis formed by Graveyard Street and Stanhope Street, with Chapel Lane and Castle Lane running perpendicularly to the east. The Square, Church Street and Bride Street represent an eighteenth century addition. There is a well defined burgage plot pattern on the east side of Stanhope Street and the Square but elsewhere it is not so apparent. There are some stone built houses and sheds on the street front of these plots but they do not have any dateable features. Part of their fabric may be of seventeenth century date but it is impossible to be certain.

The Castle
Ballinakill Castle was built by Sir Thomas Ridgeway between 1606 and

Plate 10.3   Ballinakill Castle: late nineteenth century view.

1613.[94] In 1642 it was described as 'fortified with a strong wall, and that with turrets and flankers'.[95] It was captured in the same year by Confederate forces under Preston but was recaptured after heavy bombardment by Cromwellian forces under General Fairfax.[96] The castle was then destroyed and the present ruins are those of a structure built by the Dunne family about 1680.[97] The north gable of a rectangular tower house survives in a farmyard on the east side of Market Square. Only three floors can be distinguished but it is evident from a late nineteenth century photograph that there were five floors originally (plate 10.3). The masonry consists of roughly-coursed pink shaley stone with dressed limestone quoins. The ground and first floors are featureless except for two small gunloops with internal splay whose outer jambs are missing. There is a large window on the second floor with a rounded rear-arch, but the details are not clear because it is covered in ivy. There are short returns on the east and west sides. The west return, 1.5 m long, is curved internally and has a splayed gunloop. The base of a battered wall runs westwards for 4.3 m from this point. A round arch survives on the immediate north-west, perhaps the gateway into the bawn.[98]

Parish Church

The nineteenth century Church of Ireland building, dedicated to All Saints, probably occupies the site of the seventeenth century church. There is no graveyard attached to the church and burials are carried out at Kilcronan and Dysart Gallen, outside the village. Partly buried under bushes in the south-west corner of St. Brigid's (R.C.) churchyard is a plain, octagonal, straight-sided font of pink conglomerate. Its style suggests a fifteenth or sixteenth century date and it may have been removed from Kilcronan or Dysart Gallen.

Portarlington

Portarlington is situated beside the river Barrow on relatively low-lying flat ground in the extreme north-east corner of Laois. It lies on the Tullamore-Kildare road about ten miles north-east of Port Laoise. The town is named after its founder Sir Henry Bennet, Lord Arlington. It has been suggested that the first part of the name is derived from Port na h-Innse, the Irish name for the nearby Lea Castle.[99] The origins of the town date to 1666 when Charles II granted large areas of former Ó Díomusaigh (O'Dempsey) land in the area of the modern town to Sir Henry Bennet. This formed the manor of Portarlington and created the borough with a corporation, weekly market and two annual fairs.[100] Bennet had the town laid out by George Rawdon in 1667 and presumably planted settlers there soon afterwards.[101] The town was built within a bend of the river Barrow on a site previously known as 'Beladrite', i.e. Béal Átha an Droichead, 'the mouth of the bridge ford', and Cúl an tSúdaire, 'the nook of the tanner'.[102] The town grew quickly and its basic layout was established by 1678 when it was depicted on a map, now in the National Library of Ireland.[103]

About 1686 Portarlington was sold by Bennet to Sir Patrick Trant who forfeited it by attainted at the end of the Jacobite wars. Thereupon the town was granted to Henry de Massue, Marquis de Rouvigny, created Baron Portarlington about 1691.[104] Rouvigny transformed the character of Portarlington by establishing shortly thereafter a colony of French Huguenot settlers, mainly drawn from the officers and soldiers of William III's army.[105] Around 1696 he established two churches, St. Michael's and St. Paul's, for the English and French settlers, respectively, and also two schools.[106] Rouvigny later sold his interest in the town and it passed via the London Hollow Sword-blade Company to the Dawson family who were closely connected with the town until the nineteenth century.

Street pattern and market place
The original layout of the town is shown in a manuscript map drawn-up in 1678 (plate 10.4).[107] It lay in a bend of the Barrow which acted as a natural moat on the north, east and west sides. A canal was dug on the south completing the encirclement of the town. The roughly rectangular area thus enclosed was fortified with earthworks having a bastion at each corner. In the centre of the town was a large square with a market house from which four principal streets radiated in a cruciform pattern: Bennet Street (Spa Street) to the north, James' Street (Church Lane) to the east, Queene Street (now part of Main Street) to the south, and King Street (French Church Street) to the west. The town expanded beyond these boundaries in the eighteenth century, across the Barrow into Offaly, and southwards along the present Main Street.

The cruciform axis of the seventeenth century town still survives in Spa Street, Church Lane, French Church Street and the northern portion of Main Street. The market place was a square at the intersection of these streets in which there was a centrally placed Market House. The present building of *c*.1800 is used as a garage. The north-east quadrant is now an open field used for grazing. A printed memorandum of *c*.1666 refers to the intention of building houses south of the town.[108] This is probably to be identified with Foxcroft Street and the section of Main Street between its junction with Foxcroft Street and the line of the defences. A wooden bridge over the Barrow is shown on the 1678 map. The river has changed its course somewhat in the interim and the

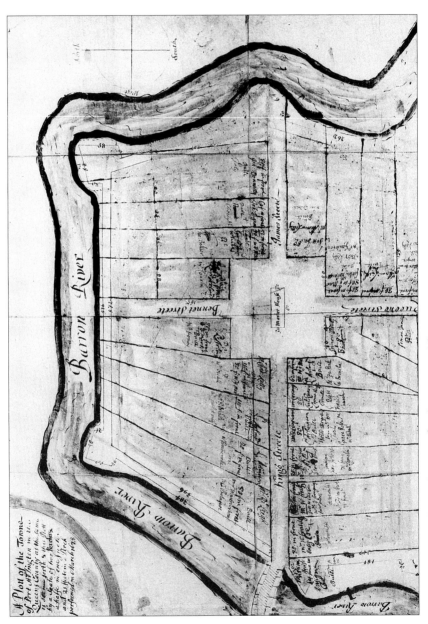

Plate 10.4   Plan of Portarlington 1678 (N.L.I. MS F.55).

foundations of the seventeenth century bridge probably lie immediately east of the Barrow Bridge.

Domestic houses

The printed memorandum of *c.*1666 was clearly used as an advertisement to attract settlers to the town. It describes the layout in great detail and notes that:

> every house to be built within the fortification is to be built at least fifty feet in front, the walls to be made of good lime and stone or mortar and stone, rough cast, and every house to be one storey and a half high at least, and every storey to be nine foot deep from floor to floor, the houses to be roofed with shingles, tiles or slates, and to have dormant windows to the streets[109]

It was also intended for houses to be built outside 'the fortification on the East side, which shall front towards the new channel', 'on either sides of the way leading from New Channel Bridge to Katherine's tower', and 'on either side of the road leading from the great bridge to Charlestown'. These houses were to be:

> at least forty feet in front, the walls to be of stone and lime or mortar and stone, and to be ten feet high from the ground to the eaves at least; and the house to have a good stone chimney[110]

None of the surviving houses in the town are of diagnostically seventeenth century form and Portarlington's 'typical' Huguenot houses belong to the early eighteenth century.

Town defences

The 1678 plan shows that the town was protected by bastioned defences enclosing an area of approximately 8 hectares (20 acres) and having a circumference of 1100m. No positively identifiable remains survive. There are some irregular features on the north-west side, however, which may have formed part of the defences. The bridge in the east wall was protected on the south by a redoubt. On the north side of French Church Street two stone walls 3 m high are set at an acute angle to one another. The western wall is broken by equidistant gaps, now filled with cement, about 2 m above ground level. The area within these walls is some two metres higher than the ground beside the river. The feature may be a remnant of the defences but it is impossible to be certain. The course of the defences north of the bridge is obscured by mounds of earth removed from the Barrow during drainage and it is possible that some remains may be incorporated in the spoil. There was a bastion at the north-west angle where the wall turned eastwards and continued without interruption to the north-east angle bastion. Here the wall turned south-east to a bastion located east of Church Lane, and from there it continued southwards to the south-east angle bastion. The south wall was given added defence by the construction of a channel whose line is still indicated by a long property boundary on the west side of Main Street. A short section some five metres wide, still filled with water, survives on the west side of the town. This is probably to be identified with the 'new channel' referred to in the printed memorandum of c.1666.[111] The south wall was also protected by a redoubt, located slightly west of Main Street and by a bastion at the south-west angle. From here the defences continued to the bridge.

St Michael's (or the English) Church

This building now functions as a badminton hall and is located on Church Lane at the north-east angle of the square. Originally constructed in 1694, it was rebuilt in 1832.[112] It has since lost its spire. The church was intended to accommodate the English speaking settlers of Portarlington. There is no associated churchyard because the parishioners used the older graveyard at Lea.[113]

St Paul's (or the French) Church

Located within its own churchyard in the south-west angle of the Market Square. The first church was built here to accommodate French-speaking Huguenot parishioners in 1696. The present building dates to 1857 and the earliest memorial is one of 1737.[114]

Later urban developments

The seventeenth century also witnessed the foundation of Mountrath, established by Sir Charles Coote, although its growth was a feature of the following century, and Rathdowney which grew commercially in the nineteenth-century largely because of the presence of Perry's Brewery. New estate villages were founded in the eighteenth century. Abbeyleix was developed by the de Vescis, Durrow by the Flowers, and Stradbally was laid out by the Cosbys. Mountmellick is also an eighteenth century creation, an important example of an industrial town, developed by the Quaker merchant community. These developments, exploiting and servicing local resources, augmented the earlier plantation towns and created the modern urban network of Laois.

Acknowledgements

This paper is largely based on fieldwork funded by the Office of Public Works in 1985-86. I wish to thank Heather A. King and Andrew Halpin for their practical help at the time and for subsequent useful discussion. I am grateful to Michael Potterton for patiently working over the text and clarifying several statements. I was first introduced to County Laois by the late Helen M. Roe who was a fount of information on all aspects of the county and a source of encouragement and help to all students of Irish archaeology. I wish to dedicate this paper to her memory.

References

1. *Ormond deeds,* i, no. 1; G. H. Orpen, *Ireland under the Normans* (4 vols, London 1911-20), i, pp 382-6.
2. A. J., Otway-Ruthven, 'The medieval county of Kildare', *I.H.S.,* xi (1959), pp 181-99.
3. G. Mac Niocaill, Na Búirgéisí XII-XV aois, 2 vols (Dublin, 1964).
4. Orpen, *Normans,* iii, p. 105.
5. A. B. Scott, and F. X. Martin (eds.), *Expugnatio Hibernica: the conquest of Ireland by Giraldus Cambrensis* (Dublin, 1978), p. 195.
6. Orpen, *Normans,* i, p. 384; *Expugnatio,* p. 350, n. 370.
7. Orpen, *Normans,* iii, p. 105.
8. *Cal. doc. Ire.,* 1251-1284, no. 1401.
9. Ibid., no. 2107; *Stat. Ire., John-Hen.* V, p. 235.
10. *Rot. Pat. Hib.,* p. 27, no. 40.
11. *Cal. justic. rolls Ire.,* 1295-1303, p. 199.
12. *Rot. Pat. Hib.,* p. 27, no. 40.
13. *Cal. inquis, post mortem,* 1347-52, p. 128.
14. Ibid.
15. *Cal. doc. Ire.,* 1302-07, pp 244-52.
16. *P.R.I. rep. D.K.,* xii, p. 31, no. 1697 (grant of Ballycaslan Omoye to John Barnyes, 1570-1); *P.R.I. rep. D.K.,* xvi, p. 64, no. 5147 (grant of Ballicaslan Omoy to John Baskerfield, 1587); ibid., p. 118, no. 5424 (lease to Edward Sutton, 1590).
17. *A.U.,* s.a. 844; W. M. Hennessy (ed.), *Chronicon Scotorum* (London, 1866), *sub anno* 845; *A.I.,* 844; *A.F.M.,* s.a. 843.
18. B. Hodkinson, The rock of Dunamase', *Archaeology Ireland,* ix, no. 2 (1995), p. 21; idem, *Excavations* 1995, p. 53; T. McNeil, *Castles in Ireland, feudal power in a Gaelic world* (London, 1997), pp 12-13; R. H. M. Dolley, *The Hiberno-Norse coins in the British Museum* (London, 1966), pp 72-4.
19. Orpen, *Normans,* ii, pp 375, 382, 217; K. O'Conor, 'Dunamase castle', *J. Ir. Archaeol.,* vii 91996), pp 101, 111, see also his chapter in this volume.
20. Ibid., p. 101; McNeill, *Castles in Ireland,* pp 33-4.
21. Orpen, *Normans,* ii, p. 265; *Cal. doc Ire., 1171-1251,* nos 644, 647, 664.
22. Otway-Ruthven, *Med. Ire.,* p. 252; *P.R.I. rep D.K.,* xlii, p. 57.
23. R. Butler (ed.), *Annals of Ireland by Friar John Clynn and Thady Dowling* (Dublin, 1849), p. 30.
24. K. O'Conor, The Anglo-Norman period in County Laois (unpublished M.A. thesis, Department of Archaeology, University College Dublin, 1986), p. 28.
25. E. O'Leary, 'Dunamase castle', *J. Kildare Archaeol. Soc.,* viii (1909-11), p. 165.
26. J. C. Erck (ed.), *A Repertory of the inrolments of the patent rolls of chancery in Ireland commencing with the reign of King James I* (2 pts, Dublin, 1846-52), ii, p. 735.

27. E. Ledwich, *The antiquities of Ireland* (Dublin, 1790), pp 200-04.

28. O'Leary, 'Dunamase castle', p. 168.,

29. Orpen, *Normans*, iii, p. 104; J. Feehan, *Laois: an environmental history* (Stradbally, 1983), p. 370; Otway-Ruthven, *Med. Ire.*, p. 252; R. A. Glasscock, 'Ireland', in M. W. Beresford, and J. G. Hurst (eds), *Deserted medieval villages* (London, 1971), p. 296.

30. *Cal. doc. Ire., 1252-84*, index; Otway-Ruthven, 'The medieval county of Kildare', p. 183.

31. Helen M. Roe, pers. comm.; O'Leary, 'Dunamase castle', p. 164.

32. *Cal. doc. Ire., 1252-84*, no. 933.

33. Ibid., no. 2028.

34. H. Wood, 'The muniments of Edmund de Mortimer, third earl of March, concerning his liberty of Trim', *R.I.A. Proc.* 40 c (1931-2), pp 335-6.

35. P. D. Sweetman, O. Alcock, B. Moran, *Archaeological inventory of County Laois* (Dublin, 1995), p. 75, no. 704.

36. *Cal. doc. Ire., 1171-1251*, no. 1950.

37. Feehan, *Laois*, p. 369; *Cal. justic. rolls Ire., 1295-1303*, p. 192.

38. *Cal. doc. Ire., 1302-07*, p. 250.

39. *Cal. Carew MSS, Misc.*, p. 134.

40. *Archaeol. inventory, Co. Laois*, p. 80, no. 738.

41. Otway-Ruthven, *Med. Ire.*, p. 252.

42. *Archaeol. inventory, Co. Laois*, p. 107, no. 934; O'Conor, Anglo-Norman Laois, pp 240-4.

43. Gwynn, and Hadcock, *Med. relig. houses* (London, 1970), p. 391.

44. *Rot. pat. Hib.*, p. 27, no. 40.

45. *Cal. inquis. post mortem*, 1347-52, p. 128.

46. *Rot. pat. Hib.*, p. 69, no. 64.

47. *Archaeol. inventory, Co. Laois*, p. 102, no. 909.

48. *Cal. doc. Ire.*, 1302-07, p. 249.

49. *P.R.I. rep. D.K.*, xlv, p. 51; *Rot. pat. Hib.*, p. 165, no. 211.

50. *Rot. pat. Hib.*, p. 256, no. 14; *Cal. pat. rolls Ire., Hen. VIII-Eliz.*, pp 52; 441.

51. *Archaeol. inventory, Co. Laois*, p. 83, no. 759.

52. Bradley, J., 'Anglo-Norman sarcophagi from Ireland' in G. Mac Niocaill and P. F. Wallace (eds), *Keimelia: studies in medieval archaeology and history in memory of Tom Delaney* (Galway, 1988), pp 86-8.,

53. H. A. King, 'A fifteenth century fiture carving from Killaban, Co. Laois', *Kildare Archaeol. Soc. Jn.*, xvi, no. 5 (1985-6), pp 492-5.

54. O'Conor, Anglo-Norman Laois, p. 27.

55. Ibid., p. 40.

56. See N. Canny, *The Elizabethan conquest of Ireland: a pattern established 1565-1576* (Hassocks, Sussex, 1976), pp 7-8.

57. J. T. Gilbert, 'Rothe's register of the antiquities and statutes of the town of Kilkenny', *H.M.C. rep.*, ii (1874), p. 261.

58. O'Conor, Anglo-Norman Laois, pp 231-3.

59. Ibid., p. 122.

60. Clyn, *Annals*, pp 32-3.

61. R. T. Dunlop, 'The plantation of Leix and Offaly', *E.H.R.*, vi (1891), pp 61-3.

62. Ibid., p. 64.

63. Ibid., p. 69.

64. Ibid., p. 82.

65. Ibid., p. 87.

66. O'Hanlon and O'Leary, *Queen's County*, i, pp 429-30; G. A. Hayes McCoy, 'Conciliation, coercion and the Protestant Reformation 1547-71', *N.H.I.*, iii, p. 70.

67. Feehan, *Laois*, pp 223-4.

68. Hayes McCoy, 'Conciliation, coercion and the Protestant Reformation', p. 162; *Cal. pat rollls Ire.*, Eliz., pp 219-23.

69. *P.R.I. rep. D.K.*, xi, nos 1325, 1327, 1348, 1351, 1396, 1406, 1544; ibid., nos 1624, 1649, 1689, 1774, 1802.

70. *A.F.M.*, s.a. 1597, Cal. C.P. Ire., 1596-1597, pp 467, 470; O'Hanlon and O'Leary, *Queen's County*, ii, pp 476-8.

71. Feehan, *Laois*, fig. 12:22.

72. Helen M. Roe, pers. comm.

73. Feehan, *Laois*, p. 397.

74. *Excavations 1996*, p. 63.

75. *A.F.M.*, s.a. 1548.

76. *Cal. pat. rolls. Ire., Hen. VIII-Eliz.*, p. 280; *P.R.I. rep. D.K.*, xi, p. 119, no. 819.

77. *Cal. S.P. Ire.*, 1596-1597, pp 467, 470; Feehan, *Laois*, p. 395.

78. Helen M. Roe, pers. comm.

79. *O.S. Letters, Laois*, i, p. 74.

80. F. Grose, *The antiquities of Ireland* (2 vols. London, 1791), ii, pl. opp. p. 45.

81. *P.R.I. rep. D.K.*, xi, p. 210, no. 1406.

82. O'Hanlon and O'Leary, *Queen's County*, i. p. 436.

83. *Cal. S.P. Ire.*, 1598-9, p. 409.

84. *Archaeol. inventory, Co. Laois*, p. 86, no. 778.

85. *O.S. Letters, Laois*, ii, p. 267.

86. *P.R.I. rep. D.K.*, xii, p. 19, no. 1625; ibid., xvi, p. 238, no. 5825.

87. *Pat. rolls Ire., Jas. I*, ii, p. 307.

88. O'Hanlon and O'Leary, *Queen's County*, i, 234; *Cal. pat rolls Ire., Jas I*, p. 236.

89. Feehan, *Laois*, p. 378.

90. *Inq. cancell. Hib. repert.*, i, com. regine: 16 Car I.

91. Feehan, *Laois*, p. 377.

92. *Census Ire.*, 1659.

93. Feehan, *Laois*, p. 378.

94. O'Hanlon and O'Leary, *Queen's County*, i. p. 234.

95. Feehan, *Laois*, p. 377.

96. O'Hanlon and O'Leary, *Queen's County*, i, pp 519-20; *Topog. dict. Ire.*, i, p. 109.

97. O'Hanlon and O'Leary, *Queen's County*, i, p. 234.

98. *Archaeol. inventory, Co. Laois*, p. 110, no. 941.

99. E. D. Borrowes, 'The Huguenot colony at Portarlington in the Queen's County', U.J.A., iii (1855), p. 62. See Hylton's chapter in this volume.

100. *Cal. S.P. Ire.*, 1666-9, pp 220-2.

101. Ibid., p. 318.

103. Borrowes, 'The Huguenot colony', p. 62.

103. Feehan, *Laois*, fig. 12:16.

104. Borrowes, 'The Huguenot colony', pp 63-4; *Topog. dict. Ire.*, ii, p. 425.

105. Borrowes, 'The Huguenot colony, pp 65-6; Feehan, *Laois*, p. 392.

106. E. D. Borrowes, 'The Huguenot colony at Portarlington', *U.J.A.*, vi (1858), p. 328.

107. Feehan, *Laois*, fig. 12.16.

108. *Cal. S.P. Ire.*, 1666-9, pp 259-61.

109. Ibid.

110. Ibid.

111. Ibid.

112. O'Hanlon and O'Leary, *Queen's County,* p. 286.
113. W. FitzGerald, 'The history and antiquities of the Queen's County barony of Portnahinch', *Kilare Archaeol. Soc. Jn.,* vi (1903-5), p. 222.
114. Ibid.

Chapter 11

THE ENGLISH SETTLERS IN QUEEN'S COUNTY, 1570-1603

IVAN COSBY

The English Settlers

Who were they? From where did they come? What was it that attracted them to settle in a territory still little known to the geographer and where the inhabitants were notoriously hostile to interlopers, although the O'Dempseys were consistently loyal and little is ever heard of smaller clans such as the O'Kellys, O'Lawlors and O'Dowlings, leaving the O'Mores of Galin and the Keatings of the Doonane mountains in Slievemargy as the notable antagonists. It is hoped that by co-ordinating some of the facts about the better known settlers to deduce their motives for coming.

The English who obtained grants of land in the county may conveniently be divided into three categories. There were those who were officers in her majesty's service and for the most part held the rank of captain; their lands were the most extensive and situated furthest from Maryborough, the focal point of the Plantation, and most is known about them as they appear more frequently in the extant state records. The second category comprises a large number of small land holders who lived in the vicinity of Maryborough and probably within the jurisdiction of the borough. Although they contributed to the militia, they were not soldiers and rarely feature in the government of the county. The third category was composed of those Englishmen who held land in the county as a reward for service elsewhere in Ireland. They spent little time in the county and although their properties there provided a source of income they could not be described as settlers.

One of the original settlers in the first category was John Barnyse of Castletown. Little is known about his origins, but by 1570 he was sufficiently old to be receiving a pension of two shillings a day for past services. He must have been a close friend of John Piggott another contemporary settler, because after the latter's death in 1570 Barnyse came to live at his home at Dysart. It is probable that while living there he married Piggott's widow, before his death in 1587. It was at Dysart that he began building a castle to prevent attacks from the O'Mores and O'Connors, but it was in 1574, when still needing money to complete it that his adversaries seized his property which included 140 cows, 100 sheep and 36 calves.

The Piggotts at Dysart were a branch of the Piggott family of Chetwynd Edgmont, in Salop. John Piggott was succeeded by a younger son, Robert in 1586, who married Anne, the sister of William Sentleger, and later, after Anne's death in 1599, Thomasine, the daughter of the auditor at war, Sir William Peyton. Robert Piggott's eldest son by his first marriage, John of Grangebeg, was married to Martha a daughter of Sir Thomas Colclough of Ballyknockan Castle, a neighbouring English settler, while his youngest daughter by his second wife married Richard Cosby of Stradbally, after Cosby's victory over the O'Mores at the battle of Aughnahilly in 1606. During the military campaign between 1598 and 1603, Robert Piggott, together with Robert Whitney, was one of the few settlers to hold out with a company of 12 horsemen for which he was later knighted.

Another of the soldier settlers was John Barrington, whose family came from Barrington Hall in Essex. Barrington was a distant relation of Sir Henry Sydney, the lord deputy. In the service since 1555, John Barrington had succeeded his father George who also seems to have held lands in the Queens County. He had two brothers in the county, although they appear not to have done anything noteworthy, Joseph being eventually killed by the O'Mores and the youngest, Robert, marrying an O'More. John, at any rate, lived at Cullenagh Castle until, after living on a pension of 4 shillings per day since his discharge in 1584, he was killed by the O'Mores in 1593. His son Alexander, a petitioner for his father's pension in 1586, married Margaret, Robert Bowen's eldest daughter, who had been previously married to Gerald Fitzgerald of Morrett and Timogue, the bastard son of the earl of Kildare and the daughter of Fergus O'Kelly of Timogue. Although both John and Alexander Barrington married into Roman Catholic families, the Barringtons were certainly a Protestant family in 1640, like the Piggots.

As for the Bowens, John ap Thomas ap Owen (Bowen), a Welsh soldier, and constable of Balliadams in 1649, was the first of that family to settle in the county. He died in 1669, leaving his eldest son Robert to succeed and to marry Alice Harpole, daughter of Walter Harpole, dean of Leighlin, the couple having a son John, presumably born in 1573, who married the daughter of Myler Magrath, archbishop of Cashel, although there is a reference to a John Bowen being intermittently a sergeant-at-arms in Munster from 1580 to 1586. Robert Bowen also had a brother, Captain William, provost marshal of Leinster in 1581, who

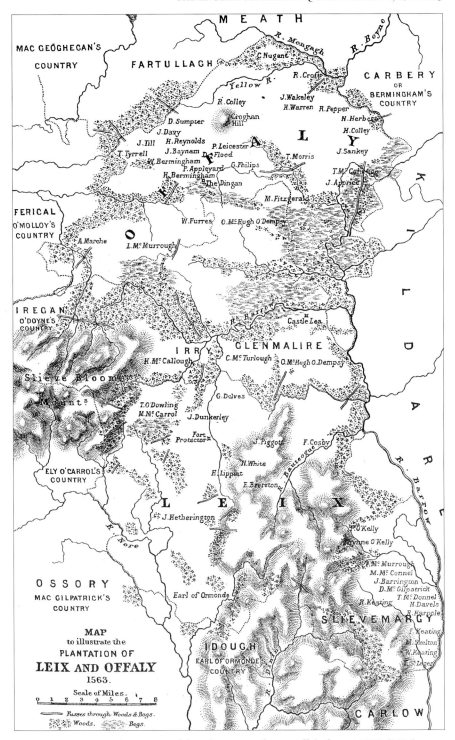

Fig. 11.1 Robert Dunlop's map of the plantation of Leix-Offaly from *E.H.R.* (1891).

spent some time in Queens County, though he held lands in Mayo, while there also existed a close relation, Mary Bowen, either the sister or daughter of one of them, who was married to Lucas Wayfare.

In March 1592, Robert, William, John Bowen and Wayfare were involved in the murder of a certain Richard Stanton, which the Lord Deputy Fitzwilliam considered too foul an act to pardon, originating in William Bowen's need for fifteen quarters of land in Mayo belonging to Stanton and for which Stanton's brother William had also been murdered in Connaught by the Bowens, according to Richard Stanton's wife Honora O'Dempsey. However, although Robert Bowen was imprisoned by Fitzwilliam who wanted to stamp out unlawful behaviour by men of English blood, the privy council brought about Bowen's release, pending an impartial commission, when it appeared that Stanton already stood indicted for treason for refusing to recognise the authority of her majesty's officers and because Sir Henry Wallop, Sir Henry Harrington and Sir George Carew had spoken in favour of Bowen, who it seems was eventually pardoned and lived until 1621. Besides John and Margaret, his other children made several marriages within the county, such as that of Margery to Henry Brereton, a settler at Loughteog near Stradbally; of Susan and Mabel to Roger Hovenden of Ballyfehin and Robert Hetherington of Bawherard, respectively, both English settlers; and of Elizabeth to Piers Butler.

In Stradbally there was the Protestant family of Cosby, descended from Francis Cosby, second son of John Cosby of Great Leak in Nottingham. Born in 1510, and married to Lady Mary Seymour, daughter of the duke of Somerset, c.1530. Francis Cosby arrived in Ireland in 1546, having served in Henry VIII's wars in the Low Countries, and was among the petitioners for a commission to plant the Queen's County in 1549. Appointed general of the kern in 1558, and also sheriff of Kildare, he was a member of the commission which shired Queen's County in 1556 and in 1565 was made constable of Maryborough, although then living at Monasterevan, a residence normally at the disposal of the lord deputy.

Killed in 1580, Francis Cosby was succeeded by Alexander who had married Dorcas Sydney. She came from Orford in Kent and had been one of her majesty's maids of honour. Such court connections made it easier for herself and her husband to obtain a large grant of land in Queens County. Such fortune changed, however, as Alexander was himself killed with his son Francis in 1596, and in 1598 their castle at Stradbally was sacked. The succession then passed to Francis' younger brother Richard.

Although the Cosbys were a Protestant family, Francis Cosby, Alexander's son, had married Helen Harpole whose family were Roman Catholic till 1640 at least. Originally from Canterbury, and first mentioned in 1556 as a gentleman and soldier at Leighlin, Robert Harpole held lands in the county as early as 1570, and was for many years constable of Carlow until his death in 1594. Walter Harpole, dean of Leighlin, whose daughter Alice had married Robert Bowen, was probably Robert's brother, who himself had married Frances O'Byrne, a clan which followed the Kavanaghs in Odrone, Co Carlow. Their eldest son, Sir William Harpole constable of Carlow, linked his family with the Davells, who were Roman Catholics at least in 1640, by marrying Eleanor, daughter of Henry Davells, the constable of Dungarvan. Sir William married secondly Mary Brereton, daughter of Andrew Brereton of Dublin and widow of Nicholas White, formerly master of the rolls. The suggestion that Sir William, who died in 1616, had married Feagh McHugh's wife or that he promised to marry Doryne, Owny McRory O'More's sister, were rumours spread by the earl of Thomond. Sir William's brother, George, who held the Harpole lands in 1622, lived at Shrule and married Mabel, the eldest daughter of Alexander Cosby.

Another Roman Catholic family were the Hovendens. Giles Hovenden had been a captain of horse in 1532. Twelve years later he was acting as one of the commissioners of the Connaught government but in 1551 had moved to the south-west of Munster. He obtained the lordship of Killabban in the Queen's County in November 1549. Giles by his marriage to Elizabeth, daughter of Sir Walter Cheevers, had six children. The eldest, John, who succeeded to Killaban, died in 1619. Captain Piers, the second son, of Tankardstown married an Anne Brett and died in 1613. His son, Thomas, married Thady, a daughter of the 4th baron of Upper Ossory. Captain Richard, the third son, was active in defeating the Spanish who landed on the west coast in 1588 where he took 800 prisoners. Captain Walter was killed when his company was lost near Maryborough in December 1597; Joanna, the only daughter, married John Barrington, while the youngest, Henry, became a follower and secretary to the earl of Tyrone. Henry subsequently married Catherine, daughter of Tirlagh O'Neill; she was to be the mother of Sir Phelim O'Neill of 1641 fame by her later marriage to Tirlagh McHenry O'Neill.

The only other family in the group of service captains about which anything is known was that of Whitney. John Whitney, the first to settle in Queen's County, was descended from a family taking its name from the lordship of Whitney in Herefordshire, and more immediately from James Whitney, the chief sergeant of Connaught and Clanricard in 1565. Living at Shean Castle, and married to a Cecilia Skerret, John Whitney's successors continued in residence there until 1661 when the then John Whitney sold the manor of Shean.

Other than that which is mentioned in the text, nothing was learnt about the origins of the English settlers in the second category above. The third category, however, did contain a number of notable characters, not least being Ludowick Bryskett of Italian, Florentine origins. A graduate of Cambridge in 1559, a literátor, and friend of Sir Henry Sydney and his son Sir Philip, Bryskett's most notable work was 'A discourse of Civill life, containing the ethical part of moral philosophy' published in 1606. He appears to have been a friend also of Dr.Long, archbishop of Armagh, Captain Christopher Carleil, Captain Thomas Norris and above all of Captain Warham Sentleger, one of the Queens County settlers. While his government offices over the years to his death in 1606 included registrar in chancery (1577); clerk of the council (1582, 93, 94); controller of customs (1579-81); collector general of customs (1583, 84, 85); clerk of the council of Munster (1583-1600) and clerk of casualties (1594); he seems to have spent very little if any time in Queen's County.

Henry Davells, who was probably a Roman Catholic, was in 1568 constable of Carlow, later becoming constable of Leighlin in 1572 and sheriff of Carlow in 1573. He was appointed constable of Dungarvan in 1574 and fulfilled commissions in Munster up to his death at Tralee in 1579. His son, Henry, was the probable holder of the Davells lands in the following century.Sir William Parsons comes under this category although not receiving lands in Queen's County until the seventeenth century. Described in 1600 as a servant of Sir Geoffrey Fenton, he got the office of surveyor general from the latter on foot of being well acquainted with crown revenue. Parsons also acquired 100 acres in Co. Longford and 1,000 acres in Co. Tyrone, as well as being patentee of 1,500 acres of escheated land in Co. Wexford in 1616.

Of the other settlers in the third category little is known other than that Captain Henry Hungerford left the county about 1583 to become constable of Dungarvan., his parents having died in 1581 after the Hungerford home had been sacked by the Irish. Hungerford was god-parent to one of Dorcas Sydney's numerous children. Little is known of Patrick Grant either, other than that he was described as a servant of Ormond who sent him with a Captain Roberts in September 1583 to conduct a priest attached to the earl of Desmond back to Kilkenny.

Besides the English settlers in Queens County there were a number of Scottish Galloglasses of the MacDonnell clan, namely Calvagh MacTirlaghe MacDonnell at Tennakill; Maelmurry McEdmond MacDonnell at Raheen; and Tirlagh MacDonnell at Castlenoe in Farnans. They were given a special grant of lands in Queen's county as a reward for their part in the wars against the O'Connors, O'Mores, O'Carrolls and O'Molloy. However, in an indenture with Sir Henry Sydney made in 1578 it was agreed that the MacDonnells should pay the crown £300 during pleasure instead of providing the usual customs of Bonnaghts and Sovrins for the maintenance of the queen's galloglasses as the queen wished to abolish these dues. Instead, they agreed to furnish 90 spears of galloglasses, for which they would receive ordinary pay plus the right to demand such victuals as were not covered by the £300. They promised not only to fulfil their duty as galloglasses, but not to serve under any but those appointed by the queen. Calvagh McTirlagh was killed in 1570 while fighting in Connaught and was probably succeeded by Alexander, who after his own death in 1577 would probably have been succeeded by Hugh Boy MacDonnell.

Mention should also be made of a number of English captains who came to the county with the army of re-occupation in 1600. Chief of these was Captain Sir Henry Power who arrived in Waterford, probably in March 1598, with 612 soldiers from Picardy. Later wounded in the relief of Maryborough while in Ormond's service, he was given at different times chief command of forces in Munster and Leinster, holding, with Warham Sentleger, special powers from Essex as a commissioner in Munster whilst there. Returned to Athy in October 1600, he was thereafter active in the re-occupation of Queen's County and still commanded 50 foot in Maryborough in 1611. By this time he had been made a privy councillor and was returned as a member to the parliament of 1613.

Another captain in the re-occupation forces was Captain Thomas Loftus, who married Francis Cosby's widow, Helen Harpole. Born in Ireland, the fourth son of Adam Loftus the lord chancellor, Captain Loftus had seen service as constable of Wicklow Castle in 1582 and 1596 before being included by Mountjoy in May 1600 in a force to defend the Pale. Receiving his knighthood in June 1600, his company of 100 foot formed part of the re-occupation force in Queen's County in July 1601. He also held lands in King's County and County Meath.

Richard Graham, a man of English birth, was another captain to feature during the occupation period. Commanding a company since 1595, his command drew fulsome praise from Mountjoy during active service in King's County and he was present at Kinsale and Carrickfergus for which he was knighted. Although his company does not appear on army lists as being present in Queen's County during this time, his estate in Laois was in addition to the 1,000 acres in County Cavan given to him in the new plantations in 1630. Edward Fisher, another captain in the forces in Queen's County in 1600, had his company of 100 withdrawn from Queen's County in 1602 and sent to Carrickfergus. In 1616 he was one of the patentees of 2,000 acres of escheated lands in Wexford.

One notable figure who did not fit into any category was Patrick Crosby who, although of Irish descent, regarded himself as an Englishman. Originally, Mac Ui Crossan, although he claimed to have the family name Crosby since the reign of Edward IV, it was charged against him in 1600 that his mother was an O'More and that his father's mother was one of the O'Kellys of Clanmalire. Ormond believed that Crosby's ancestor had been chief rhymer to the O'Mores.

Not unexpectedly, Crosby seems to have been used as a go-between between the government and the Irish and, being a fluent Irish speaker like his brother John, bishop of Kerry and prebendary of Dysart Enos, he was employed as a spy amongst the rebels in Munster at the time of Essex's arrival in Ireland. Conflicting estimates of his character suggest that there was doubt as to which side he was actually on. On the one hand he was said to have been in close alliance with the baron of Upper Ossory in planning the capture of Ormond and fostering the rebellion of Owny McRory (whose daughter was married to the baron of Upper Ossory). It was supposed that both enjoyed the protection of Rome and that Crosby had been an acquaintance of the papal legate, Archer. Crosby also was believed to have been shown favour by Captain Tyrell and having engineered the removal of Tyrell and other O'Mores from prison.

On the other hand Sir George Carew constantly eulogised Crosby, praising his faithfulness and zeal during twenty years service, particularly as he had lost all his goods in the O'Neill rebellion. Of his trustworthiness Carew wrote, 'I know no man of his Coat within this Kingdom that is better able and more unfeignedly willing to do Her Majesty's service than he is'. He is now best remembered for transporting the O'Mores to his property in Tarbert in Kerry.

From the information available certain observations can be made about the English settlers. They came for the most part from that unique group in English society – the gentry. Typically, they were representative of old, well-established but inconspicuous families but unlike the adventurers of their class who undertook expeditions to America later in the century they did not share geographical origins. Many of the gentry were motivated by a desire for personal and social advancement which later in the century would be found in New World settlements, privateering in the Caribbean, or perhaps in one of the newly formed trading companies. But in Henry VIII's, and early in Elizabeth's reign, social preferment and adventure were to be had in their majesties service in Ireland rather than further afield. Besides the similar social background of the personnel involved in these undertakings, which characterise the beginnings of English colonial expansion, another notable feature was the aura of patriotism which they invested in these enterprises.

It is hardly surprising that it is possible to discern a more than coincidental connection between the English wars in the Low Countries and the movement to extend the Pale in Ireland. They were simply the same service in two theatres of war. When Henry VIII's wars in the Netherlands ceased the members of the service looking for further employment were attracted to Ireland and when the queen recommenced war in the Netherlands in the 1580s it was not surprising to find some younger sons of settlers attracted to this new theatre of action. Sir Peter Carew had been in Henry VIII's wars but subsequently came to Ireland. Closely connected to the Carews was George Harvey, constable of Maryborough and uncle of Sir George Carew. The Sydneys were also closely involved in both arenas and the Cosbys and Barringtons were personally and genetically connected with the Sydneys. In 1585 Captain Walter Hovenden and Captain Arnold Cosby were both attracted back to the Low Countries.

If it had only been a spirit of adventure which motivated the settlers, their enthusiasm would have soon waned with the ferocity of the opposition to their occupation; but the legality of the queen's right to the government of Ireland was indisputable, and the captains in the service were a personification of that government. The leaders of the Irish, the Keatings and Rory O'More, were pursued as much for their disloyalty as for revenge and were always referred to as rebels or traitors.

Another fact to emerge is the extent to which the original settlers were of mixed religion. Indeed a religious conscience does not appear to have troubled the settlers particularly; marriages between Roman Catholics and Protestants were not infrequent, and those who were Roman Catholic do not seem to have had any difficulty reconciling their faith with loyalty to the crown. But for the fact that the Established Church became identified with the English government and the Irish adopted Roman Catholicism as a unifying hallmark, religion might have been a 'non issue' and it is probably mistaken to regard the war between the settlers and the Irish in the county in any serious sense as a religious one.

The ferocity of the war should perhaps be attributed to the inevitable conflict caused when a new civilisation imposes itself upon an anachronistic society. On the one hand there was the English community which valued the concept of the nation state, that implied central government based on the institutions of crown, lords and commons and an administration effected by professionals.In conjunction with this centralisation, there existed municipal and local government, for which purpose the county was shired; common law replaced brehon law and circuit courts replaced the ancient senchas mór and aes dána.

In opposition to the new order was the heterogeneous Celtic society whose small individual clans, based upon a certain geographical area, found the idea of a nation state a complete anathema. Each tuath or country of the Irish was theoretically independent of any other, but due to the influence of feudalism a hierarchical structure had developed which gave the chieftains, such as the O'More or the O'Connor, a protective authority over lesser dependent clans. This order gave certain individuals very considerable and undisputed spheres of influence which would not be lightly surrendered. Not unnaturally men such as Rory Oge O'More or his successor were loath to renounce this traditional order. Evidence suggests that the resistance of the Irish was the work of a few individuals rather than of the Irish as a people. There was only war between them and the settlers when there was a capable individual to lead the Irish. When he was killed peace would follow, which would not have been the case if the resistance had been a popular one.

It can be seen, therefore, that the plantation was motivated by interests other than adventure, and that it was more than a scheme to develop the land agriculturally, though this was in itself an important consideration; it was to no small extent the consequence of a socio-economic revolution in English society which had its origins in the disintegration of feudal society.

The Land Settlements in Queens County

By 1570 the eastern part of the county, which is now covered by the baronies of Slievemargy, Ballyadams, Cullenagh, Stradbally, Portnahinch and Maryborough East had been extensively settled by English planters interspersed by Irish and Scottish Galloglass grantees; but settlements did not, with the exception of a few, extend further to the west than a longitude line, running five miles west of Maryborough. Iregan or O'Doyne's Country was only settled after 1620, while the south-west part of the county comprising Upper Ossory was not shired until after Florence, 3rd baron of Upper Ossory surrendered it to the queen in 1601.

It is apparent from the fiants and the patent and close rolls of Elizabeth's reign that the divisions of land as made in the grant of 1570 or before remained little changed at least until the report of the Irish Commission of 1622 (see Appendix), though they may have been regranted to different settlers, the land having escheated to the crown due to an attainder or no male issue of a previous holder. Unless exceptions were specifically made in a particular case, grants existing in 1570 were subject to the conditions as laid down in a grant to Henry

Colley which was used as a prototype. Land according to this grant was held in tail mail by service of 1/20 knight's fee; rent was 2d per acre for seven years rising thereafter to 3d per acre; there was an array of obligations on hustings, musters, and dealings with the Irish. Although many grantees were dissatisfied with these restrictive terms and efforts were made to have grants for periods longer than 21 years and to have tenures altered from tail male to one of fee simple as an inducement to settlers to remain, grantees only began to receive their estates in free socage at the turn of the century.

Ballyadams

Taking each barony separately, therefore, it is possible to trace the settlers and settlements within the county in the period between 1570 and 1622. The English settlers who received substantial grants in Ballyadams, which included the Irish cantred of Feranclandidonil, were John Bowen in the north, whose land stretched along the county border, and John and Pierce Hovenden in the south. In February 1570 livery was made with a fine of £7.10.4 to Robert Bowen, alias Robert Thomas, son and heir of John ap Thomas Bowen of the lands of Ballyadams, Cappanafeacle, Rathfilbert, Ballintubbert, Monascreeban and other denominations, amounting in all to 902 acres. His son, John aged 48, inherited the lands on Robert's death in 1621.

John Hovenden, for his part, held in 1571 in the order of 532 acres in Killabban, Ballyfoyle, Killeen and Cullenagh and while there is no reference to this tenure in the 1622 inquisition after his death in 1619, the Books of Survey and Distribution shows it being held by John Hovenden, the grandson of Pierce Hovenden. Pierce, brother of the first John was also granted 446 acres in Coolganagh, Clonprice, Tankardstown and Ballylehane, bordering the Barrow and stretching inland along the border with Slievemargy in 1571. He received a further 100 acres of Rahaspock and Kilfeacle in 1578 out of the lands of Flynne O'Kelly, besides the tithes of corn of Coolbanagher in 1591 along with a lease of lands in Rathbrennan, Kilminchin and Clonkeen at Maryborough. Although there is no mention of Pierce in the 1622 inquisition, his son Thomas appears to have inherited Pierce's lands on the latter's death in 1613.

The only other English gentlemen to hold land in Ballyadams were Robert Harpole and Patrick Hetherington. Harpole was granted the Grange of Kilmagobock in 1577, hitherto leased by Viscount Baltinglass in 1561, and Patrick Hetherington was granted 124 acres in Tullomoy in 1563. Tullomoy passed to his son George in 1595 and was later held by William Hetherington, together with the other Hetherington lands in the barony of Cullenagh .

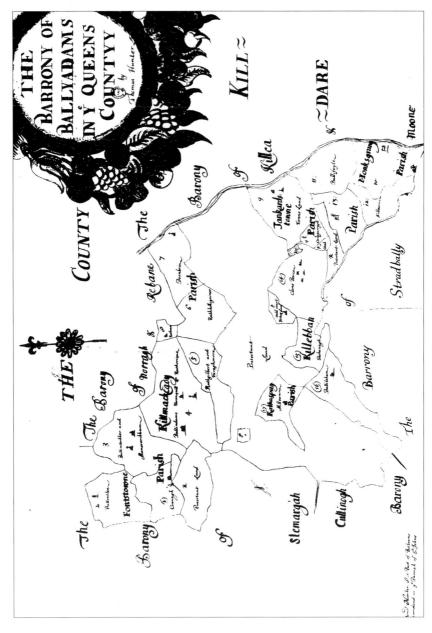

Fig. 11.2 Down survey map of Ballyadams.

Situated between the Bowens and Hovendens were the lands of Maelmurry McEdmond MacDonnell grant of 1563, confirmed in 1570, consisting of 717 acres of the estate of Rahin, Milltown, Shanganagh Bog, Aghanine and Ballylehane Upper with other denominations. Being a galloglass he was required to maintain 9 galloglasses. Escheated to the crown upon Maelmurry's attainder, along with the lands of Kedagh McPierce, Teig O'Kelly and Murtagh O'More, the estate passed by patent in 1601 to Sir Richard Graham (Greames) He still held these lands in 1622, although it should be noted that Graham's claim was disputed in 1601 by Sir Henry Power. Power writing from Ballyadams camp to Sir Robert Cecil put in a bid for the McEdmond lands: 'I understand Sir Richard Grymes (Graham), at his now being in England, hath obtained Her Majesty's grant for the same ...' which he felt would rather have been just reward for his own 20 years service and especially as:

> I have made choice to stay in Leix till these wars were finished, abandoning all my business in England, how much so ever they concern me, all which may be thought not to proceed for the lucre of the entertainment being but a noble the day, seeing that I have already been drawn from a far greater means and a greater list, all which I find not to be respected by the State, in that I am not thought worthy to hold the Lord Deputy's grant, but that it is thought fitter for such a talking fellow as he is, on whom it is bestowed. Which disgrace, pardon me, I beseech your honour if I think I have reason if you will compare us together he being one of whom the world hath taken little notice and never had better reputation in the wars than a private Captain and that but within these few years. For myself ... I do not use to vaunt myself at the killing of every churl or idle fellow, as per-adventure he doth ... For my own parte I have been at almost £200 charge in building upon those lands, and following the law upon those that formerly possessed them to entitle the Queen therein, building upon the promise of the Ld Deputy to me ... that he hath not only given me the Custodian of them but in a Caveat ... to the Remembrance, that no grant should be passed to those parcels to any but me, ... in a lease of twenty one years.

Despite Power's pleas and perhaps because of Mountjoy's patronage, Graham also acquired the lands of Fergonanym O'Kelly immediately to the west of Maelmurry McEdmond's estate. Totalling 230 acres, those lands of Corbally, Kilkefelde and Tecalme had been granted first to Robert George in 1563, had been passed in trust in 1591 to Thomas

Cahill; and had been patented to Graham in 1601 with the McEdmond lands all of which he still held in 1622.

The only other landholder in Ballyadams was the earl of Kildare who held Graigue, Shanganagh More and Inch, which were held by the same grant as those in Stradbally Barony. From the map of 1563 it may be finally observed that most of Ballyadams was cultivated with the exception of a narrow wood probably situated between Ballyadams and Killabban which would have covered McEdmond's lands around Ballylynan. There were also some woods further south covering much of Skehanagh.

Slievemargy

In Slievemargy, on the other hand, the English settlements were not very extensive and in separate parcels, which might be attributed to the rough terrain in this barony. With the exception of the Barnyse tenement, which stretched along a long narrow strip south of the river Douglas, which formed the boundary with Ballyadams, and paralleled Piers Hovenden's lands on the north bank, most of the settlements were made in the south-east part of the barony bordering on the Barrow. The Irish and Scottish lands considerably surpassed those of the English, both in total acreage and in size of individual grants held.

Terence McDonnell held large tracts of land in the north of Slievemargy, immediately south of Barnyse's narrow strip, and in the west. South of him the Keatings were entrenched while Leisagh McDonnell held the southern border with Carlow, except for a parcel held by Arthur Tomen. Terence McDonnell's lands to the west in Kilgory were separated from Leisagh's lands by the ungranted woods and mountains of Slieve Tomane. Similarly ungranted were the areas of Turra and Doonane (the Doonane Hills), as well as the forested north-east of the barony on the Barrow.

John Barnyse's estate of 186 acres in Castletown, Kilcruise, Coonbeg and Ballyfinan granted in 1571, passed on his death to John Baskerville, who still held it in 1622. Barnyse also got the wardship of Dysert in 1578, where he was in fact living. In similar fashion John Barre's 523 acre estate at Shrule granted in 1570, was surrendered to the queen's commissioners and regranted to Robert Harpole of Carlow in 1576, probably because of Barre's death. Harpole originally possessed one grant of land since 1570 in Coolbanagher and another for lands in Ballinrahin, which were surrounded by those of the Keatings, Terence McDonnell and Thady McDonagh, whilst also holding another parcel nearer to Carlow town, consisting of Garrough and Derrymoyle amounting to 65 acres. All of these lands were surrendered by Harpole in 1576 to the same commission that took

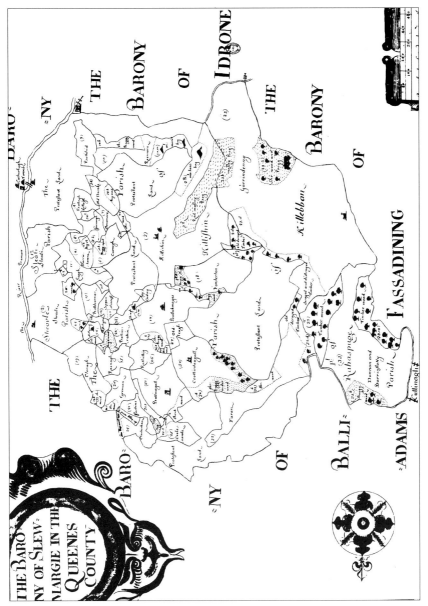

Fig. 11.3 Down survey map of Slievemargy.

Barre's lands and were regranted to Harpole along with such parcels as Ballyhormer, Clonrere, Cultwerin and Rossleaghenbeg and lands of Leisagh McDonnell in Rossmore, Ballyhide, Farrinduf and Gannenoe. Finally, Harpole got the advowson of Clownenagh, formerly granted to Robert Barber. Terence McDonnell's lands in 1570, 834 acres, in Farnans, Kilgory, Slatt, Ballynagall and other denominations were granted in 1602 upon his death without male issue to Patrick Crosby and twenty years later passed by purchase to George Harpole. Robert Harpole , by the way, had succeeded his brother William.

In the barony of Slievemargy also Matthew Skelton held land in Sleaty situated on the Barrow between the lands of Edmund Keating and the earl of Kildare, as well as a parcel sandwiched between Leisagh McDonnell and Henry Davells, both parcels totalling 218 acres. Passing on his death in 1590 to his son, Martin Skelton, alias Lynt, those lands were held still in 1640 by Martin Skelton, although he is not mentioned in 1622. By 1640, however, Derrymoyle was being held by a Protestant, Edward Harman. Sleaty was shared with a Stephen Skelton described as an Irish Protestant in contrast to Martin an English Roman Catholic. Henry Davells, for his part, held 151 acres of Curragh, Clonmore and Killeshin in 1570 but on his death in the Desmond rising in 1579 the property passed on in wardships for his son Henry and grandson Pierce in turn.

Five Keatings, namely, Thomas, Edmund, John, Walter and Richard, held parcels of land in 1570, much of it probably situated in the cultivated area between the English and Scottish lands. Thomas held 67 acres of what is now Ashfield, forming a deep enclave in Terence McDonnell's lands immediately to the west of Arless. This land was forfeited in 1598 because coign and livery had been allowed contrary to tenure and was given to Dr. Metcalf who also was granted the lands of Thady McDonagh, comprising the modern Cooperhill demesne, namely Stanelaugh and Quidneaghe, south of Harpole's property and between the lands of Edmund Keating, and previously granted after attainder to Sir Richard Graham in 1601. Edmund Keating's own lands, Oldleagh and Ballyvallaghe on the southern end of Thomas Keating's lands, and Cappabeg, wedged between McDonagh's, Davell's and Walter Keating's lands, totalling 96 acres were also surrendered in 1598 and passed by patent to Sir William Sentleger along with Richard Keating's forfeited lands on the north-east border of the barony along the Douglas river and at the eastern end of the Doonane Mountains, sandwiched between Terence's southern border and John Keating's land, 435 acres in all. In the patent and close rolls Richard Keating is referred to as being granted lands in Slievemargy in 1576 and the fiants refer to the same lands being granted to him on new terms although the 1622 inquisition states the 1578 grant to have been made to Adam, not Richard Keating.

Sentleger also in 1622 held the 48 attainted acres of Coolhenny, Shanvally and Kylveick originally granted to Walter Keating in 1563 and renewed in 1570 on new terms. A fourth parcel of forfeited Keating lands to pass to Sentleger was the 98 acres at Towlerton, Straughneugh and Ballihide, granted in 1570, where Leisagh McDonnell also held some estate. John Keating was slain in 1576 by command of the earl of Essex. Besides those lands Sir William Sentleger was passed the lands of Leagh and Mollifad, situated between Walter Keating's eastern parcel and that of Skelton, having been held since 1570 by Sir Thomas Sentleger, the last of the original English grantees in the barony of Slievemargy. These lands were held in 1622 by Sir Robert Sentleger. Sentleger's acquisitions underline the fact that all the land in the Slievemargy Barony, originally granted to an Irishman or Scots galloglass, had passed subsequently into the hands of English settlers, some of whom did not appear in the county until the end of the century.

Stradbally

In Stradbally barony, which coincided more or less with the northern part of the ancient Irish cantred of Eughterhir, whose eastern boundary adjoined that of Ballyadams and ran along the Slewton Mountains (Bankers Hill). The southern and western boundaries of the barony appear to have coincided with the cantred of Feranokelle which included Timoge, Clopook, Loughteog and Grange. Most of this barony in 1563 was cultivated apart from the not very steep grassy hills of Slewton and the area of the Great Wood between Derrybrock and the Barrow that extended northwards to the barony border on the Morrett River and south to Blackford Castle which appears to have been in a clearing. This wood cut Blackford off from Athy except for a pass at the castle itself. The great Wood probably coincided with the modern townlands of Vicarstown(Dodd), Vicarstown(Cosby), Ballymanus, Blackford, Balliikilcavan and Monaferrick with a narrow strip of wood running along the Stradbally river to the town itself. The ridge of hills from Ballymaddock to Raheenisky on the west border of the barony separated it from Dunamase and the Pigotts at Disert.

Most of the known townlands in the Eughterhir part of the barony were granted to Francis Cosby in 1563, including Stradbally, Ballynolan, Kilrory, Ballymaddock, Vicarstown, Ballyrider, Loughill Park, Ballaghmore, Upper and Lower Grange, Clonericoke in Kilrory, Derrybrock, Upper and Lower Park,Moyanna, Rathcrea, Cloduf, Oughaval, Ballaghmore,Oldmill, Ballymanus and Derrybrock. In 1569

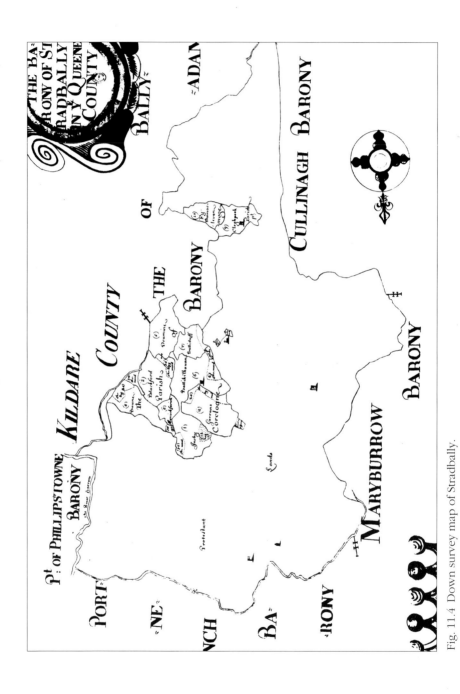

Fig. 11.4 Down survey map of Stradbally.

he also received Clopook, Guileen which sliced through the earl of Kildare's lands in the southern part of the barony. Cosby's lands joined those of Hetherington in Ballyadams. Also in this grant were the lands of Ballyknockan, Kilcolmanbane and Cappoley, Clonebrick and Cowlkhre in Cullenagh barony. The Cosby lands were regranted to Francis Cosby in 1578 who died at the battle of Glenmalure, the lands then passing to his son Alexander Cosby. A protracted law suit in which Lord Bourke of Castleconnell claimed some of the Cosby land on foot of the queen's grant of compensation for his brother's death in a duel on Finchley Common at the hands of Arnold Cosby, Alexander's second brother. The decision after complex legal wrangling finally went in favour of the Cosby family, due to its friendships in high places, Alexander being regranted all his lands in 1593.

Those lands, so wasted by the last rebellion that no-one could be found to undertake their rehabilitation, passed from Alexander and his eldest son Francis, both killed at the battle of Stradbally Bridge on 19 May 1596 at the hands of Owny McRory O'More, to an infant William. A grant of wardship was made to Dorcas Sydney and Helen Harpole, William's grandmother and mother, respectively, of his body and marriage. According to an inquisition taken at Maryborough on 18 August 1596 it was found that Francis Cosby at the time of his death was seized in his demesne as of fee tail of the site, circuit ambit and precinct of Stradbally, formerly a friary, with a watermill in the town, 3,000 acres arable and pasture in Stradbally and Shanmollen(except for 15 acres belonging to Edward Brereton). Dorcas Sydney had in dower half of all the lands and possessions and Helen had another third. By 1622 the estate had passed to Alexander's fourth son, Richard, living at Stradbally. Clopook and Timahoe had been merged by this stage in the ownership of Pierce Davells.

Another parcel of land in Stradbally barony leased to the Englishman Captain William Portas included Blackford, Monaferrick, Garrans, Ballykilcavan, Kellyville, Inch, Bawn and Dromlin (unidentified), amounting to 498 acres. The castle and lands of Blackford, one of the main routes into the county, were surrendered in 1576, possibly on account of Portas' old age, and Blackford passed into the hands of Robert Harpole and, although in 1599 the castle was reported to have been sacked, the manor was still held by George Harpole in 1622.

Most of the southern part of the barony comprising the Feranokelle lands south of the Stradbally River had been granted in 1568 to the earl of Kildare. The grant included Timogue, Ballinteskin, Ballyprior and Ballycoolan and south of Cosby's land at Clopook, the lands of Fallowbeg and Luggacurren, still held by the Kildares in 1622. Most of the cantred of Feranokelle west of the Stradbally River was occupied in

1570 by Edward Brereton, whose 426 acres comprised the townlands of Loughteeog, Loughekeo, Money, Ballenegarbanaghe (unidentified), Shanemollen in Oldmill and Raheenduff, lands which were inherited by his son Henry, who in 1610 was permitted to hold the estates as a manor.

Although Raheeniskey was the only part of the lands in Stradbally granted to John Pigott in 1563 it is intended for the sake of clarity to deal with his grant here. The other lands held by Pigott stretched south from Dunamase just west of the Grange till they met those of Francis Cosby and Barrington in Cullenagh. Piggott at Dysert was one of the captains in the service who held the territory which formed a protective perimeter around the liberties of Maryborough. Piggott's 778 acres of arable pasture were situated in Dysart, Derry, Ballyclider, Collenech (unidentified), Lamberton Demesne, Raheenanisky, Dunamase and Raheenahoran, together with Hophall acquired in 1569. John Piggott died in 1570 and his lands passed eventually in 1587 to a young son Robert, who by 1622 also held Aghalaker, granted to his father but passed in the interim to John Wakeman. One of Robert Piggott's soldiers Daniel Finney, who had previously served under Sir Warham Sentleger until his death in 1599, was allowed to have livery of Piggott's lands of Rahinnecullyman in the parish of Clonnenagh and Clonkeen in consideration of his service and of his poverty.

Cullenagh

In Cullenagh Barony were the ancient church lands of Feranoprior; the southern part of Feranolauler; Galin, the heavily wooded and hilly area that traditionally held the O'More stronghold at Rahanavanagh; and the cantred of Touachlov and Franamanagh.

Perhaps, the largest single land grant to have been made in the whole county was that made to Alexander Cosby and his wife Dorcas Sydney which extended from Timahoe, adjoining Kildare's lands in Luggacurren to the east and Barrington's lands in the west. From Timahoe, Cosby's lands extended the length of the eastern boundary of the barony, but skirting round the hills to the north-west of Moyadd. The same grant also ran along the south border of the county to a point a mile or two west of Ballinakill. Strategically this area was important as full control of it would effectively have prevented the O'Mores, who inhabited the inaccessible parts of Galin to the west of Cosby's grant, from infiltrating south to Ballyraggett, the stronghold of the Mountgarrets, or from going east across the Doonane mountains to the Keatings in Slievemargy. The townlands in this grant included Timahoe, Ballinaclough, Garryglass, Fossy, Ballintlea and Orchard, all cultivated land according to the 1563 map, while Ballycarran, in

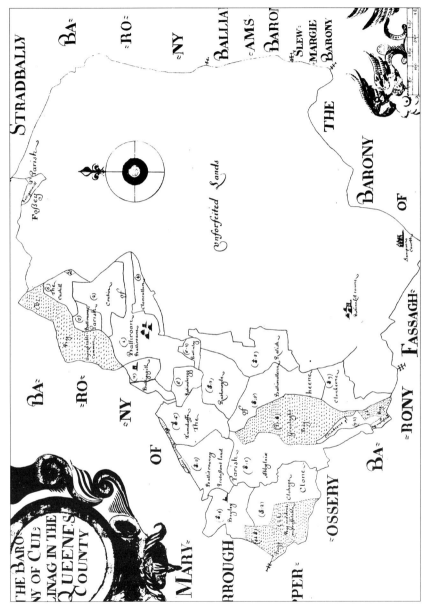

Fig. 11.5 Down survey map of Cullenagh.

Maryborough barony, immediately to the west of a similar grant made to Alexander Cosby's father, was also in the grant.

The second part of Alexander's grant comprised the forested townlands of Graigmutton, Boleybeg and Lisnacoman in the upper reaches of the river Greg, which had cultivated land namely Knockandagun, Graigenahown, Boleybawn, Kilrush and Kilcronen, on either side bordering the hills on the southern boundary of the county, Between Kilcronen and Knockandagun stood the wooded area of Cloghoge, Kilnashane and West Boleybeg, north of which lay the lands of Graigue, Moate and Ballypickas. Moyadd a small cultivated district on the border adjoining Terence O'Donnell's lands in Slievemargy was cut off from the rest of Cosby's lands in Cullenagh by hills and forest but was linked by a pass coming out to the north of Graighowen that may have lain along the route of the modern road from Graigue Cross at Blandsfort to Carlow. The remainder of the grant included Moneyclear, Ballinakill and Lisbigny which was marked on the 1563 map as Tisbegin.

The massive original grant to Cosby and Dorcas Sydney was split up over time for several reasons. In 1594 Alexander was granted a license to alienate lands including Tulmore and Ballyvicas to a certain Sir Thomas Cockelie, but the Cosby family papers record that Dorcas Sydney, not approving of Richard Cosby's marriage to Elizabeth Piggott, left all her estates except Timahoe to her second husband, Sir Thomas Zouche, from England. Timahoe was set in a long lease to Sir Thomas Loftus by Richard Cosby, Loftus being the husband of Helen Harpole, Richard's sister-in-law. Richard Cosby was described in the inquisitions as heir to Timahoe in 1622. Similarly, while Dorcas Sydney was believed to have sold Ballinakill and Dysert Gallen for silver coins, it appears that Ballinakill and Lisboin were granted in a patent of 1612 to Alexander King and Richard Sutton and their heirs, a patent that also included the lands of Tullimore and Balinas, formerly granted to John O'More in 1563 and held in 1622 by Lord Londonderry then living at Ballinakill.

West of Cosby's lands at Timahoe were the lands of John Barrington, inclusive of Raheenduff Big, Kilvahan and Bawnree, an estate of strategic importance since it straddled old boundaries between the Irish cantreds of Toumologan, Feranoprior and Feranolauler; it was situated at the eastern end of a woodland pass, along which Essex marched to relieve Maryborough in 1599; and was just north of the Cullenagh mountains behind which the O'Mores used to take refuge. Captain John Barrington died in 1593 and the inheritance passed to his son Alexander Barrington who eventually received a patent to the lands in 1622.

Directly west of Barrington were lands granted to Jenken Hetherington, comprising Balliroan, Ballyruin, Cruheen and Cloncullane, some 482 acres mainly arable between the Cullenagh mountains and the Colt woodlands. This district was of strategic importance as it commanded the route from Maryborough to Ballinakill and Ballyragget and lay immediately south of the junction to Timahoe, besides being an outpost surrounding Galin. Indeed, Jenken Barrington died in defence of his castle, while his son David, who also received Ballyroan in 1578, was unable to keep the settlement, declaring to the lord high treasurer in 1600 that 1,500 rebels had besieged his castle at Ballyroan in the rebellion, obliging him to flee to Dublin and leaving his estate completely spoiled.

On the western border of the barony which was the furthest west of the early settlements, beyond which was the unshired Fitzpatrick lordship, lands, centred round Abbeyleix and separated from Cosby's lands at Moate and Ballypickas by waste land, were granted to the earl of Ormond. These lands bordered the western extremity of Galin and cut the O'Mores off from the McGillapatricks. The Ormond grant of 1563 included the site of the abbey of Leix, Tullyroe where the old town was, now Abbeyleix demesne, besides Clonkeen, Ralish, Rathmoyle and Cloghoge some 850 acres. Ormond also held land in Clogrennan on the Kilkenny border, south of Lisagh McDonnell's original grant in Slievemargy, land held until 1610 by Arthur Toman.

Ballygormil, a small townland on the border where Cullenagh, Stradbally and Maryborough baronies meet, sandwiched between Cosby's, Murtagh O'More's , Piggott's and Brereton's lands was originally granted to Hugh Lippiat in 1563 before being divided between Francis Cosby, Alexander Cosby and Murtagh O'More. In 1640 it was divided between Thomas Davell's land at Timahoe and Thomas Daniell's land in Maryborough.

The only lands granted to the Irish in Cullenagh were those to Murtagh Oge O'More and Kedagh McPiers O'More. Murtagh was granted Cremorgan and Little Raheenduff in 1563 and 1570, land passed to his son Lisagh McMurtagh Oge O'More in 1589 but confiscated from him in 1598 when he was attainted for treason and given in 1601 to Sir Richard Graham. Graham was given a new title to the lands formerly held by the rebels, McMurtagh O'More, Kedagh McPiers, Mulmory McEdmond and Frynne O'Kelly, in 1613. Kedagh's lands at Monceagle, lying south of Hetherington's land in Galin, appear from the 1563 map to have been heavily wooded.

Portnahinch and Maryborough North

Portnahinch Barony was made up of Clanmalire and Irry. Clanmalire,

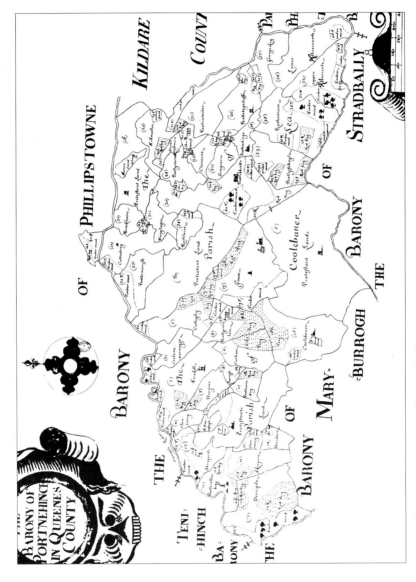

Fig. 11.6 Down survey map of Portnahinch.

Fig. 11.7 Down survey map of Maryborough, northern part.

stronghold of the O'Dempseys, extended from the Barrow in the east to Morrett and Lea Castle in the west, with the north and south borders formed by the Barrow and Morrett Rivers. Immediately west was Irry, stretching as far as Acragar and bordered on the south by the cantred of Feranodoulin and Toumologan a cultivated district originally inhabited by the McLaghlen O'Mores. Unlike Tonmologan, Clanmalire and Irry appear to have been little cultivated, having much wood especially along the banks of the Barrow and Morrett rivers. It is possible that the modern townlands of Courtwood, the Derries, Coolnoe, Rathronshin, Balleglove and Fishertown were probably areas of wood and bog and not granted in 1570.

Few English settlements were made in Clanmalire or Irry. Most of Clanmalire was a preserve of the earls of Kildare and Terence O'Dempsey. In 1570 Kildare held Cappakeel between Morett and Ballybrittas but it was escheated and passed first by patent to Sir John Davis, the attorney-general and then by purchase to Sir William Parsons. West of Ballybrittas, bordering on the lands of Calvagh McDonnell in Tinnekill, John Harres held 98 acres in Emo Park, Killinare, Irlyne and Tologhar.

Morett belonged to Kildare but passed to Oliver Fitzgerald, married to an O'More; Fitzgerald's son, Richard, got a lease of it from Kildare in 1577 and also got a grant from the queen of Harres's land above at Emo and Irlyne. However in 1585, the earl of Kildare leased Morett and Shanganagh to his bastard son Gerald, a shortlived possession since Gerald was murdered and Morett burnt in the late 1590s, leaving the property in the hands of Lady Francis Howard, widow of the twelfth earl of Kildare.

The manor of Lea, uncultivated land interspersed with forest along the Barrow's right bank, passed from the earl of Kildare to Sir Maurice FitzThomas Fitzgerald of Lackagh, Co Kildare in 1556 for a mortgage of £500 and 600 oz. of silver, before it was held in turn by Maurice's son Thomas to 1611; by the latter's wife Margery Fitzjames to 1618; by Robert Bath to 1621; and finally reverted to the earl of Kildare in 1624.

Dividing the Fitzgerald lands were those of the O'Dempsies amounting to 3,300 acres and centred on their castle at Ballybrittas. To the south-west, and probably on the Clanmalire-Irry border were Coolbanagher and Killimy granted to Robert Harpole in 1564, regranted in 1578, and held in 1622 by his second son George. Coolbanagher from the evidence of the 1563 map appears uncultivated and Killimy may have been situated on the edge of the wood covering much of Emo Park through which was a pass linking Ballybrittas with Shean Castle. Calvagh McTirlaghe McDonnell held since 1563 the 998 acre estate covering Tinnakill, Portnahinch, Clonterry, Lauragh, Dangans,

Lorrengarrett, Kilnacash, Ballinriddery, and Coolnavarnoge to Collagh, land held in 1622 by Hugh McCallowaghe McTirlaghe McDonnell's son Fergus. Hugh's grant of the 313 acres of Acragar, Derrygille, Cloncosney and Kilmolgan was also held by Fergus. Acragar was at the entrance of a pass through the dense Bann Regan forest which separated the McDonnells from Iregan and O'Doyne's country.

Dividing the McDonnell's estates were John Whitney's lands of Kilmainham and Eyre, both in Irry, although most of Whitney's lands were in Toumologan or Maryborough North. They included the lands of Shean, Eyre, Killenny, Shaboe, Killone, Ballydavis and Kilmurry, among others such as Raheenahoran, where Piggott had lands such as Killeen, Ballythomas, Derrygannon, Kilmainham and Killeen. Whitney acquired these lands in 1569 when their former resident George Delves died and they eventually passed to his second son, Robert, in 1621....

Maryborough town

During the 1560s Maryborough was more than a garrison. From a map of it in 1563 there were at least seventeen houses and messuages bounding three sides of the fort, but they were all protected by an outer ringwork. It is significant that there were no dwellings to the west of the castle. The houses for the most part were of two storeys, with central chimneys and were probably thatched as was usual in this period. Anthony Roger's house was unique in that it had a stone tower at one end which may have been used as a watchtower looking east. The house also appears larger than the others. Another feature of the town was that there was no direct access to the fort from the rest of the settlements.

In 1569 Maryborough as a corporate town received a charter which gave it the status of a borough with a burgomaster and two bailiffs to be elected annually on St Michael and All Angels day (29 September) by the burghers and commons. The duties of the burgomaster and bailiffs were: to maintain the borough; to hold courts of the town and to execute judiciously all matters connected with it, with the burgesses and the commons. On the day of their election officers had to take a corporal oath before the constable of Maryborough (or in his absence before the burgesses and commons) promising to be faithful to Her Majesty and confirming her own rights and liberties in the borough. The powers invested in the burgomaster were: to elect a sergeant to carry the mace before the burgomaster; to build with the burgesses all necessary ditches and walks for the town's defenses. All lands and tenements within 8,000 yards on either side of the castle walls were to fall within the franchise and liberties of the borough. Except by the default of the burgomaster and bailiffs, no sheriff was permitted to

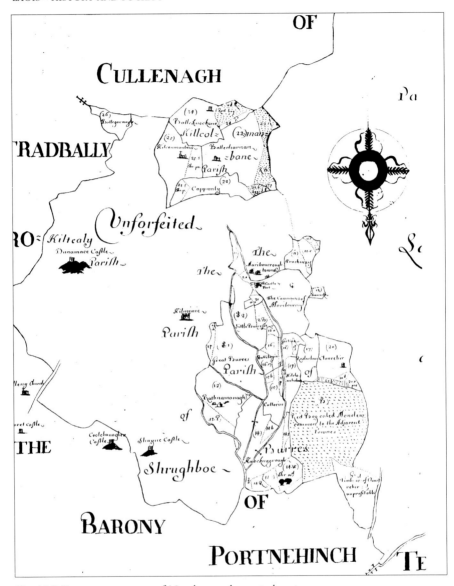

Fig. 11.8 Down survey map of Maryborough, central part.

execute any duties in the borough. All writs were returned by the burgomaster himself. He and the bailiffs had authority to hear all pleas arising within the town's jurisdiction as did the mayor of Drogheda. The profits of pleas, assizes and goods of enfangenthief were to be used to fortify the town with walls and ditches and make payments. The burgomaster was to act as justice of the peace. On Thursdays the town could hold a market within the town from 8 a.m. to 3 p.m., between which times all transactions had to be completed except those between freemen in the town. A foreigner had to have a license from the burgomaster to sell by retail any imported goods.

There was a tax on most goods sold, which also was used to improve fortifications. However, the burgomaster had to pay the exchequer 10/- for the custom, one moiety at Easter, the other on 29 September. Bye-laws made by a majority of the burgomaster, the bailiffs, the burgesses and the commons had to comply with the common law. All waifs and strays were to be used for the common benefit of the town, and inhabitants were subject only to the borough for all trespasses, contracts and other personal offences committed within the town.

About forty messuages can be accounted for during the period 1570 to 1600 and most had sustenance lands attached in neighbouring liberties such as Clonkeen, Kilminchy and Kyle Kiproe. Nicholas White held land in Kyle, Rathleig and Balliloquillock; William Fynne held lands in Raheen; and Robert Eyre held 830 acres in the areas of Kilminchy and Clonkeen. One of the larger landholders just outside Maryborough was Captain Thomas Lambyn, sometime sheriff, who held over 200 acres mostly arable, in Rathevan, Beladd and Clonkeen. To the north-west and west of Maryborough, moreover, lay the cultivated area of Pallas, Ballina, Clongower and Clonreher, which too came within the 8,000 yard radius of the burgomaster's jurisdiction. The six townlands around Pallas, 485 acres, belonged to Anthony Hungerford at first and then to Ludowick Briskett, before falling to William Browne after the O'Mores had captured it. Beyond lay forest and the great White Bog.

The cultivated lands north of Maryborough seem also to coincide with the grant to John Dunkerley in 1563 of Clonreher and other lands, later in the possession of Robert Harpole and his son George. Immediately to the west of the Piggott lands south of Maryborough were the lands of Cappoley and Cashel granted to Francis Cosby, and to the west of these the townland of Ballycarnan granted to Alexander Cosby in 1570. Ballyknockan Castle and lands, 660 acres, were eventually possessed by Pierce Davells and linked with Clopook, as they had been under Hugh Lippiat's ownership prior to 1570. Cashel passed to the Davells but Ballyknockan and Ballycarnon were held by Pierce Crosby in 1640.

In concluding a survey of the land settlements around Maryborough some observations may be made about the nature of them. Around the perimeter of the 8,000 yard radius large parcels of land were held by captains of infantry, namely Dunkerley (Harpole after 1576), Whitney, Piggott, the two Cosbys and Thomas Lambyn. Within this barrier were several parcels held in conjunction with messuages in the town by Eiers, White, Ralph and the Georges, the small holders who appear not to have been professional soldiers.

Till the end of the century a longitude line running the whole length of the county a few miles west of Maryborough marked the limit of land settlements made to either English or Irish. The failure to make land grants west of this line in the following century may be attributed to the failure to shire Upper Ossory in the south-west until after 1600; in the north, the Iregan lands were inaccessible due to thick forests. West of Maryborough there was the White Bog and as one progresses towards the Slieve Bloom Mountains the land becomes less fertile, which would also have been a disincentive.

There were, however, certain exceptions where isolated grants were made beyond the general line of the western frontier. Francis Cosby in 1569 got Mountrath, Clonenenagh, Rosekelton and Tromro, formerly David McMurragh's, lands linked by one pass between Clonenenagh and Clonkeen. This grant was strategic since it straddled a pass on the River Blackwater into Ely O'Carroll and by 1622 was held by Samuel Downing. West of the Pallas estate in a cultivated clearing in Irry was Mathew Skelton's grant and north-west of Irry, separated by Cammogh Wood, were Balifin, Rossmore and Deerpark held by Morghe O'Carroll (MacEvoy) since 1563, passing to George Thornton in 1606 and Pierce Crosby in 1622. This too controlled a pass from Ely O'Carroll to Ballyfin. Donald McGylapatrick got land between Clonkeen and Rosskelton, namely Ballynamuddagh and Coolnacartan primarily dense woodland on the eastern border of the old Irish cantred of Glandibui. Sir Barnaby Fitzpatrick got 400 acres in Derrykeane, Cronoge, Dysartbeagh and Clanndouglas which probably coincided with the cultivated areas on the 1563 map between Cosby in Mountrath and Ormond in Abbeyleix. It was not until 1620 that lands in Iregan, O'Doyne's country, were settled, despite earlier commissions in 1572 and 1576. The land, much of it in Tinnahinch barony, going to Lord Dunsane (1,020 acres), Marmaduke Nelson (600 acres), Giles Rawlins (1,602 acres) and Walter Graham (724acres). Furthermore, Ossory in Clanmallagh and Clandonagh, held by Barnaby Fitzpatrick since a 1537 indenture with Henry VIII was only shired in 1600 as part of the Queen's County when Florence 3rd Baron, surrendered and was regranted it.

To conclude this survey of lands held between 1570 and 1622, it can be seen the descendants of a considerable number of original settlers still possessed lands, although, because of the upheavals of the O'Neill rising, O'More actions especially, many settlers were forced to leave at some stage. The Barringtons, Cosbys and Whitneys were typical of such who returned, although others like the Hetheringtons of Ballyroan seemed not to. Large grants were split by 1600 it appeared, but all Irish, with the exception of the Fitzgeralds, O'Dempsies and Scottish grantees in 1570, had lost out to the English by 1622, the McDonnells of Tinnehinch also excepted. Especially noteworthy were the very large grants made to captains in the service and to Scottish Galloglasses.

By tracing the history of landholdings forward to 1622 and by using the comprehensive inquisitions of lands held at that time, it has been possible to determine the families for whom the expulsion at the end of the century was only temporary. The period of military re-occupation between 1600 and 1603 likewise explains why the composition of the English community was altered by the arrival in the county of captains of companies who as part of the re-occupation forces had settled on new or attainted lands.

The Government of Queens County 1570-1598

Until 1598 that government was carried on from Maryborough and led by a seneschal who was supported by a local militia administered by the captains of her majesty's service. Apart from assessing the inhabitants, the seneschal, Francis Cosby, carried out such tasks as putting down a rebellion in the north-west of Queen's County in 1572 stirred up by the O'Connors; planning the survey of unsettled areas, like Iregan, in 1572 and 1578 and taking the information of Mulroy O'Carroll in 1574 that the earl of Desmond was organising a resistance movement in 1574 that included the O'Mores and O'Connors with plans to enlist 600 Scots. Cosby also acted as constable of Maryborough from 1565 to 1578 and as her majesty's general of the kern, controlling in all 30 horsemen, 100 foot and 33 kern.

There seems to have been some dissatisfaction with Cosby's government. Nicholas White, master of the rolls, complained to Lord Burghley in 1573 that Cosby had been responsible for the O'More disorders by being a winker 'at rebellion'. Cosby rejected this charge when faced with it by Lord Deputy Fitzwilliam to whom the queen had complained of Cosby's inaction, on the grounds that it was not his wish to have so many O'Mores 'in Protection' within the county. The extent to which the county could be out of contact with Dublin was testified to by Fitzwilliam losing touch with Cosby throughout that year, 1573-74, but at any rate Cosby was still seneschal in 1577 when he was commissioned to take the war to Rory Oge O'More and the O'Connors. Even when removed later from that duty, Francis Cosby was listed as general of kern when killed at Glenmalure.

Henry Colley appears to have ruled both King's and Queen's county between Cosby's removal as seneschal and 1583, at which point the need to pursue the O'Mores and Keatings led to Captain Sir Warham Sentleger being given exclusive control of Queen's County as lieutenant or governor. He held this post until his death in 1600, when succeeded by Captain Sir Henry Power, despite Sir George Bouschier's wish in 1585 to have joint control of King's and Queen's County. Sentleger, it should be said, did not confine his activity to Queen's County, tracking kern under Piers Butler in 1587; making war on the rebellious Burkes in 1589-90; serving in Monaghan in 1593 and being with Sir John Norrey's army at Newry in 1595. In Kings/Queen's counties Sentleger was not to make any outward show of aggression against the O'Mores, but rather was to keep a watch on their numbers to make sure that they had no more followers than were covered by the protection. On the other hand he was to use martial law to 'cut off those idle rascals wheresoever he may find them either straggling for spoil or otherwise feeding upon the subjects'.

Under the governor of each province there was a provincial marshal and there was certainly one in Queen's County after 1597, when Robert Bowen held the post. One of the most important offices, nevertheless, was the constable to whom the grantees of land had to register the numbers of men they had under arms, pay their customs and dues. Only the major fortified forts in Leinster such as Philipstown, Athy, Carlow and Maryborough had constables. In 1578 Sir George Harvey, who already had 25 years service in Ireland, took command of Maryborough , with power of martial law over the county. Harvey 's career there was marked, however, by turmoil, being involved in George Carew's murder of Owen 0 Nasye in Dublin; being imprisoned for neglecting a court case; being an impecunious petitioner for funds and increased power; and like Sentleger combining the offices of governor and constable, a situation that continued into the new century as the new governor, Power, sought the post.

The success or failure of the settlement depended ultimately, however, whatever the character and function of the chief officers, upon the ability of the service captains to survive in their small castles and lead expeditions against the Irish. Of the settlers approximately 21 held the rank of captain or constable, but only 14 of them seem to have been on active service to any significant extent between 1570 and 1590. It appears that at least one of the chief castles in each barony had a constable in charge of troops there, although not necessarily the owner, as in Bowen's castle at Ballyadams, and it was the captains or constable's duty to make muster and array of the inhabitants, there being two or three companies for each barony. These were made frequently in the 1570s, were rare during the period of comparative quiet in the 1580s and ceased during the 1590s as this system of raising forces became impracticable with the captains being gradually expelled from their castles during the extensive resistance campaign in Queens County, which was an important arena in O'Neill's war against the English.

Licences to exercise martial law were more frequently used against felons and rebels, such as Whitney's and Francis Cosby's in 1570 and 1572; Francis Cosby's against the O'Mores in 1577; John Barrington's in 1582 and Sentleger's in 1583 upon being appointed governor. Sentleger was again using it in Carlow and Queens County in 1596-7 when defeated outside Maryborough in 1597. It would probably be impossible to determine exactly how many troops were deployed between 1570 and 1598, but theoretically 104 horse, 22 foot and 35 Galloglasses should have been available at any one time although the militia organisation was ineffective. Lambyn in 1573 reporting to the lord deputy complained that Rory Oge O'More was free to move at will and requested that 'It may please your Lordship[to leave] me with six pounds of powder and ten pounds of lead; it would stand me and FitzHarris[whose estate was wasted by O'More]in great stead, for there is not a pound of powder nor lead to be gotten in this country for love nor money, and Fitzharris is driven to a great extremity for lack of both'..

One of the settlers' complaints was that they did not have sufficient forces or equipment to deal effectively with the enemy. County Leix was allocated 100 foot, 30 horse, 33 kern under Cosby and 21 under Owney McHugh McDonnell. Offaly was only to have 100 men. However, in 1577, an additional 337 foot was provided to pursue the O'Mores and O'Connors in both counties. Nevertheless, Anthony Hungerford's command of 100 men was gone in 1582 in keeping with a general policy of reducing forces in the queen's pay in Ireland and giving O'More protection. In further pursuit of this policy, Stradbally Castle was not maintained, Maelmurry McEdmond's kern was disbanded and only John Barrington's, Ormond's, Harrington's and Barnyse's horsemen were kept, along with the footmen under George Harvey at Maryborough and Harpole at Carlow, which were few. Barrington's command of 50 horse, incidentally, had been granted by Lord Deputy Grey and had survived charges of insubordination , malfeasance of cess besides surviving disbandment in 1583.

Of other captains, it is known that Henry Cosby had a company at the Battle of Blackwater in 1598 when he was accused of disobeying orders; and that Walter Hovenden lost his life and company in the battle against Tyrell and Owny McRory outside Maryborough in 1597. Hovenden's brothers, Richard and Piers, served mostly outside the county. Such companies, it ought to be said, were paid for by a cess on the people and when Sydney tried to increase the sum to £2,500 in 1577, the Queen's County gentlemen protested on the grounds that Queens County was over-taxed, was a frontier area and lay wasted by the O'Mores during the Butler Rising. At any rate, as Alexander Cosby made clear in 1593, the whole question of pardons, surplus retainers, kerns and enlistment or presence of idle men led to both trouble and cost; the £600 p/a of 1593 representing the burden of coping with the Irish and Galloglasses, with the unreliability of the Irish being a by-word. A settler's worst fear was surprise attack from Irish they had recruited. Feagh McHugh was cited as an untrustworthy figure of that kind, yet he was in pay as a leader of kern and regarded as a reliable planter for Galin by Fitzwilliam himself. At any rate the disdain of the Irish for the English, who were at most knights compared to Irish who were often earls, bred danger.

A further injustice was the sharing of enemy spoils among captain's troops without regard to the poor or the slaughter of those same poor when they took shelter in rebel fastnesses through necessity, practises which would eventually leave no people in the settlements. In fact the O'Neill risings and the war in the late 1590s had a disastrous effect upon the settlement, with only two castles, Ballyadams and Dysart, barely holding out. That situation had been presaged in 1596 by Sentleger and Robert Piggott when English resolve was needed to prevent a total loss.

The Reoccupational War

The settlers were not in a strong position to resist the increasing pressure of the O'Mores when O'Neill supported them after 1596. Many of the original settlers had died or been killed leaving only minors to succeed. When Tyrell sacked Maryborough itself in December 1597 only Robert Whitney and Terence O'Dempsey came to Sentleger's assistance. Sentleger had ended Owny O'More's protection in 1596 with some equivocation as a grant of Galin to O'More would have been some restraint on him there, besides which O'More might be enticed to suppress rebellion in Munster, as Bowen, the provost marshal of Leinster suggested in 1598.

There were several schools of thought as to what future policy should be maintained towards the Irish in County Leix. Sentleger favoured allowing the O'Mores to settle in Galin subject to some rent as the land there was primarily waste. Such a concession would give them fixed boundaries regarded as a prerequisite for the maintenance of the colony as there was not a single secure place in the county. This 'dove theory' which would grant lands to O'More that in the plantation scheme were earmarked for settlers was re-stated two years later (1598) by the provost marshal of Leinster, Bowen. His argument was that in order to subdue Ireland, Munster would have to be first pacified. By pacifying the Leinster septs it might be possible to then enlist them in suppressing Munster, a not unlikely scenario in the shifting politics of sixteenth century Ireland. Connaught could then be quieted and the government would be able to focus on Tyrone and Ulster. The best means to weaken the enemy was to get them fighting among themselves. Owny's support could be bought with the County of Leix which had belonged to his ancestors but which now had been assigned to freeholders of which he was one. It was obvious that the patentees were unable to make a profit; the Piggotts and Bowens still had possession but their hold was tenuous. It would in Bowen's schemata be more practical to write of the Leix plantation, enlist O'More in the Munster campaign and give the settlers new lands in that province. But for this scenario to be realised the queen had to be convinced that because a man happened to be born in Ireland he could not be capable of legal service. Adam Loftus writing in November of that year spoke of all the English in the county being spoiled by the O'Mores. Sentleger noted the O'Mores's gathering strength along with Tyrell's 60 men, in the face of his own 100 men, leaving Robert Piggott and Whitney as the only captains remaining in the county.

Tripartite negotiations were opened between the lord deputy, O'Neill and O'More and Captain Kingsmill's Company was sent to Queen's County in efforts to prevent further deterioration, but to no avail as Owny wanted more than Galin, even though Callough was the rightful O'More heir. Ormond's relief of Maryborough in January 1599, where Capt. Marshall lay besieged with 150 men, and Essex's victualling of the town in May were some relief, but all the McDonnell galloglasses had rebelled, as had the O'Dunns and O'Dempsies, except for Sir Terence Dempsey and Teague Oge O'Doyne, while the rebels had 570 foot and 30 horse.

However, Essex's expedition marked a turning of the tide in favour of the crown as it reinforced the forces that remained in the county and relieved all the castles, besides stationing reinforcements at strategic points of entry into the county at Ballyraggett, Carlow and in King's County. In response, moreover, to Ormond's capture by Owny McRory in April 1600, a further 350 men were delivered to Sir Henry Power in the county and a new bellicose scheme for bringing peace there was proposed. By August, Mountjoy had marched through the county with 800 foot and 100 horse, met up with Ormond and St Lawrence at Cullenagh Castle, invaded Upper Osserie and saw Sir Oliver Lambert devastate Slievemargy. The death of Owny McRory, furthermore, led to the Keatings, O'Lalors and O'Kelly's submitting, as O'More was the heart of the rebellion, while the scheme to cut off Munster from O'Neill by winning the support of the resident Irish chiefs between the Barrow and the Shannon won the acceptance from O'Dempsey, O'Dunn, the Baron of Upper Ossorie and the Galloglass Hugh Boy McCallough.

In October, Castle Reban on the Barrow, a little north of Athy, was saved from Capt. Tyrell, who invaded the county from King's County in support of O'More's sister Doryne, while in March 1601 Tyrell was again foiled when he re-opened his campaign in King's County and on the northern borders of Clanmalire. By this stage, Mountjoy was able to trust in the midlands being strong enough to contain the O'Mores, create a cordon around Leinster which would allow him to concentrate on Ulster. Indeed, after Kinsale, forces were vastly reduced within the county to a level it had been at before the O'Neill rising. By October 1602, in fact, Mountjoy was finally able to thank God that Leinster was all quiet and 'the Mores [are] consumed', they being 'not above thirty'.

Appendix I

Planters in Leix, 1549-1552 (from W. Fitzgerald's, 'Historical notes on the O'Mores and their territory of Leix', *R.S.A.I. Jn.*, vi (1909-11), pp 29-30).

Date	Nmber of Fiant	Planter	Lands
1549	249	Brian Johns or Jonys, or Jones, Constable of Carlow Castle.	The lordship of Slievemargy.
1549	407	Gyles Hovenden, Gent.	Killabban, Tankardstown, etc.
1550	673	William Hydney, of Kilmainham, Gent.	Ballyroan, etc.
1550	674	The brothers John and William Glaceters, soldiers.	Vicarstown, Ballymanus, etc.
1550	684	Robert St. Leger, Esq., of Carlow.	The lordship of Gallen (the Parish of Dysart-Gallen).
1550	686	Humfrey Haselwood, soldier.	Killone and Kilmurry in the Barony of Stradbally.
1550	694	Robert Quycke, soldier.	Ballycarroll in the Barony of Maryborough East.
1550	695	Hugh Johns or Jones, yeoman.	"Kilnebron and Dysert", (? Dysart-Enos).
1550	696	Thomas Smythe, Gent.	Colt, Kyletabreeheen, and "Rancollenan".
1550	697	Anthony Colclough, Gent.	Ballylynan, Kilmoreny, etc.
1550	698	John Thomas, *alias* Bowen, soldier, constable of Ballyadams Castle.	Ballintubber, Derrinroe (now Kellyville), Killyganard, Balintlea, etc.
1550	699	Thomas Jacobe, of Stradbally, Gent.	The Manor of Stradbally.
1550	700	Donnell mac Shane, (? MacGillapatrick), Gent.	Roskelton, Ardlea, Trumra, etc., in the Parish of Clonagheen.
1550	701	Henry Barrett, soldier.	Clonaddadoran, etc.
1550	703	Sir Ralph Bagenall, Kt.	Eyne, Straboe, Shaen, Borris, and Ratheven.
1550	704	Thomas Croweher, soldier.	Ballynemolyn (*alias* Milltown) and "Raynroan", in the Parish of Rathaspick.
1550	709	Thomas Flody, soldier.	"Cowlrayne".
1550	710	Thomas Apoell, soldier.	Bawn, Monaferrick, and "Ballecowlyn" in the Parish of Curraclone.
1550	712	William Gerbarde.	Ballyadams, Kilmokidde (now Ballyadams Church), etc.
1550	713	John Dunkirley, soldier.	Clonreher, Parish of Borris.
1550	716	Henry Wise, Esq., Captain in the Fort of Leix.	Ballykockan, Kilcolmanbane, etc.
1550	724	Francis Cosby, Gent., of Kildare.	Moyanna, Ballynevicare, alias Vicarstown, Garrymaddock, etc.
1550	725	Calvagh mac Tirlagh (? MacDonnell).	Killeany, Parish of Clonagheen.
1550	727	Thomas Page and John Ley.	Lyaghdi . . . (? Loughteeog, Parish of Dysart-Enos).
1550	736	Edmund Fay, Captain of the King's Kerns.	Ballyfin, Clonygowan, Clonenagh, and "the Camaghe", etc.
1551	740	Walter Peppard, Gent., of Kilkea, Co. Kildare.	Dunbrin, Shanganagh, etc.
1551	741	Sir John Travers, Kt., of Monkstown, Co. Dublin.	The lordship of Timogue, *alias* Farran-O'Kelly [forfeited by the Earl of Kildare].
1551	830	John Bellingham, Gent.	Cullenagh, and Cremorgan.
1551	838	Richard Masterson, Gent.	Clontygoe, Ballypickas, Tullore, Killelan, Dooary, Cloncullane, etc., in the Parish of Ballyroan.
1552	944	Matthew King, Gent., of Moyglare, Co. Meath, Constable of Dungarvan.	Abbeyleix, Lisbigney, Cloneen, Ralish, etc., in the Parish of Abbeyleix.
1552	1131	Edward Randolph, Gent., of Carlow.	The lordship of Timahoe, *alias* Farraneprior.
1552	1145	Richard Mannering, Gent., of Dublin.	The lordship of Gallen (see No. 684).

Appendix II

Summary of Inquisition of 1622 (R. Dunlop, 'The plantation of Leix and Offaly', *E.H.R.* (1891).

Proprietors in 1622	Estates in Queen's County		Original Grantees	How acquired
Ormonde, Earl of	Abbey of Leix	820 acres	Earl of Ormonde, 5 Eliz.	Grant
Ormonde, Earl of	Stratedrussbog	25 acres	Arthur Tomen, 5 Eliz.	Grant
Londonderry, Earl of	Ballynakill	— acres	(1) Alex Cosby and Dorcas Sidney, 13 Eliz. (2) Alex King and Richard Sutton, 9 Jac.	Query
Valentia, Viscount	Rathbronnan	— acres	Robert Eyre, 11 Eliz.	Query Forfeiture of original grantees, owing to
St. Leger, Sir William	Ballymoyler	435 acres	Richard Keating, 5 Eliz.	breach of
St. Leger, Sir William	Coltehenry	48 acres	Walter Keating, 5 Eliz.	conditions
St. Leger, Sir William	Ballymoyleran	98 acres	John Keating, 5 Eliz.	in suffering
St. Leger, Sir William	Colnergen	96 acres	Edmund Keating, 5 Eliz.	coyne and livery in 1598. Grant, 19 Jac.
Metcalf, Dr.	Croughtenteyle	67 acres	Thomas Keating, 5 Eliz.	
Metcalf, Dr.	Stranelaugh	42 acres	Thady McDonough, 5 Eliz.	Grant, 19 Jac.
Crosby, Sir Pierce	Ballyfynan	48 acres	(1) Morrough M'Connel, 5 Eliz. (2) George Thornton, 3 Jac.	Purchase
Crosby, Sir Pierce	Tyrre	84 acres	(1) Thady M'Murrough, 5 Eliz. (2) Mathew Skelton, 13 Eliz.	Query
Crosby, Sir Pierce	Clonrusk	— acres	(1) Thomas Harding, 11 Eliz. (2) Patrick Crosby, 44 Eliz.	Inheritance
Parsons, Sir William	Downe and Ballyduff	— acres	William Parsons, 38 Eliz.	Grant
Parsons, Sir William	Killinkillough	92 acres	(1) Earl of Kildare, 13 Eliz. (2) Sir John Davis, 11 Jac.	Purchase
Barrington, Alexander	Cullenagh	427 acres	John Barrington, 6 Eliz.	Inheritance
St. Leger, Robert	Laawghe	88 acres	Thos St. Leger, 5 Eliz.	Inheritance
Graham, Sir Richard	Rahyne and Dere	717 acres	Mulmory M'Edmond, 5 Eliz.	Forfeiture
Graham, Sir Richard	Dowarry	184 acres	Kedough M'Pers, 5 Eliz.	of original
Graham, Sir Richard	Rahaspick	100 acres	Frayne O'Kelly, 5 Elz.	Grant, 43
Graham, Sir Richard	Cremogan	— acres	Murtagh O'More, 12 Eliz.	Eliz.
Graham, Sir Richard	Rahynduff	60 acres	Murtagh O'More, 5 Eliz.	
Pigott, Sir Robert	Dysert	760 acres	John Pigott, 5 Eliz.	Inheritance
Harpole, George	Colvanacre, &c.	488 acres	Robert Harpole, 6 Eliz.	Inheritance
Harpole, George	Castlenoe	434 acres	(1) Terence M'Donnell, 5 Eliz. (2) Patrick Crosby, 44 Eliz.	Grant, 18 Jac.
Harpole, George	Kilmagobock	— acres	Robert Harpole, 20 Eliz.	Inheritance
Whitney, Robert	Syan	1,520 acres	(1) George Delves, 5 Eliz. (2) John Whitney, 13 Eliz.	Inheritance
Brereton, Henry	Loughtyoge	411 acres	Edward Brereton 5 Eliz.	Inheritance
Donnel, Fergus	Tenekyll	998 acres	Charles M'Turlough, 5 Eliz.	Inheritance
Donnel, Fergus	Acregar	312 acres	Hugh M'Cullough, 5 Eliz.	Inheritance
Skelton, Martin	Slety	— acres	Mathew Skelton, 5 Eliz.	Inheritance
Day, Henry	Clonkyne	123 acres	Thady O'Dowling, 5 Eliz.	Query
O'Dempsey, Sir Terence	Ballybritish	— acres	Owen O'Dempsey, 6 Eliz.	Inheritance
Butler, Edmund	Arleyne	431 acres	(1) Donnel M'Gilapatrick, 5 Eliz. (2) Barnaby FitzPatrick, 19 Eliz.	Query
Butler, Edmund	Desert Beaugh	— acres	Barnaby FitzPatrick, 13 Eliz.	Query
Butler, Robert	Killine	— acres	Barnaby FitzPatrick, 6 Eliz.	Query
George, Robert	Corbally	120 acres	Ferganym O'Kelly, 6 Eliz.	Grant, 20 Eliz.

Proprietors in 1622	Estates in Queen's County		Original Grantees	How acquired
Baskerville, Walter	Ballycashan	180 acres	John Barnish, 19 Eliz.	Conveyance
Cosby, Richard	Stradbally	1,385 acres	(1) Francis Cosby, 5 Eliz.	Inheritance
			(2) Alex Cosby, 35 Eliz.	
Loftus, Sir Thomas	Tynnaho	— acres	Francis Cosby, 11Eliz.	Query
Davells, Pierce	Knockancoo	150 acres	Henry Davells, 5 Eliz.	Inheritance
Downing, Samuel	Trummoroghe	193 acres	(1) David M'Murrough, 5 Eliz.	Purchase
			(2) Francis Cosby, 11 Eliz.	
			(3) Richard Cosby, 6 Jac.	
			(4) Edmund Medderpond, 19 Jac.	
Lamden, Thomas	Lands in Maryborough	298 acres	Thomas Lamden, 11 Eliz.	Inheritance
Lamden, Thomas	Lands in Maryborough	— acres	(1) John Ralph, 11 Eliz.	Inheritance
			(2) Thomas Lamden, 13 Eliz.	
Eyre, William		70 acres	Robert Eyre, 5 Eliz.	Inheritance
Hetherington, William	Towloughe	124 acres	Patrick Hetherington, 5 Eliz.	Inheritance
Hetherington, William	Ballyroan	412 acres	(1) Jenkin Hetherington, 20 Eliz.	Inheritance
			(2) David Hetherington, 20 Eliz.	
Wakeman, John	Raleage	92 acres	Nicholas White, 5 Eliz.	Grant, 6 Jac.
Finney, Daniel	Rahynhullen	— acres	William Finney, 11 Eliz.	Inheritance
Bowen, John	Ballyadams	— acres	Robert Bowen, 20 Eliz.	Inheritance

Proprietors in 1622	Estates in King's County		Original Grantees	How acquired
Warren, Sir Henry	Ballybrittan	620 acres	Henry Warren, 5 Eliz.	Inheritance
Warren, Sir Henry	Lyennemarren	145 acres	Richard Pepper, 5 Eliz.	Purchase
Colley, Sir William	Edenderry	387 acres	Henry Colley, 5 Eliz.	Inheritance
Herbert, Sir Jasper	Monasteroris	449 acres	Nicholas Herbert, 5 Eliz.	Inheritance
Moore, Sir John	Castletown	760 acres	(1) Robert Colley, 5 Eliz.	Inheritance
			(2) Edward Moore, 20 Eliz.	
Moore, Sir John	Clonefad	90 acres	Anthony March, 6 Eliz.	Purchase
Moore, Sir John	Crutt (moiety of)	93 acres	(1) John Till, 5 Eliz.	Purchase
			(2) Brian Fitzwilliam, 31 Eliz.	
Moore, Sir John	Crutt (moiety of)	93 acres	(1) John Davy, 5 Eliz.	Purchase
			(2) Rosse Macgeorghegan, 18 Eliz.	
Moore, Sir John	Rathrumon	155 acres	Walter Bermingham, 5 Eliz.	Purchase
Leicester, Robert	Clonearl	180 acres	Peter Leicester, 5 Eliz.	Inheritance
Leicester, Robert	Kylduff	90 acres	David Sumpter (vacated)	Grant
Leicester, Robert	Killyshell	100 acres	(1) William Furres, 6 Eliz.	Purchase
			(2) Edward Furres	
Wakeley, Thomas	Ballyburly	— acres	John Wakeley, 5 Eliz.	Inheritance
Brabazon, Malby, and White, John	Marystown	255 acres	Thomas Morris, 5 Eliz.	Purchase
Moore, Viscount	Abbey of Galen	— acres	Viscount Moore, 10 Jac.	Grant
Herbert, Sir Edward	Abbey of Darain	— acres	Nicholas Herbert, 17 Eliz.	Inheritance
O'Dempsey, Sir Terence	Clonegawnaghe	3,302 acres	Owen O'Dempsey, 6 Eliz.	Inheritance
Westmeath, Earl	Ballycorbet	200 acres	Christopher Nugent Lord Delvin), 5 Eliz.	Inheritance
Offaly, Lady	Killegh	— acres	(1) Edward D'Arcy, 11 Eliz.	Grant, 18 Jac.
			(2) Earl of Kildare, 20 Eliz.	
Offaly, Lady	Raynduf	1,546 acres	Lysagh M'Murrough, 5 Eliz.	Purchase
O'Conor, Brian	Derrymollen	454 acres	(1) Thady M'Cahir, 6 Eliz.	Conveyance
			(2) Sir Francis Annesley, 18 Jac.	
Tyrrell, Maurice	Brackland	260 acres	Thomas Tyrrell, 5 Eliz.	Inheritance
Flood, Oliver	Kilclonfert	180 acres	David Flood, 5 Eliz.	Inheritance
Reynolds, John	Barneboy (moiety of)	46 acres	Humphrey Reynolds, 5 Eliz.	Inheritance
Sankey, William	Ballylaken	260 acres	John Sankey, 5 Elliz.	Inheritance
Rush, Sir Francis	Clonmore	192 acres	(1) Henry Duke, 5 Eliz.	Marriage
			(2) Wiliam Brown, 38 Eliz.	

Appendix III

Unless exceptions were specifically made in a particular case, grants existing in 1570 were subject to the conditions as laid down in a grant to Henry Colley which was used as a prototype. Land was held in tail male by service of 1/20 knights fee. In some cases the fraction of a knight's fee varied, as in the grant to John Pigot of eleven acres at Aghaleker which was held by 1/50 knight's fee, granted 1563. There was a rent of 2d per acre for the first seven years; it then rose to 3d per acre. The grantee had to attend hostings, when called upon, with the greater part of his servants and tenants armed with victuals for three days. After seven years he had to attend all hostings, maintain a specified number of English horsemen; give one plough day for each plough on his lands or to do such work as the constable of Maryborough might command. The lord lieutenant had the right to take as much wood and underwood as may be required from a grantee's land, for building in the county. The grantee was not permitted to use the Brehon law against any subject answerable to the laws of the kingdom; his sons and principal servants were to use the English language, dress and rule as far as they reasonably could. He had to appear before the constable or sheriff on the first of September each year with all the men under his government between the ages of 16 and 60, as was the case in a muster and array. No man of Irish blood was to be maintained who was accustomed to bear arms born outside the county without license granted by the constable and a majority of the free tenants of the county. He had to keep open or closed all fords on his lands as the constable ordered; no-one could destroy any castle, bridge, pavement or togher except such fords adjoining Irish country; nor could he receive pay, or attend upon or assist in incursions. All women possessing a dower or jointure out of the lands were bound to the same conditions; no alienations were permitted, except one third for life to younger sons. The grantee must live on the premises, must not marry or make compaternity with any Irish living outside the counties of the kingdom and not amenable to the laws. They were not to permit coyn or other exactions undertaken by outside persons. If any woman having a jointure were to marry an Irishman as above the jointure would automatically cease. Finally there was reserved to the lord lieutenant the power to alter water courses.

(Cosby, English settlers)

Appendix IV

A true register of all the children's names, the day of their birth the year and the names of the godfathers and godmothers by Mrs Dorcas Sydney's own hand.

1. Francis Cosby, my eldest son was born upon new year's eve between 7 and 8p.m. anno 1571 in the White Friars in Dublin. His godfathers: Sir William Fitzwilliam; the chief remembrancer in Ireland. His godmother: Mrs Fagnet (?) Agard, wife to councillor Francis Agard ,he was christened at St Patrick's Church.

2. William Cosby, my second son was born 10th June, 1573 between 3 & 4 a.m. at the fort in Leix, his godfathers were Sir Henry Fitzwilliam and Captain Meredith; his godmother was the Lady Fitzwilliam, wife to lord deputy.

3. John Cosby, my third son was born 23rd August 1574 at 10 a.m. at Stradbally, his godfathers were Mr John Whitney and Mr FitzHenry; godmother, the Lady Mary Seamour.

4. Richard Cosby, my fourth son was born 14th June 1576 between 5 & 6 in Stradbally. His godfathers my brother Arnold Cosby, Mr John Pyrse; his godmother, Mrs Burriss.

5. Mabel Cosby, my eldest daughter, born 12th August 1578 between 11 and 12 a.m. at Lupen Hall in England. Her godmothers Mrs Mabel Agard and Mrs Catherine Cotten; her godfather, Sir Henry Harrington.

6. Humphrey Cosby, my fifth son born 28th September 1581 between 6 & 7 a.m.in Stradbally. His godfathers were Capt. Marchwood and Capt. George Herney (Harvey), his godmother Mrs Hungerford.

7. Josean Cosby my second daughter born 20th November 1582 at 10 p.m. at the Queen's House in Orford in Kent. Her godmothers were her grandmother Sydney, and Mrs Walker of Orford. Her godfather Mr John (?) of Sennock in Kent – This Josean Cosby was mary'd to the Lord of Hoath.

8. Elizabeth Cosby, my third daughter was born the 8th September 1584 in Stradbally at midnight. Her godmothers were Mrs Luther and Mrs Boskernel; her godfather Edward Brereton, Esq.

9. Charles Cosby my sixth son was born 11th September 1585 at noon in Stradbally. His godfathers were Sir George Bouchier and Capt Thomas Lee; his godmother Mrs Grace Harthpole.

10. Ideth Cosby my fourth daughter, born 11th August 1588 between 9 & 10 a.m. Her godmothers were Mrs Ideth Brereton and her sister Mrs Ross; her godfather Mr Henry Cosby.

11. John Cosby, the youngest was born 11 August 1589.

12. Mary Cosby, born 10th July 1990 between 10 & 11 a.m. Her godmothers were Lady Dier and Sentleger; her godfather Mr. Bowen.

13. Ann Cosby, sixth daughter born 19th September 1591. Her godmothers Mrs Pigott and Mrs. Lambkin (Lamben?), her godfather was Mr John Harrington.

14. Arnold Cosby, ninth son, born Thursday 20th June 1594. His godfathers were Thos. Lambkin (Lamben/) Esq. and David Harrington. His godmother, the Lady White.

(Cosby Papers Stradbally, quoted in Cosby, English settlers)

Appendix V

Chief Castles

Abbeyleix (Ormond)
Acaragar (McDonnell)
Ballyarans (Bowen)
Ballybrittas (O'Dempsey)
Ballynockan (Cosby, Colcloghge)
Ballylehane (Keatings)
Ballynakill (Cosby)
Ballyroan (Hetherington)
Blackford (Portas, Harpole)
Coolbanagher (Harpole) R.
Cullahill (McGillaptrick)
Cullenagh (Barrington)
Derrybrock (Cosby)
Dunamase (O'More?)
Dysart (Biggott, Barnyse)
Gortnacleigh (Fitzpatrick)
Grantstown (Fitzpatrick)
Killebban (Hovenden)
Lea (Earl of Kildare)
Loughkeog (Brereton)
Morrett (Gerald Fitzgerald)
Pallas (Newtown,m Hungerford, Briskett. [R])
Raheen (McDonnell)
Shean (Selves, Whitney, Lamben)
Shrule (Harpole)
Stradbally (Cosby, Cooche)
Tankardstown (Hovenden)
Timahoe (Cosby, Loftus)
Timogue (O'Kelly, G. Fitzgerald)
Tinnekill (McDonnell)
Tully (Heterington)
[R] – Described as old or in ruins

Smaller Dwellings

Ballymadock
Castletown
Clonenan
Clonrehen, Dunkerley
Garrough
Garrymaddock
Kilmurry
Knockadagin
Lisboin
Moneferrick

Moyadd
Oldarrig
Rosconnil

Important Border Forts
Athy
Ballaghmore
Ballyraggat
Carlow
Castlecuffe
Cloghrennan
Monastereven
Reban

(Cosby, English settlers)

Note. This chapter is based on a B.A. dissertation presented to Trinity College Dublin by Ivan Cosby in 1969. The editors wish to thank Mr Cosby for permission to use an abridged form of his work. Those who wish to consult the sources for this article should consult the original dissertation, The English settlers in the Queen's County 1570-1603.

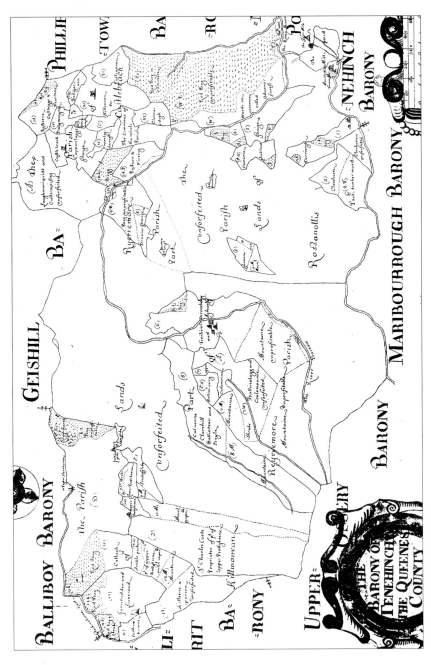

Fig. 11.9 Down survey map of Tinnahinch.

Chapter 12

THE MacGIOLLAPADRAIGS (FITZPATRICKS) OF UPPER OSSORY, 1532-1641[1]

DAVID EDWARDS

Introduction

Sometime late in 1532 Dermot MacGiollapadraig of Ballykeely, the tanaiste of the MacGiollapadraigs of Upper Ossory, was taken prisoner and placed 'in painful duress' by the earl of Ossory, Piers Ruadh Butler, the head of the Butlers of Ormond.[2] Dermot could anticipate little mercy from Earl Piers. He had recently led a series of violent attacks on Butler lands that had resulted in the death of the earl's son, Thomas Butler, who had been chased down and killed by Dermot's forces while trying to retrieve his father's property from thieves operating in MacGiollapadraig territory. The *Annals of the Four Masters* record that in revenge for his son's death the earl had Dermot of Ballykeely 'fettered'.[3] Taken literally, this merely means that Dermot was placed in chains; however, this cannot have been the end of the matter. Following his capture there is a sinister silence regarding his fate in extant sources: the heir-designate of a prominent southern Gaelic dynasty, and a proven strong man and man of war, he was evidently doomed to spend the rest of his days in confinement. He was never heard of again.

The significance of 1532

Because of these events the year 1532 is the best place to begin a discussion of the fate and fortunes of the MacGiollapadraigs (or Fitzpatricks) of Upper Ossory during the early modern period, for it has not previously been noted that Dermot MacGiollapadraig's arrest and subsequent disappearance marks a major watershed in the history of the clan – and of a lot more besides. Before 1532 the MacGiollapadraigs had been steadfast supporters of the principal force in national politics (and the main rivals of the Butlers of Ormond), the Fitzgeralds, earls of Kildare. In the recent past, for instance, Dermot's uncle, Finine MacGiollapadraig, had been killed at Durrow on the

Laois/Kilkenny border fighting for the Fitzgeralds against the Butlers,[4] and likewise Dermot's cousin Shane, ancestor of the MacGiollapadraigs of Formoyle, was a public client of the earls of Kildare, mentioned in the Kildare rental of 1513 as receiving a gift of a horse from the ninth earl, Garret Oge Fitzgerald, in return for his support.[5] The MacGiollapadraigs were Geraldines.

With Dermot's fettering in 1532, this tradition of service to the Fitzgeralds came to an abrupt end. At once the MacGiollapadraigs changed allegiance, in the spirit of Niccolo Machiavelli becoming friends to the Butlers and foes to the Fitzgeralds in order to derive immediate political benefits that might otherwise have escaped them. Dermot of Ballykeely was rendered obsolete by this sudden *volte face;* worse, he was rendered expendable too. In order to consolidate the new accord with the Butlers, it seems the MacGiollapadraigs were willing to sacrifice their tanaiste to the earl of Ossory, the father of his victim, Thomas Butler. Dermot was accordingly handed over to Earl Piers by his elder brother, the chieftain of the clan, Brian MacGiollapadraig – another former Geraldine supporter – in a dramatic exchange ceremony on the Kilkenny frontier. Further proof that the MacGiollapadraigs had deserted the Fitzgeralds came to light with Brian MacGiollapadraig's marriage, also in 1532, to one of Earl Piers's daughters, Margaret Butler; without the fettering of Dermot, the marriage – the ultimate seal of the new alliance – would probably never have taken place. Such was the stuff of dynastic politics in sixteenth century Ireland, where all too often close kindred, in this case a younger brother, were mere pawns in the schemes of their family elders.

Cynical and opportunistic though they were, the significance of these developments, long overlooked by historians, cannot be overstated. For the first time in generations events in Upper Ossory were felt far away, having a major impact on national politics. By joining the Butlers and delivering Dermot MacGiollapadraig up to the earl of Ossory, Brian MacGiollapadraig helped to sound the death toll on the political ascendancy of the Kildare Fitzgeralds. At a stroke the greater part of modern County Laois was removed from the Geraldines' grasp – for they had precious little influence over the MacGiollapadraigs' eastern neighbours, the O'Mores, most of whom supported the Butlers – and the important military corridor running from County Kildare through Upper Ossory to Glashare Castle in north County Kilkenny was closed to them. So too was access to north-west Tipperary and Limerick. The age-old Geraldine pincer around the northern frontiers of the Butler lordship was therefore sundered. Suddenly the Fitzgeralds faced a novel Butler-MacGiollapadraig-O'More triple alliance that was capable

Table 1
The MacGiollapadraigs' main line of descent, c 1450-1640

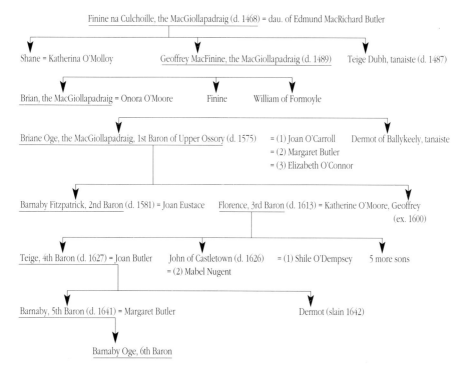

of pushing out of present-day County Laois and penetrating deep into County Kildare itself. Suffice it to say that the defection of the MacGiollapadraigs and the loss of Upper Ossory played no small part in the lead-up to one of the great watersheds of Irish history, as it helped to drive the Kildare Fitzgeralds to the brink of self-destruction in the revolt of 1534 – a revolt which, every schoolchild is taught, laid the foundations for the English reconquest of Ireland and the age of plantation. For once, events in Upper Ossory mattered.

The extent of the MacGiollapadraigs' involvement in preparing the ground for the Kildares' destruction (and all that followed) should not be underestimated. They knew what they were doing. By handing over Dermot of Ballykeely to the earl of Ossory and entering into a formal marital alliance with the Butlers, the MacGiollapadraigs consciously reinvented themselves, becoming one of the first Gaelic clans to accept the re-emergence of English power in Ireland during the reign of Henry VIII. By 1532 Piers, earl of Ossory, was firmly established as an agent of English expansion in the country; in particular, his eldest son and heir, Lord James Butler, was increasingly well connected at King Henry's court, earning the respect of the monarch himself and the trust of his chief minister, Thomas Cromwell.[6] For those in Ireland with a wary eye on the future it was manifest that the English royal government was determined to cut the Fitzgeralds down to size and promote the Butlers at their expense. For a clan leader on the borders of the Pale such as Brian MacGiollapadraig – a man who, like his brother Dermot, was an old associate of the Fitzgeralds – it was time to cut a deal with the rising Butler star or else run the risk of permanent political isolation. His brother's murder of Thomas Butler presented Brian with the opportunity he needed to demonstrate his pliability to the Butlers and their backers in London. Hence, at a hearing in Waterford late in September 1533, he gave Cromwell and the Butlers what they wanted – a detailed background to the murder, culminating with an indictment of the ninth earl of Kildare, Garret Oge, who, he said, had incited Dermot of Ballykeely to kill Thomas Butler and, the deed done, had rejoiced at the news of Butler's death.[7] The timing of Brian's deposition proved critical. Kildare had recently been summoned to London by the king to answer various charges of political misconduct; Brian's testimony against him helped to insure that the summons was not rescinded – in short, that the Fitzgeralds had little choice but to begin plotting their ill-fated revolt.[8]

Brian was eventually well rewarded for his part in driving his dynasty's former allies over the top. Once the Kildare rebellion had imploded, and the rebels crushed and scattered, Henry VIII and his government were obliged to look favourably on this hitherto obscure Irish chieftain who, it was realised, had put himself out on a limb to help the crown and oppose the Geraldines. Consequently, by the mid-1530s Brian MacGiollapadraig was readily identifiable as one of the great winners of post-Kildare Ireland, having hitched his Gaelic banner to the bandwagon of growing English power. In many respects he was the first of a new breed, the Gaelic anglophile, a type of political creature that was destined to become fairly common across early modern Ireland.

What made Brian's achievement truly remarkable was his cold-hearted farsightedness. Not for nothing had he abandoned his brother and denounced his former patron, Kildare. Perverse though it might seem, he appreciated that the only way to oppose the Butlers of Ormond effectively was to pretend to be on their side. Since early in Henry VIII's reign the Butlers had been gathering strength, and with crown encouragement they had greatly expanded the size of their army to the south of Upper Ossory in Kilkenny and Tipperary. If nothing was done to check their growth, Upper Ossory would be engulfed and overrun, dragged back into subjection by being reshired with County Kilkenny, from which it had escaped during the late middle ages. In perhaps the ultimate Machiavellian twist, Brian had only married Margaret Butler and become an open ally of her family in order to continue his independence of them. The marriage alliance was a charade and double-cross, a pragmatic means to draw closer to the Butlers' source of strength, the English crown, so as to turn some of that strength back against them. His new wife, like his brother, was just another pawn in Brian's schemes.

We should not be greatly surprised by the labyrnthine trickery shown by the MacGiollapadraig chieftain during the 1530s. A sea change was under way in Irish life with the resumption of English political and military involvement in the country. It was no time for middle-ranking dynasties such as his to stand on fine principles; rather the English reintervention necessitated the swift adoption of new survival strategies. All that mattered was retaining power. In the ensuing turmoil of sixteenth century Ireland the MacGiollapadraigs would owe a lot to Brian's skills of deception, for he set them on a steady course that allowed them to avoid the sort of pitfalls that overwhelmed many of their neighbours – the O'Mores, the O'Connors, the MacMurrough Kavanaghs – and to hold onto their territory intact, as an autonomous Gaelic lordship, until the early years of the seventeenth century.

And yet his far-sightedness had its limits. Ultimately, his plotting and scheming, and that of his successors, was all in vain, for like the rest of Gaelic Ireland Upper Ossory lost its strength and independence after the completion of the English reconquest at the beginning of the seventeenth century. In the new era of unlimited English power that dawned after 1603, the MacGiollapadraigs found themselves undone by an unscrupulousness the equal of their own, double-crossed by the crown just as they had once double-crossed the Fitzgeralds and the Butlers. The clan's long record of loyalty was disregarded as ambitious governrnent officials and growing numbers of English colonists greedily eyed their land, and in the 1620s their territory was seized (through an English legal fiction) for redistribution and plantation. Because of this, the MacGiollapadraigs' earlier machinations against the Butlers were rendered null and void, and the clan was forced to reassess its position once again. In doing so, the legacy of 1532 was finally overthrown, as the clan suddenly realised they now had more in common with the Butlers – who also had suffered at the crown's hands after 1603 – than with their one-time English protectors. And so it was that the MacGiollapadraigs ended the age of plantation as they had begun it, with another political *volte face,* in 1641 entering into a combination with their former enemies, the Butlers, to shake themselves free of the ensnaring presence of their former friends, the English. Although Irish history abounds with many similar tales of insecurity, treachery and counter-treachery, it has only been in recent years that stories involving middle-ranking dynasties – such as the O'Rourkes and the O'Reillys – have begun to receive serious historical examination, as scholars have striven to measure more accurately the impact and nature of the English reconquest.[9] The MacGiollapadraigs' story, never before told, is perhaps more instructive than most regarding the volatility of the politics that underpinned the reassimilation of early modern Ireland into the English dominions.

A debatable land

The tortuous nature of the MacGiollapadraigs' experience was reinforced by the fact that their territory, Upper Ossory, was a poorly defined space on the Irish political map as the English reintervention started. Though its boundaries had been more or less established by the early sixteenth century, embracing the modern baronies of Upperwoods, Clarmallagh and Clandonagh, it was not until after 1600 that its status as part of Queen's County (County Laois) was confirmed. Until that time it was very much 'a debatable land', existing on the fringes of two counties – County Kilkenny and (after its foundation in 1556) Queen's County – belonging equally to both, yet standing independent of both. The crux of the problem lay in the medieval past. At the time of the Anglo-Norman invasion in the 1170s the MacGiollapadraigs had been kings of Ossory, a great royal lineage commanding much of modern Kilkenny and Laois. The clan had subsequently retreated in the face of the Anglo-Norman advance, by 1213 re-establishing themselves to the north in the Slieve Bloom mountains,[10] but the Anglo-Norman colonists had continued to press and harry them. When introducing a new standard territorial unit, the county, the Anglo-Normans defined the county of Kilkenny as coterminous with Ossory, the region previously ruled by the MacGiollapadraig kings. As a result, having retreated to the northernmost uplands of their former kingdom, the MacGiollapadraigs of Ossory became the MacGiollapadraigs of Upper (northern) Ossory and their lands were deemed part and parcel of medieval Kilkenny.[11]

Over the following centuries they were never able to shake off their attachment to the county that the Anglo-Norman colonists, led by the Butlers of Ormond, had established on their lands. Whether they agreed to it or not, their new base around Slieve Bloom was accounted as Upper Kilkenny, and the Butler-approved officials of Kilkenny county sought time and again to enforce their writ over them. Periods of reconciliation with the Butlers, such as occurred, for instance, during the 1410s and 1420s,[12] did nothing to alleviate the pressures exerted on the MacGiollapadraigs' independence by the county officialdom of Nether (lower) Ossory, as Kilkenny was sometimes called. Taxation was a constant bone of contention, but still more important was the principle of lordship. The Butlers of Ormond and the Kilkenny community simply refused to relinquish their claims of jurisdiction over the clan and their territory: the MacGiollapadraigs must, they insisted, obey the summons of the Kilkenny county sheriff and appear for trial at the county court, based in Kilkenny. By the sixteenth century relations between the clan and the Kilkenny settlers had turned to near-permanent coldness. As an agent of the Dublin government observed about 1587:

> This county [Kilkenny] though it contain in it both Upper Ossory and Nether Ossory, yet such mortal mislike there is between them of the county of Kilkenny and McGilpatrick Lord of Upper Ossory that he will not suffer any trials of his country to be made in that county.[13]

Certain that their autonomy would be systematically crushed by the Butler lords of Kilkenny, the MacGiollapadraigs had eventually gone on the offensive, seeking to push the Butlers and their followers as far away from Slieve Bloom as possible. Commencing in the fourteenth century, in line with a genereal Gaelic resurgence, they had forced the Butlers and their feudal clients, the Graces, the St. Legers and the Purcells, out of the fees they held in Rathdowney, Killermogh, Offerlane, Coolbally, Gortnycross, Aghmacart, Ballygennan and Gortreny.[14] As a result of this, the clan's territory was considerably enlarged, reaching a length of 25 miles, from Slieve Bloom to the area around Durrow, and a width of 15-20 miles, and the Anglo-Norman cantreds (or baronies) of Aghaboe and Odogh had disappeared as territorial units.[15] Ironically, their failure to push further south below Durrow may have been due to the presence nearby of a friendly Kildare Fitzgerald garrison at Glashare Castle; when Glashare later passed to the Butlers in the 1530s Durrow marked the frontier where MacGiollapadraig and Butler forces met. (It is not a coincidence that Durrow remained a detached part of County Kilkenny until 1837).

It is important to realise how fluid conditions along the Upper Ossory/Kilkenny frontier were *circa* 1530. Although the spheres of influence of neither the Butlers nor the MacGiollapadraigs would ever extend much beyond their early sixteenth century perameters, this was far from clear at the time. In disputed border areas nothing was certain. Even during lengthy periods of apparent territorial stability, the possibility always existed that the frontier would change again. A MacGiollapadraig chieftain or Butler earl might die unexpectedly, creating a power vacuum from which the other might benefit. Locals on either side of the border had to be constantly on their guard lest a sudden attack caught them unawares. Fear of each other was made worse by the fact that settlement levels were low; nobody wanted to live so close to a war zone, so that there were less people available to support a defence force. Mutual mistrust led ultimately to a total transformation of race-relations in the region, producing a local form of what modern commentators would call ethnic cleansing – by the 1530s the area north of Durrow was populated exclusively by Gaelic Irish, while those living to the south were almost entirely of Anglo-Norman descent, along with some Gaelic elements traditionally hostile to the MacGiollapadraigs.[16] Separating the two communities was a man-made border (recorded in the Ormond Deeds) of trenches, fences and earthen banks that ran east to west from Coolnacrutta through Coolcashin to Loughill. This creation of a no-man's-land was further compounded by the MacGiollapadraig decision to strip the region around Durrow of all woodland, with Brian MacGiollapadraig accredited with cutting down 'the bishop's woods up to the moor for defence of his country from Kilkenny thieves'.[17]

MacGiollapadraig anxieties that they might be overrun were exacerbated by their awareness that militarily they were no match for the Butlers. Contemporary estimates of the private armies of the Leinster dynasties show that the MacGiollapadraigs (whose war-cry was 'Kerelader Aboe' – 'Fear láidir bú')[18] lagged behind not just the Butlers and the Fitzgeralds, but the MacMurrough Kavanaghs, the O'Connors, the O'Mores and the O'Byrnes as well. In all, the chief of the MacGiollapadraigs was only able to put between 160 and 180 armed men into the field, a figure that seems to have remained fairly constant across the sixteenth century.[19] By the 1530s the Butlers had boosted their army enormously, and had begun to outnumber the MacGiollapadraigs by a factor of three or four to one.[20] The fact that the MacGiollapadraigs might also anticipate trouble with pro-Butler sections of the O'Mores to the east and the O'Carrolls to the west meant that, unless they could find help from some outside source that held sway over the Butlers, the Butlers and their allies would almost certainly destroy them.

The English reintervention promised to save the clan. The monarchy of Henry VIII was opposed to aristocratic ascendancy, with the king himself usually unwilling to grant a large degree of power to his nobles: as one of his ministers commented after his death, King Henry 'was veary suspicious and much given to suspection' (sic).[21] This meant that the pre-1534 political and military expansion of the Ormond Butlers could be manipulated to the advantage of the MacGiollapadraigs after that date, i.e. the MacGiollapadraigs could seek royal protection against over-reaching Butler ambition in post-Kildare Ireland.

Brian MacGiollapadraig took his chance straightaway. Realising that the crown was willing to plot the Butlers' restriction with one hand while promoting them to high office with another, he made it known that he and his family could serve as a counterweight to Butler power in the southern midlands. Thus, just as the Butlers got their hands on the vacant Ormond title late in 1537, with Piers Ruadh becoming an earl twice over 'as earl of Ormond and Ossory', the MacGiollapadraigs also found their position strengthened by the crown. Royal agents were already reporting back to London how the Butlers were 'loath to live in subjection',[22] and as a knee-jerk response to Butler success the new lord deputy of Ireland, Leonard Grey, viscount Grane, was encouraged to consider how best to turn Brian MacGiollapadraig and his followers into an effective anti-Butler force. Ironically Brian used Margaret Butler, his wife, to initiate discussions with the deputy on this matter! For Grey, it was imperative in the interests of the crown that Upper Ossory continue as a debatable land lest it be overrun and assimilated into a greater Ormond lordship. Thus on 8 November 1537 he entered into negotiations with 'MighellPatrick' 'captain of his nation'. Brian played his part convincingly, posing as a biddable Irishman, promising to hold his lands of the king, to adopt English-style customs, and to govern Upper Ossory in the same fashion as those feudal border-lords of the Pale, barons Delvin and Slane. In return Grey agreed to recognise Brian's suzerainty over the rest of the MacGiollapadraigs and, crucially, to afford him the protection of the English law. Decoded, this meant just one thing: should Upper Ossory be threatened in future by hostile neighbours like the Butlers, the crown would use its strength to defend it. An early version of surrender and regrant, the treaty served a direct warning to the Butlers not to over-reach themselves. It also accepted that Upper Ossory was, and would remain, a borderland and potential war-zone, a place where the native rulers would need to maintain a private military force in order to survive. Henry VIII's government was applying two sets of standards simultaneously, one for the Butlers (who must curtail their military abuses) and another for their foes (who could keep troop numbers up for 'defence'). By entering into the treaty the MacGiollapadraig chief had secured his principal political goals: formal crown recognition of his lordly status and a guarantee of protection. His debatable land of Upper Ossory was accepted into the Tudor state as a crown satellite. It was not deemed part of Kilkenny.

For the moment at least he was an autonomous Gaelic lord under an English king.[23]

Preserving independence, 1537-52

But Brian had not finished plotting. The real twist to his schemes had yet to come. For all its advantages, the settlement of 1537 still left him with the thorny problem of how to handle the Butlers. Clearly, Lord Deputy Grey expected Brian to adopt an aggressive stance against his foes; easier said than done. Brian was not convinced of the feasibility of open conflict with the overlords of Kilkenny. Apart from their military might, the Butlers were politically too well placed for him to dare attack them – so well placed, in fact, that they could out-manouevre the lord deputy, and even defy him, by going over his head, utilising their contacts at the royal court in London to discredit him and get what they wanted from the king. Crucially, they had little difficulty overcoming King Henry's reservations about the extent of their power. Brian MacGiollapadraig was understandably cautious about getting too closely involved with Grey in any attack on them, and decided that it was best to let the deputy go it alone. Accordingly, once the agreement had been signed and sealed, and his independence of the Butlers guaranteed by the state, Brian cut loose from Grey, yet again demonstrating his skill in the art of the double-cross. When Grey tried to drive the Butlers into revolt in the summer of 1538 Brian (possibly having encouraged the deputy along this path) stayed aloof, content to let the governor test the ice for him. When the policy collapsed under Grey's feet, with the Butlers gaining widespread sympathy in Dublin and London, the wily MacGiollapadraig chieftain was able to survive the subsequent controversy as Grey lost first his deputyship and then his life, executed on trumped-up charges of treason in 1541.[24]

Grey's blunder taught Brian a valuable lesson: as yet the Butlers were too important to the crown in Ireland, and too sure of themselves at court, for the MacGiollapadraigs to risk offering public support against them. After all, Upper Ossory was only a bridgehead in the southern midlands; the Ormond lordship dominated most of the south. If the Butlers could destroy a lord deputy of Grey's stature, it was best for Brian to continue his preferred strategy of overt friendship and occasional covert hostility. For the rest of his active political life Brian stuck where possible to this path, seeking to discomfit the Butlers without full-scale confrontation. To this end he tried to get closer to the English monarchy, promising much to its representatives but not always delivering. Despite all his friendliness towards Henry VIII he remained an independent Gaelic lord, repeatedly refusing to appear before the nearest English law courts, in Kilkenny, lest doing so might jeopardise his independence. Outwardly an agent of anglicisation, Brian was really something quite different – a Gaelic chief seeking to preserve his Gaelic inheritance by whatever means necessary.

The opportunistic nature of his stance has been overlooked by Irish historians, who have viewed him only from the government's perspective instead of from his own. As a result he has been portrayed only as he allowed the royal authorities to see him, as one of the most 'civil' of the Irishry. It has been suggested, for instance, that by the 1540s Brian had become a mascot of the government. He is mainly remembered as the first Gaelic chieftain to be granted a peerage by an English monarch, in June 1541 (on Trinity Sunday) created 'Baron of Upper Ossory' by Sir Anthony St. Leger, Grey's successor as lord deputy. Likewise it is sometimes noted that he was the first native Irishman ever to sit as a member of the Irish parliament, taking his place among the barons in the house of lords at the opening of the 1541 assembly. Much has also been made of the fact that he travelled to London to be knighted by the king in person in 1543.[25] Though all of this was important, it does not mean that Brian MacGiollapadraig was entirely committed to the government's assimilationist policies. Some months before he was granted his peerage Lord Deputy St. Leger had to force him to enter into a second and more extensive surrender and regrant treaty, one in which he promised to renounce his Gaelic title 'MacGiollapadraig'; to hold his lands by knight's service; to use the English language and adopt English dress; to introduce English methods of agriculture; to give military aid to the deputy when demanded; and to obey the king's laws and to answer 'His Highness's writs, precepts and commandmants ... in any place where his courts should be kept.' The fact that St. Leger appeared in Upper Ossory backed up by a large royal army probably did most to persuade Brian to accept these far-reaching terms. Once the army retreated, however, he returned to character. Happy to be known as the baron of Upper Ossory in the English world, there is nothing to suggest he gave up being 'MacGiollapadraig' at home. As far as we can tell from extant sources, he never wrote or spoke a word of English, but continued to correspond with the government in Latin.[26] And he seems never to have appeared in a court of English law, only before the Irish Council in Dublin Castle. On Brian's terms, then, the 'assimilation' offered by St. Leger meant being a lord of two worlds, English and Gaelic, instead of just one; it did not mean replacing Gaelic ways with English. Hence, having promised the sky to St. Leger, he quickly cut loose of him and used his time in England in 1543 to secure an increase in his status in Upper Ossory, acquiring a grant of manorial jurisdiction, a court leet and a weekly market at Aghaboe to add to his pre-existing powers and privileges as chieftain.[27]

His relationship with St. Leger's government was far from cosy. Like Grey before, Sir Anthony St. Leger wanted to nurture Brian as an anti-Butler presence in the midlands. As before, Brian played along, extracting everything he could from the deputy but failing to confront the Butlers directly. In 1543 he tested the limits of the government's generosity. He claimed that the castle and manor of Glashare in north County Kilkenny had been unjustly taken from him by the earls of Kildare before 1534 – an outright lie – in order to discover if the crown, having bestowed Glashare on the Butlers in 1537, would now give it to him. Going further, he even inquired if the government would consider granting him the manor of Leixlip in County Kildare as compensation for the costs he had incurred when travelling to parliament in 1541 to take up his seat in the house of lords! His requests fell on stony ground.[28] Leixlip was retained by the crown and the new head of the Butlers, James Butler, ninth earl of Ormond, was never in danger of losing Glashare. In 1544 Brian went as far as he ever would for St. Leger, raising his forces to attack Ormond's ally in Laois, Rory Caech O'More, but when he subsequently found himself imprisoned in Dublin Castle on the orders of Ormond's allies in the Irish government, he decided to beat a hasty retreat and keep his distance from the deputy.[29] In the months that followed St.Leger and Ormond went full-tilt at at each other's position. As it was far from clear which party would prevail the Gaelic baron of Upper Ossory did the only thing possible – he pretended to support both sides. Thus in November 1544 he told St. Leger of 'secret combinations' and meetings between Ormond and the southern lords, while a year later he warned Ormond that the deputy and his brother, Robert St. Leger, were trying to entrap him.[30] In the end these tactics served him well, for he out-lasted both protagonists, as Ormond died in mysterious circumstances in London in October 1546 and St. Leger was eventually replaced as lord deputy in May 1548.[31]

His studied neutrality served him well. By the time of St. Leger's recall the Irish midlands were once again in turmoil with the O'Mores and the O'Connors forging an alliance against the government. The stability that had existed along Upper Ossory's frontiers was shattered, and the MacGiollapadraigs were soon drawn into the conflict. For Brian the most worrying thing was not the prospect of new border wars but the possibility of sweeping changes in the political balance of the region. Much though he loathed the power of the O'Mores and the O'Connors he was uneasy about their reduction and the rise of new, more powerful, forces along the borders of the Pale. His concern was entirely understandable. The misfortunes of the O'Mores and the O'Connors provided a major opportunity for expansion to the MacMurrough Kavanaghs, the O'Carrolls and the Butlers. As early as 1545 the Kavanaghs of Idrone had seized their chance to push out of north Carlow towards the midlands when they invaded the little O'Brennan lordship of Idough in north-east Kilkenny – barely ten miles from Upper Ossory.[32] The prospect of further Kavanagh expansion was most unsettling, but the activities of the Butlers in south Laois was even more disquieting – in 1549, after the leader of the rebel O'Mores had been taken to England, Sir Richard Butler, the acting head of the Butlers, moved his forces into O'More country and built a fort at 'Garryndenn'.[33] To cap it all, the royal government in Dublin was seemingly determined to completely destroy the midlands clans and instigate a radical new programme of coercion and colonisation, ready to establish major new garrisons in the heart of Laois and Offaly and introduce a plantation of colonists from England and Wales.[34] Should any of these expansionist forces succeed in their objectives without the active involvement of the MacGiollapadraigs then clearly the clan's future would be in jeopardy. Baron Brian had to act quickly to contain the forces of change.

His decision to marry for a third time (Margaret Butler having died in 1546) helped him to contain the situation and avoid any loss of position. His new bride, Elizabeth O'Connor, was an excellent political choice as spouse, ideally placed to further his influence among both the O'Connors and the O'Mores, for she was respectively daughter and ex-wife of the two principal midlands rebels, her father being the chief of Offaly, Brian O'Connor, and her late husband the former Laois chieftain, Patrick O'More. She became the baron's third wife sometime between 1548 and July 1551, and was soon employed as a mediator with the rebels on her husband's behalf. Evidently (if only for the moment) Brian MacGiollapadraig had decided to keep his distance from the royal authorities in Dublin, seeking to limit the disturbances along the northern and eastern frontiers of his lordship by appeasing his former enemies. Egged on by his bride he took no part in the royal campaigns against O'More and O'Connor forces, and probably offered shelter to some of the rebels, if only to prevent them combining against him. Elizabeth's role in all this should not be underestimated. According to later testimony she spent the first years of her marriage 'practising and procuring all mischief against the good and true subjects [of the crown] and raising and maintaining rebellion against the prince'.[35] The precise extent to which Baron Brian actively colluded with the midlands rebels is unknown, predictably shrouded in secrecy, but reading between the lines (a precarious thing for any historian) he was probably more for the O'More and O'Connor rebels than against them. For all their faults they represented an old established order that had suited the MacGiollapadraigs well enough; their extirpation by the state threatened something new and altogether less manageable. More than anything else, the government's projected plantation scheme was an enormous threat, especially as the MacGiollapadraigs were offered no part of it. Accordingly, one of the reasons why the original Laois/Offaly plantation failed to get off the ground in the early 1550s was because the baron of Upper Ossory, ostensibly an ally of the crown, was opposed to it. Once more Brian left his mark on the great events of his lifetime.

His resolve to move closer to the O'Mores and the O'Connors enabled him to affect political developments in another, more familiar way, a way that was much more reassuring to the crown. Free of the threat of O'More and O'Connor aggression, Brian moved swiftly in the late 1540s to block Butler expansion; had he not done so, it is possible that like the O'Mores and the O'Connors, the MacGiollapadraigs would have been declared outlaws by the government, and so shared their terrible fate. Fortunately, his opposition to the Butlers was very effective, and he and his clan retained their strategic value to the Tudor state. Beginning in the late 1540s he waged a border war against Sir Richard Butler (the brother of the late ninth earl of Ormond) that resulted in a highly satisfactory stalemate. Butler expansion was curbed and Butler client families in north County Kilkenny – the Rosconnill St. Legers and the Clonboran Graces – were forced to retreat from their outlying lands inside Upper Ossory's borders. Equally satisfying, large parts of north Kilkenny were devestated by the MacGiollapadraig forces, depopulating the region and forcing it into economic decline.[36]

The war finally ended in 1552 with neither side victorious, and as a gesture of reconciliation Brian allowed his kinswoman Johanna MacGiollapadraig to marry Robennet Purcell of Foulksrath, a senior commander of the Butler army.[37] Subsequently other marriages during the 1550s helped to consolidate a tentative Butler/MacGiollapadraig peace,[38] with Brian anxious to avoid a major reversal as it emerged that the Dublin administration could no longer back his campaign against his Kilkenny enemies, for the Butlers had once more availed of their contacts at the royal court to win the favour of the monarchy. Never one to ignore a warning sign Brian got out of the war before it was too late. Yet again he had survived a potential trap.

And so it was that the first baron of Upper Ossory entered the new decade having led his dynasty through one of the most complex and least certain periods of Irish history, at one and the same time linked to the English crown, the Butlers of Ormond, the O'Mores of Laois and the O'Connors of Offaly, an associate of all but true friend of none. It remained to be seen if his duplicitous dealings would catch up with him in the years to come.

The rise of Barnaby Fitzpatrick

For all his convoluted political gymnastics, by 1552 Baron Brian felt able to look to the future with growing confidence. In particular he was sure that the provincial dominance of the Ormond Butlers was destined inevitably to subside as a serious threat to his position in Upper Ossory. In 1543, determined to break free of the shadow of Ormond power, he had sent Barnaby, his eldest son and heir, to London to be reared as a courtier in order to break the Butlers' monopoly of court influence. By the early 1550s it seemed that this investment in the Tudor state was beginning to pay dividends. Far from disappearing into obscurity Barnaby had grown into his role with remarkable speed. In February 1547 he had been selected as one of the henchmen for Henry VIII's funeral, and when the king's body was conveyed from Westminster to Windsor for burial, Barnaby carried 'a banner of ancient arms' in the funeral procession.[39] A few months later, Barnaby alarmed the dowager countess of Ormond – and doubtless pleased his father immeasurably – when he presented Brian's petition for Leix Abbey to the master of requests.[40] He was everything Brian had wanted him to be – accustomed to palaces and the company of royalty, Barnaby had become a thoroughly anglicised Irish youth who spoke English fluently and signed himself 'Fitzpatrick' in the English manner. Delighted by his progress his father allowed him to become the main focus of his stategy for sustaining MacGiollapadraig autonomy in the future. It was Brian's single biggest mistake.

Having spent so long away from home Barnaby Fitzpatrick had little in common with his father. Even before his journey to England he had been living outside Upper Ossory, attending school in the 'Inglisshe Pale' since late 1539 or early 1540 when aged just four or five (he was born about 1535). Once in London, from April 1543 Barnaby had grown further apart from his father's world. He had formed a firm childhood friendship with Henry VIII's son, Prince Edward (the future Edward VI), who was barely seven when Barnaby arrived at Whitehall. The relationship between the two boys – one a precocious but sickly English prince-royal, heir to a powerful kingdom, the other an alien to the world of the court, the son of a middling Gaelic lord fresh from the midlands of Ireland – has long been recognised as one of the curiosities of the Tudor era and commemorated as one of the great moments of MacGiollapadraig (Fitzpatrick) history. It is not generally recognised that it was ultimately responsible for the ruin of Barnaby's father, Baron Brian. In achieving the very influence that Brian had desired for him, Barnaby had become empowered at his father's expense. It soon emerged that English statesmen much preferred to deal with the son – so familiar, so young, potentially so pliable – than with the father – so worldwise and full of trickery. In promoting his son the first baron of Upper Ossory had unwittingly sown the seeds of his own downfall.

With the benefit of hindsight it is clear that this was already manifest by 1552. By this time Barnaby had grown out of his original court function of whipping boy to the prince – in the mid-to-late 1540s he had been, as one authority put it, Edward's 'proxy for correction', beaten whenever his royal companion made a mistake at school[41] – and was instead beginning to perform altogether more adult services for the state. At Westminster major political figures such as Sir William Cecil and the radical Protestant Sir William Pickering looked to Barnaby to improve their communications with Edward – since 1547 boy-king of England – and inform them of matters pertaining to the young monarch that might otherwise have escaped their attention. Small wonder that he was made a gentleman-in-ordinary of the king's privy chamber in 1551;[42] his proven malleability made him an ideal royal companion for Edward's ministers. Barnaby further displayed his willingness to serve the state by agreeing to travel to Paris in 1552, ostensibly as a replacement for Edward during an official embassy headed by Lord Clinton, but in reality to act as a sort of open spy on the French king, Henri II, with whom the English had recently been at war. Anglo-French tensions still prevailed, and Barnaby was asked to do his bit for England, instructed to advertise Edward's ministers of occurrences in France, to improve his knowledge of the French languge so that he could listen more attentively to conversations at the French court and, if circumstances permitted, to view and report on the state of the French forts. And all this while 'gentilhomme de la chambre du Roy' in Paris! It is not known how useful Barnaby was to Edward's government, but in the event he stayed at the French royal palace for an entire year, a major undertaking for one so young (he was barely seventeen).[43]

If only because of his probable religious inclinations Barnaby should have fallen on hard times following the death of Edward VI in July 1553. Almost certainly he had been one of the first native Irish lords to embrace Protestantism: although he has left no religious testament behind, he must have found Protestantism acceptable; it would have been unthinkable for him to have been allowed to get as close to King Edward as he did had he failed to espouse the new religion.[44] For this reason the accession as queen of Edward's half-sister, Mary, a pious

Catholic, presented him with the unwelcome prospect of being forced out into the cold unless he could persuade Mary that his previous attachment to Protestantism had been an aberration. It is revealing that he seems to have had little difficulty accomodating himself to the new regime. Despite the fact that there was a rumour in Ireland that he and his cousin Thomas of Ormond had been 'both slaine in the court',[45] he did not immediately return home to reassure his family of his wellbeing, but stayed on in London to get close to Mary. According to some sources early in 1554 he helped defend Mary's rights to the throne against the Protestant rebel, Wyatt.[46] Only when his position was assured did Barnaby head for home, sailing to Ireland in the autumn of 1554. He did not return empty handed. As a token of his high standing with the Marian government he arrived in Dublin armed with a letter from the queen's husband, King Philip of Spain, recommending him to Sir Anthony St. Leger (who had been reinstalled as lord deputy late in 1553).[47]

What little evidence survives suggests that it was not a happy homecoming. In December 1554 the lord deputy noted at the end of a letter to Queen Mary's secretary of state, Sir William Petre, that Barnaby Fitzpatrick could not repair to England as he was detained by some business in his father's country.[48] Unfortunately St. Leger does not go into detail on the matter – in all likelihood he did not know what was happening – but if Barnaby's own words written seventeen years later are accurate, then it seems he had promptly fallen out with his stepmother, Elizabeth O'Connor, whom he resented as exerting too much influence over his father's policies. Outraged that his clan had loosened its ties to the crown as a result of the Laois/Offaly plantation, and that Baron Brian was offering protection to rebels, Barnaby blamed everything on Elizabeth, 'the most naughty and malicious creature alive'.[49] Barnaby's unease was entirely understandable: as a courtier he could ill afford to be associated with his father's hostility to the midlands plantation, a project that he knew Queen Mary and her ministers were determined to establish.[50]

Over the next few years a protracted dynastic struggle ensued in Upper Ossory. In 1556 Barnaby reappeared on the public stage, required by the government to take command of a band of MacGiollapadraig horsemen and kerne for a hosting against the Scots in Ulster.[51] The fact that he, not his father, was chosen to lead the detachment was highly significant. A new administration, headed by Thomas Radcliffe, earl of Sussex, had taken up office in Dublin. Resolved to seize greater control of Ireland by military means, the Laois/Offaly plantation was high on Sussex's agenda, and his administration made no secret of the fact that it wanted Barnaby to lead the MacGiollapadraigs instead of Brian.[52] To strengthen his position in Upper Ossory the government appointed Barnaby to a permanent position in the royal forces, making him a captain of 40 kerne, a post worth £300 per annum that gave him the military and financial basis he needed to break free of his father.[53] In gratitude for this support, Barnaby went on a major expedition to the north of France in 1557-8, serving in the unsuccessful English defence of Calais.[54] With each assignment he was being groomed for power. By mid-1558 Queen Mary was employing him against his kinsmen the O'Mores and O'Connors,[55] a clear sign of the crown's confidence in his ability to overturn his father and stepmother in Upper Ossory. When he met Sussex in O'Carroll's country in July, Baron Brian's fate was sealed, for Barnaby joined the deputy with a force much larger than the 40 kerne funded by the state, having recruited many extra horsemen.[56] More and more of the MacGiollapadraig clan were moving over to his side, so that finally in 1559 (sometime after 17 August)[57] he was ready to move directly against his father. A *coup d'etat* was staged in which Baron Brian was deposed as clan leader with consummate ease. His anglicised hybrid son had out-manoueuvred him, gaining the support of most of the senior MacGiollapadraigs who decided they would rather be ruled by one close to the English monarchy than by the baron and his bride, the dreaded Elizabeth O'Connor.

Brian spent most of the rest of his life confined to Upper Ossory as a virtual prisoner of his son, driven out of most of his castles and possessions as his former lordship was redefined as an anti-O'Connor and anti-O'More zone and his fellow clansmen turned favourably towards the prospect of renewed English expansion. He had little hope of getting his power back. His son and heir Barnaby Fitzpatrick was perfectly suited to the task of leading the MacGiollapadraigs forward into a new era, and having seized power Barnaby was careful everafter to retain a strong grip over the clan. It was not difficult for him to do so, for he was usually able to rely on a strong measure of state support. As late as 1564, early in the reign of Elizabeth I (the new queen of England) Baron Brian received orders from Dublin not to undermine his son's campaigns against the O'Mores and O'Connors. The missive went on to warn him that his private quarrel with Barnaby must not jeopardise the state; if it did, he would suffer the consequences.[58] All hope of Brian staging a comeback ended in 1566 when, encouraged by the Dublin executive, Barnaby declared his father old, frail and impotent, incapable of leadership, and asked the crown to confer him with regency powers in Upper Ossory. His main friends in the Elizabethan government, the new lord deputy of Ireland, Sir Henry Sidney, and the queen's chief minister in England, Sir William Cecil –

both old acquaintances from Edwardian times – intervened strongly on his behalf, so that two years later, after careful deliberation, Elizabeth I gave her consent. With a stroke of the royal pen Barnaby was granted all his father's estate, to hold directly of the crown *in capite*.[59] Thus it transpired that, though he had to wait patiently till his father's death in 1575 to succeed him as second baron of Upper Ossory, Barnaby Fitzpatrick was baron in all but name for many years beforehand.

Elizabethan Upper Ossory

Considerable though his advantages were, Barnaby was ultimately a failure. He never realised his potential to become a national figure, greater than his father had been, and under his headship the MacGiollapadraigs advanced very little.[60] Clearly, this was not because Barnaby lacked powerful friends after seizing power in 1559. Nor was it because he faced serious internal opposition in Upper Ossory: whatever challenges emerged against his leadership he usually managed to nip in the bud. Rather, his failure was due to circumstances beyond his control. Prominent though he was, he was never able to match his main rival, 'Black' Thomas Butler, tenth earl of Ormond, his cousin and neighbour, an Irish nobleman with even better connections in England. If Barnaby Fitzpatrick was a familiar face at the court of Elizabeth I, Ormond was much more familiar, not just the principal Irish courtier at Whitehall but one of the greatest courtiers of the Elizabethan period. He dwarfed Barnaby in every respect and, as Elizabeth's reign progressed, thwarted him at every opportunity too. Thanks to Ormond, the MacGiollapadraigs benefited little from their loyalty to the crown and Barnaby Fitzpatrick was transformed from a political prodigy of the 1550s to a might-have-been thereafter. Thanks to Ormond, the greatest tragedy of Barnaby's life was the death of Edward VI, his boyhood friend. Had Edward lived Barnaby, not Ormond, might have dominated Anglo-Irish relations; because Edward died, and was eventually succeeded by Elizabeth, who valued Ormond highly, Barnaby was compelled to drink the bitter brew of an under-achiever for the rest of his life.

It was cruelly ironic that 'Black Tom of Ormond' became Barnaby's principal persecutor. The Butlers and the MacGiollapadraigs had got along well enough following the conclusion of war between them in 1552. In the summer of 1553 the two dynasties had co-operated closely against the first Protestant bishop of Ossory, John Bale, their forces combining to attack the bishop's supporters and force him to flee the diocese in fear of his life.[61] Little of note seems to have happened between them in the following few years until 1559, and even then what did occur was undoubtedly of great benefit to Barnaby

Fitzpatrick. For just as he was preparing the *coup* against his father, soldiers commanded first by Richard Butler, viscount Mountgarret (Ormond's uncle) and then by Sir Edmund Butler of Clogrenan (Ormond's brother) resumed the old border war around Durrow.[62] In doing so they helped to prepare the way for Barnaby's *coup* by sapping the military strength of his father at a critical moment. It should be stressed that it is *not* clear that the Butlers attacked as part of a government-inspired plan to oust Baron Brian and install Barnaby in his stead; all that can be said is that they may have done. Whatever the case, Barnaby soon fell out with the Butlers after 1559. Unwilling to be their puppet, during the 1560s he tried to free himself of the threat they posed by challenging their dynastic head, the earl of Ormond, at court. To be fair to Barnaby, it was the obvious thing to do. Opposition to the Butlers was usually a prerequisite of successful clan leadership in Upper Ossory, and MacGiollapadraig clan members (as much as Barnaby himself) would have assumed that his personal connections at the English royal palace would maintain him against Ormond. In the event, it was a disastrous miscalculation.

Thomas Butler, tenth earl of Ormond, rose rapidly at court following the accession of Elizabeth I in November 1558. A favoured confidant of the queen, he was rapidly promoted to high office, becoming lord treasurer of Ireland and a member of the Irish Council in 1559. As was her wont, Elizabeth gave him a pet name ('Dark Lucas') and showered him with grants and favours. At times she seems to have treated him like a brother, while on other occasions she relied on him as a counterweight to her greatest favourite, the overly ambitious earl of Leicester, Robert Dudley. Barnaby should have kept his distance, but he hoped that by identifiying himself as one of Leicester's supporters he could strike down Ormond, whom he jeered as his 'hevye frende'.[63] Over the following years he made little attempt to hide his animosity towards Ormond, and in the mid-1570s he even invaded north County Kilkenny.[64] Elizabeth turned against him. Though prepared to heed her ministers' advice and confirm him as *de jure* as well as *de facto* ruler of Upper Ossory, she otherwise ignored Barnaby, treating him with cool disdain. Most obviously, she never entrusted him with major office;[65] less obvious, but equally significant, she hardly ever wrote him a personal letter, something that she was careful to do with those she valued most. Almost all the letters she sent to him were mere stock letters, identical texts that were despatched to a number of Irish lords at times of crisis.[66]

In private Barnaby complained to his friends of his unfair treatment by the queen: was he not a loyal servant of English expansion, a model subject, one whom Lord Deputy Sidney boasted about as 'valerous and loyall' (sic) ,'the faithfullest man for the queen's service in martial action'?[67] His resentment was understandable. In 1560 he had been knighted at Berwick after participating in the English invasion of Scotland and the siege of Leith.[68] In 1564 he had earned the praise of Irish government officials for his exemplary hostility to the O'Mores and O'Connors, and his younger brother Florence MacGiollapadraig had handed his infant son over as a hostage to the O'Mores in order to end their rebellion.[69] Two years later Barnaby served under Sidney in the northern expedition against Shane O'Neill,[70] and in June 1569 his forces fought off an attack by Butler rebels, thus helping to ensure that the Butlers failed to break out of the south in time to draw their O'Neill allies south out of Ulster.[71] Finally, during the mid-to-late 1570s – having succeeded to the Upper Ossory peerage as second baron – Barnaby had thrown himself into the task of exterminating the O'Mores and O'Connors,[72] fighting alongside New English captains such as Francis Cosby and Robert Harpole in a ruthless campaign punctuated by murder, treachery and atrocity. Unlike other Irish lords Barnaby, second Lord Upper Ossory, did not balk at the extremity of the measures adopted by the state in the midlands, but eagerly participated in the bloodshed as one of a growing number of martial law commissioners, possessing the authority to execute without trial all 'offenders' whatsoever.[73] In 1577 having killed some of the O'More rebels, he boasted to Sir Francis Walsingham 'I doubt not with the the help of God to kill or banish the rest in short time'.[74] He was equal to his word. In July 1578 he performed his most famous piece of service, tracking down and killing Rory Oge O'More, the 'chiefest rebel' in Leinster. According to Sidney's later testimony, when offered the reward money of £1,000 for Rory's death, Barnaby was content merely to take £100 for his trouble.[75] He might have been better advised to take what was offered. During this, the peak of his career, he received just one important appointment, in 1576 becoming lieutenant to the lord deputy of the forts in King's County and Queen's County.[76]

Efforts by Sidney and his successor, Lord Justice Drury, to have Baron Barnaby given higher responsibilities ended in catastrophe, for the state as much as for the baron himself. In 1579, having co-opted him as an auxiliary member of the Irish Council, Drury gave him the task of mediating in Munster affairs, requiring him to mend fences between the crown and the earl of Desmond, who was on the brink of rebellion. It seemed Barnaby's moment had arrived at last. Reputedly enjoying a good relationship with Desmond's wife, Countess Eleanor, Baron Barnaby travelled south to try and secure Desmond's allegiance. However, his efforts to dissuade the earl from revolt were unsuccessful, undone by the often unscrupulous actions of Sir Nicholas Malby, his colleague in the field in Kerry, who was disinclined to show Desmond any mercy. When Barnaby spoke with Desmond at Askeaton Castle the earl fell 'into an extreme rage, protesting he would never come to William Drury, nor where Malbie was a counsellor', and he promised to lay Kerry waste rather than bow down to English officialdom.[77] Given that this was his first attempt at high-level mediation, it seems fair to observe that Barnaby's failure might have been anticipated. Perhaps Drury (who was fatally ill) should have chosen someone of greater weight, such as the eleventh earl of Kildare, for such a critical mission. Whatever the case, politics is an unforgiving business, and the collapse of the Askeaton talks brought Barnaby's flirtation with Council membership to a swift end. Following Drury's death early in October, and as the Desmond rebellion spread through the country, the baron lost his influence in Dublin.

The Desmond revolt of October 1579, and the combined uprising of Viscount Baltinglass and Feagh MacHugh O'Byrne in July 1580, signalled Barnaby's final undoing for, disgarded by the central authorities, he soon found himself trapped by events. Outside Ossory, around the northern, western and eastern borders of his lordship, sympathisers with Baltinglass and Desmond proliferated, and eventually pockets of sympathy appeared inside his territory as well. Meanwhile, to the south, Ormond made the baron's predicament much worse by threatening to rally his Butler forces and invade Upper Ossory at the slightest sign of MacGiollapadraig complicity with the rebels. From where he stood, Baron Barnaby was understandably anxious to prevent members of his clan from participating in the revolt; the fact that Upper Ossory was part of a natural corridor between Limerick and Wicklow only served to undermine his chances of doing so – unless he could find a new strategy designed to minimise the dangers confronting him. The solution he chose was one of limited neutrality. When Desmond's brother, Sir John Fitzgerald, set out towards Leinster in August 1580, Baron Barnaby offered him hospitality at Coulkill Castle. It was a decision born of weakness: to have attempted opposing Sir John would have risked losing control of the MacGiollapadraig clan. Unfortunately for Barnaby, it immediately redounded against him. Having left Coulkill, Sir John of Desmond and his followers attacked the earl of Ormond's brother, Piers Butler, at Leix Abbey, as a result of which Barnaby's half-brothers Dermot and Turlough MacGiollapadraig found common cause with the rebels.[78] Within days Ormond retaliated, accusing the baron of treason,[79] and before the year was out the earl had convinced enough people in Dublin of Barnaby's unreliability. On 14 January 1581 Lord and Lady Upper Ossory were jailed in Dublin Castle.[80] They remained locked up

– evidently in unhealthy conditions – for nearly four months, until May, when they were both taken ill and had to be removed to a house in the city. Though Lady Upper Ossory recovered, Baron Barnaby did not. He died early the following November, aged about 46, one of the greatest victims of Ormond's power.[81]

Having commenced his career so brightly as a creature of the English royal court, Barnaby Fitzpatrick, second baron of Upper Ossory, ended it in disgrace, a broken man, largely because his principal adversary was more adept than he at manipulating court influence. Arguably his sole achievement of any moment was his retention of Upper Ossory's independence – an achievement that had cost him his life. Otherwise, in almost everything else that mattered, his touch had turned to mire. Most seriously, he bequeathed to his successor a lordship that was in danger of coming apart at the seams, torn between pro- and anti-English factions as the negative aspect of the government policies he had supported began taking effect around the southern midlands. In particular, sections of the MacGiollapadraig clan, including Geoffrey Fitzpatrick of Ballyowley (Barnaby's youngest brother), were concerned that the chieftain's cooperation with the state was destroying the clan's very fabric, centralising all power in the hands of the chieftain.[82] His heir had a flawed inheritance.

The Nine Years War

After 1581 the gradual fragmentation of the MacGiollapadraig dynasty began gathering pace. Having spent much of his earlier career as a border lord fighting with his neighbours, Barnaby's successor as third baron of Upper Ossory, his younger brother Florence, lacked influence with the government.[83] As a result, for the remainder of the sixteenth century Upper Ossory continued to squirm uncomfortably in the shadow of Black Tom of Ormond. Having secured the succession with government approval, Florence soon lost the support of some sections of the clan because he failed to seek revenge on Ormond for Barnaby's demise; by the same measure, in order to prevent the broad mass of the clan rebelling both against him and the crown, he needed Ormond to stay neutral. Though hardly a friend of Ormond, Florence could not afford to behave as an enemy, lest he too was crushed by the earl's overbearing influence. Accordingly one of his first actions after succeeding to the barony was to patch up a truce with Ormond and the Butlers.[84] Eventually his manifest frailty in the face of Ormond power provided a spur to internal opposition.

The MacShane MacGiollapadraigs were Florence's main opponents, acting as a fifth column element sniping away at his authority. Their leader, Shane, was reputedly a bastard son of the first baron of Upper

Ossory, i.e he was a half-brother of Baron Florence, and he and his sons were unhappy at being passed over in the MacGiollapadraig succession (table 2 below). Florence seems to have kept them under control for most of the 1580s. The support of Lord Deputy Perrot (1584-88) helped him in the short term to pose as a traditional chieftain, as Perrot was hostile to Ormond's hegemony in southern Ireland.[85] Among other things the deputy granted the baron power to execute martial law in his territory in May 1585, and he appointed Teige MacGiollapadraig, Florence's eldest son and his heir-presumptive, to a lucrative posting in the queen's military establishment, granting him a minor command and a pension of four shillings a day.[86] However, once Perrot was replaced after 1588 by a succession of chief governors overtly less critical of the earl, Baron Florence had little choice but to curtail his anti-Butler policies, in the 1590s only permitting his servants to encroach upon the boundaries of Ormond's manor at Glashare.[87]

Table 2
The MacShane MacGiollapadraigs of Ballygehin, circa 1600

Illegitimate offspring of
Brian MacGiollapadraig, 1st Baron of Upper Ossory

Teige Mac Briain (hanged 1540)	Onora O'Dunne (1) = Shane Mac Brian of Ballygehin = (2)	Ellen Butler, dau. of 1st Lord Mountgarret

Brian	Blind Teige	Shane Og	Edmund	Dermot	Turlough	Saiv	Granny

The outbreak of a national uprising from 1594 left Florence hopelessly exposed. The MacShanes committed themselves to rebellion, by 1596 entering into an open alliance with a traditional MacGiollapadraig enemy, the chief of the O'Mores of Laois, Owney MacRory O'More. Dermot MacShane permitted Ballygehen Castle to be burned rather than let it be taken by Florence, and his brothers were involved in a number of skirmishes with Florence and his followers.[88] The lordship of Upper Ossory was soon hopelessly polemicised, riven between two groups both of which had chosen for contingency's sake to become bedfellows of age-old foes, the baron reluctantly edging nearer to Ormond, the MacShanes more eagerly drawing close to O'More. In time both would live to rue their choice of allies; Florence because Ormond did not trust him, never embraced him warmly, and finally turned against him, the MacShanes because the O'Mores and the other allies they made were unable to deliver as much as they promised.

Another internal enemy whom Florence had to contend with was his half-sister Grainne MacGiollapadraig, the sole surviving child of the first baron and Elizabeth O'Connor. For many years the wife of a major Butler lord, Edmund, second viscount Mountgarret, Grainne posed a major threat to Florence. Her Mountgarret connections gave the MacGiollapadraig rebels something they might otherwise not have had, namely a strong profile in the wider world of anti-government conspiracy, for in 1596 her husband had agreed to marry their eldest son, Richard Butler, to a daughter of Hugh O'Neill, earl of Tyrone, the greatest rebel in Ireland. In the wake of this union Mountgarret became for a time 'lieutenant to Tyrone of all his forces', and his high status in the rebel confederacy encouraged the MacShanes and other dissident MacGiollapadraigs to overcome their suspicions of his Butler blood and join with him in a single conspiracy, presenting a united front against Baron Florence and the state in the southern midlands.[89] To add to the baron's dilemma Mountgarret was indisputably a more effective opponent of Ormond power than he was. The second most senior Butler lord, he hoped one day to succeed to the earldom, and since the death of Ormond's only son in 1590 he had been challenging the earl's authority in Kilkenny with increasing self-confidence. His sudden promotion to national importance after the O'Neill marriage alliance left his kinsman and neighbour the baron of Upper Ossory trapped, unable to take sides in the conflict. From where Florence stood, while failure to confront the viscount would invite the hostility of Ormond – who was made lord general of the crown forces in Ireland in 1597 – open alliance with Ormond would destroy his chances of regaining full control of the clan. In the space of a year his capacity for independent action had shrivelled. After 1596, with no obvious way forward, he sat on the fence and played for time, in the hope that his territories would be by-passed by events.

For a few years this policy promised to succeed in its purpose of keeping the war out of the area. Ormond for the most part was too busy securing Kilkenny's eastern frontier with Carlow to give much heed to Upper Ossory, and Mountgarret failed to gain enough support inside Ormond's territories to use Upper Ossory as a power-base or turn it into a battleground. Admittedly, early in 1596 Ormond had taken possession of MacGiollapadraig land lying along the Kilkenny border,[90] but this apart, he did relatively little, content to leave Baron Florence and the MacGiollapadraigs to their own devices, especially after the circa 1598 marriage of his grandniece, Margaret (daughter of Walter Butler of Kilcash), to Florence's grandson, Barnaby (son of Teige, his heir-presumptive). The arrest of Mountgarret in October 1596 and the killing of the Wicklow chieftain Feagh MacHugh O'Byrne in May 1597 robbed the rebel MacGiollapadraigs of their principal regional leaders, so that their activities were subsequently confined to a handful of relatively minor affrays.[91]

This remained the case until 1600. Even after Mountgarret had regained his freedom in 1598 little had happened in Upper Ossory, not least because after returning home the viscount had fallen out with some of his MacGiollapdraig followers who had expressed a desire that when the war was over they would be 'righted of the wrongs' that the Butlers had previously done unto them.[92] It took some time before he felt safe alongside them again; presumaby his wife Grainne and the Kilkenny-born Jesuit, James Archer, helped to patch things up. Hence it was not until April 1600 that Upper Ossory assumed an important role in the war. That month, in a plot perfectly designed to suit Viscount Mountgarret's ends, Shane Oge MacGiollapadraig combined with Archer and the O'Mores to plot the capture of the most important commander of the queen's forces, the earl of Ormond. Having seized the old nobleman at a parley in Idough, the rebels led the earl away to Gortnaclea Castle, a tower house standing between Aghaboe and Abbeyleix, and a MacGiollapadraig possession.[93] Although ultimately it proved a fiasco for the rebels, with the earl securing his freedom and returning home to Kilkenny in triumph, the kidnapping of Ormond was of major symbolic significance for the MacGiollapadraig clan. At a stroke Upper Ossory had been dragged into the heart of a countrywide conflict and identified by the royal authorities as a major rebel stronghold. It meant that Baron Florence was exposed to the cold scrutiny of the government, for at the very time that Ormond was captured and brought into Upper Ossory for hiding, the baron had been absent at court, extracting a guarantee of his territory's independence of Kilkenny from the queen.[94] His seat on the political fence was becoming highly uncomfortable.

If the Ormond kidnapping was not enough to contend with, Florence's grip on power was further endangered by the behaviour of his eldest son, Teige, who chose this moment to go over to the rebels. It is difficult to trace the underlying cause of Teige's decision – later evidence suggests there was no love lost between him and his father – but whatever his reasons, Teige's revolt caused the baron enormous embarrassment. In August 1600, on hearing of the approach of the lord deputy, he burned Castletown and the surrounding area to prevent it providing succour to the royal army in which he had once served.

Although Teige submitted after his father led a ruthless campaign against his forces early in the new year,[95] Upper Ossory remained deep in crisis.[96]

In November 1601 one Captain Richard Tyrrell added immeasurably to Baron Florence's discomfort. Now the chief rebel in the midlands following the death of Owney MacRory O'More, Tyrrell established a major new toehold in the region. Unfortunately for the baron, he allegedly did so with MacGiollapadraig connivance. As the earl of Ormond told Sir Robert Cecil, the English secretary of state, having taken Killurin Castle in O'Molloy's country, Tyrrell advanced into Upper Ossory, where he encountered no resistance; on the contrary, it transpired that instead of opposing him Teige MacGiollapadraig welcomed his arrival, and once more threw in his lot with the rebels, surrendering possession of his chief seat, Water Castle, to Tyrrell.[97] His family's reputation in government circles was irreparably damaged. For a time Water Castle became Tyrrell's main base. Tyrrell's wife, a sister of Owney O'More, set up residence in the fort, and Tyrrell himself brought his spoils back there. (It was also the place where he kept his prisoners and hostages). It was only a matter of time before crown officials began viewing the favourable treatment of Baron Florence as ill-advised lenience.

Stung by criticism, and fearful of reprisals by Ormond, Florence at last re-entered the war in late April 1602, by which time it was clear beyond all reasonable doubt that Tyrone and his confederates were doomed. Early in May he wrote to Cecil boasting of his recent service against the rebels: 'I have lately taken [as] prisoners two notable traitors who did much disturb Leinster, Dermot MacShane, a nephew of mine whom I could never rule, and William McHubert'. These, he was proud to say, were now dead, as he had handed them over to Lord Deputy Mountjoy for execution. But behind the boasts and bluster Florence was concerned to explain away his failure to act earlier, and more decisively, against his kinsmen. Offering all the usual promises of future good behaviour, he blamed his manifest under-performance in the field on the earl of Ormond, 'my potent adversary', whom he accused of working against him ever since the war began. The accusation was entirely predictable. Once more a MacGiollapadraig chieftain was seeking friends in high places by warning of the dangers of Ormond ambition in the southern midlands.[98] He was about to learn that this tried and trusted formula had run its course.

Jacobean decline

At first glance it might seem that Florence MacGiollapadraig, third baron of Upper Ossory, had emerged victorious from the trauma of the

Nine Years' War. After all, not only had he done just enough to be counted on the winning side in the conflict, but his limited support of the English crown had gained him the greatest of all prizes: a guarantee by Elizabeth I in 1600 that his territory would never be returned to County Kilkenny, but would instead be formally re-shired as part of Queen's County, 'it having been doubtful whether the country was part of any county or not'.[99] At last the MacGiollapadraigs were completely free of the threat of Ormond aggrandisement. Secondly, Florence had also secured a fee-farm grant of Aghmacart Abbey and Aghaboe Friary (as well as the reversion of several rectories in Ossory) as a reward for his fitful loyalty. Lastly, Elizabeth I had agreed to settle the MacGiollapadraig succession along the lines indicated by Florence, with his second son John (alias Shane) of Castletown recognised as his rightful heir at the expense of his eldest son, the aforementioned Teige, whom he wished to disown for his treachery in 1600.[100]

The fact that some of these decisions were confirmed after the treaty of Mellifont by Queen Elizabeth's successor, the Scottish-born monarch, James I, seemed likewise to augur well for the future. Evidently, the MacGiollapadraig clan could expect the reign of James I to be nothing more than a continuation of that of his predecessor, with the baron of Upper Ossory's status as the crown's representative remaining unchanged, his power over the rest of the dynasty still very much embraced by the state.

All was not as it seemed. The scene was set for another of those episodes of political betrayal that punctuated the annals of MacGiollapadraig history in early modern times. Unbeknownst to him, serious problems were headed Baron Florence's way so that, despite its promising start, the seventeenth century would soon mark a major downturn in the fortunes of himself and other senior members of the clan. Following the end of the Nine Years War powerful new forces were let loose in Ireland. For one thing, now that Tyrone was vanquished and the country lay conquered before it, the colonial administration in Dublin no longer needed the MacGiollapadraigs as a counterweight to the Butlers; suddenly the clan was dispensable. For another, the English soldiers who had completed the reconquest expected reward for their endeavours, and in the main they got it. After King James had established his grip on the throne a number of them, headed by Sir Arthur Chichester – appointed lord deputy in 1605 – were promoted to high political office in Dublin. They assumed the reins of command partly in the manner of conquerors in search of spoils, but also as battle-scarred ex-combatants determined now that peace had arrived to punish those – such as the MacGiollapadraigs – who had failed to adequately support the crown during the war.

The clan's religious affiliations increased its difficulties. In the cold wind now blowing from Dublin Castle the Catholicism of the MacGiollapadraigs also counted against them. Under Chichester's leadership the crown redefined loyalty along sectarian lines. Dubbed by one historian as a 'missionary Lord Deputy',[101] Chichester made acceptance of Protestantism the main badge of loyalty. Greatly disturbed by the number of major landowning families in Ireland that were publicly recusant, the Jacobean authorities would have been alarmed to note that the supposedly loyal MacGiollapadraigs had intermarried among such prominent Catholic families as the Nugents of Delvin, the Kilcash and Dunboyne Butlers, and the Eustaces of Kildare. Their connection with the Nugents was especially disconcerting for the state. Recent work by McCavitt has revealed that Richard Nugent, Lord Delvin, was one of the principal opponents of the political and religious settlement in Jacobean Ireland. In December 1605 he signed a petition of the lords and gentry of the Pale criticising the government's attempts to bring about the protestantisation of the Irish elite through coercion, and shortly afterwards Chichester had his suspicions confirmed when he learned that Delvin was involved in a conspiracy with native chieftains in Ulster such as Rory O'Donnell, earl of Tyrconnell, to overthrow the government.[102] It is not known whether Baron Florence was involved in Delvin's schemes or not, but there is no doubt that the fact of Florence's agreement to the marriage of his favoured son, John MacGiollapadraig of Castletown, to Delvin's sister, Mabel Nugent a few years earlier, only drew hostile attention upon him and his clan now that leading recusants were being targeted for punishment. As soon as Chichester was aware of Delvin's prominence among the Catholic opposition he set about crushing him and his associates. It has not previously been noted that Delvin's brother-in-law, John MacGiollapadraig, and John's father Florence, Lord Upper Ossory, were among the deputy's earliest victims.

Commencing in 1605 the government made land and taxation the focus of its assault on the MacGiollapadraig lordship. In October of that year, Chichester appointed two senior judges, Sir Nicholas Walsh and Sir Charles Calthorpe, to look into a 'controversie depending betwixte the gentlemen and freeholders of Upper Ossorie, plaintifes, and Florence, Lo: Barron of Upper Ossorie, defendant'.[103] The language of the commission is striking, with the baron's erstwhile clan subjects now suddenly afforded English legal rights under the common law as 'freeholders', i.e instead of being occupants of the land by the baron's will they were now being classified as owners in their own right, and this even before the case was heard. (This profound change in legal terminology, at a stroke replacing native standards and definitions with

English ones, was made possible by a proclamation of denization drafted by Chichester's chief legal adviser, Sir John Davies, and issued by the crown in March 1605).

Having listened to the arguments of both sides Walsh and Calthorpe did what Chichester wanted and, 'for the better settling of the said parties in a good and fairlike [manner]', they sided with the 'freeholders' against the baron and his son John. All taxes and exactions traditionally due to the MacGiollapadraig chieftains of Upper Ossory were declared to be 'utterlie extinguished and abolished', 'never to be claymed hereafter'. It was a drastic blow to Baron Florence's feudal power. Before 1605 he had been entitled to a wide range of levies and services from his underlings, such as the free carriage of his goods, free labour, and the rights to levy 'men, horses, [and] howndes' as he saw fit; henceforth he would have to do without all these cost-saving privileges and pay the going rate for service. The judgement went further. In accordance with the government's desire to engineer a new society in Ireland, replacing (uncivilised) Gaelic structures with (civilised) English norms, Walsh and Calthorpe also decreed that in future all 'freeholders' in Upper Ossory must hold their lands 'of the said Lo: Barron in *free soccage* (my italics) as of his Castle or manor of Cowlchill in the parish of AghmcArte by suite of Courte to the Courte Barron of the said mannor fowre tymes a yeare'. Tenure by free socage meant that Baron Florence's rights to the wardship of minors disappeared, and that each freehold would pass outside his control to the most senior male claimant by primogeniture.[104] No more would the MacGiollapadraig chieftains masquerade as anglophiles while clinging to ancient Gaelic sources of power and revenue. The 1605 award heralded a revolution in Upper Ossory, effectively eradicating the basis for an autonomous aristocratic lordship in the territory. To all intents and purposes the MacGiollapadraig chieftaincy was dead and buried.

Florence appealed to the lord deputy and council against the verdict of Walsh and Calthorpe, but his complaints were destined to fall on deaf ears. Chichester dismissed the case from the council table and referred it to the master of the rolls, Sir Anthony St. Leger, and the king's sergeant-at-law, Nicholas Kerdiffe, who in their capacity as 'Lords Justices of Assize' in Queen's County were authorised to make a final decision over Florence's rights at the county court in Maryborough. This they did on 13 April 1606.[105] Predictably they upheld the earlier ruling of Walsh and Calthorpe and maintained the government position that the baron's exactions had been 'unlawfullie demaunded' of the Upper Ossory freeholders, and the extension of socage tenure to Florence's former subjects was automatically confirmed. On 4 June following their decision was ratified by Lord Deputy Chichester and the

Plate 12.1   Cullahill Castle with lime-kiln in foreground (Redmond).

Irish Council in Dublin, who required it to be enrolled as an act of state in the records of chancery and in the 'Counsell Booke'.

What happened to Baron Florence MacGiollapadraig was symptomatic of the experience of other native lords at this time. On the northern borders of the Pale Lord Delvin had his claim to forfeited lands in Longford summarily dismissed by the authorities,[106] while in Ulster the experience of Rory O'Donnell, earl of Tyrconnell, was very similar to Baron Florence's, in that O'Donnell too saw some of his rights of overlordship (over two vassal lineages, the O'Boyles and the MacSweeneys) abolished in 1605 by order of the government.[107] It is well known that this sudden loss of power and prestige led O'Donnell to flee the country in 1607; Florence's reaction was less dramatic. Deprived of most of his power and a large portion of his income he turned against his former subjects, taking the MacShane MacGiollapadraigs, the O'Dullanys and others to court to disposess them of various lands around the territory.[108] After 1605-6 Upper Ossory ceased to be ruled even nominally by its traditional overlord and instead splintered into several independent component parts.

The fragmentation of the lordship continued apace with the eruption of a major succession dispute that had long been bubbling under the surface. As noted above, shortly before her demise in 1603, Elizabeth I had recognised Florence's second son, John, as his heir-apparent; significantly, however, there is no evidence that King James, having confirmed some of her other decisions, agreed to uphold this one. The upshot was a bitter internal conflict between John and his elder brother, the ex-rebel Teige, which lasted for several years. In 1612 Baron Florence, an old man in his late seventies and close to death, granted the bulk of his estate to John, evidently in the expectation that John might thereby succeed him as fourth baron as Elizabeth I had indicated.[109] The Irish administration undid his grounds for optimism, and ignoring the promises of the king's predecessor, allowed James I to make political capital out of the MacGiollapadraigs' succession dispute. In order to continue its systematic reduction of the dynasty's power, the government followed a decidely Machiavellian course, recognising Teige, the former traitor, as fourth baron of Upper Ossory on the death of his father on 3 February 1613 (fig. 12.1),[110] while simultaneously encouraging his loyal brother John of Castletown to push his claim to most of the baronial lands. Though attractively dressed up in the language of even-handed government, the policy reeked of opportunism: formal recognition of Teige's succession as baron was delayed, so that he was unable to take his seat in the Irish House of Lords (and so was prevented from joining the Catholic opposition) during the 1613-15

Fig. 12.1   Inscriptions on east and west sides of Errill Cross commemorating the
deaths of Florence Fitzpatrick and his wife Katherine More (after Carrigan,
'Wayside Cross at Errill, Queen's County', *J.R.S.A.I. Jn.*, liv (1924), pp
148/9.

parliament, while neither he nor John got much satisfaction from the
government's attempted mediation.[111]

By the middle years of James I's reign, the senior branches of the
MacGiollapadraig clan were deep in trouble. Despite reaching a private
agreement concerning the ownership of Castletown and Grantstown in
March 1615,[112] Baron Teige and his brother John had other differences
that were more difficult to settle. Equally pressing, given the fact that
neither could be sure of his income until all outstanding disputes were
settled, was a bill for arrears of composition money due to the crown
that was backdated to 1604. Irrespective of their legal and financial
problems, the government was determined to make the senior
MacGiollapadraigs pay their full share of the arrears, which amounted

to £440 (stg). In 1616 John was imprisoned for protesting against the unfairness of a decree issued by the commissioners of arrears demanding a doubling of the annual composition levy in Upper Ossory, from £25 to £50 (stg) per annum. Apparently John found the order objectionable on two grounds: (i) he could not understand why he and others of the 'chiefest freeholders' of the area were to pay for the negligence of the officers responsible for collecting the money; (ii) nor could he accept that Baron Teige and himself, who between them held 72 ploughlands *in capite* of the king, for which they paid an annual crown rent, were to pay the same as the rest of the freeholders, who held their lands rent-free by socage tenure. Eventually a compromise was reached and John was set at liberty (after Baron Teige had travelled to Dublin to support him), but the amount of money demanded of them was not reduced. Instead it was agreed that henceforth both Teige and John would hold seven ploughlands each as demesne land free of composition, the tax to be collected out of the 58 ploughlands remaining to them.[113]

In August 1618 the king ordained that Teige and John receive new patents for their lands, the dispute between them having finally been settled by order of the privy council.[114] Six months later, on 18 February 1619, when John had his estate erected by fiant into the manor of Castletown-Opherellan, it seemed that at last conditions were settling down in Upper Ossory after a lengthy period of flux.[115] In recent times, for all their setbacks, the senior MacGiollapadraigs had been showing signs of political recovery. In particular they had added to their already strong alliance with the Nugents by drawing close to the Butlers of Ormond. Ever since Upper Ossory had been formally shired with Queen's County the main cause of the enmity between the two lineages – territoriality – had ended, and as a token of good faith, Black Tom's successor, the eleventh earl of Ormond, Walter Butler, had granted a lease of Durrow manor to Barnaby MacGiollapadraig, Baron Teige's son.[116] He had also permitted Barnaby an interest in the Upper Ossory rectories in his possession at Clanowle, Rathdowney and Offerlane.[117]

But close contact with Earl Walter had its price. During the 1613-15 parliament he had taken a leading role in the Catholic opposition, infuriating the government with his behaviour, and after the assembly he became a marked man.[118] Regarding the senior MacGiollapadraigs there is reason to suspect that, just as their affinity to the Nugents had probably encouraged the state to move against them in 1605-6, so by the latter part of the reign of James I their rapprochement with the earl of Ormond may have been responsible for a new assault on their territory. The obstructionism displayed by Barnaby MacGiollapadraig in

1615, refusing while a member of a Queen's County jury to convict a well-known murderer at the Maryborough sessions, may have suggested to the authorities that he was eager to imitate Ormond's conduct. Certainly it revealed he was just as capable of causing trouble as the earl. Together with his near kinsman Donal MacGiollapadraig, Barnaby was fined £3 (stg) and imprisoned during the lord deputy's pleasure for his action.[119] Worse was to follow. In 1619 Ormond was jailed in London, having refused to accept a controversial division of his inheritance made by the king, protesting (correctly) that his legal rights had been overridden.[120] As a direct result of the earl's problems, several of the MacGiollapadraigs, including Baron Teige, John of Castletown, and John McCallough of Ballykeely, nearly lost parts of their respective estates in Ossory, due to an administrative error in the royal forfeiture of Ormond property.[121] More seriously, during 1621 – as Ormond's palatine rights to the liberty of Tipperary were being stripped from him in punishment for continuing his protest – their territory was suddenly, without warning, assigned for plantation by the crown.

The Plantation of Upper Ossory

Until the recent publication of Victor Treadwell's book *Buckingham and Ireland*[122] the plantation of Upper Ossory has been overlooked in almost all the standard academic authorities on early modern Ireland, apparently because scholars had failed to realise that it actually took place.'[123] This oversight is entirely understandable, for very little documentation has survived about it, and it began after the establishment of most of the other plantations. The following brief outline attempts to augment Dr. Treadwell's treatment; where he is primarily concerned with the planters and with the high politics of the plantation, this present study concentrates on the planted and on the local impact of the scheme. It is based on a few scattered items from a variety of sources and records only the barest details of what occurred.

The crown was able to proceed with a plantation in Upper Ossory as a result of establishing its title to the territory at a court of inquisition held at Maryborough on 17 September 1621. The court declared that James I was lord of the area by descent (via the Mortimers and Edward IV) from its medieval conquerors, the Marshalls and the de Clares, claiming that it had passed to Elizabeth de Clare as part of her purparty following the death of her father Gilbert in 1318.[124] This was a fiction, mere pseudohistory. Elizabeth's property had included the two demesne manors of Offerlane and Formoyle and various feudal fees, including the great fee of Rathdowney – but nothing else.[125] As such the crown had a claim to, at best, no more than half the territory, a claim which in any event had surely been undermined since the end of the middle ages by a string of royal grants to the MacGiollapadraigs. Indeed, under James I, the present monarch, Baron Teige and John MacGiollapadraig of Castletown had had their lands (comprising the greater part of the territory) confirmed to them by royal patent; equally important, in 1613 many of the lesser members of the clan had had their lands recognised as theirs 'by ancient possession'.[126]

Yet the spurious nature of the crown's title mattered little. As elsewhere at this time – in Longford, Leitrim, north Wexford, O'Dunne's country in Queen's County, O'Melaghlin's country in Westmeath, and the Ormond lordship in Kilkenny and Tipperary – flawed legal title was no barrier to a government determined to reduce the power of the Irish lords through the confiscation and redistribution of land.[127] On 5 October 1621, barely three weeks after the territory had been pronounced as part of King James's de Clare inheritance, the lord deputy and council informed the privy council in London that the baron of Upper Ossory and the senior MacGiollapadraigs had 'willingly surrendered to the king's pleasure'.[128] It is not difficult to understand why the clan leaders were so compliant: having witnessed the transportation of combative Wexford natives to America and the state's ruthless reduction of the earl of Ormond, wisely they had no desire to make a stand over points of law. All that counted was survival. Thus by February 1622 the rumour was abroad of another potential land bonanza in Ireland for well-placed officials. Among those who are known to have petitioned for grants of Ossory land at this time was the Ulster colonist, Sir Ralph Bingley (who hoped to receive between 1,500 and 2,000 acres),[129] and Henry, Lord Docwra, a former soldier who had served against Hugh O'Neill and had since been treasurer of Ireland.[130] As the vultures gathered, the king penned a letter to Baron Teige and his brother John full of sanctimonious praise for their worthy co-operation.[131]

Everything moved forward smoothly during 1622 and 1623. On 21 August 1622 the king ordered the certification of the total number of acres in Upper Ossory,[132] and by November he had agreed to pass three-quarters of the escheated territory to the natives and former inhabitants (as in Leitrim). The remaining quarter was to be reserved for the crown as a royal custodiam. Eventually, almost a year later to the day, on 8 November 1623, the real mover behind the plantation emerged to take his reward – the king's favourite, George Villiers, duke of Buckingham, who it was revealed was to receive all of the custodial land, having 'undertaken the plantation of it'.[133] Once Buckingham declared himself, John MacGiollapadraig ceased co-operating with the state, and early in the new year there were disturbances in Ossory.

However, following the swift deployment of troops to the region by the government,[134] John changed his tactics, deciding that a less confrontational course might succeed in cushioning the impact of the plantation scheme.

Towards this end, in 1624 John called on the help of his brother-in-law Richard Nugent, earl of Westmeath (formerly Lord Delvin), to try and extract concessions from King James in London. Westmeath had recently emerged as the undisputed leader of the loyalist Catholic community of the Pale. He was engaged in a high-level initiative at court to force a relaxation of the government's anti-recusant policies in return for an assurance of the Catholics' continued fealty and a promise of money. For a while, as James I moved towards war with France, Westmeath seemed perfectly placed to gain favourable terms for the likes of the MacGiollapadraigs and others affected by the threat of plantation in Ireland. But in the event, however, his capacity to extract concessions from the crown was severely limited. His influence was systematically eroded by Dublin officials, who resented him greatly, and the Lord Deputy, Henry, Lord Falkland, denounced him as 'very busy and ambitious', a 'minion of the Jesuits and priests', a troublemaker too 'eager in pressing of grievances'. Falkland specifically tried to anticipate any objections the earl might have had to recent events in Upper Ossory by pointing out that MacGiollapadraig of Castletown, Westmeath's kinsman, had failed to submit to the plantation commissioners 'against all reason, as if animated to obstinacy in despight of duty'.[135] Falkland need not have feared for the plantation – Buckingham, its main beneficiary, was much too powerful for it ever to be called into question. Looking ahead, even when he was threatened with impeachment by the English Parliament in 1626 he managed to insure that his patent for Ossory land remained hidden from view, so that his enemies could not investigate the devious way it had been acquired. The plantation was stalled (until the reissue of his patent in August 1626); it was not abandoned.[136]

For a brief period it must have seemed that their ties to the earl of Westmeath had succeeded in gaining the senior MacGiollapadraigs some worthwhile concessions. On 28 March 1625 (the day after James I's death), the privy council drew up a set of orders for the Ossory plantation in which it was agreed that Baron Teige, his son Barnaby, and his brother John of Castletown, as 'the principal men of the country', would *each* receive grants of a manor, courts leet and baron, and 2,000 acres in demesne, along with power to create tenures and freehold estates and 'other reasonable privileges'. It looked as though under the new king, Charles I, the plantation would preserve their territorial supremacy in Ossory.[137]

It was only a mirage, however. Despite royal promises that Upper Ossory would be treated the same as Leitrim, where senior clan members received land at the expense of their inferiors, it was not. Surviving evidence indicates that, after the appointment of new plantation commissioners on 4 September 1626[138] the crown set out to humble the senior MacGiollapadraigs (and thus intimidate Westmeath)[139] through large-scale land seizure. A plantation grant that was made to Barnaby MacGiollapadraig on 20 November 1626, shortly before his father's death – Baron Teige died in 1627 – was in fact a grant for a new, much diminished, estate for the barons of Upper Ossory.[140] Thus, where the barons had once controlled circa 25,000 acres, after agreeing to the plantation they were required to exist on just 10,500 acres (table 3 below). The plantation was a double-cross, reducing the barons – with their own consent – to the level of the poorest peers in the country.

Table 3
Plantation Grantees, 1626-32

(Acreage in brackets. Asterisks denote recipients of additional plantation grants)

Principal grantees
> *Villiers manor*
>> George, duke of Buckingham (10,788)
> *Coulkill manor*
>> Barnaby, 5th Baron of Upper Ossory (10,560)
> *Ballyraghan manor*
>> Geoffrey MacGiollapadraig of Ballyraghan (3,831)*
> *Corrane manor*
>> Morgan O'Cashien of Corran (2,162)
> *Castlefleming manor*
>> Edmund MacGiollapadraig of Castlefleming (1,442)

Miscellaneous native grantees
> Philip Dougan (1,971)
> Brian McShane McTeige MacGiollapadraig (1,774)
> Augustine McCostigane (1,291)
> Patrick McDonogh Oge O'Connor, hereditary physician (1,246)
> Geoffrey MacGiollapadraig of Tintour (994)
> John McCallough MacGiollapadraig of Ballykeely (841)*
> Thomas Hovendon (764)
> John MacGiollapadraig (761)
> Edmund Oge MacGiollapadraig (729)
> Brian MacGiollapadraig of Garran McConly (694)
> William Gilbert of Maryborough (639)
> Cosney O'Doran and his heirs, brehons (498)

Donal MacGiollapadraig of Gortnaclea (405)
Teige McFinine MacGiollapadraig of Archerstown (349)*
Patrick Oge O'Dullany (329)
Dermot McFinine of Derrilosky (293)
Edmund McShane MacGiollapadraig of Ballygehin (537)
Teige McDonill McDermot MacGiollapadraig (291)
William Fynan (261)
Donill McShane MacGiollapadraig of Ballytarsney (250)
Moriagh McDonough, Connor (235)
Owney O'Cashine (213)
Donnill O'Dullany (202)
Patrick McFinine (199)
Donogh McWilliam O'Phelan (182)
Shane McEdmund MacGiollapadraig (181)
William O'Phelan (178)
William MacCallough MacGiollapadraig (171)
Dermot McTeigh Oge MacGiollapadraig of Akipp (159)
Thomas Carey (149)
Teige Oge MacGiollapadraig (127)
Dermot MacGiollapadraig of Clonib (123)
Piers Doogin (116)
Katherine Mainwaring (115)
Carroll O'Phelan and Geoffrey McCostigane (85)
Roger Masterson (70)

(Sources: *Cal. Patent Rolls, Ire., Charles 1;* N.A.I., Lodge MSS, records of the rolls, v).

Perhaps because of advice from the earl of Westmeath, the Castletown family escaped the barons' fate by continuing to withhold their estate from the plantation area. John of Castletown died on 25 July 1626 still unwilling to submit to the plantation commissioners. His successor, his eldest son and heir, Florence (alias Finine) MacGiollapadraig, followed the same path as his father, arguing that the Castletown estate could not be included in the plantation having been lawfully assured to his family by Elizabeth I. Unsurprisingly, the Castletown family were forced to spend much of the following decade disputing the entitlements of would-be beneficiaries of the plantation to part of their land. The MacGiollapadraigs of Formoyle joined the fray, apparently supporting the Castletown position that the plantation was unlawful. Consequently, they likewise spent the 1630s in a legal limbo.[141]

The plantation insured that henceforth the territory was no longer dominated by the barons of Upper Ossory alone. After 20 January 1627 – the date of his grant – they had to cede territorial supremacy to the duke of Buckingham. His estate was a carefully crafted jewel, a new axis of power in the region, designed to rival the barons' seat at

Coulkill. Based at Borris Castle, formerly MacGiollapadraig property, and one of Ossory's principal stongholds, Buckingham's estate – dubbed Villiers manor – contained almost 11,000 plantation acres. The crown insured the duke was afforded every advantage, with Lord Deputy Falkland instructed to lay out his land in a 'convenient place all together'.[142] The duke also got a higher proportion of profitable land than most of the other grantees. As much as 65 per cent of his Borris estate was prime arable and pasture land. In contrast, many of the native grantees only received what might best be described as marginal land, full of bogs and woods. It is all the more interesting to note, therefore, that in the final analysis he and his family got rather more out of the territory than the Irish government that backed him. Though he had promised to plant his estate with settlers from England, very little English colonisation ensued. Perhaps this was due to the duke's untimely death – he was assassinated in London in 1628. More likely, however, he and his family may never have intended to colonise Upper Ossory. If this was so, then from beginning to end, the plantation had been a sham, a ruse to provide a leading courtier with the opportunity to seize a large Irish estate at the expense of an irksome native dynasty. The MacGiollapadraigs and their clients underwent plantation only to enrich Buckingham and his family, not to advance the English colonial presence in Ireland.

The 1641 Revolt

The onset of the plantation coincides with the survival of evidence concerning the economic condition of leading members of the clan – evidence which tends to suggest that the MacGiollapadraigs were increasingly impoverished by their experiences. Among other things it is recorded that in the late 1630s Barnaby, 5th baron of Upper Ossory, Florence of Castletown, and others were in debt to merchant families of Kilkenny, while Thady MacDonnell MacGiollapadraig of Kilpurcell owed money to a New English landowner in County Kildare.[143] Some, such as the Castletown and Palmershill families, had to mortgage or sell part of their possessions to raise money.[144] More revealing is the last will and testament of the dowager Lady Upper Ossory (Baron Barnaby's mother), dated September 1631. According to this, although she was of full noble status, she was nonetheless quite poor, unable to pay arrears of rent totalling a mere £23 to her kinsman, the eleventh earl of Ormond. She possessed only a small number of livestock on her lands, 'in [horses] garranes and maers twelve head, in cowes, nine great cowes with six calffes'.[145]

It has been suggested that harsh economic conditions as much as loss of political power drove the Ulster Irish out into revolt in October

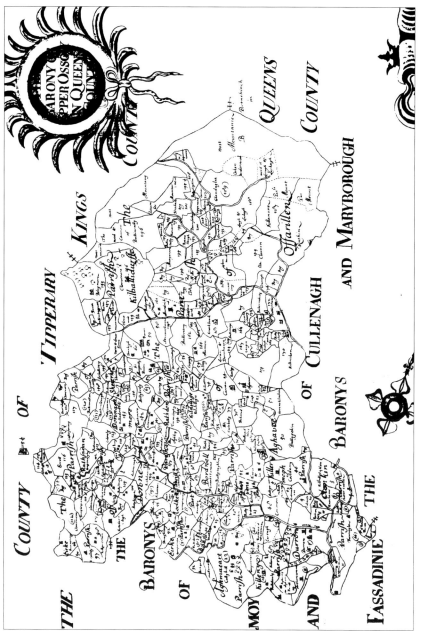

Fig. 12.2   The barony of Upper Ossory from the Down Survey.

1641.[146] The MacGiollapadraigs support this line of interpretation for the southern midlands.[147] However, crude economic indicators are not enough to explain the strong anti-Protestant sectarianism that characterised the clan's rebellion. At Mountrath on 30 November forces commanded by Florence MacGiollapadraig of Castletown went about claiming that the Queen of England, the French Catholic Henrietta Maria, had authorised them 'to banish all Protestants out of this kingdom', while others ripped up bibles and shouted 'begone English dogs'.[148] Unlike the neighbouring revolt in Kilkenny, in Upper Ossory and Queen's County a number of Protestants were 'cruelly beaten' for their faith, and others were killed, i.e. the Hill family at Leix Abbey.[149] Part of this sectarian animosity was doubtless due to the encouragement of priests such as Paul O'Cashine, who repossessed Leix Abbey and celebrated mass there as soon as the Hills were killed, and the friar, John MacCostigane, who accompanied the local troops into battle.[150] But the violence was also vengeance for past wrongs. During the mid-1630s part of the Ossory plantation area – at Skeirk, Rathdowney, Castletown and Donoghmore – had been set aside by the Dublin administration towards the maintenance of newly installed Church of Ireland rectors.[151] Chief amongst these Protestant clergymen was Richard Olmstead, who received more than 500 acres of former MacGiollapadraig land in and around Castletown. Olmstead was an apocalyptical preacher, a severe man who detected only sinfulness and obstinacy in his Catholic Irish neighbours. His sermons had probably served to increase sectarian tension in the region.[152]

Vengeance was also sought for other reasons. When Mountrath was raided some of the MacGiollapadraig soldiers went in search of 'the English churl' that had allegedly killed a local man and his wife.[153] A few weeks later, on 23 December 1641 the sixth baron of Upper Ossory, Barnaby Oge, wrote to the earl of Ormond in Dublin to denounce the behaviour of the lord president of Munster, Sir William St. Leger, in the midlands and south. The president, he said, was 'so cruell and mercilesse that he caused honest men and women to be moste execrably executed', and he went on to accuse St. Leger of precisely the sort of atrocities that the English believed of the Irish rebels. The war in the midlands was an ugly business, affording no room for neutrality. Shortly afterwards Baron Barnaby Oge went over to the Catholic rebels, and the following year he took a prominent part in the foundation of the Catholic Confederation in Kilkenny. By September 1642 he was out in the field with his uncle Dermot McTeige, Florence of Castletown, and many of his family's former clients, including the MacCostiganes, O'Connors and O'Cashines, at the head of a large Catholic army that tried to take Borris Castle back from Buckingham's servants.[154]

Ultimately, of course, one reason more than any other served to reunite the MacGiollapadraigs and the other local families outside the walls of Borris under the leadership of the sixth baron of Upper Ossory: together, they all rejected the plantation and the arbitrary nature of land confiscation that had prevailed in Ireland throughout the early seventeenth century. No surer testament of this was the fact they found common cause with the O'Brennans of Idough. In 1635 the O'Brennans had had their lands at Castlecomer in north-east County Kilkenny forfeited through a legal fiction very similar to that which had earlier made way for the Upper Ossory plantation. As in Ossory, the land had gone to a favoured servant of the crown, Christopher Wandesford.[155] Accordingly, it seems fitting to end this paper by simply noting that the O'Brennan attack on Castlecomer of late 1641 was aided by MacGiollapadraig forces, and that, in return, the MacGiollapdraig attack on Protestant English settlements near Upper Ossory had O'Brennan support. Given that the MacGiollapadraigs had spent centuries defending their separateness from north Kilkenny, mutual aid such as this was no small development.

References

1. I wish to record my thanks to my colleague Kenneth Nicholls for generously allowing me access to his genealogical notebooks. This paper would have been much poorer without his help and encouragement.
2. For dating the event see the letter of 21 Dec. 1532 by Walter Cowley to Thomas Cromwell in *S.P. Henry VIII, Irl.*, iii, pt. ii, no. 62.
3. *A.F.M.*, s.a. 1532.
4. *Ir. Mon. and ep. deeds*, no. 134.
5. Gearoid Mac Niocaill (ed.), *Crown surveys of lands, 1540-1, with the Kildare rental begun in 1518*, (Dublin 1992), p. 324. The earls of Kildare were entitled to a tax of 4d for every cow, and other similar tributes, in Formoyle at this time (Ibid., p. 268).
6. For instance, as early as July 1528 Henry VIII informed one of his ministers that the defence of Ireland should be left in the hands of either Earl Piers or his son: *L. & P. Hen. VIII*, iv, pt. 11: 1526-8, no.4541. For the rise of the Butlers at this time see David Edwards, 'The Ormond lordship in County Kilkenny, 1515-1642' (Ph.D. thesis, Trinity College, Dublin, 1998), pp 124-49, and C.A. Empey, 'From rags to riches: Piers Butler, earl of Ormond, 1515-39', *Butler Society Journal*, ii, no. 3 (1984). '
7. The text of the indictment is given in full in James Graves & J.G. A. Prim, *The history, architecture & antiquities of St. Canice's Cathedral* (Dublin 1857), pp 239-41; an edited version can be found in *Ormond Deeds, 1509-47*, no. 191.
8. Laurence McCorristine, *The revolt of Silken Thomas: a challenge to Henry VIII* (Dublin 1987), pp 53-4, and Steven G. Ellis, *Tudor Ireland: crown, community and the conflict of cultures, 1470-1603* (London 1985), pp 122-3.
9. Ciaran Brady, 'The O'Reillys of East Breifne and the problem of Surrender and Regrant', *Breifne*, vi (1985); Hiram Morgan, 'Extradition and treason-trial of a

Gaelic lord: the case of Brian O'Rourke', *Irish Jurist,* xxii (1987).

10. G.H. Orpen, *Ireland under the Normans* 4 vols. (Oxford 1968 edn), ii, pp 223-4; Katharine Simms, *From kings to warlords: the changing political structure of Ireland in the late Middle Ages* (Dublin 1987), p. 119; Kenneth Nicholls, *Gaelic and gaelicised Ireland in the Middle Ages* (Dublin 1972), pp 168-9.

11. C.A. Empey, 'The cantreds of the medieval county of Kilkenny', *R.S.A.I. Jn.,* Ci (1971), pp 128-9.

12. E.g., in 1421 the chief of the MacGiollapadraigs united with forces led by one Freney of Kilkenny (a leading Butler supporter) to raid into Laois: *A.F.M.* s.a. 1421; Art Cosgrove, *Late Medieval Ireland, 1370-1541* (Dublin 1981), p. 88.

13. Alnwick Castle, Duke of Northumberland Papers, MS. 476 (GC 26), f. 32v. My thanks to Brian C. Donovan for lending me his notes on this source.

14. Brooks, *Knight's fees,* pp 227, 265 and 270-2.

15. Empey, 'Cantreds', p. 132.

16. In 1577 aged witnesses on the bishop of Ossory's lands at Durrow dated the deterioration of cross-border relations to the later years of the episcopacy of Bishop Oliver Cantwell (d. 1527) and the early years of his successor, Bishop Milo Barron (1528-51): *Ir. Mon. & ep. deeds,* no. 134.

17. Ibid; *Ormond Deeds, 1584-1603,* app. 1. For a detailed discussion of the Kilkenny/Laois borderlands during the sixteenth century, see Edwards, 'Ormond lordship', pp 12-26.

18. *Cal. S.P. Ire., 1601-3 & addenda 1565-1654,* p. 683.

19. James Buckley (ed.), 'A viceregal progress through the south and west of Ireland in 1567', *Waterford & S.E. of Ire. Arch. Soc. Jn.,* xii (1909), appendix B, p. 184, which states that 'McGilpatrick is lorde of Osserie and wilbe xl horsemen, a battle [i.e. 60-80 galloglasses] and iii score kerne'. For troop numbers circa 1490, see Liam Price, 'The armed forces of the Irish chiefs in the sixteenth century', *R.S.A.I. Jn.,* 7th series, ii (1932); for a 1580s estimate, see Alnwick Castle, Duke of Northumberland Papers, MS.476 (GC 26), f. 18v.

20. E.g., H.F. Hore & James Graves, *The social state of the southern and eastern counties of Ireland* (Dublin 1870), pp 98, 109, 121; N.L.I., MS. 2507, f. 65.

21. Diane Willen, *John Russell, first earl of Bedford. One of the king's men* (London 1981), p. 32. For the best summary of Henry VIII's attitudes towards noble power see Helen Miller, *Henry VIII and the English nobility* (Oxford 1986).

22. *Cal. Carew MSS, 1515-14,* no. 96.

23. *S.P. Henry VIII,* ii, pp 514 -5.

24. For a provocative new account of Grey's deputyship and downfall see Ciaran Brady, *The chief governors: the rise and fall of reform government in Tudor Ireland, 1536-88* (Cambridge 1995), pp 13-25.

25. Brendan Bradshaw, *The Irish constitutional revolution of the sixteenth century* (Cambridge 1979), pp 238-40, where he is misidentified (p.238) as 'MacGillapatrick of Carlow'.

26. E.g., as late as 1564 the government wrote to him in Latin: Lord Justice Arnold & Council to Upper Ossory, 5 Aug. 1564 (P.R.O., S.P. 63/11/61).

27. *S.P. Henry VIII,* iii, pp 464 and 475.

28. Ibid., pp 463-5.

29. Ibid., pp 490-3.

30. *Cal. S.P. Ire., 1509-73,* pp 70-1; A.F.M., s.a. 1545.

31. For the Ormond-St.Leger dispute see David Edwards, 'Malice aforethought? The death of the ninth earl of Ormond, 1546', *Butler Soc. Jn.,* iii, no. 1 (1987), and idem, 'Futher comments on the strange death of the ninth earl of Ormond',

ibid., iv no. 1 (1997).

32. R. Butler (ed.), 'The Annals of Thady Dowling', *Irish Archaeological Soc.* (1849), s.a. 1545.

33. Jones to Bellingham, April 1549 (P.R.O., S.P 61/2/35).

34. Dean G. White, 'The reign of Edward VI in Ireland: some political, social and economic aspects', *I.H.S.,* xiv (1964-5).

35. J. T. Gilbert, *Facsimiles of the national manuscripts of Ireland* (London 1884), p. 172.

36. As note 17 above.

37. *Cal. Fiants Ire., Edward VI,* no. 950.

38. At about this time Brian's daughter Honora was married to Piers Oge Butler of Lismalin, Co. Tipperary, while his bastard son Shane MacGiollapadraig of Ballygehin was married to Sir Richard Butler's base daughter Ellen.

39. *Cal. S.P., Dom., Edward VI* (London 1992), pp 5-7.

40. Joan, countess of Ormond, to Cecil, 6 July 1547 (P.R.O., S.P. 61/1/4).

41. Thomas Fuller, *Church history,* ii, p. 3; Patrick F. Tytler, *England under the reigns of Edward VI and Mary* (2 vols., London 1839), ii, p. 85; Philip Wilson, *The beginnings of modern Ireland* (Dublin 1914), p. 384.

42. John Murphy, 'The illusion of decline: the privy chamber 1547-58' in David Starkey (ed.), *The English court from the Wars of the Roses to the Civil War* (London 1987), p. l29.

43. Gilbert, *National manuscripts,* pp 169-71; J.G. Nichols (ed.), *The literary remains of Edward VI* (Camden Soc., 1851); B.L., Cotton MSS, Caligula E.IV, ff 284-9.

44. The fact that he was quite highly regarded by Cecil, a man who throughout his long career made Protestantism a badge of political acceptability, also suggests this.

45. *The vocacyon of Johan Bale to the bishoprick of Ossorie in Ireland,* ed. Thomas Parke, Harleian Miscellany, vi (London 1765), p. 415.

46. Gilbert, *National manuscripts,* p. l71.

47. C. Gilblin, 'Catalogue of Irish material in the Nunziatura di Fiandra', *Collectanea Hibernica,* i (1958), p. 46.

48. St. Leger to Petre, 18 Dec. 1554 (P.R.O., S.P. 6211/8).

49. Gilbert, *National manuscripts,* p. 172.

50. One of the O'Connor leaders returned to Ireland in the same ship as Barnaby in 1554 – in the care of William Fitzwilliam, O'Connor was to be placed in custody in Dublin Castle as a hostage for the submission of his clan (Giblin, 'Catalogue of Irish material', p. 46).

51. H.M.C., *Haliday MSS: The Irish privy council book, 1556-71* (London 1897), p. l8.

52. This was surely the underlying reason for the government's temporary imprisonment of Baron Brian in Dublin in 1556 – ibid., p. 4.

53. H.M.C., *De L 'Isle & Dudley MSS,* i (London 1925), pp 366, 376 and 384.

54. B.L., Cotton MSS, Caligula E.I., ff 28-55.

55. Mary to Barnaby, 12 March 1558 (P.R.O., S.P. 62/2/18).

56. *Cal. Carew MSS,* 1515-74, p. 274.

57. On 17 August 1559 the baron was in control of Upper Ossory and engaged in peace discussions with Sir Edmund Butler of Clogrenan, negotiations which make no mention whatsoever of Barnaby (H.M.C., *Haliday MSS,* pp 71 -3). Barnaby was probably at this time absent in England to attend the celebrations following the accession of Queen Elizabeth I: see Travers to Sussex, 27 Jan.

1559 (P.R.O., S.P. 63.1/12).

58. Lord Justice & Council to Upper Ossory, 5 Aug. 1564 (P.R.O., S.P. 63/11/61).

59. Petitions of Sir Barnaby Fitzpatrick, 1566 (ibid., S.P 63/19/88-9); Lord Deputy & Council to Privy Council, 13 April 1566 (ibid., S.P. 63/17/8); Notes by Cecil, Dec. 1567 (ibid., S.P. 63/22/61); Cecil's memorandum of Ireland, 24 April 1568 (ibid., S.P. 63/24/16); Elizabeth I to Sidney, June 1568 (ibid., S.P. 63/25/12).

60. Brady, *Chief governors,* pp 287-8, has some useful comments on his career.

61. As note 45 above.

62. For Mountgarret, R.I.A., MS. D.5.3, item 4; for Sir Edmund Butler, H.M.C., *Haliday MSS,* pp 71-3.

63. B.L., Cotton MSS, Titus B Xlll, f. 142; Conyers Read, *Mr. Secretary Cecil and Queen Elizabeth* (London 1955), p. 286; while at Calais in 1557-8, Barnaby had served under Leicester's brother, John, Lord Dudley (note 54 above).

64. I have discussed the invasion elsewhere: Edwards, 'Ormond lordship', pp 196-207.

65. Under her rule he received only a handful of minor commissions and grants: *Cal. Fiants Ire., Eliz. I,* nos 2113, 2115, 2117, 2345, 2370, 2843-4, 3047; N.A.I., Lodge MSS, records of the rolls, i, pp 385-6.

66. E.g. *Acts of the privy council,* 1578-80 (London 1895), p. 256. Ironically, one of the only times Elizabeth sent a letter specifically to Barnaby – praising him for killing Rory Oge O'More – it went missing, and he had to wait six months for a second version of the message (ibid., pp 21 -2).

67. Herbert Hore (ed.), 'Sir Henry Sidney's memoir of his government of Ireland', *U.J.A.,* viii (1860), pp 188-9.

68. G.E.C., *Complete Peerage,* sub 'Upper Ossory, 2nd baron'.

69. J. O'Hanlon & E. O'Leary, *History of the Queen's County* (Dublin 1907), ii, p. 450.

70. H.M.C., *Haliday MSS,* p. 167.

71. David Edwards, 'The Butler revolt of 1569', *I.H.S.,* xxviii (May 1993), pp 231 and 249-50.

72. Ormond even suggested that Barnaby provoked Rory Oge O'More into revolt in 1575 in order to wage war against him: Ormond to Fitzwilliam, 6 Aug. 1575 (Oxford University, Bodleian Library, Carte MSS, Vol 55, fol 330).

73. For the dramatic spread of martial law as an agent of state repression in Elizabethan Ireland, see David Edwards, 'Beyond reform: martial law and the Tudor reconquest of Ireland', *History Ireland,* v, no. 2 (Summer 1997), pp 16-21.

74. Upper Ossory to Walsingham, 30 Jan. 1577 (P.R.O., S.P. 63/ 57/8).

75. Sidney, 'Memoir', p. l89.

76. *Cal. Fiants Ire., Eliz. I,* nos 2843-4.

77. For Malby's behaviour see Ciaran Brady, 'Faction and the origins of the Desmond rebellion of 1579', *I.H.S.,* xxii (Sept. 1981), pp 310- 11. Barnaby had taken preys of cattle in Kerry with Malby and the earl of Kildare at the beginning of Sept. 1579 (James Hogan & N. McNeill O'Farrell (eds.), *The Walsingham letter-book, May 1578 – Dec. 1579* (Dublin 1959), p. 167); for his subsequent attempt at mediation see ibid., pp 167-8.

78. Examination of Sir James Fitzgerald, 25 Aug. 1580 (P.R.O., S.P. 63/76/25, inclosure i).

79. Ormond to Lord Grey, 28 Aug. 1580 (ibid., S.P. 63/75/73); see also Ormond to Walsingham, 28 May 1580 (ibid., S.P. 63/73/30).

80. Wallop to Walsingham, 14 Jan. 1581 (Ibid., S.P. 63/80/5); Ormond to Wilson,

15 Jan. 1581 (ibid., S.P. 63/80/11); Offenders indicted by Ormond, 15 Jan. 1581 (ibid., S.P. 63/80/12); *Cal. Carew MSS, 1575-88,* no. 489.

81. D. B. Quinn (ed.),'Calendar of the Irish council book, 1581-6', *Anal. Hib.,* no. 24 (1967), p. 117; Lord Grey to the privy council, 6 Nov. 1581 (P.R.O., S.P. 63/86/51).

82. In 1578 Geoffrey Fitzpatrick had rebelled against Baron Barnaby and joined the Butlers: Edwards, 'Ormond lordship', pp 208-9; John was almost executed as a traitor in 1582-3, but received a pardon before the execution could take place (Executed traitors, 1 Dec. 1582-30 Sept. 1583 (P.R.O., S.P. 63/1/108/34)).

83. E.g., Sidney to Elizabeth 1, 20 April 1567 (P.R.O., S.P. 63/20/66).

84. Grey to the privy council, 6 Nov. 1581 (ibid., S.P. 63/86/51).

85. *C.S.P.I., 1586-8,* p. 293; ibid., *1588-92,* p. 235; see also B.L., Cotton MSS, Titus B XII, f. 78.

86. *Cal. Fiants Ire., Eliz. I,* no. 4640; Thomas Williams' book of the Irish garrison, 30 Sept. 1586 (P.R.O., S.P. 63112713, enclosure i).

87. *Ormond Deeds, 1584-1603,* app. 1, p. 133.

88. John C. Erck, *Repertory to the Irish patent rolls of James I* (Dublin 1852), i, Pt. 2, p. 515; see also *Cal. S.P., Ire., 1596-7,* p. 156, where Ormond complains of Shane, whom he calls 'John'.

89. Mountgarret's participation in Tyrone's rebellion is discussed in detail in Edwards, 'Ormond lordship', chapter 4.

90. Ibid., and N.L.l., D. 3242, a deed of 24 January 1596 in which John Butler of Kiltinan, Co. Tipperary, conveyed lands inherited from his mother, Margaret Fitzpatrick (sole daughter and heiress of Baron Barnaby) at Clonboran, etc., to the earl of Orrnond for ever. It is revealing that in the document the lands are referred to as ' in Upper Ossory in the County of Kilkenny (sic)', and that none of the MacGiollapadraig clan acted as parties to the deed.

91. For O'Byrne's instigation of a Leinster revolt in support of Tyrone, and the significance of his death, see David Edwards, 'In Tyrone's shadow: Feagh McHugh O'Byrne, forgotten leader of the Nine Year's War' in C. O'Brien (ed.),T*he Wicklow firebrand* (Rathdrum, 1998), pp 212-48.

92. Sir James Perrot, *The chronicle of Ireland, 1584-1608,* ed. H. Wood (Dublin 1933), p.150.

93. James Graves, 'The taking of the earl of Ormond, 1600', *Kilkenny Arch. Soc. Trans.,* iii, Pt. 2 (1860-1), pp 393, 395, 407, 412. It is possible that in 1600 Gortnaclea – which then belonged to Florence's grand-nephew, Donal MacGiollapadraig – was uninhabited, as Donal's father Brian had died five years earlier, while Donal was young.

94. He was at court, 'newly come out of Ireland', by 10 May 1600: N.E. McClure (ed.), *The letters of John Chamberlain* (2 vols., Philadelphia, 1939), i, pp 93-4. *Cal. Fiants Ire., Eliz. I.,* no. 6610. He also extracted a fee-farrn grant of Aghmacart Friary: N.A.I., Lodge MSS, records of the rolls, i, p. 333.

95. *Cal. S.P. Ire., 1600-l,* pp 173, 177.

96. Ibid., *1600,* p. 396.

97. Ibid., *1601-3 & addenda 1565-1654,* p. 195.

98. Ibid., p. 385.

99. *Cal. Fiants Ire., Eliz. I,* no. 6610.

100. N.A.I., Lodge MSS, records of the rolls, i, pp 333 and 336.

101. John McCavitt, 'Lord Deputy Chichester and the English government's "Mandates Policy" in Ireland, 1605-7', *Recusant History,* xx (1991), pp 320-31.

102. John McCavitt, 'The Flight of the earls, 1607', *I.H.S.,* xxix (1994), pp 159-73,

esp. pp 162-3; *C.S.P.I., 1603-6,* pp 362-5.

103. The main source for the following paragraphs is N.A.I., Paulet (Fitzpatrick) Papers, M. 2660 – Baron Florence's copy of the government's ratification of the proceedings in Upper Ossory up to June 1606. The original court roll of the proceedings of October 1605, containing the signatures of all the freeholders and gentry of Upper Ossory, was unfortunately destroyed in the Public Record Office fire of 1922: *Eighth report of the Irish Record Commission,* p. 518.

104. *Oxford English dictionary,* sub 'socage'.

105. This judgement 'by the Justices of Assise in the Queenes County' helps to fill out our knowledge of the workings of the Irish assize circuit in 1606, which is otherwise not very well recorded: John McCavitt, ' "Good Planets in their several spheares': The establishment of the assize circuits in early seventeenth century Ireland', *Irish Jurist,* xxiv (1989), pp 265-6.

106. J.P. Farrell, *History of the County Longford* (Dublin 1891), pp 35-41; Raymond Gillespie, 'A question of survival: the O'Farrells and Longford in the seventeenth century', in R. Gillespie & G. Moran (eds.), *Longford: essays in county history* (Dublin 1991), pp 15-16.

107. Hans Pawlisch, *Sir John Davies and the conquest of Ireland: a study in legal imperialism* (Cambridge 1985), pp 68-71.

108. Erck, *Repertory,* pp 514-7; N.A.I., C.P., parcel Q, no 33; ibid., parcel X, no. 33.

109. N.A.I., D. 19304-5. In 1611 he had his estate confirmed to him by the royal commission for defective titles, on payment of £23 (*Cal. S.P. Ire., 1611-14,* p. l04).

110. For the correct date of Florence's death see William Carrigan, 'The Wayside Cross at Errill', *R.S.A.I. Jn.,* liv (1924), pp 147-51.

111. Ibid., pp, pp 346 and 408-11.

112. N.A.I., D.19307.

113. Ibid., Ferguson MSS, Abstracts of revenue exchequer orders (2nd Remembrancer), 1592- 1657, pp 216-8.

114. *Cal. Pat. Rolls. Ire.,* James I, p. 413.

115. N.A.I., M.2661.

116. According to extant Ormond rentals Barnaby held Durrow between *c.* 1610 and 1615: N.L.I., MS. 2506, ff 37v and 81v.

117. *N.A.I.,* MS. D. 5285A.

118. *Cal. Carew MSS, 1603-24,* p. 273; *C.S.P.I., 1611-14,* p. 405; H.M.C., *Downshire MSS,* iv. p. l 28.

119. H.M.C., *Egmont MSS,* i, p. 44. It is not clear whether his accomplice was Donal of Tintour or Donal of Gortnaclea.

120. Edwards, 'Ormond lordship', pp 94-110; Victor Treadwell, *Buckingham and Ireland, 1616-28: a study in Anglo-Irish politics* (Dublin, 1998), pp 124-5.

121. *Ormond deeds,* vi, app. iv, pp 179-80.

122. As note 120 above.

123. For instance, a map of 'Irish Plantations, 1609-25' in T.W. Moody, F.X. Martin & F.J. Byrne (eds.), *N.H.I.,* iii (Oxford 1976), p. 220, omits Upper Ossory completely, as does a recent survey article written for the school curriculum (Raymond Gillespie, 'Plantations in early modern Ireland', *History Ireland,* i, no. 4 (Winter 1993), pp 43-7). It receives two sentences and a footnote in W.F.T. Butler, *Confiscation in Irish history* (Dublin 1917), p. 87.

124. *Inq. Lagenia,* Queen's County, Charles I, no. 19.

125. Orpen, *Normans,* iii, p. 96.

126. *Inq. Lagenia,* Queen's County, James I, no. 3.

127. Aidan Clarke, 'Pacification, plantation and the Catholic question', in N.H.I., iii, pp 219-22; Butler, *Confiscation*, chap. 3.
128. *C.S.P.I., 1615-25*, p. 336.
129. Ibid., p. 344.
130. Docwra to Buckingham, 1622 (Kent Archives Office, Cranfield Irish Papers, MS. Hil 19).
131. *Cal. Pat. Rolls, Ire., James I*, pp 572-3.
132. *Cal. S.P. Ire., 1615-25*, p. 389.
133. Ibid., p. 435; Cal. *Pat. rolls Ire., James I*, p. 569.
134. B. L. Sloane MS. 3827, ff 35-7.
135. *Cal. S.P. Ire., 1615-25*, p. 475; see also ibid., pp 477-8; for Westmeath's post-1625 machinations at court see Aidan Clarke, *The Old English in Ireland, 1625-42* (London 1966), pp 36, 38, 41-3.
136. Treadwell, *Buckingham and Ireland*, p. 273.
137. *Acts of the privy council, June 1623-March 1625*, p. 511.
138. N.A.I., Lodge MSS, records of the rolls, v, pp 15 and 72.
139. Falkland continued to denounce Westmeath during 1626-7: Bernadette Cunningham (ed.), 'Clanricard Letters', *Galway Archaeological & Historical Soc. Jn.*, xlviii (1996), p. 200.
140. As no separate grant was made to Teige, so Barnaby's grant became the plantation grant for the barons of Upper Ossory when he succeeded his father to the title.
141. *Inq. Lagenia*, Queen's County, Charles I (33).
142. *Cal. S.P. Ire., 1615-25*, p. 435.
143. B.L., Add. MSS, 19,843, pp 62, 68, 106 and 107.
144. *Inq. Lagenia*, Queen's County, Charles I (5); N.A.I., MS. M4683.
145. St. Kieran's College, Kilkenny, Carrigan MSS, vol. 83, pp 212-3.
146. Raymond Gillespie,'The end of an era: Ulster and the outbreak of the 1641 Rising', in Ciaran Brady & Raymond Gillespie (eds.), *Natives and newcomers: the making of Irish colonial society, 1534-1641* (Dublin 1986), pp 191-213.
147. For New English aggrandisement and economic expansion in the original Queen's County plantation area, see Nicholas Canny, 'The marginal kingdom; Ireland as a problem in the first British Empire', in Bernard Bailyn & Philip D. Morgan (eds), *Strangers within the realm: cultural margins of the first British Empire* (London 1991), pp 43-8.
148. T.C.D., MS. 815, ff 19r, 21r-v, 22v-23r, 31v.
149. Ibid., ff22r, 60v.
150. Ibid., f. 62r; William Shaw Mason, *A statistical account of Ireland* (3 vols., Dublin 1814-19), i, p. 24. '
151. N.A.I., Lodge MSS, records of the rolls, v, p. 340.
152. Alan Ford, 'The Protestant Reformation in Ireland, 1590-1641', in Brady & Gillespie (eds.), *Natives & newcomers*, pp 68-9.
153. T.C.D., MS. 215, f. 23v.
154. Shaw Mason, *Statistical account*, i, pp 23-4; Thomas Carte, *The life of James, duke of Ormonde* (6 vols., Oxford 1851), v, p. 279; J. T. Gilbert, *History of the Irish Confederation* (7 vols., Dublin 1882-91), ii, pp v-viii, 50, 154, 222.
155. Edwards, 'Ormond lordship', chapter six. For a discussion of the O'Brennan case see W. Nolan, *Fassadinin: land, settlement and society in south-east Ireland, c. 1600-1800* (Dublin, 1985), ch. 2.

Plate 12.2   Ballagharahin Castle (courtesy Con Brogan).

Chapter 13

WARFARE AND ARCHITECTURE IN COUNTY LAOIS THROUGH SEVENTEENTH CENTURY EYES

ROLF LOEBER

Sometimes more is known about Irish architecture from historical sources than from surviving remains. This is especially true for Co. Laois, which, compared to other counties, has suffered terribly from warfare, changes in ownership, and, presumably, neglect. Furthermore, older sites in the county have been rarely drawn or engraved before the twentieth century,[1] and as a consequence the appearance of many sites is mostly known from documentation rather than from drawings. The publication of the Archaeological Inventory[2] has greatly contributed to the identification of castle sites in the county, documenting 32 remains of castles, and another 42 known from documents only. In addition, other obliterated sites are known from maps made of the eastern portion of the county during the 1560s, with the exclusion of the barony of Upper Ossory.[3] To my knowledge, only one castle, Ballaghmore (#15, see Gazetteer), is roofed and inhabited.

Archaeological surveys of the surviving castles, although highly valuable, often are a mere shimmer of the complexities of sites that may have had auxiliary buildings, bawns, gardens, orchards and so on. Moreover, many of the sites were once centers of population with villages or hamlets, only a few of which the Archaeological Inventory identifies.

Further, archaeological surveys do not usually indicate the successive families who owned the estate, nor whether the families were Gaelic, Anglo-Norman, or New English. Consequently, the interpretation of sites in a cultural context is often frustrating.

The castles in Co. Laois, like elsewhere in Ireland, have diverse origins. Some date back from the Anglo-Norman invasion of the area (e.g., Dunamase), and others were built by native Gaelic septs, such as the FitzPatricks (e.g., Grantstown, plate 13.1). A third group of castles were built by seventeenth century settlers (e.g., Castle Cuffe, plate 13.2 and Rush Hall).[4] The word castle is used here in a loose sense,

377

Plate 13.1   Grantstown Castle (from Grose, *Antiquities*, i).

Plate 13.2   Castle Cuffe (courtesy of IAA).

referring to both tower houses and fortified houses. This chapter focuses on seventeenth century descriptions of castles in the county, particularly those recorded during sieges following the outbreak of the rebellion of 1641.

Plantations and Settlements

To understand the building of castles in Co. Laois, it is essential to understand the history of natives and settlers of the county. The influx of the Normans in the county from the twelfth century onwards led to some castle building as at Dunamase, which like a secular cashel, towers over the countryside. As to the Gaelic Irish, it is not clear when they started to build stone castles, and to what extent they and possibly the Normans built wooden castles as well. During the fourteenth century, the Irish were able to regain ground and expel the Normans from the county.[5] It is clear that in the fifteenth and sixteenth centuries, if not earlier, Irish septs in the county increasingly built stone castles, mostly on a square plan, but round towers were also built (see Grantstown). The FitzPatricks erected a number of castles, which prompted the Lord Deputy Sidney in 1575 to praise the valour and wisdom of Sir Barnaby FitzPatrick, the 2nd baron of Upper Ossory, and to tell the lords of the council that no country could be better governed and defended.[6] Compared to other septs, the FitzPatricks probably held the largest number of castles in the early seventeenth century: a law suit of 1613 mentioned that the seignory of the barony of Upper Cross (presumably Upper Ossory) contained 57 castles. Of these, at least nine belonged to the chief of the FitzPatricks.[7]

The political situation in the county changed dramatically with the introduction of settlers in the sixteenth century. The history of plantations in the county has been reviewed elsewhere and is only summarized here.[8] Lord Deputy Bellingham founded a fortified garrison in 1546-8, called Fort Protector (later Maryborough, now Portlaoise), and another fort at Daingean in Co. Offaly (called Fort Governor, later known as Philipstown). The fort at Maryborough survived when the O'Mores revolted. Upon the suppression of the rebellion, a plantation was instituted with the native inhabitants keeping about a third of their former territories: the remaining two thirds went to new planters, who arrived in three waves.[9] A first wave of settlements took place under the third deputyship of St. Leger (1553-6), when the government was prepared to grant freeholds in County Laois to residents from the Dublin Pale and to soldiers who had been instrumental in suppressing the local rebellion. Letters patent were issued to twenty nine planters from 1551 onward. The letters patent included the clause that planters had to reside on their estate, to arm their tenants, and to exclude the O'Mores. St. Leger tried to strike a balance between New English, Anglo-Irish, and loyal Gaelic Irish proprietors in the choice of grantees. Not all the grantees occupied the lands and government soldiers were stationed in some castles, such as Stradbally and Ballyknockan (#7).[10]

By 1564, the second wave of letters patent had been issued for the plantation in County Laois. These grants of land were in fee farm rather than leases for years, which better encouraged settlements. About twice as many planters were in the second wave of grants (37) compared to the first wave and included most of the former grantees. Half of the grantees were soldiers (five came from Scotland and four from Wales). Most of the settlers were Roman-Catholic. About a third were New English, another third were Irish, and only 17 per cent of the settlers came from the Dublin Pale. Even in this diluted ethnic form, the plantation was a novel approach to settlement, relying heavily on new blood but also on co-operation among individuals from diverse backgrounds. The extent of the land grants did not amount to more than about half of the county. The O'Mores, the original principal inhabitants, were forced to transplant to the west; they settled in an area in Offaly adjoining the Shannon.

The western parts of Co. Laois and O'Dunne's country in Iregan, O'Dempsey's country in Clanmalier, and FitzPatrick's country in Upper Ossory were excluded from the plantation. Most of the new settlers inhabited and improved older castles on their estate; few built new dwellings. For instance, Francis Cosby built a large house out of the materials of the friary at Stradbally. A surviving example of a new settler castles is at Shrule, while Timahoe might have been a rebuilding of an earlier ecclesiastical structure. Some of these buildings (Timahoe), were built on an oblong plan rather than the traditional squarish castle plan. Timahoe measured about forty feet by seventy-eight feet.[11]

It is notable that many new plantation estates were grouped within a radius of six miles of the plantation fort of Maryborough. Another concentration of castles was situated along the river Barrow, the strategic north-south corridor, including Shrule (1576), Monksgrange (1588), both built by members of the Hartpole family, and Tankardstown (1583), built by a member of the Hovenden family.[12] To protect this corridor, a third fort was built by the government at Blackford in 1560.[13]

Further west, a small village, incorporated in 1569-70, arose in the immediate vicinity of the fort at Maryborough. Its charter stipulated that the burgesses were to fortify the borough with ditches and stone walls for the defense of the settlement. A contemporary plan of Maryborough prior to 1570, shows a rectangular, walled enclosure of the town with a moat. The fort for the garrison (measuring about 135 by 113 yards) was surrounded on three sides by the enclosure, and had a castle on one corner and a blockhouse diagonally across.

The Laois-Offaly plantations had a dramatic existence. Eighteen separate risings took place between 1563-4 and 1603. As early as 1575, Lord Deputy Sidney reported that Counties Laois and Offaly 'are much spoyled and wasted, by the Race and Offspringe of the old natyve Inhabiters...' Two years later he took pledges of the O'Dempseys 'and other doubtful Neighbours upon that Border...'[14]

The unrest continued as late as 1599, when Moryson reported that

> In the County of Leax... Owny Mac Rowry Omore, and all the Sept of O Mores, and the chiefe of the Galloglasses in that County, of the Sept of Mac Donnel, the Sept of O Dempsies (except Sir Terence O Dempsey) the Sept of O Doynes (except Teig Oge O Doyne), were all in rebellion... Master Hartpol, Master Bowen, and Master Pygot [Pigott], were the onely English Inhabitants, by whom and some others, certain Castles were kept for the Queene, besides the Fort of Mariaborough kept by the Queenes Garrison.

As we see later, this situation of a few isolated castles and a single governmental garrison trying to withstand Irish forces would repeat itself after the rebellion of 1641. Moryson also reported that English forces extensively burnt the corn to destroy the livelihood of the rebels and their hired soldiers, but parts of the country not visited by the English army, remained free from the massive destruction[15] (see below). Peace returned to the county after the general defeat of the rebels. In 1604 Sir John Davies wrote that public peace was well established in the Pale, Leix, and Offaly, and that the English families planted there governed the country; remaining Irish, such as the MacCoghlans, O'Molloys, O'Dunne's, O'Dempseys lived peacefully and dutifully attended the assizes.[16]

From the late sixteenth century, several initiatives were taken to thin out the Irish in the county and transplant them to the west of the island. In 1594 Ralph Lane, a soldier (and subsequently a planter in Virginia), with the Lord Deputy Perrot's approval, communicated a proposal to the queen to transplant the entire sept of the O'Mores to some uninhabited part of Munster. The plan, originated by a member of the O'More sept, speaks of its advantages for the planters and the more humane consequences for the O'Mores,[17] but did not materialize. However, Sir Piers Crosby (of Stradbally) offered, in return for a grant of the 4,000-acre Tarbert estate in County Kerry, to transport the troublesome 'seven septs of Leix' to this remote place (including the

Mores, Kellies, Lalours, Dorans, Clandeboys, and Dowlins). The transplantation was not a success and many of the members of the septs filtered back to Counties Laois and Offaly over the subsequent decades.[18] The unrest accelerated from the winter of 1622 onwards. Two years later the 'rebels' were noted at Ballaghmore (#15) on the border of counties Laois and Offaly. In September 1626, the continued unrest caused by the returning septs culminated in the government issuing a proclamation that banned the septs from Co. Laois and appointed Sir Charles Coote to enforce the proclamation. In a publication of 1630, Richard Olmstead, the minister of the Mountrath settlement, thanked Coote and expressed:

> That memorable worke of your Honour worthy to be recorded in pillars of Marble, cleansing & purging (like a happy Physitian) this countrey... fro[m] those cursed vipers, & Cockatrices the rebellious kearne, who so infested the Countrey, that no man had any security . . . for four years space . . .

Emanuel Downing, the owner of the Mountrath (#2) estate in the 1620s, referred to the transplantation in one of his letters written in 1631 to Sir John Coke, principal secretary of king Charles I, and recommended the repetition of the time-honored method of uprooting the leaders of the Irish and transplanting them to an area further out west.[19] Thus, there was a considerable presence of restive, native elements in the county, which may have hastened the outbreak of the 1641 rebellion.

The size of the native population which survived the plantations and transplantation is not fully clear, but a few contemporary documents give some insights as to the number of native freeholders at the beginning of the seventeenth century. An inquisition of Iregan in 1607 showed that there were many freeholders of the name O'Dunne, O'Melane and other Gaelic Irish, most of whom owned 5 to 10 acres.[20] Further, according to one of the FitzPatricks, Upper Ossory had 180 freeholders in 1613.[21]

The third plantation in the county took place in the early 1620s when portions of the lands in Iregan, Clanmalier, and Upper Ossory, belonging to the septs of the O'Dunnes, the O'Dempseys, and the FitzPatricks, respectively, were confiscated and distributed to English settlers. Castle Cuffe (#1) and the revamped castles of Borris-in-Ossory (#6) and Ballinakill (#10) date from this period.

The landscape
Maps of County Laois from the 1560s show vast woods and bogs, and

little clearings. However, settlers and probably natives also, must have cleared large areas of the woods. The English soldier Moryson who travelled through Laois in 1600 noted that

> It seems incredible, that by so barbarous inhabitants, the ground should be so manured, the fields so orderly fenced, the Townes so frequently inhabited, the highwaies and paths so well beaten... The reason whereof was, that the Queenes forces, during these warres, never till then came among them.[22]

The county was basically rural with small villages that hardly qualified as towns. The appearance of the villages is very elusive, since only a sixteenth century plan of Maryborough is known.

The landscape varied greatly from barony to barony. The Civil Survey of the mid-seventeenth century, mentions that the barony of Ballyadams had good arable and pasture land and no wood of note, and had many enclosures. In contrast, the northern part of the barony of Upper Ossory was heavily wooded and had 'high boggy' mountains.[23] Although precise comparisons are not feasible, it appears that between the late sixteenth and the mid-seventeenth century, large portions of the woods, due to the enormous need for fuel for the iron works, were cut down.

A visitor in 1610 noted that between Philipstown and Maryborough

> prettye castles & howses may be seene... som that weare newly built, and som old wales repayred & in some places in the fields English people making harvest, but not so aboundantly as wold be looked for.[24]

The peacefulness of the county was also stressed in 1622 when Sir Francis Blundell called Leix because of its plantation 'the civillest countie.'[25] This conception, however, was illusive as can be judged from the events following the outbreak of the rebellion in 1641.

Military Activities between 1641 and 1650

The following text briefly deals with the course of the military campaigns between 1641 and 1650.[26] Table 1 gives an overview of all the sieges, including recurring sieges of the same sites, while figure 13.1 shows the geographic distribution of the documented sieges. Details of selected sieges can be found in the appended gazetteer.

Sieges and Seizures by the Irish Irregulars of Towns and Castles in 1641

Soon after the outbreak of the rebellion in Ulster in October 1641,

TABLE 1
Overview of the sieges in Co. Laois from 1641 to 1650

	Attacking forces and castles/towns besieged and/or seized				
Year	Irish irregulars	Ormond	Confederate	O'Neill	Cromwell
1641	Castle Cuffe (1) Mountrath town (2) Mountmellick town (3) Maryborough town (4) Fermoyle (5) Clogrenan Castle Lea				
1642	Borris-in-Ossary (6) (a) Timahoe	Unidentifed places	Borris-in-Ossory (6) (b)		
1643	Ballynockan (7)		Ballylehand (8) (a) Ballyadams (9) (a) Ballinakill (10) (a) Ballybrittas (11) Dysart (12) (a) Kilminchie (13) (a) Morett Castle Ballyroan Clogrenan*		
1644					
1645					
1646				Cullenagh (a) Kilminchie (13) (b) Dysart (12) (b) Martyborough Fort (14) (a) Ballaghmore (15) Ballyadams (9) (b) Stradbally	
1647					
1648				Ballyehane (8) (b)	
1649		Maryborough Fort (14) (b) Cullenagh (b)			
1650		Castletown/ Gash			Maryborough Fort (14) (c) Ballinakill (10) (b) Dunamase

Note: Numbers after the names of castles and towns refer to entries in the gazetteer in the text. Sites without entries are, because of lack of relevant information, not included in the gazetteer. Letters in parentheses indicate the order of sieges for those sites besieged more than one time.
* = date unclear.

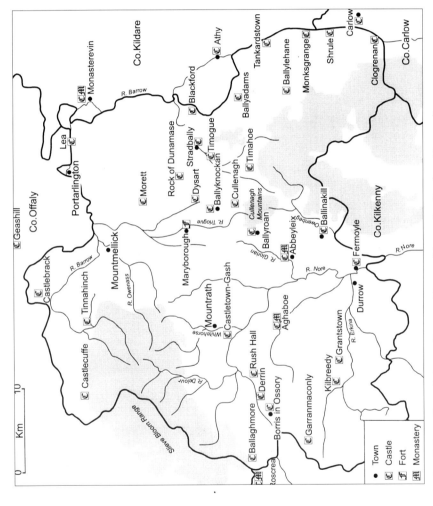

Fig. 13.1   Sites of sieges discussed in text (drawn by Stephen Hannon).

unrest in Co. Laois was followed by the Irish attacking many towns in the county (e.g., Mountrath #2, Mountmellick #3, and Maryborough #4). They successfully seized most of the towns in a short span of time, especially when such towns lacked a strong castle. Some towns held out longer, but only because of the presence of a garrison in the adjoining castle (Borris-in-Ossory #6, Ballinakill #10). The Irish also attacked many castles (e.g., Castle Lea, plate 13.4), and fortified country houses (including Castle Cuffe #1, and Clogrennan, plate 13.4), and numerous small farms. They were not always able to capture a castle,[27] and were least successful in capturing government garrisons (e.g., Borris-in-Ossory #6, Ballinakill #10).

As the countryside fell into the hands of the Irish, the garrisons became isolated outposts and difficult to defend for several reasons. First, military supplies were interrupted and often enormously delayed. Second, strongholds attracted the bedraggled tenants, labourers, artificers, and merchants from surrounding areas who had been chased away from their own dwellings. The large influx of refugees became a heavy burden on the inhabitants of the castles, leading to disease and shortages of food.

The Irish did not appear to always have occupied castles they won. For example, they only looted Castle Cuffe (#1). On the other hand, after they seized the castle of Timahoe (a seat of the Loftus family), they garrisoned this castle under the command of Col. Lewis Moore.[28] It should be pointed out that several castles were not besieged by the Irish irregulars – Timogue and Ballyadams (plate 13.5 #9), owned by Garret Fitzgerald and Sir John Bowen, respectively. Witnesses to later depositions accuse the owners of fraternizing with the Irish.[29]

First Series of Sieges by Ormond's Forces

In April 1642 Ormond and his troops relieved the garrisons of Borris-in-Ossory (#6) and Maryborough (#4), and further-away outposts in Co. Offaly, including Birr. 'In our march thither', wrote one of the officers, 'we fired two hundred villages. The horse that marched on our flanks fired all within five or six miles off the body of the army; and those places that we marched through, they had the rear of the army always burned.'[30] The incursion, however, did not materially change the position of the outposts. Occupants of the remaining castles were short of food and undertook armed forays into the country to collect corn and cattle, attacking the Irish whenever possible and prudent.

Sieges by the Confederate Army of English Castles in 1642-43

The formation of a Confederate army in Leinster in 1642 increased the pressure on Co. Laois, with the earl of Castlehaven, in particular,

Plate 13.3   Lea Castle (from Grose, *Antiquities*, i, between pp 76-7).

Plate 13.4   Clogrennan (from Grose, *Antiquities*, ii, p.10).

Plate 13.5   Ballyadams (courtesy of IAA).

undertaking many successful sieges. After the army of General Preston arrived with heavy artillery, the remaining strongholds surrendered (Borris-in-Ossory #6, and Ballinakill #10). When the cessation of hostilities was concluded in September 1643 all of Co. Laois was in the hands of the Confederate forces.[31] The Catholic hegemony may also explain why so many places are not mentioned as having been besieged, such as Shrule Castle, owned by Robert Hartpole, because its owner was a member of the Irish Confederation.[32] One of the implications of the cessation was that peace returned to the county. Presumably some rebuilding of private residences damaged during the hostilities took place, and taxes were levied for the Confederacy of Kilkenny.[33] Furthermore, tillage returned to some degree of normality, even on the estates that had been taken over from the English. In 1646 several castles were used by the Confederates as garrisons: Ballinakill (#10), Ballyroan, Aghaboe, and Borris-in-Ossory (#6).[34]

Sieges by O'Neill's forces

The threat of rifts among the Confederates was recurrent and culminated in June 1646 when Owen Roe O'Neill, the commander of the Ulster army, declared war on the Supreme Council of the Confederates. In 1646, O'Neill's forces penetrated Co. Laois, seizing several strongholds, including Cullenagh, Maryborough Fort (#14), Kilminchie (#13), Dysart (#12), Ballylehane (#8), Ballyadams (#9), and Stradbally.[35] By 1649, General Hugh O'Neill still held three garrisons in the eastern midlands: Maryborough Fort (#14) in Co. Laois, and Reban and Athy, both in Co. Kildare, which 'brought under contribution all the Queen's Countie.'[36]

Second Series of Sieges by Ormond's Forces

A second wave of incursions by Ormond's troops took place in 1649. Ormond took some 'petty' garrisons in the county, but it is unlikely that he was able to completely dislodge O'Neill's forces. Around this time, Edmond Roe Butler, son of Lord Mountgarrett, took the castle of Cullenagh.[37] The earl of Castlehaven, who had switched his alliance from the Confederates to Ormond, took Maryborough Fort (#14) in 1649, and, after the fall of Kilkenny, made his headquarters at the principal FitzPatrick stronghold of Castletown (also called Gash) in 1650.[38] By that time, Ormond and Owen Roe O'Neill reconciled their differences in October 1649, but O'Neill died in the next month.[39]

Sieges by Cromwell's forces

English Parliamentary forces undertook the initial phase of the reconquest of Ireland in 1647. However, the major campaigns between that year and 1650 did not include forays of the main army into Co. Laois, and were limited to smaller forces attacking the main garrisons.[40] For example, Maryborough Fort (#14) was seized in 1650, but not before the Irish fired the fort and several of their garrisons in Co. Laois.[41] Likewise, Ballinakill (#10), after an artillery siege, surrendered to General Fairfax. In that year, Colonels Hewson and Reynolds also took the hilltop castle of Dunamase.[42] This concluded the reconquest of the county, and no further military activities took place until the outbreak of the Williamite war thirty-seven years later.

Architecture

Accounts of sieges in the period 1641-1650 highlight the diverse nature of architecture of castles and houses in Co. Laois. The typical architecture that survived into the seventeenth century was tower houses, but halls were also noted (see below). Sometime during the late sixteenth and early seventeenth century, fortified country houses emerged. The development from tower houses to country houses probably had several intermediate steps, such as tower houses on an oblong plan (e.g., Shrule, Garranmaconly, Kilbreedy, and possibly Dysart (#12). Probably slightly later country houses on an oblong plan emerged (e.g., Clogrennan and Rush Hall), alongside more elaborate plans such as an U-plan enclosing a small court-yard, as at Castle Cuffe (#1).[43] It is more difficult to reconstruct the development of facades of country houses because of lack of surviving drawings. However, the Butler house of Clogrennan is known from a late seventeenth century drawing by Thomas Dineley, showing a large house of five floors with three curvelinear gables, which, replacing an earlier castle, was probably built before 1628.[44] This and other semi-fortified country houses, stood within the protection of defensive bawns with corner towers (also called flankers). For example, the square bawn at Rush Hall, measuring 64.5 metres each way, partially survives with several of its five-sided corner towers and a 3.7 metre high wall.[45] The flankers with their gunslits were essential to field fire along the curtain walls and thus thwart the scaling of the walls by attackers. Among all settler castles, possibly the castle of Ballinakill (#10) was the most defensible with its water-filled moat, gatehouse and, presumably, a drawbridge. The building was also exceptional in that it had a 'clock tower', which must have served as a bell tower.

The development of castles and other principal houses inhabited by the chief members of the principal Gaelic septs is still poorly understood. Despite confiscations, many castles remained in Irish hands, and Gaelic political culture at several locations survived well into the seventeenth century. For example, a schedule of the division of the O'Dunne estate in 1607-8 mentions two of the principal castles, Castlebrack and Tinnahinch. Each consisted of a hall, and a parlour or 'chamber' at the end of the hall. Although not specifically mentioned, each of the castles, according to the Down Survey, also had a keep. Castlebrack dated back to the early part of the fifteenth century, while Tinnahinch dated back to the second half of that century.[46] Castlebrack, apart from the hall, also included a kitchen, a brewhouse, a 'Backhouse,' and other houses within the bawn. The account also mentions that there was a haggard (a place of storage for corn) and barns, situated on the south side of castle. On its west side were the gardens, the orchard, the park, the stable, and the 'houses' for cattle. On the north and west sides were situated 'the houses and tenements for tenants and other uses.' At Tinnahinch, the account mentions 'the stone wall of an hall' which joined the castle, presumably the keep. Thus, there may have been two halls at this site, one of which certainly was constructed of stone. Within the walls there were the kitchen, the brewhouse, the backhouse, the stable, and the porter's lodging. The latter may have been situated at the gate house. In addition, mention is made of two gardens, three orchards, a park and a meadow on the south side of the castle. Furthermore, there were a mill and 'all the houses,' presumably of the tenants in the village, on the east side of the river Barrow. However, the Down Survey shows a small village on the west side of the river. Nowadays there are no substantial remains of either Castlebrack or Tinnahinch.[47]

There is some evidence that castle building by the native Irish, like the settlers, developed from square and vertical keeps to oblong and more horizontal castles. Examples are Garronmaconly Castle, built by a member of the FitzPatrick sept, and Kilbreedy, owned by a member of the O'Phelan family.[48] Almost always the Irish castles were protected by fortified, stone bawns. However, in at least one case, an Irish house, shown on the Down Survey, stood within a pallisaded enclosure.[49]

The examples illustrate the relative complexity of each of these Gaelic sites and their survival into the seventeenth century. How these and other Gaelic sites fared during the subsequent warfare is not clear.

Sieges of Castles

The following accounts of sieges reveal much about techniques of warfare by the respective parties. The Irish practiced two types of attacks. The first type consisted of attacks by the locals on their Protestant neighbours (e.g., in the case of the siege of Castle Cuffe #1, and the seizing of the towns of Maryborough #4, Mountrath #2, and Mountmellick #3). These encounters were characterized by a lack of organized army involvement and the absence of artillery (Castle Cuffe

#1, was taken with the aid of an imitation cannon). In addition, the attacks were directed at the lesser, non-defensible dwellings inhabited by English settlers and their tenants. Presumably, the Irish, by virtue of sheer numbers, were able to press the English to leave their homesteads. As a consequence of these attacks the English and their families fled to strongholds nearby. This resulted in an enormous concentration of people at the strongest places such as Ballinakill (#10), Ballylehane (#8), and Maryborough Fort (#14).[50]

The second type of attack by the Irish on the English consisted of more formal sieges by army units to gain possession of strongholds, often situated at strategic locations (e.g., Borris-in-Ossory #6, Ballinakill #10). In rare instances, castles were taken by assault (e.g., Dysart, #12), which must have occurred either because attackers did not have field guns, because sites were strong enough to withstand field artillery, or because sites were inaccessible to heavier artillery. For example, the siege of Ballinakill, with field guns remained unsuccessful only until very heavy artillery was brought in by General Preston. The inhospitality of the terrain of the county with its extensive woods and bogs must have made it hard to bring all but the lightest artillery to some parts of the country. In such instances, the Irish used ladders to scale walls, built sows (contraptions of heavy wood on wheels that could withstand musket fire and which could be moved toward the walls to protect individuals undermining the walls), and assaulted a castle by the digging of trenches (e.g., Borris-in-Ossory, #6). Mining and countermining were undertaken during the siege of Ballinakill (#10). That siege also saw the use of bombs (called grenadoes) and incendiary devices fired from cannons.

Military sieges following 1641 were qualitatively different from sieges during the preceding century. More cannons and of a larger caliber were brought into the field, both by the English and the Irish. With few exceptions (e.g., Ballyshannon, Co. Kildare), Irish strongholds, even when built as late as the early seventeenth century, could not withstand the impact of an attack by means of artillery. Thus, all the known artillery sieges of castles in Co. Laois eventually led to surrender, although some held out for quite some time. In a rare instance defenders were able to outwit attackers with artillery (see Ballyadams, #9).

Contemporary accounts probably are not exhaustive in listing all castles that were besieged. For example, Castlehaven turned from Monasterevan (Co. Kildare) into the northern portion of Co. Laois in the summer of 1643, and 'took three or four small Places,' including Morett Castle, with the other castles remaining to be identified. However, this activity ceased with the cessation that took place in September 1643.[51]

The county, unlike many coastal counties, did not have substantial, walled cities that needed to be besieged (the town of Maryborough #4 with its wall and moat was basically non-defensible). Neither was the county the site of any of the major battles. Remarkably, even though there were several crannogs in the county,[52] as yet no sieges of crannogs have been identified.

It should be kept in mind that not all English settlers were opposed to the Confederation of Kilkenny. In fact, several members of the sixteenth century settler families, including the Hartpoles, Hovendens, Darvells, and Cosbys were either Catholics or joined the Irish rebels after 1641. For example, Robert Hartpole assembled a troop of soldiers, and manned his castle of Shrule for the Irish.[53] On the other hand, several individuals of Gaelic stock, such as Barnabee Dunne of Brittas, had become Protestant and had English tenants.[54]

The conquest of castles was in fact a conquest of estates and economic resources. Not surprisingly, once castles had fallen, the custodianship of the castle and the adjoining lands was granted to individuals of the victorious party. For instance, Ormond granted a custodiam of the Ballyknockan (#7) estate to Jonathan Hoyle, minister at Dysart.[55] One of the goals of this custodiam was to assist the government in keeping the castles in the hands of the victors at no charge to the state. Successive parties used custodiams to their advantage. For instance, after the Confederates had successfully besieged Ballinakill Castle (#10) in 1643, the custodianship of its estate became available, but a dispute broke out among Confederates concerning who would receive it.[56]

Part of the value of the estates consisted of industries such as the manufacture of cloth and iron. Iron ore was mined at Dysart (#12), Mountrath (#2), and probably other sites. Iron mills were situated at Mountrath (#2), Ballinakill (#10), and Mountmellick (#3). Cannons were cast at Ballinakill (#10) in the 1630s. It is probable that some of the knowledge of cannon casting was shared with members of the native population, because after the outbreak of the rebellion Lewis O'Dempsey, Viscount Clanmalier, ordered two cannons to be moulded by an Englishman, i.e., one field piece and one 'batterer.'[57] Given the great technical skill and equipment needed for this (casting and boring the cannons), it is quite probable that he might have drawn from the expertise of craftsmen from the cannon foundry at Ballinakill rather than from artisans from the nearby ironworks of Mountmellick (#3). Clanmalier's cannons were used at the siege of Geashill (Co. Offaly), but both broke and were useless.

At the outbreak of the rebellion, there probably was a supply of ready-made iron available in the county that could be used for the manufacture of hand weapons. One of the depositions of that time mentioned that two smiths, Francis Jackson of Castletown and Alfred Smyth, of Newforge, both close to Mountrath (#2), made darts, swords, and mended some gunlocks for the Irish, while George Silly of 'Londonhowse' (not located) made pikestaves.[58]

A Gazetteer of Sieges

The next part of this chapter focuses on seventeenth century descriptions of structures, villages, and their industries in order to reconstruct the appearance and economy of Co. Laois. Ironically, the information is mostly drawn from military accounts of sieges subsequent to the outbreak of the 1641 rebellion in which sieges and destruction of castles are described. In addition, the depositions by victims of the 1641 rebellion further present eye-witness accounts, albeit not impartial, of the devastation brought about in the military campaigns. Whenever possible, other contemporary accounts were consulted. Because of the unevenness of the source material the chapter does not present an exhaustive survey of sieges of all castles in the county. The following order of sieges is roughly chronological, but some sites went through more than one siege spaced over several years.

1. **Castle Cuffe** (former Ballintaggart). One of the grandest country houses of the early 17th century in Co. Laois. Sir Charles Coote probably built this large U-shaped house sometime between 1617 and 1621. Castle Cuffe was named after Coote's wife Dorothea, who he married in 1617 and who was the daughter of Hugh Cuffe. At Coote's creation of baronet in 1621, he was styled of 'Castlecuffe'. Coote developed the Mountrath estate and ironworks (#2), on the other side of the Slieve Bloom. However, most of his estate was situated in Connacht, where he served as provost marshall and was appointed vice-president in 1621.[59] Serving in these various activities implied that he only occasionally resided at Castle Cuffe.

In 1641 Daniel Dunne and others attacked Castle Cuffe by using a piece of half burned timber yoked to six or eight oxen, as a fake cannon which tricked the defenders (Coote was absent) into believing that they would inevitably have to surrender; the rich booty of the house, 'all the furniture, household stuff and armes,' was plundered and then the house was 'demolished.'[60]

Castle Cuffe appears to have had few defenses, with only a blocked-up pistol loop guarding the entrance.[61] However, the house probably stood in a bawn, but evidence of this part of the structure is not now apparent. A considerable amount of the ruins survive. They show the existence of tall, massive early seventeenth century chimney stacks, and indicate that the main house was plastered on the outside with decorative quoins, which were still visible at least a few years ago.

2. **Mountrath town**. The most populous town of Co. Laois in the late 1650s.[62] The lands of Mountrath originally were part of the demesne lands of Rory Caech O'More, chief of Leix, who rebelled against the English and was slain in 1545. Although granted to Englishmen in the late sixteenth century, the site does not seem to have been settled. Around May 1620, Richard Cosby sold the lands of Mountrath to Emanuel Downing, a Dublin attorney from Suffolk, who had married a sister of James Ware Junior. Upon the death of his wife in 1621, Downing married Lucy, the sister of John Winthrop Senior. Subsequently, Winthrop, was associated to some degree with the development of the Mountrath estate. However, for several reasons Downing sold the estate to Sir Charles Coote some years later. He and Winthrop collaborated in London before they became involved in the Massachussets Bay Company. It is quite likely that the Mountrath plantation constitutes a trial on Irish soil of a scheme that eventually led to the massive removal of puritans from East Anglia in England, across the Atlantic, to New England in the 1630s and 1640s.

Mountrath, certainly under Coote's regime, but probably already under Downing, had several industries, primarily cloth works, and iron manufacture.[63] The latter was facilitated by the presence of large woods In the neighborhood. The operation of iron works at Mountrath was only possible because the iron deposits were in reasonably close proximity to extensive forests, which could supply the charcoal necessary for the works. Boate mentioned that the white iron ore was mined two miles from Mountrath, and that the rock iron ore came from Dysart (#12), near Maryborough (just over 7 miles), while later sources indicate that bog iron ore was present in bogs north of Mountrath.

Mountrath was attacked by the Irish in November 1641, resulting in the English losing all their property.[64] The absence of a stronghold inside of the town or fortifications around it had made it an easy target.

3. **Mountmellick town.** This was the estate of Sir Adam Loftus, Viscount Ely, Lord Chancellor of Ireland, and was the fourth largest town in the county in the late 1650s.[65] Loftus founded ironworks at this location in 1630 on the river 'Ownasta,' a tributary to the river Barrow.[66] The works are shown on the Down Survey and included a large mill pond, watermill, and an iron furnace immediately north of the village. The carpenter at the works was David Dempsie, and it is quite possible that other Irishmen worked at the ironworks. The town was attacked by the Irish in November 1641, and the English were driven out.[67] Subsequently, some O'Dempseys, perhaps craftsmen from this site, attempted to cast a cannon. They molded two pieces successfully, but at the first shot the barrel burst, and the attempt was a failure.[68]

4. **Maryborough town** (now Portlaoise). This was the third largest town in the country in the late 1650s.[69] Soon after the outbreak of the rebellion, the Irish besieged Maryborough, then housing about 350 persons, and according to one eye-witness 'plundered diverse howses there, and killed many protest[ants].'[70] The fort, but not the town, was able to resist the attacks. In April 1642 Ormond's troops brought relief,[71] but the site probably surrendered to the Irish sometime afterwards.

5. **Fermoyle** (ffarmoyle). Originally a FitzPatrick castle. Before 1641, the 'house and castle' was owned by William Gilbert, 'Esq.,' probably a relative of Sir William Gilbert, governor of Maryborough Fort. In a deposition dated 11 June 1642, William Gilbert stated that the house was surprised by the Irish in the owner's absence (he was in Dublin at the time). He claimed the usual losses such as cattle and corn, but also household goods to the value of £100, consisting of 'Plate, Pewter, Brasse, Ironware, Beddinge, Lynnen... [and] howshould stuffe, meaninge apparell, bookes & Armes. . . "[72]

The site was marked on the Down Survey as a castle in ruins. Remains on the site consist of a three-storey house with parts of a bawn.[73] The features of the house with its tall and narrow windows are more characteristic of the early eighteenth century than of the early seventeenth century.

6. **Borris-in-Ossory** (also called Manor Villiers, Villiers manor, and Villiers Fort). A strong plantation castle with a bawn and deerpark. Originally a FitzPatrick castle, built in the fifteenth century. The estate was confiscated in the early 1620s and granted in 1624 to George Villiers, 1st Duke of Buckingham, the confidant of King Charles I. The foundation charter mentioned the older castle and bawn on the site, which was 'much for the Defence of the Countrey,' but which had been destroyed in the troubles of the late sixteenth century, after which it had been, to a measure, rebuilt.[74] According to James Ware, the estate consisted of one quarter of the barony of Upper Ossory, which in the letters patent consisted of a total of 10,788 acres of which 7,003 acres were arable. (These quantities were usually an underestimate of the true acreage). The grant stipulated that Buckingham was a to build a stone castle with a bawn 14 feet high and 150 feet square, to be made defensible with flankers and to be guarded with a garrison.[75]

Tenants were to build close to the castle. Possibly, the small, early seventeenth century semi-fortified house of Derrin Castle, just one mile ENE of Borris, was one of the tenants' houses.[76] This T-plan house shows pistol loops on each side of one of the two main fireplaces.

The 1624 grant of Borris included the right for Buckingham to enclose a deerpark of 1,200 acres for hunting. However, he never came to Ireland and leased the estate to Sir William St. Leger, the Lord

President of Munster. According to the Lord Deputy Wentworth in 1637, St. Leger 'bestowed a very great sum in planting, building, and improving the lands...'[77] This included the creation of a deerpark which was stocked with deer from Munster donated by Richard Boyle, the earl of Cork.'[78]

At the outbreak of the rebellion in 1641, the castle on the site was garrisoned with a constable (Capt. John Pigott) and 30 wardens because of its importance for guarding the main road to Roscrea (Co. Tipperary).[79] It was besieged in the next year mostly by the Fitzpatricks. According to a contemporary account, lacking artillery they harmlessly fired at the 'spike holes' and windows of the castle. The attackers occupied the houses of the town close to the castle and bawn, but the defenders set fire to the houses to eliminate any threat from those sites. The rebels returned with many scaling ladders and two sows. The defenders, not having artillery, developed a remarkable strategy to build a cannon. They removed a wide leaden pipe from the castle wall, bound ropes and tallowed hides around it and mounted the device upon a carriage so as to be able to fire on the sows. When the attackers heard about this, they retreated with their sows. The siege continued until Easter 1642 (having lasted 17 weeks) until the castle was relieved by a force of Ormond's army under Sir Charles Coote. The castle then housed about 300 people, most of whom had fled from indefensible sites in the neighborhood. However, the respite was temporary. Once Coote had left, the FitzPatricks returned, and prepared 'straight & crosse works' of retrenchments, which allowed them to come closer to the castle than ever before (this indicates that the defenders did not have cannons that could thwart the progress of such trenches). Another relief party arrived, but again the relief was temporary. The FitzPatricks returned with an iron field piece, operated by their gunner, David Broe, which had been used to protect their own stronghold at Castletown. However, fortunately for the defenders, the piece burst when fired. This did not signal the end of the siege, though, because General Preston of the Confederation of Kilkenny arrived with his army and artillery.[80] The castle, then known as 'one of the strongest fortes in Leinster,' surrendered on December 11, 1642.[81]

The castle may have subsequently been taken in 1646 by O'Neill's forces. In the next year, a Capt. Hedges, was stationed here.[82] Apparently, there are no remains of the castle above the ground.[83] However, on the 6-inch Ordnance survey map its site is indicated north of the main road through Borris-in-Ossory, opposite to the crossroad to Donaghmore.

7. **Ballyknockan.** The castle and lands had been granted to Henry Davelle in 1563.[84] It must have been situated in a strong position

because it was surrounded on all sides by bogs,[85] and may have been accessible by a causeway only. This was one of the castles close to Maryborough, which may have served as a defensive buffer for the fort. According to testimony in 1644 by Jonathan Hoyle, minister of Dysart, Thomas Davelle by being in rebellion had forfeited the castle.[86] Sometime in 1642, when there was a pause in the hostilities, Hoyle occupied the castle, shingled the roof and mended the breaches. After some problems, Hoyle received a custodiam from the lord justices for the estate, in order to keep the castle out of the hands of the Irish without a charge to the government. However, Hoyle was severely tested in this, because on 27 January 1643, several of the Irish tenants on the estate disputed the harvesting of corn on the nearby lands, and introduced rebels to their houses, 'which were built neare unto the castle.' The rebels were able to pull the chain that locked the gate and entered the castle, but the occupants were able to beat them down the stairs. Succour arrived from Maryborough, but the rebels were able to rob the castle's ward of their horses and provisions.

The history of the castle during the subsequent warfare is not clear. Remains on the site consist of the lower portions of a tower house.[87]

8. **Ballylehane** (also known as Ballylenan, Ballihenan, and Lynanstown). This was a large but poorly defensible castle. A castle already stood at this location in 1346. The site must have been occupied by the O'Connors of Offaly, perhaps in the middle ages, because an armorial panel with the O'Connor coat of arms, formerly located in the castle, was later built into a gate-pier. In 1563, the earl of Ormond received a grant in this border area of the abbey at Leix (Abbeyleix) and planned the construction of several castles, including Ballylehane.[88]

In the sixteenth and seventeenth centuries, the castle was owned by the Hovendens, an English family.[89] However, from at least 1619 onwards it was held by members of the Greame (also called Graham) family, who were Scots and who were related to the Hovendens. Christian, daughter of Sir Richard Greame, knt., died at this castle in 1624, then called 'Linnastonne.'[90]

The castle was taken by the earl of Castlehaven in 1643, when it was defended by George Graham, who kept a garrison, who Castlehaven described as 'English and Scottish mungrells, the best horsemen in them parts...' Presumably, the castle's bawn was large because the site was said to have held over one thousand Englishmen and Protestants. However, other accounts mention 250 to 300 or 500 refugees. Castlehaven's cannons breached the walls. One contemporary account stated that 63 shots of their 'great Ordinance' were fired at the castle, yet none of the besieged were materially hurt, which indicates that the attackers must have used field artillery only and did not have fire bombs in their arsenal. Partly because of lack of water, the garrison surrendered in August 1643 on condition that they could march out with their arms. One account relates that the castle was demolished, but this appears to be incorrect.[91]

The Hovenden family returned to reside at the castle, for we find that in 1648 Thomas Oge Oventon [sic, Hovenden], presumably a Catholic, held the castle, but that it then was captured by General O'Neill in one hour. Probably the siege was short because the castle had no defenses against O'Neill artillery. A contemporary account mentioned that the castle was 'verie rich of malte, corne, brasse, armes, ammunition, and the matter of £3000 of money and plate...'[92] O'Neill, presumably because of lack of manpower, decided not to keep the castle as a garrison, and ordered it to be burned.[93]

Castlehaven's account of 1643 mentions a togher close to the site, probably in the direction of Athy (Co. Kildare), which 'was a great way cut through a Bog, and I believe about half a Mile in length.'[94] It is not clear whether the castle was only accessible through the togher; the site of the togher has not yet been identified. Nowadays, there are no remains of a castle other than the armorial stone mentioned above.[95]

9. **Ballyadams.** A castle at this site belonging to the O'Mores was taken by the lord justices in 1546. Government soldiers were stationed here from at least 1556-8 onwards. It was granted to a Welshman, Robert Bowen, son of John Ap Thomas Bowen, in 1570.[96] The castle is situated about three miles north of Ballylehane (#8). After Castlehaven had conquered Ballylehane in 1643, he moved to Ballyadams, then occupied by the Provost Marshal Sir John Bowen, 'an old soldier' and Castlehaven's 'long acquaintance.' Castlehaven requested permission to put a garrison in the castle, which Bowen refused. As Castlehaven recounted, Bowen called his wife and two

> very fair daughters... [and] desired one favour, that in case I was resolved to use violence, I would shew him where I intended to plant my Guns, and make my Breach. I satisfied his Curiosity, and asked him what he meant by this question? because (saith he) swearing with some warmth, I will cover that part or any other your Lordship shoots at, by hanging out both my Daughters in Chairs.

Castlehaven relented and noted that 'Tis true the place was not of much Importance, however this Conceit saved it.'[97] However, the castle was captured by O'Neill's forces in 1646.[98] Remains on the site contain a six-storey high, late medieval structure with rounded towers at the south-west and north-west angles.[99] However, stylistically the castle is very similar to the castle at Castlejordan (Co. Meath), dating from the sixteenth century.[100] At Ballyadams, two wings were added, one on each side of the tower, probably sometime in the seventeenth century. One was never finished. When Austin Cooper visited the castle in 1782, he noted that

> The inside of the Case [Castle], exhibits a scene sufficient to excite compassion from every lover of ancient grandeur – the boarded floors all torn up – the plaistered walls & ceelings threatening the observer with destruction, & to complete this grand scene of desolation, the great state room still remains hung with elegant Tapestry now let to rot away.[101]

Remains at the site consist of the full tower and one of the wings.

10. **Ballinakill** (also Ballynakill). This was a large castle and bawn mostly built in the early seventeenth century, adjoining a plantation town and an iron works. The town was the second largest in the county in the late 1650s.[102] Originally part of the Cosby estate, it was granted to assignees of Thomas Ridgeway, earl of Londonderry in 1611 under the name of the manor of Gallen-Ridgeway. The grant included the nearby ancient anchoritic site of Dysart Gallen and the motte of Castle Gallen.[103] A year later, when a provost and burgesses were appointed, the town of Ballinakill was incorporated.[104] Richard Billings described the settlement there in 1643:

> Ballinekilly was a collony of English, planted there by Sir [Thomas] Ridgeway... It is seated among woods, in a place soe watered with springs, as afforded the Earle conveniences to make many fish-ponds neare the castle hee built there, which hee likewise fortified with a strong stone wall, and that with turrets and flanckers...

The castle had a deer park, which in the early 1630s contained 700 acres (English measure) and was 'impaled and rayled.'[105] Adjoining the castle was a well inhabited town. The town's sovereign, Walter Curry, also acted as Lord Ridgeway's attorney in about 1641.[106] Remarkably, one of the servants of Capt. Richard Steele, defender of the town in 1642-43, was John Fortune, an Indian, probably from Patagonia in South America.[107] According to Steele, Ridgeway invested £10,000 in the creation of the town and, presumably, its castle and iron-industry.[108]

Close to the town, there was an iron mill, which kept 'many lusty men at worke...'[109] The iron works were probably already in operation in 1613 when Ridgeway requested Sir Richard Boyle, himself a developer of iron works and a cannon-foundry in Munster, to send Ridgeway 'presently (but be secrett) a skilful groundman or miner & hammerman.'[110] The iron works were situated south-east of the town on the Ironmills River, a tributary to the Owenbeg River, where the Ironmills bridge spans the river. There is also a location called Iron-mills, near Kilcronan.[111] Eventually, the iron works at Ballinakill received, by royal patent, a monopoly of producing iron ordnance in Ireland.[112] The iron may have been mined locally, but prior to 1641 specialists from Liege in the Low Countries operated the foundry.[113] Lord Deputy Wentworth wrote in 1633 about 'Blagnal's Works', where some ten minions were cast, 'which, upon Trial, prove passing smart and fine Pieces.'

Minions were small cannon able to fire 3 1/2 pound balls. Blagnal refers to Richard Blacknall, who had been employed by Sir Richard Boyle, earl of Cork, at the earl's ironworks in Munster. Wentworth mentioned that Blacknall brought four minions to Dublin, 'which I saw tried here myself in Kilmainham; they are very good, and doubtless as good Mine as in the World, it casts the smoothest, and with the closest Grain I ever saw...'[114] The castle was situated in an area dominated by the Confederates. Its strength was alluded to in Richard Belling's description of the site, mentioned earlier. In addition, cannons manufactured here probably were used for its defense.[115] The situation became perilous, however, because upon the outbreak of the rebellion large numbers of Protestant tenants and other settlers had flocked to Ballinakill for succour. Richard Bellings recounted that with the aid of the additional labour force, Ballinakill Castle was reinforced with:

> many new workes, filling them with water, which the ground naturally afforded them in great plenty; soe as there being noe want of provisions of all kinds, the place might have well beene judged impregnable against an armie that without ordinance came to beseige it.[116]

Furthermore, the water moat probably would have made it difficult for foot soldiers to scale the walls. However, the castle, with its garrison of 60 horse, became isolated from outside support in 1642. Over-crowding in the castle had become desperate, and a contemporary report states that of the 600 Protestants at the site 140 were lost to 'flux and disease.'[117] The situation was temporarily relieved by Colonel George Monck, who was sent by Ormond to Ballinakill in December of that year.[118]

The castle successfully withstood the initial attacks. The defenders burned the tanhouses, which provided cover to the attackers outside of the gate. Afterwards the attackers started to use small field artillery, which did little harm other than an eight-pound shot falling through the roof, killing one person and wounding another. The next day, Capt. Tirrell (probably Tyrrell) and his men made an assault on the town, but the defenders successfully opposed him. Tyrrell was killed; his head was cut off by the defenders and hung 'on the top of the Clock howse.' This is one of several mentionings of a clockhouse, presumably in the town.

The next assault consisted of the attackers mining their way to the north-east turret of the bawn and firing faggots at the castle, but a countermining operation by the defenders successfully dealt with this. A similar mining and countermining operation took place at the east end of the garden and successfully thwarted the attack, thanks to the 'industry of John Cornelius [one of the miners of iron ore?] who hath skillful myners whoe countermined & meeting them, broke downe their timber work, [and] had a skirmish with them underground with a small piece, musketts & pistolls...,' killing several of their pioneers, 'and because 'god disappointed them in blowing us up.' Until that time, the attackers had used their field artillery with little success, especially when aiming at the gate house and its drawbridge.

The siege intensified when General Preston arrived with his army, but this force was also unable to capture the castle. The prospects of the siege dramatically changed upon the arrival in Dungarvan (Co. Waterford) of two iron guns for twenty-four pound bullets each, and an iron mortar piece, both of which had been shipped from Spain.[119] One or more of these pieces of artillery were carried overland, first to Kilkenny and then to Ballinakill. A Dublin letter writer noted that 'Preston hath amongst his other great peeces a demycanon against which none of our castles can hold out.'[120]

On 4 May, the heavy artillery started 'to play' without intermission from five o'clock in the morning until two o'clock in the afternoon. The cannonade was directed at the castle's staircase, which was the weakest part of the castle, causing it to collapse. In addition, the attackers fired 'granadoes' (which is a hollow bullett filled with powder and small bulletts) to set fire to combustible areas. One fell 'on a great beame on the gallery to the clock howse, broke it into two..., & fell upon a stone ye top of the Castle.' This attack may also be subject of another account that mentioned that when the cannon fired at the castle, it 'unexpectedly... beat down p[art of the castle, and... a bomb [fired by a mortar] falling directly on the top of the roof, broke it and the planks, partitions and beams, two lofts under it...'[121] Another account of the siege also mentions the use of grenadoes, consisting of long fistulas or pipes filled with powder and burnstone stopped with tarre and pitch at the one end, & in the middle having their little touch holes with muskett bulletts tyed in little baggs which falling amongst the multitude [of people] would doe much harme.

The defenders in the court were able to quickly cover them with clay to make them harmless. However, Ridgeway, fearing for the lives of so many people, decided to negotiate a surrender, which was accepted.[122] In the meantime, troops sent out to relieve the castle were intercepted, and the place was forced to surrender, 'leaving their magazines stored with provisions of all sorts.'[123] In all, the siege had been long, from 20 November 1642 to 5 May, not counting the arrival of relief in December 1642. However, the actual final siege by Preston's forces took five weeks, from 1 April 1 to 5 May, with the great artillery only firing from 4 May. The town must have been without walls or embankments and, consequently, was defenseless. A contemporary account relates that the town of Ballinakill was destroyed by the rebels at this time.[124] However, the castle was not fully demolished during the siege, and subsequently served as a Confederate garrison, at least until 1646 when Capt. Barnwall's troop was stationed there.[125] It was finally besieged by the Cromwellian army under General Fairfax, who cannonaded it from Warren Hill, adjoining the present Heywood demesne, presumably in 1650. The garrison was subsequently forced to surrender the castle.[126]

11. **Ballybrittas.** This was the main seat of the O'Dempseys. A castle on the site was marked with auxiliary buildings on the Laois/Offaly map of the 1560s. In 1622 the estate was owned by Sir Terence O'Dempsey (later elevated to Viscount Clanmalier), who then held 3,300 acres.[127] In 1642, Colonel Crawford, a commander in Ormond's army, besieged the castle. Castlehaven, who was then attending to the siege of Ballinakill (#10) by the Confederate general Preston, successfully relieved Ballybrittas.[128] In June 1643, however, Sir Michael Ernely and his troops took several castles in this area, including Ballybrittas, where they found the best pillage.[129]

No remains survive at the site of the old castle. However, a photograph most likely taken at the turn of the century shows a fortified house of three stories, probably on a T-plan, with three massive chimney stacks crowned by diagonally placed flues, which were typical for the seventeenth century.[130] It is highly likely that this house replaced an older castle.

12. **Dysart.** Probably an oblong castle with a large hall. Originally a medieval castle stood on this site owned by the O'Lalor family. After its confiscation, it was granted to John Pigott in 1577. The castle had a

large hall, and most likely a large bawn. An iron mine was nearby. Iron works were in operation at Dysart in the sixteenth century.[131] Boate, at the middle of the seventeenth century, mentioned that rock iron ore came from Dysart, which was one of the types of ore used to make iron at the iron works at Mountrath. He mentioned that the iron ore deposits were close to the surface and were sufficiently large enough to supply several ironworks.[132] He does not mention, however, that iron was manufactured at this site.

At the outbreak of the rebellion in 1641, Major Pigott was appointed governor of Athy (Co. Kildare). According to one report, in his absence, the castle had to surrender to the earl of Castlehaven in 1643, even though the cessation had been concluded. Pigott did not want to serve against Parliament and retired to Dysart, which he repossessed and where he lived for some years.[133]

In 1646, however, the castle was attacked by O'Neill's Irish forces under Colonels Farrell and Rory Maguire. Pigott refused to surrender, believing that the castle could not be captured without the use of cannons. However, the commanders of the attacking troops, who indeed lacked guns, gave orders to storm the castle. The soldiers first set on fire the haggard, which caused the smoke to envelop the castle. While attacking musketeers fired on the defenders, 'the pikemen carrying on the pointe of theires conflamed shefes, throwing them as thicke as haile unto the castle windowes...' kindling the wooden castle door through the grate. Another account mentions that the attackers 'first sacked the portion outside the gate, and then scaled the barricaded walls. The large hall, the stables and the immense haggard were burned. Captain Pigott and over 80 soldiers were killed.' The bounty for the soldiers must have been good, because 'the house was very riche.'[134]

The remains of the monastery church at Dysart were still in evidence in 1782 when visited by Austin Cooper, who also noted part of a tower on the summit of the hill, which must have served as a windmill, and lower down, the 'Butt of another tower.'[135] Nowadays, the remains of the castle consist of only a north-east angle tower of a curtain wall.[136] The Pigott family later lived at nearby Cappard.

13. **Kilminchy.** The site had been granted to Robert Eirer in 1569,[137] but by the beginning of the seventeenth century was in the hands of Sir William Gilbert, the governor of Maryborough (now Portlaoise). A sketch on the Down Survey of the mid seventeenth century shows an oblong structure, which may have been similar to Garranmaconly Castle in the same county. In 1643 Gilbert was forced to surrender the house to Lord Castlehaven after putting up some resistance. As usual, the soldiers plundered the goods of the castle. When Castlehaven received the message of the cessation, Lady Gilbert and her family re-

entered into possession of it and were restored of the goods that were found among the soldiers.[138] However, the castle was taken again, in 1646 by O'Neill's troops.[139] Subsequently, the house was occupied by these forces and hosted the Nuncio Rinnucini after his flight from Kilkenny.[140]

The castle is obliterated (the surviving gateway dates from the nineteenth century), but a small single-storey outbuilding NW of the 19th century Kilminchy House remains. It has a distinct batter and may belong to the original castle.[141]

14. **Maryborough Fort** (the Fort of Laois, also Lease, and now Portlaoise). Soon after the outbreak of the rebellion, the Irish besieged Maryborough, which then housed about 350 persons, and according to one eye-witness 'plundered diverse howses there, and killed many protest[ants].'[142] The fort, but not the town, was able to resist the attacks. Ormond's troops brought relief in April 1642,[143] but the site surrendered to the Confederate Irish sometime afterwards. In 1646, O'Neill's army occupied the fort. According to Castlehaven, 'ONeales Troops... had Fortified..., the Fort of Lease, and all other places capable of strength...'[144] In 1649, however, Castlehaven, then allied with Ormond, was sent into Co. Laois with 5,000 footmen and 1,000 horsemen, and some cannons 'to reduce the Fort of Lease... Athy and other Garrisons, possessed by ONeals People.' He successfully executed these orders.[145] Upon arrival at Maryborough, Castlehaven summoned the governor Sir Phelim O'Neill to give up the castle. O'Neill refused, but was then forced to surrender.[146]

Early in 1650 the fort was attacked by Cromwellian forces under Col. Hewson, who with artillery and a strong force had entered Co. Laois. The occupants of the fort, however, set fire to the fort, and surrendered it on 16 February.[147]

15. **Ballaghmore.** This castle, situated between the lands of the FitzPatricks and the O'Carrolls of Ely O'Carroll, served as a border castle. Built around 1480, it was disputed between the two septs in 1565.[148] It was situated on an important pass between the counties of Laois and Offaly, along the main road between Maryborough and Roscrea (Co. Tipperary). In 1642 the pass probably consisted of a stone causeway through the bogs. Mention of it is made in an English document stating that near the castle of Florence FitzPatrick, between Borris-of-Ossory and Birr, there was

a stone Cause-way through a Bogg, where but two Horses could march in Front, where the Rebels had cast up a ditch on each side of the Cause-way, and cut off some two yards in length at the entrance on the Cause-way, so to hinder our mens passage.

The English eventually gained the passage.[149]

In 1647, Capt. Hedges, who was in garrison at Borris-in-Ossory and possibly a commander in O'Neill's forces, attacked Ballaghmore. After a stout resistance, the castle surrendered, and Hedges blew up some part of it and filled the entrenchments.[150]

Conclusion

We set out to view warfare and architecture in Co. Laois during the seventeenth century through contemporary eyes. On the one hand, warfare in the county was rather conventional, ranging from forays, burning of corn, and assaults without cannons on castles and strongholds. On the other hand, warfare differed from preceding rebellions and wars because of the use of artillery. None of the castles was able to withstand bombardments of heavy artillery. Warfare in Co. Laois probably was somewhat representative of warfare in other landlocked counties without major cities, but this awaits similar studies on other counties.

Several contemporary accounts provided detailed descriptions of sieges and provide glimpses of castles, bawns, and adjoining towns and villages. Inevitably, the descriptions are useful complements to the *Archaeological inventory* of the county, but at the same time are insufficient to reconstruct lost castles.

Acknowledgements

The author is much indebted to several individuals, especially Maurice Craig, Elizabeth FitzPatrick, Jane Ohlmeyer, and Geraldine Stout, for information about sources and sites. In addition, Magda Stouthamer-Loeber and Ailana Winters provided helpful comments on an earlier draft.

References

1. An exception is E. Ledwich, *Antiquities of Ireland* (Dublin, 1790).
2. D. P. Sweetman, O. Alcock, & B. Moran, *Archaeological inventory of County Laois* (Dublin, 1995).
3. There are three versions of this map (British Library (BL), Cotton Ms Aug. I, ii, 40; Trinity College Dublin (TCD), Ms 1209, f.9; National Maritime Museum, Greenwich, Ms P. 39). Information kindly provided by Dr. John Andrews. For printed copies of the various maps, see T. W. Moody, F. X. Martin, & F. J. Byrne (eds.), *A new history of Ireland* (Oxford, 1976), opp. p. 78; E. O'Leary and M. Lalor, *History of the Queen's County* (Dublin, 1914) II, frontispiece; and, A. P. Smyth, *Celtic Leinster* (Blackrock, 1982), pp viii-ix. All the extant versions were published in J. H. Andrews and R. Loeber, 'An Elixabethan map of Leix and Offaly: cartography, topography and architecture' in W. Nolan and T. O'Neill (eds), *Offaly: history and society* (Dublin, 1998), pp 244-5, 246, 247.

4. Possibly Sampsons Court, shown near Ballynakill on the Down Survey of the barony of Cullenagh, should be added to this list of fortified country houses. It probably was situated near the Ballynakill iron works. *Census Ire. 1659*, p. 499.

5. Feehan, *Laois*, p. 249. NLI, Ormond deeds D. 1357. I am indebted to Aoife Leonard for the latter reference.

6. F. Grose, *The antiquities of Ireland* (London, 1791), ii, p. 73.

7. *Cal. S.P. Ire., 1611-14*, p. 409. The following FitzPatrick castles are mentioned by Sweetman et al., *Archaeological Inventory*, pp 110ff.: Aghmacart, Ballagharahin, Ballaghmore, Ballygeehin, Ballykealy, Castletown, Clonburren, Galesquarter, Garranmaconly, Gortnaclea, Grantstown, Tintore, Ballynahimmy, Coolkerry, Grenan, Harristown, Killanure, Roskeen. Several of the castles, belonging to the chiefry domains, are mentioned in the letters patent granted to Florence FitzPatrick, 3rd Lord Upper Ossory, in 1600: Cowlchill [Cullahill], Formoyle [Fermoyle], Grace-Castle, Water-Castle [Watercastle], Tentoure [Tintore], CastleTown [Castletown], Burrishe [Borris]. Donnaghmore, Flemingstown [Castlefleming], &c. Sir. E. Brydges (ed.), *Collin's peerage of England* (London, 1812) iv, p. 339.

8. R. Loeber, *The geography and practice of English colonisation in Ireland' from 1534 to 1609* (Athlone, 1991).

9. Most of the following is based on R. Dunlop, 'The plantation of Leix and Offaly, 1556-1622' in *Engl. Hist. Rev.*, vi (1891), pp 61-96; D. White, 'The Tudor plantations in Ireland before 1571', unpublished Ph.D. thesis, Trinity College (Dublin, 1968).

10. *Cal. Carew MSS, 1515-74*, p. 267.

11. H. S. Crawford, 'The round tower and castle of Timahoe' in *R.S.A.I. Jn.*, liv (1924), pp 34-45.

12. For Tankardstown, see O'Leary and Lalor, *Queen's County*, ii, p. 766.

13. *Cal. Carew MSS, 1575-88*, p. 93.

14. A. Collins (ed.), *Letters and memorials of state* (London, 1744), i, p. 241.

15. F. Moryson, *An itinerary* (Glasgow, 1907), ii, pp 230-31.

16. *Cal. S.P. Ire., 1603-6*, p. 159.

17. Dunlop, Leix and Offaly, pp 86-7.

18. H.M.C., *4th report*, p. 566; BL, Add MS 4756, f. 81ff; A. Clarke, 'Sir Piers Crosby, 1590-1646' in *I.H.S.*, xxvi (1988), p. 149; W. Knowler (ed.), *The earl of Strafford's letters and despatches* (London, 1739) i, p. 69; J. Crawford, earl of Lindsay, A *bibliography of royal proclamations...* (Oxford, 1910), ii, p. 30; R. Loeber, 'Preliminaries to the Massachusetts Bay Colony: the Irish ventures of Emanuel Downing and John Winthrop Sr.' in T. Barnard, D. Ó Cróinin, & K. Simms (eds.), A *miracle of learning* (Cambridge, in press); BL, Sloane MS 3827, ff. 35, 37, 94, 96.

19. Loeber, 'Preliminaries to the Massachusetts Bay Colony', in press.

20. K.W.Nicholls (ed.), *The O Doyne manuscript* (Dublin, 1983), pp 2-29.

21. *Cal. S.P. Ire., 1611-14*, p. 409

22. Moryson, *Itinerary*, ii, p. 330.

23. R. C. Simington (ed.), *The Civil Survey 1656-6* (Dublin, 1961), x, pp 22-3.

24. *HMC, 4th report*, p. 566;

25. BL, Harl. MS 3292, f.40-45.

26. For more details on the military campaigns in Ireland, see O'Leary and Lalor, *Queen's County*, ii, R. Loeber and G. Parker, 'The military revolution in seventeenth century Ireland' in J. H. Ohlmeyer (ed.), *Ireland from independence to occupation 1641-1660* (Cambridge, 1995), pp 66-88; P. M. Kerrigan, *Castles and fortifications in Ireland 1485-1945* (Cork, 1995), pp 85-103; T. Bartlett & K.

Jeffery (eds.), *A military history of Ireland* (Cambridge, 1996); J. Burke, 'The New Model Army and the problems of siege warfare, 1648-1651' in *I.H.S.,* xxxii (1990), pp 1-29.

27. Clogrenan was subsequently relieved by Col. Sir P. Wemys (O'Leary and Lalor, *Queen's County,* i, p. 217; ii, p. 515), but served as center for Confederate troops in 1647 *(Cal. S.P., Ire., 1633-47,* p. 606).

28. O'Leary & Lalor, *Queen's County,* ii, p. 514; the will of Sir Thomas Loftus of 'Tymochoe' was proved in 1639 (A. Vicars, *Index to the prerogative wills of Ireland 1536-1810* (Dublin, 1897), p. 289).

29. TCD, MS 815, ff. 65-65v.

30. M. Ashley, *General Monck* (Towata, 1997), p. 30.

31. S. Wheeler, 'Four armies in Ireland' in Ohlmeyer, *Ireland from independence to occupation 1641-1660,* p. 49.

32. J. T. Gilbert (ed.), *History of the Irish Confederation and the war in Ireland, 1641-1643* (Dublin, 1882), ii, p. 216.

33. Gilbert, *Confederation,* v, p. 228.

34. Gilbert, *Confederation,* vi, p. 84; *Cal. S.P., Ire., 1633-47,* p. 758.

35. J. T. Gilbert (ed.), *A contemporary history of affairs in Ireland from* A.D. *1641 to 1652* (Dublin, 1879), i, p. 128; Gilbert, *Confederation,* vi, pp 23, 30; O'Leary & Lalor, *Queen's County,* i, p. 195; J. I. Casway, *Owen Roe O'Neill and the struggle for Catholic Ireland* (Philadelphia, 1984), passim and map on p. 220.

36. Gilbert, *Contemporary history,* ii, p. 18

37. O'Leary & Lalor, *Queen's County,* ii, p. 529.

38. *Castlehaven's memoirs,* p. 155.

39. Wheeler, *Four armies,* p. 64.

40. Ibid., p. 57.

41. Gilbert, *Contemporary history,* iii, part 1 p. 369.

42. O'Leary & Lalor, *Queen's County,* i, pp 234, 272.

43. Sweetman et al., *Archaeological inventory,* pp 124-25. Stylistically, Rush Hall is from the early seventeenth century. It was probably built by Sir Francis Rushe, who with 50 foot was stationed at the fort at Philipstown in 1606 *(Cal. S.P. Ire., 1606-8,* p. 1). He died in 1629 in the same year as his only son Thomas, leaving a few daughters ([C. T. Lamacraft], *Some funeral entries of Ireland* (n.l., Association for the Preservation of the Memorials of the Dead, n.d.), pp 109-110).

44. NLI, MS 392, f. 81. Stylistically, the house dates from the early seventeenth century, which is supported by the fact that by 1628 Capt. Thomas Butler had bestowed 'great charge upon the house' (J. Morrin (ed.), *Calendar of the patent and close rolls of Chancery* (Dublin, 1863), ii, p. 379; *Cal. S.P. Ire., 1625-32,* p. 368).

45. Survey by Elizabeth FitzPatrick, 1993, for the Office of Public Works. The addition to the main house may be of a later date.

46. Nicholls, *ODoyne manuscript,* pp xiv-xv, 40, 186; Sweetman et al., *Archaeological inventory,* p. 111.

47. The remains at Castlebrack include a pile of rubble, about 20 metres in length (perhaps representing the remains of the hall) and part of the bawn wall with an external fosse. The remains of a deserted settlement are on the south-west and downslope from the ruined tower house, where slight traces of earthworks are visible. Surviving at Tinnahinch are a circular mound or platform with a diameter of 25 metres, and with two enclosures (Sweetman et al., *Archaeological inventory,* pp 57, 67, 106, 111).

48. Sweetman et al., *Archaeological inventory,* pp 114-15. Garronmaconly Castle is known from a drawing by Beranger, who named it Garron (RIA, MS 3C30, f. 48).

49. Barony of Maryborough map, house shown at Cloanadogaste (probably Clonadacasey, about 2½ miles east of Mountrath).
50. TCD, MS 815, f.103.
51. *The earl of Castlehaven's memoirs* (Delmar, NY, 1974), p. 78; Gilbert, *Confederation*, iii, pp 48, 56, 59, 60.
52. Feehan, *Laois*, pp 259-60.
53. O'Leary and Lalor, *Queen's County*, ii, p. 515; Gilbert, *Confederation*, vi, p. 85.
54. TCD, MS 815, f. 103
55. TCD, MS 815, f. 121.
56. Gilbert, *Contemporary history*, ii, p. 13.
57. Gilbert, *Contemporary history*, i, pt. 1, p. 28.
58. TCD, MS 815, f. 41.
59. Loeber, 'Preliminaries to the Massachusetts Bay Colony', in press.
60. Gilbert, *Contemporary history*, i, pt. 1, p. 18.
61. Sweetman et al., *Archaeological inventory*, p. 124; author's survey, July, 1988. Remains also include an octagonal garden house in the rear of the enclosed garden, and eighteenth or early nineteenth century outbuildings.
62. *Census Ire. 1659*, p. 498. Most of the following is taken from R. Loeber, 'Preliminaries to the Massachusetts Bay Colony', in press.
63. TCD, MS 815, f. 46
64. See e.g., TCD, MS 815, ff. 25v, 26v, 28v, 30v.
65. *Census Ire. 1659*, p. 505.
66. *Cal. S.P. Ire., 1625-32*, p. 505; Simington, *Civil Survey*, x, p. 23; in 1634 Loftus paid a merchant of Dublin in iron from this area as part payment of a debt (*HMC, Var. Coll.*, iii, p. 185).
67. TCD, MS 815, ff. 7-7v, 8v-9, 10v-11, 16.
68. Gilbert, *Contemporary history*, i, pt. 1, p. 28.
69. Pender, *Census*, p. 497
70. TCD, MS 815, ff. 38v, 110.
71. Ashley, *Monck*, p. 30.
72. TCD, MS 815, f. 55.
73. Sweetman et al., *Archaeological inventory*, p. 125.
74. Feehan, *Laois*, p. 381.
75. *HMC, 12th rep.*, app. IX, p. 161; *Cal. pat. roll Ire., Jas. I*, pp 569, 586; Public Library, Pearse St., Dublin, Gilbert MS. 169, f. 116; Feehan, *Laois, p.* 381, citing the original charter, mentions the obligation to enclose the bawn with four flankers.
76. Sweetman et al., *Archaeological inventory, p.* 127.
77. Knowler, *Strafford's letters*, ii, p. 97; *Cal. S.P. Ire., 1647-60*, p. 130.
78. A. B. Grosart (ed.), *The Lismore papers* (London, 1886-8), series 1, iii, p. 54.
79. *Cal. S.P. Ire., 1633-47*, p. 774; *HMC, 11th rep.*, App. viii, p. 127.
80. Public Library, Pearse St., Dublin, Gilbert MS. 169. f. 227; *A full relation, Not only of our good successe in general. . . (London*, 1642); *A true relation of the divers great defeats given against the rebells in Ireland, by the Earle of Ormond...* (London, 1642), p. 4; TCD, MS 815, ff. 323-27.
81. Gilbert, *Confederation*, ii, p. 126.
82. Grose, *Antiquities*, ii, p. 38.
83. Feehan, *Laois*, p. 382.
84. BL MS 4756, f. 87; Fiant 511.
85. O'Leary and Lalor, *Queen's County*, i, p. 245.
86. TCD, MS 815, f. 120ff.

87. Sweetman et al., *Archaeological inventory*, p. 111.

88. Loeber, *Geography and practice*, p. 42.

89. White, *Tudor plantations*, p. 452; Sweetman et al., *Archaeological inventory*, p. 118.

90. [Lamacraft], *Funeral entries*, p. 119; NLI, Report on Private Coll., xii, p. 2510, 1 Mar. 1618-9, 16 Ja. I., Lease by Sir Richard Greame of Lynanstowne, Queen's Co., knt., to several individuals in Co. Wicklow. On the Greame or Graham family in Co. Laois, see Sir B. Burke, *Vicissitudes of families* (London, 1863), 3rd series, pp 139-59; Ballylynan, also known as Lynanstown, is situated about 2 miles NE of Ballylehane, but no castle is indicated at that location.

91. *Castlehaven's memoirs*, pp 65-66, 68; TCD, MS 815, ff. 112, 338v, 344; J. Hogan (ed.), *Letters and papers relating to the Irish rebellion* (Dublin, 1936), pp 101-2; Gilbert, *Aphorismical discovery*, i, p. 68; *A full relation, Not only of our good successe in general...* (London, 1642); slightly different information in *A true relation...*, pp 2-3.

92. Gilbert, *Contemporary history*, i, 246-47.

93. O'Leary and Lalor, *Queen's County*, ii, p. 529.

94. *Castlehaven's memoirs*, p. 66.

95. Sweetman et al., *Archaeological inventory*, p. 38. O'Leary and Lalor, *Queen's County*, ii, opp. p. 552, show a photograph taken at the turn of the century of a possible, round flanker at the site.

96. White, *Tudor plantation*, p. 452.

97. *Castlehaven's memoirs*, p. 68; Gilbert, *Confederation*, ii, p. 195; O'Leary and Lalor, *Queen's County*, i, p. 184.

98. Gilbert, *Confederation*, vi, p. 23.

99. Sweetman et al., *Archaeological inventory*, p. 110.

100. Loeber, *Geography and practice*, p. 11.

101. L. Price (ed.), *An eighteenth century antiquarian: the sketches, notes and diaries of Austin Cooper* (Dublin, 1942), p. 88.

102. Pender, *Census*, p. 498.

103. *Cal. pat. rolls Ire., Jas. 1*, pp 199-200; TCD, MS 815, f. 114v. Also called the 'Mote of Castle towne Gallen Ballynekill' in 1630 (Nottingham University, Willoughby MS Mi Da 57/1 (e); Feehan, *Laois*, fig. 8.15.

104. *Cal. S.P. Ire., 1611-15*, p. 299.

105. Nottingham Univ., Willoughby MS Mi Da 57/1 (e), 2 April, [1630], marriage agreement between Sir Robert Ridgeway, Lord Ridgeway, and Lady Elizabeth, daughter and heiress of Sir Simon Weston of Litchfield, which included the Ballinakill estate as dowry. The Willoughby papers contain lists of mostly English tenants on the estate in 1631 and 1633 (MSS Mi Da 57/1 (b) and (d)).

106. TCD, MS 815, f.110v-111.

107. See Fortune's deposition in TCD, MS 815, f. 322.

108. TCD, MS 815, f. 117

109. Gilbert, *Confederation*, i, p. 149

110. Grosart, *Lismore papers*, series 2, i, p. 161; Loeber & Parker, *Military revolution*, p. 70.

111. O'Leary and Lalor, *Queen's County*, ii, p. 519.

112. Grosart, *Lismore papers*, series 1, iii, p. 209.

113. W. Nolan, The historical geography of the ownership and occupation of land in the barony of Fassadinin, Kilkenny, c. 1600-1850. Ph.D. thesis, NUI (UCD, 1975), p. 76; *Anal. Hib.*, ii, (1931), p. 77.

114. Knowler, *Strafford's letters*, i, pp 144, 163.

115. Sir Thomas Ridgeway also had cannons to defend his castle at Augher in Co. Tyrone (R. Loeber and G. Parker, *Military revolution,* p. 67).

116. Gilbert, *Confederation,* i, pp 149-50.

117. *A full relation, Not only of our good successe in general...* (London, 1642). The total number of people in the castle (740) agrees with the account by John Carpenter, who counted 753 men, women, and children in the castle (TCD, MS 815, f. 77v). However, another account mentions 900 people, which may have included people from the town (TCD, MS. 815, f. 114).

118. Hogan, *Letters,* p. 71; Ashley, *Monck, p.* 35; Gilbert, *Confederation,* ii, p. 254, where mention is made of 100 men in the garrison under Capt. William Ridgeway.

119. O'Leary & Lalor, *Queen's County,* i, p. 520; Loeber & Parker, *Military revolution,* p. 75.

120. *HMC, 13th rep., app.* i, pp 115-6; *Castlehaven's memoirs, pp* 64-65; TCD, MS 815, ff. 116v-118.

121. TCD, MS 815, f. 77-

122. TCD, MS 815, f. 77v.

123. Gilbert, *Confederation,* i, pp 150-51; TCD, MS 815, f. 111.

124. TCD, MS 815, ff. 76-77v, 117.

125. Gilbert, *Confederation,* vi, p. 84.

126. O'Leary and Lalor, *Queen's County,* I, p. 234.

127. BL, MS 4756, p. 86

128. *Castlehaven's memoirs,* p. 64.

129. Gilbert, *Confederation,* ii, p. lxiv.

130. Sweetman et al., *Archaeological inventory,* p. 118; O'Leary and Lalor, *Queen 's County,* ii, opp. p. 521. Curiously, a drawing by Beranger shows only one of the three chimney stacks and gables (P. Harbison, *Beranger's views of Ireland* (Dublin, 1991), no. 30).

131. E. McCracken, 'Charcoal burning ironworks' in *U.J.A.,* xx (1957), p. 132.

132. G. Boate, *Ireland's naturall history* (London, 1652), p. 105.

133. Gilbert, *Confederation,* ii, p. cxiii.

134. *HMC, 6th rep.,* p. 189; Gilbert, *Contemporary history,* i, pp 128-29; Gilbert, *Confederation,* vi, p. 23.

135. Price, *Cooper,* p. 87.

136. Sweetman et al., *Archaeological inventory,* p. 108.

137. White, *Tudor plantation,* p. 450.

138. Gilbert, *Contemporary history,* i, p. 73; Gilbert, *Confederation,* iii, pp 35, 43.

139. Gilbert, *Contemporary history,* p. 128.

140. O'Leary & Lalor, *Queen's County,* ii, p. 526.

141. Sweetman et al., *Archaeological inventory,* p. 120.

142. TCD, MS 815, ff. 38v, 110.

143. Ashley, *Monck,* p. 30.

144. *Castlehaven's memoirs,* p. 131; O'Leary and Lalor, *Queen's County,* i, p. 195.

145. *Castlehaven's memoirs,* p. 136.

146. Gilbert, *Contemporary history,* ii, p. 220.

147. Ibid., pp 162, 369; O'Leary and Lalor, *Queen's County,* i, p. 195. The governor at this time probably was Colonel Lewis Moore (Ibid., iii, pt. 2, p. 99)

148. Feehan, *Slieve Bloom,* p. 187; *HMC, 15th rep., app.* 3, pp 149-50.

149. *A true relation...,* p. 4.

150. Grose, *Antiquities,* ii, p. 38.

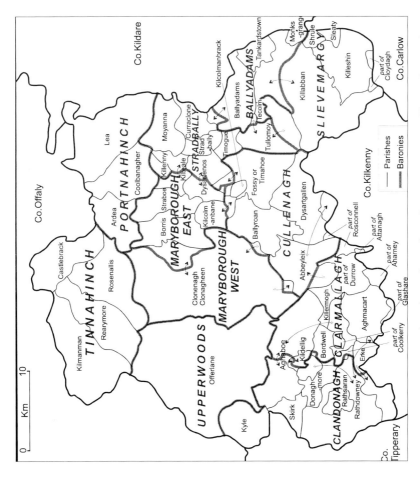

Fig. 13.2   Baronies and civil parishes of modern county Laois (drawn by Stephen Hannon).

Chapter 14

PORTARLINGTON AND THE HUGUENOTS IN LAOIS

RAYMOND PIERRE HYLTON

The Huguenots did not found Portarlington. Instead, they revitalised a partially-destroyed, moribund townland settlement; dominated it through half a century; imbued it with their language, culture and traditions, and bequeathed the myth of the 'Irish Athens', which persists to the present day.[1]

What was to become the territorial boundaries of Portarlington included acreage from both County Laois and County Offaly, along a sharp bend in the River Barrow. That portion of land on the Laois side had the old townland name of Cooltedoora, or 'woody nook',[2] and included the venerable market village of Lea, which, at one time, held a castle, a parish church, and a court baron.[3] Cooltedoora was part of the O'Dempsey holdings until Lewis O'Dempsey, Viscount Clanmalire, was attainted for treason, and his forfeited estates were granted to Henry Bennet, earl of Arlington, by letters patent on 27 July, 1666.[4] Arlington, who formed part of Charles II's governing cabal of the 1660s-70s, held 10,837 acres upon which he intended to plant a colony composed predominately of English settlers.

The Portarlington borough charter was enrolled in chancery on 3 August, 1667.[5] That Portarlington was indeed named after Henry Bennet and not after Henri Massue de Ruviguy, Baron Portarlington (and later, earl of Galway) is now too well-established as fact to admit of contradiction, though the derivation of the prefix 'Port' is a much more debatable question. An early view, still held by many, puts forward the possibility that this might refer to the Castle of Lea (being taken from the Irish for 'fort').[6] The castle, however, was located a full mile from the town limits, a fact which, while militating against this theory, does not necessarily preclude it. Moreover, the River Barrow could be navigable and a small riverside quay existed at one time – whether built by Arlington or not is uncertain.[7] Arlington is, however, asserted to have been responsible for draining the low-lying terrain and, one year later, to have completed the work sufficiently to have begun construction.[8]

The borough sent two members to the Irish parliament, and was administered by a sovereign elected from amongst twelve burgesses, who were elected by the freemen.[9] The burgesses themselves were to determine upon the designation of new freemen who would, on the first Sunday after Michaelmas, swear their oaths and make a public declaration against such 'superstitions and idolatrous' Catholic practices as: the cult of the saints; veneration of the Virgin Mary; and transubstantiation. The burgesses could also appoint two portreeves; authorise two fairs *per annum;* a court baron; a court of record; and maintain a prison. Officers for the upcoming year would be elected at a 'sovereign court' held on the first Monday following the Feast of St. John the Baptist. This governmental structure was maintained throughout Arlington's time, and beyond – well into the eighteenth century.[10]

Curiously, amidst all the English surnames, there is one that is Huguenot, and that is de Hennezel. The Huguenot presence in Ireland was barely significant until the 1680s, though scattered families may have arrived as early as 1569. Ananias de Hennezel from Lorraine had immigrated to Birr, County Offaly, where he married a member of the de Bigault family, who had operated a glass manufacture there since 1623.[11] By 1670, Ananias set up a glassworks at Portarlington, though with what success is difficult to determine.[12] By 1691, both the Hennezels and their glassworks had vanished, though the family obviously lived on in Ireland into the early nineteenth century.[13]

The earl of Arlington ultimately abandoned his grandiose plans for Portarlington borough; the financial benefits proved to be negligible, the soil was not of the best quality, and a great many of his tenants had simply packed up and left.[14] The townland may therefore have been virtually derelict by the time Arlington sold the Portarlington holdings to Sir Patrick Trant. Trant seems to have made few tangible improvements and, in any case, the political upheavals of the late 1680s intervened. Reputedly, the area was ravaged during the War of the Two Kings, and the Jacobite Trant was, in turn, attainted on 26 April, 1689.[15] The forfeiture was awarded by King William III, to his Huguenot supporter, Henri Massue, Marquis de Ruvigny.

In France, Ruvigny had held a pre-eminent position within the French Calvinist church as its Depute-General. In his capacity as Depute-General, Ruvigny served as the representative-at-court for his co-religionists. In the wake of King Louis XIV's decision to revoke the Edict of Nantes in 1685, Ruvigny was conscientiously compelled to choose exile, over conversion to Catholicism.[16] At this point in time, however, he was allowed to maintain ownership of the Ruvigny estates in France. At the same time, thousands of Ruvigny's less-eminent fellow Huguenots were desperately making their way out of France: some 50,000 would find asylum in the Netherlands; while 35-40,000 made their way to Britain. Ruvigny hesitated to join the Williamite military effort during the War of the Two Kings; it was only after the battle of the Boyne, and the deaths of Huguenot Marshal Frederick, duke of Schomberg, and his own younger brother, Pierre de la Caillemotte, that the marquis entered active service at the head of a squadron of calvary.[17] Ruvigny's brightest moment as a military commander occurred during the clash at Aughrim, when he launched an audacious cavalry charge at the decisive instant, bringing about a Williamite victory. Thereafter, having gained King William's confidence, the marquis rapidly advanced in royal favour. On 2 March 1691, Ruvigny was created Baron Portarlington and Viscount Galway, and was granted the fee simple to Trant's 36,148 acre forfeiture as a first step towards obtaining the title "in custodiam" (1693), then permanently (1696).[18] The grant was, by this time, larger than that initially held by the earl of Arlington, and took in townlands extending along both banks of the River Barrow, and parcels of land in Counties Kildare and Kerry.[19] At the apex of his political influence, 1697, Ruvigny was named lord justice of Ireland, and conferred with the title earl of Galway.[20]

The earl of Galway's original scheme envisioned a commercial-industrially-based colony, much along the same lines as what had been attempted during the 1660s-70s with Huguenot craftsmen, artisans and entrepreneurs under the auspices of the duke of Ormond and Colonel Richard Lawrence.[21] The first of Galway's leases at Portarlington date from 1692, suggesting that he already held the fee on a *de facto* basis.[22]

Before too long, however, the project assumed a militaristic orientation. Portarlington was situated in the path of two projected invasion routes from France, which called for landings at Cork and Waterford and for a Franco-Jacobite convergence in the midlands.[23] It was of the utmost importance, from a strategic angle, to maintain a tried-and true military presence in the vicinity. To this end, Galway transformed his plan to encompass the formation of a garrison colony, composed of veterans in the Huguenot regiments enrolled in the Williamite army, who could be pensioned on the Irish or English establishments. Rents were placed at a nominal rate with funds to go towards the maintenance of a French church, a classical school, and a French school. Lord Galway himself saw to the further construction of both a French and an English Protestant church, and anywhere from 100-150 dwellings.[24]

The basic plan for the actual town area of Portarlington was not altered by Galway. A central market sector was set off to form a rectangular axis from which four thoroughfares would fan out in different compass directions: King's Street; Queen's Street; Bennet Street; and James Street.[25] Land was parcelled into lots that remained in basic conformity to those of the Arlington-Trant years: the Huguenot Joly family assuming title to a tract once held by John Donnelly; the De Choisys taking over the former holdings of John Bignon; De Bostaquets replacing the Warburtons; and those lands which had been reserved for the earl of Arlington (and/or Patrick Trant) himself were to pass, under the aegis of the earl of Galway, to the Camelins, de Lavals, and Du Clousys.[26]

In late 1692, the first families and individuals within the Huguenot community who were to reside in what was being proposed as a model settlement began to arrive. Life was not luxurious, and as is the case in most such enterprises, difficulties arose almost immediately. Housing appeared to be the most pressing concern; the Arlington-Trant colony had been the scene of depredation during the years 1690-91 and many, perhaps all, of the old dwelling structures had been destroyed, heavily-damaged, or abandoned to poor repair. Though the earl of Galway did begin to undertake the work of rebuilding, progress was often slow and erratic, necessitating the lodging of settlers at Cloneygowan, Monasterevan, Lea, Doolagh, and, perhaps, Birr. Construction would not be finished until 1698.[27]

The original forty individuals/family-heads who arrived at Portarlington during the first year were officers of the four Huguenot units who had been discharged on pension after the Treaty of Limerick (the 'Limerick veterans'). Of the forty, twenty-two were aged and/or disabled ;eight of these received serious wounds at the first Battle of Limerick, where the Huguenot regiments suffered their highest toll of casualties. By rank they include: one lieutenant-colonel; twelve captains; sixteen lieutenants; one cornet; six ensigns; two of unlisted rank; one non-commissioned; and one exceptional case. These were mainly *noblesse d'epee,* members of the lower noble orders who had traditionally entered military service.

One of the early community-leaders was a member of the upper nobility: Jacques Belrieu, Seigneur de St. Laurens, Baron De Virazel, who had been pensioned on the Irish establishment as 100 per annum, although he saw no military service.[28] De Virazel had been a close friend of Lord Galway's having served as a judge on the Parlement of Bordeaux prior to being imprisoned in the Bastille from 14 March 1686 - 12 May 1687 for refusing to abjure his Protestant faith.[29]

As a member of Lord Galway's éilte inner-circle, De Virazel wielded political influence at Dublin Castle and spent as much of his time there as he did at his official home at Portarlington, dying at Dublin in 1719.[30] The family, however, continued to reside and own property at Portarlington until, at least, 1809.[31]

The ranking officer among the Limerick pensioners, Lieutenant-Colonel Daniel Le Grand Du Petit Bosc, also emerged as a leading force within the Huguenot community; like De Virazel, he was among a handful of Huguenot settler families with sufficient means to be classified as wealthy.[32] Most of the veterans could not say the same for themselves and their families; having arrived at their new home in straitened financial condition. Two of the officers never enjoyed the luxury of living in the homes that had been promised them: Ensign Josias de Castlefranc died in rented accommodation at Lea on 15 July 1695 and Lieutenant Moise Fermet in similar circumstances in Doolagh at the home of Lieutenant Jean Procureur des Champs (1697).[33]

Of the forty Limerick pensioners only twenty-six were married, or would marry shortly after their arrival at Portarlington. Seventeen would start families. The pensioners would soon be augmented by non-noble colonists who arrived during the course of the following five years, 1692-97. These particular families and individuals came from Central-Southeastern France, from: Burgundy; Provence; and, especially, Dauphine. The mountain passes and wooded acreage along the Swiss border afforded fleeing Protestants a greater degree of concealment over more numerous escape routes than elsehwere available. Consequently, thousands poured into the Swiss cantons (some 10,000 from Dauphine alone between 1685-92);[34] and problems of overcrowding, accommodation, and relief – so familiar to future refugee situations – reached acute proportions. As a means of alleviating these problems; a massive relocation scheme was devised. Most of these Huguenot families were to be settled in Ireland, with at least 400 designated as future residents for Portarlington.[35] The proposal could by no means be considered to have been excessively grandiose and, with the backing of King William and Lord Treasurer Sidney Godolphin, abetted by Galway intimates/agents: Charles de Sailly; Jean Nicolas; and Jean David Boyer (all of whom resided at one time or another at Portarlington), there was every likelihood for success.[36] That it foundered is due in so small measure to the incompetence and defeatism of Galway agent Henri de Mirmand, who set his face against the entire project from the very beginning. Losing no opportunity to openly denigrate the scheme at every juncture, and deliberately accentuating the difficulties involved, Mirmand facilitated the self-fulfilment of his own prophesies of failure.[37] In spite of this, some families did find their way to Portarlington. The exact number cannot be determined precisely, though it fell far short of the 400 originally envisioned. We may be certain of at least 13 families comprising some 32 individuals by 1700: Freau; Vincent; Poussete; Bonin; Champ; Pastre; Bourget (all from Dauphine); Comte; David (Burgundy); Esperiat (Provence); Ouly; Marthe and Vuilly (simply designated as "Swiss").[38] Six additional families were probably of Dauphinois origin: Liotard; Bonnet; Neuache; Jordan; Serre; and Guiot.[39]

Portarlington's early pioneering years may be conveniently divided into two periods: 1692-97, which saw a slow, haphazard increase in population and the years 1698-1702, which witnessed a dramatic upturn and the demographic zenith of the French Protestant community.

Despite subsequent, persistent romanticizations, about the genteel and luxurious nature of the life of the Huguenot colonists,[40] the documentary evidence limns a picture of hardship and difficulty. By 1694, the French worshippers had formed a consistory under the leadership of Pastor Jacques Gillet, which conducted itself along stringently Calvinist lines; and the church registers were begun. In 1694, the Portarlington colonists addressed a petition to the French Church at the Lady Chapel of St. Patrick's Cathedral in Dublin. In it, they described themselves as being in dire straits: with the greater portion of their assets exhausted on travelling expenses; in taking up leases; and in everyday costs of necessities. With charitable funds depleted, they pleaded that the Dublin congregation's consistory might appeal to the lords justice that each colonising refugee might receive seed and whatever else necessary to give him and his family to provide for his family. The response, in this instance, was favourable.[41]

In 1695, another petition drawn up by the Huguenot community complained about the lack of a schoolmaster; a surgeon; and the fact that construction of the French Church was behind schedule.[42]

In 1697, the War of the League of Augsburg came to an end with the Peace of Ryswick and Parliament, over royal opposition, ordered the general disbanding of all Huguenot units; and another wave of military pensioners arrived at the Midlands settlement.[43]

Unlike the Limerick contingent, these Ryswick pensioners included a far smaller proportion of veterans designated as 'aged', 'sickly', or 'disabled' (a bare total of seven out of forty-eight); fourteen were pronounced fit for service at the outbreak of the War of the Spanish Succession in 1702.[44]

The Ryswick veterans were, in the main, younger, more vigorous men than the Limerick group, and included many future community leaders who were to set the course in borough politics into the late 1730s. At least thirty married and reared families, and twelve of these had more than four surviving offspring. The Ryswick veterans were to infuse Portarlington with its legendary character and facilitate its identification with the values and gentility of the French provincial *noblesse d'epee* – and its translation into folklore.[45]

The rapid growth in population that followed soon upon the arrival of the Ryswick veterans, while desirable, had its drawbacks. A typically high Ancient Regime mortality rate (particularly amongst infants and women of childbearing age) necessitated the setting up of a permanent burial ground. Until 10 October 1698 the bodies of deceased refugees were taken to Lea.[46] On that date the first interrment occurred in land behind the French Church which the earl of Galway donated for cemetary plots.[47] Noble status and comparative isolation did not, of course, preclude visitations of severe epidemics. One such, termed *'la grande infection'* by Pastor Benjamin De Daillon is recorded as raging through the settlement in early July 1698.[48]

There were certainly more than the usual portion of tension, anxiety, animosity and division; given the extraordinary, stressful situation engendered by diverse individuals being thrust together in an artificial environment, where they had, for the most part, no desire to be in the first instance. That negative emotions bubbled occasionally to the surface is not to be wondered at; contrarily, it is amazing that overtly violent (verbal or physical) manifestations occurred as infrequently as they did. Despite the ridiculously idyllic picture concocted by future apologists, these Huguenots had little to unite them other than religion (the exercise of which, ironically, gave rise to the most vitriolic internecine squabbling in the history of the Portarlington refuge) and the common misery of exile.[49] Here was a group of families and individuals who had survived horrendous persecution, endured imprisonment, hardship, diseases, travelled hundreds of miles, and were thrust together in the middle of Ireland amongst a population whose language was different, whose religious orientation was hostile, and who saw the newcomers as an arm of Protestant ascendency. Even within the Portarlington community itself, the effects of regional divergence should not be underestimated. In a semi-isolated environment, Languedocians were juxtaposed to Normans, Poitevins, Lorrainers Dauphinois, Parisians, etc. Class, on the other hand , was a negligible factor. Though the social spectrum there encompassed everything from *haute noblesse* to *laboureur,* the leadership of the *écuyer* (minor *noblesse d'épeê*) was accepted as a matter of course, and perhaps even served as a cement for the community. A survey of family surnames in old Portarlington yields an extraordinary proportion of noble houses: 44 per cent of the total.

Passions exploded most spectacularly in a duel, between two retired military officers in late August 1700. One of the antagonists, Captain

Clause Sermant, was killed , eliciting posthumous censure from Pastor Daillon and letters from Lord Justice Galway to the secretary of war, asking that pension payments be provided for his widow and five surviving children.[50] In 1702, the settlement was to be forever altered over the question of conformity to the Church of Ireland, and a demographic regression from which the French community never truly recovered, plagued the colony for decades to come.

French Protestantism as practiced by the Huguenots was Calvinist and, hence, basically at odds with the notion of conforming within an episcopal, Anglican establishment. However, there had always existed an influential element within the Huguenot exilic community in the British Isles which saw no moral difficulty (and even political advantages) to some measure of compromise entailing a degree of conformity to the official faith of the host country.[51] Others, however, viewed any such accommodation as a betrayal of the pure, traditional form of Calvinist worship for which they had weathered such suffering and sacrificed so much. Portarlington was one of the communities that insisted upon pursuing an independent, non-conformist course; and maintained it from 1694-1702, under its first two ministers; Gillet and Daillon.

Politics was to change all this. At Westminster in 1699, the Whig junto lost control of parliament and, the following year, an Act of Resumption was tacked unto a land tax bill. Royal opposition notwithstanding, the Act cleared the commons and lords. This was but one episode in a long-brewing power struggle between the crown on one hand, and a vaguely-defined coalition of anti-royalist, anti-foreign parliamentarians on the other. In the case of the earl of Galway, there was a deeper fear: that as a foreigner, whose loyalty was apparently more of a personal one to King William himself rather than to England (i.e. parliament); and as the virtual viceroy over Ireland, who commanded the allegiance of a potentially influential minority (not the least of which would be the military nobility of Portarlington, Dublin, Carlow, Waterford, Youghal, Kilkenny, Cork and – perhaps – Birr), might prove to be a subversive instrument in royalist hands if his power were not curtailed. Accordingly, the Act of Resumption of 1700 placed the forfeited estates previously granted by the King and Queen into the hands of a seven-member commission appointed by the house of commons. In the case of Galway's forfeiture, the commission's report was unfavourable; thereby reverting to the Trustees for Forfeited Estates.[52] Faced with the real possibility of being once more deprived of domicile and investments of time, property and energy, the plight in which the refugees found themselves must indeed have proved 'deplorable'.[53] And from what might be gleaned concerning

Portarlington's socio-economic topography around the years 1701-1703, the settlers did have something to lose. The community was beginning to establish an identity and some degree of cohesion – even a modest air of – prosperity. There were around 150 new dwellings, townhouses and farm cottage, on which rent was being paid. There were at least 30 farming/artisanal families who would require the building and maintenance of barns, workshops, stables, fences, mills and wells; and whatever might pertain to the well-being and upkeep of their livestock, poultry, apiaries, and orchards. There would have been a great deal of time and effort expended in the draining of land, much of which was too low-lying and prone to flooding to be naturally arable.[54] Among refugee families who engaged in business we may have evidence for the presence of: blacksmiths, maltsters, bakers, butchers, wig-makers, retailers, linen manufacturers, and carpenters.

It was the Anglican Bishop of Killaloe who was to take the unlikely role of rescuer when he addressed an ardent petition to parliament on the refugees' behalf. The petition was favourably received, read and virtually incorporated into a bill confirming the titles of all present Portarlington tenants, the passage of which was accomplished without incident on 25 March 1702.[55]

That the bishop of Killaloe was not motivated by purely altruistic consideration was evidenced by a seemingly inconspicuous clause in the parliamentary relief bill which would 'convey, assign and make over' to William Moreton, Bishop of Kildare, the two churches, the schools, and the right to appoint ministers and schoolmasters 'from time to time'.[56]

Bishop Moreton lost no time in parlaying his recently-derived authority into the leverage he required in order to enforce Anglican conformity upon the Portarlington congregation. He had a reputation as a high-churchman who was aggressive against dissent, and sympathetic towards Roman Catholicism. This had perhaps blocked his ambition to be considered for an archbishopric, but had facilitated his reinstatement to the privy council after the Peace of Limerick.[57] He soon clashed with the learned, passionate and articulate Daillon, who defied the bishop's attempts to dismantle Calvinist forms and tradition. Accordingly, when the final deed of conveyance was safely signed and delivered on 20 September 1702, Moreton artfully drove a wedge between the dissenters and the moderate accommodationists within the congregation (and perhaps played on personality issues as well), painting his adversary as a stubborn, embittered old fanatic; replacing him in the pastor's chair with Antoine Ligonier de Bonneval, a former chaplain in the Williamiate regiments.[58] A superficial measure of conformity was ultimately achieved, but at an appalling cost to the community. The congregation split; close to perhaps 60 per cent siding with Daillon, who stayed on for a further six years as moderator of the consistory. The tension inherent in the situation, saw two ministers and their mutually-antagonistic followers engaged in constant, sullen confrontation. Daillon departed in 1708 to accept the pastorate over the non-conformist French congregation at Carlow,[59] but the schism endured, and persisted in both overt and subtle forms far beyond the time of Bonneval's tenure as well. At least one of the community leaders felt strongly enough about the situation to vacate his position as church elder. This was Robert d'Ully, Vicomte de Laval, who was perhaps the highest-born individual in the settlement, claiming descent from King Henry IV of France.[60] He was replaced by the Norman veteran, Captain Isaac Dumont de Bostaquet.[61]

In 1702, the French colony was at its peak, demographically-speaking. Perhaps 500 individuals resided in and about the vicinity of Portarlington. After the Daillon-Moreton debacle, the population begins a decline; at first gradual, and then precipitous: by 1720, the number of Huguenot residents numbered barely over 200. Some sixty-seven families defected; most of these for reasons of conscience: they could not abide with the degree of compromise that the new arrangement seemed to require. The non-conformist temples in Dublin benefited from this: sixteen former Portarlington settlers re-emerge as members of either the Lucy Lane or Peter Street congregations.

The War of the Spanish Succession had its impact. Casualties in combat and, more significantly, lengthy separation of couples, had further adverse effects on the population. Eighteen of the veterans were recalled to active service; most were dispatched to the Spanish-Portuguese theatre of war, where the earl of Galway had assumed command of the Allied forces. Three went to Flanders and/or Germany. Captain Noe Cadroy, whose father Joseph had leased a house, garden plot amd malthouse from Galway, was killed at the Battle of Almanza.[62] It is not entirely certain what happened to Lieutenant Guy Auguste dela Blachiere, Sieur des Coutiers: he is simply described as having died in Portugal in 1707.[63] In 1709, two Portarlington veterans lost their lives at sea when the ship on which they were sailing was attacked by a squadron of French vessels: Captain Lieutenant Pierre de Chizadour, Sieur de Bette; and Joseph d'Ully de Laval.[64]

For Portarlington, the year 1703-1720 marked a period of uncertainty and transition: families arrive, and depart (mainly the latter). Differences as to the practice of religion deepened, if anything. No sooner had the danger passed, as far as France and the War of the Spanish Succession were concerned, than the threat of a Jacobite invasion in favour of James Edward, Chevalier de St. Georges became a certainty. To assure the Anglo-Protestant hold on Ireland, the earl of Galway was recalled for a final term as lord justice. In an attempt to downplay and/or gloss over the continuing rancour between conformist and dissenting Huguenots, Galway engineered the presentation, by the Prince and Princess of Wales, of an engraved communion plate and church bell to the *'eglise conformiste'*[65] Bonneval needed all the buoying that he could get, for the presence, at Portarlington, of the legendary Canisard guerrilla leader Jean Cavallier was a constant thorn in his side. Cavallier, who had fought royal troops to a standstill and had been rescued from under a mound of corpses at Almanza, enjoyed a unique position within the refugee communities. Remarkably, this son of a journeyman baker from Ribaute in the Cevennes married into the exclusive ranks of the Portarlington *noblesse*, taking as his bride Elizabeth Marguerite, daughter of Captain Charles de Ponthieu, who had retired on pension in 1692, but was reactivated for service in 1706.[66] Cavallier's views were radical – even eccentric; certainly anathema to an arch-establishmentarian like Bonneval – who, insofar as it was possble, snubbed the Cavalliers.[67] One could not, however, ignore Cavallier's prestige, nor his influential family connections (he was a cousin-by-marriage to the community leader, Josias de Robillard, Seigneur de Champagne).[68] In 1726, Cavallier was able to muster an impressive array of subscribers for the Dublin publication of his *Memoires of the Wars of the Cevennes* (including Champagne). The book itself has been subject to criticism for certain inaccurate statements and for its putative purposes of progaganda, and the retroactive justification for some of the more controversial aspects of Cavallier's career. It is in the preface, of the *Memoires*, however, that the deepest, most enduring significance of the work is contained. In its advanced message of religious tolerance, the preface establishes Cavallier and, by association, the Huguenots of Portarlington, in a precursorial role vis-a-vis the Enlightment. In earnest, impassioned language, Cavallier pleads, not only for the removal of all politically-imposed liabilities on the free exercice of religion amongst denominations of Protestantism, but extends his advocacy to Catholics and, by implication, even beyond Christianity itself.[69] In and of itself, Cavallier's preface stands as an effective rebuttal to the historically unjustified characterisation of the Huguenots as advocates of the Penal Laws in Ireland.[70]

The mid-late 1720s witnessed the return of a certain degree of stability, and even a renewed vigour within the Huguenot community, occasioned to some degree by the advent of a third wave of noble veteran families (15 surnames may be positively identified). The leader of the Portarlington community was indisputably Josias de Champagne, who belonged to a new generation of refugees who were much less exclusive in their outlook; much more amenable to associating and working with their Anglophonic neighbours, and to whom their exile, and new surroundings were becoming a more permanent reality. This was a generation which would greatly advance the process of assimilation, of the acceptance of the reality of their situation, and the gradual fading of the dream of a return to a purified, Protestant French homeland. Certainly, the French settlers did not hesitate to exercise political power, and thus dominated borough politics throughout the 1730s and into the 1740s.

Champagne, son of Josias Champagne and Marie de La Rochefoucauld, was born in Saintonge on 17 November 1673 and escaped, with his father, to Holland in 1687. His political talent may have been inherent in his family; the elder Champagne was elected by his brother officers in the Huguenot regiments of the expeditionary forces as their spokesman to the king and parliament. Regretably, he was not to serve for long in his capacity, dying at Belfast in 1689 of "fatigue".[71] The father had held the rank of captain, but the son was to surpass his achievement: serving for 30-odd years in the military; seeing action in three conflicts; and retiring on half-pay with the rank of major in 1718.[72] An affable, engaging personality, he began modestly enough on money borrowed from his brother, François Auguste with which he purchased a plot of ground on King Street from Lieutenant-Colonel Daniel Le Grand Du Petit Bosc in 1703; by 1709 he had built a dwelling-house for his family.[73] His marital/personal connections indicate an ambitious young man on his way upwards: in 1705 he married Lady Jane Forbes, daughter of the second earl of Granard.[74] He even maintained himself on good terms with Dean Jonathan Swift – no easy task.[75] Champagne gradually prospered, and later was able to buy three additional town plots and 115 acres of land from Le Grand Du Petit Bosc.[76] On 29 April 1729, Champagne was elected burgess in place of the deceased Lancelot Sanders, and on the following 3rd June was elected borough sovereign.[77] Champagne's three consecutive terms as sovereign mark a period of renewed dynamism in borough affairs, in which there appears to have been a great deal of apathy and neglect. Overseers, who were predominately French in the initial years, were appointed to regulate certain areas impacting upon safety and public health, the upkeep and repair of foot pavements (which included the bringing of action against those who left dung in the streets and market square for longer than one week); the inspection of butcher-stalls; the driving of swine from the streets and commons; the draining and scouring of ditches; the inspection and repair of faulty chimney-stacks; regulating the weight of butter and the size of bread-loaves; and the maintenance of two community turf-kishes.[78]

During the late 1720s, to the end of the 1740s, it was the French noblesse which in many ways still directed policy at the local level. Perhaps it was their role during these decades which most contributed to the pervasive legend of gentility. Champagne aside, the leading luminaries were: Jean David Boyer; Pierre Goullin; Charles Gaspard Le Grand Du Petit Bosc; Charles De Quinsac; Claude Le Blanc; Dr. Josue Pilot; Jean Micheau; Pierre, Henri, Josias and Francois De Franquefort; David D'Arrippe; Isaac and Hector Hamon; Jean De Clausade; and Jacques de Crosat, Seigneur des Pruniers.[79]

Boyer and Champagne are the figures who most effectively bridge the gap between the old and the new. Boyer might for lack of a more accurate term, be labeled a 'founding father'. He was born at Civry in Poitou in 1655; entered into a military career, serving a four-year's stint in The Netherlands, then in Ireland, where he sustained a severe wound at the first Siege of Limerick. Boyer was among the first group of veteran colonists at Portarlington, being retired on half-pay with the rank of lieutenant; leasing a cabin and 88 acres from the earl of Galway.[80] He was a member of the earl's intimate circle, on whom he relied when dealing with Irish matters; along with Virazel, Elie Bouhereau, Nicolas and Charles De Sailly. His intensive involvement in the day-to-day affairs of establishing Portarlington as a viable community earned him the designation of 'Galway's steward'.[81] He thus enjoyed a residual prestige which translated into political influence long after the earl himself had passed on.[82] Boyer was a perpetual fixture as burgess and held the post of sovereign from 1725-28, and again in 1735. And, from 1728 to the time of his death in 1744, apart from his term as sovereign, he was always deputy-sovereign, presiding over the sovereign court an extraordinary numbers of time, during the frequent absence of certain sovereigns. In effect, Boyer seems to have been the borough's actual working administrator up to the end. That he was so active to the ripe old age of 89, is a tribute to an astoundingly vigorous and varied career.[83]

In terms of physical longevity, however, none among the community's refugee population could equal Lieutenant-Colonel Daniel Le Grand Du Petit Bosc, one of the borough's wealthiest landowners, and an incorrigibly outspoken hypochondriac and critic of the medical profession. On a Dutch pension of 700 guilders per annum, which he received on top of his Irish military stipend, he built Arlington House on King Street alongside the River Barrow. Generations later, it was at Arlington House that the Reverend Thomas Willis and his wife maintained one of the more noteworthy French boarding schools –

theirs was attended by, among others, the Wellesley brothers.[84] Daniel died in 1737, at the age of 95 years, his son, Charles Gaspard embarked upon a productive career in local politics which was highlighted by his election to two terms as borough sovereign (1742-3; 1746-7).[85]

The Micheau family had been retainers to the Champagne family in Saintonge, and chose to join their feudal overlords in exile. Accordingly, Jean Micheau entered borough affairs at the same time as Josias de Champagne, and held the post of town clerk from 1726 until his death in 1752; also being appointed to the office of portreeve more frequently than any other individual (1726-8; 1730-32; 1736-7; 1743-5; 1747-8; 1752).[86]

A cavalryman, Claude Le Blanc, who retired on half-pay from Miremont's squadron of Dragoons, opened a butcher shop; became, in 1732, inspector for butcher-stalls throughout the borough, and sired nine children before his death in 1754. Le Blanc and his family (some of whom Anglicized their surname to Blong) have secured immortality for themselves in the lines of Joyce's *Finnegan's Wake*.[87]

During the 1740s and early 1750s, however, the trend was unmistakeable: many more Anglophonic names were entering the ranks of borough freemen, and far fewer French surnames are mentioned in any capacity whatever. By July of 1754, the first and even the second generation of Huguenots had faded, and Dr. Josue Pilot, son of a veteran who served during the War of the Two Kings and himself a former veteran of the War of the Austrian Succession (as a military surgeon in the service of the duke of Cumberland), remained the sole Huguenot representative on the sovereign court.[88] Pilot retired from the court in October, 1771 in favour of Joseph Dawson; shortly thereafter, on 10th November 1771, the last surviving Portarlington veteran of the War of the Spanish Succession, David Daniel David D'Ully de Laval, passed on at the age of 76.[89]

By this time, Portarlington's French heritage had become more nostalgic than actual: in 1771 there were at least 28 families of demonstrably pure French stock and perhaps 309 individuals who had at least one Huguenot parent. This statistic may be qualified by the fact that, out of this total, at least 109 individuals were over sixty years of age (among them, eight widows of pensioned veterans). Assimilation with the Anglophone Protestant community was already well under way, and many of the younger descendants of noble French refugees were leaving the Portarlington area for greater opportunities in Dublin or London.

Portarlington casts its most enduring shadow, perhaps, in its residual reputation for culture and gentility – the basis for which has legitimate roots. However, it is necessary to penetrate the overlay of legend and outright exaggeration which has been carefully nourished and embellished by amateur nineteenth century antiquarians, Whiggish myth-makers, and assorted enthusiasts for whom, in certain cases, the Huguenot stereotype could be employed both for didactic and literary effect.[90] Portartlington's relative isolation and its unique position as the only Huguenot settlement in Ireland wherein the French Protestant population proved for a long time dominant over the Irish and/or English element in the locality, perhaps acted as an effective brake on the rapid deterioration of French culture and language.

The fabled (or, allegedly-fabled) schools of Portarlington are the focus of considerable controversy. Illiteracy certainly did exist: between the years 1694-1734 there are 57 documented cases in the French Church registers. These individuals are all non-noble, nine of these were Anglophones. *Labourers,* at 13-21 instances out of 45, form the largest single grouping of illiterates among the French population (the balance being composed of: three weavers; one mason; one butcher; one gardener; and one shoemaker). Twenty-three originated from Southern French provinces (Languedoc, Dauphine, Burgundy, Saintonge, Auvergne, and Guyenne). Instances of illiteracy drop sharply after 1711, coinciding perhaps with the defection of many non-noble families during this time. The fact that from this point of time on and throughout the 1720s-30s the overwhelming proportion of remaining families were noble (close to 44 per cent), would tend to lend support to the idea of the continued existence of high educational standards within the community as a whole. The extent to which this acted to preserve the vestiges of the community's French identity into the 1850s is debatable. Apart from the original, officially-endowed French and classical schools, private establishments may well have been established quite early on. In the midst of all the rumours, myths and half-truths, there is the testimony of no less a personage than Elie Bouhereau, the earl of Galway's personal secretary. Anxious to make sure that his grandsons Elie and Richard ('Dicky') spoke fluent French, and concerned by what he perceived as linguistic debasement within the Dublin Huguenot community, Bouhereau contributed generously to the costs and boarding of the young men at Portarlington. Elie stayed at the home of retired Lieutenant Armenault de Machinville from 29 May - 24 October 1712; and Dicky from 28 May 1716 - 7 January 1717.[91]

The first schoolmasters for whom we have an accurate record are: Etienne Durand, who supplemented his income by plying his craft as a bootmaker; and the shopkeeper/church elder Louis Buliod.[92] One of the oldest nineteenth-century legends credits a 'Monsieur Faurel' who allegedly admitted boarding students, and whose son was a pensioned lieutenant, with being Portarlington's first pedagogue.[93] 'Monsieur

Faurel', however, is probably totally apocryphal; he appears in no record whatever, and his entire existence at Portarlington is open to question. There was a Lieutenant Jean Faurel, who lived as a pensioner at Portarlington, in a state of quasi-poverty; he lived in sparse, rented accommodation (a 15-foot long room).[94] No family members are mentioned. This Lieutenant Jean Faurel was further alleged to be the model for Laurence Sterne's ailing Lieutenant Le Fevre in *The life and opinions of Tristram Shandy, gentleman*.[95] It is just possible that Sterne may have met Faurel in his extreme youth (Sterne's date of birth was 24 November 1713 and Faurel died at Portarlington on 22 March 1718)[96] but there are too many disparities between what is known of the real Lieutenant Faurel and the descriptions of the fictional Le Fevre to admit of any valid comparison.

It is certain that, in 1714, the wife of the pensioned veteran, Ensign Marc Thibaut de Champlaurier did keep a (private) school. Isaac Benin La Ferriere (1704-1758), whose mother was Anglo-Irish, was *'chantre et maître d'école de l'église Francoise'*.[97] Until he died in 1775, the French parish clerk, Guillaume Macarel doubled as the schoolmaster.[98]

Ironically, it was only after the first two generations of Huguenot immigrants had waned that the private boarding schools of Portarlington entered into their era of greatest repute (*c.* 1770-1800). During these years there might have been no fewer than sixteen such establishments accepting children of the gentry from all corners of Ireland with the purpose of, hopefully, endowing them with the Gallic 'polish' and sophistication desired in gentlemen and ladies. The fashion began to come apart, as the events of the French Revolution began to tarnish all things French with the blemishes of radicalism and in time – treasonous insurrection.[99] The schools suffered an irreversible decline because of the linkage of France with the 1798 Risings (Portarlington itself had been the scene of a bloody clash, and some of the insurgents were executed in the market square afterwards), and because of the continual threat of Napoleonic invasion.[100]

Though the schools, which were no longer a feasible financial proposition, disappeared, the French Church and its pastors lingered well into the reign of Queen Victoria. French was, by momentum of tradition, the language of worship until at least 1817. The pastorate remained a strong focus. Two of the French ministers were eminently accomplished men of letters, and, though they had received Anglican ordination, were dissenters by sympathy, and conducted their congregational worship in an appropriately independent manner. The first of these ministers, Gaspard Caillard was appointed to his post by King's letter in 1739, after having served as the pastor of the French non-conformist church at Peter Street, Dublin, from 1720-1739.[101]

Caillard gained a reputation throughout the Irish midlands as a fiery, forceful preacher in the evangelical tradition, eliciting the admiration of no less-eminent a visitor than John Wesley.[102] Caillard published some of his sermons at Dublin in 1728 *(Sermons sur divers textes de l'Ecriture Sainte);* two of the sermons therein mark the pastor as a man of advanced ideas vis-a-vis the principles of religious toleration.[103]

In his final years, Gaspard Caillard became quite feeble and his sucessor-designate, Antoine Vichon Des Vouex, assisted him in day-to-day affairs until the older man passed on in 1767.[104] Des Voeux was, undoubtedly the most scholarly of all the French ministers at Portarlington: his literary oeuvre included a detailed commentary on the *Book of Ecclesiastes; Trois Sermons;* and the editorial/publication of *The Compendious Library.*[105] Des Vouex died in 1792, to be succeeded by Jean des Vignoles, the last French pastor to utilise the ancestral language to any appreciable degree. By the time of his death in 1817, Anglophonic names were replacing the French surnames to an increasing degree as families married exogamously, or moved away from the region. Jean's son Charles des Vignoles, was the last independent French pastor and relinquished the post in 1841, to take up the appointment of dean of Ossory.[106]

Nothing so enhances the past as the fact of its being lost forever and when the antiquarian, Sir Erasmus Borrowes visited Portarlington in the 1850s with the purpose of writing the first historical accounts of Huguenot Portarlington for the *Ulster Journal of Archaeology,* he arrived at that propitious moment when vestiges of the French heritage had all but vanished.[107] In such situations, a certain degree of romanticisation often follows in its wake. In its glamourisation, initiated by Borrowes and adorned over the years, the idyllic quality of the Portarlington legend has assumed a particularly seductive glow – a glow which shows no signs of diminishing over the past century-and-half.

References
1. James Floy, 'The Huguenot settlement at Portarlington' in *P.H.S.L.*, v, (1892), p. 19.
2. Sir Erasmus D. Borrowes, 'Portarlington' in *U.J.A.*, v (Belfast, 1855), p. 65.
3. Portarlington, N.A.I., Caulfield MS 4976, 1A, 53-87.
4. Floy in *P.H.S.L.*, v, p. 19.
5. Original patent of Portarlington Borough, 1669, N.L.I., MS 90, ff 1-6.
6. Borrowes, 'Portarlington', p. 62.
7. O'Hanlon and O'Leary, *History*, p. 283.
8. Ibid.
9. N.L.I., MS 90, f3.
10. Minutes of the Sovereign Court of Portarlington, N.L.I., MS 90.

11. Grace lawless Lee, *The Huguenot settlements in Ireland* (London, 1936), pp 135-6.

12. Hennezel to Robert Leigh, 10 November 1670, *C.S.P.I., 1669-70*, p. 302.

13. *Gentlemen and citizens' almanac* (1820), p. 86.

14. Sir George Rawdon's account of Arlington Estate, 16 March 1667, *C.S.P.I., 1666-68*, p. 318.

15. Warburton's petition to William III, 11 December 1690, *C.S.P.I., Dom. 1690-9*, p. 185.

16. David Carnegie Agnew, *Henri Massue, Marquis de Ruvigny* (Edinburgh, 1864), p. 36.

17. Samuel Smiles, *Huguenots in England and Ireland* (London, 1889), p. 230.

18. Galway to William III, *C.S.P.I., Dom.1691-2*, pp 550-1; J.G. Simms, *The Williamite confiscation, 1690-1703* (London, 1956), p. 88.

19. David Carnegie Agnew, *Protestant exiles from France in the reign of Louis XIV* (London, 1871), i, pp 163-5.

20. Coat of Arms to the earl of Galway, 1697, G.O.I., MS 104, f.13.

21. King to lord deputy, May 1669 - two drafts, *C.S.P.I., 1669-70*, pp 635-6.

22. Borrowes, 'Portarlington', p. 66.

23. Sir Charles Petrie, A French project for the invasion of Ireland at the beginning of the eighteenth century, in *The Irish Sword*, v, (1949-53), pp 9-13.

24. *Jus Regnum, or the King's right to grant forfeitures* (London, 1701); Borrowes, 'Portarlington', p. 218; Floy, 'The Huguenot settlement', p. 18.

25. Portarlington, 1678, N.L.I., MS 21F (55)1.

26. Ibid (glosses on the original map).

27. At the very soonest, it would have to have been after the death of Lieutenant Moise Ferment late in 1697. See note 33.

28. *Hiberniae notitia* (Dublin, 1723).

29. Dublin and Portarlington veterans in *P.H.S.L.*, v, p. 72.

30. Ibid.

31. Portarlington church registers in *P.H.S.L.*, v, xix, p. 149.

32. The others who fit into this category would certainly include: Robert d'Ully, Vicomte de Lavl; Josias de Robillard, Seigneur de Champagne; Jean-David Boyer; Francois Daulnis de Lalande; Jean Armenault de Machinville; and (perhaps) Isaac Dumont de Bostaquet.

33. Portarlington Church Registers in *P.H.S.L.*, v, xix, pp 5, 14.

34. Bernard Bligny, *Histoire du Dauphine* (Toulouse, 1973), p. 71.

35. Quoted in Smiles, p. 213; from: Galway to David Barbut in the *Bulletin de la Societe de l'Histoire du Protestantisme Francais*, v (1868), p. 69.

36. Baronne de Chambrier, Projet de colonisation in *P.H.S.L.*, v, vi, p. 380.

37. Ibid., p. 390. Mirmand's negativism was so persistent and pervasive that researchers may be tempted to probe the entire fiasco and Mirmand's role in it.

38. Portarlington Church registers, pp 2, 3, 7, 11, 14, 18-19, 26, 37, 56.

39. Eugene Arnaud, *Historie des Protestants du Dauphine* (Geneva, 1970), 3 vols, iii, p. 361.

40. Mainly: Borrowes; Agnew; and Smiles; but perpetuated in later works.

41. Portarlington Church registers, p. xi.

42. Ibid.

43. Smiles, p. 231.

44. Dublin and Portarlington veterans, v, xli, p. 6.

45. Borrowes, v, vi, pp 337-8.

46. Portarlington registers, p. 18.

47. Ibid.
48. Ibid.
49. The excessive de-emphasis of the oft-bitter confessional divisions within the Huguenot community that developed into an established myth until the 1980s has been countered by recent research; see Forrest, G.A., 'Religious controversy within the French Protestant community in Dublin, 1692-1716: an historiological critique' in Kevin Herlihy (ed.).*The Irish dissenting tradition, 1650-1750* (Dublin, 1995), pp 96-110; Raymond P. Hylton, The Huguenot communities in Dublin, 1662-1745, N.U.I., U.C.D., unpublished Ph.D thesis (1985), pp 264-8.
50. Galway to Blathwayt? October 1700; Galway to Blathwayt 24 October 1700, B.L., Add. MSS 9718, ff 122, 126; Portarlington Church registers, p. 28.
51. The earl of Galway, in fact, was himself often to act as one of the most persistent advocates of the accommodationist (conformist) tendency; an ironic departure considering his role in establishing Portarlington's early, non-conformist settlement.
52. William F.T. Butler, *Confiscation in Irish history* (Dublin, 1917), p. 227.
53. *Jus Regium.*
54. This had indeed been a possibly decisive factor contributing to the demise of the earl of Arlington's English colony (see above).
55. Bishop of Killaloe's bill, *H.M.C., H.L. MSS*, v, v, pp 49-50.
56. Ibid.
57. Nottingham to Sydney 24 July 1691, *H.M.C.*, Finch MSS, v, iii, pp 176-7; Capel to Shrewsbury 12 April 1694, *H.M.C.,* Buccleuch and Queensbury MSS, v, ii, p. 62.
58. Title book of the diocese of Kildare, 1678-1737, N.L.I., mic. n.4565, p. 4531; *Formulaire de la consecration et dedicace des eglises et chapelles selon l'usage de l'Eglise d'Irlande* (dublin, 1702).
59. Lee, p. 132.
60. Borrowes, 'Portarlington', p. 226.
61. Dumont de Bostaquet was the author of an autobiography, *Memoirs inedits de Dumont de Bostaquet, gentilhomme Normand* which however, ends its narrative at 'Bray' (Bride) Street,'Dublin, in 1692 and does not shed light on his final years at Portarlington.
62. 'Dublin and Portarlington veterans', p. 24.
63. Ibid., p. 30.
64. Agnew, *Protestant exiles,* ii, pp 167-8.
65. The inscribed bell is maintained, to this day, at St. Paul's Church at Portarlington.
66. Portarlington registers, pp 84, 88.
67. Ibid.
68. Agnew, *Protestant exiles,* ii, p. 64.
69. Jean Cavallier, *Memoires of the wars of the Cevennes* (Dublin, 1726), pp i-xxiv.
70. This assumption was effectively refuted in Patrick Kelly, 'Lord Galway and the Penal Laws' in H. Caldicott, H. Gough and Pittion, *The Huguenots and Ireland: anatomy of an emigration* (Dun Laoghaire, 1985), pp 239-54.
71. T.P. Le Fanu, 'The Children of Marie De La Rochefoucauld' in *P.H.S.L.*, v, xii, no.6 (1929), p. 6.
72. Ibid.
73. Ibid., p. 8.
74. Agnew, *Protestant exiles,* ii, pp 125-6.

75. Jonathan Swift, *Unpublished letters* (ed., George Birbeck, London, 1899), pp 51, 61.
76. Le Fanu, 'The Children of Marie De La Rochefoucauld', p. 8.
77. Original patent and minutes, N.L.I., MS 90, f.18.
78. Ibid., pp 22-3.
79. Ibid., pp 18-83.
80. 'Dublin and Portarlington veterans', p. 42.
81. Ibid.
82. Galway died at Stratton Park near Micheldever in England on 3 September, 1720. Though he returned to Dublin Castle and served a second term as lord justice (1715-17), his political influence and even his prestige within the Huguenot community itself, had been much eroded.
83. Original patent and minutes, N.L.I., MS 90, ff 9, 17-19, 22, 42, 50.
84. 'Portarlington registers', p. 135.
85. Original patent and minutes, ff 68-74.
86. Ibid., ff 7-15; 25-33; 53-58; 71-76; 83-89; 100.
87. James Joyce, *Finnegan's wake* (New York, 1966), pp 405-6.
88. Smiles, p. 421; Original patent and minutes, f.107.
89. Original patent and minutes, p. 145; 'Portarlington registers', p. 128.
90. Smiles, in particular, holds up an idealisation of the Huguenots as being prototypical to his Victorian self-help philosophy.
91. Diary of Elie Bouhereau, Marsh's Library, Dublin, MS 3072, ff 31, 122, 124.
92. 'Portarlington registers', pp 61, 75.
93. 'Portarlington' (Dublin, P.R.O., Caulfield Ms. 49761 I.A.), pp 53-87.
94. 'Dublin and Portarlington veterans', p. 37.
95. 'Portarlington' (Dublin, P.R.O., Caulfield MS 4976 I.A.); Laurence Sterne, *The life and opinions of Tristram Shandy, gentleman* (London, 1886), pp 205-15.
96. 'Portarlington registers', p. 84.
97. Ibid., p. 125; Lee, p. 173.
98. Ibid., p. 129.
99. Lee, p. 172.
100. Thomas Pakenham, *The year of liberty* (London, 1972), p. 151.
101. 'Portarlington registers', p. xviii; 'Non-conformist Church registers' in *P.H.S.L.*, v, xiv, pp 61-2; 84; 99-100; 108-113.
102. John Wesley, *Journals* (London, 1872), ii, pp 194-5.
103. 'Sur l'Intolerance' and 'Sur les Justes Bornes de la Tolerance', pp 1-61.
104. 'Portarlington registers', p. 126.
105. Published in London (1760) and at Dublin (1751-2), respectively.
106. 'Portarlington registers', p. xviii.
107. At the same time, and in much the same way, Thomas Gimlette was doing the same thing, as regards the Huguenots in Ireland, as a whole, and particularly, the community at Waterford.

Chapter 15

LOCAL OFFICE HOLDING AND THE GENTRY OF THE QUEEN'S COUNTY *c.* 1660-1760

D.M. BEAUMONT

Introduction

Until the latter half of the eighteenth century the network of local office holders, from the High Sheriff to the humble churchwarden, did not in any sense resemble a bureaucracy or even an administration. In order to understand the organisation and behaviour of the 'state' in the seventeenth and eighteenth centuries we need to set aside our modern preconceptions about what actually constitutes effective government.

Seen simplistically the Kingdom of Ireland had a relatively centralised structure – it was governed by the English Crown's representative, the lord lieutenant, who consulted with the Irish Parliament which had the ability to legislate (subject to the approval of the English Privy Council), and their tasks were carried out by government officials, who were the core of the central apparatus in Dublin. They in turn had tentacles of command in the provinces in the form of the local magistracy, principally the sheriffs and justices of the peace, who were appointed by the centre and owed their allegiance to it. This local superstructure was solidified by the threat of coercive forces when required – a formidable army, which could be reinforced by troops from elsewhere and by raising the local militia.

However, it has been suggested that the 'centre' was diminutive in size, ramshackle in terms of organisation and manned by staff lacking the qualities required for a professional civil service.[1] This archaic and personalised form of government also existed in England, described as, 'an extraordinary patchwork of old and new, useless and efficient, corrupt and honest mixed in together ... administrative anomaly was the norm'.[2] It is perplexing how such a system with poor lines of communication and lacking an adequate form of surveillance over its officers managed to perform any of the principal tasks of government such as collecting public revenue and maintaining law and order. In an Irish context the ruling elite's problems were compounded by being a small Protestant minority, and they had to execute predominantly English statute law in a differing environment with religious and racial tensions, against a backdrop of regular rebellion and re-conquest. Whereas the English state after 1689 changed gear and quickly expanded to meet the demands of waging war on the continent on an unprecedented scale the Irish civil establishment did not expand to the same degree and was dwarfed by the manpower and expenditure of the army.[3] With such a deficiency in 'infrastructural power' one wonders how the Irish state was able to survive at all.

The same questions need to be tackled at a local level, especially since the day to day business of ruling Ireland remained overwhelmingly in the hands of the local gentry, who were in effect the source and substance of the Irish 'body politic'.

By focusing on a small sample of the office holders in the Queen's County I shall attempt to give an impression of the haphazard and informal nature of local administration and by dealing with issues of honour and status will give an indication of the complex social contours and subtle gradations within the gentry in an Irish county from c. 1660 to c. 1760.

There are difficulties in using the county as an interpretative tool.[4] There is a temptation to take the structure of local government in the nineteenth century and apply it to this earlier period – to describe the network of officers who enmeshed the countryside in terms of institutions such as the grand jury and the corporations.[5] But it was not a neatly ordered and multi-layered system.

Another way of outlining a local administration would be to draw a series of concentric circles – parochial, baronial and county jurisdiction – especially in the context of England's precocious system which developed before the Norman conquest and because of the striking resilience of certain offices (e.g. sheriff) and of the county as a unit of government. Even this is not fully satisfactory since the elite operated in many circles simultaneously – many were absentees or had estates scattered over Ireland and further afield with multifarious commitments and loyalties. Even the core gentry families belonged to a network encompassing the King's and Queen's counties or a particular segment of west Leinster. In economic terms 'the region' can be more useful in trying to identify the subtle gradations within this ruling group.[6]

I would argue that one could describe this government in terms of a complex network of interdependent relationships between individual gentlemen and the centre. Patronage and family tradition, as opposed to ability, played an important part in securing offices but this was not a semi-feudal or even a strictly master-servant relationship. The elite endeavoured to create and maintain an economic order that would aid and protect their estates and incomes, yet one must not exaggerate the reductionist view of human motivation.[7] Office was not primarily held for material gain, there was less clamouring for pay and pension than in other states (indeed office could be a financial liability). Instead honour, local prestige and social advancement helps to explain why a large proportion of the gentry volunteered themselves for such positions.

I shall discuss (i) what could be termed the 'official magistracy' – the duties of the sheriffs and the j.p.s who were appointed by royal charter or commission (ii) urban government – taking the example of two boroughs and (iii) the additional office holders appointed by the centre who had particular fiscal and defence functions – the revenue collectors and the militia. With these overlapping themes in mind I shall address four questions: who were the local officers (in terms of numbers, social composition and background)? What did these men gain from such positions? What utility did the state derive from their activities? And finally how did this system change over the period?

Size of the magistracy

Given the small proportion of the population who were Protestants and the even smaller number of gentlemen eligible to become magistrates the task of maintaining law and order in a whole county seems at first sight to have been an extremely daunting one. A sheriff and his j.p.s peering over one of their 'grand jury' maps at assizes would have to consider eight baronies and fifty parishes – the 367 square miles which made up the Queen's County.[8] The population therein comprised of at least 38,000 souls in the early eighteenth century (rising to as high as 82,000 by the early nineteenth century). This was a scattered and predominantly rural community with perhaps, on average, just 20 people per square mile.[9]

The destruction of the rolls of magistrates and peace books means that one is reliant upon pre-1922 antiquarian transcripts and the very occasional 'Commission of the Peace' warrant which makes it difficult to make assumptions about the relative expansion of the magistracy in different counties. In the Queen's County, according to one list (probably incomplete), there were just 54 new commissions in the period 1662-1714 and between 1715 and 1765 this number increased to 98 new j.p.s (81 per cent increase).[10] But when compared to a county like Cork, admittedly with a larger population, there were 131 new commissions between 1661 and 1719 and in the period 1720-1769 the increase is especially striking – no fewer than 362 j.p.s appointed (176 per cent increase).[11] In Wexford the number of commissions also far exceeds those for Queen's, but in the latter period there is actually a reduction (by 18 per cent) in the number of new j.p.s.[12] In the Queen's County there were typically 1 or 2 commissions each year although in certain years (e.g. the beginning of a new reign) this figure could rise significantly. At the accession of King George I in 1714 a cluster of 14 new j.p.s. were commissioned.[13] A commission of William Flower in 1747 names 57 j.p.s..[14] Thus as a starting point one can suggest that for for the latter part of the period under question there were approximately 50-60 j.p.s. at any one time.

Though a very small number in terms of the county population the members of the magistracy comprised of a high proportion of the county gentry. A rough count using a variety of indexes puts the number of Queen's County families at 125 (those described as gent. or esq.).[15] This compares to some figures referring to early eighteenth century Ulster – one list mentions 81 landowners in Antrim and 110 in Down with incomes over £100.[16] The Queen's County appeared to have a larger than average number of minor or petty gentry so that the relatively low income qualification that was needed to become a magistrate (usually £100) meant that there were far more potential candidates than the desired number of places. There might have been one j.p. for every 800 people,[17] in addition there were the constables, churchwardens, watchmen and town officials (both Catholics and Protestants could become constables). Numerically then, the administration was reasonably well manned, even by English standards.

It is more difficult to ascertain the number of magistrates who took an active as opposed to a passive role in local law enforcement. It has been suggested that of the 2,024 j.p.s in the whole of Ireland in a return of 1760 as few as one fifth were actually active.[18]

Social background of the J.P.s

What type of gentleman became a j.p.? According to Matthew Dutton in 'The office and authority of a justice of the peace in Ireland' (1718)[19] candidates must be,

> men of the best reputation, the most prevalent men in the county, as they were formerly called, together with some lawyers, they must be substantial persons, dwelling also in the county, they must be of good governance, and must not be steward to any lord.

Members of the Piggot family from Disert kept an extensively annotated book containing 'Extracts of Common Law' (c. 1745).[20] In this highly litigious age an understanding of law could not be left to the avaricious vipers and pettyfogers. Dutton states that under the Tudors there were great many problems with the office, 'but how prodigiously have they encreas'd since, and yearly continue to do so'.[21] Early statutes provided for just 8 j.p.s per county but by the early eighteenth century, 'the number of Justices is greatly encreased in every county'.[22] An expansion of the number of titles/positions (e.g. the selling of baronetcies in James I's reign) can in some instances lead to an 'inflation of honours'. With j.p.s, the large growth (especially after c. 1714) must in part be attributed to the need for Protestant manpower in implementing the burgeoning statute book and perhaps a growth in the size of the gentry without any diminution of the esteem in which the position was held. There remained a great demand for commissions, for the prestige and local status which it carried, by members of established county families as well as newcomers.

In his autobiography Pole Cosby, whose family had settled at Stradbally in the mid-sixteenth century, looked down upon some of the more recent settlers and those without pedigrees. He described Judge Parnell as a, 'so so judge he had neither the parts nor knowledge that his high post required, he was but a mushroom, a man of no family at all at all'. The Parnells, originally from Cheshire, appear to have arrived in Ireland during the Cromwellian period.[23] Ephraim Dawson (who became a j.p. in 1714) was similarly disdained, 'he got a very great interest into this county though he was quite a newcomer into this county and a very mean upstart, for his father kept an ale house the sign of the cock in Belfast'. In reality Dawson's father was a revenue collector for Carrickfergus with very respectable relations in Dublin. Cosby's criticism is not consistent since he welcomes John Bland (who also became a j.p. in 1714) as a, 'very polite, well bred man, had read a good deal and well versed in books and knew mankind very well, he was a sensible and cunning artful man'. Bland, who had fought alongside Cosby on the continent, had only just arrived in the county.[24] Such examples help to show that the handful of families with sixteenth-century pedigrees, such as the Bowens or the Piggots could not dominate the magistracy. A j.p. was as likely to come from Restoration or Williamite settler stock. Personal qualities and contacts in Dublin, their politics, and not just the size of the estate and the antiquity of the family, were as important in securing office.

Magistracy in action

The pattern of war and crisis in Ireland meant that titular head of the county was often a noble who held a martial position. For instance in 1699 Charles Coote, the earl of Mountrath, was the 'Governor' of the county with two deputies, Colonel Fitzpatrick and Denny Muschamp and two muster masters.[25] But the real power was firmly placed in the hands of the gentry.

The position of the high sheriff, though prestigious, was not seen as a glittering prize. One senses that it was an office that any noted gentleman within the very small group of grand jury men could obtain at some point. In describing the appointment of Captain Nathaniel Mitchell in 1734 Cosby remarked that he was, 'made High Sheriff [which a weavers son had no pretensions to] this year to serve this turn'.[26] Dutton wrote,' The King's Majesty [by his dignity royal] is the principal conservator of peace within his dominions and sheriffs were conservators of peace within his county'.[27] The high sheriff had the responsibility of choosing juries and convening the quarter sessions and the assizes, the custody of prisoners, to collect some casual revenue of the crown and during parliamentary elections had the important task of acting as returning officer for the shire.

Though the magistracy formed a full time arm of the law it was in many senses a 'problem orientated' system. Crime waves and dearth mobilised local elites into ad hoc committees and they took action at their own discretion. Where evidence survives it tends to relate to the more sensational, such as the posse that set out to hunt down notorious robber, and the reports of rapparees, houghers and highwaymen, rather than the routine civil law and the internecine legal battles over land between gentlemen which took up far more time.

Though the Queen's County was not a main theatre of war between 1689-1691 it did not escape the pressures of heavy troop movements. The 1641 depositions record the serious losses of certain individuals and give a patchy picture of atrocities during the Rebellion,[28] whereas during the Williamite War the far larger number of soldiers involved in the campaigns caused a more general upheaval. The Dutch troopers billeted at Castle Durrow in 1690 were badly behaved and attracted the attention of rapparees who carried out incessant guerrilla warfare stealing 350 head of black cattle and burning stables.[29] The Queen's County magistracy had a quasi-military function in dealing with the problems of lawlessness directly related to the instability and suffering of warfare some time after 1691. Initially they had to liaise with the victorious army in mopping up operations such as one in 1691, 'upon intelligence that a party of rapparees were troublesome about Castle Cuff', 70 of them were alleged to have been killed.[30] There was also an attempt to preserve order among Protestants. In June 1690 there was an order from Col. Walter Butler commanding, 'those of Protestant religion within the said counties [Wexford, Carlow, Kilkenny and Queen's] within ten days to deliver into the hands of the respective High Sheriffs what arms of what kind soever'.[31]

In times of relative 'peace' there was the occasional outlaw who galvanised the gentry into action. 'Mr. King' who owned estates in the midlands reported in November 1728, 'there is soe much noise in this county at one Paul Lyddy a notorious robber that our mighty men keep watch every night has put me in fear of my little share of this world'.[32]

The other instances in which one gets a picture of the magistracy in action is when they punish religious non-conformists, particularly the Quakers who are well documented in the Queen's County. Accounts of the 'sufferings' of Quakers often name the officer who 'persecuted' them. For instance in 1672 'Thomas Pigot of Disert, the High Sheriff, gott at the last sumer assizes an order to distraine friends goods for non-payment of fees'.[33] The j.p.s busied themselves in an attempt to extract tithes and other levies from these recalcitrants. In 1680 John Gilbert was described as being especially zealous with one woman, 'he threw down the shop window upon her head which being heavy hurt her'.[34] One intriguing case is that of William Morris 'lately a Justice of the Peace', who in 1658, 'for speaking a few words in love ...was put it to the stocks and afterwards committed to the gaole in Maryborough'.[35] County officers assisted by churchwardens, constables and so called 'tithe mongers' seized what ever they could including stooks of hay, peas, turf, livestock, pewter and rugs.[36]

Parliamentary elections provided further opportunities for the sheriff and his deputies to flex their muscles in tackling, or in some cases adding to, the malpractices and corruption in boroughs. 'Double returns' of candidates (when it is was not clear who was legally elected) meant that the sheriff, who checked the votes, had a decisive role in the outcome. His impartiality was often doubted. In a petition to the commons in November 1715 John Barrington argued that, 'Launcelot Sands Esq. High Sheriff was prevailed to accept the indenture of William Wall Esq. (who pretends to be Sovereign of the Corporation)', for candidates who achieved less votes than he did.[37] There was often a recourse to violence, in December 1727 another petitioner, William Trench Esq. wrote that during an election,' Robert Piggott struck and insulted the petitioner in open court and several of his accomplices drew their swords so that the petitioner's friends were obliged for their own safety to quit the court and the petitioner was thereby deprived of their vote'.[38] In August 1754 an election held in Maryborough was described as a, 'vast riot of party' between 'Gilbert supported by Dawson and Westenra against Pigott that you made high sheriff of this county'.[39]

The grand jury men, whom the sheriff chose, assembled during the Spring and Summer Assizes ostensibly to meet the judges on circuit to try those accused of the more serious crimes. But there was also a political and administrative function. They decided on how the county cess should be allocated between competing uses such as roads, bridges and the poor. Pole Cosby received grants at the Lent Assizes in 1733 and 1735 for widening bridges.[40] It was also an important social gathering for the county gentry as shown by their expenditure on such occasions. Colonel John Fitzpatrick of Castletown noted in his 1713 account book the amount, 'expended on a treat for the Gentlemen at sessions'.[41] In England the assizes was a real spectacle with great pomp as the judge and his entourage arrived into the court room. In Ireland this could not always be achieved. Robert Molesworth in 1707 wrote to his wife, 'I remember for many years together that the judges lodged in cabins in Philipstown'.[42] It was also an opportunity for central government to keep an eye on their local officers. Dublin Castle used informers and the county correspondence to the under secretary that was forwarded onto the lord lieutenant or the lord justices. In addition the presence of the judges served to remind the magistracy that malpractices and failure to enforce the law would not go unnoticed.

Much of the time of the officers was spent in settling disputes between gentlemen. Though only a small proportion of the population had full access to the law the gentry were highly litigious as shown by the sheer volume of cases brought before the courts. In Dutton's work the section on 'forcible entry' is one of the longest. The interests of the individual and of a familial or political faction could have a stronger pull than loyalty to the county. In November 1734 Pole Cosby's tenant was ejected from Timahoe by Colonel Murray and a jury of twelve men was set up to find, 'whether Col. Samuel Freeman had a right to make leases in the Lordship'. At least five of the jurors lived outside the county. In Cosby's opinion only one of the twelve men was impartial – 'one was led by the nose of the Sands' (Launcelot Sands), one was owed money by Freeman, another was in the same regiment as Freeman and wanted favour and six were, 'devotees of Dawson' (Ephraim Dawson, who undermined Cosby's political hold over the county). As a result he lost his case and consulted lawyers in England.[43]

Internecine arguments could be further encouraged by the blurring of the officers duties and the unequal application of the law. Magistrates in some neighbouring counties had the reputation for being more zealous than others. Tradition has it that in the mid-sixteenth century Durrow became part of County Kilkenny because it was thought that a dangerous outlaw would be punished by the diligent sheriff who resided across the border rather than in Queen's County. As late as 1770 it was argued that in the town of Ballinakill, 'the residence of an active magistrate is much wanted, he must be in commission of the Peace of Queen's County and County Kilkenny where from its neighbouring situation offenders might be sheltered from justice'.[44] Dutton identified other areas of friction, he said that, 'all sheriffs, mayors, sovereigns and constables are at all times to be aiding and assisting unto the commissioners of the Excise'. In a dispute would the word of an officer employed by the revenue outweigh that of a county j.p.? He goes on, 'in some cases, as in forcible entry his (the j.p.s) single testimony is of a greater authority than an indictment of a jury'.[45] The picture becomes even more confused when one takes into account the overlapping jurisdiction of town and county.

Town magistrates

To some degree urban dwellers had their own institutions which were separate from and on occasions a rival to the county magistracy. Towns were important foci for economic activity and beacons of improvement for the rest of the country. The numerical weakness of Protestants in the countryside (in the Queen's County one estimate is of a ratio of one Protestant to twelve Catholics)[46] was in part compensated by their stronger position in the towns. At times of rebellion Protestants, vulnerable on their estates, used towns as a place of refuge to consolidate their forces and repel encroachments made by the Catholic armies. Despite being very small, certainly by English standards, towns organised their freemen into corporations and were able to appoint their own magistrates (where a charter with the great seal was provided – rather than by commission at the discretion of the lord chancellor), and if they were parliamentary boroughs they could elect members to sit in the commons. Thus Irish towns had an administrative importance that was far greater than their physical size.

By taking the surviving corporation books of Maryborough[47] and Portarlington,[48] the first a product of the mid-sixteenth century plantation and the other a creation of the 1660s (which has long been a source of fascination on account of the Huguenot settlement),[49] one can compare and contrast the successes and shortcomings of the officers in dealing with similar problems of law, order and improvement.

The role of the corporations

The lists of officials, ordinances and minutes of the corporations gives the impression of a highly organised and efficient local body. The Portarlington patent of 1669 provided for a sovereign and deputy, assisted by a clerk and a dozen burgesses who were the basic unit of government. In addition there were two portreeves or bailiffs and overseers in a number of areas – for the North and South Commons, for the river, foot pavements, the poor, stalls for the butchers and all manner of activities within this one hundred acre site.[50] Accounts of the cut and thrust of borough politics in the early eighteenth century and the way in which municipal office and patronage were used by gentlemen jostling for power can obscure the routine and mundane activities of these bodies.

Their primary role was to regulate economic affairs. At Portarlington the twice-yearly fair and the weekly market were monitored by overseers who clutched measuring containers to check the size and weights of bread and butter and to inspect the butcher's stalls and fine those who, 'sold unmerchantable or blown meat'.[51] No butcher could sell, 'hind quarters of mutton without having the kidney and the kidney suit [suet] in the same'.[52] The commons were source of constant complaint. Both towns issued ordinances to punish those who transgressed the rules laid down for grazing, at Portarlington in 1728 'any person that cuts sods or commits waste on it' was fined[53] and in 1731 Maryborough officials made particular pains to prevent Catholics from using the commons.[54]

Closely connected was the task of punishing petty crime and tackling problems created by the impotent and idle poor. The expansion of statute law in this area (e.g. the Vagrancy Acts of 1714 and 1744) meant that by 1750 their official duties had become more onerous. Portarlington made provision for a prison and there were many drives to 'take up vagabonds and beggars in order to have them punished'.[55] In May 1733 the corporation decided to act against 'a person who was disorderd in his senses and had done much mischief'.[56] Three years later another 'mad man' was turned out of the town . The stocks were maintained to humiliate boys playing ball on the Sabbath and there was a drive to 'take up and impound carrs and horses travelling on Sunday til after the evening service'.[57] The threat of licentious behaviour meant that in 1737 'no play could be put on without the special leave of the sovereign',[58] and at Maryborough in the previous year an ordinance prevented the erection of 'tents, huts and booths' on the commons.[59] Faulty chimneys were repaired or pulled down to meet the fire regulations – this was a recurrent problem for in 1748 Portarlington's corporation complained that still 'several persons in the borough do make fire in low cabbins that have no chimneys which may endanger the burning of the town'.[60]

Repairs to the fabric and the general 'improvement' of the town were the other officers' preoccupations. Maryborough made provision in 1731 for maintaining the commons 'to make a large double ditch ... quick planted with ornamentale trees ... a large gate with two pillars made of limestone and mortar..and clearing away several cottages or cabbins bordering on commons which caused obstruction to free and comon passage thro'.[61] In 1728 Portarlington sought to repair all of the foot pavements and make them all at least four feet wide and four years later tried to prevent 'dung being left in heaps in the streets, bridges or market places'.[62] Maryborough ordered that 'every housekeeper in the said town shall hence on every Friday or on every Tuesday in each week sweep or cause to be swept and cleaned the streets'.[63] Both groups of officials tried unsuccessfully for decades to prevent hogs from roaming the streets and both endeavoured to create a convenient course for horse racing and to repair bridges, roads and meeting places. A similar pattern of expenditure can be found in other provincial Irish towns.[64]

Electoral politics

In order to carry out these duties successfully the urban administration needed to be composed of a hard core of diligent and skilled men, chosen by a relatively stable population of freemen, who were resident in the locality and owed their first loyalty to the town, who participated actively and strove to improve by collaborating with the official magistracy (without excessive personal interest and outside patronage) and whose work was backed up by a regular and adequate form of local revenue. Both Portarlington and Maryborough lacked nothing of these attributes.

The freemen who elected the officers were an extremely volatile group. Maryborough stipulated that in addition to the five shilling qualification they had to have lived within the land and liberties of the corporation for at least a year; yet the actual number of men fluctuated greatly. Just before parliamentary elections, corruption and/or the bending of the rules often led to the hurried admittance of groups of new freemen. It has been shown that similar malpractices operated in England[65] but in Ireland things were further complicated by religion. Burgesses and freemen would have had to read out their oaths and declarations in favour of the established church, such as in 1727,

> I do swear from my heart, I do abhorr and detest and objure as impious and hereticall that damnable doctrine ... I do believe there is not any transubstantiation of the elements of bread and wine at or after the consecration.[66]

This provided no guarantee of excluding Catholics.

In 1733 at Portarlington it was reported, 'information has been made to the court that several persons as to the number of 13 have been illegally admitted and sworn freemen in this corporation'.[67] In Maryborough a group of freemen were admitted in 1747 and much to the chagrin of the officials 'were afterwards found to be Papists and others pretending to be Protestants were marryed to Papists'. From then on the corporation was 'determined to the uttmost of our power hereafter to hinder or prevent any Papist ... or any person suspected of being a Papist from being admitted'. A list of the legal members was drawn up and the applicants had their names posted up in advance in a public place for the scrutiny of townsfolk.[68]

Many freemen failed to satisfy the residence requirements. Two hand lists of the voters in the period 1728-1760 – which provides an invaluable aid for constructing a prosopographical analysis of clusters of gentry families – shows that a large proportion lived outside the corporation and many resided in other counties. Of a sample of four hundred freemen just 77 (19 per cent) lived in Maryborough, while 127 (32 per cent) resided outside the county a handful were well out of reach in America and Gibraltar.[69] There was an attempt to tackle this problem in Maryborough in 1731 when it was reported that

> the greater part of the burgesses and freemen reside out of the liberties of the said borough and do not pay or contribute to any public taxes to the great prejudice of the said borough ... by reason of such great number of voters not resideing severall votes and tumults have arisen.[70]

Thenceforth no non-residents were to be admitted. However, the hand list shows that this aim was never achieved and only a small proportion of the freemen would have actively participated in the towns affairs.

Office holders seemed to feel that they and the members of the local Protestant community were surrounded and outnumbered – at best this manifested itself in the drive for corporate unity by purging outsiders and at worst their behaviour bordered on paranoia. Portarlington's freemen read oaths, 'not to be abbeting to any confederacy or conspiracy against the said town and burrough or my neighbours and not to be retained by any man but the said sovereign'.[71] At Maryborough in 1731, 'no Papists or persons professing the popish religion are able to put or graze any horse or other cattle or beast whatsoever on the said commons'.[72]

It has been suggested that, 'to judge from corporation books and petitions the electoral system was being abused on a grand scale ... extraordinary even by eighteenth century standards'.[73] The Queen's County evidence reinforces this view. William Flower for example became an M.P. for Portarlington in 1727 yet had only been made a freeman in the same year.[74] In a fierce dispute over the election of burgomaster in Maryborough in 1754 between Bartholomew Gilbert and John Pigott the minute books had been confiscated by Anthony Trench for safe-keeping. It was only in 1758 that both parties, 'after much expense were reconciled and Mr. Dawson unanimously elected burgomaster', that the books were finally recovered 'but during the interval no entry was made in either of them of the corporation acts'.[75]

Town improvement and the gentry

Municipal office in the two corporations was not on the whole sought by substantial gentlemen. The position of sovereign or burgomaster tended to go to a prominent townsman like Josias Champagne who unusually was re-elected five times in Portarlington. A place on the grand jury which met in the principal towns at assizes probably carried more prestige than presiding over a corporation court. Gentlemen could influence affairs more indirectly through patronage. Ephraim Dawson acquired the manor of Portarlington in c.1708 and in return for political support (e.g. he was M.P. for the borough in 1713-14 before becoming M.P. for the county and was unanimously elected sovereign in 1727) the family acted paternalistically. In 1751 when the corporation decided to build a new tholsell it was minuted that, 'W.H. Dawson (Ephraim's son) has been so good as to propose advancing so much money as shall be necessary'.[76] Magnates could also avoid tarnishing their reputations at borough level by employing their stewards and other agents to act on their behalf.

The activities of the officers were severely limited by inadequate funds. There was a continual patching up – insufficient work funded by *ad hoc* payments – which meant that buildings and roads soon fell into disrepair. The bridge at Portarlington was broken so many times that finally in 1732 it was planned to 'allow some neighbouring mason a yearly salary and that some reward be offerd to the person that discovers them that brake it.'[77] In 1752 the tholsell at Portarlington was 'in so dangerous and ruinous condition' that it was deemed unsafe for the sovereign and freemen to hold an assembly there.[78] In 1749 the quarterly tax, the cess, barely provided enough to pay the clock keeper his 30 shillings salary, to pay the clerk his expenses and to make a few repairs.[79] Monies from fines tended to be distributed among the poor. In Maryborough it was ordered that any one who did not pay the cess could not use the commons. This problem was exacerbated by the idleness and incompetence of some of the overseers. At Portarlington in 1733 there were complaints about the 'cow boy of the South Commons' who had, 'not performed his office as he ought to do' and should be discharged and a 'fine be imposed on them if they do not punctually perform what they are enjoined to do'.[80] The 'hog roaming' problem for instance showed that it was difficult to reform the manners and behaviour of townsfolk. In 1749, 'the order having proved ineffectual the corporation decided to levy a 1 shilling fine for every pig or hog that is seen'.[81] Officers were well aware of their shortcomings. At a meeting in 1732 the Portarlington officers announced 'Gentlemen, notwithstanding several good orders that have been made in this corporation from time to time for the publick good thereof it is found that most of the chieftest things are left undone'.[82] This contrasts with the impressions of travellers like Samuel Molyneux who passed through the town in 1709 and thought it to be, 'a pretty new town well planted', or the rose-tinted views of some historians who thought the French settlers had created a flowery idyll on the banks of the River Barrow. Molyneux was less impressed by Maryborough, 'a sad dirty town tho the county town of the Queen's County'.[83]

While urban officials with their limited funds quibbled about re-pointing a crumbling bridge or gilding a clock face, great strides were being made in the area of rural as well as town improvement by private landed gentlemen. William Flower, an M.P. for Portarlington and a freeman had single handedly laid out a market place and erected sturdy stone houses at Durrow. Not only did he build a fine new seat in 1715-16 and extended his gardens, he also put up walls, repaired adjacent roads and the parish church. The demesne branched out into the locale symbolised by the new avenue which linked, 'the Great house towards Durrow town'.[84] Similarly Pole Cosby, who was a freeman of Maryborough, describes in his autobiography how he erected bridges and houses in the town of Stradbally. At the Lent Assizes of 1733 the grand jury gave him £20 to build a bridge, 'because it being so near my seat I had a mind to have it a somewt Handsome', so Cosby laid out a further £40 of his own money to complete the task.[85] Some of the new houses can be seen in an estate painting of c.1740.[86] It was men like these in the countryside and not the civic officials who set the pace for improvement. Only towards the latter part of the eighteenth century does one see the emergence of institutions such as 'houses of industry' which required a large degree of collective organisation and which would not have been taken on single handedly by landowners. A pamphlet of 1776 shows that a plan for a 'humble habitation for the poor' in Maryborough was funded entirely by subscriptions from local gentlemen and clergymen.[87]

Revenue Collectors

In addition to the magistracy there were a number of office holders appointed by the centre who performed more specialised tasks. Though the crown used sheriffs to collect certain fees and fines the bulk of the revenue – hearth tax, tunnage and poundage, and the excise – was administered by separate agencies that were directly accountable to officials in Dublin. The servants of the revenue board, in comparison to the *ad hoc* structure of county officership, achieved a greater degree of internal organisation and professionalism. They were also under closer surveillance.[88]

By the second quarter of the eighteenth century the structure of the revenue office was organised as follows: the headquarters was the Custom House in Dublin, commissioners and sub-commissioners had jurisdiction over particular areas or districts, these in turn were sub divided into divisions and foot walks. The 'Maryborough District' covered the King's and Queen's Counties and within it there were 13 foot walks and each had its own 'gauger' who was accompanied by a surveyor (there were two in the district in 1730).[89] Both men would visit the retailers and breweries in each walk – there were between 10 and 24 brewers within a riding distance of 4 to 16 miles – armed with appropriate measuring instruments, journals and stock books they would sniff out unlicensed ale houses and secret caches of undeclared liquor.[90] In a report by Edward Thompson on the conduct of the officers in 1733 some of the men are commended for their duties. Richard Boyland (a gauger) was 'well enough qualified for his post, having been 22 years imployd in the revenue', and Edward Blurton 'has been fifteen years in this division and is verry well qualified for a walk of better business'.[91]

Though efficient by the standards of the day there were many difficulties. In comparison to the maritime districts such as Cork and Wicklow which generated a far greater volume of work (and therefore more money) for the collectors, landlocked Queen's County was under less scrutiny. Edward Thompson in his report admits that 'I have touched lightly on Maryborough District and pas'd Naas without surveying it'.[92] The surveyors did not always live near to their 'walks'. It was noted that William Phelan the gauger of the Mountrath Walk 'is a native of this county and spends too much time with his wife and family who live at Ballyroan, three miles distant from his residence and out of his walk'.[93] In the Queen's County there was a distance of between 4 and 20 miles between the gauger's residence and the surveyor's office. With the non-gentry status of the junior officers there was also the danger of too much familiarity with the tax payers. At Ballinakill the report says 'there are three persons in this division who sell wine constantly, yet there is no charge made upon them this year in any book whatever, the officer says that they are very poor', as a result he was 'severely reprimanded'. In the same town it was found that 'the surveyor has not been in his residence ... and that he had forged that survey'.[94] There are other instances where it appears that the officer turned a blind eye to private cellars, perhaps for a liquid reward.

In order to check up on the officers all manner of tactics were employed. One of Thompson's inspectors got the officer of Ballinakill out of bed and demanded to see his stock book. At Mountrath the officer was pursued while on his walk 'and having surveyd two houses by check met with him took his books and in it surveyd the remainder of his work', it was found that,' such persons returned for wine license, pay but triffles'.[95] One of the 'general observations' of the report was that there, 'were great opportunities to the officer to act dishonestly in their stations if so minded'. Information was received that Mr. Henry, the gauger of Mountmellick 'kept a shop and three brewing pans'.[96] Perhaps one of the reasons for these problems was that the lower grade revenue offices were not held in high esteem. A list of new freemen for Portarlington in 1732 shows that among the many esqs. and gents. 'Mr. Arthur Palmer', was described as 'Officer of Excise',[97] which was a recognition of his status. Yet this salaried post which required a degree of intelligence and training and offered opportunities for promotion (and therefore ideal for a younger son of a gentleman) never quite achieved the same status as the more established offices or the glamour and respect that went with the more martial offices.

The Militia

The Queen's County gentry preferred to be listed as 'Ensign', 'Captain' or 'Colonel', even if their claim to such a title was exceedingly tenuous. Ireland contained the bulk of the British army (12,000 out of 19,000 men in 1701) and was used as a strategic reserve during the many continental campaigns.[98] In England very few troops were housed in barracks. So as not to be seen as an instrument of autocracy the military mingled with civilians in ale houses up and down the country. In Ireland by contrast there was a massive programme of barrack building. In 1704 the 'Annuall charge for maintaining and upholding the Barracks' shows that some troops of horse were based at Maryborough.[99] Philip Rawson esq. was paid a yearly rent of £60 by the 'Trustees of the Barracks' in 1737 for the barracks at 'Donomore' containing two troops of horse.[100] There was a very strong military tradition in many Irish gentry families. Col. Humphrey Bland for example was delighted when all his nephews chose military careers in the 1750s, 'provided that they may lose their Irish brogues which they contract at the country schoolls'.[101] By comparing the few surviving lists of militia and army officers from the King's County there is a striking continuity of service in some families.[102]

For those anchored on their estates there was an opportunity of joining the militia. Though technically a trained peace-keeping force which was periodically mustered at times of crisis it was as much a source of local pomp and display for the gentry and it overlapped with their civil duties.[103] Of the c. 220 individuals that Pole Cosby mentions in his autobiography at least 25 have a military title. John Loveday on his tour of Ireland in 1732 was very aware of this martial air, 'he disliked the pretensions which dubbed the squires colonels and their houses castles'. When visiting William Flower at Castle Durrow he remarked, 'He, according to the general affected custom of the country is called Colonel, because he has that rank in the Militia'.[104] Flower was made a lieutenant colonel of a militia regiment of dragoons in 1727.[105] The Irish gentry tended to keep these titles long after their regiments were disbanded.

Of the methods of raising and administering the militia we know very little save a 'Book of rules and orders of the commissioners of Array in the King's County' (1678-81) which lists all of the officers and shows how charges were levied on the landowners, it is also provides an illuminating insight into the workings of Dublin Castle and the effectiveness of its chains of command in the provinces.[106]

Conclusions

This rather sketchy outline of local office holding has, in the absence of grand jury records, relied upon the scraps quarried from estate papers. The picture has been further distorted because the main body of material relates to the latter end of the period under review. Some key areas, such as poor relief, local reactions to dearth and the implementation of the Penal Laws have hardly been touched upon because there is little documentation. Although it has been shown that the much of the officer's business was 'internecine' – between members of the Protestant elite – my angle has been unwittingly skewed towards the attitudes of those who were in the saddle rather than to the bulk of the population in their cabins.

The admirable work of O'Hanlon et al chronicles the sequestration of lands and the fate of Catholic priests, but they were less interested in themes covered in this chapter. They wrote, 'The History of the Queen's County in the 18th century [in so far as it can be said to have any history] is the history of the Penal Laws'.[107] Dissenters in English counties faced similar hardships. On reading the accounts of Congregationalists and Quakers in Suffolk in the latter half of the seventeenth century who were chased by office holders down secret tunnels and out into barns and fields (like 'mass pits') one might think – if it were not for the more complicated racial tensions – that there were few fundamental differences between the two kingdoms.[108] Suffolkers, living in a highly populated and intensively cultivated county might have found parts of the Queen's County very English (e.g. the barony of Stradbally), as was commented upon by observers,[109] but would be less familiar with the 'martial air' – an undercurrent in office holding that can be followed throughout the period.

In the context of local government the idea of 'the county' is in many senses an artificial one because the office holders who jostled together had differing units of jurisdiction – e.g. many freemen were enrolled in different boroughs and lived outside the county, the revenue commissioners looked to the 'District', the clergy to their diocese and the turnpike trustees repaired lengths of road intersecting more than one county. Then there are the ambiguous loyalties of men on the county border like William Flower who seemed to embrace County Kilkenny in every way (he was an M.P. for the city of Kilkenny, sheriff and colonel of the militia) but also secured a parliamentary borough in the Queen's County. Like other midland counties the Queen's County is bounded by five others, and on its own was perhaps lacking in geographical integrity.

However, there does seem to have been a backbone of families who could be said to have made up a 'county gentry', individuals whose name crop up again and again – whether it be on parliamentary petitions, in estate correspondence, maps or tradesmen's bills – and the many 'captains' and 'colonels' who peopled Pole Cosby's immediate habitat. Further prosopographic study should enable one to give a better idea of the number of individuals concerned. One county study of Tipperary describes the 'landed society' only in terms of an economic equilateral triangle – with the nobles at the apex and the freeholders at the base.[110] By looking at the relationship between office holding and status one begins to build up a more three dimensional and less schematic view of social structure.

The benefits that the state gained from this type of local government are less obvious than those that were accrued by the gentry. It gave discretionary powers to the magistracy and, despite the increasing work load, a great degree of prestige was derived from holding office . There were many advantages in being inside 'the law' rather than on the edge of it. For instance by pressing certain cases at grand juries (e.g. for repairing roads adjoining their estates) they could consolidate first and foremost their own economic interests.

The revenue may have provided a more 'modern' role model but this organisation was achieved at a price, namely the salaries and expenses that were needed to keep the bureaucracy running.[111] This is the key reason why the centre did not attempt to make any far reaching institutional reforms at a local level over this hundred year period. With the exchequer's lack of liquidity, and rising debts (due to the demands of the military establishment) it was even more necessary that the gentry at a local level could provide a relatively inexpensive service. In return for a modicum of power they gave impetus to the physical improvements in the town and country almost always at their own expense. Viewed from the top this was a very workable system.

Acknowledgements

My principal debts are to Toby Barnard (Hertford College, Oxford) and David Dickson (Trinity College, Dublin) for their comments and constant encouragement.I gained further insights from Prof. Cullen's Modern History Graduate Seminar group, where I gave a paper on this subject.

References

1. One of my principal sources is D.W. Hayton's unpublished D.Phil. thesis (Oxford, 1975), Ireland and the English Ministers 1707-1716'.

2. G. Aylmer, 'From office holding to civil service: the genesis of modern bureaucracy' in *T.R.H.S.* (fifth series), xxx (1980), p. 96.

3. For figures relating to England see J. Brewer, *The sinews of power: war, money and the English state 1688-1783* (London, 1989), pp 65-66. For Ireland see Hayton, 'English ministers', pp 48-51.

4. This area has also been explored by T.C. Barnard in 'The political, material and mental culture of the Cork settlers c.1650-1700' in P. O'Flanagan and C. Buttimer (eds.), *Cork: history and society* (Dublin, 1993), ch.9, pp 309-65 (esp. pp 311-15).

5. There have been some useful studies of the evolution of local institutions, e.g. B. Donnelly, 'From grand jury to county council: an overview of local administration in Wicklow 1605-1898' in K. Hannigan and W. Nolan (eds), *Wicklow: history and society* (Dublin, 1994), ch. 22, pp 855-95.

6. For e.g., D. Dickson, 'An economic history of the Cork region in the eighteenth century' (T.C.D. unpub. Ph.D thesis 1977), for the concept of 'hinterland' see p. 419.

7. A point made by S.J. Connolly, *Religion, law and power: the making of Protestant Ireland 1660-1750* (Oxford, 1992), pp 86-7.

8. For e.g. one grand jury-type map is that made by Oliver Sloane of Hillsborough, c.1765 (printed), showing the churches, castles, seats, farmhouses, roads, rivers, bogs, woods and hills, N.L.I. map. 16.h.19. (fol.2).

9. Figures for 1706 from Molyneux's 'Number of houses from the Hearth Money of 1706', on the basis of 5 heads to one hearth gives the figure 37,908 for the Queen's County. This is probably a very conservative estimate, T.C.D., MS. 893/2. The later figure derives from Beaufort's 1792 computation and re-used in William Wakefield, *An account of Ireland statistical and political* (London, 1812), i, pp 272-3.

10. A list of magistrates in, O'Hanlon and O'Leary, *History*, ii, app.iv, pp 777-88. The relatively low number of j.p.s suggests that this list is not complete.

11. H.F. Berry, 'Justices of the peace for the County of Cork, 1661-1800', *Journal of the Cork Hist. Arch. Soc.*(2nd Series), iii (1897) pp 58-65, 106-112. Figures used by Dickson, 'An economic history of the Cork region', p. 65, table 2:1.

12. J.P. Swan, 'The justices of the peace of County Wexford 1661-1800' in

T.R.S.A.I., Series iv (1894), p. 65. For the period 1664-1714 there were 166 commissions and for 1715-1765, 136.

13. See 'O'Hanlon list', p. 787.

14. Commission of the Peace for Lord Castle Durrow, 6 June 1747, N.L.I., MS 20,230. He appears on the O'Hanlon list as a magistrate in 1707.

15. My gentry data base covers the period 1650-1765 and is still being compiled.

16. P.R.O.N.I., MS 24.K.19/1.

17. Using the 1706 Hearth Tax figures, see note 9.

18. See Hayton, 'English ministers', Ch. 6, p. 198.

19. M. Dutton, *The office and authority of the justice of the peace for Ireland* (Dublin, 1718), T.C.D., E.B. NN.gg.59.

20. Extracts of Civil Law, belonging to the Piggott family, *c.*1745, N.L.I., MS 19,484.

21. Dutton, 'Justice of the peace', p. 1.

22. Ibid., p. 75.

23. Genealogical notes (modern typescript) on the Parnell family of the Queen's County, P.R.O.N.I., D289/1.

24. 'The autobiography of Pole Cosby of Stradbally, Queen's County 1703-1737' in *Kildare Archaeological and Historical Society Journal,* 5 (1906-1908). Parnell, p. 254, Dawson, p. 174 and Bland, p. 253.

25. P.R.O.N.I., ENV/HP/24- Q.C., which cites, H. Upton, 'List of the governors and deputy governors of Ireland in 1699' in p. *R.I.A.* (1924).

26. 'Cosby autobiog.' p. 312.

27. Dutton, *'Justice of the peace',* p. 75.

28. The 1641 depositions for the Queen's County, T.C.D., MS 805.

29. Flower Papers, N.L.I., MS 11,473 (1-3).

30. *An account of the defeat of the rebels by their Majesty's forces in the Queen's County, 4 May 1691* (printed, E. Jones, 1691), N.L.I., Thorpe Coll. p. 12.-no.704.

31. H.M.C. O'Connor MSS report 2 (1874), p. 227.

32. King papers, Ballylin 1681-1819 (mainly Roscommon estates), N.L.I., p. C. 308-312. Box1. To King from W. Piers, 27 Nov. 1728.

33. Mountmellick monthly meeting records, records of the sufferings 1656-1686 and *c.*1726-1735, Friends Historical Library, Dublin, Ref. G.2.

34. As above, M.M. V.G. *1 (Friends Lib.).

35. Ref. G.2 (Friends Lib.).

36. As above, M.M. V.G. *1 and M.M. V.G. *3 (Friends Lib.).

37. Commons Reports, iii, p. 17, 17 Nov. 1715.

38. Ibid., p. 482, 8 Dec. 1727.

39. H.M.C., Stopford-Sackville MSS, i, p. 222.

40. 'Cosby autobiog', p. 311.

41. Rental book of Capt. John Fitzpatrick 1700-1719, N.L.I., MS 3000.

42. H.M.C., Clements and various collections MSS viii, 1913, p. 273, 11 June 1707.

43. 'Cosby autobiog', pp 311-4.

44. Mr Frederick Trench's memo of Ballynakill in Stanhope Papers (Irish estate), P.R.O.N.I., T.186/1 (transcript).

45. Dutton, *'Justice of the peace',* for the excise see p. 67.

46. Wakefield, *An account,* i, p. 620.

47. Maryborough: List of the burgesses in the early eighteenth century, N.L.I., MS 1727. Minute book and charter 1728-1760, N.L.I. MS 1726. By-laws and acts of the assembly of Maryborough, 1731, Portlaoise County Library.

48. The corporation book for the borough of Portarlington *c.*1727- *c.*1765, N.L.I.,

MS 90.

49. For e.g. R.P. Hylton, 'The Huguenot settlement at Portarlington, 1692-1771' in *The Huguenots and Ireland: an anatomy of emigration*, ed. C.E.J. Caldicott, H. Gough and J.P. Pittion (Dublin, 1987), pp 297-320. See his chapter in this book.

50. Portarlington Corp. Book contains an abstract of the 1669 patent at the beginning of the volume, N.L.I., MS 90.

51. 'Port. Minute', 7 May 1730.

52. Ibid., 4 May 1738.

53. Ibid., 1 June 1728.

54. 'Acts of Maryborough' 1731.

55. 'Port. Minute', 7 May 1730.

56. Ibid., 26 May 1733.

57. Ibid., 21 Oct. 1732 and 7 May 1730.

58. Ibid., 13 Nov. 1737.

59. 'M/B Acts', 1731.

60. 'Port. Minute', 1 June 1728 and 10 June 1748.

61. 'M/B Acts' 1731.

62. 'Port. Minute', 1 June 1728.

63. 'M/B Acts' 1731.

64. For e.g., the town of Wicklow see Donnelly, 'From grand jury to county council', esp. pp 859-60.

65. See F. O'Gorman, *Voters, patrons and parties: the unreformed electoral system of Hanoverian England 1734-1832* (Oxford, 1989), esp. pp 38-68.

66. Oaths for the justice of the peace, the recorder, sovereign and for the freemen, N.L.I., MS 90, pp 1-4.

67. 'Port. Minute', 11 July 1727 and 1 Oct. 1733.

68. 'M/B Acts' 23 July 1747.

69. Hand list of the voters of Maryborough, 1760 N.L.I., MS 1726. See also H.F. Kearney, 'Select documents': xiii in *I.H.S.*, viii, no.33 (March, 1954), pp 53-83.
    In my sample of 400 (total number of 623 in N.L.I., MS 1726): main categories are, Maryborough, 77 (19 per cent), elsewhere in the county, 186 (47 per cent), King's Co., 25 (6 per cent), Dublin, 43 (11 per cent), other Irish counties, 46 (12 per cent), the army, 10 (3 per cent), England and the Isle of Man, 3 (1 per cent), N.L.I., MS 1727, a handlist of c.1750 also lists the 'place of abode'.

70. 'M/B Acts' 1731.

71. Oaths at the front of the Portarlington minute book, N.L.I., MS 90.

72. 'M/B Acts' 1731.

73. Hayton, 'English ministers', p. 146.

74. Port. Minute Book', 21 Oct. 1727. Flower was previously M.P. for Kilkenny 1715-1727, and held the Portarlington borough until his elevation to the Irish House of Lords, see 'Port. Minute', 29 Nov. 1733.

75. 'M/B Acts' 1754-58.

76. 'Port. Minute', 30 Sept. 1751.

77. Ibid., 21 Oct. 1732.

78. Ibid., ? Oct. 1752.

79. Ibid., 10 Aug. 1749.

80. Ibid., 26 May 1733.

81. Ibid., 21 Dec. 1749.

82. Ibid., 21 Dec. 1732.

83. For e.g. of romantic view of Portarlington, T.P. Le Fanu, 'The French veterans at Portarlington' in *Kildare Arch. Soc.*, ii (1930-33), pp 179-200. Molyneux's

Journey to Kerry 1709, T.C.D., MS 883, ii. He passed through the King's and Queen's Counties in July 1709: for Portarlington, p. 107 and Maryborough, p. 129.

84. Flower papers, N.L.I., MS 11,455-11,456.

85. 'Cosby autobiog.', p. 311.

86. The painting (sold by Sotheby's in 1986) was hung at Stradbally Hall now in private Irish collection. Illustrated in Knight of Glin and Edward Malins, *Lost demesnes: Irish landscape gardening 1660-1845* (London, 1976), p. 23.

87. Edward Ledwich, *First annual report of the corporation instituted for the relief of the poor and punishing vagabonds and sturdy beggars in the Queen's County* (printed pamphlet, Kilkenny 1776), N.L.I., 1, 6551 Kilkenny.

88. For an English context see Brewer, *Sinews of power*, p. 102.

89. Information from, 'The register of reports on the state of the revenue and the conduct of its officers, 1733', by Edward Thompson, commissioner of the revenue and excise', N. Arch. Ire. 2c.36.1.

90. Ibid., p. 108, in the whole district there were 194 brewers in all the walks amounting to 128 miles.

91. Ibid., p. 106-7.

92. Ibid., p. 98, figures for amounts collected from inland excise, ale licence, wine licence, quit rents and hearth money on p. 104.

93. Ibid., p. 106.

94. Ibid., pp 89-91.

95. Ibid., p. 89, 106.

96. Ibid., p. 992 and p. 105.

97. Portarlington Minute Book, 2 Oct. 1732, N.L.I., MS 90.

98. See figure for the military establishment in Hayton, 'English ministers', p. 213.

99. 'The civil and military establishment, 1704' (with a list of the barracks at the end of the volume), N.A.I., M.2940.

100. Indenture between Philip Rawson Esq. and the trustees of the barracks 1737, N.A.I., M.5754 (3).

101. The correspondence of Humphrey Bland *c.*1751- *c.*1758 (private collection, Ireland).

102. For e.g., List of the Militia officers of the King's Co. *c.*1690, B.M. Add. MSS 34,766. The army reviewed at Birr and Tullamore in 1770, N.A.I., M.4901.

103. For a resume of the different arrays of the militia see Connolly, *Religion, law and power*, pp 201-2.

104. 'A tour in Kildare in 1732' (William Loveday), printed extracts edited by T.U. Sadleir in the *Journal of the Kildare Archaeological Society*, vii (1912-14), pp 168-177, for Flower, p. 168.

105. Certificate from Lord Carteret commissioning Flower, 16 Sept. 1727, N.L.I., D.20,237.

106. Militia Book, Birr Castle Archive, MS A/19. I am most grateful to Rolf Loeber, see 'The reorganisation of the Irish Militia in 1678-81: documents from Birr Castle', in Irish Sword (forthcoming).

107. O'Hanlon and O'Leary, *History*, p. 558.

108. For e.g., The Whitingstreet Independent Congregational minute book 1646-1988, Suffolk Record Office, Bury St. Edmunds, FB3/3 SO2/1 178   .

109. For e.g. of view of the county: Commentary on a journey between Kildare, Carlow and the Queen's County (esp. Stradbally) of 1782, N.L.I., MS 773 (6) (modern typescript).

110. T.P. Power, *Land, politics and society in eighteenth century Tipperary* (Oxford,

1993), p. 75.

111. Of the monies received by the revenue in the Queen's County between 25 March- 15 August 1733 around 10 per cent of total was disbursed on salaries (see 'Thompson report', p. 104). At a national level Hayton states that in 1715 (50,000 was spent on salaries, 'English Ministers', pp 50-51.

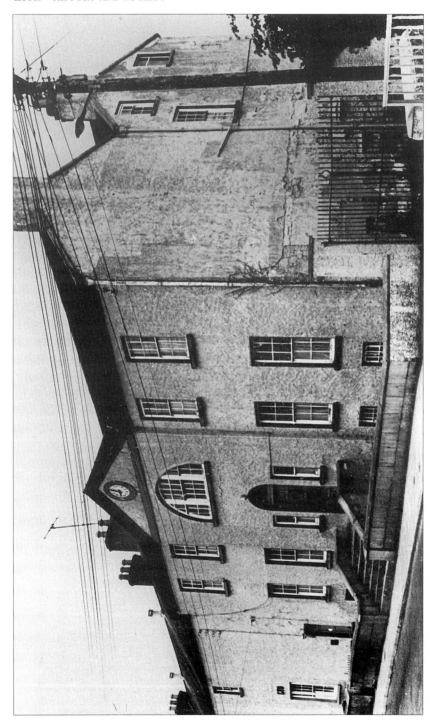

Plate 15.1   Late eighteenth century house, French Church Street, Portarlington (IAA).

Chapter 16

BISHOP DANIEL DELANY (1747-1814)

SR. MARY O'RIORDAN (BRÍGÍDINE SISTER)

Family Background

The Delanys & Fitzpatricks were ranked among the 'Seven Tribes of Laoighis', where the O'Delany, 'a man of hospitality', once ruled over 'the delightful Coill Uachtarach' (now Upperwoods), one of the eight baronies of the Queen's County.[1] There were no fewer than eight branches of the Delany Clan, all deriving their surname from 'Dubh-shlaine', the original 'Dark Man of [the River] Slaney.[2]

The Fitzpatricks, claimed descent from Heremon, son of Milesius, and were chiefs of Ossory. Noted for religious zeal and generosity to the clergy, the family adopted the surname Mac Giolla Phádraig (Son/Servant of Patrick) out of respect for the Apostle of Ireland.[3] A Mac Giolla Phádraig, Prince of Ossory, rebuilt in the twelfth century, the Celtic monastery of Aghaboe and gave it to the Dominicans 'under the invocation of St. Canice'.[4] The clan territory was named from Aonghus Osraighe. The marriage of Aoife, daughter of Diarmaid na nGall, to Strongbow, which eventually brought the province of Leinster under Anglo-Norman dominion, resulted in the displacement of the Fitzpatricks when, about 1192, 'a general sentence of eviction was issued against the clan by its Norman overlord'.[5] Moving northwards they made common cause with the Delanys of Upperwoods, captured the foreigners' castles at Aghaboe and Castletown, and established themselves at Borris-in-Ossory. In the latter half of the fourteenth century Mac Ghiolla Phadraic expelled the remnant of the foreign settlers and brought the O'Phelans and Delanys into subjection.[6]

More than two centuries later another man of the clan left a mark on history. This was Bishop Daniel Delany (1747-1814) (Plate 16.1), son of Daniel Delany and Elizabeth Fitzpatrick of Paddock, Upperwoods, Laoighis. Though he may not have been aware that the blood of chieftains ran in his veins, and could never have heard the Fitzpatrick war-cry, *'Fear Láidir Abú'*, it may be significant that when he had to choose an episcopal motto he should fix upon *'Fortiter et Suaviter'* (*'Firmly and Gently'*).

Plate 16.1   Right Rev. Dr. Delany, Bishop of Kildare and Leighlin.

Birth, Schooldays

Paddock lies in the parish of Castletown, two miles from Mountrath by the Ballyfin road. Here, in February 1747, the first of two sons was born to Daniel and Elizabeth Delany, tenant-farmers on the Castlecoote Estate. The child was given his father's name, and grew to attend the local hedge-school at Briosclagh.[7] It may not be amiss to quote here a description of such establishments, written as early as 1814:

> The school-houses are, in general, wretched huts built of sods, in the highway ditches. They have neither door, window nor chimney, – a large hole in the roof admits light and lets out the smoke from a fire in the middle.A long narrow hole in the mud wall affords ingress and egress. Fully attended in summer, half-empty at Spring and Harvest, they are utterly deserted in winter.[8]

Daniel Delany, senior, died young and his elder son went to live at Mountrath with his mother's sisters, the Misses Fitzpatrick, shopkeepers in the town. There, one of his aunts took charge of his education, since his mother would not permit his attendance 'at a proselytising school'.[9] Daniel was considered talented, 'a boy, endowed with a pious and amiable disposition, uncommon quickness and a great cheerfulness'.[10] The Fitzpatricks and Delanys were respected among their Protestant neighbours. and one of these, 'a young gentleman who had just finished his schooling in England'[11] gave Daniel a Latin grammar and some private assistance with the study of it. In spite of his aptitude for learning and love of books Daniel was careful not to carry his reading material out of doors, lest he draw unwelcome attention on friends or relatives.[12]

> The place of Catholic worship was a rough thatched house, built on a sandbank in the river Nore. To this day, the road nearby is known as 'Chapel Lane'. Lord Castlecoote inserted in every lease a clause prohibiting the tenant from providing a site for a Catholic chapel, school or priest's residence. In heavy rain the sandbank flooded, and people sometimes spent all of Saturday night in an effort to have the chapel ready for Sunday Mass.[13] There Dan received his First Holy Communion when about ten years old.[14] He visited the chapel, dusted the altar, arranged candlesticks, locked and unlocked the door, brought other boys of his own age there and taught them hymns.[15]

These hymns, with the serving of Mass, he learned from the Rev Denis Lawler who lived in a mud hut on a nearby bog.[16]

The Brigidine Annals also attribute a love of Irish history to the young Daniel, describing how he heard the stories of Celtic schools and monasteries from his aunts. Clonenagh and Aghaboe were almost on his doorstep. His character had its less serious side too, for he was exuberant and fun-loving, like any growing boy. One of his aunts would sometimes save him from a scolding with the remark: 'Let the boy alone. He will yet be a great man'.[17] His kindness, and his power with his elders, appear from the story of his begging a meal for a poor and hungry man whom he had brought home at an inopportune time. Yielding to the boy's plea the aunt sat the unexpected guest down in her kitchen and plied him with food. So relieved was Daniel that he began one of his noisy games and was rebuked for it.

Before leaving the old man returned thanks to God and his hostess, then crossed to the boy and placed both hands on his head saying 'This head will one day wear a mitre'.[18]

Though aware of the difficulties under which Catholic clergy laboured Dan decided to become one of them. This involved leaving his mother alone, since John, her only other child, had died when scarcely out of infancy. By 1763, when he was 16, it had been settled that he should go to France 'for his priesting'. The influence of Protestant friends enabled him 'to cross safely over, without being noticed or registered'.[19] For fourteen years thereafter a mantle of silence enveloped him, until his return in 1777.

France

James Warren Doyle, Bishop of Kildare & Leighlin 1819-1835, was personally acquainted with Daniel Delany and states that the latter studied at Paris, exhibiting there 'evidence of rare endowments and brilliant talents'.[20]

Pre-Revolution Paris would have presented a culture-shock to most Irish students. The language-barrier apart, there was the identification of church with state, splendid religious ceremonies, and academic challenges in plenty. All training in philosophy and theology radiated from the Sorbonne, which by universal consent held pride of place among the great academies of christendom.[21]

Houses of residence had sprung up, named usually from the regions from which they originally drew their students. The Irish were for long a floating population, scattered among various institutions, until the first 'Irish House' was opened on the Rue St. Thomas[22] on a date unknown. A papal brief of 1626 authorised the Irish bishops to ordain students *before* sending them abroad for study, enabling many to maintain themselves on their Mass stipends.[23] In 1677 a house formerly used by Italian students[24] and now derelict was given to the Irish. By 1750, 100 priests and 60 ecclesiastical students depended on this establishment.[25] Such was the position, more or less, when Daniel Delany arrived in 1763. Where he studied is not clear, probably at one or more of the other city colleges connected with the Sorbonne. A register of St. Nicholas du Chardonnet, preserved in the Archives de la Seine[26] indicates that he received diaconate there in 1770. St. Nicholas's had many links with Irish and other foreign students.

In 1768 the Lombard students represented to the king the poor conditions obtaining in their college consisting of:

> Two small buildings, dark and half-crumbling. The 100 students are so tightly packed that they have not a single room for their common exercises, and must take their meals in a damp underground place surrounded by cardboard boxes and exposed to unhealthy and disgusting odours; all which has caused the deaths of several during their Humanity Course and compelled others to abandon their studies completely and return home in the hope of regaining their health.' [27]

There is nothing to indicate with certainty how long Daniel Delany continued on in Paris after ordination. One Brigidine source said he 'was attached to the teaching staff of one of the great Colleges in Paris'.[28] Another places him at St. Omer.[29] A third quotes him as claiming to have been the only person who could make the grave and learned Dr. Alban Butler laugh and that he had read the latter's 'Lives of the saints' in manuscript form.[30]

Home Again

About 1777 Daniel Delany returned to Ireland, as quietly and as secretly as he had left fourteen years earlier since his legal standing as a papist and as a priest educated abroad was open to question.[31]

Whatever may be said of the joy of his mother and aunts on his return, and it must have been great, it is apparent that he again faced something of a culture-shock. The sandbank chapel would be in utter contrast to the cathedrals, churches and college oratories of France, the secretive ritual of the Mass house could do little to raise heart or mind to Heaven by comparison with the feastday processions of 'sixty encensers, sixty flower-throwers, one hundred copes, ... the music of the French National Guard, .. and each (cleric) bearing a lighted candle'.[32a] There were also the effects of two hundred years of social and political intolerance. Catholics suffered under Penal Laws; Protestants resented restrictions on trade. Despairing of justice, each formed secret societies to fight the system and each other.[32b] A contemporary account by a Queen's County landlord describes the plight of the people as deplorable in the extreme because of restrictive and tyrannical leases, abuse of the tithe system and landlord absenteeism. Of housing conditions it says:

> As to the houses of the people... few deserve to be classed better than hovels. The hogs of England have more comfortable dwellings than the majority of the Irish peasantry. In many cases the whole stock of domestic animals and the peasant's family herd together in one miserable shed, with no better roofing than sods or weeds.[33]

In the Ireland of the time three distinct struggles proceeded at once: that of parliament for statutory independence; that of the Catholic Church for freedom of religion; that of the tenant farmer (and the landless labourer) for agrarian justice. The first commenced in mid-century with the 'Patriot Party' of Lucas and Grattan, and by 1782 achieved a temporary success with the Statute of Renunciation. The first stirrings of the second had been felt with the formation of a timid and tentative 'Catholic Committee' in 1757 when Daniel Delany was just ten years old. Progress was slow, Emancipation came in 1829, and the Church Disestablishment Act in 1870. The struggle between landlord and tenant was even more protracted, being carried on into the early twentieth century. In such a maelstrom, where justice too often went to the strong, Fr. Delany decided, after just a month at home, on a return to France. He saw it as a simple matter of his soul's salvation. When told of his intention Elizabeth Delany begged him to remain, at least for her lifetime, saying that it had long been her prayer to have her priest son with her at the end. In the event he yielded and opted for the home mission. The example of his paternal uncle in neighbouring Castletown probably influenced him too. The Rev William Delany was accustomed to say in the face of disillusionment that he had been ordained for the suffering Irish and that he would not turn his back on his vocation.[34] Shortly after taking his decision Fr. Delany contacted Bishop James Keeffe and was asked to assume a curacy in Mountrath. There he rented a small house from a Mr. Hawkesworth, Lord Castlecoote's agent.[35]

Tullow

Fr. Delany's stay at Mountrath can have been but brief since he was curate at Tullow before the end of 1777. The appointment would hardly have excited him. Conditions in south Carlow would not differ greatly from those in the midlands, nor would the people be much more fortunate. In truth, he found 'excessive drinking, faction-fighting, gambling, card-playing and unseemly brawls' to be commonplace occurrences.[36] The town was also a focal point for certain of the Bible Societies, who sought 'to attract the young to their schools, and adults to conventicles where the Church of Rome was slandered, and priests held up to derision and ridicule'.[37] Tullow was a mensal parish, – the bishop living in a secluded spot some three miles from the town, but before Daniel had been two years with him Dr. Keeffe moved to Kildare for one of his many prolonged sojourns there.[38]

Coping with conditions as best he might, Fr. Delany tried sermons, house to house visitation, personal intervention and every means open to a young priest in his position. Personal taste and foreign training rendered much of his work repugnant and he might have given up many times, before he began to see something of the cause, at least the root cause, of the evils which repelled him. The degraded state of his people, as of Catholics elsewhere, and of many of the poorer Protestants, he came to attribute to mass ignorance. Much of the poverty, prejudice, violence and vice which prevailed across parish and country, prevailed because neither perpetrator nor victim knew better.

Penal enactments forbade Catholics to keep schools, or to teach anyone any species of literature or science under pain of banishment. To return from banishment was to court the gallows.[39] Only Protestant schools were permitted, many of which, maintained by Bible Societies, were proselytizing institutions. Here, almost unknown to him, Daniel's main concerns came together. Degradation, violence and vice were about him every day, but most of all on Sundays. Profanation of the Lord's Day 'tortured his soul' and nothing he could do seemed to have effect.[40] Change iniquitous laws he could not, improve public morality he seemed unable to do, but he could influence the minds of some, and this, he began to do when he drew a few children about him to sing. He had done this in boyhood, and did it now for the same reason, a love of music and song.[41] What began as a leisure-time occupation for Sundays and an attempt to keep some children out of the reach of evil on the holy day, grew as more and more began to attend 'till they flocked to him in crowds'.[42] From hymn-singing it was a natural progression to prayer and religious instruction. The more gifted he taught to play whistle or flute; and from these emerged a band of sorts, further enlivening proceedings. As helpers were found, the work developed; classes grew, and the beginnings of a 'Sunday School' system took shape in his ramshackle parish chapel behind Mill Street.

Music and singing, hitherto impossible in the suppressed state of Catholicism, attracted others to chapel: 'Young men and women, and even some of the older generation, wanted a share in the Sunday Instruction'.[43] Classes were provided for 'those of more mature age and for married persons'[44] and as the demand grew, more helpers had to be trained. Gradually 'the profane amusements had been abandoned by many, Sunday was spent in an edifying manner and the whole face of the parish was changed'.[45]

It is probably well to insert here an account of the form *the* 'Sunday Schools' came to take, as described by Brigidine sources:

> At an early hour every Sunday crowds wound their way to the Parish Chapel. At a given signal they knelt and sang 'O Salutaris Hostia', and then 'Veni Creator' for light and grace. Standing they sang the hymn of the season (in English) and this was followed by Morning Prayer which all recited together aloud. A reflection from Challoner's 'Meditations' followed until an hour had been spent thus. Instruction in classes followed until noon when Mass was offered. At 2 p.m. classes were resumed, and at 4 p.m. all sang Vespers together before returning home.[46]

Bishop

In 1783 Richard O'Reilly, who had been co-adjutor to Bishop Keeffe from 1781, was translated to Armagh, and Daniel Delany was appointed to succeed him in Kildare & Leighlin.[47] Consecration followed on Sunday, 31 August 1783, in Tullow parish chapel. This new responsibility weighed heavily, particularly as the diocese was extensive and the bishop was over eighty years of age. Not that Dr. Keeffe contemplated immediate retirement. He was, in fact, seeking a site for a diocesan college, and when he had found one at Carlow he moved his residence there.[48] A lease was secured in 1786 and building work had begun before his death in September 1787. Daniel continued to live at Tullow, (at a spot still known as 'Bishop's Cross'), and his succession to the diocese was confirmed early in 1788.[49] We should now, perhaps, survey his episcopate under specific headings, rather than hold to any chronological approach with its many intertwining (and possibly confusing) strands. Let us begin with the diocese.

Kildare & Leighlin was a large diocese covering much of the midlands and south-east of the country, with a predominantly rural economy and no really large towns. Covering parts of seven counties it had 43 parishes from two to six, eight, or more unions.[50] In the late eighteenth century travel was slow, difficult and often dangerous. A Roman Catholic bishop would have more than the ordinary perils of the highway to fear, religious intolerance, the extreme poverty of his clergy and people, misunderstanding of his mission or actions, the moral, spiritual and temporal problems of a far-flung flock to whom he was often a stranger. Everywhere were savage laws, inequality, discrimination, crass ignorance, brutal violence, poverty, drunkenness, clergy in terror of their lives – often from those of their own religious persuasion, – chapels nailed up, and a wretchedness almost unparalleled in Europe. Daniel describes one day's journey when he had been visiting 'seven or eight parishes in: Kildare and King's and Queen's Counties':

> From about 11 in the forenoon, a hungry, harassed and joyless November ride of about 30 miles without the smallest refreshment or company.[51]

One of his closest disciples was Judith Wogan Browne of Clongowes Wood who actually moved to Tullow so as to avail more readily of his spiritual direction. She describes him as 'going through the diocese to put down faction-fighting, pointing to the sinfulness and barbarity of such behaviour'. She adds that in this 'he took people quietly, went to homes to enlist wives and mothers on his side. He dreaded assemblages, people were too excitable, the greater number having had very little religious training, and no secular teaching'.[52] He would himself declare that no hard word should be directed against the people in their excesses, due largely to their lack of education. He grievously felt his people's need and his own inability to respond adequately. In a sermon he said:

> Straitened as I am in time, and distracted by a variety of objects crowding in on me, each contending, eagerly demanding preference, by which I am beset, overwhelmed, as I stand before you in the present peculiarly trying and arduous moment.[53]

In his work he had need of all his endurance, of his spiritual resources, and of the experience of better things which he had gained in France. On this last point, it is perhaps worth noting what Lecky has to say of Irish clergy educated overseas:

> They possessed a foreign culture and a foreign grace which did much to embellish Irish life ... They came to their ministry at a mature age and with a real and varied knowledge of the world ... They had the manners of cultivated gentlemen, and a high sense of clerical decorum.[54]

Though gifted with humour, Daniel Delany could be diffuse and tedious in his sermons and letters. In conversation he was brilliant and engaging, more formal communications found him using an involved and prolix style. The sermon extract quoted above may serve as an example. In writing he piled image upon image, so that it is sometimes difficult to follow him. Writing for his Brigidines he derides his own document as 'diffusely prolix and minutely detailed'. Even that self-criticism might have been more simply couched.

Other Clergy

Daniel Delany's feeling for his clergy emerges in an early report to Government in which he makes special allusion to three parishes:

> In Edenderry the parish priest is very old and quite blind. At Philipstown ... besides his old age, the parish priest is rendered utterly incapable, by his infirmity, of assisting in his chapel. The parish priest of Kill, a poor lame old man turned of 90 years, would need a second assistant, were there means to support him.[55]

In November 1788 he received a rather pompous letter from Lord Aldborough declaring:

> I, some time since, troubled you with my sentiments respecting the late Parish Priest of ..., and that I thought his requisition of a trial but just, fair and reasonable, to which I received no answer. I have since received a letter from him. .. On finding substantialer [sic] justice from you than he did from Dr. Keeffe, who degraded him 'sine foro et strepitu'.[56]

Writing again that month, to Archbishop Troy, Delany alludes to the correspondent and says:

> A pleasant fellow this said Earl appears from ye complexion of the winding up of his letter, notwithstanding ye formidable mien our doughty hero affects to exhibit in ye commencement. Like the scorpion, there is a cure in the tail for the bite in the head.[57]

Two letters to Archbishop Bray, newly appointed to Cashel, show a fund of goodwill towards the recipient and a prayerful affection for his brother bishops. In the second, written from Portarlington on 12 Oct 1792 he assures his friend 'I most certainly shall not fail (to attend) in spirit at Thurles next Sunday', and goes on to send good wishes to 'Drs Egan, Moylan, Teehan and Coppinger, 'with best respects also to Dr. McMahon and to their Lagenian Lordships'.[58a] In a postscript he offers apologies for the use of black sealing wax, adding that the family he is with, are in mourning.[58b]

Soon after becoming bishop he had adopted Mountrath as a mensal parish, but a clergy conference which he attended there on 12 March 1793 had to be abandoned when the house was invaded by Orange Yeomanry on the pretext that the assembly was plotting treachery.[59] Later he had to withdraw catechists from the town because of danger from the same source. In 1805 he sent his friend, the Rev. Thady Dunne, there as administrator, but three years later the priest was forced to flee in his night attire from an Orange mob. Failing to find other shelter he took refuge under a bridge. The cold and wetting he endured there, and possibly the terror he experienced, brought on a fatal illness.[60] In a letter of 18 Nov 1808 to his friend Bishop Moylan in Cork Daniel wrote that an official at Dublin Castle was disposed 'not to let this outrage go unpunished, or at least to prevent a repetition of similar atrocities'. In the same letter he deplores a difference at Kilkenny, where 'all the great or respectable Catholics, as they denominate themselves, forsooth, are pitted against Dr. Lanigan, his clergy, etc., the little ones in the Lord. Violent attacks on the bishop in the Kilkenny Paper. Aye, aye, newspaper, newspaper, the tribunal of the public!'[61]

The next Administrator at Mountrath, Rev. M. P. Malone begged after a few years to be relieved of the parish. Writing on 19 March 1813 the bishop told him:

> I am very glad you have determined on coming down yourself as matters can be treated of with infinitely more satisfaction in a personal interview than by letter, in deciding on a business of this nature. I am engaged to attend precisely on the day [you suggest] at a Month's Mind in the parish of Graigue, Carlow. You will be sure to meet me there, and this will curtail your journey by eleven miles, [and] I shall have an opportunity of stating fully and distinctly to you all matters that may enable us to come to a final determination touching the vacant parish; which shall, I need not add, remain in *'statu quo'* till I have the pleasure of seeing you. I feel much obliged for your kind expressions of acknowledgement &c., &c., of my dispositions in your regard...[62]

To the above was added minute directions on how to locate the house at which the bishop might be found in that area. The result of the interview may, perhaps, be surmised from the fact that Fr. Malone remained at Mountrath until his death in 1835. Attendance at that month's mind in Graigue may well have been the last pastoral visit Daniel Delany was able to make. He died the next year.

Blessed Sacrament Confraternity

One of Daniel Delany's first acts as co-adjutor bishop was the establishment of the Confraternity of the Blessed Sacrament at Tullow. That was in 1783.[63] He saw the Confraternity as a means of spiritual formation, and was exact on admissions, accepting only those who were well instructed in the meaning and aims of the devotion.[64] In 1784 he surprised everyone, and horrified many, by announcing a public procession through the town for the feast of Corpus Christi.[65] No such display of 'Popery' had been seen there for at least a century. Would this 'unnecessary provocation' be tolerated? If asked, Daniel would have said that honour should be paid to the lord in public and in private. On the day he carried the monstrance, many came only to watch. Yet there was no interference from magistrates or from hostile mobs, or any untoward incident, despite the assembled crowds.

The next decision was the ringing of the angelus bell, something which caused Bishop Keeffe to exclaim that 'that young hothead will get us all into trouble'.[66] The procession became an annual event thereafter and 'people came from far and near to see and to take part'.[67] Soon the celebration had been extended to eight whole days, with continuous exposition of the blessed sacrament in the chapel, and three processions, one on the feast, another on the Sunday, a third on the octave day. The Confraternity provided adorers, the women taking the daylight hours and the men the nights.[68] Daniel recommended his 'intentions' to the prayers of the worshippers, and in after years would have Exposition whenever a major problem presented itself. No matter what business engaged him, he was never absent from Tullow at Corpus Christi. When he had a convent, he laid out the grounds with an eye to facilitating the procession, and erected there, first 'a station' and later a temple for benediction. Clergy and lay people came from 'distant parts, even from England' for these occasions[69] and a description of one Procession mentions

> the delight of the old people ... who remembered the time when a bishop or priest who dared to perform any function of his sacred office in public would risk the most severe penalties.[70]

Between 1784 and 1797 the processional route was from the chapel at Mill St. to Bishop's Cross and back,[71] about a mile-and-a-half each way. In 1798 and for some years thereafter the processions were not held, but were resumed from 1805 when the new church had become available.[72] Only a few weeks before his death in 1814 Daniel rose from his sick bed to carry the host for the last time in public.[73]

When he had established the Confraternity at Mountrath, he also introduced the Corpus Christi celebrations there. It is worth noting that Tullow and Mountrath were the only parishes in the diocese to have the Confraternity, though of course the processions gradually became widespread. Both exposition and procession were huge innovations at a time when religious intolerance was rife, and when reservation of the blessed sacrament in Catholic churches was unknown in Ireland. From among the members of the Blessed Sacrament Confraternity Daniel Delany later drew the teachers and religious he needed.

Christian Doctrine Confraternity

When he first began his Sunday Schools Fr. Delany was the sole instructor, but as volunteers appeared and helpers were recruited he saw the need to organise and train, all the more as adults began to come for instruction.[74] Neither was it overlong before the difficulty of maintaining a supply of teachers was borne in upon him, 'some grew tired of the labour entailed by frequent attendance.... When the novelty wore off and early zeal declined, the number of helpers grew less.'[75] He came to believe in the spiritual formation attaching to membership of the Blessed Sacrament Confraternity, and began to select his teachers from it, forming first a Sodality of Christian Doctrine which he trained and instructed himself. In 1788 he associated this group with the Church-wide 'Confraternity of Christian Doctrine', and through Archbishop Troy applied to Rome for the grant of the usual indulgences. In writing to thank the archbishop for his aid, he asked:

> What is the meaning of 'piorum hominum' in [the formula of] the Indulgence? Females are not, surely, thereby excluded? They have certainly been characterized as 'the devout sex'; and would be found to come forward with ten times more ardent zeal and true piety in promoting this most excellent Institution, than the men. Besides – how commit the instruction of girls to male catechists or teachers? But my grammar should remind me that 'homo' is of ye common of two genders...[76]

A scrap of paper in the bishop's hand and dated 'Holy Innocents 1790' describes the objects and operation of the work in Tullow. It was

> lately established ... to promote the Kingdom of Our Lord Jesus, and to spread the saving knowledge of His Adorable Name among the lowest and most abandoned of our poor people..., facilitating the mode of instructing the ignorant and forlorn ... in principles of Religion'. Instruction was to be given, not in the catechism alone, but in the reformation of 'vicious manners and corrupt habits', going on to assist in 'advancing to Christian justice,

471

the science of the saints and habits of Gospel virtue'.[77]

The Confraternity members were also to assist and direct their families and neighbours 'according to their opportunities and abilities as far as evangelical prudence, enlightened charity and discreet, well-regulated zeal' deemed it prudent or necessary.[78]

The Sunday Instruction was given in the chapel, with two teachers for each of the many schools, so as to 'relieve each other, and to supply for absence when necessary'. This system also allowed for the disengaged teachers to receive instruction 'according to their specific religious knowledge or perfection of life'.[79] The general roll of learners and teachers was to be called by the president twice in the day, and 'all absences to be accounted for'. In addition there was provision to have 'the illiterate or wholly unlearned taught the use of letters, so far as may qualify them for reading the Catechism, Prayer Book or other pious productions'.[80] Perhaps the thing most worthy of notice in all this is the desire to foster ongoing spiritual advancement.

Children, once they knew their prayers and catechism, were classed into 'small schools' to prepare for first communion. Daniel always presented a prayer book to each first communicant with the child's name and the appropriate date entered on it.[81] All who had been confirmed were admitted to 'Reading Schools', specially designed for the Blessed Sacrament Confraternity, or for the teachers who had been selected from that Confraternity.[82] In time a circulating library was added.[83] In all, there were four divisions of instruction, with a president and vice-president at the head of each,[84] and in every Division a number of schools, each provided with two teachers.[85]

Later, the Sunday instruction was also made available on week-days, in evening schools, and even in home instruction for those unable to come to church.[86] This last was to cater for those house-bound by illness or age, and for those who did not possess the clothes which would permit them to appear in town.

The crux of the system was to provide the number and quality of teachers needed. The system was voluntary, the work unpaid, the duties far from light. Daniel was to lament in later years that though he had personally trained 'an almost infinite number' the greater part 'did not long continue. Some married, others died or left the parish, many fell away'.[87] Again, all this was to provide religious instruction and the ability to read, but there was need for secular instruction also, for which the majority could not pay.

Catechists at Mountrath

Despite the difficulty of maintaining a supply of teachers the bishop wished to extend the Sunday instruction scheme to Mountrath which he had taken as a mensal parish soon after his succession to the diocese. This last step may have been the result of necessity as much as of any feeling of *pietas'* for the place where his boyhood had been spent. The parish was in a sad state, riven by political and religious divisions, torn by prejudice, a hotbed of hatred and violence.[88] In 1792 he sent six of his women catechists there from Tullow, having rented a cottage for them in the town.[89]

It was a bold, almost a foolhardy step, taken as the result of long consideration and much prayer[90] and an account of the results survives from Daniel's own pen:

> A dozen priests would scarcely suffice to hear, between now and Easter, the General Confessions which these six poor Mistresses have, under Heaven, been the cause of, since they went up there. And that in a place where as many clergymen, assembled by me not long since, to give a General Station, would not have as many penitents as one priest could with ease dispatch. Nor was there ever such thorough and universal reformation brought about in any parish, at least to my knowledge, in so many years as they have spent months in that town. A very regular and proper clergyman told me, before they went up, that he absolutely despaired of ever seeing the people do any good. And yet they now attend thrice a week [adults for the most part] in such numbers and with such a hunger for Instruction. And on Sundays the chapel was never more crowded by scholars of every denomination. Indeed, the Day of the Lord's Visitation seems to have approached that people on whom, young and old, He is pouring out His Spirit most abundantly. The priests contend that they [the girl-teachers] are a soul-saving supernatural power, such wondrous effects have their humble but zealous and persevering exertions produced.[91]

In the mysterious way of God 'tragedy' intervened, as the letter goes on to explain, and one of the girl catechists, Mary Dawson, died suddenly. The bishop had her body brought back to Tullow and interred in the chapel there, 'her favourite dwelling while alive'. That was merely the first 'tragedy'. Soon afterwards, before the catechists had been nine months in Mountrath, the remaining five (none of their names are known to us) had to be withdrawn for fear of Orange hostility to their work.[92]

Carlow College

Though begun by his predecessor the work of completing Carlow

College devolved upon Daniel Delany. Intended for the education of laymen and clerics many delays prevented its opening, even when ready for occupation. During this period an Englishman wrote of it that it was an institution of national importance, observing that:

> It is natural that Catholics should wish to give their children the advantages of a liberal education, and it is impolitic, unjust and cruel to drive them to the expedient of seeking it abroad. An evil like this cannot be speedily remedied, and the man who made the first essay towards checking it merits the thanks of the Legislature. The person I allude to is Dr. Delany, than whom no man can be more enlightened or humane, a man of exemplary piety whose character truly resembles the disinterestedness of the primitive Christian fathers.[93]

Carlow might, with hindsight, be seen as the offspring and successor to the Irish Lombard College at Paris, since its opening in October 1793 followed closely on the confiscation by the Revolution of the last vestige of that institution – its seminary on the Rue du Cheval Vert.

Carlow's original purpose, however, was to respond to the need occasioned by the non-return of some priests ordained abroad for Ireland. The difficulty involved in a secret return to an unattractive mission, the allure of French conditions, and the opportunity for academic advancement combined to reduce greatly the number who returned to Ireland after ordination. Bishop Conway of Derry, writing to his counterpart in Kilfenora, remarked that in forty years he had not known 'a parish priest or missionary, either in Derry or in five or six neighbouring dioceses,' who had begun in Paris as an unordained student. Dr O'Gara of Tuam stated that only three such had come to his diocese in 27 years.[94] The Rev. Philip Rouse, parish priest of Kildare, established in 1780 a burse at Paris, but with the stipulation that if after three years' study the holder decided against ordination for the home-diocese, he forfeited his claim.[95]

Daniel Delany is quoted as declaring that Carlow College had been planned 'many years prior to the destruction of our Irish Colleges on the Continent, long before the most distant surmise of their impending ruin', and that its founders preferred 'a comparatively expensive domestic education to a foreign, though gratuitous, one'.[96]

Carlow's first president was its co-founder, Dean Henry Staunton. There were six professors, of whom three were French emigrés, and who remained until the French Concordat of 1801 with Pius VII. The opening of Maynooth in 1795 was a grievous blow since the latter enjoyed a state grant, while Carlow depended almost entirely on the fees of its students. In a letter to Lord Castlereagh in 1800 Bishop Delany describes the college as 'a large handsome edifice, 120 ft. long, consisting of four floors above the surface' and appeals for financial assistance (which was not forthcoming). He also mentions the application made to him personally by a well-to-do farmer to name his son to a (free) place in Maynooth, (Carlow College's 'younger but highly favoured sister') and adds: 'Needless to say, his prayer was rejected with indignation'.[97]

A New Direction

The impracticality of depending entirely on volunteer helpers for the work of his Christian Doctrine Confraternity, and the need to extend that work, convinced Bishop Delany of the necessity for a group which would be both a leaven of sanctification in the parish and a force committed to the education of its people.[98] He needed assistants who would devote their lives to the work already begun.[99] Naturally, his mind turned to a Congregation of Teaching Sisters, especially as such a group had recently been established in the diocese of his friend Bishop Moylan. Inquiries brought an invitation to go to Cork and see the work for himself.[100] However, at Nago Nagle's South Presentation Convent he was told that a lack of numbers must preclude all expansion for some time. A second difficulty was that he also envisaged both pay and boarding schools, while the sisters there felt that their apostolate was to the children of the poor exclusively.[101]

Vividly aware of the good done by his catechists, and knowing that among them there were others like Mary Dawson, mystics who wished to consecrate their lives to God in a religious state, 'he decided to provide for them, to begin, and trust that God would find others to continue the work'.[102] He first proposed to provide convents at Tullow and Mountrath, and to begin in whichever place a long lease might be had.[103] The need for new churches in both parishes, intolerance, the Rebellion of 1798 and its aftermath delayed his plans until, acting on a verbal promise, he had actually built a church at Tullow and begun work on a small convent beside it.[104] All this was ventured after endless prayer, many expositions, novenas and processions, each directed to the seeking of guidance.[105] Then on 1 February 1807 he established six women in the little house he had built and called them the Sisters of St. Brigid.[106] It is to be noted that he named this foundation from the patroness of his own diocese, and there is other evidence to indicate that he saw his little group as a revival of the Brígídine first established at Kildare. One year later, on 2 February 1808, he brought together four of his male catechists and established them as the Society of St. Patrick; giving them the old penal day chapel as a residence. In April 1809 he sent some of his women religious to Mountrath, and the following year three of his 'monks'. He had made a beginning.

None of the pioneer religious was in a position to offer financial assistance towards these projects, and none had more than a modicum of education.[107] They did share their founder's simplicity of heart; and thus equipped, faced a very uncertain future with a faith which was soon to be tried in many ways. Daniel Delany was himself already 60 years of age, and for him time was running out. His health soon failed and he died in 1814; but after two hundred years his congregations still work in ten lands spread over four continents.

Church Building

After the completion of Carlow College Bishop Delany moved to replace the sand-bank chapel at Mountrath. Because of Lord Castlecoote's policy, acquisition of a site seemed hopeless, but Mrs Hawkesworth, wife of the estate agent, prevailed on her husband to give a plot in his own possession,[108] and so work could commence about 1795. The people 'amazed at the extensive dimensions of the new building .... came to call it 'Delany's Folly'.[109] Orange hostility to the work manifested itself in threats to the masons, but a Fr. Dunne, then serving in the parish, defied opposition, worked on the building himself and, it is said, accompanied the carters 'armed with a stout blackthorn to repel aggressive Orangemen'.[110] By about 1800 the parish had a new cruciform church with three galleries.[111] An inscribed chalice, which Daniel had presented to the old chapel was transferred to the new, and has remained among the church plate ever since.

From about 1792 attempts were made to acquire a site at Tullow, and the bishop discussed the question with the landlord at the latter's home in Wexford. His account of the interview, written to Dr. Troy, shows his disappointment:

> I took down the leases at his own instance, and had no doubt of getting a long time on the terms agreed on four years ago. He received me ... very well, but most peremptorily told me that for a lease of 100 years he would expect – I know not what extraordinary rent, for he would not specify it, ... but he would make the most of it..., not in reference to situation or extent.., but with a view to our wants. He would have the place valued... and so let us bid accordingly. Here are our Protestant brethren for you.[112]

A few years later Daniel described the Tullow chapel:

> A ground rent of £10. 4s. 6d. is paid for the town chapel, actually

for the most part reduced to a heap of ruin, without our being able to obtain a lease to rebuild the same.[113]

About 1800 he again tried to negotiate a lease, but a verbal promise was the best he could secure. On the strength of this, he marked out foundations, began to build, and by 1805 had completed a simple cruciform building[114] from which he resumed the Corpus Christi processions. It was not until 1814, shortly before his death, that he secured the long lease he desired.[115]

Slowly, Dr. Delany succeeded in obtaining leases from landlords throughout the diocese, and even the use of woods and quarries, for the building of churches and schools. It was said of him that he drew out the best in Protestants, and that they never refused anything he asked of them.[116]

The Political Scene

Catholics and Presbyterians alike felt themselves aggrieved by Chief Secretary Orde's proposals for the revival of the plan for parish schools mooted in 1787. Shortly after, Bishop Delany wrote to Archbishop Troy that the idea was

> a most sinister, invidious and illiberal business, an inhuman and impious scheme, [whose] primary, if not sole, aim is the utter extirpation of our holy religion. Philanthropy forsooth! What egregious fudge, what nauseating stuff, what provoking nonsense!.[117]

In the same letter, he declared that he had already written to seven influential centres in his diocese stressing the dangers of Orde's plan, and urging that the 'wolf be kept from the door'. Strong action from a man providing some 80 teachers for his own Sunday instruction classes, and from one who eschewed politics as much as might be, believing himself short-sighted in such matters.[118]

Neither did he much approve of Catholics participating in the Volunteer movement, seeing the ensuing intermingling of politics and religion as 'leading to Latitudinarianism', since emulation in patriotic ardour would be quickly succeeded by 'transports of religious enthusiasm'; and since the offering of joint vows at the one shrine of liberty led 'by easy transition to joint action in the religious domain'. He was particularly pained that a Volunteer Assembly had not found 'another school than a Presbyterian Meeting-House to resort to for [religious] instruction'; and he protested that recently:

Whole bodies of Catholics marched in open day in ye metropolis to places where, a few years since, the strong arm of the law had been employed in vain to drag ye weakest member of ye Corps, publicly boasting on their return.. of their resolution to profit again by such wholesome instruction, in spite of .. an ignorant and tyrannical priesthood; proclaiming indifference to religious distinctions [as] the only true criterion of benevolent, superior, and open minds'.[119]

Neither could he have been enthusiastic for the mingling of religious denominations in the Society of United Irishmen, even if that body had remained strictly constitutional and had not so assiduously espoused the ideals of the French Revolution.

In the Queen's County, Protestant and Papist were said to be more inveterately divided than in any other place. 'Gentlemen wore Orange ribbons, and some barristers sported Orange rings with emblems; ensigns of enmity, not conducive to conciliation'.[120] By the late seventeen-nineties Dublin Castle had decided that an armed rebellion was to be provoked; it courted the Catholic Bishops and other conservatives hostile to 'French ideas'; it granted an endowed seminary at Maynooth in 1795, and held out prospects of the removal of penal disabilities in return for support. When the armed uprising came, it was fragmentary and ill-prepared, and the south-east of the country suffered heavily. The counties of Wexford, Wicklow, Carlow and Kildare were 'deluged with the blood of their people'.[121] Bishop Caulfield of Ferns added a postscript to a letter sent to Archbishop Troy in late summer 1798:

Only this moment a letter from my ever-dear brother at Tullow. I had been told by one of the Carlow students that he was in a miserable way, his chapel filled with soldiers and horses, himself insulted, and could not venture home, but remained in town with Miss Browne, and was much emaciated. However, he writes in good spirits, has his chapel free now. The Yeomanry in that quarter had killed at least one hundred of the United wretches the Wednesday and Thursday before.[122]

The Brigidines have always held a tradition that Father John Murphy made his way to Bishop Delany the night before his capture near Tullow.[123a] The little chapel at Ardattin was burned by the Yeomanry, and the bishop's man-servant was arrested and sent to a Dublin prison.[123b] In the aftermath of the Rebellion, Daniel travelled much through the diocese, quietly exhorting his people to patience and the avoidance of secret societies.[124] A story told of him may illustrate his understanding of the times. He is said to have been asked during the early eighteen-hundreds at a dinner at the Curragh to account for the origin of the pike used by the rebels. His reply was succinct: 'Government, sirs, supplied the material, the Orangemen blew the fire, and the smiths forged them'.[125]

In 1799 Castlereagh availed of a meeting of the Maynooth trustees to sound out the church on the possibility of giving the king a voice in the nomination of Irish bishops. This had already been rejected in 1795, at the time of the Maynooth grant, and was renewed now that the morale of Irish Catholics was at a particularly low ebb. On 17 January 1799 the three archbishops and seven bishops who were trustees, gave it as *their* opinion that the king might justly be given the right to satisfy himself of the loyalty of any appointee to a see. In their reply they also sought to safeguard church discipline, to limit the extent of government interference, and stressed that no agreement could be reached without the prior sanction of the Holy See. Had they rejected the idea out of hand, they would have left the entire Catholic body open to a charge of disloyalty. Unfortunately, none of these facts prevented the question from being angrily debated for years afterwards, with much distrust on both sides and much abuse of all bishops. The dispute became particularly sharp with the involvement of English Catholics, who were more prepared to allow a measure of influence to the crown. When in 1808 some influential advocates of Catholic rights, made concrete proposals for a form of veto, the Irish bishops officially protested. At that time a visitor raised the matter of an 'Address' with Daniel Delany, who (as he said himself):

> Immediately started back, as if from a serpent, vehemently protesting against any measure calculated to censure the reverse decision of the bishops at their late meeting.[126]

In the same letter Daniel condemns 'this audacious innovation of the Laity, great or small, profanely intermeddling with the Divine Constitution of the hierarchy', and goes on to deride the idea of a voice for the Crown. He writes:

> Had the Veto passed, I did indeed apprehend that as Salic Law excluding females from dynastic succession is not applied in Britain, the Church might on a future day be again subject to the Pettycoat Government of a Pope Joan; but little did I dream of seeing one start up here at home.[127]

The letter concludes with an expression of confidence in the 'preponderancy of the Body of Bishops, and the great mass of the truly orthodox faithful' who were, he believed, 'all to a man, at least in the humble sphere of life, on our side'.

A question of discipline in the English Catholic Church resulted in the Irish Bishops meeting in synod at Tullow on 9 June 1809. L'Abbé Blanchard, a French emigré, had called in question the Concordat reached with Napoleon in 1801, and, when condemned by the English vicars apostolic, had appealed over their heads to the Irish bishops, declaring that he would take silence as approval of his stance. Eighteen bishops attended the Synod of Tullow[128] where they refused to entertain the appeal, affirmed allegiance to Pius VII, and condemned eleven of Blanchard's theses. Eleven other prelates also approved the synod's statement.[129]

By 1809 Daniel Delany had firmly decided against all further involvement in the political scene. The spiritual warfare in which he was engaged could not, he affirmed, be advanced by such means. To Dr. Moylan of Cork he wrote in December, 1809:

> To the deuce with these secular manoeuvres .. The Kingdom of our Master is not of this world. Away with Politics, with Committees, .. with Conventions and Addresses and Petitions, and the plague-knows-what Applications and diplomatic negotiations at ye seat of Empire, with in-or-out Ministers and Professional Speechifiers. The trials of Bishops, Archbishops, and PRIMATES are in future, it seems, to be adjudicated on, and disposed of here, at the Bar of a Gifford, or some orthodox Editor of an Orange Journal. Bravo! Talk of the once-boasted liberties of the Gallican Church.

He then goes on to tell of an approach made to him in the matter of an address:

> I entered an earnest protest against signing the proposed Resolution of Thanks, against putting my name in future to any papers of a similar nature, or to any Petition, or any Application whatsoever. To which the Manager replied that it was not expected that I would sign it, but they hoped that I would have no objection in a general way to ye measure of returning thanks. In short the object of [their] application to me seemed to be merely to engage me NOT to give a veto, which I accordingly withheld. You see to what a pass we are brought by our Politics, our Petitions, our Addresses, our Conventions, our Aggregate Meetings, our Parliamentary Negotiations, our Boards, our Secular

Discussions, our Emancipations and the deuce-knows-what. Good heaven, where will it end, or whither lead us?[130]

In 1813, as infirmity increased, Daniel was induced to take up residence in Tullow convent where he was given a room overlooking the chapel, into which a small door leading into a balcony was opened for him. He left the convent for the Corpus Christi procession in 1814, and died in the convent on 9 July of the same year. A century later, two papers addressed to '*RT. REV D. DELANY, C.B.*' were found in a small wall-cupboard in the convent; one, an uncut copy of Plowden's *Historical letter to Columbanus* (1812); the other, an unopened propaganda leaflet on the veto question: two 'burning issues', which had aroused no answering spark in a bishop with more lasting things on his mind.

Appreciation

On 18 March 1783 James Keeffe took up his pen to explain to Propaganda, (which three years before had given him a guardian instead of a co-adjutor) why he wanted Daniel Delany as his assistant in the diocese. He urged as reasons for his choice:

> His blameless life and pastoral vigilance. Almost every Sunday and feastday he has preached to great effect and with such distinction that even Protestants have flocked to hear him. He formed a choir of 30 boys who assisted him constantly in singing Solemn Mass and Vespers. Three days each week he gave Catechetical Instruction in his own church. He is humbly pious, and adorned with all the Virtues which the Apostle requires in a bishop.[131]

Nearly 30 years later, James Warren Doyle, who had come to the see five years after Daniel Delany's death, wrote of him:

> He rendered virtue attractive and vice abhorrent. This bishop laboured unceasingly to rebuild chapels, to increase the number of clergy, to promote Instruction by means of Schools, Confraternities and the Circulation of useful Books. He built and endowed two Convents of Nuns and laid the foundations of two Monasteries of Men, which he partially endowed. His labours were unceasing.[132]

These are weighty tributes, paid by two outstanding bishops. When foresight and hindsight are in agreement it is likely that the judgement may be relied on.

Plate 16.2   An aerial photo of the house (with the porch) where Dr. Delany lived for three years before he moved to Tullow Convent in 1813. It was then taken over by Masseys (of Massey Ferguson fame); Dr. Kidd came next and his grand-children then Centons. The present owner is Mrs. Agar.

Many have described Daniel Delany as an idealist. He was that, and much more, for he was someone who took God at his word, at the Word which became flesh, and he ventured to make his own flesh available for 'those things which have yet to be undergone for .., .. the Church' [Col 1:24]. From where did he get such faith? Brought up by mother and aunts in extraordinarily difficult times he learned that 'there is no cheap faith', but learned also how to be generous. His early teaching and his studies abroad taught him piety, his pastoral work formed him in the furnace of affliction; schooled him to feel for, and with, his neighbour; his experience of God's leading taught him the paradox of a success gained through the cross. He found others who believed in him, supported him, shared and suffered with him, and by their example led him to God. In his daily prayer he found God Himself; and going out from there, he discovered God again in his neighbour. His native abilities and his youthful formation indicated to him certain root causes of the evils which bedevilled his times, and he concentrated on doing what he could, where he was, to improve things. Where wrong-doers lacked opportunity for knowing better, he did not know how to condemn. In that he was extraordinarily like his God.

The 'Returns' made by Dr. Doyle to the Commissioners of Education Inquiry, 1824, indicate that ten years after Daniel Delany's death more than eleven hundred people were receiving instruction from 129 teachers in Tullow parish church every Sunday.[133] That alone was no small thing, yet it represented only one visible aspect of his legacy. People have wondered how he can have remained so little known, almost forgotten, one of whom James Doyle could say in 1813:

> I have seldom seen a figure so striking. I listened to him for about an hour, left him with regret, and did not cease to think of him all the way home.

Daniel Delany, however, would not have us centre on himself. Rather, with Moses, his message would be 'Would that all the Lord's people were prophets' [Num 11:29].

THAT, I believe, remains his legacy.

Brígídine Sources
1. J. O'Donovan (ed.), [G. Ó hUidhrín and S. Ó Dubhagáin] 'Tribes and territories of ancient Ossory' in *Kilkenny Archaeological and Celtic Society Trans* (1950-51), p. 51. See also O'Hanlon Queen's County, i, p. 1
2. O'Byrne, *History of The Queen's County* (Dublin, 1856), p. 122

3. O'Hanlon, *Queen's County,* i, p. 57

4. M. J. Brenan, *Ecclesiastical history of Ireland* (Dublin, 1864), p. 83

5. Carrigan, *Ossory,* i, p. 71

6. Idem.

7. T • II • 12. Brígídine sources are referenced as follows: the initial letter refers to the convent, i.e. T = Tullow; M = Mountrath; G = General; R = Regional; C = Central; the Roman numeral indicates the section; the alphabetical sequence indicates the sub-section (if any); the Arabic number indicates the actual document.

8. W. Shaw-Mason, *Statistical account or parochial survey of Ireland,* i, p. 598. Dublin 1814

9. M • II • B • 2

10. M • II • A • 30

11. M • II • B • 4

12. M • I • D • 7

13. Comerford, *Kildare & Leighlin',* iii, p. 300.

14. M • I • D • 4

15. M • II • B • 3

16. M • I • D • 5

17. M • II • A • 30

18. M • II • B • 4

19. M • I • D • 10

20. M • I • B • 19/20

21. J. Dubreuil, *Le théâtre des antiquités de Paris* – supplement p. 40 (Paris 1639)

22. A.N.P. (Archives Nationales Paris) • M • 147 • II

23. A.N.P. • F19 6237C M• VIII • I • Pìece 1

24. A.N.P. • M • 147 • I

25. A.N.P. F19 6237A • I • 229 Pìece 8

26. A.S.P (Archives de la Seine, Paris) • 38 • D • J

27. A.N.P. • F19 • 6237B. • U

28. G • I • A • 3

29. M • I • B • 19

30. M • I • B • 20, M • II • A • 31

31. M • II • B • 7

32a. R • I • 85

32b. M • II • B • 8

33. Coote, *Queen's County,* p. 53

34a. M • II • B • 8

34b. T • II • 33

35. M • II • B • 8

36. T • VI • Z • 1, G • I • A • 4

37. G • I • A • 4

38. T. McGrath, Unpublished lecture, 'Three Bishops' 1987

39. M • I • B • 10

40. G • I • A • 4, T • V • A • 1, T • VI • Z • 22

41. M • I • B • 23.

42. Ibid.

43. G • I • A • 10

44. C • VI • 7, T • VI • 24

45. T • VI • A • 1, C • VI • 7, T • VI • 25

46. G • I • A • 9, M • II• B • 16, T • VI • 25, C • VI • 6

47. G • I • A • 5
48. T • II • 19
49. Ibid., I, p. 165
50. Comerford, *Kildare and Leighlin,* i, p. 286
51. D.D.A., Troy Correspondence, Delany to Troy, 23 Nov 1788
52. R • I • 118
53. R • I • 204
54. W. Lecky, *History of Ireland in the 18th Century* (London, 1892), four vols., iii, p. 354
55. Comerford, *Kildare and Leighlin,* i, p. 256
56. G • I • B • 6 (Full text)
57. G • I • B • 7 (Full text in G • I • B • 12-14 from D.D.A., Troy Correspondence)
58a. G • I • B • 20
58b. Photostat of full original manuscript in G • I • B • 19a-22a
59. Comerford, *Kildare and Leighlin,* i, p. 301
60. Ibid.
61. G • I • B • 26 Photostat of full original manuscript in G • I • B • 27-30
62. G • I • B • 38 Full text in M. Gibbons, pp 308-9
63. T • II • 23
64. M • I • D • 26, G • I • A • 6
65. T • II •37
66. M • II • B • 20
67. G • I • A • 7
68. M • II • B • 40
69. M • I • B • 44
70. R • I • 89
71. G • I • A
72. C • VI • 21; M • II • E • 11; Troy Correspondence, 14 Nov. 1788/AB2/116/4
73. G • I • A • 8
74. T • VI • A • 2, M • II • B • 15, G • I • A • 10
75. G • I • A • 10
76. D.D.A., Troy Correspondence, 16 Nov 1788
77. Gibbons, pp 146, 149
78. Ibid.
79. Ibid.
80. Ibid.
81. M • II • G • Z • 1
82. M • II • E • 3; T • VI • Z • 6
83. R • I • 151
84. M • II • E • 4
85. M • II • B • 17
86. R • I • 151-152
87. C • VI • 9
88. T • II •38
89. T • II • 29, M • II • E • 4
90. C • VI • 8
91. D.D.A., Troy Letters 1793
92. T • II • 38
93. C. Topham-Bowden, *A tour through Ireland* (Dublin, 1791), pp 96-9
94. R • I • 147, 148

95.   A.N.P. F 17. 14764, I, .9, 1-5
96.   Idem
97.   Marquis of Londonderry (ed.), *Correspondence of Viscount Castlereagh* (London, 1848-53), 12 vols., iv, p. 143
98.   T • VI • A • 4
99.   G • I • A • 10
100. M • II • B •21
101. M • II • B • 22; C • VI • 10; T • VI • A • 4; T • VI • Z • 11
102. C • VI •10, 11
103. M • II • E • 1
104. C • VI • 12, M • I • B • 42
105. G• I • A • 12
106. G • I • A • 11
107. G• I • A • 11, 12
108. C • VI • 13
109. Comerford, *Kildare and Leighlin,* iii, p. 300
110. Ibid, p. 301
111. M • II • B • 14.
112. Comerford, *Kildare and Leighlin,* i, p. 286
113. Idem
114. T • II • 39
115. C • VI • 36
116. M • II • B • 26, M • II • G • 31
117. G • I • B • 4-5
118. G • I • B • 4
119. D.D.A., Undated letter to Troy
120. Quoted in O'Hanlon, *Queen's County,* p. 162
121. M • I • D • 57
122. Moran, Spic. Ossor. (Dublin, 1874-84), iii, p. 566
123a. M • I • E • 3
123b. Ibid.
124. M • II • G • 24
125. R • I • 103
126. Letter to Dr. Moylan, 18 Nov 1808 in Moylan Correspondence, Cork Diocesan Archives, *Kildare and Leighlin,* i, app.
127. Ibid.
128. Full text of the 1809 Synod of Tullow report in Comerford
129. Comerford, ibid., pp 303-6
130. C.D.A., Moylan Correspondence
131. Irlanda 1783-1804, file of Propaganda Archives, Rome
132. M • I • B • 19, 20
133. Returns of 1824 education enquiry are taken from Brenan, *Schools of Kildare and Leighlin,* p. 940

Chapter 17

CAPTAIN ROCK IN THE QUEEN'S COUNTY

STEPHEN RANDOLPH GIBBONS

In the spring of 1832 an anguished petition went up to the House of Commons, asking for special provisions to be made for the maintenance of order in the Queen's County. It was signed by no less than the lord lieutenant of the county, its high sheriff, the grand jury and the body of magistrates. This assemblage of Queen's great and good explained their concern succinctly and powerfully, maintaining

> that a system of intimidation intrudes itself into all the concerns of life so that a man is not at liberty to dismiss a servant or labourer, to employ a tradesman, or to take a farm, without permission from self-constituted legislators, who carry on their plans, by anonymous threats and notices, which if not obeyed, are carried into effect by the vengeance of daily and nightly marauders . . .[1]

The county had been badly disturbed for about a year, but the problem of 'self-constituted legislators' and 'daily and nightly marauders' was far from new. Queen's had often previously had its share of such agrarian crime, though it is clear that 1831-1832 saw the phenomenon reach a new, local peak. Not only was there almost universal resistance among small farmers to making tithe payments, but also assaults, riot and affray were frequent throughout the county, and were especially common in the Castlecomer coalfield and adjacent areas, which extended across the Kilkenny-Queen's border in the south.

Agrarian crime of the 'Whiteboy' type became prominent from about 1760 onwards. There were several quite distinct periods of agitation. Arthur Young's account would have it that such crimes began in Tipperary, and certainly, two generations or more later, some Queen's residents before parliamentary inquiries specified Tipperary, or the areas adjacent to it, as the source of outrage spreading into their districts.[2]

One contemporary, the Irish attorney general, gave a detailed account of this Whiteboy activity to the Dublin House of Commons in 1787. Whilst confirming Young's picture that it was concerned with regulating rents and the inheritance of land, he also enlarged considerably on the objectives of these early groups. They include, he says, the reformation of tithes so that only the rector should receive the payment, cutting out any proctor or middleman; and the restriction of the tithe payment itself. In addition, he says, they aim for the reduction of parish cesses or vestry taxes. All these grievances recur in the course of the next eighty years or so.[3]

The depredations of these early groups went well beyond the Tipperary borders, and they were particularly active in Kilkenny and Queen's Counties in 1775. Some, from the areas around Abbeyleix and Durrow, took part in determined attacks on tithe proctors in 1774 and 1775; groups from the same districts, uniformed in white and urged on by horn-blowers, joined other contingents in a sizeable and sustained assault on Ballyragget in the spring of 1775. Their anger was directed against the local magnate, Robert Butler, who had been instrumental in organising local gentry and tenants into an anti-Whiteboy association. Butler's servants and neighbours were well-prepared for the assault, but the initial attack was followed by a series of further attempts which lasted over some months.[4]

The following year twelve Whiteboys were sentenced to death at Maryborough Assizes, their crimes including the ear-cropping and burying alive of tithe-proctors. Although the county appears to have become much quieter after 1776, John Troy, bishop of Ossory, felt it needful to excommunicate Whiteboys in October 1779. This seems to have had little effect, for there were further condemnations from the same source five years later:

> They have lately assembled at unseasonable hours and in different parties, sounding their riotous horn. They have presumed to administer oaths of combinations and proceeded to barbarous acts of violence against the persons and property of several individuals . . . [5]

Queen's did not escape some further disturbance when Caravats and Shanavests were active in Munster in the years after 1808, or the Carders and other groups made themselves felt over a wide sweep of country, from Roscommon to Waterford, from about 1813 onwards. Cases of committals for riotous assembly and 'shooting at persons' do indeed occur for most of the years between 1805 and 1812, the numbers finding their way into the assize statistics for the county varying from one to ten. In the latter year there are also two reports of 'riotous assembly, appearing armed by night, and attacking dwelling houses.' Tipperary's total for the same year was twelve.[6] It was notoriously difficult to bring cases as far as trial, and frequently we find that a majority of cases were either abandoned or resulted in acquittals; in 1814, for example, the eight cases of riotous assembly at the county assizes were all acquitted before juries. The clerk of the crown whose task it was to produce these returns was moved to comment somewhat petulantly that

> many other indictments against persons in custody were prepared in this county . . . which were ignored by the Grand Jury; and many more were prepared by him against persons also in custody, which by reason of the absence of prosecutors, were not disposed of . . .[7]

The actual number of 'riotous assemblies,' including those before lesser courts and those which did not result in legal process, was undoubtedly very far in excess of eight. What proportion of these were 'agrarian' in origin is a matter for speculation.

The lord lieutenant, Whitworth, reported to Sidmouth on disturbances throughout Ireland in the four years to 1816, and listed separately events in Queen's. There were cases of 'assembling in arms' for each of the years from 1813 onwards, as well as a case in 1813 of conspiring to murder a tithe proctor. He also, however, comments on the small proportion of convictions obtained, a state of affairs he attributes to 'widespread intimidation' and 'the disordered state of society'.[8] The Rathdowney area, for example, was reported to be badly disturbed, with numerous violent outrages, in 1816.[9] More than one witness before a parliamentary inquiry was later to testify that the new phase of disturbances in Queen's had commenced about 1815, and James Doyle, bishop of Kildare and Leighlin, connected this with the consolidation of farms which, he said, had been carried on since that period.[10]

One feature common among the secret groups was the effort to obtain arms. Mail coach guards were robbed of their weapons; soldiers were attacked, and the houses of gentry raided for the guns they possessed. Yeomanry weapons were one obvious target, and a member of the Durrow Infantry, Charles Alley, had an anonymous letter posted on his house in January 1814:

> Dear Charles, I favour you, I a friend, letting you know of the woeful complaint that is lately lodged to our captain and company. I would severely suffer for it if it be found out. We must

pay you a visit shortly I do not know how soon. We are informed that you have fire arms and charge you to make no resistance for if you do they would consume you and yours. The visitation will be by night. We have to our company 5 carders 6 shearers 12 pick'd men and 60 armed. We must attend all complaints as we are sworn we must fulfil, so far 5 carders 6 shearers pick'd men armed 60. Woe, woe, woe, we are sworn to this mark and that we must fulfil or die. Woe, woe, woe to such as we visit.

I. of the Carovats[11]

Over much of the country the landless labourer was vitally dependent on obtaining conacre on which to grow vegetables. And to the landless labourer we must add many others. One Queen's resident commented that conacre was general in the county; some people, he said, had an acre of their own, but it would not support them, and they were thus forced to meet the high rents of conacre in order to support themselves.[12] These rents could go as high as £10 or £12 the acre if the position were good and the land to be prepared by the farmer, but it was much cheaper in less favoured areas. And in some country districts no rent at all was charged, the manuring and cultivation done by the taker being considered sufficient recompense to the farmer. Where this applied in the Queen's county it was known as 'a free crop'.[13] Thus, year by year, the amount of conacre ground available and the price at which it might be let were both items of pressing, urgent interest, particularly during the February-April period when agreements for the coming season were normally made. One threatening notice warned a landowner

> You are to charge no more than 6 guineas per acre for potatoe land and . . . you will not or shall not set that ground in the farm way but the poor must have it . . .[14]

The Reverend Marcus Monck, of Johnstown, let out a parcel of land near Rathdowney, almost certainly for conacre. In 1815 he received a letter from his obedient servants Captains Knockabout and Fireball:

> Ballingarry, Febry 20th 1815
> Revd. Mr Monks I hope your honour wont be offended at these few lines, we understand that you are a gintleman we hope you will act as a gintleman, there is not a gintle in the Queens County but is fawling their ground but you alone and were it not for the goodness of your lady we would visit you. Before now. We are informed that you have some of your ground set at an

unreasonable Rent, and if you dont fall the highest rented ground you have to 40s per acre, Captain Knockabout and Capt fireball with their little army will sertainly visit you. We would not wish to put you out of your Court, or have your Lady a Widdow, and if your determined to fall the Ground let it be Published on the Sunday following in the Chappel of Grogan. We are informed that there is a great many bad actions done on your Glebe which is Incouraged by Yourself and if you dont Amend from oppressing the Poor in every Respect you will be sorry, and that Very Soon
No More at Present from your Obt Servants
Capt Knockabout and Capt Fire Ball.[15]

The general background to the frequent robberies of arms, mentioned above, is undoubtedly the unsettled and unpredictable state of much of the country; but there were some quite specific features which aggravated the situation. One was the deepening of sectarian animosities in the eighteen-twenties, and another was the popular perception of the new bodies of police which appeared from 1814 onwards, and more particularly after 1822.

Queen's had a larger-than-usual proportion of Protestants. A survey by Church of Ireland ministers in 1814 gave a figure of one in four; Edward Wakefield, however, puts it at one in twelve.[16] Whatever be the true figure, we find contemporary references to 'the protestant town of Mountrath', to Mountmellick 'much inhabited by Quakers', and to the intensity of sectarian feelings there.[17] John Dunn of Ballinakill claimed in 1824 that 'Orangeism has got into almost every town in the Queen's County,' but specified Mountmellick and Mountrath as the 'grand depot' of the local Orange party.[18] To this must be added the bitterness stirred up on one hand by the New Reformation and on the other by the primitive millenarianism of much of the peasant population in the 1820-1825 period. One threatening notice in Co Cork closed with the remark 'In my opinion there will not be a Protestant living in the year 25'.[19] There are clear parallels which occur in Queen's, so that one resident was later to describe how the Protestants of his area all sat up throughout Christmas Eve 1824, fearful that their lives might be in danger from some sudden Catholic rising.[20]

Equally significant was the appearance of the new police forces. Contrasting so clearly as they did with the old and inefficient baronial constables, they were another factor making for resentment, at least among some sections of the population. Well-armed and organised, the establishment of their barrack quarters throughout Ireland can only have spurred on the secret societies in their frantic searches for arms.

The town of Durrow was nominally a part of Kilkenny in 1823, only returning to Queen's a few years later. In June 1823 the head of the new constabulary in the area, Captain Kelly, received an anonymous notice which not only demonstrates both anti-police and anti-Orange feeling, but has vaguely political overtones as well:

> KELLY – I request you will call home your Peelers out of Durra and Cullohill; if you do not, I will send them to Hell or the North in a few days; there is a friend of mine at Ballyragget that will settle your boys there also, and put their skins on poles for Orange flags. We are the boys that will soon let you see we are not afraid of your Orange rascals; we will soon let you see we will soon put an end to the vermin . . . Huzza for Erin's Sons for ever - we were long enough chain'd under your cruel yoke. Yours &c
> CAPTAIN O'CONNELL[21]

The Rockite disturbances of 1820 onwards were centred in the Munster counties, but Queen's also experienced a very turbulent period. Bishop Doyle, whose diocese largely extended through Queen's, issued his first pastoral against secret societies in 1819, after some instances of arson and violence; and Upper Ossory was proclaimed in May 1821, as the problems in the south and west continued.[22] They were not, however, confined to the southern and western areas of the county. The retired General Dunne, writing from his home, Brittas House near the King's Co border, claimed he had struggled to keep his area tranquil, 'though surrounded by disturbance on every side,' and asked for a party of the Tinnehinch and Ballyboy Yeomanry Corps to be stationed at Clonaslee. Dunne's own party, patrolling that area, had been fired on; and parties of Rockites had assembled in order to card men obnoxious to them.[23]

One captured Rockite at this time stated that he had taken an oath to 'subvert government and all Protestants,'[24] and there is evidence of a belief in some parts that 'the extinction of Protestantism foretold by Pastorini is to be accomplished by Captain Rock.'[25] However that may be, most of the agrarian nocturnal crime is clearly aimed at those who took land. Thus a Quaker called Neil was ordered by anonymous letter to quit his holding at Pike of Rush Hall, near Mountrath. He and his family were threatened with destruction unless he complied. This was on 28 December 1821. Neil, despite his profession, was quite determined to defend himself, his family and his property, and asked for police help. This was given, a detachment remaining in the immediate locality until the danger was past. Land, we may assume in the light of scores of similar threats, was the prime issue; Neil's religion an incidental.[26]

Henry Goulburn, secretary to the lord lieutenant, expressed a hope early in 1822 that the Rockite disturbances were dying down: 'We have the satisfactory assurance of the revival of family feuds which are in this country the pretty sure indications of returning peace . . .'[27] He was to be disillusioned. The valley of the Nore and its tributaries was badly disturbed by the spring of the year, and a search for arms was made among the peasantry of Upper Ossory. In Maryborough the parish priest, having received information that illegal oaths were being taken among his parishioners, went individually to those concerned:

> All except two, who were strangers, promised me they would abandon their bad practices; they admitted that an oath could not be a bond of iniquity, and I was very glad to hear them say so. The two persons who infected the parish denied their misconduct; all the others acknowledged every thing. As I could have no hopes whatever of the conversion of the two strangers I allude to, I denounced them on the Sunday following in the chapel.[28]

Bishop Doyle renewed his exertions to check the secret societies. In 1821 he had issued a lengthy address 'to the deluded and illegal associations of Ribbonmen'; in his pastoral in 1822 he asked

> . . . how are your wants to be remedied and your distress removed by these associations? Is it by the breaking of canals, by the destroying of cattle, by burning houses, corn and hay, and establishing a reign of terror throughout the country that you are to obtain employment? Is it by rendering the farmer insecure in the possession of his property that you will induce him to increase his tillage? . . . Is it by causing a heavy police establishment to be quartered throughout the country, to be paid by taxes collected from the holders of land, that you will enable them to give you employment? No . . . Your conspiracies . . . are calculated not to relieve, but to augment your distress an hundredfold.[29]

Doyle's biographers claim some lessening of disturbance as these words were read from altars throughout the disturbed districts in Queen's and neighbouring areas. Nevertheless, the Rockite activities continued. Houses and farms were burned, houses attacked for weapons, and threatening notices posted ordering that farms should not be taken by new tenants. The winter of 1822-1823 proved particularly black. Joseph Nicolson, superintendent magistrate of police, reported from Rathdowney on 'a most desperate gang infesting this part of Ossory';[30] and Marcus Monck, from the same area, requested an increased police force to deal with the frequent 'nocturnal depredations.'[31] Gentlemen were plundered of arms, sometimes repeatedly- Peter Roe's house at Killdellick being attacked two nights running in January 1823.[32] In a despatch to Peel in April 1823 Wellesley, the lord lieutenant, acknowledged 'an increased spirit of outrage' in Westmeath and Queen's. He added the comment that the expiry of leases at that time of year usually led to disturbances; but, alas for his implied hopes, Captain Rock showed no sign of relaxing his activities as the year progressed.[33]

Wellesley had said in his despatches that the troubles in Queen's had spread in from Tipperary; but when John Cosby, of Stradbally Hall, wrote to the Castle in May 1823 he reported that there had been houses burned in the parish of Lea, barony of Portnehinch, and gave his opinion that the bad influences were from the King's County and Co Kildare.[34] At the same time Lord Portarlington, at Emo Park, was affronted to become himself a target of the Rockites:

> Having received a threatening letter signed Captain Rock, desiring me to prepare a coffin, if I attempt to plow some land on my estate which is lately come out of lease, and stating that 500 men well armed will rise up against me, & having had a plow which I employed to till this land, cut into pieces, a few nights ago, I have arranged with Major Powell . . . to make a search for arms at an early hour on Tuesday morning with 100 men of the Queen's County police who happen to be stationed at Maryborough during the Assizes . . .[35]

The search at first yielded only inferior results, but it must have been a continuing and an extensive one: by June some 200 stand of arms had been collected 'from unqualified people in and about Portarlington.'[36]

The outrages continued. John Hoban's house near Borris was attacked, his son injured and his son-in-law's ears cut off. The family were suspected of giving information about illicit distillation, though it seems probable that no one could have been certain of this. Eight persons made up the attacking party, saying they were the men of Captain Rock and Lieutenant Starlight; they were armed with 'a scythe, a hurl, wattles and firelocks.'[37] A man named Monaghan was carded, and a police detachment attacked, near Emo.[38] Joseph Mulhall's house, and Michael Weaver's house, both at Coolnacart, were burned at night.[39] For one outrage, committed near Rathvilly, the only cause which could be suggested was that the victim had incurred his neighbours' wrath simply because he had honestly paid his rent.[40] Among the many notices reported was one from Lea parish, addressed to an inhabitant of Jamestown:

Sir
We now caution you against occupying the widow Kings house on the Portarlington road as wee will knot a low aney strangers to com in to this side of the parish . . . if you do mark the consiquence Mount Etena never emited such flames as will be seen in [Clensentry? Clonany?]

Signed

15th May 1823   Captain Rock[41]

In the south of the county the situation was at least as bad. Cosby, in one of his frequent letters to the Castle, alluded to

a very extensive district in that part of the country including parts of the County Kilkenny, Tipperary and Queen's County- reaching from Johnstown by Durrow to Balinakill (sic), indeed, I may add, to the collieries that is quite without a resident magistrate . . . I fear that part of the country will never rest peaceable unless a stipendiary magistrate or two be appointed . . .[42]

John Dunn of Ballinakill supports this picture of the colliery district and the south west of the county, adding detail as to the wretchedness of most of the inhabitants: 'I believe there is not above one man out of six that has constant work, I might say one in ten . . .'[43] The colliers themselves, in or out of work, were notoriously ungovernable. When an attempt was made in July 1824 to increase the tolls levied on loads of coal the colliers attempted to force the gate at Tollerton just west of Carlow, and to destroy the 'ouncels'- presumably a weighing machine. The resultant affray was one of many in the area, some of which involved serious injuries; they were the forerunners of much worse to come within a few years.[44]

J S Rochfort lived on the Queen's-Carlow border and was familiar with the area mentioned by Cosby. In April 1825, when pressed to estimate an average wage for the area which would cover both employed and unemployed he settled for a figure of fourpence a day. That alone might go far to account for the appalling misery, and the Rockite activity, of the area. There was, he said, a tendency to remove tenants from farms as leases fell in, in an attempt to clear land which had become heavily over-populated by subdivision. When asked how such tenants then managed to exist he declared:

I really scarcely know: but I suppose with what little they can run away with from the landlord, and afterwards with the charity of the neighbours; they generally find work somewhere or other, or perhaps they join the Rockites.

Perhaps they did. Rochfort had been deterred from causing evictions on his own property:

They would have resisted in every way they could . . . and if I had got any tenants to take it, I am sure they would have run the risk of their lives.[45]

There were further attacks to end the year, and further attempts at robberies of arms; typical of the latter being the occasion when four men, with faces blackened, entered the house of a Mr Burnett of Fisherstown – about two miles from Monasterevan and took away 'one double gun, one case of pistols, two swords and one powder horn full of powder.'[46] But 31 December proved a date like any other, despite Protestant fears; and 1825 was at last to see the end of the most extreme Orange demonstrations in the county. The redoubtable Bishop Doyle renewed his attack on the Rockites in his pastoral of February 1825, and visited many parishes in Queen's to denounce them: we are told that heaps of old guns, swords, and blunderbusses were brought in and flung at his feet.[47] The disturbances continued, but their incidence lessened. By 1827 the county was comparatively peaceful.

Agrarian disturbance was back again with something of a vengeance by 1829, so much so that the magistrates of the county set up their own fund in March of that year, to be applied to 'peace preservation purposes.' Their secretary describes that period as a time when 'the county was disturbed by nocturnal meetings of ill-disposed persons in arms . . . and . . . various attacks were made on the habitations of individuals.' The funds were to be used for rewards and especially to encourage and recompense those who

being engaged in their usual labours, and accosted by strangers with a view to deter them from proceeding therein, or to impose arbitrary regulations on the farmers or their men, shall seize and bring such persons before the magistrates . . .[48]

William Despard, living between Abbeyleix and Mountrath, later regarded the 1828-1829 period as a sort of watershed, since which time the previous understanding between the classes had disappeared. His explanation for this was that 'there were meetings in the year 1828, which the lower orders attended, and at those meetings there were speeches made by perhaps some of the farmers . . .' This had produced agitation. His workmen had, in fact, been driven away, like those of some other major landholders.[49]

A number of other Queen's residents concurred with Despard that this was the start of a new wave of problems for the county. John Cahill, landowner and 'surveyor of large estates,' living down towards Carlow, pointed out in 1832 that four years earlier a series of evictions had left many people 'strollers in the place ever since.' He added some detail about local evictions to the information he had already supplied about unemployment among colliers:

> There was one gentleman evicted 89 persons; there was another gentleman evicted 96; there was another gentleman 95; there was another gentleman eight; there was another gentleman eight; in all, with the colliers left idle, 1,126.[50]

When numbers of the county's gentry and clergy gave evidence before the Poor Inquiry which reported in 1836 they were asked about disturbance in their districts. By and large, they testified to the new wave of problems from 1829 onwards. Dysart Galen had been under Whitefoot influence in 1828 and 1829, according to James Delany, its parish priest; Peter Lalor, parish priest of Clonenagh, stated that his area had been very much disturbed from November 1828 onwards. Others give a picture consonant with this, the period of disturbance starting variously in the years between 1828 and 1831. Rathdowney, Rathsaran, Ballyroan, Killabban, Killiney, Moyanna and Abbeyleix were among the areas said to be very disturbed. The old General Dunne, living out his retirement near Clonaslee, dismissed the problems in his parish as 'trifling', but added

> at the same time agitation has been carried forward, and Carders, Blackfeet, Whitefeet, have been organised, and attended by the giddy and young, and those who have nothing to lose.[51]

John Delaney, parish priest of Ballinakill, gave an account of the hard times which afflicted his area in 1829. He spoke of three families, the heads of which were fined for stealing switches of wood, which they needed for thatching their cabins. They were given the option of being forgiven the fine, but being ejected instantly – in November – or of paying the fine but taking six months notice to quit. They chose the first alternative, and the three families became scattered over the parish:

The next summer, 1830, was one of famine with us; we were obliged to introduce a sort of poor-rate, to keep the people from starving and dying in the ditches: two of those families were thrown upon the parish, and I had to support them myself . . . one of the poor men lost his cow. Some time after being turned out, a series of calamities befel him; he took ill, and after lingering a long time in a state of the utmost destitution and misery, died of a broken heart. The sons of this man, together with the second family above mentioned, became leaders in this system of Ribbonism . . .

Delaney also described evictions locally on the Cosby estate: a vast number, he said, in the previous seven years. Some of those displaced had come to Ballinakill, and Delaney had done his best to prevent their settling locally. This, however, was no easy matter, 'for if they found an outhouse unoccupied they would literally force themselves into it.'[52]

There is no fundamental change in the activities of 1828 onwards from those of four or more years earlier. Thus, in October 1828 two houses were maliciously burned near Maryborough. Both had recently changed hands, and the new owner of one had been ordered by anonymous letter to quit the premises. There were three cases of rescue of distrained property reported that month from Carlow Graigue; and from Borris-in-Ossory, among cases of cattle and sheep-stealing, the police reported two threatening letters which had come to their notice. In the one case which is recorded in detail the land had been taken after a former tenant had been ejected.[53]

H B Wray, an active and efficient sub-inspector of police in Queen's, was asked by the Poor Inquiry Commissioners for details of outrages connected with land. He provided the following:

7 Feb. 1829 A number of armed men attacked the house of the widow M'Daniel, of Ballyknocken, who forced her son in-law (Robin) to swear that he would have nothing to do with a farm he had lately taken from Major Cassan, from which the former occupant was ejected.

15 Mar 1829 On the night of this date a house, the property of a man named Huslam, on the estate of Major Cassan, was maliciously consumed at Lalor's Mill, he having recently taken same together with a farm.

20 Mar 1829 On the night of this date the houses of James Sutcliffe, Martin Whelan, and Peter Dunn, near Poorman's Bridge, were attacked by a party of armed men, who swore them to quit their farms in 21 days.

Wray followed these with twelve similar examples, and added an interesting comment:

> These crimes and outrages were not generally perpetrated by persons in distressed circumstances, although the cause assigned by those who committed them was to avenge the persons who were ruined or injured by being ejected from their farms, to prevent others from taking them, and to protect the general interests of the poor.[54]

O'Hanlon and O'Leary, in their classic history of the county, recount other outrages from this period, one of which involved thirty-eight men attacking a house; on that occasion a police detachment was lying in wait for them.[55]

Over the following two years, 1830 and 1831, the troubles rose to a crescendo, with Queen's often occupying the place in the journals which previously had been taken by Limerick, Cork or Tipperary. John Price, magistrate, land agent, and farmer at Westfield Farm near Mountrath, described 1830 as a period of very great disturbance throughout Queen's, and more particularly in the whole of the colliery district.[56] The county's reports have to be seen in the wider setting which included similar turmoil in King's, Tipperary and Kilkenny. Galmoy barony in the latter county had its own troubles which reached northwards in their effects at least as far as Rathdowney and the hurlers of Kilkenny brought agitation, excitement and riot to the south-east of Queen's.

In addition to all this, the tithe agitation in the county was reaching a peak. Patrick Lalor of Tenakill told a public meeting at Maryborough in February 1831 that that he would pay no further tithes, and to such a pitch had the general agitation been carried that there was a near universal refusal to pay the impost by about the autumn of that year. William Despard, asked about tithe in June 1832, declared that no tithe had been paid recently in the county, and when asked whether it was ever likely to be paid his reply was 'Never; they will never pay tithe.' He included Protestant farmers in this comment.[57] John Cahill's statement in July 1832 was equally to the point:

> I have not paid my own tithe for the last year; for if any person was to pay, they would be visited by nightly parties, and would be in danger of death, for it is nothing less than that.[58]

Rockite and Whitefoot had moved from seeking to regulate tithe to a determination to abolish it.

This widespread, renewed activity brought with it a spate of threatening letters. In June 1831 William Scarlett of Ballyfin received a warning to depart immediately from the schoolhouse he inhabited; the letter was concluded with the signature 'Captain Rock' and the words 'Long Live O'Connell and Reform.'[59] The same month John Baillie, a shopkeeper whose entrepreneurial activity extended to leasing the tithes of Stradbally from the rector, found a notice fixed to a nearby tree.

> Notise to the inhabitants of Ballybritis and every other person that shall be seen to go in to John Bailly's for to buy from him or to sell to him and in particular manner to his servants to quit him not to be seen in his service from this day out if the be the will find my vengance to over take them and that soon He is an enemy to his country and deserves that chastisement that is in our hands he is but a branch and we are the thrunk cut him off and he will decay-
>
> Let no person pull this down.

According to Thomas French, the Castle's informant, the result of this notice was that 'none of the lower class, who are his principal customers, can venture to enter the shop.'[60]

On the morning of 25 September it was the turn of the Roman Catholic chapel at Maryborough to bear a notice. John Souther and William Hugs, it said, had the tithe decrees in their possession and were determined to execute them without delay. The anonymous author felt it needless to go into detail:

> It is unnecessary to mention to the public how they are to threat them and dont spear them one hour & let his seven baul pistol not deter ye boys . . .[61]

In October a number of cows were cruelly killed in the colliery area near Newtown engine (parish of Killabban, barony Slievemargy). On the horn of one of them was left a notice cautioning John Edge to take no further arrears of rent from his poor tenants; those who had taken land to give it up; and attempting to enforce a payment of 22 pence daily for colliers. Edge was closely involved with the changes which were being introduced in much of the colliery area, and which involved a move away from the small-scale 'one pit one collier' system. The writer, in ordering 'let them have now pit but one' is trying to stem the change to a more intensive, capital-based system. He concludes a lengthy series of threats with 'I am Captain Rock, that was never afread to travel by night or day'.[62]

A few days after these threats in Newtown a notice was posted some miles away, on Mayo chapel. It cautioned land jobbers and land holders against taking the land of any person 'unless with their good wishes,' and set a maximum of £6 an acre for conacre. Those who should demand more, and those who should pay more, were equally promised extinction. 'It touches his Honrs feelings very much to hear the manner in which numbers are oppressed by tyrants' said the author, before signing himself 'Capt. Rock & Starr'.[63]

At the end of October Philip Roberts of Stradbally was ordered by notice received through the post, signed simply 'Rock,' to put out of his employment a man named Dunne. The latter was alleged to be an informer, but according to the *Leinster Express* this was quite untrue.[64] It is of course possible, as another newspaper commented on a similar occasion, that 'the fellow took advantage of the state of the times, to write as from a banditti, while he meant merely to serve a private purpose.'[65]

Outrages which involved extreme violence also increased. Among the worst were the attempted murder of the Scots steward of the Lyster family at Grenan, near Durrow, in May, and the actual murder of a stone-cutter working on the Mount Henry estate in October. In the latter case fifty-five tenants subscribed amounts varying from two shillings and sixpence to one pound towards a reward; the general belief was that the unfortunate man had shown a little too much loyalty to his landlord, intending to join the celebrations at the coming-of-age of the estate's heir the following day.[66] Mountmellick and Mountrath fairs were both disturbed by Whitefeet and Blackfeet, behaving simply as factions.[67] There were attempted rescues of prisoners from police or military custody near Mountrath, and, much more seriously, on the Newtown-Castlecomer road, where four deaths occurred.[68] Robberies, arson and anonymous threats seem to have become virtually daily experiences in the whole colliery district.[69] More than 100 stand of arms were robbed from the county's residents in the course of the year 1831. It comes as welcome light relief to read of one group of 'nightly marauders' who, having entered the house of Lancelot Jackson at Bocca, near Mountrath, then demanded to be served with supper, 'which request was immediately complied with.'[70]

The experiences of the Lysters at Grenan give some inkling as to the effect produced by the general rise in outrage and lawlessness.

> [Captain Lyster's] lady and family were lately obliged, in consequence of having received threatening letters, to leave Grenan and reside elsewhere- his labourers were driven from the fields . . . Captain Lyster is brother-in-law to the Bishop of

> Dromore . . . He is a resident gentleman and spends upwards of £1000 a year in giving employment to labourers on his estates . . .

Their Scots steward who had been attacked in May, no doubt thinking himself lucky to recover, left the area; Lyster himself was fired at on the open road in November 1831. In the following spring another steward of the family was murdered.[71]

If the disturbances were greater than ten years previously, so was the means available to resist them. The county constabulary proved much more effective than during the earlier period, and both prosecutions and convictions for Whiteboyism increased. The Spring Assizes at Maryborough in 1832 saw forty-three convictions for Whiteboy offences, for example; and the assizes were shortly to be followed by a special commission at which more Whiteboy convictions were to be obtained.[72] Typical of the tighter control being exercised by the police was the incident when the four-man police patrol operating out of Abbeyleix intercepted a party of Rockites as they were in course of attacking a house near Durrow; five were made prisoner.[73] There were other, similar successes.

In addition to the ordinary police, the county had eighty men of the Peace Preservation Force (PPF) in 1832; their distribution giving some indication of the main problem areas:

> 21 constables at Wolf's Hill; 9 constables at Hollymount; 10 constables at Garrindenny; 10 constables at Carlow Graigue; 10 constables at Knockardagur; 10 constables at Milford; 10 constables at Tolerton (sic).

This distribution was varied slightly for 1833, Mayo, Kilmoroney and Maidenhead becoming stations for the PPF, and Wolfhill, Garrindenny and Towlerton losing their detachments. The numbers were also reduced, to a total of 48.[74]

The Queen's County's two members of parliament, Sir Henry Parnell and Sir Charles Coote, moved for a select committee of inquiry into the state of the county on 31 May 1832. Though the scope of this inquiry was broadened to cover the whole country, its report nevertheless made good use of the evidence of various Queen's residents, and is ample confirmation of the scale of the county's problems.[75]

By the middle of 1832 the *Dublin Gazette* was offering rewards for information about seven attacks in the county.[76] A policeman was then murdered in July, and a land steward in November, besides numerous woundings.[77] Some of these crimes were related to goods distrained for rent, and increasingly, some were related to tithe. Thus in April John

Bayley (Baillie), a tithe proctor at Inch who had endured many previous threats, was badly wounded, and the following November W Browne, keeping some corn distrained in default of rent, was fired at and injured.[78]

Two hundred and twenty six illegal notices were reported to the police in Queen's in 1832, and 215 attacks on houses. The corresponding figures for 1833 were 320 and 622: Queen's had become the most disturbed county in Ireland.[79] The police establishment, and the extent of military units available, were both increased. Ballyadams, Slievemargy and the parish of Tullamore were proclaimed in June 1832.[80] And in July, Myles O'Reilly produced to a Commons committee a copy of an 'Oath of a Whitefoot . . . as it is practised at present in the Queen's County, and all over Ireland.' It not only bound takers to a strict code of mutual support, but also contained one vow to wade in Orange blood and another to cut down 'Kings, Queens and Princes, Duks, Earls, Lords and all such with Land Jobin and herisy.[81]

Bishop Doyle, it is said, finally broke his heart over the recrudescent Whitefeet outrages in his diocese. He commenced an address during one visitation at this time with the words 'Men of the Queen's County, my blood is upon you!' On another occasion:

> resolved to inflict some indelible mark of reprobation on certain Blackfeet whom he had hopelessly tried to convert, Dr Doyle, during a visitation at Mountmellick, commanded them to leave the house of God. While the men were moving towards the door, Dr Doyle repeated the word "Depart" three times; exclaiming, "And if I might venture to anticipate the judgment of the Almighty, I would add- into eternal fire."
>
> His burning words seared their way into these guilty hearts. The men fell on their knees and sought and obtained pardon.

Doyle's influence, as on other occasions, resulted in the surrender of some arms, and there were affecting scenes of repentance as small groups of Rockites and Whitefeet capitulated to his powerful presence and personality; but though he was frequently commended for this, his outspoken opposition to tithe ensured that he could never be an establishment figure. He died in June 1834.[82]

The core of Rockite and Whitefoot concerns might not have changed, but it is possible that their efforts to prevent transfer of lands began about this period to become increasingly ambitious. Many threats relate to lands transferred within two, three or four years previously, but one also finds increasing numbers which refer back over longer periods. Thus one Thomas Clarke sent his son to Ballylinan to arrange for a piece of land to be ploughed. The property had been in Clarke's possession for ten years. The son, on his arrival, found a notice attached to a stick thrust into the soil:

> To Thomas Clarke
> Sir- you are requested to take notice to resign the four acres of land formerly held by Andrew Byrne of Mullamore to his son Dennis Byrne and never dare to put a plough on the same land again this is the first and last notice remark if you do not comply with this you will be sorry when too late for, if not plenty of powder and ball awaits you .
>
> Captain Rock

The Andrew Byrne referred to had in fact sold all interest in the land not ten, but twenty years previously, the purchaser on that occasion being at least one owner anterior to Clarke. On the next morning the notice was followed up. Four men called at the house where the younger Clarke was staying. He was told in no uncertain terms to leave the area that day and warned that the threats in the notice would indeed be executed if the instructions were not heeded. One of the men drew a pistol and fired it into the air, after which they departed. This may have been a blatant attempt to coerce someone out of his property: alternatively, there may well be an implication that land is something inalienable, despite any intervening commercial transaction.[83]

The *Annual Register* was moved to comment at unusual length on the 'turmoil in the county' and found some comfort in reporting that the special commission sent to the county to try offenders had managed to some extent to remedy the notorious legal delays which, many claimed, allowed Rockism to flourish. The commission's activities had, it said, produced a considerable improvement in the state of the county.[84] Some amelioration did indeed take place, but disturbance was slow to die away. The many outrages of 1833 and 1834 show an immense range of concerns; Patrick Kinehan, of Roskelton, for example, was peremptorily ordered not to allow 'that Orange thief, Dick Ince, to draw turf through his land;' while a threatening notice from Spring 1834 condemned 'all land jobers', ordered that two farmers should not 'give grass' to someone disliked locally, and promised that retribution would come from a distance if necessary: 'to twenty miles off.'[85]

When a general report was made as to the state of Leinster in 1834 its verdict was that

> The cases of crime are so numerous . . . A complete system of legislation, with the most prompt, vigorous, and severe executive

power, sworn, equipped and armed for all excesses of savage punishment, is established in almost every district.[86]

A case of arson at Inch on 30 December 1835 indicates that Rockite concerns might well intermingle with family jealousies. A house, out-offices and a ton of hay were destroyed. They were in the possession of one Mary Moor. The prime suspects were also Moors: they had been dispossessed of the lands some time previously, and had been pressing to have them back.[87]

1836 ranks as a much quieter year, yet the record of agrarian crime is still considerable. Charles Kemmis, of Rossnaclonagh near Borris, issued sundry notices to his tenants to quit and also summoned various neighbours to give evidence as to shots fired in the vicinity. His house was attacked and he was warned to leave before March 1836. 'Capten Rok' accused him:

> You are nothing but a blodey tirant and perciquter to your tenents you have noticed them to quit but you must quit first . . . You think the police will sav you but as soon as the thath is fit to burn you may then look to your hous you will get a hot supper . . . [88]

Near Clonaslee a threatening letter warned Edward and Pat Murray to have nothing to do with the lands of John Heydon 'or if ye do ye will be put out of the care of this world.' This letter was illustrated with a drawing of a coffin, in the best Rockite style.[89] At Ballyduff, parish of Kyle, a herdsman was warned to leave his work in March 1836; in this case it appears that the job was simply wanted for another.[90] When a Church of Ireland minister dispossessed a certain tenant at Aghmacart, Peter Mahoney joined in a plan to shoot him. He later confessed that the group concerned in this enterprise was accustomed to meet nocturnally, drink whisky, kill sheep and commit various larcenies-thus providing an insight into the *modus operandi* of at least some Rockite groups.[91] One illegal notice of this period, signed by 'Captain Starlight,' warned its recipient- a partner in a mixed marriage- not to have his child christened by the Church of Ireland minister; another threatened a man who had obtained a road contract previously expected by others.[92] One man whose outhouse and stock were destroyed by fire in March 1836 could suggest only one possible reason for this: that 'he had voted for his landlord, Sir Charles Coote, at the last election'.[93] At Grenan, in August, where payment by the task had been introduced for the mowing, there was a serious assault on a mower.[94] Captain Rock, the Rev Henry Smyth of Lea tells us, did not approve of the system of payment by task; hence its rarity.[95] There are, however, yet other cases of Rockites attempting to increase the rate of payment for task work.

Mention has already been made of the fate of one Scots agriculturist, at the Lysters' Grenan estate. Improvers trod a difficult path. In March 1834 one such 'commenced running new lines of fences, and laying out improvements on a comprehensive and extended scale', adjacent to the Erril crossroads, west of Rathdowney. Overnight a gallows was erected there, from which 'an unfortunate old gander was . . . suspended.' His bill contained a 'last speech and dying declaration' in the best tradition of the ballad and long-song singers of the day, to the effect that he had been hanged as a warning to all innovators. If the proposed works were not discontinued, it said, he would not be the only victim of Captain Rock.[96]

Those who brought in new tools might also be discouraged by the direct methods favoured in England at this period: ploughs were destroyed in the county, for example, like that of Lord Portarlington, mentioned above, and one at Mayo in 1839.[97] When used for the ridge cultivation of potatoes the new iron ploughs inevitably displaced labour.

Finally, after the county had become much less disturbed, John Price, agent for Lord Lansdowne on the estate at Luggacurren, attempted to rationalise the chaotic holdings there. Many who were dispossessed were aided to emigrate, and the remainder were given proper leases on reasonably-sized farms. In 1843 Price introduced the Deanston system of thorough-draining, bringing in for the purpose 'a very clever Scotch agriculturist,' named M'Clitchie. The arrangements appear to have been made in a sensitive and careful way, and gained a wide degree of approval. But M'Clitchie received an anonymous letter through the post:

> Sir- At four days' notice, we the undersigned persons forthwith request you to quit this country and go home, and not be the cause of destroying old honest tenants' by your making of drains . . .

The notice made sundry threats, and of course no names were subscribed to it. M'Clitchie went back to Scotland.[98]

The range of activities involving Rockites, Whitefeet and the like was enormous, and any simple explanation of their activities is likely to be inadequate. That they were most frequently concerned with land, the need to retain possession of it, and the many charges upon it, is clear. 'While land was a necessary of life, there was a struggle to the death for the possession of it.'[99]

Oliver MacDonagh is clear that

> the official view of land in Ireland, as it hardened in the statutes and judgments during 1801-1865, was English-derived . . . land was ultimately like goods, a common-or-garden commodity . . .[100]

But this concept, he points out, was at variance with custom, and to the peasant it represented an unmistakeable threat. Barrington is one son of the Queen's county who confirms that such custom did indeed prevail during his youth: he tells us that in those days about 1760-

> no gentleman . . . ever distrained a tenant for rent . . . The greatest abhorrence, however, prevailed as to tithe proctors . . .[101]

Of course the secret societies of the county regularly opposed the distraint which had become a frequent feature of peasant life by the 1820s, and sought also to curb the worst excesses of tithe proctors, using murder if necessary. Their actions indicate that to them land was anything but a common-or-garden commodity; and whatever else they did, they fought fiercely to prevent its slipping away into new hands. To examine large numbers of their often highly explicit threatening notices is to see some of the detail of this concern for existing or established holdings, down to the occupation of particular farms, the rents for conacre or farmland which passed in particular locations as 'fair', and even the changing attitudes over the 1820s and 1830s to tithe payment.[102]

The Rockite threats in Queen's also have an occasional political or religious element. The former is some indication that the political turmoil of the times had its effect rather more widely than the limited franchise might suggest; the latter reflects the sectarian animosities of the period, especially in the Mountrath and Mountmellick areas. But neither religion nor politics appear to be the central concern of the authors. This writer's impression is that they constitute an occasional, background gloss on more urgent concerns.

The availability of employment, the influx of 'strange' labourers, the wages of labour, all feature in Rockite notices, as do dairying and any sort of land improvement or improved method which appeared to threaten tenure or jobs. There are indeed instances elsewhere of Rockites forbidding the use of cradle scythes for mowing, and specific prohibitions of ploughs for the ridge-culture of potatoes.

The Rockite attitude to the police suggests a sometimes frantic determination not to come under any strong, central control. Queen's saw both attacks on police patrols, and on police barracks. Robberies of arms presumably derive from similar attitudes. And when one considers the mayhem and intimidation, the frequent gratuitous cruelties and the misery often caused by Rockite attacks, they sometimes resemble nothing so much as a lawless, callous and reckless banditti. It is perhaps true that 'communal violence is peculiar to societies in which a deep malaise is present.'[103]

Of course, this is only part of the picture. Rockite groups served a variety of ends and were 'leagues for communal defence . . . trade unions . . . vehicles for ordinary criminal activity'.[104] And undeniably, many of the groups in the Queen's county took upon themselves the redressing of the real grievances of the peasant community. 'Tyranny' is a concept their threatening letters often use: and it is usually applied to farmers, agents or proctors, and sometimes to parsons. Beames's contention is that the secret societies were engaged in a desperate struggle against the many changes which were transforming a close-knit peasant culture, rooted in the land and dependent on it, into something based on commerce and money. They thus championed older, traditional values as against those of a wider and apparently harsher world.[105]

How organised were the Rockites? Despite the use of occasional Ribbon oaths, like that mentioned above, and reports in the county of 'swearing-in,' it seems likely that local groups were mostly evanescent and had only the most rudimentary organisation. Outrages were carried out by groups gathered for the purpose, but also by men acting with no more than one or two others- and indeed, alone. The report of 1834, mentioned above, which saw 'a complete system of legislation' and 'a severe executive power' in Leinster Rockism was exaggerating: the disparate groups which made up the Rockites and Whitefeet lacked such cohesion, though their widespread activities and common objectives might well have seemed like the same thing to contemporaries. Unlike the true Ribbonman, the Rockite was not part of any widespread, connected organisation. He was, however, part of a widespread protest against cultural, social and above all economic changes which were relentlessly obliterating a way of life.

At his worst, the Rockite committed abominable crimes. Some of these were quite gratuitous; and some were part of a struggle against the emerging, ordered society of nineteenth century Ireland. At his best, however, in the words of the man who was probably his most implacable enemy in the Queen's County, Hugh Boyd Wray, he was 'protecting the general interests of the poor . . .' in the only way he knew how.[106]

References

1. PRO, HO/100 f 176.

2. e.g. Evidence of J. R. Price, *Select committee to examine into the state of the disturbed counties in Ireland, into the immediate causes which have produced the same, and into the efficacy of the laws for the suppression of outrages against the public peace* (cited hereafter as *Select committee on disturbed counties*), 1831-32 xvi (677) p. 419, No. 6676.

3. Cited G. C. Lewis, *Local disturbances in Ireland* (London, 1836, reprinted Cork 1977), p. 16.

4. The topic is fully covered in J. S. Donnelly 'Irish agrarian rebellion: the Whiteboys of 1769-76' in *RIA Proc.*, 83c (1983), and by M. J. Bric 'The Whiteboy movement 1760-1780' in W. Nolan and T. G. McGrath (eds), *Tipperary: history and society* (Dublin, 1985); see also *Annual register*, 18 (1775), Chronicle, p. 92.

5. W. Carrigan, *History and antiquities of the diocese of Ossory* (Dublin, 1905), i, p. 186 ff and *Fourth report from the select committee to inquire into the state of Ireland, more particularly with reference to the circumstances which may have led to disturbances in that part of the United Kingdom,* 1825 (129), viii, p. 664 (680).

6. *Return of the number of persons, male or female, committed to the several gaols in Ireland for trial . . . etc.,* in *1805-12,* 1813-14, xiii, pp 125-128 (341-344).

7. *Return of the number of persons, male or female, committed to the several gaols in Ireland for trial . . . etc.,* in *1814,* 1814-15, xi, p. 29 (391); *Indictments and trials at assizes and special commissions,* 1823, xvi, p. 11 (635).

8. *Return of the number of persons, male or female, committed to the several gaols in Ireland for trial . . . etc.,* in the year *1813,* 1814-15, xi, p. 33 (345); *Statement of the nature and extent of the disturbances which have recently prevailed in Ireland, and the measures which have been adopted, etc.,* 1816 (579), ix, p. 11 and appendix 4, p. 16.

9. H. D. Walsh, *Borris-in-Ossory, Co. Laois: an Irish rural parish and its people* (Kilkenny, 1969), p. 119.

10. *Minutes of evidence from select committee on the state of the poor in Ireland,* 1830 (589), vii, p. 391 (567), no. 4352.

11. NA, SOC, II (1814).

12. Evidence of Wm. Despard in *Select committee on disturbed counties,* 1831-32 (677), xvi, p. 38, No. 446.

13. *First report of the commissioners for inquiring into the condition of the poorer classes in Ireland,* 1836, xxxiii, Appendix F, p. 18.

14. SOC, 1767/17.

15. SOC, 1712-92.

16. *House of Lords Journal,* lvii, 1825, p. 1262; E. Wakefield, *An account of Ireland, statistical and political* (London, 1812), ii, p. 620.

17. Evidence of J. Price in *Select committee on disturbed counties,* 1831-32, xvi, p. 436, no. 6909; Article 'Mountmellick' in N. Carlisle, *A topographical dictionary of Ireland,* London 1810; cf O'Hanlon and O'Leary, *Queen's County,* p. 631.

18. *Minutes of evidence taken before the select committee appointed to inquire into disturbances in Ireland, in the last session of parliament,* 1825 (20), vii, p. 278 (278).

19. *Ballina Impartial,* 9 June, 1823.

20. Evidence of J. S. Rochfort in *Third report from select committee to inquire into the state of Ireland, more particularly with reference to the circumstances which may have led to disturbances in that part of the United Kingdom,* 1825 (129), viii, p. 440 (454).

21. *Ballina Impartial,* 30 June, 1823.
22. W. J. Fitzpatrick, *The life, times and correspondence of the Rt. Rev. Dr. Doyle, Bishop of Kildare and Leighlin* (Dublin, 1880), i, 115-116; NA, Privy council order book 6, 1818-1822, p. 364.
23. Dunne to Lord Castlecoot, 7/12/21 in SOC, 2292/26.
24. SOC, 2371/17.
25. J. G. Purcell to Lord Arden, 11/12/21 in HO, 100, 100/202, f337.
26. Nicolson to Gregory, 2/1/22 in HO, 100/203, f6.
27. HO, 100/203, f1.
28. Evidence of N. O'Connor in *Select committee on disturbed counties,* 1831-32, xvi (677), p. 179, No. 3168.
29. Fitzpatrick, *Doyle,* i, p. 200-203.
30. SOC, 2503/21.
31. SOC, 2503/24.
32. *Dublin Correspondent,* 18 January, 1823.
33. Wellesley to Peel, 8 April, 1823 in HO, 100/107, f123.
34. SOC, 2503/26.
35. Portarlington to Gregory, 21 March, 1823 in SOC, 2503/40.
36. Major Powell's report, 14 June, 1823 in SOC, 2503/35.
37. SOC, 2503/29; *The Warder,* 9 August, 1823.
38. SOC, 2503/32.
39. SOC, 2503/39.
40. State of the Country precis: Leinster, in SOC, II 47 (1823).
41. SOC, 2503/32.
42. Cosby to ?, 20 April, 1823, SOC, 2503/30.
43. *Minutes of evidence before select committee (session 1824) on the disturbances in Ireland,* 1825 (20), vii, p. 283-284.
44. *The Warder,* 24 July, 1824.
45. *Third report from select committee on the state of Ireland,* 1825 (129), viii, p. 440.
46. SOC, 2609/12; *The Warder,* 24 December, 1824.
47. W. J. Fitzpatrick, *Doyle,* i, p. 393.
48. *Select committee on disturbed counties,* 1831-32, xvi (677), appendix ii, p. 62.
49. Ibid., p. 37, nos. 417-419.
50. Ibid., p. 471, nos. 7249-7253.
51. *First report from commissioners for inquiring into the condition of the poor in Ireland,* 1836, xxxii, supplement to appendix E, p. 122 (234), et al.
52. Cited G. C. Lewis, *Local disturbances,* p. 65-6.
53. Monthly report, October 1828, in SOC, 2881/51.
54. *Appendix to first report of commissioners for inquiring into the condition of the poorer classes in Ireland,* 1836, xxxiii, appendix F, p. 55 (57).
55. O'Hanlon and O'Leary, *Queen's County,* ii, p. 646.
56. *Evidence taken before the commissioners appointed to inquire into the occupation of land in Ireland* (hereafter *Devon report),* 1845, xxi, p. 717, no. 4.
57. *Select committee on disturbed counties,* 1831-32, xvi (677), p. 40, Nos. 498-499.
58. Ibid., p. 477, no. 7370; for the course of the anti-tithe movement in Queen's at this time, see P. O'Donoghue, 'Causes of the opposition to tithes, 1830-38' in *Studia Hibernica,* no. 5 (1965).
59. SOC, II 178 (1831).
60. French to Stanley, 27 June, 1831, in SOC, II 177 (1831).
61. SOC, II 178 (1831).

62. *Leinster Express and General Advertiser* (hereafter *LEGA*), 22 October, 1831.
63. Ibid.
64. Ibid., 29 October, 1831.
65. *Ramsay's Waterford Chronicle*, 15 December, 1821.
66. *Westmeath Journal*, 26 May, 1831; *LEGA* 22 October, 1831.
67. *LEGA*, 1 October, 1831.
68. *LEGA*, 22 October, 1831; *Times*, 2 December, 1831 3 (f); *Westmeath Journal*, 8 December, 1831 and 10 December, 1831; cf *Return of persons killed or wounded in affrays with the constabulary force in Ireland since December 1830*, 1846 (280), xxxv, p. 16.
69. cf *Westmeath Journal*, 3 November, 1831.
70. *LEGA*, 15 October, 1831.
71. *Westmeath Journal*, 24 November, 1831; *Dublin Gazette*, 10 May, 1832.
72. Report from Lt. Col. D. O'Donoghue to Sir W. Gosset in *Select committee on disturbed counties*, 1831-32 (677), xvi, Appendix 1, p. 40.
73. *Westmeath Journal*, 10 November, 1831.
74. *A return of the Peace Preservation Force in Ireland, during each of the last three years . . . etc.*, 1834, xlvii, p. 10 (408).
75. *Parliamentary debates*, 3rd series, 13 (24 May to 3 July, 1832), col. 262; *Select committee on disturbed counties*, 1831-32, xvi (677), 1.
76. *Dublin Gazette*, 19 April, 1 and 10 May, 5 and 16 June, 1932.
77. *Dublin Gazette*, 7 August and 22 November, 1832.
78. *Select committee on disturbed counties*, 1831-32, xvi, appendix 1, p. 41; *Dublin Gazette*, 25 November, 1932.
79. *A return of the number of offences against the law, which have been committed in Ireland, etc.*, 1833, xxix, p. 6 (416) and p. 16 (426).
80. Privy council order book PB7, 14 June, 1832.
81. *Select committee on disturbed counties*, 1831-32, xvi (677), p. 345, no. 5834.
82. W. J. Fitzpatrick, *Doyle*, ii, 407.
83. *Carlow Standard*, 15 March, 1832.
84. *Annual Register*, 1832, History, p. 288.
85. *LEGA*, 1 November, 1834; ibid., 15 March, 1834.
86. *Papers relating to the state of Ireland*, 1834, xlvii, p. 5 (421).
87. J. Moreton to H. B. Wray, 31 December, 1835, in Outrage papers, 1836, Box 44.
88. W. Williams to H. B. Wray, 29 February, 1836, ibid.
89. Ibid.
90. Leinster Constabulary report dated Mountrath, 11 March, 1836, ibid.
91. J. Stoker to H. B. Wray, 5 January, 1836, ibid.
92. W. Williams to H. B. Wray, 12 January, 1836; Queen's Co. reports in ibid. The threatening notice in the latter case was in blank verse.
93. Report dated Maryborough, 4 May, 1836, ibid.
94. Report dated, 9 August, 1836, ibid.
95. *Supplement to appendix D, First report of commissioners for inquiring into the condition of the poorer classes in Ireland*, 1836, xxxi, p. 119 (135).
96. *LEGA*, 12 April, 1834.
97. HO, 100/231, f269.
98. *Devon report*, 1845, xxi, p. 719, no. 1026.
99. Evidence of Sir M. Barrington in *Select committee on outrages (Ireland)*, 1852, xiv, p. 487, No. 4815; cf *Select committee on disturbed counties*, 1831-32, xvi (677), Evidence of William Despard, p. 49, no. 715; and of J. R. Price, p. 425, no. 6736.

100. O. MacDonagh, *States of mind. A study of Anglo-Irish conflict 1780-1980* (London, 1983), p. 36.

101. Sir J. Barrington, *Personal sketches and recollections of his own times* (Glasgow and London, 1876), p. 4.

102. Cf S. R. Gibbons, *Rockites and Whitefeet Irish peasant secret societies, 1800-1845;* unpub. Ph.D. thesis, Southampton, 1982.

103. M. Chesnutt, *Studies in the short stories of William Carleton* (Gothenburg, 1976), p. 118.

104. T. Garvin, 'Defenders, Ribbonmen and others: underground political networks in pre-famine Ireland' in *Past and Present,* no. 96, August 1982.

105. M. Beames, *Peasants and Power: the Whiteboy movements and their control in pre-famine Ireland* (Brighton, 1983).

106. *Appendix to first report of commissioners for inquiring into the condition of the poorer classes in Ireland,* 1836, xxxiii, appendix F, p. 55 (57).

Chapter 18

MEDICAL CHARITIES IN QUEEN'S COUNTY, 1765-1851

LAURENCE M. GEARY

Medical charities, comprising voluntary hospitals, county infirmaries, fever hospitals, dispensaries and district lunatic asylums, evolved during the eighteenth and early nineteenth centuries to provide free medical aid to the sick poor. The earliest were the voluntary hospitals, which were established in the main urban centres, Dublin, Cork, Waterford, Limerick and Belfast. These institutions were built, equiped and maintained by private endowment and public subscription. An Act of the Irish parliament, dated 1765, attempted to provide for the rural population, by enabling an infirmary to be established in each county. The inspiration was a compound of charity, and self-interest. The legislators aspired to the restoration of health and the prolongation of life but the preamble to the Act expressed the additional hope that the county infirmaries would promote labour and industry and increase productivity in the kingdom.[1]

County infirmaries were funded by a combination of parliamentary grants, county presentments and voluntary contributions. Theoretically, admission was restricted to poor persons suffering from non-infectious diseases and to those requiring surgery. Less serious cases were attended in out-patient clinics. Individuals who could afford to pay for medical care, and incurables, irrespective of their financial standing, were debarred but, as we shall see later, the medical charities were grossly abused in this respect. The rules governing patient admission and conduct were strict and there were several offences for which they could be summarily discharged, including smoking, dirtying the floors or walls, swearing, blasphemy, drinking, gaming, filthy conversation, disobedience, or impudence to the officers of the house.[2]

An infirmary for the Queen's County was opened at Maryborough (now Portlaoise) in 1766. Its early years were unimpressive. John Howard, the English prison reformer, who visited the institution in April 1788, recorded that there were only twenty patients. He noted the general filth and dilapidation of the building and the fact that it was only partly roofed. There was no water supply and the bedding was dirty and inadequate. The basic diurnal diet was a threepenny loaf and two pints of diluted milk. The surgery consisted of a tiny closet, which contained ten vials, some without corks, a little salve stuck on a board, some tow, and pieces of torn paper scattered on the floor. In one of the four wards he saw a patient, whom he described as a 'naked, pale object', tearing his shirt to make bandages for his fractured thigh.[3]

A new infirmary, consisting of two storeys over basement, was opened in 1808. Each floor contained water closets and was abundantly supplied with spring and river water. There were eleven wards, each thirteen feet high and sixteen feet square, with ventilators in the ceiling and over the doors. Patients were thoroughly cleaned and fitted out in institutional garb before they were admitted to the wards. Those who were dangerously ill were allowed the company and assistance of a female relative. It was thought that such an arrangement would help to remove the prejudices which many country people entertained towards hospitals and other institutions, prejudices which were partly fostered by separation from their family. The infirmary was directed and controlled by a board of governors, who appointed a sub-committee to manage the institution. An individual who subscribed a guinea became a governor for one year, while ten successive subscriptions or a single one of twenty guineas made the donor a governor for life.[4]

The staff consisted of a surgeon, an apothecary, a secretary, who acted as providor and house-steward, an unpaid treasurer, a housekeeper, a male nurse, who doubled as barber, a female nurse, a porter, three female servants, and a janitor, who did the whitewashing and assisted with the cleaning. In 1829, the secretary, John Robinson, and the housekeeper each received an annual salary of £27-13s-10d. The porter, who was provided with a house and garden, was paid £14-15s-4d, while the nurse and the female servants shared £67-15s-9d between them. The housekeeper and nurse were also supplied with fuel and candles.[5]

In 1827, John Jacob, who was then twenty-two years of age, succeeded his father as surgeon and apothecary to the infirmary. Jacob was a medical graduate of the University of Edinburgh, a Fellow of the Royal College of Surgeons in Ireland, and destined to become one of the most prominent and influential provincial medical practitioners in the first half of the nineteenth century. He was the younger brother of Arthur Jacob, professor of anatomy and physiology at the Royal College of Surgeons in Ireland, and joint-founder and editor of the *Dublin Medical Press*, a weekly polemical journal, whose editorial columns reflected the uncompromising stance of the Jacob brothers on the bitter and divisive medical politics of the early Victorian era.[6]

John Jacob was subsequently appointed surgeon to the county jail and physician to the district lunatic asylum which was opened at Maryborough in 1833. He was also the proprietor of the Midland Retreat, a private lunatic asylum near Maryborough, which was advertised 'for the reception and treatment of the insane and of persons suffering from a disturbed state of the nervous system'.[7] Jacob received a total annual salary of £284 for his various public appointments, a salary unmatched by any of his colleagues, and one to which the medical inspectors attached to the Whatley poor inquiry commission in the mid-1830s took exception. This reservation aside, the inspectors were very impressed with the commitment, integrity and professionalism of everyone connected with the county infirmary. They were struck by 'the high grade and striking importance of the medical education' and by 'the very superior tone of the professional care devoted to the sick'. Queen's was the only county hospital in which the inspectors found any organised system of medical education. Each of Jacob's nine indented apprentices was placed in charge of a certain number of patients and was obliged to keep detailed case notes. The students also took turns to clerk for the physician and to perform the apothecary's duties. The inspectors concluded that Jacob's educational system would almost certainly produce 'good practical men' and would redound to his credit.[8]

Jacob attended more than 11,000 intern patients at the infirmary during the decade ending 1851. The year 1844 has been excluded from the calculations as I was unable to locate the relevant report. In addition, some 35,000 individuals were treated in the out-patients' clinic and another 2,500 in their own homes (see table 1).

The numerical variations that occurred from year to year did not necessarily reflect fluctuations in the prevailing levels of illness but were due, in part at least, to the funds and the number of beds that were available, to the nature of the ailments and the length of time individuals spent in the hospital. According to Jacob, surgical cases outnumbered medical ones because the poor were less inclined to seek hospital treatment for chronic illnesses and continued to work in order to support their families. He attributed much of the illness among the poor to dietary factors, to their almost exclusive dependence on potatoes, which, he said, were seasoned only with a little salt and washed down with water.[9]

Unlike some of his colleagues, Jacob did not debar individuals suffering from venereal disease from the county infirmary. He never mentioned the condition specifically but referred to it coyly as the consequence of irregularity and dissipation. In his opinion, the best way to check the spread of venereal disease was to hospitalise the

Table 1

Table showing the number of intern patients treated at the infirmary between 1841-3 and 1845-51

1841	Surgical	Medical	Fever	Total
Male	400	209	145	754
Female	183	165	158	506
1842				
Male	489	213	175	877
Female	164	126	203	493
1843				
Male	487	203	176	866
Female	197	135	226	558
1845				
Male	370	154	152	676
Female	209	108	210	527
1846				
Male	403	164	207	774
Female	183	100	227	510
1847				
Male	276	214	287	777
Female	148	92	353	593
1848				
Male	385	87	127	599
Female	150	57	138	345
1849				
Male	343	90	56	489
Female	156	56	71	283
1850	509	153	131	793
1851	522	138	165	825
Total	5,574	2,464	3,207	11,245

Source: *Dublin Medical Press,* 29 June 1842, pp 407-8, 24 May 1843, pp 325-7, 26 June 1844, pp 409-411, 11 March 1846, pp 149-151, 18 August 1847, pp 98-9, 9 August 1848, pp 84-6, 2 May 1849, pp 275-6, 27 March 1850, pp 195-7, 5 March 1851, pp 150-2, 3 March 1852, pp 133-5.

carriers. The refusal of some county surgeons to treat venereal patients increased the pressure on the Maryborough hospital and Jacob was eventually compelled to limit admissions. He did so in order to prevent what he termed the undue interference with the relief to which 'more moral characters' appeared better entitled. Those who were refused treatment sometimes committed a petty criminal offence in the expectation of being sent to prison, where they would receive medical attention. According to Jacob, venereal patients presented an example of 'squalid destitution' which was utterly disgraceful to a so-called civilised country. Additional centres for diagnosis and treatment were required and, to prevent recidivism, post-recuperative employment. As things stood, their chances of getting any sort of meaningful work were non-existent. Their options were limited. If denied admission to the workhouse, crime or the resumption of 'their former habits of misery and vice' seemed inevitable.[10]

Dispensaries

In practical terms, county infirmaries were only of use to those who lived within an accessible distance. Those who resided in remoter areas were effectively excluded because of transportation costs and difficulties. This fact was acknowledged by the establishment of dispensaries under an 1805 Act of parliament. These institutions were intended to complement the county infirmaries, to bring relief to the door of the sick, as a parliamentary committee of inquiry phrased it in 1846.[11] There was no standard principle on which dispensaries were established. They could be opened anywhere, irrespective of need or demand. Once local subscriptions were raised, the county grand jury was legally obliged to sanction a similar amount from taxation. The combined sum was placed at the disposal of a committee elected by the subscribers to use at their discretion to provide medical relief to the sick poor.

Dispensaries generally opened for a couple of hours on two or three mornings of the week but there was great variation as it was left to each dispensary committee to determine the times at which the doctor attended. In general, the understanding between the medical officer and the subscribers was that all the sick poor who attended the dispensary would be supplied with medicine and advice and that domiciliary attendance would be undertaken where necessary. However, the medical officer was not obliged to visit beyond a fixed and moderate distance from the dispensary and generally received extra payment if he did so. By the 1840s, there were eighteen dispensaries in Queen's County (see appendix B).

Fever Hospitals

Fever had terrified and killed countless thousands in Ireland for generations. The vector of the disease was not discovered until the early years of the twentieth century but people had long been aware from practical experience of the contagiousness of fever. The general acceptance of this principle led to the establishment of special hospitals for the isolation of the infected. Three different types of institutions evolved during the first half of the nineteenth century, county, district and poor law union fever hospitals. The latter were the most recent, dating from 1843. They derived their financial support from the poor rates and were open to all who resided within the union. County fever hospitals, which admitted the infected from all parts of the county, were entirely funded by local taxation. District fever hospitals, which dated from the 1816-1819 fever epidemic, were dependent on a combination of local philanthropy and local rates. Unlike county fever hospitals, there was no limit to the number of district hospitals which could be established. However, their method of funding, not least the necessity of raising local subscriptions on an annual basis, retarded their development.

In the mid-1830s, the only fever hospital in Queen's County was a small, privately-funded one at Abbeyleix, which limited its patient intake to the immediate neighbourhood of the town. The shortage of accommodation was so acute that Dr John Jacob felt obliged to admit fever patients to the county infirmary, contrary to regulations. Such infringements were justified by the alternative of almost certain death for the individuals involved. The situation was regularised by the establishment of separate fever wards in the hospital in 1838.[12] Fever hospitals were subsequently opened at Mountrath, Newtown and Mountmellick.[13]

District and Private Lunatic Asylums:

Asylums, to cater for the lunatic poor of one or more counties, were provided for under an 1821 Act of the imperial parliament. Ten such institutions were opened in Ireland in the succeeding years, including one at Maryborough in 1833, for the admission of lunatics from Queen's County, King's County, Longford and Westmeath.[14] The ubiquitous John Jacob was appointed physician. He sought advice from the medical superintendents of the various public and private asylums in Britain and Ireland and visited mental hospitals in Dublin, Belfast, Armagh, Carlow, Limerick, Liverpool, Manchester, Derby, Nottingham, Wakefield, York Retreat, Newcastle, Perth, Edinburgh and Glasgow. Jacob appears to have read extensively on the subject of insanity and to have been familiar with the latest theories and writings on the treatment of the insane and on asylum management.

Jacob incorporated his findings as well as his ideas on the future management of the Maryborough asylum in a pamphlet which he published in 1833.[15] In the preamble, he advised the governors that his intervention should not be ascribed to 'a meddling disposition', nor interpreted as a criticism of the asylum's current management. He was paid from public funds and as such felt duty-bound to make the institution as useful as he could. Jacob claimed that the position of the insane was hopeless until relatively recently times. They were regarded and treated as sub-human and, to use his own phrase, consigned to the dungeon and the lash. Medical intervention, beyond the empirical administration of 'universally applicable anti maniacal nostrums', was rarely attempted. Little effort was made to explore possible organic causes and the mentally afflicted were largely abandoned by medicine and society. Their safe-keeping and attention to their physical needs was all that was deemed necessary or desirable. However, by Jacob's time, a more sympathetic and interventionist approach was in vogue, the so-called 'moral treatment' of the insane. Jacob was committed to this policy and was very much opposed to the harsh, disciplinary practices of earlier times. At the Maryborough asylum, patients would be treated as gently and indulgently as possible and, while restraint could not be entirely dispensed with, it would be used on the 'most improved plan' and only when the physician deemed it necessary.[16]

Jacob was concerned at the exclusion of 'epileptic lunatics' from Irish district asylums, including Maryborough. He regarded epileptics as the most unpredictable and dangerous of all lunatics, and most in need of institutionalisation and professional supervision. 'Their propensities are very destructive and their outbreaks of violence particularly alarming', he observed. Jacob also objected to the patients being locked in their cells from 6 o'clock each evening, an hour he considered far too early for those who were capable of feeling 'the least enjoyment in their lives'. He regarded smoking as offensive and potentially dangerous and was strongly opposed to the habit among patients or staff. He objected to the practice of 'drugging' noisy patients with tobacco to keep them quiet, claiming that the habitual use of large quantities of such a 'powerful herb' was deleterious to health. It was a well known fact, he said, that some individuals would continue smoking until they fell down 'in a state of profound intoxication'.[17]

The admission procedure at the Maryborough asylum was cumbersome and regimented. A relative was obliged to swear an affidavit before a magistrate that the prospective patient was a pauper and a lunatic and without sufficient means to enter a private asylum. In addition, a magistrate, parish minister and churchwarden had to certify that they were convinced that the individual involved was 'a fit subject for the lunatic asylum'. A medical certificate, to similar effect, was also required. Two relatives had to agree before a magistrate or parish minister to remove the patient from the asylum on recovery or when requested to do so. Personal details such as name, age, religion, occupation and marital status were entered on the medical certificate and, for women, the number of their children and the date of birth of the last. There was a comprehensive list of medical queries, including incidence of insanity among the patient's relatives; the frequency and duration of the patient's bouts of insanity; the apparent cause of the present attack; possible links with child-birth or lactation; the patient's health and circumstances prior to the attack and currently; symptoms and features of the attack; habits, whether temperate or otherwise; any change in the patient's moral condition, conduct, temper or disposition; any unusual excitability or depression; eccentricity or weak-mindedness; frequency and duration of previous committals; medical treatment and its effect; destructive tendencies.[18]

The patient could be admitted once these bureaucratic hurdles had been surmounted. The entire administrative procedure was one of petty officialdom, epitomised by the expectation that the patient's friends or relatives would provide him with a good strong suit of clothes and a change of linen. This was superfluous as the patient was stripped of his own clothing on admission and obliged to don the garb of the institution. It was also expected that the patient would be accompanied by an intelligent relative who could provide the necessary information on the case.

One hundred and nineteen patients were admitted to the institution between 14 May 1833 and the end of September 1834. The ratio between the sexes was fairly evenly balanced, 62 males as opposed to 57 females. Ten deaths were recorded during the period. A further 28 patients were discharged, 2 as incurable, and 4 were re-admitted. There were 85 inmates on 31 December 1834, 28 from Queen's county, 25 from King's, 23 from Westmeath and the remaining 9 from Longford. Of the total, 38 had some form of work, either in the premises or on the grounds, and 4 were under restraint.[19]

Diet was regarded as an integral part of treatment. It was nutritious and generous, and certainly far superior to that available to the non-institutionalised poor of the time. For those on ordinary rations, daily breakfast consisted of one quart of stirabout and one pint of new milk, while supper was 8 ounces of bread and 1 pint of new milk. Dinner on four days of the week was 3. 5 pounds of potatoes and one pint of new milk; on another two days, it was 1 quart of soup and either 2 pounds of potatoes or half a pound of bread. Sunday dinner consisted of 12 ounces of beef, with cabbage, and 2 pounds of potatoes. For those on full diet, breakfast and supper were similar to the ordinary fare, while dinner consisted of 1 pound of meat, 2 pounds of potatoes and 1 pint of beer.[20]

The functions and duties of the different officers and servants were precisely delineated by Jacob. The attendants, or keepers, were forbidden to subdue or struggle with any patient, except in self defence, or to confine, deprive or punish them in any way, without express authority and specific instructions from the physician or manager. 'No keeper shall at any time deceive, terrify or irritate by harsh language, by mockery, by mimicry or by allusions to anything ludicrous in the present appearance or past conduct of any of the patients'. They were not to act vindictively but to forgive the patients their foibles and to treat the most and least troublesome with the same consideration. The attendants were to encourage and participate in the patients' 'harmless amusements' and to report their peculiarities to the physician or manager. Failure to do so would be regarded as proof of incapacity and unfaithfulness. Keepers and servants were forbidden to discuss religious or political topics with the patients, to accept money from patients or visitors, on pain of instant dismissal, or to smoke within the institution.[21]

It is reasonable to assume that the same conditions and expectations applied to Jacob's private asylum, the Midland Retreat. This institution consisted of two separate buildings, Anne Brook for women and Woodville for men. According to Jacob, neither house presented any of the usual features of a lunatic asylum. They were handsome, well furnished country residences, with large enclosed gardens. Restraint was not practised under any circumstances and, the advertisement concluded, the closest attention was paid to the medical treatment and general health of the patients.[22]

The Irish medical charities were not a poor law, although before the late 1830s they were the principal form of public poor relief available in the country. They were not intended exclusively for the destitute but for a broader, equally ill-defined collective, the poor, who might be regarded as those who could support themselves, however marginally, through their own labour and productivity but who would have been reduced to the level of paupers if prevented by illness from working for any length of time. Those at risk included small farmers, cottiers, agricultural labourers, artisans and domestic servants and it became the custom to provide these individuals with gratuitous medical relief. Jacob became even more concerned with distinguishing the industrious poor from the destitute after the introduction of the poor law in the late 1830s. He regarded the former as 'decent' people, who deserved preferential treatment and hospital care which was superior to that available in the workhouse infirmary. He added that those who supported themselves and their families by their own industry should be protected from what he termed 'the contaminating, the socially demoralising influence of the workhouse'.[23]

There was an even more fundamental problem than Jacob's

perceived need to distinguish between the destitute and the working class and that was the difficulty of defining the industrious poor, of deciding just who was entitled to gratuitous relief. Such a distinction was necessarily flexible and was often determined by time and circumstance. For instance, Jacob reported early in 1844 that there was an increased number of more substantial farmers and shopkeepers seeking relief at the county infirmary. These individuals had been able to pay for medical treatment prior to this but their circumstances had clearly deteriorated. This development was not unique to Queen's county. By the early 1840s, the Mayo county hospital was no longer regarded exclusively as 'an asylum for paupers', according to the infirmary surgeon, who added that many of the inmates in 1843 had 'commanded medical aid at a serious expense when in the enjoyment of better circumstances'.[24]

The problem of defining entitlement, of establishing the parameters of gratuitous medical relief, was virtually unresolvable and there was gross abuse of the entire medical charities system by 'unfit objects'. This was the less than complimentary term applied to those who availed of gratuitous medical relief, although they could afford to pay for private treatment. The blame was partly attributable to the over-zealousness of some governors in issuing tickets of recommendation to individuals who were not entitled to such relief.[25] Jacob and his colleagues constantly railed against this and other abuses but to little avail. One of their main concerns was the perennial uncertainty and inadequacy of funding. Complaints were frequently levelled at land-lords, particularly absentees, and other supposedly affluent individuals, for not providing a more secure financial and moral base for the county infirmaries and other medical charities.[26] The financial and other deficiencies of the system were tragically exposed during the Great Famine.

The impact of the Great Famine on the medical charities in Queen's County

In the late 1840s, the entire medical charities system was submerged in a tidal wave of sickness and disease. Between 1845 and 1849, general starvation and famine-related diseases were responsible for more than 1,000,000 excess deaths in Ireland, most of them attributable to fever, dysentery and smallpox. These three highly contagious diseases, which had long been endemic in Ireland, swept the country epidemically and with great malignity during these years. Their destructiveness was intensified by the presence of other epidemic infections, especially tuberculosis, bronchitis, influenza, pneumonia, diarrhoea and measles. The arrival of Asiatic cholera as a pandemic in 1848-49 exacerbated the situation. This fearsome disease added to the physical and mental suffering of the beleaguered population and increased the overall mortality.

The starving, the sick and the destitute besieged the country's hospitals, workhouses and dispensaries. Those who were too ill or weak to crawl, or who were unable to procure transport of their own, were carried by their relatives and abandoned outside the most convenient institutional wall. Such an act of despair and finality was indicative of the plight of the starving poor. Patients were placed two, three and occasionally four to a bed and hospital managers and others often went to the greatest shifts to provide additional accommodation.[27]

The partial failure of the potato crop in 1845 gave little indication of the apocalyptic events that were to follow. The country passed through the autumn and winter of that year relatively unscathed. None of the 362 fever cases treated in the Queen's County infirmary during 1845 was attributed to famine or food shortage. However, Dr Jacob was far from sanguine, experience having shown the close relationship between famine and fever in Ireland. Like many of his colleagues, he attributed the prevalence of fever to dirt and neglect, to the careless habits of the poor and their disregard of personal and domestic hygiene, which for him was epitomised by the common practice of keeping pigs and other farm animals in the home. He also railed against the ubiquitous manure heap, the 'pestilential effluvium' from which was responsible for much of the prevailing sickness and disease. The relationship between dirt and disease was well known but little effort had been made in Ireland to encourage cleanliness among the poor. He stressed the necessity of attempting 'to inculcate, encourage and enforce habits of cleanliness and due regard for domestic decency and comfort'.[28]

Despite his foreboding, neither Jacob nor anyone else could have anticipated the sheer scale of the tragedy that befell the country in the late 1840s. Fever appeared epidemically in many areas in the autumn of 1846 after the complete failure of that year's potato crop. A very malignant form of the disease struck the town of Abbeyleix at the beginning of September. According to Dr Swan, it was 'the poor, the dirty and the starved' who were primarily affected, although no one was immune. Swan's account of the Abbeyleix experience was graphic and gripping, the staccato reportage emphasising the horror:

> Pulse weak, 80 to 100; tongue dry, often glazed; skin dry and dirty looking; appetite often very keen; patients in hospital for some days, in several instances eating a moderate meal voraciously and dying in a few minutes after: as the nurse said, "the hunger was in

their hearts". Vomiting not common but diarrhoea very; seldom delirium; in some cases purpura, others scurvy, and again in others gangrene of extremities and terrible sloughing from pressure, the sacrum and occipital bone being laid bare in several cases ... The most common sequelae were oedema of the legs, chronic diarrhoea, and in some instances phthisis'.

The primary infection was relapsing fever, rather than the more malignant typhus, and more males than females were affected.[29]

A similar pattern of relapsing fever occurring disproportionately among males was detected by Dr Walsh at the Ballinakill dispensary, where dysentery was also very prevalent. In the six months ending 1 November 1847, Walsh treated 320 cases of fever, 198 males and 122 females. The death rate was much higher among the middle and upper classes than it was among the poor, a phenomenon noted in other parts of the country also.[30]

Fever raged on an unprecedented scale in Maryborough, according to Dr Jacob. He recorded the physiological effects of starvation, as he witnessed them in pestilential 1847. He noted the steady physical deterioration, from perfect health to emaciation and debility. Individuals seemed to burn more easily in the sun and the hands, feet, face, and other exposed parts of the body became covered in blisters and ulcers. Bowel complaints degenerated into uncontrollable and often fatal bouts of dysentery. Oedema caused great physical weakness and invariably ended in what Jacob termed 'the release of death'. Physically shrunken individuals staggered about, their wasted muscles unable to support them. An incalculable number of survivors of famine and starvation-related diseases were left permanently infirm, mutilated and scarred, he said, while the mortality was on an almost incomprehensible scale. 'In another world only will stand recorded the number of lives that were lost', he noted despairingly.[31]

In February 1847, Samuel Edge, MD, surgeon to the Newtown dispensary and physician to the Doonane fever hospital, informed Sir Philip Crampton, one of the key members of the Central Board of Health in Dublin, that the locality in which he resided was 'neither more nor less than one large hospital'. Starvation and disease had claimed many victims. In the previous week alone, ten inquests had been held and a verdict of death by starvation returned in each case. Fever, diarrhoea and dysentery were rampant and many were suffering from oedematous swellings of the extremities. To make matters worse the fever hospital was grossly overcrowded and deeply in debt.[32]

The Mountrath fever hospital in Mountmellick union also faced a financial crisis. In late December 1846, Dr Henry J. Smith informed the

McCarthy's Ironworks, Mountrath (Redmond).

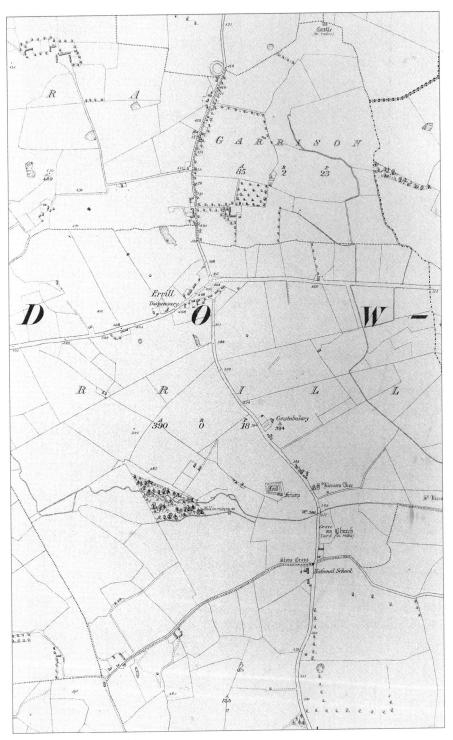

Errill, Sheet 27, O.S. 1841.

Errill (Redmond).

Bogland edges near Portlaoise (Redmond).

Goose Green, Timahoe (Redmond).

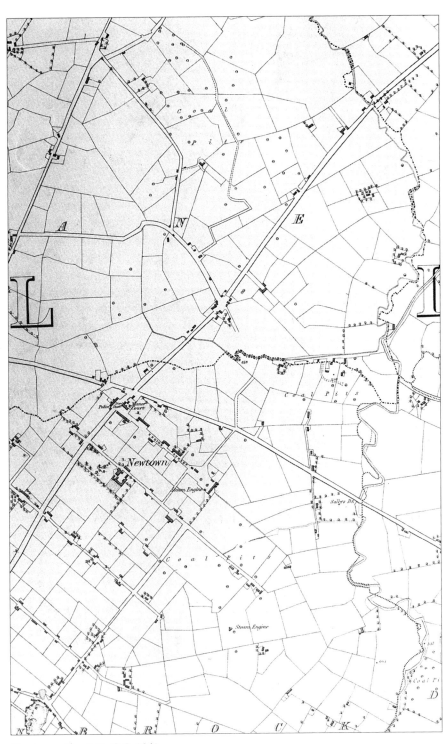

Newtown, Sheet 31, O.S. 1841.

Fleming's Fireclay, The Swan (Redmond).

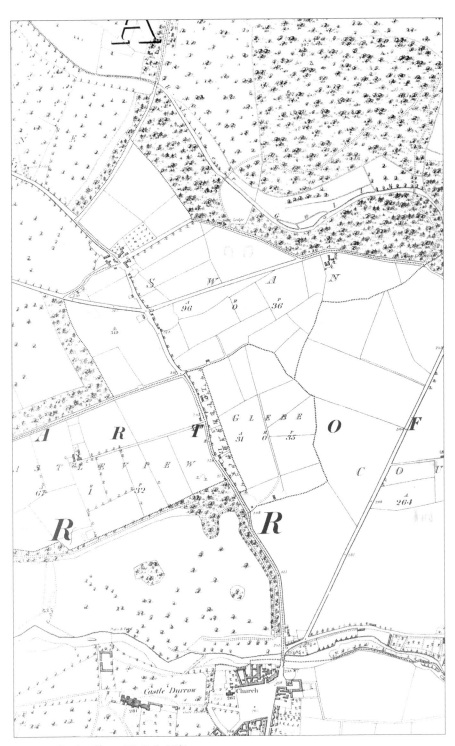

Durrow district, Sheet 29, O.S. 1841.

Durrow (Redmond).

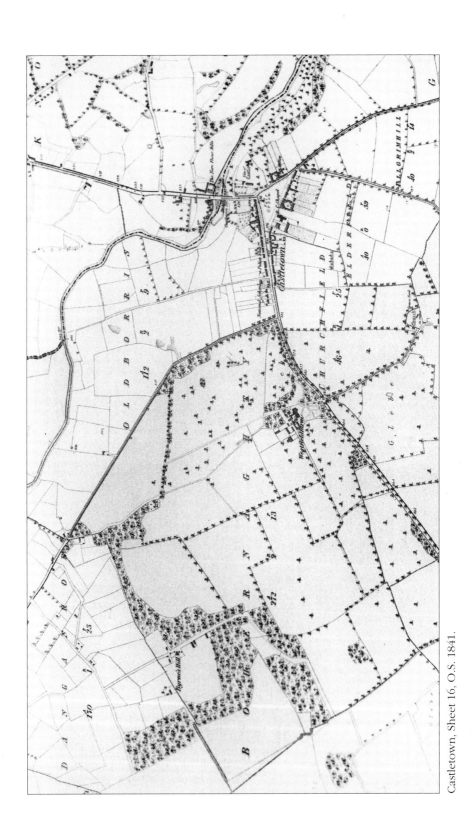

Castletown, Sheet 16, O.S. 1841.

Castletown (Eason, NLI).

Cottages at Stradbally (Redmond).

St. Michael's church, Portarlington, with cabins adjacent (Lawrence, NLI).

Donaghmore and River Nore (Lawrence, NLI).

Forest track in Slieve Blooms (Redmond).

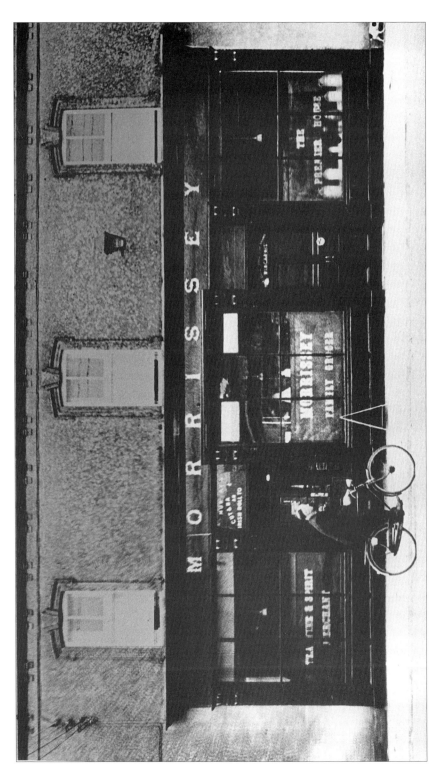

Morrisey's, Abbeyleix (Redmond).

Lord Lieutenant that the hospital was overcrowded, almost bankrupt and threatened with imminent closure. Medical charities throughout the country faced a similar prospect. There was a sharp and general fall in subscriptions and as these determined the level of county presentments, many hospitals and dispensaries found themselves under severe financial strain, and this at a time when there was an unprecedented and ever-spiralling demand for their services. Smith urged the lord lieutenant to make funds available to maintain the Mountrath hospital, adding that the resident gentry could not be expected to meet all the charitable demands currently being made upon them.[33]

The government rejected this and all similar appeals for additional funding for permanent fever hospitals and dispensaries. Instead, they proposed to establish temporary institutions wherever they were needed, subject to the approval of the Central Board of Health. In all, the board sanctioned 373 emergency hospitals and dispensaries, the first in February 1847, the last in October 1849.[34] Under the enabling legislation, the establishment and maintenance costs, together with those of patient care and medicines, were provided from the poor rate, while the Treasury paid the doctor's salary. Under the same legislation, existing fever hospitals and dispensaries could, if authorised by the Central Board of Health, be brought under the aegis of the local board of poor law guardians and financed in the same way.

Such a transfer was effected in the case of the Mountrath fever hospital in June 1847. The Central Board of Health was anxious to maintain the hospital because of the amount of fever in the locality. The Mountmellick guardians, who were just as concerned about the possible spread of disease, agreed to co-operate. They were also influenced by the fact that the doctor's salary was the treasury's, rather than the rate payers', responsibility and, finally, they believed that the arrangement would be temporary. There was only one other emergency fever hospital established in the county, at Ballyroan in Abbeyleix union, in July 1847. The relatively small number of temporary hospitals in Queen's County suggests that the impact of epidemic disease, while severe, was not as great as in other areas. The county also appears to have escaped relatively unscathed from the cholera pandemic that struck Ireland between December 1848 and August 1850. During this period, a total of 45,698 cases were reported to the Central Board of Health, of which 19,325 proved fatal. This represents a mortality rate of 42.3 per cent.[35]

William Wilde regarded the board of health figures as an underestimate for the country as a whole and in the 1851 census attributed 35,989 deaths to the disease.[36] However, Wilde's returns are also unreliable, as he conflated cholera and some dysentery and diarrhoea mortality. There were only thirteen reported cases of cholera in the three towns in Queen's County which had a population of more than 2,000, eight in Mountrath, five in Mountmellick and none in Maryborough. Of the total, four proved fatal, a percentage that was again below the national average if the figures of the board of health are taken as the benchmark.[37]

The conversion of the Mountrath permanent fever hospital into a temporary one placed it on a more secure financial footing. The institution was supported by the poor rates and no longer dependent on uncertain local philantrophy and county presentments. This development guaranteed the continued existence of the hospital but it also created marked social tensions and divisions in the Mountmellick union. The maintenance charge fell on all the rate payers and many of them objected to supporting a hospital which was of local use only and which did not benefit them or their families.

At the beginning of December 1849, some two and a half years after the hospital's change of status, the Mountmellick poor law guardians complained to the Lord Lieutenant that what was perceived of as a temporary arrangement was proving less finite than anticipated. They referred to the continued existence of the Mountrath fever hospital 'at a great expense to the union at large'. Furthermore, recent legislation had returned responsibility for the doctor's salary from the treasury to the rate payers. The guardians resented the imposition of such charges on the union generally and argued that it would be more equitable to make each electoral division responsible for its own patients. However, in this instance, the guardians went even further and requested that the Mountrath fever hospital be closed altogether. They contended that such a move was warranted by the decline of fever and other infectious diseases in the district and the unlikely possibility that they would recur epidemically in the immediate future. This tension between local requirements and concerns and those of the poor law union as a whole was reflected in other parts of the country also.

About forty residents of Mountrath, including the Catholic and Protestant clergy, poor law guardians, ratepayers and magistrates signed a counter petition, advocating the continuation of the existing arrangements. They argued that the town was eleven and a half miles from the union hospital at Mountmellick and that the removal of fever patients over such a distance would be difficult, expensive and potentially dangerous. They also claimed that the Mountrath hospital had helped to curb the spread of infection in the district. Their final argument was that the local poor had the greatest confidence in Dr Smith and wished to remain under his care.

The Mountrath petition was supported by the Central Board of

Health who had been informed that fever still existed in the district. In response, the Mountmellick guardians offered to establish and maintain a permanent fever hospital at Mountrath under the provisions of the poor law amendment act of 1843,[38] if the temporary arrangement were discontinued. This proposal would mean that the cost of maintaining patients would devolve on the electoral divisions which benefited from the hospital rather than on the union as a whole. The Central Board of Health reacted strongly. They argued that the guardians did not have the authority to take such a step and that they were impinging on the board's legitimate area of responsibility. The government rejected the board's defensiveness, maintaining, quite justifiably, that a permanent fever hospital was a greater prospective good that a temporary one. They ordered that the hospital be restored to permanent status from 25 March 1850.[39]

Epilogue

There was a decided lack of medical and lay consensus regarding the usefulness of pre-Famine medical charities. Some contended that they were very beneficial institutions, others that they were potentially so, while a third strand believed that they were almost useless because of the many abuses and defects attached to them. The perceived defects of the medical charities and concern over the misuse of public funds led to several official inquiries in the 1830s and '40s. Each had its own agenda and solutions, none of which proved acceptable to the various, often competing, interests involved. There were two main areas of concern, finance and management. With regard to funding, there were some who advocated a continuation of the system of voluntary contri-butions and local taxation, primarily because they wished to maintain what they saw as the charitable connection between the higher social classes and the medical facilities of the poor. Increasingly, however, those who were concerned with and involved in the medical charities came to accept that a more reliable system of funding was essential and they called for some form of compulsory taxation, similar to the poor rate.

The question of control and management, at local and national level, presented a far greater difficulty. In the late 1830s, the poor law com-missioners emerged as possible contenders for the overall supervisory role. For a variety of reasons, such a prospect was anathema to the majority of Irish medical practitioners. The debate was interrupted and overshadowed by the Great Famine, a catastrophe which almost completely overwhelmed the country's medical resources. In its wake, the Medical Charities Act of 1851 established a state-funded dispensary service, to provide free medical relief to the sick poor.[40] The system was administered by the poor law commissioners, who were also given responsibility for the fever and county hospitals, as well as the workhouse infirmaries. With some modifications, this system survived until relatively recent times.

Appendix A

Medical practitioners in Queen's County in 1843 and 1846

1843	1846
Abbeyleix	**Abbeyleix**
Boxwell, William. LRCSI	Swan, Thomas P. MD (Edin., 1844), FRCSI
Doxey, Thomas. MD (Edin), LKQCPI	Sheppard, John H. MFPSG, Lic. Apoth
Sheppard, John H. MFPSG, Lic. Apoth	
	Aughavoe
	Hanrahan, William. MRCS, 1843
Ballacolla	**Ballacolla**
Drought, Robert. LRCSI	Drought, Robert. LRCSI
Ballickmoyler	**Ballickmoyler**
Bolton, Ebenezer N. MD (Edin., 1834)	Bolton, Ebenezer N. MD (Edin., 1834)
Ballinakill	**Ballinakill**
Green, Samuel, Lic. Apoth	Green, Francis W.
Walsh, James Nelson. MRCS, 1831,	Walsh, James Nelson. MRCS, 1831, FRCSI,
Lic. Apoth	1844, Lic. Apoth
	Ballyroan
	Doxey, Thomas. MD (Edin), LKQCPI
Borris-in-Ossory	**Borris-in-Ossory**
White, William. MD (Glas, 1837), MRCS	White, William. MD (Glas, 1837), MRCS,
	FRCSI, 1844
Castledurrow	**Castledurrow**
Kennedy, George. Lic Apoth	Ormsby, Robert. MRCS, 1832, Lic. Apoth
Ormsby, Robert. MRCS, 1832, Lic. Apoth	Swan, John. MRCS, 1835, Lic Apoth
Swan, John. MRCS, 1835, Lic Apoth	
Clonaslee	**Clonaslee**
Dundas, Lorenzo. LRCSI	Alloway, George H. LRCSI
Cruttyard	**Cruttyard**
Edge, Samuel. MD (Glas, 1837), MRCS,	Edge, Samuel. MD (Glas, 1837), MRCS,
1828	1828
Emo	**Emo**
Clarke, Joseph R. MD (Glas), LRCSI	Clarke, Joseph R. MD (Glas), LRCSI
	Errill
	Dunne, George V. MD (Glas), FRCSI
Maryborough	**Maryborough**
Fitzpatrick, Archibald. MRCS, 1833,	Fitzpatrick, Archibald. MRCS, 1833,
Lic Apoth	Lic Apoth
Jacob, John. MD (Edin), MRCSI	Going, Henry. LRCSI
Martin, Joseph T. LRCSI	Jacob, John. MD (Edin), MRCSI
Pilsworth, Thomas. Lic Apoth	Pilsworth, Thomas. Lic Apoth
Wright, Thomas B. MD (Edin), LRCS	

Mountmellick
Croly, Henry. MD (Edin, 1832), FRCSI
Dowling, James. Lic Apoth
Owens, George B. Lic Apoth
Thornell, William, MD (Glas, 1837),
MRCS, 1831

Mountrath
Knaggs, Robert. MRCS, 1830, Lic Apoth
Lewis, William H. MRCS, 1836, Lic Apoth
Pim, Thomas, MD
Smith, James. MRCSI

Rathdowney
Delaney, Kyran. MRCS, Lic Apoth
Harte, John F. LRCSI
Kenah, ?. Lic. Apoth
Kennedy, William R. LRCSI

Stradbally
Bailey, Thomas H. Lic Apoth
Lawlor, William D. MD (Edin), LRCSI,
MRCS

Mountmellick
Croly, Henry. MD (Edin, 1832), FRCSI
Dowling, James. Lic Apoth
Hipwell, Thomas. MRCS, 1844
Thornell, William, MD (Glas, 1837),
MRCS, 1831, FRCSI, 1844

Mountrath
Carey, Joseph K.
Knaggs, Robert. MRCS, 1830, Lic Apoth
Lewis, William H. MRCS, 1836, Lic Apoth
Pim, Thomas, MD
Smith, James. FRCSI
Smith, Henry J. LRCSI

Rathdowney
Delaney, Kerr W. MRCS, 1821, Lic Apoth
Harte, John F. LRCSI

Stradbally
Bailey, Thomas H. Lic Apoth
Gray, John P.
Perceval, William. MD (Glas), LRCSI

Timahoe
Hobson, Abraham, MD (Glas, 1843),
MRCS, 1837, FRCSI, 1844

Key: L = licentiate; M = member; F = fellow; MB = bachelor of medicine; MD = doctor of medicine; Lic. Apoth. = licensed apothecary; TCD = Trinity College Dublin; RCSI = Royal College of Surgeons in Ireland; RCS = Royal College of Surgeons, London; FPSG = Faculty of Physicians and Surgeons, Glasgow; Glas. = Glasgow; Edin. = Edinburgh.

Source: Henry Croly, *The Irish medical directory for 1843* (Dublin, 1843), pp 281-3; Henry Croly, *The Irish medical directory for 1846* (Dublin, 1846), pp 281-4.

Appendix B

Medical charities in Queen's County in 1843 and 1846

Dispensaries	Medical Officer 1843	Medical Officer 1846
Abbeyleix	Boxwell, William	Sheppard, John H.
	Sheppard, John H.	Swan, Thomas P.
Aughavoe (est., 1845)		Hanrahan, William
Ballacolla and Swan	Ormsby, Robert	Ormsby, Robert
Ballacolla private dispensary	Drought. Robert	
Ballickmoyler	Bolton, Ebenezer N.	Bolton, Ebenezer N.
Ballinakill	Walsh, James N.	Walsh, James N.
Ballybrittas	Fisher, Maddison W. MD	Fisher, Maddison W. MD
	(Glas), LRCSI	(Glas), LRCSI
Borris-in-Ossory	White, William	White, William
Castledurrow	Swan, John	Swan, John
Clonaslee	Dundas, Lorenzo	Alloway, George H.
Errill	Kennedy, William R.	Dunne, George V.
Mountmellick (est. 1814)	Croly, Henry	Croly, Henry
Mountrath (est. 1818)	Smith, James	Smith, James
Newtown	Edge, Samuel	Edge, Samuel
Offerlane	Knaggs, Robert	Knaggs, Robert
Raheen	Walsh, James N.	Walsh, James N.
Rathdowney	Harte, John F.	Harte, John F.
Stradbally and Luggacurren	Lawlor, William D.	Perceval, William
Timahoe		Hobson, Abraham

Fever Hospitals
Abbeyleix

Doonane and Cruttyard		Edge, Samuel
at Newtown		
Maryborough (fever wards	Jacob, John	Jacob, John
of county infirmary)		
Mountrath		Smith, Henry J.
Mountmellick		

County infirmary

Maryborough	Jacob, John	Jacob, John

District lunatic asylum

Maryborough	Jacob, John	Jacob, John

Workhouse infirmaries

Abbeyleix	Boxwell, William	Swan, Thomas P.
Mountmellick	Croly, Henry	Croly, Henry

Source: Henry Croly, *The Irish medical directory for 1843* (Dublin, 1843), pp 131, 175-6, 181, 281-3; Henry Croly, *The Irish medical directory for 1846* (Dublin, 1846), pp 127, 149, 281-4.

References

1. 5 Geo. 111, c. 20, 'An act for erecting and establishing public infirmaries or hospitals in this kingdom'.

2. *Poor Inquiry (Ireland). Appendix B, containing general reports upon the existing system of public medical relief in Ireland; local reports upon dispensaries, fever hospitals, county infirmaries and lunatic asylums; with supplement, parts 1 and 2, containing answers to questions from the officers etc. of medical institutions,* B.P.P., 1835 (369) xxxii, part 1, pp 358-9 and supplement, p. 166.

3. John Howard, *An account of the principal lazarettos in Europe; with various papers relative to the plague: together with further observations on some foreign prisons and hospitals; and additional remarks on the present state of those in Great Britain and Ireland* (Warrington, 1789), pp 86-7.

4. John Jacob, 'Report of the Queen's County infirmary for the year 1835', *Dublin Journal of Medical Science,* 9 (1836), pp 177-9, 188.

5. *Report on the county infirmaries of Ireland, most respectfully submitted to his grace, the Duke of Northumberland, Lord Lieutenant General and General Governor of Ireland, by the General Board of Health* (Dublin, 1829), pp 16-18, 58.

6. See Jacob Papers, Archives, Royal College of Surgeons in Ireland. For John Jacob, 1805-1864, see obituary in *Dublin Medical Press,* 9 March 1864, p. 261. See also 16, 30 March, pp 283, 337-8, 346. For Arthur, see Charles A. Cameron, *History of the Royal College of Surgeons in Ireland and of the Irish schools of medicine, including a medical bibliography and a medical biography* (Dublin: Fannin & Co., 2nd ed, 1916), pp 453-5.

7. Henry Croly, *The Irish medical directory for 1846* (Dublin: Fannin and Co., 1846), pp 282-3.

8. *Poor inquiry (Ireland). Appendix B,* part 2, pp 3-15.

9. Jacob, 'Report of the Queen's County infirmary for the year 1835', pp 177-9, 188.

10. *Dublin Medical Press,* 26 June 1844, p. 410, 11 March 1846, pp 149-150.

11. *Report from the select committee of the House of Lords on the laws relating to the destitute poor and into the operation of the medical charities in Ireland; together with the minutes of evidence taken before the said committee,* B.P.P., 1846 (694) xi, part 1, p. xxvi.

12. Jacob, 'Report of the Queen's County infirmary for the year 1835', p. 185.

13. *Dublin Medical Press,* 11 March 1846, p. 150.

14. Henry Croly, *The Irish medical directory for 1843* (Dublin: William Curry, Jun. & Co., 1843), pp 136-7.

15. John Jacob, *Observations and suggestions on the management of the Maryborough District Lunatic Asylum* (Dublin, 1833).

16. *Ibid.,* pp 3-19.

17. *Ibid.,* pp 21-5.

18. *Ibid.,* pp 45-50.

19. Denis Phelan, *A statistical inquiry into the present state of the medical charities in Ireland; with suggestions for a medical poor law, by which they may be rendered much more extensively efficient* (Dublin: Hodges and Smith, 1835), pp 231-2, 236.

20. Jacob, *Observations and suggestions on the management of the Maryborough District Lunatic Asylum,* pp 50-2.

21. *Ibid.,* pp 60-2.

22. Croly, *The Irish medical directory for 1846,* advertising section.

23. *Dublin Medical Press,* 11 March 1846, p. 149, 2 May 1849, p. 275, 27 March 1850, p. 196.

24. *Dublin Medical Press,* 26 June 1844, p. 410.

25. *Ibid.*
26. Jacob, 'Report of the Queen's County infirmary for the year 1835', p. 179; *Dublin Medical Press*, 18 August 1847, p. 98.
27. *Dublin Medical Press*, 9 August 1848, pp 84-5.
28. *Ibid.*, 11 March 1846, p. 150.
29. *Dublin Quarterly Journal of Medical Science*, 8 (1849), pp 41-2.
30. *Ibid.*, pp 3, 8, 11-12, 15, 18, 24-5.
31. *Dublin Medical Press*, 9 August 1848, pp 84-5.
32. CSORP 1847 H 3420, N.A.I; *Dublin Medical Press*, 7 July 1847, p. 15.
33. CSORP 1847 H 363, NAI.
34. *Report of the commissioners of health, Ireland, on the epidemics of 1846 to 1850* (Dublin, 1852), pp 60-6.
35. *Ibid.*, pp 28-42.
36. *The census of Ireland for the year 1851*, part V, tables of deaths, i, B.P.P., 1856 [2087-1], xxix, pp 251-2.
37. *Report of the commissioners of health, Ireland, on the epidemics of 1846 to 1850*, pp 34-8.
38. 6 & 7 Vic., c. 92, 'An act for the further amendment of an act for the more effectual relief of the destitute poor in Ireland'.
39. CSORP 1850 H 1366, NAI.
40. 14 & 15 Vic., c. 68, 'An act to provide for the better distribution, support and management of medical charities in Ireland; and to amend an act of the eleventh year of her majesty, to provide for the execution of the laws for the relief of the poor in Ireland'.

Chapter 19

JAMES FINTAN LALOR OF TINNAKILL

MICHAEL G. O'BRIEN

I

Nineteenth and twentieth century accounts of Irish history are permeated with enigmatic references to James Fintan Lalor. Acclaimed as a revolutionary land reformer, a physical force nationalist and a socialist by Davitt, Pearse and Connolly, Lalor was presented, retrospectively, as the founding ideological father of multifarious movements. Portrayed as an 'isolated thinker', intensified mystical fascination, while facilitating the branding of James Fintan as a means of establishing respectable pedigrees. Twentieth century works have generally complicated interpretation of Lalor's life. Repeatedly, romantic delusions and personal philosophies have compensated in the absence of reliable data. Without any supporting documentary evidence, evocative accounts, such as Fogarty's description of Lalor's continental experiences,[1] frustrate interpretative efforts. Furthermore, to suppose that access to James Fintan's private papers would mitigate against further misinformation is a dangerous assumption. For in the second edition of Fogarty's work, though the author did have access to extant family and personal papers, the temptation to indulge wayward romanticism, though mollified, persists.[2] Admittedly, Fogarty's texts did include valuable biographical material and laid the foundations for further evaluations of the subject's life and theoretical influence. Disappointingly, despite more recent works, Lalor has largely remained a captive of rigid ideological interpretations, which have shied away from gauging the significance of the symbiotic relationship between James Fintan and the place where he spent most of his life, Tinnakill. Similarly, personal philosophies have conveniently overshadowed the intrinsic ideas, which underpinned his actions and the range of ideas which characterised Irish politics generally in the 1840s. In the most recent analysis of Lalor's life, the binding shackles of nationalist and socialist have been replaced by the umbrella label, 'radical'.[3]

II

Located in the townland of Tinnakill, in the extensive united parishes of Clonenagh and Clonagheen, wherein lay the ruins of a monastery founded by St. Fintan in the sixth century, in the barony of Maryborough West, lies Tinnakill House. The Lalor family's asssociation with Tinnakill originated in the mid-eighteenth century when Fintan's grandfather, Patrick, a tenant farmer in the adjacent townland of Doon, entered a thirty year lease with John Preston Esq., for 86 acres and 30 perches, in June 1767.[4]

By 1805, when Patrick Lalor signed his last will, his accumulated agricultural holdings exceeded three hundred acres. Combined with property in Mountrath, his investments accrued sizeable profit rents.[5] Through wise investment, which formed the basis of his career as a middleman, Patrick Lalor succeeded in bridging the gap between tenant and gentleman farmer. All his property, with the exception of Tinnakill, he bequeathed to his eldest son James (James Fintan's uncle and godfather). Tinnakill, passed to his second son, James Fintan's father, Patt, who had farmed the holding with Patrick senior. However, in January 1813, Patt purchased from James, his (James') life interest for the sum of £2,911-8-11, which facilitated the latter's emigration to America.[6] Patt Lalor between 1814 and 1832 continued and emulated in practice his father's career as a land speculator and middleman. By the latter date, Lalor estimated that he had accumulated between six and seven hundred Irish acres.[7]

Prosperity at Tinnakill differentiated the Lalors from the surrounding tenant masses. Though distinguishable from the majority of their less fortunate neighbours, they were combined with them in what Sam Clark describes as the most powerful source of social integration even beyond the local group, namely religion, which served in the one instance to bridge class divisions and on the other to set people of different religions apart.[8] Privileged position conferred social responsibilities on families like the Lalors, who within the context of nineteenth century politicisation, were expected to provide leadership to the inarticulate masses. Accordingly, throughout the nineteenth century, starting with Emancipation and culminating in the Home Rule movement, Tinnakill was the seat of popular politics in the Queen's County. Likewise, Tinnakill provided the material resources which facilitated the development and sustenance of family members careers, including James Fintan's. While rebelling against his lack of independence, it is instructive to note, that his opposition to the Repeal movement, ideas on agrarian reform and first letters to the *Nation* were all penned in Tinnakill. Or to be precise, maintaining the characterisation of an isolated conspirator, Lalor retreated to his 'attic-like room under the eaves of the old house. Stuffed close with books and papers, scantily furnished, this "den" under the roof, was Lalor's place of escape'.[9] Hardly conducive environs for a person of delicate constitution. Even accepting the strained relationship between Patt Lalor and James Fintan, the latter surely had the opportunity to develop his ideas in more comfortable circumstances. By the mid-1840s several family members had left home to pursue careers in America and Britain, leaving a number of Tinnakill's twenty-two rooms empty. Towards the end of his life, during his enforced absences from Tinnakill, Lalor remained in regular contact with family members from whom he secured ongoing financial and moral support.

III

As the eldest of Patt and Anne Lalor's twelve children, born on 10 March 1807, James Fintan (Plate 19.1) might have grown up to anticipate a grand inheritance. However, through either a cruel twist of fate or the vagaries of nature, he had to cope with a spinal injury and general poor health throughout life. Other family members experienced similar bronchial problems. Brothers John (b. 1815) and Richard (b. 1823) both suffered from chronic asthma, which rendered the former a valetudinarian long before his death in 1874.[10] James Fintan's spinal injury, which may have been the outcome of an undocumented domestic accident, when a family nurse dropped him as a child,[11] had a significant bearing on his personal development and family relationships, while sapping his energy and frustrating his efforts in public life.

Accordingly, William (b. 1810), the third born and second son, assumed household responsibilities, which would ordinarily have fallen to the first born son. Known to neighbours and friends as Master Billy, William actively supported his father during the tithe campaign and on the election hustings of 1832 and 1835. During Patt Lalor's short parliamentary career, William relished the responsibility of managing the family's agricultural holdings, while also collecting information from local tenant farmers, which his father used in parliamentary debates.[12] William was the undeclared heir to Tinnakill. However, Patt Lalor's reluctance to reward William's abilities and loyalty with a significant holding, precipitated the latter's departure to America. Though Patt Lalor regretted his favourite son's departure and endeavoured to secure his return by promising 'to divide' his property with him, William who established a thriving farm in Wisconsin was never to return to Tinnakill.[13] Throughout the 1840s each of the Lalor children imitated the bold precedent of contesting and violating paternal directives, which had been most clearly established by William and James Fintan.

While William rebelled against the paternal yoke, unlike James

Plate 19.1   James Fintan Lalor (from frontispiece to L. Fogarty, *James Fintan Lalor patriot and political essaysist 1807-1849* (Dublin, 1918)).

Fintan, he had enjoyed a fond relationship with his father during his years at Tinnakill. The earliest extant communication between Patt Lalor and James, emphasises the strained relationship between father and eldest son.[14] Contrasting sharply with this unhappy relationship was the close bond which existed between James and his mother, Anne Lalor. His delicate constitution obliged him to spend much of his first seventeen years at home, where he received private tuition.[15] In February 1825, mid-way through the academic year, James was admitted to Carlow Lay College, where he studied for one year. While poor health checked his studies, attendance at the college's courses in political economy and elements of law, were to have a bearing on his later theories. The unusual time of his arrival in Carlow may be attributable to both his own state of health and perhaps to events at Tinnakill. Anne Lalor after the birth of her eleventh child, Richard, in 1823, became seriously ill and was unable to nurse the infant, who was cared for by Catherine Delaney, the wife of neighbouring farmer, Michael Delaney of Mountfead.[16] Likewise, it was in the mid-1820s when his father's political career commenced. By 1825, 'the Honest Patt Lalor' was fully immersed in galvanising support for Emancipation. Correspondence between Lalor and Daniel O'Connell in 1825 indicates that Patt Lalor had the important function, in the wake of disaffection generated by Burdett's Relief Bill, of conciliating local clerical opinion in the diocese of the influential James Doyle.[17]

James' invitation to his mother to visit Carlow College at the start of the summer vacation, would seem to indicate an improvement in her wellbeing.[18] During the short vacation, James spent only a few days at Tinnakill, returning to Carlow on 8 August for the commencement of the new academic year.[19] However, failing health brought him home again in February 1826.[20]

Little is known of his immediate subsequent activities. Upon his recovery it seems that his father secured an apprenticeship for him in Maryborough with Dr. Jacob, where he was to study with the intention of gaining a place in the Royal College of Surgeons. Given Patt Lalor's understanding of parenthood,[21] his efforts to plan a medical career for James were indeed likely. However, his plans backfired in 1827 upon the death of Jacob. Possibly because of a disagreement with Jacob's son, James quit his medical studies and according to traditional lore undertook a continental journey:

> His life abroad was a restless one. He was covetous of experience, action, adventure. The parts of France whose associations attracted him, he explored quietly with something of a devotee's ardour. Around the capital especially he found countless footprints

which he followed with passionate interest, living the crowded days and months of 1789.

His travels we are told were financed by his mother:

Though his tastes were not those of a grand seigneur, his travels cost a considerable sum, and but for frequent remittances from home he might often have come to a stand-still. His mother, however, kept him supplied regularly – his father naturally refusing to encourage him morally or materially.[22]

However, in view of James Fintan's literary instincts and 'penchant for hoarding letters', the absence of any correspondence between him and Tinnakill at this time implies that he was at home in the period from 1827 to the early 1830s.[23]

These years coincided with the pinnacle of Patt Lalor's political career and the transfer of routine farm and household responsibilities to his sons William and Joseph. In the anticlimatic atmosphere following Emancipation, the prospect of rallying support for a Repeal campaign was daunting. However, the Repeal issue provided Lalor with the platform for his most memorable agitation. At a Repeal meeting in Maryborough on 10 February 1831, Lalor launched the programme of resistance to tithes in the Queen's County.[24] Lalor's prime motive in opposing the payment of tithes has been attributed to personal pecuniary interest rather than altruistic concern for the interests of the people.[25] Certainly a complex combination of peculiarly local and general factors account for Lalor's unwillingness to pay tithes. The parish's entry into composition in 1829, vestry abuses and of particular relevance, the change in the mode of collection[26] strenghtened the prevailing perception of tithes as an inequitable and badly administered tax. Furthermore, arbitrary interpretations of Lalor's motives must acknowledge his role as the conductor and overseer of popular politics, whose perception of self was that of a leader in a class struggle between the 'aristocracy' and the 'democracy'.[27]

In view of James Fintan's later theories on agrarian issues, Patt Lalor's programme of opposition to tithes is particularly instructive. As befitted a follower of O'Connell, Lalor's opposition was carefully tailored to remain within the law. The system of passive resistance advocated by him and started in Graiguenamanagh the previous year, ensured widespread support from adherents of different faiths and persons in varied economic circumstances. In his evidence before both select committees appointed to enquire into the collection and payment of tithes in Ireland, Patt Lalor's interpretation and recourse to the law, stumped the commissioners, who regarded the law as absolute, immutable and hence unassailable.[28] A further hallmark of his campaign against tithes was his advocacy of a progamme of exclusive dealing and boycotting of those who failed to support the agitation.[29] Finally, in Lalorite tradition, Patt Lalor set out his own proposal for the maintenance of the established church. His tendency to issue didactic treatises, which include terminology used by James Fintan, would seem to indicate a significant paternal influence over the eldest son. Thus, what have been referred to as 'idiosyncratic neologisms – such as "overplus"'[20] were in use at Tinnakill.[31] Patt Lalor's popular efforts were crowned in glory with his return for the county in the 'Tithes or No Tithes' electoral contest of 1832. Unlike William, James offered no public support to either the tithe or election campaigns. Despite this apparent indifference, his life and that of the household generally, continued to revolve around the activities of Patt Lalor.

James apparently took advantage of his father's parliamentary absence to join the entourage of William Conner of Inch, county Kildare. Conner was an agrarian radical whose views on the land issue went beyond mere tithe commutation. His ideas demonstrated both an appeal to law and a concern for economic principles. Lalor undoubtedly viewed his apprenticeship to Conner as a furthering of his education and an opportunity to improve his grasp of 'applied' law and economics.[32] How long this apprenticeship to Conner lasted is uncertain, it had certainly ended by 1840 when James was immersed in the activities of the Raheen Temperance Society, close to Tinnakill. James was secretary to this society, renamed the Shamrock Friendly Society in 1841, which had as one of its principal aims, the provision of free legal advice to the poor.[33] Much to his annoyance, neither the activities of the local society, nor his concern with the implementation of land reforms aroused his father's interest. Indeed their relationship remained brittle and deteriorated further after the death of Anne Lalor. Agrarian issues had been displaced by the tithe act of 1838, when popular politicians became pre-occupied with the workings of an Irish poor law and the revitalised campaign for Repeal.

IV

By the late 1830s dissatisfaction with O'Connell's apparent 'Whig Alliance' was mounting. Due to the intransigence of the Tory House of Lords, the Whigs failed to effect their major Irish reforms. Anticipating Tory victory under Robert Peel in the 1841 election, O'Connell launched a new association for Repeal. The Association attracted and benefited from the prominent membership and philosophical contributions of Thomas Davis, Gavan Duffy and John Dillon. This triumvirate founded the *Nation* in 1842, where they espoused a new nationality which extended beyond O'Connell's utilitarian constitutionalism and distanced them increasingly from the Repeal Association. Yet, in the 'Repeal Year' of 1843 and monster meetings, the *Nation* essentially supported the O'Connellite line. Similarly, Patt Lalor was orchestrating public support in the Queen's County, where he utilised his position as a poor law guardian for both the Abbeyleix and Mountmellick unions to promote Repeal.[34]

Contrary to public opinion, James Fintan identified the Repeal movement as an undesirable diversion and potential obstacle to tackling the country's most pressing need, fundamental agrarian reform. Agrarian reform, which would be founded upon 'an agricultural peasantry – not grass farmers or gentleman farmers, not breeders of stock or feeders of fat cattle; not gentlemen who try to be farmers, nor farmers who try to be gentlemen'.[35] In short, not through the efforts of those in his father's position or at the helm of the Repeal movement. Ironically, such discreditable characteristics were reinvoked as positive attributes in James Fintan's letter to Robert Peel. He informs Peel, that as the son of a gentleman farmer, he enjoys a station in life, which places him at a 'point of contact, where all ranks of Repealers touch'.[36] His motive in writing to Peel is to exploit his position at Tinnakill to assist in the suppression of the Repeal movement. He expresses his intentions in forceful terms: 'I am most anxious that the present Repeal movement should be speedily and safely suppressed, not imperfectly and for a period, but fully and forever'.[37] Lalor poured scorn on the Repeal agitators and looked to the landed proprietors for an improvement in Ireland's condition. 'To them alone, that Ireland can look with any real and rational hope, – with any hope that can stand one cool moment's examination – of amendment in her social condition; of deliverance from her present state of poverty, disturbance and insecurity; and of the establishment, on a settled and solid basis, of tranquillity, industry, order and prosperity.... It is worse than vain to be looking – as too many in Ireland are looking – to what is called Agitation'.[38] He continues to dwell on the paramount role of the landed proprietors, who finally as a result of their inaction, are the recipients of Lalor's most venomous attacks. Thus, in 1843, he perceived membership of Peel's Conservative party the optimum means of achieving his goal.[39] By 1847, he had defected to the Young Irelanders. Essentially, Lalor perceived parties as potential vehicles for realising agrarian change, rather than concentrating necessarily on ideological distinctions. Whether Patt Lalor knew of his son's treacherous correspondence with Peel is uncertain. James did take precautions to ensure that his father remained ignorant of this duplicity and used a Miss Butler's house in Maryborough as his forwarding address. However, his disparaging remarks on gentlemen farmers, implicitly criticising his father, marked a nadir in family relations, which hastened James Fintan's departure from Tinnakill (Plate 19.2).

Away from home, James was preoccupied with efforts to establish an independent career. Securing a respectable position took precedence over the composition of political expositions. Coinciding with heightened internecine conflict within the Repeal Association over a range of issues from federalism to the Peace Resolutions, James Fintan seemingly viewed the fracas with detached bemusement. Alternatively, and somewhat more charitably, his silence may be associated with his continuing poor health. Somewhat ironically, Patt Lalor repeatedly forwarded monies to James during his illnesses. Other family members, notably Jerome,[40] who emigrated to America in March 1845,[41] acted as intermediaries between father and eldest son. When James had recovered his strength he became involved in a scheme with William Blood, to establish a bank which would provide loans, at reasonable rates, to the poor.[42] James travelled from Dublin to Belfast in the late spring of 1845 to study the bank scheme under Fr. Finn, who was supervising a similar project. Fortunately James remained in contact with home, through his brother Richard.[43] When his health deserted him once more in late June, the regular remittances from Tinnakill, paid for his lodgings and keep. During this illness, James remorsefully pondered over the anguish he and other family members had inflicted on their father. He ruminated over his own grievances, while expressing regret on the subject of his sister Mary's marriage to her long time fiance, the Episcopalian, Joe Foxe.[44] At this time James made a voluntary promise to God, that upon his recovery, he would write to his father begging forgiveness for the past and reconciliation for the future. A conciliatory letter, effecting a distinct rapprochment followed.[45]

Remaining in Belfast, James next applied for the post of librarian and chemistry lecturer at the city's Mechanics Institute. Among an impressive set of testimonials we are objectively informed that:

> his reading has been most extensive and his habits having been at all times studious he possesses an acquaintance with books upon almost every subject far beyond what I have experienced with well educated men in general – His mind I consider clear, practical, and conceptive marked with strength and originality....[46]

As Mr. Millar, the incumbent librarian did not vacate the position and James stipulated demanding conditions before accepting teaching

Plate 19.2   Tinnakill (also written as Tennakill) House (courtesy IAA).

reponsibilities, he was forced with 'very bitter feelings' to leave Belfast and return to Dublin, where he took lodgings in Trinity Street. During the winter his health deteriorated sharply. Though reluctant to return home, continuing illness made his journey to Tinnakill on 15 March 1846, with his brother Thomas inevitable.[47]

V

My object is to repeal the Conquest – not any part or portion but the whole and entire conquest of seven hundred years – a thing much more easily done than to repeal the Union. That the absolute (allodial) ownership of the lands of Ireland is vested of right in the people of Ireland – that they, and none but they, are the first landowners and lords paramount as well as the lawmakers of this island – that all titles to land are invalid not conferred or confirmed by them – and that no man has a right to hold one foot of Irish soil otherwise than by grant of tenancy and fee from them, and under such conditions as they may annex of suit and service, faith and fealty, etc. these are my principles.[48]

Freed from the drudgery of daily independence, the stability of home life provided James with an environment conducive for the formulation of policies aimed to reduce the tenant's plight. While his health remained precarious for much of 1846, the spectre of famine and growing assertiveness of the Young Irelanders propelled him towards a more active role in public life. In anticipation of resolutions in support of Repeal being passed at the inaugural meeting of the formally established Irish Confedration in January 1847, James expressed his reservations to Gavan Duffy. Essentially, he outlined the folly of committing the new found association to the mere seeking of Repeal or to 'the use of none but legal means as any means and all means might be made illegal by Act of Parliament'.[49] In subsequent months, James expounded a series of arguments which portrayed the famine as a catalytic watershed in Irish history. For he identified 'the failure of the potato, and consequent famine' as 'one of those events which come now and then to do the work of ages in a day, and change the very nature of an entire nation at once'.[50] As a result 'society stands dissolved... and another requires to be constituted'.[51] For James Fintan, land was the fundamental cornerstone of any new social constitution. Thus, he challenged the foreign garrison of landowners to become a 'national guard' overseeing the introduction of a system of tenant proprietorship.

In essence, James perceived Repeal as the question of the town population and the land tenure issue the concern of the country peasantry. According to his developmental theory, which confirmed the indefeasible rights of property, 'until an affluent husbandry shall have first been created, no manufacture can be established on a secure foundation'.[52] The basic seed for social and economic reconstruction he refers to as a numerous and efficient agricultural yeomanry. Yet, using his own data, his developmental theory is inherently flawed. Dispossessing the lands of the eight thousand aristocrats and dividing same among the existing occupiers would soon have created grossly uneconomic holdings. As a recent biographer has noted: 'how this could lead to anything but subsistence agriculture – by definition unable to accumulate surpluses for the urban sector – is not elucidated, is not even recognised as a problem by Lalor'.[53]

Until 1847 O'Connellite repealers had borne the brunt of James Fintan's disdain. However, O'Connell's death and the decline of the Repeal Association focussed Lalor's contempt on the aristocracy. None but the landed proprietors continued to thwart the realisation of his blueprint for a new social constitution. Increasingly he was convinced that the deteriorating condition of tenant farmers as detailed by his father before the Devon Commission,[54] had been alarmingly exacerbated by famine conditions. He argued that the famine was been used by the government as a means to pursue the active policy of clearance. The landlords were assisting the process through evictions, emigration programmes, compulsory surrenders and forced sales. Much of this criticism was founded upon his vehement detestation of the family who represented the bastion of conservatism in the Queen's County, the Cootes of Ballyfin.[55]

During the first half of 1847, Lalor expressed his views in a series of letters to the *Nation*. In his correspondence with Duffy, Mitchel, Doheny and D'Arcy McGee, James proposed the organising by the newly founded Confederation of a rent strike by the smaller tenants. However, the Confederation was musing over policy and its failure to adopt an official programme of action precipitated his decision to form a Tenant's Association, which ultimately led to the tenant meeting at Holycross in September. The attempt to form a Tenants Association was not novel,[56] but the scheme was greeted by Patt Lalor as 'wild and visionary, and unsound in principle'.[57] The meeting itself was an unmitigated disaster. During a heated exchange between James and William Conner of Inch, the platform collapsed and the crowd dispersed after a show of hands in favour of the proposed Association. The Conservative *Leinster Express* reported how Conner had thrown the meeting into disarray with the allegation that: 'when Mr. Lalor and his father were taking the last penny from their tenants, I gave mine a perpetuity in the land'.[58] Not surprisingly the Tenant Association of Tipperary was forgotten and the proposed rent strike never materialised.

<h1 style="text-align:center">VI</h1>

After the Tipperary debacle, James favoured the printed medium over grass roots activism to propagate his ideas. The Confederation had by 1848 become hopelessly split between Duffy and the moderates on the one hand, who advocated the union of classes to ameliorate conditions in Ireland and the radicals led by John Mitchel who sought to ferment class conflict. With Patt Lalor's appointment to the magistracy in October 1847[59] combined with his insistence that the country's lamentable condition could only be ameliorated when all political, sectarian and class differences were set aside; not forgetting the seeming indifference of the ascendancy: it was to be expected that James Fintan was to be found among the radicals.

John Mitchel had founded *The United Irishman* when it became clear that the differences between him and Duffy were insurmountable. Mitchel invited James to write for the new publication. His refusal to do so was apparently related to Mitchel's unacknowledged adaptation of Lalor's rent-strike policy, rather than any ideological differences. Thus, after Mitchel had been transported for his militant articles in *The United Irishman*, Lalor stepped into the breach as co-founder and editor of John Martin's *Irish Felon*. The *Felon* ran for five issues, Lalor contributing seven articles. Predictably the first articles reaffirm the supremacy of the land issue:

> Repeal is not an armed man, but a naked beggar. You fail in finding the first and fundamental element of military force – you fail in finding men. The only martial population that Ireland possesses – the small farmers and labourers – will never wield a weapon in favour of Repeal.[60]

The above hints at the increasingly militant tone of Lalor's contributions, which reach a despairing crescendo or emotive rallying call in the final lines of his ultimate article entitled, *Clearing Decks*:

> Meanwhile, however, remember this that somewhere, and somehow, and by somebody, a beginning must be made. Who strikes the first blow for Ireland ? Who draws first blood for Ireland? Who wins a wreath that will be green forever?[61]

Unsurprisingly, the *Felon* offices were raided and a warrant for

Lalor's arrest was issued on 26 July.[62] He was arrested at Ballyhane, near Nenagh, prior to the outbreak of hostilities at Farrenrory, Ballingarry. Brought to Nenagh gaol, where Fr. Nicholas Power was able to inform Patt Lalor of his son's well-being,[63] he was later transferred to Newgate Prison in Dublin. James remained incarcerated until November 1848, when he was released because of ill-health. After his release, despite previous rhetoric, he attempted to found another journal, *The Newgate Calendar,* as a successor to the *Felon.* He even wrote to Duffy asking him to be the proprietor of the new journal.[64] However, Duffy had no interest in Lalor's proposed publication while Joseph Brennan, editor of the *Irishman,* opposed the founding of a rival journal. Brennan extended his opposition to James' paper by increasing his influence in the secret clubs, which Lalor had helped to establish in 1849. Thus, James failed to found his own paper, while also losing control of policy in the clubs. A simultaneous uprising was planned in the southern and western counties of Kilkenny, Tipperary, Waterford, Cork, Limerick and Clare in September. Apart from a minor skirmish at Cappoquin, the remainder of the country remained tranquil, including Cashel, where James was entrusted with the task of attacking the local barracks.[65] Though he had a force of some one hundred and fifty volunteers, 'not badly armed', he did not lead the expected assault but returned instead to Dublin, where he revived his plans to start his own paper. The scheme never reached fruition, his health once again failing and he died on 27 December 1849.[66]

VII

From this overview, two factors, which the *Nation's* obituary in 1850 refer to, are highlighted as central influences on James Fintan's life: Tinnakill and poor health.[67] While the latter was a persistent frustrating constraint, the former was fundamental to the development of his theories. Despite the well-documented strains in family relationships, many of the core beliefs of Patt, James and Richard (the most politically active family members) are notable more so for their similarities than differences. In the context of James Fintan's theories, the triumvirate were all exponents of the principle that the land of Ireland belonged to the country's tenant-farmers, 'its people'. But, the Lalors, a prosperous middle-class family were not advocating land nationalisation, but conversely the indefeasible rights of property. While Patt and Richard Lalor acted as local leaders of the inarticulate masses, James propagated his advocacy of a new social constitution through the national popular press. His persistent efforts to instigate change through the power of his writings, rather than through physical force, could be ascribed to his ill-health, but the strong impression is, that he preferred the role of ideologue to that of activist.

The *Nation's* obituary provides further insightful material upon this theme. The appraisal includes a section which asserts James Fintan's central tenets:

> the result of all that he had read or thought of the history of other countries, and the condition of his own, was a firm belief that Ireland's misery was mainly attributable to one great social cause – the false relation existing between landlord and tenant; that the entire system by which land was held in this country, was radically and morally wrong and that until it was superseded by an arrangement which would secure all men the possession of their equitable rights, there could be no reasonable hope of Irish independence or prosperity.[68]

An unjust and inequitable land tenure system had created an impoverished and vulnerable people. The suffering in the 1840s starkly illustrated the pressing need for fundamental social and political changes. Identifying and rallying support for an effective response to Ireland's immediate plight, concentrated Lalor's mind in the 1840s. A popular transformation of social relationships rather than a prolonged agitation for Repeal was the most direct means to arrest and remedy Ireland's ailing condition. The corollary of such a new 'social constitution' was the redefinition of power relations. Agrarian and political transformations were not mutually exclusive. These central tenets were developed in Lalor's mind by the early 1840s and did not undergo any fundamental change thereafter.[69] Throughout the 1840s his personal crusade led to flirtations with virtually every available political credo of the decade. Seemingly, party politics were valued not for their philosophical characteristics, but as potential patrons for the expedient pedalling of his principles. Undoubtedly, his writings are riddled with literal supporting material for those who sought or seek to label Lalor as a nationalist or socialist. Likewise, the extent of Lalor's influence on the land movement in the 1880s must be considered with the knowledge that his writings were not made available in collected form until 1896, though a selection was published in 1882. Davitt, may have been familiar with Lalor's ideas prior to the New Departure. Certainly, he was familiar with the ideas of Richard Lalor, whose views on the land issue though more moderate than James Fintan's were not entirely dissimilar. Ultimately, it is crucial that Lalor's life, writings and political impact are interpreted within the twin contexts of mid-nineteenth century Ireland and the influence of Tinnakill.

References

1. L. Fogarty, *James Fintan Lalor – patriot and political essayist* (Dublin, 1918), p. xxi.
2. Ibid (Dublin, 1947), p. xiv.
3. D. N. Buckley, *James Fintan Lalor: radical* (Cork University Press, 1990).
4. Lalor Papers, MS 8570/3.
5. Ibid.
6. Assignment of profit rents, 1813, Lalor Papers MS 8570/3 Patt Lalor to J.M. Loughnan, 27 Aug. 1848, Lalor Papers MS 85 62/3.
7. *Second report from the select committee of the House of Commons appointed to enquire into the collection* and *payment of tithes in Ireland.* H.C. 1831-2 (508), xxi, q. 3918, p.379.
8. S. Clark, *Social origins of the Irish Land War* (New Jersey, 1979), pp 63-4.
9. Fogarty, *Lalor* (1947 ed.), p. xiii.
10. On the back of Tinnakill lease, 1767, appear the names, birth dates and sponsors at baptism of Patt and Anne Lalor's seven eldest children: James Fintan (10 Mar. 1807), Margaret (5 Aug. 1808), William (23 July 1810), Joseph (8 May 1812), Patrick (1814), John (1815) and Mary (1817). Lalor Papers, MS 8570/3.
    For the years of birth of the youngest five children, Jerome(1818), Thomas(1820), Catherine(1821), Richard(1823) and Peter(1827) see Catholic register of baptisms and marriages for the parish of Raheen, N.L.I., pos. 4202.
11. D. N. Buckley, 'James Fintan Lalor, radical', unpublished M.A. thesis (UCC, 1981), p. 23.
12. *Leinster Express* 21 Sept. 1833.
13. William to Patt Lalor, 12 May 1843, Lalor Papers MS 8567/2.
14. James to Patt Lalor, 9 Mar. 1834, Lalor Papers MS 8563.
15. Buckley, *Lalor,* p. 23.
16. Lalor Papers, MS 8573/3.
17. Daniel O'Connell to Patt Lalor, 30 Nov. 1825, Lalor Papers, MS 85 62/ 1.
18. James to Anne Lalor, 22 July 1825, Lalor Papers, MS 8563/1.
19. Buckley, *Lalor,* p. 24.
20. Ibid.
21. William to Patt Lalor, 12 May 1843, Lalor Papers, MS 85 67 /2.
22. Fogarty, *Lalor* (1918 ed.), p. xxi.
23. Buckley, *Lalor,* p. 16.
24. *Carlow Morning Post* 14, 21 Feb. 1831.
25. Buckley, *Lalor,* p. 16
26. M. G. O'Brien, 'The Lalors of Tinnakill 1767-1893', unpublished MA. thesis (N.U.I. Maynooth, 1987), pp 20-5.
27. *Leinster Independent* 14 Mar. 1835.
28. Patt Lalor gave evidence before both select committees. On 27 Feb. 1832 he was a witness before the House of Lords committee and on 6 Mar. 1832 he testified at the House of Commons enquiry. For his recourse and interpretation of the law see: Second report... H.C.... on tithes 1831-2(508) xxi, qs. 4063-4066, p.388.
29. Second report... H.L.... on tithes 1831-2 (663) xxii, p.70.
30. Buckley, *Lalor,* p.70.
31. Second Report ...H.C.... on tithes 1831-2 (508) xxi, q. 3908, p. 379.
32. Buckley, *Lalor,* p. 16.
33. James Fintan Lalor Papers, MS 340.
34. *Leinster Express* 6 May 1843.
35. James Fintan Lalor Papers, Address to the Landowners of Ireland 24 Apr. MS 340.

36. James to Peel, Frank Gallagher Papers, MS 18,390.

37. Ibid.

38. James Fintan Lalor Papers, Address to the Landowners of Ireland 10/1/1844, MS 340.

39. MS 18,390.

40. Jerome to James, 13 Feb. and 8 Mar. 1845, Lalor Papers, MS 3 40.

41. Ibid., 8 Mar 1845.

42. William Blood to James, MS 340.

43. James to Richard, 19, 25 June 1845, Lalor Papers, MS 8563.

44. Ibid., 19 June.

45. James to Patt Lalor, 7 Aug. 1845, Lalor Papers MS 8563.

46. Reference from Jas. N. Walshe M.D., James Fintan Lalor Papers, MS 340.

47. James to Patt Lalor, 13 Mar. 1846, Lalor Papers MS 8563.

48. Fogarty, *Lalor* (1918 ed.), p. 44.

49. Fogarty, *Lalor* (1947 ed.), p. 4.

50. Ibid., pp 8-9.

51. Ibid., p. 1 0.

52. Address to the Landowners of Ireland, 24 April, James Fintan Lalor Papers, MS 340.

53. Buckley, *Lalor*, p. 67.

54. *Devon Commission*. H.C. 1845 (657), xxi, q.55, p. 331.

55. Buckley, *Lalor*, pp 74-5.

56. William Trenwith was secretary to a similar tenant's association in Cork and had been in communication with James before the Holycross meeting. See Trenwith to James, 21 Apr., 7 May and Sept. 1847 in James Fintan Lalor Papers, MS 340.

57. *Leinster Express*, 25 Sept. 1847.

58. Ibid.

59. A return of Magistrates appointed and superseded in Ireland in the month of October 1847 (CSORP, A 11563).

60. Fogarty, *Lalor* (1947 ed.), p. 72.

61. Ibid., pp 114-5.

62. Warrant for James' arrest, 26 July 1848, Lalor Papers MS 85 63.

63. Fr. Nicholas Power to Patt Lalor, 14 Aug. 1848, Lalor Papers, MS 8562/3.

64. Fogarty, *Lalor* (1918 ed.), pp xxxvi-xxxvii and pp 154-5 for details of the proposed journal, *The Newgate Calendar*.

65. See T. P. O'Neill, 'Fintan Lalor and the 1849 movement' in *An Cosantoir*, x, no. 4 (Apr. 1950), pp 173-9.

66. *Nation*, 5 Jan. 1850.

67. Ibid.

68. Ibid.

69. Buckley, *Lalor*, p. 28.

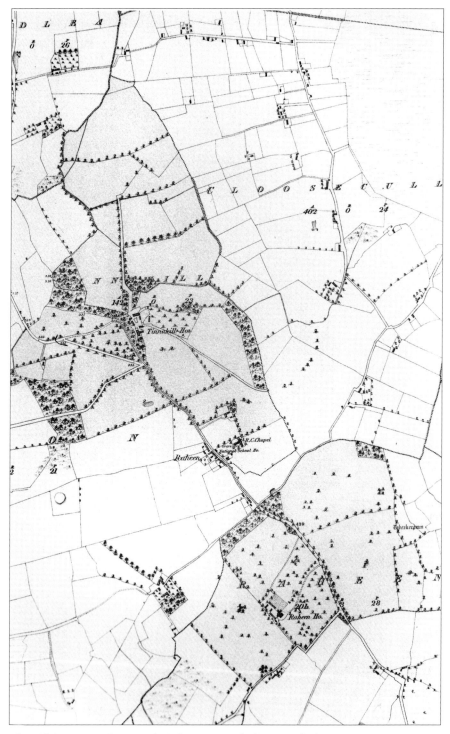

Plate 19.3   James Fintan, Lalor's homeground, sheet 17, 6" sheet Laois.

Chapter 20

THE LAND WAR OF 1879-82 IN QUEEN'S COUNTY

J. W. H. CARTER

The land war of 1879-82 is an important, disorderly, clamorous and sometimes violent period in Irish history. Yet until relatively recently Queen's County was neglected in the impressive body of scholarly literature resulting from the intensive investigation of the land war over the last twenty-five years. Of course, there is something seductive about the national leaders and the dramatic places and episodes. Even so, a concentration on one county does more than simply illuminate one piece of the complicated mosaic of the land war, it contributes towards a more satisfactory understanding of the land war in the country as a whole.

The traditional picture of rural life in the county before the land war as painted by many Land League leaders in the county – especially on public platforms – was a simplistic one. The mass of the people was portrayed as insecure in their holdings, living permanently on the verge of starvation and being preyed upon by parasitic landlords – *the fons et origo omnium nostrum malorum*[1] – who rack-rented, evicted-at-will, and who were habitually absent spending their ill-gotten gains abroad. Then, when harvests failed and prices collapsed in the late 1870s, a desperate land war, born of the need to survive, was fought by tenants against a landlord class supported by a 'barbarous code of laws'.[2]

Such a stark picture is inaccurate. Before the late 1870s, the county was not in a ferment of discontent ready to explode into a land war. Since the early 1850s the mass of its population experienced a marked increase in its standard of living: tenants' incomes and savings increased; the quality of houses improved; there were more traders confidently granting credit and selling a greater range and quality of goods. At the same time, landlord and tenant relations were generally satisfactory. The great majority of the landlords were not absentee, and while they invested little in their estates, they were unwilling to evict, and their rents fell significantly behind the growth in tenants' gross agricultural income.[3]

That there was depression, debt, and discontent in the county at the end of the 1870s is incontrovertible. But harvests and low prices reduced all farm incomes. With this reduction, farmers' indebtedness increased. The larger tenants found themselves not only owing mounting arrears of rent to their landlords but were also in debt to banks, which refused to give them any more credit. Shopkeepers were also in crisis: not only were they owed large sums by the mainly small farmers but they, in turn, were in debt to their own suppliers. By the end of the 1870s the credit system was paralysed. However, farmers reliant on livestock and livestock products fared better than farmers reliant on tillage. And, while the checking of their rising expectations might explain the disposition of some farmers, in a county where livestock and livestock products accounted for 75 per cent of its income from agriculture conditions were not as extreme as to impel the tenant farmers into a widespread land war orchestrated by the Land League.[4]

All the farmers in the county were not affected in the same way by the bearable 13 per cent drop in gross farm income from the triennial period 1874-6 to the triennial period 1877-9.[5] The hardest hit were the broken small farmers, the habitually distressed, the unemployed tradesmen and labourers, and their dependants – perhaps 15 per cent of the population of the county.[6] Most were precluded from emigrating because the economic slump in America and England in the years 1873-9 reduced the employment opportunities in the two major destinations of Irish emigrants. And bad harvests in Britain at the end of the 1870s curtailed even that source of seasonal employment. (During the years 1854-73 a yearly average of 1,096 persons emigrated from the county. The yearly average fell to 513 during the years 1874-9.)[7] Consequently, it is likely there was a 'pool of potential activists'[8] in the county who were left with time on their hands. But these paupers did not have the experience, social status or ability necessary to organise any cohesive action. In any case, because there was a perceptible gathering of momentum in agrarian agitation as privation receded after the autumn of 1880, it is reasonable to suggest there was no simple connection between the land war and distress in the county.

It was mainly due to the impressively effective and dominant leadership of Parnell and Davitt, and their inspiration of middle-class local leaders such as the tenant-farmers Patrick Cahill LL.B, William Fitzpatrick, Michael Carroll and John Redington, and the shopkeepers Patrick Murphy, Patrick A. Meehan, Martin Delaney, and Patrick Doran, that a radical transformation was effected in the county's parliamentary representation. Kenelm T. Digby and Edmund Dease, lukewarm home-rulers and members of Roman Catholic landowning families, were replaced by the middle-class Parnellites Arthur O'Connor and Richard Lalor.[9] This was accomplished in the face of bitter opposition by Roman Catholic priests such as Frs. James Sinnott of Raheen, John McGee of Stradbally, Thomas Nolan of Abbeyleix and John Doyle of Maryborough. Then, also inspired by Davitt and Parnell, veteran cleric and lay tenant-right agitators combined with young and energetic shopkeepers, farmers and Catholic curates to organise a small majority of the farmers and labourers (the mass of whom had no experience of formal organisation) into twenty-four branches of the Land League. (Four branches – Knock, Clough, Galmoy and Athy – which were outside but near the county boundary, also had many members from the county.)[10] While some of these local leaders may have been altruistic, and others were stimulated only by the desire for power, it is likely that many – particularly the shopkeepers and large tenant-farmers – were simply mercenary opportunists who appropriated a land movement which had started more than a year earlier among the small tenant-farmers in Connacht.

Until the winter of 1880, while noise, rhetoric, and some incidents accompanied the election of Lalor and O'Connor and the establishment of some branches of the Land League in the county, its population generally were still law-abiding – from 1 January 1872 to 1 November 1880 only thirty-three agrarian crimes were reported by the police in the county.[11] Nevertheless, the county was regressing steadily into disorder. Lawyers engaged by the Land League were increasingly active in defending tenants' interests in court. Predictably, this galvanised landlords and agents into a more vigilant handling of estate legal matters. At the same time, although there were noted exceptions such as Viscount Ashbrook and the much-vilified John George Adair,[12] most landlords probably granted selective abatements in rents – which had little effect on either landlords' or tenants' incomes – or accepted tenants' promises to pay rent at the autumn gale of 1880.

Then, as the summer of 1880 closed and the autumn gale neared, relations between landlords and their tenants worsened perceptively. Landlords, who believed they had been generous in their response to the flood of demands for rent reductions to the Griffith valuation by permitting abatements, and the growth of arrears (in some cases, to as much as half their annual income from rent), felt they were entitled at least to the rent due. They were also showing a greater willingness to evict than any time since 1863. On the other hand, tenants viewed the autumn gale of 1880 with predictable trepidation: though less likely to· starve because of the bumper potato crop (5.1 tons per statute acre in 1880 in contrast to the previous year's 2.1 tons),[13] most were heavily in debt to a variety of pressing creditors including their landlords, and since the total annual value of agricultural output in the county in 1880 increased by less than 3 per cent,[14] their ability to pay their rents improved negligibly.

As demands for rent reductions multiplied, accompanied by resolutions for tenant solidarity and against land grabbers, there was an understandably enthusiastic response from most tenants. Landlordism *per se* was execrated by tenant leaders as a 'system that had robbed and plundered and beggared and murdered the natives of Ireland'[15] as they appealed to the spurious historic rights of the 'people' and set clearer lines of demarcation between the tenants and their landlords. 'Good and bad landlords' were described as sailing 'in the same boat' and 'should go down together'.[16] (Significantly, there is no evidence that shopkeepers in the county like Matthew Dunne from Ballyfin and Mark J. Codd from Mountrath – both officers in branches of the land league, and to whom tenants were as deeply in debt as they were to landlords[17] – were subjected to any opprobrium.) From December 1880 newspaper reports show an appreciable increase in incidents – such as a crowd chasing and ducking a bailiff near Rathdowney,[18] and 'rough-looking men' in Borris-in-Ossory sustaining a boycott[19] – from which one might deduce that tenants in the county were growing more confidently and menacingly militant. These incidents might be taken to signal the start of the land war in the county – perhaps twenty months after it had started in Connacht.

On the surface, the county seemed to support Davitt's claim in 1903 that the Land League leaders had lost a 'great opportunity' through their failure to launch a no-rent strike in that spring of 1881, when 'landlordism would have been easily smashed . . . , disciplined and prepared as the country was then'.[20] However, when Richard Lalor proposed 'a strike against the payment of all rent' in a letter published in the *Freeman's Journal* on 7 April, 1881 there is no evidence that it elicited any widespread enthusiastic response in Land League branches in the county. In the central office, in Dublin, Anna Parnell's was the only concurring voice commenting 'I was very glad to see your letter in the *Freeman* today. It is terrible to me to see the league folding its hands and standing by while the people are being butchered'.[21] In any case, it is clear that at no time during the land war were most land-leaguers in the county either 'disciplined' or 'prepared'. Meetings and demonstrations, with their bands, banners, cavalcades, and bombast from caparisoned platforms, created the impression of tenant solidarity, but it was an illusion.

Almost half of the farming population over twenty years of age in the county, however, were not land-leaguers.[22] Even so, debilitating discord and disunity were prevalent in the land league branches, and deteriorated as details of Gladstone's land bill became more widely known. The moderate elements probably welcomed most of the bill but were discreetly silent, while the die-hards were ungrateful and publicly critical. At the same time, the much publicised and costly policy of tenants paying rent 'at the point of the bayonet' was fundamentally fraudulent. Tenants who could pay their rent did so for fear of being evicted, isolating their less solvent fellow tenants, and perversely breaking the 'rule' of the Land League with the sanction of the Land League. No wonder then that Anna Parnell and her colleagues in the central office in Dublin should conclude that the Land League was a fraud when they discovered that the applications for relief from branches of the league were all on behalf of tenants evicted because they were unable to pay their rents.[23]

It was perhaps predictable that by the autumn of 1881, the Land League in the county should be *in extremis* – a condition precipitated by Gladstone's second land act, which became law on 22 August 1881. Even Parnell's attempts to keep the divided Land League together – his masterly performance at the Land League convention in Maryborough on 26 September 1881 was an important instance[24] – were hopeless.

On the other hand, the 'action' of many of the landlords in the county was demonstrably 'weak, defenceless and disunited'.[25] Of course, by the late 1870s, landlords' incomes had been drastically reduced. This narrowed the margin of their possible response to tenants' demands for reductions in rents, and self-reliance and pride dictated that they should act independently when managing their estates. Nevertheless, given their resources and small number (161 owners of five hundred acres or more owned 88 per cent of the county),[26] it should not have been too difficult for them to mount some sort of collective action against the Land League. As it was, when landlords evicted or threatened eviction they intensified the insecurity of tenants, and when they gave concessions to their tenants they indicated their own weakness. Both forms of landlord response encouraged the tenants to join the Land League, which was opposed to landlords remaining in existence at all, and ironically helped to spawn and spread the land war in the county.

While it must be conceded that after March 1881, with the passing of the Act for the Better Protection of Person and Property in Ireland[27] and the Peace Preservation Act,[28] and the first appearance in Queen's County of agents of the Property Defence Association[29] many landlords in the county were steeled in their determination to collect their rents, and appeared more ruthless in their dealings with recalcitrant tenants. They made increasing use of the sheriff, protected by the RIC and the military, to evict, seize and auction stock, crops and tenants' interests in their farms. When *habeas corpus* was suspended in the county on 6 May 1881[30] it seemed to herald a more clamorous and combative phase of the land war. It is clear most landlords perceived the county as increasingly in the grip of terror and outrage fermented by the spreading Land League, and still seemed intimidated by the apparent strength of their organised tenantry.

The evidence from the county supports Gladstone's speech in Leeds on 7 October 1881, when he castigated 'all the classes who possess property' for their 'general cowardice', and complained that the government was 'expected to preserve the peace with no moral force behind it'.[31] Though both the Property Defence Association and the Orange Emergency Committee were founded in December 1880, it was more than ten months later – when the Land League was in disarray – that three branches of the Property Defence Association were established in the county.[32] 'Very few' of the magistrates, who were landlords, had 'the courage [publicly] to back their opinions',[33] while, at the same time, though they were in a strong position to penalise publicans who supported the Land League, they faint-heartedly signed all the certificates of renewal of publicans' licences.[34] Despite their lack of confidence in Gladstone's government – especially since Forster's unsuccessful compensation for disturbance bill in July 1880[35] – landlords turned to the government for protection, and demanded draconian measures to restore law and order in the county. It is notable that after October 1881 the magistrates seemed more determined to uphold the law, and even 'good' landlords were less willing to bargain with their tenants.

The no-rent manifesto initially inspired alarm and pessimism among some landlords and their agents in Queen's County. At the same time, despite the best efforts of die-hard land-leaguers and the ladies' land league, the manifesto was denounced by most Roman Catholic clergy and ignored by most tenant-farmers, and was a conspicuous failure. Tenants in large numbers, who were not disqualified from the benefits of the Land Act of 1881 resorted to the land court, which had started its operations on 20 October 1881, the same day the Land League was proclaimed. (During the first seventeen weeks of its operation the Irish Land Commission received 578 applications from tenants in the county to have 'fair rents' fixed on their holdings.)[36] On many estates in the county the autumn gale of 1881 produced the usual wrangling over rents, but this was not what the manifesto envisaged. During the winter of 1881-2 there seemed to be a waning of public interest even in such token resistance as paying rent 'at the point of the bayonet'. The Ladies' Land League was left on its own in an impossible position: the police were clearly an effective deterrent, but what was more telling was that the men, while grateful for succour, could not and would not permit the women to direct the course of the land war. (The last published reference to any of the sixteen branches of the Ladies' Land League in the county was in *United Ireland* on 9 September 1882, which reported the dissolution of the Graigue & Killeshin branch.)

Whatever reservations one might have about the official statistics for agrarian crime, it is clear that after October 1881 the county endured its most violently disturbed period. Significantly, during this period, Martin Rogers, the one-armed, twenty-eight year-old 'attorney's clerk' was murdered on a boreen called Srahlane near Rathdowney while serving civil processes on tenants;[37] John Redington, who was suspected of being involved in a plot to rescue Parnell from Kilmainham, was gaoled for the second time – the only one of the twenty-two suspects from the county to be gaoled twice;[38] a campaign by land-leaguers succeeded in forcing the Queen's County Hunt to suspend fox hunting in November 1881 for almost two years;[39] Fr. Thomas Feehan, the vitriolic Catholic curate from Rathdowney, was prosecuted and gaoled for almost two months.[40]

It is worth observing here that, while agreeing with Paul Bew that 'it is a mistake to inflate the purely Catholic determination of the land war',[41] it would be wrong to ignore the sectarian dimension. In Queen's County, most Protestants stayed aloof from the Land League, though there were notable exceptions (such as the tenant-farmers Alfred Salter from Stradbally and Hulton J. Harrison from Ballyroan, Willam Henry Cobbe, a merchant from Portarlington, and William Jr. and William P. Odlum, flour millers in Maryborough and Portarlington) – thereby inviting censure from Land League leaders – and some had a siege mentality. Nor should one ignore the explicit sectarian violence in the environs of Rathdowney and Mountmellick where the action and pronouncements of acerbic Catholic curates such as Frs. Edward Rowan and James Connolly seemed to legitimise attacks on Protestants.

It must be conceded that with Gladstone's Land Act of 1881, followed by the Arrears Act of 1882, a radical change had been made in the land law of Ireland in the interests of the tenants. Nonetheless, it would be an exaggeration to describe the land war as a triumph for the Land League and the tenants in Queen's County for several reasons: First, though after the success of Richard Lalor and Arthur O'Connor in the 1880 general election two lukewarm home-rulers were supplanted and the county's parliamentary voice was identified not with the landed interest but with Parnell and the Land League, nevertheless, this new voice was rarely heard speaking in parliament for the county. Because of ill-health, and to his great embarrassment, Lalor was frequently absent from the House of Commons. Although he was popular with most of his constituents, and commonly described on public platforms as 'honest', throughout most of the 1880s he seriously contemplated applying for the Stewardship of the Chiltern Hundreds.[42] O'Connor was described by William O'Brien, the M.P. for Mallow, as one who 'to the terror and dismay' of the House of Commons 'fights them [the government] with their own forms, and . . . stews them in their own gravy'.[43] But although he may have been an effective advocate of the 'national cause', nevertheless, on his own admission, he had little correspondence from his constituents, and was an infrequent visitor to the county.[44]

Second, judicial rents, which were of special interest to most tenants, meant a reduction of less than 19 per cent – a level, described by the veteran tenant-rights leader, Fr. Matthew Keeffe, the parish priest of Aghaboe, as a 'cruel mockery', and fell far short of the reductions expected by most tenants' leaders. Moreover, judicial rents were fixed on only about one sixth of the holdings over one acre in the county. On the other hand, it is arguable that the landlords were financially better off in 1882 than they were in 1879, even though their legal powers were restricted by the Land Act of 1881, and then, under the Arrears Act of 1882, the Irish Land Commissioners 'extinguished' more than £30,000 arrears of rent for the tenants on more than 1,600 holdings in the county. At the same time, rents were stabilised under the Land Act of 1881, and when 'fixed' they were at a level higher than they might have had been had they been index-linked to the falling gross income from agriculture in the county during the 1880s.[45]

Third, although during the land war dismayed landlords were confronted for the first time with what appeared to be the collective strength of defiant tenants, it is clear that confrontation provoked many landlords into a more vigorous and collective response to their tenants' demands. By Christmas 1881 three branches of the Property Defence Association had been established belatedly in the county. And when Arthur MacMurrough Kavanagh, the landlord and magistrate from Borris, County Carlow, proposed the formation of the Land Corporation 'to meet the difficulty of cultivating boycotted farms from which tenants have been evicted', landlords in Queen's County were early and generous supporters – investing more than £9,000 by the end of June 1882.[46]

Fourth, as a result of the land war, the policing of the county intensified at substantial cost to its cess payers. There was an impressive fall in the number of reported agrarian crimes in the county from the summer of 1882, yet that year its cess payers still had to pay an extra £1,376.10s.0d. – half the cost of forty extra police.[47]

Fifth, while doubtless the many instances of discord and disunity in branches of the Land League left a residue of recrimination among its members, the land war must have left many tenants in the county discontented and disillusioned for several reasons: (1) Leaseholders – more than a fifth of the tenants in the county[48] – could not enjoy the benefits of the Land Act of 1881 until 1887. (2) Die-hard land-leaguers, who would have been satisfied with nothing less than the destruction of landlordism and the total transfer of the 'land to the people', must have been galled to see resilient landlords in the county evicting more tenants in 1882 and 1883 – predominantly tenants of small holdings – than at any time since the great clearances of the early 1850s. (In 1882 and 1883 a total of 522 persons were evicted without re-admission in the county.)[49] (3) Agricultural labourers in the county, who numbered more than fourteen thousand and were the poorest of the rural population, had been fobbed off by land-leaguers with assurances that their demands would be attended to when the 'farmers' question' was settled, were incensed when the land war ended. As Parnell admitted in Maryborough on 26 September 1881, they had gained nothing but the remote possibility that farmers – whom they distrusted – would do their 'duty' and give them 'employment and better wages'.[50] More than a year after the Labourers Act of 1883,[51] the police were noting the 'smouldering discontent' and 'ill-feeling' among labourers 'caused by the manner in which they have been treated by the farmers'.[52]

Finally, there were indications that, despite the public triumphalism of some tenant leaders after the land war, the tenants were less enthusiastic. When the Irish National League was inaugurated by Parnell in October 1882 – with 'land law reform' second to 'national self-government' in its list of five main aims[53] – the response in the county, and throughout Ireland, was apathetic. By 12 June 1883, it was in such straitened financial circumstances, that a clerk in Dublin Castle noted, 'were the league not supplied with funds from sources outside of Ireland, the contributions 'for the cause' sent from the branches in this country would not pay the office expenses'.[54] By the end of 1883, despite the best efforts of many leading land-leaguers – whom the police described as 'ex-suspects, bankrupts and desperadoes'[55] – it still had only 243 branches in the country, while in Queen's County there were only ten branches[56] – a vivid contrast to the twenty-four branches of the Land League which had existed in the county. (Not until January 1886 with 1,261 branches in the country as a whole – of which twenty-nine were in Queen's County – did the branches of the Irish National League outnumber the branches of the Land League.)[57]

In 1990, when the old secretary of the Maryborough branch of the Land League, Patrick A. Meehan, was speaking about the Land League and the land war he claimed that 'the tenants were at the mercy of the landlords, but the people banded themselves together and the power of the landlords melted away like snow in the midday sun'.[58] As Meehan must have known, this was simply make-believe. Landlordism may have been undermined by 1882, but it was far from destroyed by 1882. Throughout the remainder of the nineteenth-century landlords continued to play an important role in the affairs of the county. On 28 August 1887, Captain Robert A. G. Cosby, bemoaning the 'state of affairs as regards landlords' in a letter he intended to send to the *Dublin Evening Mail* and the *Morning Mail*, wrote: 'I do not intend to die without a struggle'.[59] In a land war which had still to be won in 1882, many landlords in Queen's County would have voiced a like determination.

References

1. Fr John McGee, parish priest of Stradbally, to editor *Leinster Express* (hereafter abbreviated to L.E.), 1 Feb. 1879.
2. From the description of the 'laws supporting landlordism' by Fr James Cosgrave, the Aghaboe Catholic curate (L.E., 15 Jan. 1881).
3. J. W. H. Carter, *The Land War and its leaders in Queen's County 1879-82* (hereafter designated Carter, *Land War*), pp 1-26.
4. Ibid.
5. Ibid., appendix 1, p. 295.
6. Ibid., p. 284.
7. W. E. Vaughan and A. J. Fitzpatrick (eds.), *Irish historical statistics population, 1821-1971*, p. 288.
8. Joseph Lee in his *The modernisation of Irish society* (p. 66) suggests that in Mayo by the end of 1879 there were 5,000 extra young men – 'a pool of potential activists'. Adopting the rough method Lee may have used, there may have been about 1,500 young men in Queen's County in 1879 who were precluded from emigrating (Carter, *Land War*, p. 25, n. 4).
9. Carter, *Land War*, pp 37-52.
10. Ibid., pp 53-77.
11. *Return of [agrarian] outrages . . . 1 January 1844 to 31 December 1880* [C2756], H.C. 1881, lxxvii, 887-914 (8 Jan. 81); *Return . . . each month of 1878 and 1880 . . .* H.C. 1881 (5), 793-8. (6 Jan. 81).
12. *L. E.*, 1 Nov., 1879.
13. *Returns showing the number of agricultural holdings in Ireland and the tenure by which they are held by the occupiers* [C32], H.C. 1870, lvi, 737-56.
14. Carter, *Land War*, appendix 1, p. 295.
15. Fr John McGee speaking at public meeting in Clough (*L.E.,* 9 April 1881).
16. Fr James Connolly, curate in Mountmellick, speaking at public meeting in Mountrath (*L.E.,* 20 Nov. 1880).
17. Papers relating to Matthew Dunne's bakery, shop, agency for butter, manure and seeds (in private ownership); *L.E.,* 8 Jan. 1881.
18. *L.E.,* 11 Dec. 1880.
19. Ibid., 1 Jan. 1881.
20. Michael Davitt, *The fall of feudalism in Ireland: or the story of the Land League revolution,* pp 309-10.

21. NLI, Lalor papers, MS 8566 (10).

22. Carter, *Land War*, p. 76.

23. Anna Parnell, *The tale of a great sham*, pp 88-102.

24. *L.E.*, 1 Oct. 1881.

25. Description by 'old fox-hunter' in letter to editor (*L.E.*, 22 Oct. 1881).

26. *Return of owners of one acre and upwards in the several counties, counties of cities, and counties of towns in Ireland . . .* [C1492], H.C. 1876, lxxx, 75-81. [20 Apr. 76].

27. 1881 Protection of Person and Property Act, 44 & 45 Vict., c. 4, 2 Mar.

28. 1881 Peace Preservation (Ireland) Act, 44 & 45 Vict., c. 5, 21 Mar.

29. *L.E.*, 19 March 1881.

30. Letter dated 9 May 1881 from Thomas H. Burke, the under-secretary for Ireland, to Lord Castletown, the lieutenant of Queen's County (NLI, Fitzpatrick papers, MS 13752 (8).

31. *Nation*, 15 Oct. 1881.

32. *L.E.*, 15 Oct., 22 Oct., 31 Dec. 1881.

33. Letter from Edward S. R. Smyth to his father-in-law Lord Castletown (NLI, Fitzpatrick papers, MS 13752 (8).

34. Carter, *Land War*, p. 166.

35. 1880 A bill to make temporary provision with respect to disturbance in certain cases of ejectment for non-payment of rent in certain parts of Ireland, H.C. 1880 (232), i, 427-30 (18 June); 1880 [the foregoing as amended in committee], ibid., 431-4 (19 July); 1880 [the foregoing as amended in committee and on consideration as amended], ibid., pp 435-8 (22 July).

36. *Return . . . of originating notices lodged in the court of the Irish Land Commission and in the civil bill courts of the counties, up to and including 28 January 1882* [C3123], H.C. 1882, lv, 366.

37. Carter, *Land War*, pp 271-4.

38. Ibid., pp 238-42.

39. Ibid., pp 223-33.

40. Ibid., pp 242-53.

41. Paul Bew, *Land and the national question in Ireland 1852-82*, p. 217.

42. NLI, Lalor papers, MS 8566 (12).

43. O'Brien speaking to a public meeting in Rathdowney on 25 Nov. 1883 (*Weekly Freeman*, 1 December 1883).

44. O'Connor's speech to a public meeting in Maryborough on 28 May 1882. (*L.E.*, 3 June 1882).

45. Carter, *Land War*, pp 290-1.

46. *L.E.*, 24 June 1882 citing the *Freeman's Journal*.

47. Carter, *Land War*, p. 238.

48. *Returns showing the number of agricultural holdings in Ireland and the tenure by which they are held by the occupiers* [C32], H.C. 1870, lvi, 737-56.

49. Carter, *Land War*, appendix II, p. 300.

50. *L.E.*, 1 Oct. 1881.

51. 46 & 47. Vict., c. 60, 25 Aug.

52. Papers recording the 'progress' of the Irish National League (NA, C.S.O., I.N.L.L. & I.N.L. papers, cartons 6, 7, 9).

53. Ibid., carton 6.

54. Comment appended by R. E. Beckerson (a clerk of the lower division in the chief secretary's office) on 12 June 1883 to progress report on I.N.L. from 1 Mar. to 31 May 1883 (ibid.).

55.   Progress report on I.N.L. dated 26 Jan. 1883 (ibid., carton 9).
56.   List of branches 'established and collapsed' between 1 Oct. and 31 Dec. 83 (ibid., carton 6).
57.   List of branches 'existing' (ibid., carton 7).
58.   The poems and writings of P. A. Meehan (NLI, MS 19159, i, p. 38).
59.   Papers relating to the Cosby estate in Queen's County (in private ownership).

Chapter 21

COUNTRY HOUSES OF COUNTY LAOIS

DAVID J. GRIFFIN

Introduction

Edward Walford author of *The county families of the United Kingdom* lists almost ninety county houses and owners in the then Queen's County in the 1887 edition of his work. *The Georgian Society Records of eighteenth century domestic architecture and decoration in Ireland, vol. iv* published in 1913 lists only nine then considered to be of architectural interest. This essay includes a list which does not claim to be exhaustive, but attempts to include most of the important country houses of the eighteenth, nineteenth and early twentieth centuries (fig.21.1).

Laois is rich in country houses of all periods of which the most important are Castle Durrow built between 1716-18 by Col. William Flower M.P., later first lord of Castle Durrow, one of the best documented country houses of the early eighteenth century in Ireland; Brockley Park built in 1768 for second Viscount Jocelyn, later first earl of Roden to the designs of Davis Duckart which had important interiors unfortunately stripped in 1944; Abbeyleix built from 1773 was designed by James Wyatt for Thomas Vesey, Second Lord Knapton, despite nineteenth century alterations it contains important neo-classical interiors; Haywood built in 1773 was designed by its owner Fredrick Trench, an amateur architect with the help of James Gandon. Originally a compact villa, the house was much altered externally before its demolition following a fire in 1950. Emo Court or Park was designed by James Gandon, architect of the Custom House, Dublin, it was begun circa 1790 for John Dawson, first earl of Portarlington and remains his largest and best surviving country house.

Turning to the early nineteenth century, John Nash designed Gracefield an important example of a picturesque villa in 1817 for Mrs. Morgan Kavanagh. Ballyfin is one of the most important Regency country houses, not only in Laois but Ireland. Partially built to the designs of Dominick Madden, but completed to the designs of Richard and William Vitruvius Morrison in 1822 for Sir Henry Coote, ninth baronet. It remains their classical masterpiece. Richard Morrison

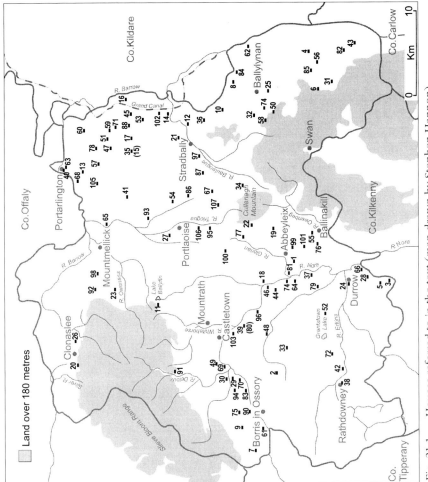

Fig. 21.1   Houses referred to in the text (map drawn by Stephen Hannon).

probably also designed Mount Henry, a villa, for Henry Smyth who died in 1838 and Farmley, another villa, now demolished.

Stradbally Hall while it incorporates an earlier house of 1772 can fairly be considered the most important and largest house of the Victorian period in the county, having been remodelled and enlarged between 1866 and 1869 to the designs of Sir Charles Lanyon. The most important survival from the early twentieth century is the elaborate formal gardens at Haywood designed by Sir Edwin Luytens.

It should be pointed out that the majority of houses listed are in private or institutional ownership and are therefore not open to the public. However some may be open from time to time. Haywood (gardens) and Emo Court are now in the care of the Office of Public Works and are therefore regularly open to visitors.

1. Abbeyleix house (plate 21.1)
A very fine three storey, seven bay house designed by James Wyatt, 1772. Built by William Colles of Kilkenny, foundation stone 1773. Very fine interior, decorative plasterwork, dining-room with grisaille paintings in the manner of de Gree. Exterior refaced in 1859 to the design of T.H. Wyatt who probably also added the library wing. The study was remodelled later by Howard Ince and further work was carried out by Detmor Blow in 1920.

2. Aghaboe
A seven bay, two storey early eighteenth century house incorporating the remains of a late seventeenth century house. Attractive mid-eighteenth century pedimented door-case. Originally linked to two flanking wings one of which has been demolished.

3. Aharney
An interesting mid nineteenth century single storey house built of brick with cut stone details, two storey tower at one end. Now a ruin.

4. Anneville
A small plain house having a small two storey folly tower in the grounds.

5. Archerstown
Five bay, two storey late Georgian house now in ruins.

6. Ashfield
Attractive three bay, two storey eaved house with Gothic style gate lodge.

Plate 21.1   Abbeyleix House (courtesy IAA).

7. Ballaghmore

An interesting two storey four bay late seventeenth century gable ended house. Door-case removed. Now a ruin.

8. Ballyadams

Rendered Gothic house of *circa* 1850.

9. Ballyduff

Small two storey three bay early nineteenth century house having a segmented headed door-case with fanlight.

10. Ballintubbert House

Two storey, five bay gable ended house dating from the early eighteenth century. Modern glass porch.

11. Ballyfin (plate 21.2)

The most important early nineteenth century house in Ireland. Built between 1821 and 1826. Dominick Madden produced designs for the house and built the library end of the house before Richard Morrison assisted by his son William Vitruvius were called in and completed the house according to a modified plan. A very fine interior featuring outstanding plasterwork, inlaid floors and chimney pieces. Thomas J. Cullen, architect designed additions in 1928 when the house became a boarding school.

12. Ballykilcavan, Stradbally.

A two storey seven bay pedimented house of early to mid-eighteenth century date having a Doric pedimented door-case. Interesting internal plasterwork. Additions made to the rere in the lateeighteenth century. Very fine stable-yard.

13. Ballymorris

Small two storey three bay house with hipped roof.

14. Ballymanus

A long two storey house probably dating from the early nineteenth century.

15. Ballyshanduffe (alias The Derries)

Castellated house built in 1810 remodelled in the mid-nineteenth century.

Plate 21.2   Ballyfin (courtesy IAA).

16. Belan

Interesting two storey three bay house of two dates, the rere being earlier. The round headed rusticated door-case is flanked by Venetian windows with Gothic glazing.

17. Bellegrove

A large nineteenth century house. Very fine winter garden added later in nineteenth century to the design of Thomas M. Deane. Burnt 1922.

18. Blackhill House.

A plain three bay, two storey house of *circa* 1800. Later glass porch.

19. Blandsfort

A two storey early eighteenth century house built in 1715. A third storey and porch were added later. Interior has some original panelling and a very fine staircase. The stables were designed by Patrick Farrell in 1792. Landscape by James Frasar (1793-1863). A Mr. Dunn, architect provided designs for additions in 1821.

20. Brittas Castle

A castellated house faced in limestone and sandstone designed by John McCurdy in 1869. Extended and altered by Millar and Symes 1879. A ruin now mostly demolished.

21. Brockley Park

A three storey, seven bay house built in 1768 to the design of Davis Duckart. A single storey Doric portico was added in the first half of the nineteenth century also a top lit billiard room. Outstanding interior having very fine decorative plasterwork and an imperial staircase similar to that at Lota, Co. Cork also designed by Duckart. Stripped in 1944 though some ruins remain.

22. Bunny's Bridge

Small three bay house.

23. Capard House

Very fine large early nineteenth century pedimented two storey cut stone Greek revival house having a single storey Doric portico. Very fine interior recently restored. The elevation is very similar to that of Aclare House, Co. Meath. Very fine two storey stables.

24. Castle Durrow (plate 21.3)

A large and important nine bay two storey house built between 1716-

Plate 21.3   Castle Durrow (courtesy IAA).

1718. Castle Durrow is perhaps one of the best documented country houses of the early eighteenth century. The door-case bears the date 1716. The builder was Benjamin Crawley. Much added to and altered in the late eighteenth and nineteenth centuries.

25. Castletown House.
Two storey, three bay house of early nineteenth century appearance.

26. Clara Hill House
An attractive gabled nineteenth century house.

27. Clonreher
An early eighteenth century five bay, two storey gable ended house with dormer windows (altered in the nineteenth century). Simple round headed doorway.

28. Clonageera House.
A square three bay, two storey wide eaved late Georgian house having a single storey Grecian Doric portico of cut stone. Rare nineteenth century external sliding shutters.

29. Coolrain
A most interesting two storey, five bay gable ended house probably dating from circa 1750. Very fine pedimented rusticated door-case. Now a ruin.

30. Coolrain House
Two storey, three bay early nineteenth century house.

31. Cooper Hill
Five bay, three storey gable ended late Georgian house having rusticated arched headed door-case.

32. Corbally House
Much altered but having an eighteenth century door-case with sidelights.

33. Cuffesborough
A three storey cut stone faced house dated 1770. Very fine rusticated pedimented door-case. The entrance hall has shouldered door-case with triple keystones in arched recesses. Recently restored.

34. Cullenagh
Much modernised. Very fine yards and stables.

35. Derries, The
(see under Ballyshanduffe)

36. Drumneen
A plain two storey, four bay gable ended early eighteenth century house.

37. Dunmore (plate 21.4)
A three storey gable ended early eighteenth century house projecting two storey wings. A ruin for many years, now demolished.

38. Eastholme
House demolished but late Victorian gate lodge and stables converted into a house survive entered via a conservatory salvaged from the convent of Abbeyleix. Built in 1870 by John Perry of Rathdowney.

39. Edmondsbury, (Formely Newtown)
An attractive two storey, five bay early eighteenth century house sprocketed roof.

40. Elms, The
Old Georgian house having three bay three storey centre flanked by lower asymmetrical wings.

41. Emo Court or Park (plate 21.5)
The most important large late eighteenth century house in county Laois. Thomas Sandby provided unexecuted designs *circa* 1780 at around the same time as James Gandon who was responsible for the general arrangement of the house as built. Work stopped in 1798 to be completed in the nineteenth century by A & J Williamson of Dublin and Louis Villramy of London. A wing was added 1857-61 by William Claderbeck of Dublin. Magnificently restored 1969 onwards under the well known firm of Sir Albert Richardson and Partners when purchased by Mr. C.D. Cholmely-Harrison who recently presented it to the Irish people. The property is now in the care of the Office of Public Works.

42. Erkina
Early nineteenth century three bay two storey house with veranda to front.

43. Everton house
Strange late eighteenth early nineteenth century two storey bow fronted house.

Plate 21.4 Dunmore House (courtesy IAA).

Plate 21.5 Emo House (courtesy IAA).

44. Farmly

Very fine two storey villa of *circa* 1810-20 displaying the influence of James Gandon but most probably designed by Richard Morrison. Doorcase was similar to that at Rochestown, Co. Tipperary, (now a ruin). Demolished.

45. Fisherstown

Attractive two storey rendered gable ended late Georgian house with off centre full height bow front and attractive fanlight above door.

46. Fruitlawn

Two and a half-storey box like house with round headed doorway in later glass porch.

47. Glenmalire House

Important early nineteenth century cut stone house having very fine entrance hall.

48. Gortnaclea

An attractive three bay, two storey house besides which are the remains of a very fine tower house.

49. Goss Brook

A small three bay, two storey over basement house, with single chimney stack, probably dating from the early nineteenth century.

50. Gracefield

An important picturesque villa of 1817 designed by John Nash and carried out by William Robertston of Kilkenny. Very fine landscape park designed by John Sutherland.

51. Graiguverne House

Very fine five bay, two storey wide eaved house of cut limestone having a single storey Greek Doric Portico. Attractive staircase.

52. Granston Manor (alias Oldglass)

Very large late eighteenth early nineteenth century house of three storeys with single storey Doric portico. Interiors much altered in the late nineteenth and early twentieth centuries. Badly damaged by fire in 1977.

53. Grattan Lodge

Very fine two storey Victorian house built in 1882.

54. Heath House

Very fine long two storey mid-eighteenth century house incorporating an earlier building. Very fine cut stone pedimented Doric door-case in the style of Richard Castle. Recently restored.

55. Haywood (plate 21.6)

Originally a most attractive three bay, two storey villa said to have been designed by its owner Frederick Trench, an amateur architect, in 1773, who seems to have had some assistance from James Gandon who provided designs for the house in 1771. The house had a two storey basement and very fine interiors. Engulfed and spoilt by huge additions including a port couchere designed by Thomas Drew in *circa* 1875. Destroyed by fire in 1950. Ruin demolished. However the splendid eighteenth century landscape park with its follies and the early twentieth century formal gardens designed by Sir Edwin Luytens now beautifully restored are open to the public and are in the care of the Office of Public Works.

56. Hollymount House

A three bay, two storey rendered house dating from the late eighteenth century. Round headed door-case.

57. Huntingdon

Two storey square eaved house with a later porch and an attractive gate lodge.

58. Inch

A long low five bay, two storey gable ended house probably dating from the eighteenth century.

59. Jamestown

Two storey, three bay gable ended house probably dating from the early nineteenth century. Single storey Doric porch. Much extended *circa* 1858.

60. Kilmullen

Large two storey, seven bay house having a very fine single storey cut stone Grecian Doric portico flanked by full height low windows. Built *circa* 1810. Later wide eaved roof.

61. Kilmartin House.

Two storey, three bay house of about 1840.

Plate 21.6   Haywood House (courtesy IAA).

62. Kilmoroney House

Five bay, two storey house of *circa* 1800. Early cast iron bridge over the river Basins.

63. Kilnacourt

A large plain five bay, three storey rendered house with a parapet probably dating from the late eighteenth century. A late nineteenth century porch obscures the door-case.

64. Knapton

Very fine late eighteenth century house having good plasterwork. Older structure at rere. Demolished.

65. Knightstown

A two storey, five bay early eighteenth century house remodelled *circa* 1760. Nineteenth century wide eaved roof. Very fine late eighteenth century entrance gates with Coade stone plaques and urns.

66. Knocknatrina House

Very large two storey gabled Tudor revival house. Burnt *circa* 1940. Now a ruin.

67. Lamberton Park

A plain two storey Georgian house. Now demolished.

68. Landowne Park

A large plain two storey early nineteenth century gable ended house.

69. Larch Hill

A simple five bay, two storey house of *circa* 1820 having a good fanlight and door-case. Very fine gates and gate pier.

70. Laurel Hill

Five bay, two storey with pedimented breakfront. Probably dating from the late eighteenth century.

71. Lea House

Plain two storey, three bay late Georgian house having recessed arched headed doorway.

72. Middlemount House

Very fine house with two storey canted bays. Attractive mid-eighteenth century door-case.

73. Millbrook House
Attractive large two storey brick built late nineteenth century house.

74. Milltown
Three bay, two storey house with round headed door-case.

75. Mondrehid
Attractive simple, five bay, two storey gable ended house with round headed door-case.

76. Moneycleare
Three bay, two storey house of *circa* 1820.

77. Mount Eagle
Pleasant two storey house.

78. Mount Henry
An attractive two storey, three bay bow fronted villa with a single storey pedimented Ionic portico. Attributed on stylistic grounds to Richard Morrison and dating from circa 1820s. Very fine richly decorated interiors.

79. Moyne
A very fine five bay, two storey pedimented house of *circa* 1750. Reconstructed and extended following two fires in 1989 to the designs of James Rawson Carroll.

80. Newtown
(See under Edmondsbury)

81. Noefields
A three storey five bay gable ended house probably dating from *circa* 1750.

82. Olderrig House
A three storey, gable ended, early eighteenth century house with a very fine pedimented door-case. Now demolished.

83. Peafield
An attractive early nineteenth century three bay, two storey house with a segmental headed door-case.

84. Popefield
A single storey Georgian House.

85. Providence Lodge
Two storey house with central round headed door-case.

86. Raheenahoran
A three bay, two storey gable ended house formally of three storeys. Flanked by two small barns one having a date stone inscribed 'D.F.G. 1733'.

87. Raheenduff, Stradbally
An attractive interesting five bay, two storey gable ended house. Massive projecting chimney stacks. Attractive round headed door-case. Possibly a late seventeenth century house rebuilt in the early eighteenth century.

88. Rath House
Very fine two storey, seven bay house of limestone ashlar having a single storey semi-circular Doric porch. The low pitched wide eaved roof has a huge central chimney stack. Very fine interior featuring an oval entrance hall. A very fine circular domed cast iron conservatory was added *circa* 1850.

89. Rathleague Lodge
Plain two storey late Georgian house.

90. Rockview
Attractive nineteenth century three bay, two storey house with arched door-case flanked by Venetian windows.

91. Roundwood
A three storey pedimented house of *circa* 1760 probably incorporating, at the rere, an earlier house. Five bay entrance front faced sandstone. Rusticated pedimented door-case of limestone. Window cases have scrool keystones as at Damer House, Roscrea, Co. Tipperary. Most attractive two storey entrance and staircase hall having staircase and first floor landing with balustrade in Chinese taste. Restored by the Irish Georgian Society from *circa* 1970 onwards. Sold and now a guest house.

92. Rynn
A classical house with portico built in 1855 to replace an earlier house which had been burnt. Demolished.

93. Shaen
Very fine large nine bay, two storey Grecian house having a very fine

Grecian Ionic porch. Designed by William Dean Butler who exhibited his designs at the Royal Hibernian Academy in 1831.

94. Shanaderry.
Very good plain five bay, three storey house of late eighteenth century date.

95. Sheffield House
A three storey five bay eighteenth century gable ended house having an attractive Gibbsian door-case.

96. Shanahoe
Interesting Italianite house of *circa* 1850 rendered with limestone dressings. Door-case under a veranda.

97. Stradbally Hall (plate 21.7)
A nine bay, two storey house built in 1772. Remodelled and enlarged between 1866 and 1869 to designs of Sir Charles Lanyon in the Italianite style. Very fine Victorian interiors including a first floor top lit picture gallery. The main ground floor reception rooms still retain fine eighteenth century decorative plasterwork. This house replaces an earlier house on a different site.

98. Summergrove
A most attractive medium sized house of *circa* 1760 probably incorporated at the rere an earlier house. Five bay pedimented enterance front having a rusticated pedimented door-case above which is a Venetian window. The interior has a very fine wood carving and rococo plasterwork dating from circa 1760.

99. Thornberry House
A five bay, two storey rendered house of *circa* 1800 with a half hexagon bow.

100. Tinnakill or Tennakill
Two storey, three bay mid eighteenth century house with pedimented breakfront.

101. Valleyfield
A three bay, two storey house having a good fanlighted door.

Plate 21.7 Stradbally House (courtesy IAA).

102. Vicarstown Rectory
Asymmetrical house designed by J.F. Kempster dating from 1877. Top lit central hall.

103. Westfield House or Westfield Farm
Fine three bay, two storey classical house built in 1929 to replace an eighteenth century house destroyed by fire.

104. Woodbine Cottage
Single storey wide eaved house.

105. Woodbrook
A two storey five bay early nineteenth century house. Doric door-case. Three storey wing and tower at rere demolished in recent years. Very fine interior. Vaulted entrance hall. Drawing room decorated with murals in the style of Watteau probably carried out by the Edinburgh decorator, David Ramsey Hay who visited Ireland many times during the 1830s. These were recently restored with the help of the Irish Georgian Society.

106. Woodville
Two storey, five bay house dating from *circa* 1810. Later glass porch. Good gates and lodge.

107. Yellow House, The
Attractive two storey house with recessed door-case.

Plate 21.8   Folly in grounds of Ballyfin (IAA).

Chapter 22

CANON O'HANLON: HISTORIAN OF THE QUEEN'S COUNTY

DONAL McCARTNEY

John O'Hanlon was born in Stradbally in what was then called Queen's County on 30 April 1821, the son of Edward and Honora Hanlon.It is believed that his father owned a tanyard in the town. He was educated locally before going at thirteen years of age to the endowed Preston School at Ballyroan. In his *History of the Queen's County* he has described this school as follows:

> In the village [Ballyroan], there was a Protestant school, endowed by Alderman Preston with lands at Cappaloughlan. The school was a large slated building erected at a cost of £500. The schoolmaster was a Master of Arts from Trinity College, Dublin, who, with an usher, gave a classical and English education in 1834, 1835, 1836, to about fifty boarders and day scholars. His stipend was £55 per annum. In subsequent years the school was removed to Rockfield House near the village; while a Police Barrack and Dispensary have been built on the former site. The Preston foundation of late has been removed to Abbeyleix, where a new school has been provided, under altered regulations.[1]

During the years when the Preston School was attended by John O'Hanlon the headmaster was Mr. Arthur Hutchins M.A.The Protestant day-boys, according to the stipulation of the founder, received their education free; Roman Catholics paid £1 a quarter for their day schooling. Alderman John Preston of the city of Dublin had been granted 1,737 acres of land in 1686 on trusts, one of which was to pay a salary to a Protestant master at Navan, and another was to pay a master at Ballyroan.[2] By the time young O'Hanlon attended the school, the estate had been vested in the Commissioners of Education. While at the Preston School, he stayed, at least for some of the time, with his granduncle, John Lalor of Pass House, who left his grand-nephew £30 in his will.

He entered St. Patrick's College, Carlow, the diocesan seminary in

1840. Opened in the 1780s it boasts of being the oldest Catholic college in Ireland to come into operation after the passing of Gardiner's Second Relief Act (1782) allowing Catholics to open their own schools. O'Hanlon wrote of Carlow College:

> The Ecclesiastical and Lay College of Carlow is dedicated to Ireland's great Apostle. It was founded in the last century, and it has served its educational purposes during the present as well for the home as for foreign missions.[3]

And in an autobiographical footnote he added:

> The author's former student life, in this college enables him to pronounce with some degree of authority, on the excellent system of discipline and course of studies adopted; nor have these declined in any single particular under existing arrangements and academic government.[4]

O'Hanlon stayed for only two years in St. Patrick's College before emigrating in May 1842 with members of his family, first to Canada and then to Missouri in the United States. He carried with him references from his ecclesiastical superiors, and after a short time working as a river fireman was admitted to the diocesan seminary in St. Louis to continue his studies for the priesthood. He was ordained in 1847 by Dr Kenrick, a Dublin man, who was the bishop of St. Louis. O'Hanlon's father appears to have died in the early 1840s, but his mother died in St. Louis in 1887 aged 93 years.

After ordination he began his missionary work in the extensive prairie lands of north-east Missouri. Simultaneously with this pastoral work he also pursued his life as an author, publishing in 1849 an *Abridgement of the history of Ireland from its final subjection to the present time*, and then two years later, *The Irish emigrant's guide for the United States* (1851). He had been deeply touched by the scenes of sorrow, misery and illness of the Irish emigrants flocking into America in the appalling aftermath of the Great Famine. He worked hard to alleviate their sufferings and used his influence with his friend, Judge Brian Mullanphy, Mayor of St. Louis, who had financed O'Hanlon's education in the seminary, to provide hospital facilities for the emigrants. The *Irish emigrant's guide* provided valuable information for those starting a new life in the United States.

The ten years between 1843 and 1853, which he spent in the seminary and as a young missionary in Missouri, were later described by him in his *Life and scenery in Missouri: reminiscences of a missionary priest (1890)*. It is an engaging picture of the happy life he spent in the Vincentian seminary in St. Louis. The superior was an American of French descent, two of the professors were Spanish, one was Italian and another was German. There was only a handful of students – ten Irish, two French, one Italian and one American from Kentucky. The life seemed idyllic for this happy few until floods left the region reeking of malaria to which O'Hanlon fell victim. For a change of air he was allowed to accompany a newly ordained Irish friend to a frontier parish where again much of his work was among the Irish emigrants.

Because of persistent attacks of bronchitis he was advised in 1853 to return to Ireland to recuperate. He was first assigned light duties as chaplain to the Carmelite brothers in Clondalkin and then to the Carmelite convent in Rathmines, and then to the South Dublin Union. From 1861 to 1880 he served as curate in the parish of SS Michael and John, where another well-known historian, Fr. C.P. Meehan, was also a curate. Meehan and O'Hanlon were not only colleagues, but assisted each other in their researches. In thanking Fr. O'Hanlon for his valuable assistance given during the progress of his labours on the life of Hugh O'Neill and Rory O'Donnell in exile, Meehan described his fellow curate as the author of a life of St. Malachy and a life of St. Laurence O'Toole and 'other works of rare merit.'[5]

The two books of O'Hanlon's, referred to by Meehan, were his first of the many works he was about to devote to the lives of the Irish saints, and no doubt gave him the idea for his major historical work.His *St. Laurence O'Toole* was published in 1857 and *St Malachy* in 1859. During the half-century which he spent in the ministry in the archdiocese of Dublin he served under three archbishops – Cullen, McCabe and Walsh – all three of whom held the priestly-scholar in the highest regard. The biography of St. Laurence O'Toole was dedicated to Archbishop Cullen, 'the exemplary successor' to the 'illustrious' St. Laurence. The proceeds from its sale were to go for the benefit of the new church of St Laurence O'Toole in Dublin. That Father O'Hanlon belonged to what he himself described as 'the patriotic priesthood of Ireland'[6] was already clearly established in his biography of St. Laurence. He stated that if he had 'in the most remote degree contributed to increase the veneration due to the memory of this patriotic and sainted prelate'[7] he would feel gratified.

From the start, history, for Fr. John O'Hanlon, especially hagiography which concerned him most, was primarily for the purposes of spiritual edification. In this he was no different from the great contemporary historians in their attitude to the past as an arsenal of lessons for the present. But O'Hanlon had also been touched by that tradition of a critical approach to the lives of the saints which had been begun by the Bollandists in the seventeenth century with their *Acta sanctorum*. These clerical scholars, motivated by the sheer quest for truth, had given themselves the task of rewriting the lives of the saints on a critical basis. They had shown themselves ready to purge from the saints' lives all exaggerated accounts of the miraculous. Their approach was to give systematic attention to reconciling the statements of different authorities; to examine the problem of sources; to dissect traditions and legends; and to allow for the distortion through which these traditions and legends had been handed on to later ages. Unlike the Enlightenment critics of the Church, they did not reject out of hand everything written by the medieval chroniclers and annalists, but sought to extract from these sources the truly historical.

O'Hanlon had also come under the influence of Romanticism which from the late eighteenth century had altered radically the approach to history. Romanticism at one level had created a nostalgia for the past leading to the fictional works of a Walter Scott or the melodies of a Thomas Moore. But it also gave rise to the spirit of antiquarianism evident in the work of a Petrie or a Eugene O'Curry interested in the task of reconstructing the obscure and remote past from the remains that had survived. Both the Bollandist and the Romantic traditions were in evidence in O'Hanlon's first publication on the life and career of an Irish saint. He wrote in the preface to the *Life of St. Laurence*

> While critical accuracy has been ambitioned in all cases, the desire of producing a work of a popular character has not been underrated or overlooked. . . [8]

He acknowledged the assistance he had been given by living Irish scholars – Eugene O'Curry, John O'Donovan, J.H. Todd and William Reeves pioneers who were labouring away trying to establish a more scientific approach to early and medieval Irish history. On the other hand, the extensive footnotes (some giving Latin or French quotations) in which he discussed his sources, made few concessions to 'a work of a popular character'. An appendix to his book gave a prospectus of a new work being prepared for publication to be entitled *The lives of the Irish saints* in twelve octavo volumes.

He produced separate biographies of three more saints – *St. Dympna* (1863), *St Aengus the Culdee* (1868) and *St David* (1869) – before the volumes entitled, *The lives of the Irish saints*, began to appear. In the meantime he had published a more general history of Ireland under the title, *Catechism of Irish history: from the earliest events to the death of O'Connell* (1868). Because of its nature this comprehensive but brief outline of the major events of Irish history exhibits the author's general attitude to the past more sharply than do his specialised narratives of the saints. Fr. O'Hanlon claimed that in no other country did patriotism take 'a less practical course for social and political amelioration' than in Ireland.[9] Indifference, neglect and the failure to cultivate a study of Irish history were, in his view, the most obvious cause for such a state of things. He regarded instruction in the history of the country as all important and indispensable. But, he complained, it had been eliminated from our schools. From the pages of history should be gathered wisdom for future guidance; and history was 'a powerful means for shaping the future prosperity, power and greatness' of the people. Yet he did not treat history in the manner of a bare-faced propagandist; nor did he seek to draw crude political lessons from it. He recognised that it was almost impossible to write or study history especially of one's own country, without some degree of political or religious bias. But, he wrote, if we desired to study it with advantage and to profit by its lessons we should endeavour to divest our minds of prejudices. Historical records should be examined with patience, care and reflection; we should rise from their perusal 'earnest, philosophic and patriotic students, and not heated, impracticable or thoughtless visionaries'.[10]

O'Hanlon showed an awareness of the great contemporary debate between those, like Carlyle, who would reduce all history to the biographies of great men, and those who emphasised the long chain of causes that precede and prepare revolutionary changes in society. He accepted a middle way between these two opposite exaggerations. He believed that the causes that lead to the ultimate rise or fall of peoples 'are usually of slow but clearly perceptible growth'[11]. On the other hand, he was convinced that:

> Those great men, who by their learning, eloquence, energy, valour and virtue have laboured in the cause of country and religion, furnish the best and brightest examples for imitation. Their memory and actions should ever be presented to our recollection and afford incentives.[12]

What is interesting about this is the emphasis Fr. O'Hanlon placed on the men of learning and eloquence and not the patriotic kings and princes and rebel leaders. It will explain his interest in the lives of the saints in early Irish history and his hero-worship of O'Connell and respect for the scholarship of O' Curry in more recent times.

The catechetical method of instruction in elementary education was widespread in the nineteenth century. It was employed in biblical, religious and moral instruction and overflowed into the teaching of secular subjects. Catechisms of Irish history followed the format used in church catechisms, and could be equally dogmatic in their pronouncements. Such a catechism, written by Sister Mary Ursula Young of the Ursuline convent in Cork, was condemned by the Chief Secretary, Sir Robert Peel, as 'infamous', 'most mischievous and inflammatory'.[13] For his abridgement of Irish history, O'Hanlon also adopted the catechetical method, but applied it more in substance than in form. So as not to disrupt the narrative, the abridgement was written in consecutive paragraphs, and not in the style of question and answer. Each paragraph was numbered, and at the end of each chapter (or lesson), questions with corresponding numbers were appended. While the lessons were comprehensive they were also concise so as not to fatigue the pupil or reader.

The objectives were to make available from 'our rare, expensive or voluminous chronicles' the salient dates, persons and events in a 'cheap, clear, concise and consecutive form', to bring them within reach of 'nearly every Irish peasant'; to provide a manual for the use of elementary schools, private tuition or fireside reading; and to direct the more advanced reader to the best sources for further study.[14] It could be argued that the aims of the volume were over-ambitious and perhaps even contradictory. The questions appended did focus the mind on the information provided in the narrative, and to that extent were of great benefit to the beginner. The bibliography, on the other hand, was 'a very considerable array of the most interesting tracts on Irish history, both printed and yet remaining in manuscript.' It was more appropriate as a list of sources for a seminar paper of a university student than for the pupil of an elementary school. The patience and care which he preached, he carried out in practice in his own writing. Nor in his case could the charge be levelled of heated and mischievous propaganda. For the pre-Christian period he acknowledged the 'friendly suggestions and advice', and the painstaking criticism that he had received from Eugene O'Curry, the professor of Irish History and Archaeology in the Catholic University, whom he described as 'this thoroughly honest, judicious and noble-hearted man'. O'Hanlon admired O'Curry for not venturing to pronounce an opinion on many issues relating to early Irish history. In this, he said, O'Curry showed 'that characteristic modesty, inseparable from true learning and worth.'[15] It was a quality possessed in no small measure by O'Hanlon himself.

The *Catechism* is the work of a nationalist, but a nationalist of the constitutional variety in the tradition of his hero, O'Connell. At first glance this is, perhaps, a little surprising for Fr. O'Hanlon had been deeply moved by the Famine emigrants to whom he had ministered in

Missouri; and even more to the point, his own maternal grandfather, Denis Downey, had been among those rebels, in some sources numbered at 350, who had been massacred at Gibbet Rath on the Curragh on 29 May 1798. Fr. O'Hanlon's account of his grandfather's involvement in the rebellion describes how the insurgents having surrendered their arms were slaughtered indiscriminately. He tells of how his grandmother turned over about 200 bodies before finding her dead husband; he also recounts the ill-treatment of his 'broken-hearted', 'desolate' grandmother at the hands of the 'ruffian soldiery', and how she could never afterwards 'regard a soldier without feelings of deep aversion'.[16] Despite the tragedies suffered by his own family he concluded his account by describing it as furnishing 'a dark illustration of baneful events connected with the Irish Rebellion of 1798'.He added:

> It is no isolated episode, for many other family afflictions, equally deplorable and tragic in results, must have chequered the lot in life of thousands who became victims during this sad period of civil commotion and disorder.[17]

Phrases such as 'baneful events' and 'civil commotion and disorder' were an indication of the views of Fr. O'Hanlon on '98. His grandfather, he said, had been 'induced' by a relative to take up arms and join the insurgent ranks. He believed that the arbitrary and atrocious measures of a reign of terror by the government goaded the people to madness and revolt. While he did not spare the government, neither did he support or imply support for the physical force methods of the United Irishmen or their latter-day disciples. His emphasis was very different from that of his friend and fellow historian, Fr. Anthony Cogan, who in his *Diocese of Meath: ancient and modern* (3 vols, 1862-70), saw the '98 Rebellion as a heroic struggle against tyranny by a patriotic peasantry. Although O'Hanlon could condemn such atrocities on the insurgents as the 'heartless and deliberate massacre' at the Gibbet Rath on the Curragh, his final verdict on '98 was:

> Thus ended a rebellion, which was rashly undertaken, prematurely commenced, unsystematically conducted and unsuccessfully terminated. In these civil broils, it was conjectured, that no less than 70,000 persons perished. A very considerable number of the country people were cut off in cold blood or without the benefit of a legal trial. Property to the amount of millions was also destroyed. What is still more deplorable, a breach was effected in the union of Irishmen that subsequently worked the downfall of their country, and even yet continues to distract it with party and

sectarian divisions.

The question which was appended to this paragraph of the *Catechism* read: "How are its doleful results to be estimated?'[18] The stress was on the tragedy and misery and disastrous social and political outcome of a policy of violence.

O'Hanlon's attitude to the physical force tradition of Irish nationalism was no doubt greatly influenced, on the one hand, by his hero-worship of O'Connell and his pacifist policies, and on the other, by his regard for Archbishop Cullen and his strong condemnation of the evils of secret societies and, in particular, of the contemporary Fenian conspiracy. That is why Robert Emmet's rebellion in O'Hanlon's Catechism got less space than did the Veto question; and why the Young Irelanders were described as 'talented and public spirited but somewhat intemperate', and 'a discontented party'.[19] By 1848 'discontent and disaffection' had reached 'a dangerous degree'. The Confederate leaders and their followers 'broke into open violation of the law' but 'these premature, and ill-conceived attempts' were suppressed.[20]

In contrast with the Young Irelanders and the insurgents of 1848, O'Hanlon's admiration for O'Connell was without qualification. In O'Hanlon's book O'Connell was 'this wondrous public man', 'this illustrious pilgrim', 'a man of transcendent genius and patriotism', ' this uncrowned monarch' of the people's affections. 'It would be difficult, he wrote 'to over-estimate the qualifications of mind and body this extraordinary moral force leader possessed.' He then went on to list the Liberator's superlative virtues, and concluded his adulation by saying: 'The nation is signally favoured that can claim the possession of such an illustrious individual'.[21]

O'Hanlon's devotion to O'Connell took on very practical expression with his deep involvement in the O'Connell Monument project. From the first moment in 1862 when it was publicly announced in the *Freeman's Journal* that funds were being appealed for to raise a national monument in honour of O'Connell in Dublin, until the unveiling ceremony on 15 August 1882, Fr. O'Hanlon played a pivotal role. Over the twenty years he acted as honorary secretary to the O'Connell Monument Committee; organised the confraternities of the Dublin churches to assist in the collection of funds at the doors of the city churches; received donations on behalf of the Committee and carried out its correspondence; and in the end it was he who as the result of a resolution of the Committee, wrote the detailed *Report of the O'Connell monument committee* which was published in 1888. The whole enterprise, despite protracted set-backs, was for Canon

O'Hanlon (as he had become since 1886) a labour of love. Here again, in this *Report*, he expressed his agreement with O'Connell's policy for 'Repeal of the detested and disastrous so-called Union of Ireland and Great Britain', while at the same time condemning 'those dangerous elements which combine in secrecy to create widespread disorder.'[22]

An even more impressive labour of love for Canon O'Hanlon (parish priest of Sandymount since 1880) was his *Lives of the Irish saints*. This was to be his finest historical work, and that for which he became most widely known. It was intended to be published in twelve volumes, nine of which and a part of the tenth had appeared between 1875 and the author's death. Each volume was devoted to a month of the year; and under each day of the month an account was given of the saint or saints associated with the particular feast-day: The festivals thus chronicled were compiled from the calendars, martyrologies and various other sources relating to the ancient ecclesiastical history of Ireland. He had already noted that:

> Lives, acts and calendars of the saints of Ireland, with poems and tracts attributed or relating to them, are very numerous but not usually accessible.[23]

Amongst the published work directly related to the task O'Hanlon had set himself was the *Acta sanctorum... Hiberniae* of the seventeenth century Irish Franciscan friar, John Colgan. By the time O'Hanlon had completed volume III, he had already presented more in English than Colgan had in Latin; and further, he had the benefit of a good deal of additional, valuable work done in the meantime by Ware, Lanigan, Lynch, Todd, Reeves, Petrie, Whitley Stokes, Archdall, O'Donovan O'Curry, Hennessy, Brennan, Cogan, Comerford and others. Indeed, the extensive array of footnotes given in the *Lives* is a sparkling display of learning.

Volume III, dealing with the feast-days of the month of March, was the largest volume, extending to 1036 pages. 432, the date traditionally associated with the coming of St. Patrick, was by an odd coincidence also the number of pages devoted by O'Hanlon to his life of the national saint. His life of St. Patrick provides a good illustration of Canon O'Hanlon's cautious, methodical approach to his daunting task. He wrote:

> The authentic facts of his life are few as compared with the cloud of fable which has served to obscure them. A just estimate of those almost superhuman labours and trials our great patron surmounted is hardly possible at the present time, so imperfect

are some of those records which profess to reveal past events, and so ill-digested are many of the ancient tracts that have special reference to St. Patrick. Modern criticism and research have done much to clear the field of vision;and it must be allowed that a wide scope has been left for conjecture and speculative opinions, nor have writers been able wholly to reconcile or explain many divergencies of statement which intrude too frequently in his Acts ... We shall endeavour, therefore, to investigate the facts relating to his biography with a caution and diligence the subject itself requires.[24]

In a review of volume III, John Healy (later archbishop of Tuam) said that there was no question of importance connected with the life of the national apostle which O'Hanlon had not discussed. Healy himself was later to publish *The life and writings of St. Patrick* (1905), which was the last of the traditional or 'pre-scientific' biographies of St. Patrick before the publication that same year of the first of the modern philological scientific studies with J. B. Bury's *Life of St. Patrick* (1905). What O'Hanlon had succeeded in doing was to gather together the variety of strands of traditional Patrician scholarship as they existed in the early 1880s. In his review, Healy wrote:

> We only regret that he frequently leaves it uncertain what opinion he adopts himself. On the vexed question of St. Patrick's birth-place Fr. O'Hanlon inclines to join those who say that he was born in the district of Strathclyde. But he puts all the other theories before the reader in great fullness, and leaves him to form his own opinion.[25]

What to Healy was a weakness, was in fact one of O'Hanlon's virtues as a historian: It was the same 'modesty, inseparable from true learning' which O'Hanlon had admired so much in O'Curry. Healy, however, spoke for many other reviewers when he heartily congratulated 'the learned and painstaking author' on the success of his labours, which he said, entitled him 'to a high place in the roll of those illustrious Irishmen, whose greatest pride was to illustrate the history of their native land'. Healy ended his tribute to O'Hanlon's *Lives*, by describing the volumes as 'an enduring monument to his own fame and to the glory of God and of Ireland'.[26] Although the *Lives of the Irish saints* have long become dated, they still retain a certain value. In his obituary of Canon O'Hanlon in the Kildare Archaeological Journal (1905), Rev. Edward O'Leary, a life-long friend who completed the *History of the Queen's County* after O'Hanlon's death, said that he knew for a fact that the *Lives,* had left O'Hanlon a poorer man by £900.

During many years before he had finished the *Lives,* O'Hanlon had already begun collecting material from manuscript and printed sources for his *History of the Queen's County.* He had also been visiting, describing and sketching the many ecclesiastical and other archaeological remains in the county. While local diocesan history had been well served in Rev. M. Comerford's, *Collections relating to the dioceses of Kildare and Leighlin,* and in Rev. W. Carrigan's, *History and antiquities of the diocese of Ossory,* the county itself, divided between the three dioceses, had yet to find its historian. The subject had a special interest for O'Hanlon, a native of the county, who had long been researching the lives and foundations of saints associated with the area. He was also attracted to the subject by the fact that the county was divided between 'the seven tribes of Leix' whose territories 'probably continued for centuries without much change of boundary'.[27] It is not impossible that O'Hanlon may also have been unconsciously responding to that pride in county which the GAA had lately aroused.

To cover the history of a county from pre-historic times right down to the end of the nineteenth century was a massive undertaking. The practice today is to assign such a task to as many as twenty to thirty specialists. O'Hanlon, recognising his limitations, tackled the work sensibly. The first volume, bringing the narrative down to 1557, was divided into four books – I. Natural history; II. Antiquarian and pagan history; III. Ecclesiastical, diocesan and parochial history; IV. General history. The Natural history section dealt with the geography, geology, climate, mountains, rivers and lakes, botany and zoology of the county. For this section O'Hanlon acquired the assistance of specialists including scientists from the College of Science, Trinity College, the Geological Survey of Ireland, and the National Museum. He also had the assistance of Robert Lloyd Praeger, the leading Irish naturalist, who contributed 'a very complete description of the Flora of the Queen's County'.[28] Arthur Mac Mahon of Colt Stud Farm, Abbeyleix, wrote the section on the rearing and keeping of horses in the county; and James A Mulhall of Pass House, Maryborough, provided an account of farm and domestic animals and poultry. O'Hanlon also had the help of competent Irish scholars in attaching to the trees, plants and birds of the county the Irish version of their names.

The social historian will regret that O'Hanlon did not devote more space, to this part of his volume. The glimpse one gets of the kinds of horses, cattle and sheep that were found in Laois would whet the appetite of those who are less interested in the dates of petty kings and more concerned with life on the farms of the county.

The greater part by far of volume one is devoted to the section on the ecclesiastical, diocesan and parochial history. This was perhaps inevitable, given the author's dedication to researching the lives of the saints. The history of each parish, in alphabetical order ranging from Abbeyleix to Tullowmoy, is outlined. Some of the smaller parishes are dealt with in a single page. The author's native parish receives thirteen pages. The emphasis always is on the ecclesiastical with very little attention given to the secular.

The section entitled 'General history' is intended to deal with the secular history of the county. It consists of fourteen short chapters from the fifth to the sixteenth centuries. The chapters are entitled the 'annals' of the century under discussion; and indeed 'annals' is the accurate description given that each chapter is written very much in the tradition of the medieval Irish annals. Canon O'Hanlon was akin to the annalist sitting in his monastic cell and painstakingly recording every bit of information gleaned from several sources. The result was an avalanche of unfamiliar names of kings, tentative dates of battles, and difficult place-names all guaranteed to overwhelm even the interested Laois reader. The *History of the Queen's County* is a veritable mine of information, but more a reference book, or a book to be dipped into rather than read through from beginning to end.

When Canon O'Hanlon died at the age of eighty-four he was only midway through his work on Laois. He had completed volume one and written the preface, but had not seen it through the press. He appealed to his friend, Rev. Edward O'Leary parish priest of Portarlington, to continue with the project; and Fr. O'Leary endeavoured to carry out the work in harmony with the views of Canon O'Hanlon and in accordance with his final instructions from his death-bed. The first volume was published in 1907, two years after O"Hanlon's death, and ascribed to Canon O' Hanlon and Fr. O' Leary. The second volume was not published until 1914. It was described in its title page as being 'compiled chiefly from the papers of the late V. Rev. John Canon O'Hanlon P.P. M.R.I.A., by Rev. Edward O Leary P.P. M.R.I.A., and Rev. Matthew Lalor, P.P.[29]

In the preface to volume II, Fathers O'Leary and Lalor described themselves modestly as editors of the volume. But the reasons they gave for the seven year delay in the appearance of the second volume was the necessity of securing a sufficient number of subscribers to make the publication possible; and the insufficiency of the material collected by Canon O'Hanlon. They admitted that they were thus obliged to undertake the duties of compilers rather than mere editors. Since, they said, they had no pretensions to pose as historians, or to write anything that might be out of harmony with O'Hanlon's well earned reputation as an accurate and impartial historian, they chose instead to add 'lengthy extracts from Blue-books, newspapers etc.'[30] One of the advantages that ensues from this method is that we are given a great deal of quotation of valuable source material, in, for example, the chapters dealing with the nineteenth century. On the other hand when the footnotes lead us to believe that we are getting original material on 1798 from the Irish state paper office, or from the newspapers, we discover that the passages have been transcribed from Lecky. In the second volume, in particular, it is impossible to tell how much of the work was O'Hanlon's and how much was added by his two friends. One thing, however, is clear from their acknowledgements: Lord Walter Fitzgerald placed at their disposal 'Notes on the O'More's of Leix' which he had published in the *Journal of the Kildare Archaeological Society*. These 'Notes' and their appendices were used almost *verbatim* in the *History of the Queen's County*. Martin J Blake supplied the editors with the lists of landowners *by fiant* during the sixteenth and seventeenth centuries. Dr Carrigan, the historian of Ossory, wrote part of the chapter on 'The Mass-places of penal times'.

Given Canon O'Hanlon's characteristic modesty he would have been the first to agree that he should be described not as the sole author of the *History of the Queen's County* but more accurately as the planner and editor. In this his work has some similarities with the present volumes of county histories, except that there were far fewer contributors to the two volumes on the *Queen's County*, and that O'Hanlon not only planned and left instructions as to how it should be completed but, indeed, wrote much of volume I and compiled a quantity of the material for volume 11.

Despite its blemishes, *O'Hanlon's History of the Queen's County* was quite an impressive achievement. One of its most valuable features were the illustrations with which the two volumes were lavished (a total of almost 170). These included sketches and photographs of archaeological sites, churches, monastic settlements, schools, convents castles, mansions, crosses, and holy wells. A number of the photographs were taken by Fr. O'Leary. Canon O'Hanlon's concern for the physical remains of the early Irish church can be judged from one of the rare personal comments which he allowed into his historical writing. In his *Lives of the Irish saints*[31] he gave a detailed description and illustration of the ecclesiastical ruins at Ougheval (Ochmills) in his native parish of Stradbally. The origin of this place he traced back to St. Colman of Laois whose church formerly stood within the cemetery of Ougheval. O'Hanlon expressed his indignation at the damage that had been done in their ignorance by the poor law guardians:

by the removal of the very ancient and interesting *cashel*, once faced on the outside with lichen-crusted and large lime-stones, and breasted on the interior by a wide supporting mound of earth. While enlarging the boundaries, or while extending gravelled walks, or planting yew and cypress trees for ornament within, it would have been possible to serve every useful purpose and to have added greatly to picturesque effect, had the historic *cashel* – possibly constructed in part by the hands of St Colman in the sixth century – been suffered to remain. In the absence of commissioners for the preservation of our ancient monuments, our local Boards should learn not to perpetrate what Cobbett called 'improvements for the worse'.Not alone the peasantry, but the gentry of Ireland have yet to learn and feel regarding the irreparable mischief of destroying sacred and ancient monuments which should be so greatly prized as relics and evidences of the past.[32]

O'Hanlon returned to this complaint in his *History of the Queen's County,* where he wrote:

The original church erected here has long since disappeared, but down to our own times remained the old *caisail* or circular fence of ... Ougheval monastery; it has now been removed, and even completely obliterated by the Poor Law Guardians in late years. A square and tasteless stone wall has been built to enlarge the graveyard's dimensions; but, it has detracted also from the former archaeological and scenic interest of this place. This vandalism is greatly to be regretted; nor do our commissioners for the preservation of historic monuments exercise sufficient vigilance or effort to prevent many similar dilapidations in several other parts of Ireland, and which the writer has witnessed.[33]

As it happened O'Hanlon died at Irishtown (Sandymount) on the feastday of St. Colman of Ougheval (15 May). It was also the feast of St. Dympna to whose life he had devoted one of his earlier monographs. A Celtic cross was raised over his tomb in Glasnevin by his parishioners, and a marble tablet with a sculptured likeness was placed in the Star of the Sea in Sandymount where he was parish priest for twenty-five years. Archbishop McCabe, when he had appointed O'Hanlon as parish priest said to Dr William Walsh (who was to succeed McCabe as archbishop):

People who do not know him will think that he cannot make a good parish priest, for, as we all know, he spends hours almost every day of his life in compiling materials for the writing of books and in writing them. But for us who know him, what a model priest we know him to have always been. . . Did his work as an author cause him to be absent from his confessional when it was his duty to be there? Did it ever lead him to neglect a sick call?[34]

And McCabe added that people outside the parish who knew Fr.O'Hanlon only from his name on the title pages of so many books that could not have been written without great labour, must think either that he had no work to do, or that he neglected his work as a priest. On the other hand, the poor people of SS Michael and John (where he had served for about twenty years) who knew him only as a hardworking curate probably considered that so far from his having anything to do with the writing of books, he could hardly make out even time to read one.

Commenting on his predecessor's remarks, Archbishop Walsh said:

It was high praise, and it was well-deserved praise. Those who know him [O'Hanlon] only as the laborious student and writer of books might have thought that he devoted to his literary labours all his time and all his thoughts. Those who know him only as the zealous missionary priest might well have supposed that outside the sphere of those ecclesiastical duties he had no other cares.[35]

Canon O'Hanlon's was truly a life of dedication – dedication to his church, to his country, to his Irish saints and to his native county. He had authored more than twenty works – one of these, the *Lives of the Irish saints*, extended to over nine volumes, in which he outlined the lives of some 3,500 saints. Typical of his industry and resoluteness was when in his late seventies the manuscript of his *Irish-American history of the United States* was destroyed in a fire in the printing works, he started all over again and published this book at the age of 82.[36]

What Canon O'Hanlon wrote about his friend, Dean Anthony Cogan, would serve as an epitaph for himself. He described Cogan as a man:

so untiring in labour, so simple in habit, so unassuming, and yet so excellent in character, so true a lover of his church and his country.[37]

References

1. O'Hanlon, *Queen's County*, i, 187.

2. Ibid., ii, 545.
3   *Lives of the Irish saints*, iii, 809-810.
4. Ibid., 810.
5. C.P. Meehan, *The fate and fortunes of Hugh O'Donnell, Earl of Tyrone and Rory O'Donnell, Earl of Tyreconnell* (NewYork,1868), p.xii.
6. *Report of the O'Connell Monument Committee* (1888),p. xiv.
7. *Life of St Laurence O'Toole*, preface.
8. Ibid.
9. *Catechism of Irish History*, preface, iii.
10. Ibid., p. iv.
11. Ibid., p. v.
12. Ibid.
13. J.W. Croker, *The Croker Papers : the correspondence and diaries of the late Right Honourable John Wilson Croker,* i, 89.
14. *Catechism of Irish history,* p. viii.
15. ibid., pp vii – viii.
16. O'Hanlon's account was written for Wm J Fitzpatrick's *Sham Squire* (1865), p. 321.
17. Ibid.
18. *Catechism,* pp 502,503.
19. Ibid., p. 565.
20 Ibid., p. 568.
21. Ibid., pp 554, 569 – 571.
22. *Report of O'Connell Monument Committee,* p. x.
23. *Catechism,* p. 39.
24. *Lives of the Irish saints,* iii, 399.
25. John Healy in Irish *Ecclesiastical Record,* 3rd series, iii (June 1882), 321-32.
26. Ibid, 332.
27. *History of the Queen's County,* i, 75.
28. Ibid., 35-38.
29. *History of the Queen's County,* ii, title page.
30. Ibid., ii, preface.
31. *Lives of the Irish saints* i, 330.
32. Ibid., i, 332. This passage was quoted with approval by Comerford in his *Collections relating to the dioceses of Kildare and Leighlin,* iii, 358.
33. *History of the Queen's County,* i, 324-5.
34. *Irish Monthly,* xxxviii, no. 447 (Sept 1910), 503-5 reporting Archbishop Walsh in *Freeman's Journal,* 25th. July 1910.
35. Ibid.
36. *Irish Monthly,*(1905), p. 363.
37. *Drogheda Argus,* 1 Feb. 1873 (Quoted in Alfred P. Smyth, *Faith, famine and fatherland in the Irish midlands,* p, 179.

Chapter 23

GOVERNMENT SURVEILLANCE OF SUBVERSION IN LAOIS, 1890-1916

PÁDRAIG G. LANE

It is the purpose of this study to trace the concerns of British Intelligence within the county during the years 1890 to 1916 and to thereby relate Laois to trends on the national stage. Police reports to Dublin Castle throughout the period on incidents, individuals and movements testified to the constant operation of surveillance and while they do not present a complete picture, the value of their use as a source for measuring Government perception of the county's affairs has been acknowledged.[1]

The county experienced the ebb and flow of national movements and the transposition of mind from constitutional politics to militant activism that affected the country at large during that period. As a microcosm of the larger stage, Laois in the 1890s, for instance, reflected the throes of Parnellism and of the land question, as well as encompassing nascent trade unionism, the cultural nationalism of the G.A.A. and Gaelic League and the democratic opportunities provided by the Local Government Act of 1898. Such issues, moreover, carried forward into the new century, albeit under new guises and sometimes with a shift in emphasis, as the re-united Irish Party pursued Home Rule, as the United Irish League encouraged the break-up of grasslands and as both Sinn Fein and the Irish Volunteers emerged in time as new nationalist factors. The one constant, however, was the diligence with which the police kept the incidence of such activities under review.

That diligence arose from the even greater concern that extremist elements would infiltrate such public movements and the activities of secret societies, especially the I.R.B., were even more carefully monitored when opportunities for making trouble, such as the 1798 commemoration, the Boer War and the outbreak of World War I, presented themselves. However, it was also true that moderate opinion within the county, be it Unionist or Nationalist, clerical or lay, was used on every occasion as a measure of the perceived significance of these developments.

From the Land War to the Parnellite crisis

During the early 1880s, when Dublin Castle, following upon the agrarian outrages of the Land War, was concerned at the reappearance of political secret societies, Laois gave no evidence of subversive activity, although the county did have a Fenian legacy.[2] While the printing of intimidatory 'No Rent' notices did draw attention from the authorities in February 1882, there were no references to I.R.B. activities in the county in either October 1882 or February 1883 when subversive societies were reviewed.[3] Their continued existence, nevertheless, was proved by the evidence, from the police informant 'Quentin', in the mid-1880s that both the National League and the G.A.A. were in the hands of I.R.B. men, a level of control noticeable in the agrarian campaign against evictions during the Plan of Campaign.[4] Agrarian agitation presented a continuing source of unrest for the constabulary to contend with – Laois by 1885, having developed a reputation for lawlessness and being ranked as the sixth most disturbed region in the country. Focused, although not exclusively so, on Lord Lansdowne's Luggacurren estate, agrarian agitation in the county led to a considerable incidence of outrages and a large police presence as the Plan of Campaign intensified.[5]

The role taken by the I.R.B. in the formation of G.A.A. clubs in the county was of greater interest to the police. The memorandum of Bourchier, the division inspector for the South-Eastern Division, on 18 July, 1887, made it clear that there was a suspicion that athletics were not the primary concern of the G.A.A. within the county.[6] The presence at that juncture of J. B. O'Reilly , the G.A.A.'s secretary, Frank Dineen, P. N. Fitzgerald and P. T. Hoctor, all known I.R.B. men, for the purpose of organising clubs within the county added to that suspicion, given the incentive of the physical force men to advance their cause in the wake of the failure of Home Rule in 1886. While the G.A.A. was acknowledged to be starting almost from scratch in Laois, with the number of clubs being relatively few to begin with, Bourchier referred to the great strides being made there, the information being that the Fenian organisers had set a target of twenty-one clubs for the county.

The prime mover locally was known to be P. A. Meehan, a man recognised to be the principal organiser of all political and other national movements within the county, although assisted in the formation of G.A.A. clubs by Thomas Harrington of Johnstown, Co Kilkenny, and by P. T. Hoctor. In fact, by November 1887, police information was that Hoctor and the others were busy canvassing the clubs for support for the I.R.B. bid to challenge clerical control of the organisation at the upcoming G.A.A. Convention in Thurles.[7] That challenge was successful, due to the efforts of Hoctor and Fitzgerald, but the I.R.B. was to lose control again at the later convention held in January 1888, leaving a legacy of bitterness between the rival factions within Laois, as elsewhere.[8] The presence of delegates from Knockaroo, Clough, Durrow, Abbeylaois and Rathdowney at both Thurles Conventions bore testimony to the strength of the I.R.B. element for the police were certain of the Fenian credentials of Knockaroo's J. J. Mc Evoy and T. Berry, Clough's P. J. Maher and J. J. Walsh, Durrow's D. O'Rourke and J. Conroy, Abbeylaois's J. Kelly and M. Hayden and Rathdowney's D. Carroll and P. Ryan, as well as being certain that the I.R.B. was not short of money in its promotion of control of the G.A.A. within the county.[9]

Certainly, the growth of the Fenian element at the expense of the clerical faction was confirmed for the police on the occasion of a G.A.A. Convention in Portlaoise in September 1888, attended by William O' Brien M. P., a patron of the organisation, and by both Dr O'Higgins of Luggacurren and P. A. Meehan.[10] The I.R.B. credentials of several of the leading delegates, most notably J. P. Doran from Portlaoise, Martin Delaney from Borris-in-Ossory, John Kennedy from Knockaroo and H. I. Herrihy from Ballyroan, were noted by the police and it was accepted that the Fenians, Pat Ryan from Rathdowney and John Mc Evoy from Knockaroo, were absent simply because they had travelled to the United States with the American Tour. The march of seven G.A.A. clubs through the town on the way to the meeting was interpreted, moreover, as a show of strength by the I.R.B. element, if not as a gesture of military capability.

Whereas the I.R.B. backed organisation made further gains in 1889, with the county remaining loyal to the I.R.B.-dominated G.A.A. executive when other counties wavered or seceded, nevertheless, Fenian control of the movement in Laois had been badly damaged by 1890, the clergy being firmly in control.[11] At the beginning of that year the general enthusiasm of the young men for the G.A.A. was acknowledged, and the close ties between the I.R.B.-backed G.A.A. and the Tenants Defence League in the agitation over evictions at Luggacurren established, police reports, nevertheless, spoke of a slowing-up in the organisation's progress, of misuse of funds and affrays at matches, and of a general opposition to the movement by both strong farmers and clergy in the county.

Whatever about political antipathy to it, the police reported that the affrays and drinking associated with the games had made the clergy very opposed to the organisation, with the bishops of both Ossory and Kildare and Leighlin issuing strong denunciations and ordering the faithful to keep away from the games on Sundays. Indeed, on the occasion of a G.A.A. tournament in Portlaoise in September 1890, Fr

Dempsey, the parish priest, ordered shopkeepers to take down advertisements for the match from their windows, while he himself stood at an important cross-roads ordering spectators to get back to their homes.[12]

The G.A.A., of course, had not been the only channel for the expression of disillusionment with the constitutional movement after 1886, as the police were quite aware that disaffection had been the motivating factor in the formation of the Democratic Trade and Labour Federation in 1889 and in the spread of trade unionism among general labourers.[13] Impetus for those developments, according to the police, came from the discontent of the labourers, both urban artisans and rural workers, at the little benefit brought to the working class from the land struggle. While farmers had benefited, the labourers had found resistance to any provision for them of plots of ground and better cottages, and lack of employment in the rural towns had created a pool of discontent that drink and idleness exacerbated. The readiness of Fenians and dynamiters, according to the authorities, to fall in with any disorderly movement explained the I.R.B.'s promptness in using this new labour movement for its own purposes.

From the moment labour clubs emerged in Laois, especially in the Mountrath, Castletown, Camross, Coolrain, and Stradbally areas, the police began to monitor the organisation of branches and to assess total membership. The county had experienced attempts to organise the labourers before but it was the presence now of labour organisers, who were known or suspected to have I.R.B. links, that constituted a cause for police anxiety.[14]

The police did, however, find a measure of reassurance in the knowledge that there were inherent difficulties involved in organising dispersed rural labourers within the county and in the opposition of the clergy and farmers to any such organisation. It became apparent, for instance, in the Castletown area that their joint opposition would give the labourer's movement there 'little chance of success', the clergy suspecting the Fenian organisers of the movement and fearing the whiff of socialism that went with it and the farmers fearing any encouragement of the demands among the labourers for better conditions.[15] Reports, therefore, in the early months of 1890, stressed that the labour movement was either inactive altogether, or waning, despite the efforts of organisers, Fenians from both Athy and Dublin, to make inroads among the workers.[16]

The Fall of Parnell
It was, however, the catalytic effect of the Parnellite split on both moderate opinion and the I.R.B. within the county that dominated

police reports in the following years, as labour, agrarian, political and sporting movements came under the influence of that event. It soon became apparent that both sides to that dispute sought to win the support of the labourers. The formal labour movement was never in terms of its numerical support, according to police estimates, a great cause for alarm. Membership was registered as fifty in 1889, one hundred and ninety in 1891 and two hundred and thirty at the end of 1892, and with rarely more than four active branches. But, nevertheless, a political appeal could be made to the greater body of both rural and urban labourers that constituted an electoral force since 1884.[17] Meetings, therefore, in Mountrath, Coolrain, Clough and Portarlington were seen by the authorities as simply efforts by both the Parnellite National League and the anti-Parnellite National Federation to muster electoral support and funds for their factions, there being little substance in their concern for the labourers.[18] The attendance of three thousand at a meeting in Coolrain, in fact, was given little credence by the constabulary, other than that there, as at Mountrath, where Davitt presided over a supposed Democratic Labour Federation meeting which was clearly anti-Parnellite, the very presence at all of the agricultural labourers, traditionally supporters of Parnell, was considered unusual. Their presence in support of the National Federation gave the authorities grounds for concern at the social breakdown of the classes supporting or opposing the rival factions.[19]

It appeared obvious to the authorities that clerical influence had a part in this political change and that it was bound up with the pro-Parnellite stand taken by the I.R.B. The activity of J. J. Whelan, William Foreman and James Coleman, known I.R.B. men and Parnellites, in organising the labour movement in Portarlington and Portlaoise in early 1891, had attracted police notice, Whelan's movements, whenever he came into the county, being particularly watched since he was classed as 'a rabid Fenian'. When, in April of that year his role in organising a Parnellite Labour Union meeting in Rathdowney became apparent, the police view was that clerical opposition to the Fenian sponsors of the meeting would ensure that it would be of little consequence.[20]

That clerical opposition, moreover, was manifested throughout the county. In Portlaoise, where P. A. Meehan chaired the labourers' meeting in April, attended by William Foreman, secretary of the Amalgamated Society of Railway Servants, the resolute opposition of the clergy to Parnell, and their support for Justin McCarthy since the end of 1890 ensured, according to the constabulary, that the labour movement there was making very little progress.[21] In January 1891 the authorities supposed that the people were generally with the clergy in opposing Parnell, thereby ensuring that the labourers would not confront their pastors by supporting suspect trade unions.[22]

Such clerical influence also had an impact on agrarian agitation *per se,* it being noted that the Evicted Tenants League in the county was also sitting on the fence on the Parnellite issue because it was unwilling to go against the clergy by taking a pro-Parnellite stand.[23] Intelligence, it should be said, appreciated that the Evicted Tenants League had a more mercenary reason for such moderation, it being acknowledged that no money was being collected for that cause in the current political climate and that the League was waiting to see which political faction would win out, or, as the constabulary phrased it, waiting 'to follow the money'.[24] Accordingly, in March 1891, new tenants on the Luggacurren estate had been at Ballinakill fair and had neither been noticed nor boycotted by the vigilance men of the National League, the progenitor of the Evicted Tenants League, supposed source of all agrarian agitation since it had fallen into the hands of I.R.B. extremists in the mid-eighties.[25]

The National League, in fact, was in decline as a pro-Parnellite political force, as well as exerting little influence as an agrarian movement, as police reports to Dublin Castle in May and June 1891 indicated.[26] In May, in such disparate areas of the county as Stradbally, Clonaslee and Camross, the National Federation was being consolidated, while in June it was reported as having replaced the National League as the major force in the county, being now stronger than either the League or the Parnellite leadership. This too was due in no small measure to clerical influence exercised by such as the parish priest of Ballyfin, regarded by the police as a significant figure in shaping public opinion.[27] In Stradbally, arrangements for a Parnellite meeting to oppose Dr O'Higgins, Tim Healy's brother-in-law, and the clergy, were likewise not expected to have widespread support, although 'it could be bad work', because of the commanding influence over the people of Stradbally's parish priest, Fr Foley.[28]

The constabulary remained especially concerned with the activities and the influence of the I.R.B. during the Parnellite crisis. Bishop Lynch's pastoral letter in May 1891, aimed at secret societies within the county would according to police intelligence have little effect because the work of those secret societies, in essence the I.R.B., 'exists in a very limited measure in Queens County'. After 'careful enquiry' at year's end the police held the view that 'at present no move is being made to organise the I.R.B.'. The significance of that report, however, lay in the constabulary's reason for that lack of momentum within the I.R.B., namely that 'people are too afraid to trust each other too far in the present crisis', in other words the Parnellite split.[29] It bore out the surmise of an earlier police report in January of that year that was 'to find the men listed in the I.R.B. list in this locality very evenly divided in opinions on the Parnell crisis'.[30] Indeed, we now know that the I.R.B. did draw back from its partisan position on appreciating that it had lost ground because of its clearcut support for Parnell.[31]

Such conclusions by the police had not prevented what at times became an obsessive vigilance about the movements of particular individuals, most notably P. A. Meehan, or, as we saw earlier, J. J. Whelan. Already under scrutiny in December 1890 for his activity in organising the G.A.A. in Portarlington,[32] Meehan's activity in support of Parnell became a primary concern following upon his presence at the Kilkenny election and his support for Parnell at a meeting in Crettyard in January 1891.[33] Later that month, Meehan's meeting in Kelly's Hotel (Plate 23.1) in Portlaoise with the Parnellite M. P. for the county, McDonald, and P. J. Kelly, warranted referral to Dublin Castle, as did Meehan's efforts to arrange a welcome in the town for Parnell as that leader passed through on his way south, efforts that produced little public support according to the constabulary.[34] The decision of a meeting later in the month to send Meehan to represent the county at the Parnellite rally in Waterford was similarly noted.[35]

Meehan, however, came under even greater scrutiny when political and private interests appeared to come into conflict. By May 1891, the police were perplexed at Meehan's apparent objection to the arrangement of a Parnellite meeting for Portlaoise, especially since doubts emerged afterwards as to his whereabouts and since great confusion, according to the police, existed in the aftermath of this turn of events. The general belief was that he was defecting to the anti-Parnellites, given that his business concerns at the Heath and in Abbeylaois had lost customers since the political split had occurred.[36] It was not an altogether surprising surmise since Intelligence, in January 1891, had already referred to Patrick Doran, an 'ex-suspect', being named as a delegate to the anti-Parnellite rally in Dublin, and bears out that same Intelligence opinion that the I.R.B. was split over the Parnell affair.[37]

Meehan was not the only I.R.B. suspect watched at this juncture for any reports of Fenians in the county, particularly when the individuals were returned Irish-American, produced extra vigilance. William Phelan, for instance, from Ballaghmore, aroused constabulary suspicion until it was appreciated that his sole objective in being home was the purchase of a farm near Borris-in-Ossory; while the presence of the Irish-Americans, Flanagan and O'Connor, occasioned equal suspicion, particularly as they showed great interest in the Parnellite split, until, equally in their case, it was accepted that they were simply touring the country on holiday.[38]

Plate 23.1   Upper Main Street, Portlaoise, with Kelly's Hibernian Hotel (Lawrence Collection, courtesy NLI).

As for the I.R.B. influence on the G.A.A. and the impact of the Parnellite split it was accepted that the recruitment potential for the extremists through that body by the end of 1891 was weakened due to clerical opposition, even though Laois was the only county from the South-Eastern Constabulary Division to have had delegates at the G.A.A. Convention that year in Thurles.[39] Nevertheless, the impact of the Parnellite split upon the G.A.A. was of more concern than the boycott of the C.Y.M.S. billiards room in Portlaoise because of the election to the C.Y.M.S. Committee of a Parnellite Fenian suspect.[40]

The decline of the G.A.A. was in evidence, according to the police at the beginning of 1891, due both to the earlier clerical opposition to it and to the Parnellite crisis. The G.A.A. County Convention in Portlaoise had to be postponed for three weeks on account of the Parnell split and then found itself in disarray when R. D. Fennell, the county secretary, proposed a motion opposing support for Parnell. Police reports of February 1891 spoke of little public interest in the G.A.A.'s affairs, of the organisation being a dead letter in Portlaoise itself, and of parts of two clubs having to be amalgamated when the club in Portlaoise broke up.[41]

Certainly, deep division existed within the G.A.A. within the county at this juncture, and these spilled over onto the playing fields. In March, a general row broke out after a football match in Ballyroan, while at Stradbally a free-for-all broke out among the players and spectators at the game between Wolfhill and the Kellyville team from Portlaoise.[42] The outbreak of fighting at a match in Courtwood in October between Ratheniska and Portlaoise, that arose from similar divisions, left bitter feelings. Constabulary opinion was that even within the G.A.A. there was considerable enmity on the issue of Parnell, a division that coupled with the clergy's suspicion of I.R.B. involvement led to the decline of the G.A.A. .[43]

From the Parnellite Crisis to the 1789 Centenary

While political divisions are supposed to have left a vacuum for other manifestations of national spirit throughout the remainder of that decade, the absence of a properly focussed Home Rule Party did not gainsay the continued presence of other issues and the appearance of new movements. The general political apathy and decline in agrarian agitation that marked the Parnellite crisis manifested itself, indeed, for most of the nineties. By 1892, the strength within the county of the anti-Parnellite National Federation was deemed by police to have risen from six branches to twenty, with a corresponding decline of the National League from eighteen branches to six, appearing to confirm the hold over the county of the conservative elements within it.[44] This situation still obtained at the beginning of 1897 when Dublin Castle was advised that all political organisation by constitutional politicians was at a standstill within the county due to apathy towards both factions by the people in general.[45]

Agrarian agitation was also at a standstill for most of the decade as confirmation came from the police of a decline in boycotting of tenants and others associated with difficult estates in tandem with the decline of the National League. By 1895 the Tenant League Association in the county was noted as having only two branches and ninety members and at the beginning of 1897 political apathy was linked by the police to the progress on purchase negotiations being made by tenants on the Luggacurren, Cosby, Drogheda, Bowe and Portarlington estates.[46] Indeed, the only excitement that year was a dispute in the bacon trade in which farmers aligned themselves with the bacon merchants while shopkeepers sided with the pig buyers.[47]

That was not to deny that underlying grievances persisted and had the potential for renewed unrest at a later date. The visit of Fr Maher C. C. of Luggacurren to the United States in 1895 to raise funds for the evicted tenants there was noted by the police and it was acknowledged in 1897 that the running sore of thirty six evicted tenants and eight derelict farms still rankled in the affected areas.[48] It was not, however, until the early months of 1899, in the wake of the formation of William O'Brien's new agrarian movement, the United Irish League, that agrarian peace was again threatened. Aimed at giving a new urgency to the unresolved problems of the land war, primarily the breaking up of grasslands, it appeared to find a response within Laois even before the organisation was properly established within the county for violent speeches on the twin issues of evicted tenants and landgrabbing were made at a meeting in Luggacurren.[49] The attendance of Frs Curry and O' Mara at a meeting addressed by Purcell of the *Midland Tribune,* and at which 1,200 disaffected tenants congregated, seemed, indeed, to signify the willingness of the clergy to support such a cause whereas they had resolutely opposed other movements and other issues. Such an alignment of tenants and the clergy in a district encompassing Arles, Killeen and Ballylinan where the anti-Parnellite National Federation was acknowledged by the police to be in a position of strength since mid-decade would, in fact, have been an expected occurrence.[50]

The agricultural labourers, for their part, mirrored in terms of their general inactivity during the decade the apathy that prevailed elsewhere in the wake of the Parnellite crisis. In January 1893, four branches of the Fenian sponsored and pro-Parnellite Labour Union were noted by the police in Mountrath, Stradbally, Camross and Portlaoise, while an anti-Parnellite Labour Federation branch was recorded in Mountmellick, but their existence was regarded as having little import, not least because the farm labourers were comparatively well-off in a period when the rural economy was buoyant and indifferent to the solicitations of either political factions or agitators.[51] Indeed, when a new labour movement, the Knights of the Plough, was organised throughout the Midland counties from late 1893, constabulary opinion was that 'it never was powerful'.[52] Although it had I.R.B. links through William Field, the movement could only muster an attendance of two hundred at a meeting in Portlaoise in January 1894 and the police were convinced that any labour organisation would never achieve any importance in the county because the labourers were too few in numbers.[53]

By 1896 the authorities accepted that the total strength of labour membership within the county was only one hundred and twenty members, where there had been two hundred and seventy nine members in 1893.[54] Police opinion was that even in terms of urban labourers, whose squalid living conditions, precarious wages and propensity for drink afforded opportunitites for the I.R.B. to recruit support, Laois was not at all comparable to the neighbouring counties of Carlow, Kilkenny, Tipperary and Kildare as a source for concern.[55]

The I.R.B., however, was another matter and surveillance of it was maintained throughout the decade. Attributing inactivity to the political upheaval that followed the fall of Parnell, the police certainly discerned no I.R.B. activity within the county by July 1892 and no suspects within the area were listed in the ongoing review of those needing surveillance.[56] Such was again the position in October 1895 when no evidence existed of I.R.B. activity although I.R.B. organisation was being carried out elsewhere in the South-Eastern Division to which Laois belonged.[57] However, by December of that year I.R.B. activity within the county was again being reported, an undoubted spillover from the considerable activity in the surrounding counties. At the same time, the Irish National Association was surmised to have made no progress at all in Laois.[58]

The latter body, also known as the Irish National Brotherhood, had originated in Fenian circles in the United States to promote a more vigorous nationalist policy in Ireland. It succeeded, however, only in stirring up a power struggle within the I.R.B. that began in 1895 and explained the revived organisation within Laois, as elsewhere. Central to that recruitment drive, moreover, was the G.A.A. within the county. By June 1896, the G.A.A. had a well-established club system within Laois and tournaments at Stradbally in May, that brought an attendance of 1,400, and Kilkenny in November, that included teams from Laois and Dublin, were acknowledged to have been arranged by the I.R.B. for its own purposes.[59]

It was the continuance of this activity in 1897 that alarmed the authorities, P. N. Fitzgerald was observed in January as travelling throughout the county 'advising and encouraging the organisation of the I.R.B.' through the G.A.A.[60] That activity, moreover, was linked to the I.R.B. rivalry with the I.N.A. for, despite the earlier assumptions that the I.N.A. had made little progress within the county due to the arrest of P. J. Tynan and his associates, P. T. Hoctor's long-standing influence within the G.A.A. there had secured a measure of control for the Irish National Association over the G.A.A., even though Fitzgerald had the support of thirty of the G.A.A. clubs for the I.R.B.[61]

Concern increased when the police found Hoctor and Fitzgerald travelling together through the county by June 1897, and supposed the latter had joined the I.N.A. with the aim of making it and the G.A.A. a united front with which to impress the 'American visitors' or Fenians, who would come for the 1798 Centenary celebrations, presumed by the police to be 'opposed to Government opinion'.[62] While the accord between Hoctor and Fitzgerald would be shortlived, the objective of the constabulary was to watch carefully the fruits of the two men's association in the short term for although 'respectable people' suspected the revolutionary intent of the '98 plans and although R. N. Blake, secretary of the G.A.A., had appealed at the Laois G.A.A. County Convention on 16 May against politics and secret societies, it was accepted that there were powerful forces working in the other direction.[63]

The gathering of I.R.B. suspects at a G.A.A. tournament in Castletown in July, at which ways of promoting the '98 Centenary (Plate 23.2) were discussed, and a tournament in Portlaoise in August under the aegis of I.N.A. suspects, John McEvoy and P. Wall, former I.R.B. members, attended by 1,200 supporters, at which the same objective was pursued, worried the police.[64] Although Blake and J. P. Dorris of Portlaoise, Laois's G.A.A. supremo, had opposed the politics of the '98 event and Dorris had reportedly vetoed tournaments in the Rathdowney area because of secret society involvement, their opposition mattered less with the police than the manner in which the General Council of the G.A.A. had come out in favour of the '98 Centenary.[65] Dorris, at any rate, stated the police, would have had little influence over the secret societies since they at once feared and suspected him.

A further tournament on 14 November in Portlaoise lead to the formation of a '98 Committee, a product of the attendance of both Dublin-based I.R.B. members of the 1798 Executive Committee and local I.R.B. and Parnellite organisers, although Government Intelligence suspected joint I.R.B. and I.N.A. involvement in what was deemed a

Plate 23.2   Wolfe Tone Street. Mountmellick with '98 memorial (Eason Collection, courtesy NLI).

latent act of disloyalty.[66] Despite the likelihood that internal dissension and the opposition of loyalists and clergy would eventually threaten the '98 preparations, with the clergy already checking the movement's 'fiery spirits', they already seemed at the end of 1897 to be assuming a 'revolutionary tendency'.[67] As it was, stated the constabulary, the movement was taking hold of three classes within the county, namely the 'bellicose' secret society members, the moderates who were in it through fear, and those, such as hoteliers, who were in it for gain.

The authorities watched with caution, therefore, anything untoward despite the belief that the movement in the end would not make any great progress because of the spasmodic efforts that lay behind it. There was little interest in politics in general in the county and the clergy had failed to identify with it.[68] The visit of Pat O'Brien, the county's M.P., on 19 November, was watched with the same degree of interest, accordingly, as the suspicious activity of a G. S. W. R. clerk at the Portlaoise station or the visit of the Irish-American suspect, Denis Walsh of Grand Rapids, while the important and immediate import of reports of I.R.B. activity, which led to increased fear among the loyalists in January 1898, warranted serious appraisal.[69] Certainly, the formation of a '98 Committee in Castletown at the hands of Parnellites and I.R.B. suspects and the creation of similar bodies in Arless, Stradbally, Ballinakill and Ballyroan between January and March of that year gave the police grounds for believing that the '98 movement was gathering momentum.[70]

The success of the I.R.B. in having R. N. Blake removed from the pivotal position of secretary of the G.A.A. on the grounds that the was 'not likely to keep its secrets', that is to say the I.R.B.'s secrets, served to confirm this anxiety which was further excaberated by a report in June that the I.R.B. was steadily using the G.A.A. and the '98 Committees for its own disruptive purposes.[71] The gravity of the situation was added to when D. P. Seery, a well known Dublin I.R.B. organiser associated with I.R.B. suspects in the Mountrath area in November and December of 1898 and visited Mountrath, Castletown and Abbeylaois in the course of a general organisational tour in Laois, Limerick and Clare.[72] Further supportive evidence for the seriousness of the situation was to hand in P. T. Hoctors's visit to Rathdowney in November to meet local suspects and in the furtive behaviour in Portlaoise, in December, of James O'Brien of Castletown, a suspected principal organiser for the I.R.B., where he was supposed to have had secret business to transact with P. A. Meehan.[73]

The potential for trouble remained apparent in 1899, even if the police continued to find some consolation in the wariness of the clergy, in places such as Arless and Stradbally, of the '98 movement, where they had assented to the presence of the movement in their parishes only on the condition that it was not affiliated to the I.R.B. backed United Ireland Centenary Association.[74] While James O'Brien might have earlier been considered 'not a very valiant organiser', he was noted visiting Stradbally between 11 and 12 February and reported on as having been well pleased with the state of the I.R.B. there, and in the county at large, where an attempt was obviously being made, stated the police, to revive the organisation.[75]

That impression received credibility when O'Brien was seen with I.R.B. suspects from Kilkenny and Tipperary at a G.A.A. tournament in Errill on 19 March, attended by some 800 people, the majority of them, according to the police, I.R.B. sympathisers.[76] By May the I.R.B., though not believed to have been generally adding to its membership, was acknowledged to be doing so in Laois and Kilkenny, where funds for recruitment had increased substantially.[77] The I.R.B., the authorities believed, was using the G.A.A. to foster its aims, even though there was a small attendance at a G.A.A. Convention in Abbeylaois, at which no secret society business was reportedly done, and despite the continued opposition of the clergy to the sporting body.[78] While it was further acknowledged that the I.N.A. was now inactive in the county, and likely to remain so, and while the '98 movement appeared to be dying out, the election of an I.R.B. suspect to the County Council in the Local Government elections, in which the I.R.B. had canvassed assiduously among the labouring classes, served to show the underlying support for Fenianism among the people.[79]

Clerical opposition, however, stated a police report, certainly had the effect of keeping down the attendance at the unveiling in August of the '98 Memorial in Ballinakill, but there was no grain of comfort in P. T. Hoctor's presence during that same month in Rathdowney and Upperchurch, visiting local suspects and circulating the *United Irishman* newspaper, or in his contact in Rathdowney, later in October, with the suspects John Fitzgerald and Daniel Quigley, in order to develop assistance for the Boers should the war in South Africa continue.[80] Likewise, the meeting in Portlaoise for the raising of funds for a Wolfe Tone memorial there, at which J. P. Dunne, the I.R.B. suspect and Dublin based secretary of the '98 movement, attended, demonstrated that the '98 Centenary still had an element of momentum in it that could, and would, be exploited for anti-British purposes.[81] The conjunction of this latent potential for trouble with the resumption of agrarian agitation gave the authorities real grounds for concern, therefore, as the new century dawned.

The Early Twentieth Century
Agrarian unrest continued to present a problem for the police for the

decade 1900-1910, although its intensity and its focal points varied. Renewed agitation began with the presence of United Irish League organisers, John Cullinane and J. P. Rahilly, in Laois in December 1899 and January 1900 and the report to Dublin Castle that the young men were swinging towards it and prepared to give the 'political men' of the reunited Irish Party, of which the United Irish League was an integral grass-roots organisation, a second chance.[82] That rural support had its rationale, moreover, in the prospects of further land legislation, for constabulary belief in 1903 was that the 1903 Land Act, Wyndham's, was being looked upon with such favour by the farmers that even the I.R.B. sympathisers among them were developing an apathy towards secret societies.[83]

Agrarian unrest *per se* continued to manifest itself within the county. By 1905 the sale of the Caldbeck estate was generating discontent among agricultural labourers who felt their interests ignored in the distribution of land by the Estates Commissioners, while by 1907 cattle driving in a campaign to break-up grasslands had spread into Laois from the east-riding of Galway, with four drives being reported.[84] Laois reportedly peaceful up to March 1907, had become disorderly along with Meath, Westmeath, Offaly and Kildare as cases before Stradbally Petty Sessions for the Stradbally, Abbeylaois and Ballypickas areas attested.[85] Trouble on the Kinch estate of Castlegrogan at the beginning of 1908 was followed by unrest in Wolfhill, Timahoe, Durrow, Abbeylaois, Cullohill, Rathdowney, Balacolla, Borris-in-Ossory and Clonaslee in the years 1908-1912 over grazing, evictions and boycotting and the strength of feeling engendered by the land question was indicated by the existence of twenty-four branches of the United Irish League in the county by 1909.[86]

Throughout that period, however, agrarian agitation never became linked with I.R.B. activity although its activities in other areas did not go unobserved. So, while, in January 1900, police perceptions were that the general population had little time for the Fenians and that the work of secret societies was making little progress within the county. By November of that same year it was acknowledged that the I.R.B. was still holding to its hard stand on nationalism in spite of the new support given by the young men to constitutional politics.[87] Pat 'Rocky Mountain' O'Brien's visit to his sister in Portarlington in August was read less as a social visit than the visit of a Clan-Na-Gael emissary, while the efforts of Laois Fenians in hindering recruitment for the Boer War was recognised as the I.R.B.'s old game of keeping alive the spirit of disloyalty to England, a role now also being fulfilled within the county by the I.R.B.-sponsored Young Ireland Society.[88]

Disloyalty was self evident also for the police in the unveiling of the

'98 Memorial in Mountmellick when, despite John Daly's misgivings about Maud Gonne performing the honours, violent speeches by J. P. Egan, J. P. O'Brien and the Tullamore man P. F. O'Loughlin, known I.R.B. suspects, were deemed to have crowned the subversive work of J. K. Bracken of Templemore, and of the Laois Fenians, in having the monument erected.[89] Such subversion, in police eyes, found an echo furthermore in I.R.B. activity within the G.A.A. and other organisations and the conclusion in 1902 was that revolutionary ideas were very much in evidence at every national gathering within the county, including meetings of the Gaelic League and the Celtic Literary Society.[90] While Intelligence had earlier noted the collapse in September 1901 of the only Gaelic League class within the county, that same Intelligence in 1902 believed that the League was progressing fairly well and likely to provide an 'evil influence' hostile to England.[91] At the same time, meetings in September and November of the Celtic Literary Society under the direction of the Tullamore I.R.B. suspect P. F. O'Loughlin were deemed to be those of another movement infiltrated, if not founded by, the Fenians.[92]

It was through the G.A.A. as always that I.R.B. efforts were most channeled and in July 1901 a hurling tournament in Abbeylaois between teams from Laois, Offaly and Kilkenny, attended by some 2,500 supporters, was avowed by the police to be an occasion for fraternisation between I.R.B. suspects from the three counties.[93] Similarly, a football match in Portlaoise in February 1902 between the Kildare side, Newbridge, and the Laois side, Stradbally, occasioned the forging of a strong Fenian movement in Portlaoise.[94] Indeed, the G.A.A. was acknowledged to be making great strides within the county at that juncture and to be in league with the revolutionary programme of the extremists, a point made at the G.A.A. Convention in Abbeylaois in April 1903, attended by delegates from Portarlington, Portlaoise and Abbeylaois at which J. J. Purcell of Abbeylaois, a 'prominent' I.R.B. suspect played a major role.[95] The links between the I.R.B. and the G.A.A. within the county were again emphasised in a police report in 1904.[96]

The propagation of physical force ideas at national gatherings stemmed, the police believed, from the organisational drive made by the I.R.B. in Laois, Tipperary and Limerick in 1902.[97] At the same time, the police view was that the I.R.B. was not likely to be particularly troublesome because of lack of funds, which were not likely to increase in the foreseeable future, and because the apathy of farmers towards secret societies that arose from confidence in Wyndham's Land Act had confined I.R.B. activity to the towns where it had always a level of support.[98]

In fact, for the rest of the decade a degree of inactivity prevailed, at least on the surface, on the part of both open and secret political movements. In 1908 political societies were generally reported to be at a standstill, with both the G.A.A.'s forty six clubs and the Gaelic League's supposedly inactive nine branches free of secret society influence and Sinn Féin's solitary branch showing little signs of life.[99] Even the United Irish League's twenty-four branches remained dormant, despite meetings in Wolfhill, Stradbally and Abbeylaois addressed by Meehan, except for whatever agrarian disputes existed. In January 1910, moreover, political activity remained dormant, with Fenianism in no way proving a threat to political peace.[100]

Suggestions, however, that a flame still burned beneath the surface did appear. In August 1908, for instance, the disqualification of a Stradbally tug-of-war team at a G.A.A. athletics meeting because it had earlier pulled against a Queens County Militia team on the Heath was readily interpreted as a gesture by extreme nationalists against army recruitment, an interpretation that found substance in Sinn Féin's protest in February of the following year against the attendance of P. A. Meehan and other Parliamentary Party supporters at a military entertainment in Portlaoise's Town Hall.[101]

Meehan had already inflamed nationalists during the previous November by accusing G.A.A. sponsored sports meetings of diverting attention away from important political issues, namely Home Rule, a remark sparked off by the calculated staging of a sports in Abbeylaois and football matches in Stradbally on the same day as a United Irish League meeting in Portlaoise. Meehan's complaint brought the spirited rejoinder from a Fr. Ramsbottam in the *Leinster Leader* that Gaelic sports helped to foster Irish distinctiveness.[102] Whether this intervention marked the emergence of a new responsiveness by the clergy to nationalism is open to conjecture. Sinn Féin through its many activities, such as a collection in Portlaoise for Griffith's newspaper in October 1908, recruitment of additional members and production of its own anti-recruitment posters, was well able to fan the flames of nationalism.[103]

The Years Leading Up to 1916

Agrarian agitation lingered in the county in the years leading up to, and after, the Easter Rising although not to the extent that caused any great alarm for the authorities. In the Wolfhill area, for instance, in 1911, there was some unrest over the holding of an evicted farm but this unrest was considered to be waning. The two cattle drives reported for the county that year increased in number to four recorded instances in 1912, moreover, but the general situation was acknowledged to be satisfactory in terms of agrarian unrest except for the areas of Durrow and Balacolla where an anti-grazing agitation existed because of unrest among the landless at what seemed to be a policy of keeping estates for division among tenants in congested areas.

By 1913, it seemed to the authorities that agitation on the grazing issue in the Durrow and Cullahill districts was also easing off and the police view in 1914 was that there was a general sense of order within the county, except for sporadic cattle drives and some disturbances on the Sweetman and Weldon estates. It was not to say, however, that agrarian agitation would not again surface when the occasion offered and some agricultural friction was in evidence in 1915. The general consensus, however, was that the county was peaceable and orderly and in 1916 this continued to be the view of the authorities although it was accepted to 'be still necessary' to keep a body of police at Lisduff in order to protect a Mr Fairbrother, the holder of land on the Castletown Estate at Grantstown. That report, filed in January 1916, was unchanged throughout the following months and on the eve of the 1916 Rising, Intelligence could only find traces of agricultural friction, the latter the product of both unrest over the pace of sales of property and of some prompting by the United Irish League.

The formation of the Irish Volunteers created some change in the content of the police reports to Dublin Castle for while the absolute quietude of political societies, both constitutional and subversive, was recorded as usual in January 1914, by June of that year the 'considerable progress' made by the Volunteers movement within the county was noted by the authorities, even though it was acknowledged it had not started there as early as in most other places.[104] By July membership stood at 2,290 men; by August this had grown to 4,038 men; and by September enrollment stood at 3,978 men, representing 36 branches.[105]

It appears clear that the immediate growth of the Volunteers within the county, as in the rest of the country, was linked to the Gaelic Athletic Association, with the Gaelic clubs in Mountmellick, for instance, being among the first in the county to form Volunteer units and while the authorities were not unaware of the more public manifestations of this link between sport and physical force nationalism it seems probable that Intelligence was unaware of the undercurrents that accompanied it. The close links between the G.A.A. and physical force nationalism were to be further proven during 1916, by the Ballyroan club.

If, however, gatherings of Volunteers such as that in Portarlington on 14 June, attended by 1,200 men and addressed by Tom Kettle and P. A. Meehan, but unaccompanied by parades or drilling, engendered a watching brief by the constabulary, there was a mixture of contempt and concern in the appraisal that the Volunteers came from a corner-boy class with no stake in the country, in other words from towns like Portlaoise with which the extremist elements had long been associated by the police.[106] This did not prevent a review of the Volunteers in Portlaoise on 16 August which John Redmond M.P., and some influential Unionists attended.[107]

By the year's end, however, the new movement had begun to lose momentum and the nominal membership of 3,776 had ceased drilling, leading police to believe the movement was dead 'for the time being'.[108] Of greater significance was the creation of an independent branch, numbering thirty, of the Volunteers in Portlaoise by those opposed to Redmond, the nucleus, in other words of the Irish Volunteers that emerged in the wake of Redmond's Woodenbridge speech. Numbering 166 by the year's end, but devoid of weapons, the breakaway movement was, indeed, already equated with the Sinn Féin organisation in the county.[109]

Even so, despite Piaras Beaslai's visit to Portlaoise on 19 December, 1915, the Irish Volunteers numbers remained at 166 in January 1916, at which point Sinn Féin was deemed to have no extant branch.[110] This appeared to confirm the May 1915 report that Laois presented no evidence of I.R.B. or Sinn Féin organisation, or August's report that no secret societies were active in the county.[111] In fact, it had taken Sinn Féin, in other words I.R.B. men on the G.A.A. Executive, to block the Laois proposal at the annual Congress in May to lift the ban on British forces being members of that organisation.[112] By that stage it should be said, Redmond's National Volunteers were a lifeless body, despite efforts by Meehan and Thomas Esmond to give the movement new life at reviews in Durrow and Balacolla in July and August.[113] The Great War, in fact, was deemed to have had an effect on political activity. Recruitment had flagged because shop boys and farmers sons were disinclined to follow corner boys and landless labourers into the army and the ending of political violence was indeed linked to the flight of many of the young men to America.[114]

Conclusion

In almost every sense, therefore, the events of the Easter Rising and the transposition of mind from constitutional to militant politics that accompanied it found their reflection in Laois and similarly caught the would-be-vigilant authorities unawares. At the beginning of 1916, indeed, as has already been indicated, Intelligence had been that both the Volunteer movements had ceased to exist and that no secret societies were known to exist, or efforts to 'promote disloyalty and sedition'.[115] The Intelligence review, in fact, at the end of 1916 stated that there had been no evidence of Sinn Féin, in other words I.R.B., activity before the rebellion.[116]

All that could be established by Intelligence at the year's end was that when the Rising broke out, seven of the Sinn Féin, or I.R.B., members left Portlaoise and were not found to have returned by the year's end, it being added that 'their movements during the rebellion could not be ascertained' although it was believed that they were involved on the eve of the outbreak in tearing up the railway line between Portlaoise and Abbeylaois.[117] While this information indicated the degree of the authorities general surveillance of suspects before the event, it also conveyed the inability of those same authorities to assess the real level of activity of the physical force nationalists.

Indeed, the actions taken by the I.R.B. on that occasion seemed to have been underestimated in terms of their intended significance by the local police, an underestimation that also attached itself to the similar attempt to demolish part of the Kildare-Carlow line. In fact, the activity of the Laois I.R.B. circle in providing explosives for the Rising in Dublin, in seeking to disrupt the movement of British forces that would counter-strike against the Rising, and in co-ordinating with other provincial units from Leinster for a convergence on Dublin, were all elements of the Military Council's plans that escaped the knowledge of the authorities at that time for no mention of Eamonn Fleming's, the co-ordinator with Pearse and Headquarters, movements surfaces in the police reports.[118] Indeed, Laois was not included in the list of five counties reported as being involved in the rebellion.[119]

There was some suspicion attached to the actions of an unnamed postal worker in Portlaoise, probably Patrick Muldowney, but this apart, the incident at Wolfhill R.I.C. barracks, in an attempt to seize arms, was the sole other action that warranted or attracted police notice.[120] In fact, police reports testified that people 'generally remained perfectly quiet' and that 'the feeling at the time was decidedly against the rebellion'.[121] Conservative opinion within the county remained the touchstone of concern so that even when, after the executions and deportations, sympathy with the rebellion began to 'awaken' the police were satisfied that it remained privately expressed and that no movement hostile to government, beyond the wearing of Sinn Féin badges in a few cases, was apparent. In fact, the end of the year report noted that the county was peaceable and orderly and showed no evidence of political activity other than that of a United Irish League led by a local M.P. who was 'a strong advocate of constitutional methods of agitation'.[122]

Sympathy had, nevertheless, noted the police, moved away from

Home Rule and had come round to the views of 'the energetic opponents' of that policy, even if the clergy were able to maintain a quiet attitude among the people. The evidence of support for the physical force policy was, indeed, most manifest in the level of G.A.A. activity promoted in support of the rebellion. It would take the events of the following years to reach the position of January 1920 when the influences of Sinn Féin and of the Irish Volunteers would be regarded as powerful factors within the county and when fresh outbreaks of agrarian agitation in the Borris-in-Ossory and Rathdowney areas would testify to the continued existence of other deep-seated discontents.[123]

It should be said that Government surveillance of all activity within the county that might have led to subversion over the years 1880 to 1916 provided a mirror image of all the more public manifestations of agitation, political, agrarian, social and cultural, that engaged the broadly nationalist population of Laois during that time. Even accepting the fact that this work of gathering intelligence was not as intense as in the earlier days of Fenianism and the Land League, the information gathered served as a valuable touchstone both of the levels of intensity and the personalities within the county attached to such agitations. It helped, therefore, to prepare for the government, when collated with the information arriving from other counties, a general picture of trends within the country at large and a first line of reaction to possible trouble.

In that respect it endeavoured to establish, within the limits of the analytical skills and disciplines of the time, a geographical and social breakdown, of the classes, issues and locations most prominent in those agitations, as well as those opposed to them. The work of more recent historians in assessing those economic, social, cultural and geographic factors in the composition of revolutionary activity helps to understand the interrelationship between I.R.B. organisation and agrarian, labour, clerical, loyalist and electoral factors within the county in those years.[124]

References

1. B. Mac Giolla Choille, *Intelligence notes, 1913-1916* (Dublin, 1966), pp xxxviii-xl; T. D Williams (ed.), *Secret societies in Ireland* (Dublin, 1973), pp 5-6.
2. P. G. Ó Laighin, *Finíní Laoise* (Baile Átha Cliath, 1990).
3. N. A., CBS 3/716 ctns. I, 2, B. Files : B. 8, 134, 251.
4. W. F. Mandle, *The Gaelic Athletic Association and Irish Nationalist politics* (Dublin, 1987), pp 43, 45, 68, 77-8, 80-86. See also R. Hawkins, 'Government versus secret societies", in Williams (ed.), *Secret societies*, pp 100-111; T. Garvin, *The evolution of Nationalist politics* (Dublin, 1981), pp 96-113.
5. L. M. Geary, *The Plan of Campaign, 1886-1891* (Cork, 1986), pp 48-9; L. P.

Curtis, *Coercion and conciliation in Ireland, 1880-1892: a study in Conservative Unionism* (Oxford, 1963), p. 258.

6. N. A., CBS, Reports of Div. Inspectors on Secret Societies, S/E Div, Ctn. 3, 1887-1895.

7. Ibid.

8. Ibid.See also Mandle, *The Gaelic Athletic Association,* pp 29-90; M. de Búrca, *The G. A. A.: a history* (Dublin, 1980), pp 37-63; S. Ó Riain, *Maurice Davin, 1842-1927: first president of the G.A.A.* (Dublin, 1994), pp 111-98.

9. N. A., CBS, S/E Div., Ctn 3.

10. Ibid.

11. Ibid.

12. Ibid.; Mandle, T*he Gaelic Athletic Association,* pp 77-8.

13. P. G. Lane, 'Land and Labour in Laois', in *Liberty,* I.T.G.W.U. Jn., 36, No.4, Nov., 1981; P. G. Ó Laighin, 'An poblachtánachas agus an soisialachas', *Agus,* Feb.-Nov., 1980; N. A., CBS, Reports on Secret Societies, S/E & S/W.Divs, Ctns. 2,3; especially 8 Oct., 1887, 7 Mar., 8 May, 1888 and 521/2225s, 3058s, 3621s, 4557s, 10,359s, 10,606s, 11,356s, 1889-91. Also N. A., Irish National League Proceedings, Ct 7, 1885-90, for Ins. Generals Reports on tensions between farmers and labourers and fears that the National League had fallen into the hands of agitators, especially Jan-June, 1885 and July, 1887.

14. N. A., CBS, Reports on Secret Societies and Police and Crime Reports, Ctns. 2, 3, 4, 5, 6, covering the years 1887-1895 form the primary sources.

15. N. A., CBS, Ctn. 3, S/E Div.; 520/1144s, 521/141s, 333s, 2351s and Ins. Jones's assessment of the labourers movement in the S/W Div, Feb. 1890-May 1891, Ctn 2., S/W Div.

16. N. A., Police and Crime Reports, Ctn. 3, 52/2351s, 520/1144, 523/3612, 521/4752; Ctn. 5, 520s/11,372, Jun, 1890, 520s/1646, 14 Oct., 1890.

17. N. A., CBS, Police and Crime Reports, Ctn. 5; 501s/1016s, 28 Feb., 1893; S Files, Ctn. 8, 501s/11,799.

18. N. A., Police and Crime Reports, Ctn. 5; 7, 20 Jan., 11, 15 Feb., 18 Mr., 1891.

19. Ibid.

20. N. A., Police and Crime, Ctn. 5, 3, 1, 20 Apr., 2, 11 May, 1891.

21. Ibid., 7 Jan, 18 Mr., 3 Apr., 1891.

22. Ibid., 7, 9 Jan., 1891.

23. Ibid., 13 Jan., 1891.

24. Ibid., 7, 13 Jan., 1891.

25. Ibid., 25 Mr., 1891.

26. Ibid., 18 Mar., 16 Jun., 1891.

27. Ibid., 31 Dec., 1890.

28. Ibid., 20 Jan., 3 Feb., 1891.

29. Ibid., 11 May 1891.

30. Ibid., 23 Jan., 1891.

31. de Búrca, *The G.A.A.,* p. 67; W. Mandle, pp 91-7.

32. N. A., Police and Crime, Ctn. 5, 14 Dec., 1890.

33. Ibid., 2 Jan. 1891.

34. Ibid., 18, 19 Jan., 1891.

35. Ibid., 20 Jan. 1891.

36. Ibid., 2, 11 May, 1891.

37. Ibid., 23 Jan., 1891.

38. Ibid., 11 Mar., 1891.

39. N. A., S. files, 1892, Ctn. 4, 716/3 (State of G.A.A. Dec., 1891 v/v end of 1889).

See also Mandle, *The Gaelic Athletic Association,* p. 92.
40. N. A., Police and Crime, Ctn. 5, 25 Mar., 1891.
41. Ibid., 13, 20, 23 Jan., 15 Feb., 18 Mar., 20 Apr., 11 May, 23 Jun., 1891.
42. Ibid., 13 Apr., 11 May, 1891.
43. Ibid., 11 May, 1891.
44. N. A. S. files, Ctn. 4, 1892, 5393s.
45. Ibid.; C.B.S., Chief Insp. and Div. Commissioners Reports Ctn. 6, Jan. & May, 1897.
46. N. A., C.B.S. C/Insp. &D/C.Repts., Ctn. 6, Jan. & May 1897.
47. Ibid.
48. N. A., Intelligence Notes, Ctn. I, July-Aug. 1895-1913, 1895. (Misc. Notes).
49. Ibid., Jan.-Feb., 1899 (Misc. Notes).
50. Ibid., July, Aug., 1895.
51. Ibid; and C.B.S., 1894, Ctn. 8, 4/246; Ctn. 3, S/E Div. 1893, 501s/6218
52. N. A., Div. Com. Reports, Ctn. 3, Feb.- July, 1894.
53. Ibid., Feb.- July, 1894.
54. Ibid., 1893, 501s/6218.
55. Ibid., Feb.- July, 1894.
56. N. A., S. Files, Ctn. 4, 6 July, 1892 and 5006s.
57. N. A., Home Office Precis Reports, Ctn. 1, 12 Feb., Oct., 1895.
58. N. A., H/O Precis, Ctn. 1, 12 Dec., 1895, Apr., Nov., 1896.
59. Ibid., 16 May, 22 Jun., 22 Nov., 1896.
60. Ibid., 18 Feb., 17 Mar., 1897.
61. Ibid., 17 Mar., 10, 15 Apr., 27 May, 1897.
62. Ibid., 18 Feb., 17 Mr., 15 Apr., 12 June, 1897.
63. Ibid., 17 Mar., 15, 27 May, 1897.
64. Ibid., 24 July, 16 Aug., 1897.
65. Ibid., 27 May, 24 July, 16 Aug., 28 Oct., 1897.
66. Ibid., 16, 20 Nov., 6 Dec., 1897.
67. Ibid., 13 Oct., 20 Nov., 6, 16, Dec., 1897.
68. Ibid., 15 May, 13 Oct., 16 Nov., 1897 and C.B.S., Div. Comm.Reports, Ctn. 6, Nov.-Dec. 1897.
69. N. A., H/O Precis, Ctn. 2, 5 Feb., 1898; Ctn. 1, 19 Nov., 1895, 22 Jun., 1896.
70. Ibid., 7 Feb., 11 Jun., 1898.
71. Ibid., 22, 24 Jan., 10, 17 Feb., 31 Mar., 1898.
72. Ibid., 22 Dec., 1898.
73. Ibid., 9 Nov., 21 Dec., 1898.
74. Ibid., 24 Feb., 1899.
75. Ibid., 25 Mar., 1899.
76. Ibid., 25 Mar., 1899.
77. Ibid., 12 May,1899.
78. Ibid., 22 Apr., 12 May, 1899.
79. Ibid., 12 May, 1899.
80. Ibid., 19 Aug., 16, 28 Sept., 3 Nov., 1899.
81. Ibid., 28 Sept., 1899.
82. Ibid., Dec. 1899.
83. Ibid., 6 May, 1903.
84. N. A. Intelligence Notes, 1907; and Insp. Gen. Const. Reports, 1905 A, 29 Jan..
85. N. A. Intelligence Notes, 1907-1908, Oct. 1908.
86. N. A. Ins. Gen. Repts, 1908-1912; also Intelligence Notes, 1907-1908.
87. N. A., H/O Precis, Ctn. 2, 15 Jan., 1, 13, Aug., 13 Nov., 1900.

88. Ibid., 13 Nov., 1900.
89. Ibid., 28, 30 Aug., 1900.
90. Ibid., Feb., 2 May, 17 Sept., 1902.
91. Ibid., 17 Sept., 1901, Feb., 1902.
92. Ibid., 17 Sept., 1902.
93. Ibid., 19 Jul., 1901.
94. Ibid., 19 Feb., 1902.
95. Ibid., 3 May, 1902, 6 May, 1903.
96. Ibid., Jan., 1904.
97. Ibid., 19 Feb., 1902.
98. Ibid., 6 May, 1903, Jan., 1904.
99. N. A., Insp. Gen. Reports, Oct., 1908.
100. Ibid., Dec., 1910.
101. P.R.O., 904/118, Aug., 1908, Feb., 1909.
102. Ibid., Dec., 1908.
103. Ibid., Oct., 1908, Feb., 1909.
104. Mac Giolla Choille, *Intelligence Notes*, pp 94, 109-12, N. A., Insp. Gen. Reports, 1914; and S. Files, 24, Intelligence Assignments.
105. Mac Giolla Choille, *Intelligence Notes*, pp 109-12.
106. Ibid., pp 94-5; P.R.O, C/O 904/120 Precis of Information, June, 1914.
107. Mac Giolla Choille, *Intelligence Notes*.
108. Ibid.
109. P.R.O., C/O 904/120, Oct., 1914.
110. Ibid., 15 Dec., 1915; C/O 904/99, Jan., 1916.
111. Ibid., Apr., 1914; C/O 904/99, Jan., 1916.
112. Ibid., May 1915; C/O 904/97 (Ins. Gen. Repts.), May, Aug., 1915.
113. Ibid., July, 1915.
114. P.R.O., C/O 904/120, Jan., 1917; also N. A,. C.B.S., S. Files 24 (7).
115. P.R.O., C/O 904/120, Jan., 1917; C/O 904/99, Jan., 1916.
116. P.R.O., C/O 904/120, Jan., 1917; and Mac Giolla Choille, *Intelligence notes*, pp 210-11.
117. P.R.O., C/O 904/120, Jan. 1917.
118. See J & B Fleming (ed.), *1916 in Laois* (Swan, 1996), P. R. O., C/O 904/99, April 1916; C/O/904, 120, Jan. 1917.
119. N. A., Insp. Gen. Reports, April, 1916.
120. N. A., S. Files, Ctn. 24, 1916; C/O 904/120, Jan. 1917.
121. P.R.O., C/O 904-120, Jan. 1917.
122. Ibid.
123. N. A., Insp. Gen. Reports, Jan., 1920.
124. D. Fitzpatrick, 'The Geography of Irish Nationalism' in *Past and Present*, lxxvii, 1978, pp 113-44; T. Garvin, 'Great hatred, little room: social background and political sentiment among revolutionary activists in Ireland 1890-1922'; J. O'Beirne Ranelagh, 'The Irish Republican Brotherhood in the revolutionary period, 1879-1923' both in D. G. Boyce, *The revolution in Ireland, 1879-1923* (Dublin, 1988), pp 91-114, 137-56.

Plate 23.1   Towns, villages and topography of Co. Laois (drawn by Stephen Hannon).

Chapter 24

KEVIN O'HIGGINS, IRISH REPUBLICANISM AND THE CONSERVATIVE COUNTER-REVOLUTION[1]

JOHN M. REGAN

At the entrance of what is now a small estate of houses on the junction in south Dublin of Cross and Booterstown Avenues one can find, under the debris thrown from the nearby road, the trace of a cross made in setting concrete with the tip of a workman's spade. Such is the memorial to the place where Kevin Christopher O'Higgins, the first Vice-President of the Irish Free State, fell on Sunday 10 July 1927 after being assassinated by three members of the Irish Republican Army. The fact that such an event, the first and only assassination of a cabinet minister in the history of the state, is so marked appears on discovery a curious omission. There is however no utility in commemorating Civil Wars. Societies, for the most part, do their best to forget them. That the place and moment where the democratic legitimacy of the new state was most blatantly challenged is ignored. That there exists no national monument to O'Higgins. That he is memorialized nowhere other than on an obelisk dedicated to him in his native Stradbally remains a silent and collective acknowledgment that O'Higgins too was a casualty, perhaps the last such, of the Irish Civil War which ended officially four years before his death.

In contrast to official amnesia O'Higgins, under a variety of epithets 'super policeman', 'moral architect of the Free State', 'strong man of the early Cosgrave Governments', is far from forgotten in the public imagination. This despite not having received a rigorous biographical treatment in over fifty years.[2] Sinead McCoole's work on Hazel Lady Lavery[3] and the disclosure of O'Higgins' private correspondence with her has in recent years enlivened a further interest in him which has been rather more prurient than political or historical.[4] After Michael Collins, O'Higgins remains the most important and intriguing political personality of those who accepted the Anglo-Irish treaty in 1921-2, and went on to create the Irish Free State. With both his political and private lives exposed the student of O'Higgins is confronted with a series of fascinating and seemingly irreconcilable contradictions.

O'Higgins enjoyed remarkable revolutionary and political careers. He did not participate in the 1916 rising but despite the handicap of a late entry into revolutionary politics he was an Acting Minister in the Dáil Government by December 1920. By the December of 1921 he was attending cabinet meetings and by December 1922 he was Vice-President of the Irish Free State, Minister for Home Affairs and emerging as the most distinctive public voice of the new state. He was just thirty years of age. Even by the standards of the most volatile of revolutionary movements his advancement was startling. But for a moderate in a movement dominated by hard-nosed republican-militarists his achievement was spectacular if not something of a surprise.[5] When he became one of the chief advocates of the treaty during December 1921, he seemed to some within the revolutionary movement who had served more conventional revolutionary apprenticeships to have risen without trace.

Desmond FitzGerald, his fellow minister and close ally in the treatyite governments, recalled of August 1922 and the deaths of both Arthur Griffith and Michael Collins 'It seems almost miraculous that Kevin O'Higgins should have appeared in our midst to guide us through the most crucial period of our history.'[6] O'Higgins, of course, did not receive the public mantle of leadership, but FitzGerald's eulogy betrayed the contention that O'Higgins not William T. Cosgrave was indeed the chief architect of the early Free State. That O'Higgins was the *de facto* leader of post-revolutionary independent Ireland was also the glaring subtext of Terence de Vere White's 1948 biography. This proposition remains a matter of debate among professional historians and political scientists alike. Brian Farrell in his study of the office of Taoiseach has argued that the influence of O'Higgins has been exaggerated at the expense of Cosgrave.[7] In a more comprehensive survey J. J. Lee has argued that O'Higgins set the style and tone of the early Cosgrave Governments while arguing that O'Higgins' influence was waning toward the end of his political career.[8] The contention here is that both interpretations tend toward an underestimation of the role and influence of Kevin O'Higgins on the post-revolutionary governments and the treatyite settlement. O'Higgins established himself as the controlling influence of the post-Collins treatyite governments in the new state shaping domestic as well as foreign policy and reforming the treatyite party and government for the purpose of imposing his will on the post-revolutionary order.

The received O'Higgins in as much as he exists as a historical figure rests squarely on the work of de Vere White. Written after a decade and half of Fianna Fáil in office, de Vere White's *Kevin O'Higgins* was in part an antidote to the republican ascendancy which after 1932 had done so much to obliterate the memory of the first decade of construction. O'Higgins emerged from these pages of biography as the patron saint of the new administration, democracy, civilian government and law and above all the new order. Both he and the first adminstration were imbued in the forties with values which at that time seemed to many old-treatyites to represent the antithesis of Fianna Fáil government amid contemporary accusations of corruption and jobbery.[9] In this sense the O'Higgins which de Vere White created, whether intentional or not, served the needs not alone of a moribund Fine Gael party, but that part of Irish society, nationalist as well as unionist, which found itself alienated from the Fianna Fáil regime and what for the sake of brevity is sometimes referred to as "de Valera's Ireland". De Vere White regenerated a dead hero to challenge de Valera's ascendency, because in 1947-8, there appeared to be no more live ones. The life of O'Higgins as the lost leader was a reminder of an antediluvian state, and suggested that there would have been, if only he had lived, an alternative future to the one de Valera offered to an increasingly disillusioned public in 1948. The received O'Higgins remains therefore very much the man de Vere White created in co-operation with the survivors, ministers and senior civil servants, of the treatyite regime. The question which nags the historian when confronted with this Kevin O'Higgins is the extent to which de Vere White produced a hagiography or simply set forth an alternative interpretation of the first decade of independence where the influence of O'Higgins was paramount if not all defining.

O'Higgins came from what can best be described as the Irish Roman Catholic establishment in waiting. His mother, Anne Sullivan, was the daughter of Timothy Daniel Sullivan, the Young Irelander, editor of the *Nation*, nationalist MP and Lord Mayor of Dublin. Sullivan was also the leader of the west Cork nationalist group within the Irish Parliamentary Party known as the 'Bantry band' whose political alliances were reinforced by an elaborate series of inter- and intra-family marriages.[10] O'Higgins' mother's sister married her first cousin Tim Healy the anti-Parnellite MP and later, at the invitation of O'Higgins, the first Governor-General of the Irish Free State. Another aunt married the successful London barrister George Gavan Duffy, later Sinn Fein plenipotentiary in 1921 and President of the Irish High Court 1946-51. O'Higgin's uncle, Timothy Sullivan, was called to the bar in 1918, married Tim Healy's daughter, and preceded Gavan Duffy as President of the Irish High Court, 1936-46. Another cousin, Alexander Martin Sullivan, the son of the nationalist writer and politician of the same name, was the last Serjeant-at-Law in Ireland. The Sullivan-Healy family were among the very upper echelons of the new Catholic middle class who had risen through the professions and business in the second half of the nineteenth century. They were also part of an extended political family which embraced Tim and Ned Harrington, and another Bantryman made good in Dublin the entrepreneur William Martin Murphy. 'Uncle Willie' as Serjeant Sullivan later referred to him 'Technically he was not my uncle, but he was my father's brothers' brother-in-law, and amongst Bantrymen that was close enough.'[11] The genealogy is complex, but what mattered was that O'Higgins was connected to a Catholic nationalist political and legal elite which spanned Cork, Dublin and London.

By the time of his birth in 1892, O'Higgins' father had become a Roman Catholic pillar in what remained an ascendancy dominated society in Stradbally. Dr Thomas Francis Higgins[12] studied medicine at the Royal College of Surgeons becoming a fellow by examination in 1887.[13] In 1882, the young Dr Higgins succeeded William Clark, a Protestant gentleman farmer, as County Coroner; a post he held until his death in 1923.[14] Dr Higgins, as a justice of the peace, sat on the bench at Stradbally sessions with the local great and the good and dispensed justice to poachers, trespassers and the local minor criminality. To underpin his rising social stock, and to house and finance an expanding family he purchased an eighty acre farm with a modest dwelling nearby at Woodlands which eventually replaced the dispensary house in town as the family residence. The young Kevin Higgins followed his brothers to Clongowes Wood College in 1903, but whereas they went into the professions of medicine and banking, he pursued a religious vocation. For his efforts he was rusticated by not one but two seminaries: St. Patrick's Maynooth, and St. Patrick's Carlow, where an addiction to nicotine caused him to fall foul of the deans of discipline. Dejected at his personal failure he fell into, as opposed to taking up, the study of law at University College, Dublin and took a lazy third class degree, after which he studied as a solicitors' apprentice in the Cork office of Tim Healy's brother, Maurice.

It was at University College Dublin that O'Higgins first displayed radical tendencies. During Michaelmas term of 1915 he was arrested for 'obstructing the recruiting authorities' which translated into burning offending posters off walls.[15] O'Higgins rejoiced in his seditious tendencies and recounted his brush with the law throughout 1915, in the auditorium of University College's Literary and Historical Society the 'L&H'. The social world of college societies provided him with a congenial alternative to study. O'Higgins at UCD was a wag. In contrast to his later abstemiousness – typical of the teetotal proclivities of the Sullivans – his UCD days were filled measure for measure with long and late drinking and sleeping. The 'L&H', and the Dublin varsity debating circuit introduced him to a world of ambitious young lawyers whose legal skills and the demands made of them by the independent state after 1922 ensured that they would have important public lives alongside their chosen careers. Patrick McGilligan, his contemporary at Clongowes and later at O'Higgins' invitation Minister for Industry and Commerce, was still on the debating circuit when O'Higgins arrived at Earlsfort Terrace in 1914. As were John Costello, later Taoiseach; Cecil Lavery a future Attorney General, Cahir Davitt, later Judge-Advocate-General of the Irish Free State army, Arthur Cox sometimes adviser to the Free State Governments on industrial policy and George O'Brien later professor of economics in UCD.[16]

Quite apart from being a social outlet the debating societies gave O'Higgins and his contemporaries a parliamentary training. The culture of the 'L & H' and UCD more generally, in O'Higgins' time, was that of a new and optimistic nationalist elite consciously preparing for a home rule Government in a society they expected to dominate. Parliamentary procedure and language were used at College debates. John Redmond and other Irish Parliamentary M.P.s were invited to address the membership. O'Brien summed up the ebullient atmosphere of the pre-war 'L &H' when he wrote

> We all took for granted that, if Home Rule was achieved, we would be among the politicians of the new Ireland...Debating took such a large part of our energies that I remember Arthur Cox saying to me that there were only three positions for which we were being fitted by our education- prime minister, leader of the opposition and Speaker of the House of Commons.[17]

Long before the Sinn Fein movement was to flounder in the confusion of 1922, on issues of legitimacy, democracy, and sovereignty, O'Higgins and his contemporaries were cogitating on these concepts part in good humour and part in earnest. When O'Higgins rose to address the motion for acceptance of the treaty in December 1921 he could have been forgiven for experiencing a sense of *déjà vu* recalling his own contribution to the 'L & H' in February 1915 on the motion 'That questions of war and peace should be submitted to a referendum'.[18] The debating societies were part of an important educational as well as social process which ensured that when parliamentary democracy began to assert itself over militarist revolution he and those of that small select group of fellow collegians who found themselves in the upper tiers of Sinn Féin would be at a distinct advantage within the revolutionary Dáil. That transformation began with the signing of the treaty on 6 December 1921 and its acceptance by a small majority in the Dáil on 7 January 1922.

During the treaty debates O'Higgins distinguished himself as one of its most able proponents speaking fourth after Arthur Griffith, Sean MacEoin and Michael Collins during the public session of the debate on 19 December 1921.[19] He followed Griffith's and Collins' lead that the treaty could be developed into greater freedom and argued that the Dáil had to take into consideration the whole Irish nation and not just the Sinn Féin constituency that the assembly represented. It was an able and lucid contribution, but not the least remarkable aspect of it was O'Higgins' enthusiasm for membership of the new Common-wealth. He said in the course of his speech .'...Yes if we go into the Empire, we go in not sliding in, attempting to throw dust in our people's eyes, but we go in with our heads up.'[20] The speech according to one contemporary jeopardized the more cautious argument Collins in particular was developing, in the hope of winning the support of moderate republicans.[21] Nevertheless the speech publicly established O'Higgins' seniority within the leadership of the emergent treatyite wing of Sinn Féin. There remained however, a contradiction between such a high-profile and what were perceived by both opponents and supporters of the treaty as deviant imperialist sympathies. O'Higgins articulated a moderate and accommodationalist brand of nationalism which had been cowed into silence by the dominant militarist-republican wing of the revolution. What remains unclear however, is the extent to which O'Higgins suppressed his sympathies for the Empire during his ascent or whether they were tolerated or just ignored by the leadership all too aware of his intellectual and political abilities.

O'Higgins had been both careful and fortunate in the friends he had cultivated in the course of his short revolutionary career. In Belfast Jail where he was imprisoned after the 'German plot' roundup in May 1918, he came to the attention of Austin Stack and was put forward and returned as the Sinn Féin candidate for Queen's County in the general election in December of that year.[22] During 1919, he became a collector for the Dáil loan in his constituency under the direction of the Dáil Minister of Finance, Michael Collins. O'Higgins quickly proved himself not alone a good collector but an excellent organiser and administrator.[23] Following on this Collins decided that O'Higgins would be best deployed at the centre of the Dáil counter-administration and he was brought to Dublin by his mentor and deposited in digs in a policeman's house in Synge Street[24] before joining the Dáil Department of Local Government the most important of the emerging revolutionary departments, as Assistant Minister to Cosgrave. The appointment was as sudden as it was strategic and O'Higgins in effect became Collins' man in Local Government.[25] To consolidate this new arrangement he was sworn into the Irish Republican Brotherhood: probably by one of

Collins' closest associates Diarmuid O'Hegarty.[26] In one move O'Higgins became one of the inner brothers – if not quite one of the boys – who surrounded Collins. Collins' sponsorship of O'Higgins was crucial to his elevation but he was also wooed by de Valera who in the Autumn of 1921 invited O'Higgins to attend and contribute to cabinet meetings but without the right to vote.[27]

With the treaty passed by the Dáil, O'Higgins was made Minister of Economic Affairs in Griffith's Dáil and Collins' Provisional Governments in January 1922. The deaths of Griffith and Collins in August, created a vacuum in the leadership of the party which Cosgrave, previously Acting Chairman of the treatyite Provisional Government, filled without challenge. O'Higgins became Minister of Home Affairs in Cosgrave's September 1922 ministry, and Vice-President and Minister of Justice in the first Free State Government formed on 6 December. The reasons for Cosgrave's decision to make O'Higgins his deputy in the new Government are not immediately clear. Though O'Higgins had established himself as an outstanding minister in the Dáil and Provisional Governments the fact remained that O'Higgins and Cosgrave enjoyed what was at best may be termed an uneasy relationship.[28] When Cosgrave succeeded Collins, O'Higgins had commented to Richard Mulcahy that 'Dublin corporators would make this land a nation once again.'[29] Their relationship in the Department of Local Government had also undergone some strain when O'Higgins countered Cosgrave's orders to close down the department when the latter was forced to go into hiding in late 1920. Seizing the opportunity to display his ministerial mettle O'Higgins carried on without the authority or goodwill of his minister.[30]

O'Higgins and Cosgrave's respective styles of politics, despite the friction they created complemented one another. O'Higgins was decisive, compulsive and at times obsessional about the causes he championed and occasionally transmogrified into personal crusades. Cosgrave was affable, charming, good humoured and a fixer of the old political school. After joining Griffith's Sinn Féin in 1905 he followed his father into Dublin municipal politics and became a member of the Corporation in 1909. Cosgrave was a skilled negotiator able to reach compromises sometimes by the most deftly engineered political stunts.[31] He was in a curious sense a private politician: his real politics were practised in the lobbies and dining rooms of Leinster House or in the seclusion of his home at Beechpark near Templeogue. He may not have had the flourishes of O'Higgins' better oratory, but Cosgrave had his compensations. O'Higgins in contrast was a brilliant self-publicist and ensured that his speeches were circulated to friends and published. In these he employed a *chiaroscuro* vision of public and political life in which he reduced all things to antithetical absolutes: right against wrong; good against evil; probity against corruption; and ultimately civilisation against anarchy. While such a world view, often brilliantly expressed with the zeal of a missionary priest had the advantage of a thundering clarity it was not ideally suited to the less absolute business of managing party politics. Most especially when the party in question was a broad coalition of Collins and Griffith's construction embracing moderates and militarists, republicans and monarchists and every shade of political thought in-between.

For all O'Higgins' ability and vitality as a parliamentarian Cosgrave overshadowed him in this one respect. Cosgrave proved in the crisis of 1922 that he had the capacity to hold together a treatyite party which like its revolutionary forebear was extraordinarily heterogeneous and contradictory in its composition. The new party contained sections which had an ambiguous relationship with both the treaty and the new state. Collins in creating a treatyite party had forged a coalition between moderate Sinn Féin and militarist-republican elements who through personal loyalty to him directly or indirectly through the IRB had been persuaded to accept the treaty as a means to – or as Collins put it a 'stepping stone' towards – political advancement.[32] Many of Collins' followers rallied to the cause of the Free State and would indeed use force of arms to put down what they saw as the anti-treaty IRA's rebellion against the will of the majority. Treatyite militarist-republicans within and without the army, remained a threat to the civil government and more pointedly O'Higgins' moderate constitutional nationalism. The treatyite militarist-republicans had been reconciled to the Free State regime through personal loyalties, promises and assumptions about what the post-revolutionary settlement would yield in terms of sovereignty and the republic. If the new order failed to meet the aspirations of revolutionary soldiers, as it most likely would, then there was the possiblity that they would revert to revolutionary politics or less euphemistically the politics of the gun.

Beyond this threat to the state's institutions and the nascent democracy growing under them, there existed the issue of defining the direction the new state would take. There existed within Collins' coalition at least two competing interpretations of revolutionary politics. The one militarist-republican the other moderate-constitutional and as yet undefined in its ultimate outlook. What was to set O'Higgins apart and facilitate his gaining hegemony over the treatyite regime was his belief that Collins' coalition held no long-term place for his brand of moderate nationalism and that ultimately if his politics were to survive militarist-republicanism and radical nationalism would have to be defeated. The clarity of this vision joined to the precision of his political scalpel meant that when the opportunity to act presented itself in March 1924 O'Higgins was able to alter significantly the direction of the treaytite regime and for that matter the new state. However, in August 1922 no one, least of all Cosgrave, expected that he would fill the void left by Griffith and Collins. Whatever about his charismatic and other shortcomings Cosgrave was a conciliator, and had the essential qualification of occupying something approaching the political centre of gravity of the treatyite coalition: O'Higgins for the moment at least remained an antipodean.

O'Higgins did however play an essential role in reconciling the new regime to elements which lay outside the Sinn Féin constituency. O'Higgins, following in Griffith's footsteps, was determined to affect an inclusive state and nation and not one which was defined by revolutionary rhetoric and exclusive notions of race and culture.[33] He told the Dáil in December 1922

> We being the majority and strength of the country...it comes well from us to make a generous adjustment to show these people are regarded, not as aliens or enemies, not as planters, but that we regard them as part and parcel of this nation, and that we wish them to take their share of its responsibilities.[34]

When Andrew Jameson, the unofficial spokesperson of the southern Unionists, approached Cosgrave during the campaign for the 1923 General Election and promised to underwrite his party's elections costs on the condition 'that certain ministers would be retained' it is difficult to believe that he did not have O'Higgins in mind.[35] O'Higgins' demeanour and voice were vaguely recognisable and at the same time also reassuring to both the former southern unionists and old parliamentary nationalists alike. In his writings during the period of disintegration in the weeks preceding the outbreak of Civil War, O'Higgins amplified the desire for a return to some form of stable Government. He wrote in the treatyite organ the *Free State* in March 1922:

> Where there was order chaos rears its head, friendship and trust give way to bitterness and suspicion, the will and the welfare of the people, formally supreme, have now become trifles light as air, the guns which did such good service against the usurper, are now flourished in the faces of Irish citizens. To the frenzied tune of "the existing Republic" this sorely tried land is drifting into anarchy, is being hurried to a condition of things which one's mind has come to associate most readily with Mexican politics.

> The "plain people" look on in dismay and deep depression. The
> economic life of the country is ebbing. The very social fabric is
> threatened. What are the conflicting issues that are convulsing the
> nation? Formulas, phrases, creeds: doctors are wrangling over a
> patient whose chief need is rest and time to recuperate after an
> operation for the removal of the deep-seated cancer of a foreign
> tyranny. While they wrangle life is ebbing and dissolution is at
> hand.[36]

Such breathless polemic captured what were already his political
axioms: that disorder in the absence of the rule of law would bring
about a breakdown of the 'social fabric': or in other words the spectre
of social revolution. In his speeches and journalism during the Spring
of 1922 O'Higgins became convinced that the republican experiment
had not alone failed but it had been turned on its head. Writing again
in the *Free State* he recorded:

> The increased contempt of these rabid Republicans...for the
> opinions, rights and interests of the "plain people" is certainly
> remarkable. In his innocence the writer was accustomed to
> associate Republicanism with robust democratic principles. He
> fancied that it eliminated both autocracy and junkerdom...[37]

From early 1922 O'Higgins became increasingly disillusioned and
hostile toward republican politics and this sense of betrayal fuelled an
attack on revolutionary republicanism which was to become the *leit
motif* of the rest of his career.

O'Higgins' relationship with republicanism had been ambiguous
from the commencement of his revolutionary activities. He had told the
special crimes court which convicted him in May 1918 that

> ... most of us who support Sinn Féin in these days (sic) are out
> only for the independence of Ireland and not necessarily for the
> destruction of the British Empire; our ideal would be if the British
> Empire behaved itself.[38]

This was perhaps an indication of the accommodationalist approach
to Empire which later emerged during the treaty debates. In-between
times O'Higgins had enjoyed a dalliance with the IRB, but O'Higgins,
even as republican brother, remained aloof and fiercely independent.
Membership of the brotherhood was a necessary accoutrement for an
ambitious rising star within the revolution and not a declaration of a
doctrinaire political faith. Gearóid O'Sullivan and Seán Ó Murthuile,

both senior IRB men, visited O'Higgins at his flat on the evening the treaty was published to find him entertaining friends. They were told curtly that it was his intention to support the treaty '...even against the wishes of the IRB.'[39].

In the last week of June 1922 O'Higgins submitted a memorandum to the Provisional Government 'in the hope of stimulating thought' and the document serves as an exposition of his thinking on the crisis which was escalating. Though there were to be modifications, the June 1922 memorandum sketched what were to be the two major principles of his political thought over the last half-decade of his life. Fundamental to his thinking was the abandonment of revolutionary aspirations in favour of a reductionist interpretation that the Government's only priority was to have its writ run unhindered throughout the state. The other substantive point the memorandum addressed was the issue of partition. O'Higgins believed that with a Civil War in southern Ireland, Sir James Craig's Northern Government would be amenable '...to any suggestion, even remotely calculated to alleviate conditions in their area and in our ours.'[40] O'Higgins argued that if some advancement could be made on the issue of unity it would undermine the anti-treatyite opposition and allow some of its leadership to extricate itself from the republican fundamentalists.

> It is clear that they hoped for such an opportunity in the Constitution, but British suspicion was roused to such a pitch by the "Pact" that every unpleasant form was insisted on, and even Mr de Valera could not find a loophole through which to slip away from his "rock".[41]

'I wonder' wrote O'Higgins '...if anyone here or in England, or in North-East Ulster believes very strongly in the Boundary Commission as a piece of constructive statesmanship. I don't.' He preferred instead to suspend it in the event of the northern Government coming to an understanding with its southern counterpart. O'Higgins elaborated:

> On an immediate cessation of hostile activity against his [Craig's] Parliament, and a general acquiescence in its jurisdiction by Nationalists resident in his area, met on his side by ameliorative measures to be defined later (disbandment of Specials, release of prisoners, etc.) he would undertake within six months of the confirmation of our Constitution by the British Parliament to take and abide by a plebiscite of the Province of Ulster on the question of whether the six counties should or should not come within the Free State, such plebiscites to be taken at intervals of say a year

until unity is reached. In consideration of this the Boundary
Commission proposal to be waived.

O'Higgins saw the 'in built' majority of 200,000 Protestant unionists in
the nine county province of Ulster as offering the unionists and the
northern Government an assurance of fair treatment. The proposal,
however, betrayed a naiveté about unionist politics and identity which
was typical of revolutionary nationalist politicians. What O'Higgins
knew of the north had been glimpsed through iron bars of the Crumlin
Road Jail during his short imprisonment there in 1918. Moreover, he
seemed blissfully ignorant of the fact that Ulster Unionists in 1920 had
rejected a similar proposal put to them by the British Government
during the preparation of the Government of Ireland Act, so as to
ensure their unassailable majority within a six country state.[42]

During the course of the Civil War, O'Higgins secured a reputation
for being the most resolute and intractable of the treatyite ministers.
The reality of the situation was more complex. The treatyite position
was founded on the belief that the Provisional Government had
received an unquestionable majority mandate at the 'pact' General
Election on 16 June 1922. Support for the treaty as expressed in the
result of the election enabled the treatyite Governments (Dáil and
Provisional) to go to war on their interpretation of democratic
legitimacy and not the treaty itself. It also allowed Collins to claim that
those who opposed his Government in arms were in rebellion against
the democratically elected Government of Southern Ireland.
Consequent to this was the treatyites pursuit of a policy of
criminalisation which denied the anti-treatyites or 'Irregulars' (as they
were styled by the treatyites) prisoner-of-war status. The criminalisation
of the anti-treaty IRA was crucial in the first weeks of the war to both
expedite the processing of prisoners and to further reinforce the
legitimacy of the Provisional Government. It also enabled the treatyite
Government to pass special powers legislation in October to execute
'Irregular' prisoners and ultimately, in their eyes, legitimised the reprisal
executions of 8 December 1922.

In the public and more especially in the republican imagination
O'Higgins was given disproportionate responsibility for the treatyite
Governments' procrustean policies. O'Higgins may have been the most
articulate voice within the Civil War Government but he was
nevertheless amplifying an agreed policy and not his own agenda. It
has to be admitted that he did believe himself to be more resolute than
others in the Government and feared some would seek settlement with
the anti-treatyites in bringing the war to an end thereby compromising
the regime and ultimately his position within it.[43] The total destruction

of revolutionary republicanism both inside and outside the regime was essential to O'Higgins' continued survival and the assertion of moderate constututional nationalism over its revolutionary counter-part.

One of many ironies of O'Higgins' murder in July 1927, was that it was witnessed only by Professor Eoin MacNeill the former Minister for Education who had been forced to resign in November 1925. MacNeill had sat at the same cabinet table, ordered the same executions and sanctioned the same policies as O'Higgins but for whatever reasons he was spared by the assassins even when they had him in the sights of their revolvers.[44] Joe McGrath the first Minister of Industry and Commerce, and also Director of Free State military intelligence service – an institution with a less than savoury record – could within a decade be found playing a hand of poker with Seán Lemass.[45] The existence of an intense personal hatred for O'Higgins among those who opposed the treaty – de Valera included[46] – came not from his position or any rational interpretation of his political role during the Civil War. O'Higgins was different to his comrades because he was emblematic of the triumph of moderate-nationalism over revolutionary -republicanism. Professor Michael Hayes, the Ceann Comhairle of the Dáil (1922-32), articulated

> ...In a curious way there were people who said (although they were anti-treaty themselves and violently against Mulcahy)...Mulcahy had a right to be anything he liked and who didn't agree that O'Higgins had a right to say what he said. Now I think that is not logical or philosophical but it is true.[47]

O'Higgins in the eyes of the anti-treatyites was not alone guilty of national apostasy he was also perceived as an interloper and an *arriviste* in a revolutionary movement to which he never truly belonged. Therefore, unlike Mulcahy or more appositely MacNeill whose revolutionary origins lay in the IRA, he had no right to be absolved of his sin of compromising over the treaty and all that it entailed. Whether or not this rationale was applied on Cross Avenue on 10 July 1927 it is impossible to say. But O'Higgins' fellow ministers, like MacNeill, and the senior soldiers, like Mulcahy, were permitted to grow into old age without serious molestation.

If O'Higgins did not articulate an individual position on the fundamental principles on which the Civil War was fought he did at times give voice to an identifiably different emphasis for the justification of the Government's ruthless counter-insurgency policy. Central to his conceptualisation of the war was the idea that it was in essence a struggle against criminality merely masquerading behind political principle. In particular he articulated with considerable energy a perception that the war was not alone a threat to the social but also the moral stability of the nation. He wrote in the blackest month of the Civil War January 1923 '...there is a great deal of greed and envy and lust and drunkenness and irresponsibility...we are dealing with anarchy under cover of a political banner.'[48] O'Higgins repeatedly identified in militarist-republicanism, both pro- as well as anti-treatyite, an implied threat to the sexual morality of the people. Nowhere were these inter-connected themes of sexual deviance, republicanism, and moral corruption better exposed than in what became known as the Kenmare case. In June 1923, two daughters of the local doctor Randal MacCarthy in Kenmare, County Kerry, were allegedly violently – and implicitly sexually – assaulted by three Free State army officers after attending a dance in their home.[49] When the incident was apparently ignored by the army authorities and the Attorney-General the matter was brought to O'Higgins' attention. O'Higgins was doubly enraged on the grounds that the uniform and reputation of the new state had been besmirched in the incident and also that the officers' guilt had he believed been covered up by an IRB conspiracy within the army's General Headquarters presided over by Mulcahy and his senior officers. O'Higgins went so far as to write to Cosgrave threatening to resign in August 1923 concluding '...Lady Lavery spoke to me about it having heard of it in London from Lord and Lady Kenmare and you can imagine the use that will be made out of it there.'[50] Such matters of sexual impropriety proved to be of considerable embarrassment to both the O'Higgins and Healys. Maurice Healy wrote to his brother Tim in October 1922 reporting the moral decline in Cork '...There is a good deal of drinking. The [Free State] sentry at South Mall post is sometimes seen with a girl on his knee. The scenes between soldiers and women beat anything seen even in the halcyon days of the British Tommy. The demoralisation of women is appalling.'[51] As late as 10 November 1924 Tim Healy wrote to his sister-in-law Annie in scandalised tones following a visit from O'Higgins' mother and sister Irene who relayed 'the Kenmare business...was generally known.'[52] The alleged moral degeneracy which had accompanied revolution and Civil War had particularly shocked the cultural mores of the Irish nationalist middle class.

O'Higgins' reaction to the Kenmare incident though apparently genuine can be only partly explained in terms of genuine moral indignation. He manipulated the incident to undermine the Minister for Defence Richard Mulcahy in cabinet and used the case and the army's handling of it as proof that the IRB influenced the judgement of senior army officers. In this and in other similar episodes O'Higgins exposed a tendency to superimpose moral arguments on political disagreements and in the case of the army he used the association of sexual crime and deviance to undermine its senior officers. In the Kenmare case he linked the IRB and Mulcahy to what was allegedly a heinous crime. In the absence of hard evidence – and against the repeated advice of the Attorney-General – O'Higgins, the Minister for Justice, contented himself with his own verdict stating at the Army Inquiry in April 1924 'I believe them [the three officers allegedly involved] guilty without any trial further than such inquiry as has been held.'[53] As has already been noted O'Higgins could on occasion identify 'lust' as being a motivation for anti-treaty criminality. On the day before Erskine Childers' court martial commenced O'Higgins, in an infamous and much cited speech implied Erskine Childers had been party to 'rape'.[54] The insinuation was long remembered.[55] Apart from the Kenmare case O'Higgins also used the rapid spread of venereal-disease in the new army to undermine Mulcahy in the cabinet. Mulcahy later recalled

> ...O'Higgins was influenced that way by Freil his secretary – they set up a V.D. committee and this was another of the things used against us, simply because we set up a proper Army Medical Service and we set up prophylactic provisions for various things.[56]

During the Army Inquiry in April-May 1924 the incidence of venereal disease was used by O'Higgins' chief informant on the military, Colonel Jephson O'Connell, a Roman Catholic priest from the Diocese of Salford in England, to substantiate the point that the army was a morally corrupting institution.[57] However, O'Higgins pre-empted such statements to the Inquiry by supplying the cabinet with tables of dubious scientific value indicating serving and ex-Free State soldiers involvement in crime with special reference to sexual misdemeanours.[58]

The use of moral arguments and specifically sexual inneundo in the absence of direct accusation was a vicious and effective weapon designed to damn the reputation of the army before the Cabinet. There was, however, yet a further subtext to the Kenmare case. The three officers allegedly involved, General Paddy Daly and Captains Edward Flood and James Clark, had been implicated in and were in fact responsible for the reprisal executions at Ballyseedy on 7 March 1923. Niall C. Harrington a junior officer serving in Kerry had supplied information relating to the atrocity to Kevin O'Higgins: though it remains unclear whether or not he actually supplied the names of the officers involved. Following an inquiry over which Daly presided, the Kerry matter was closed though O'Higgins and his ministry remained less than convinced that the issue had been resolved. O'Higgins believed, and it was an assumption reinforced by the Kenmare case, that Daly and the other officers were protected by Mulcahy and by implication the IRB at Headquarters. This appeared to be further confirmed when Mulcahy recommended that Flood and Clark should not be demobilised in early 1924: O'Higgins had the decision overturned by the Executive Council.[59] The Kenmare case gathered an importance which transcended the crimes allegedly committed against the MacCarthy sisters. It became for O'Higgins a test of the army's and more especially Mulcahy's commitment to the application of justice. At every faltering step O'Higgins became further convinced of an IRB cover up protecting Brothers against prosecution. The accusations of sexual crime against the army were born in part out of a frustration that no evidence could be found of IRB interference. O'Higgins understood that a cabinet which was apparently unmoved by the manifest cover-up following the Kerry reprisal murders could be forced to take action on the grounds of sexual impropriety. The implication of sexual misconduct real or invented had more effect within the Government than any other disciplinary or criminal misdemeanour and thus O'Higgins used it to effect.

Notwithstanding O'Higgins' obsession with and manipulation of accusations of sexual immorality in the new state for his own political purposes up to the end of the Civil War, he prosecuted policies which were acceptable to all of the ministers of the treatyite Governments. It was, however, on the issue of the rationalisation of the defence forces which the consensus of treatyite politics – as it might properly be described – was to flounder and most notably on the reorganisation of the Criminal Investigation Department and army. Divisions in the cabinet opened up between Mulcahy who defended his demobilising policy and McGrath who became the spokesperson for a group of disaffected officers who formed a pressure group based on IRB structures but styling itself the Irish Republican Army Organisation (IRAO). Mulcahy had also to defend himself against a constant barrage of scathing criticism from O'Higgins who believed, like the IRAO, that the army was under the influence of the IRB presided over by Mulcahy and his staff officers at Headquarters.

The army mutiny of 6 March 1924 did not come as a surprise to the Government. Intelligence reports indicated that the IRAO might stage a coup and in response Cosgrave and his Government, somewhat nonchalantly, sat and waited.[60] On the night of the 7th the army authorities ordered that the house of Joe McGrath, the Minister for Industry and Commerce, be searched.[61] Furious at this action McGrath resigned from the Government the next day. The fact that the army had taken such action against a member of the Executive lost Mulcahy and the army authorities any remaining sympathy they might have had in the cabinet and General Eoin O'Duffy, Commissioner of the Garda Síochána, was placed in charge of the army but not over the senior officers of the army council nor Mulcahy as Commander-in-Chief as both derived their authority from the Department of Defence.[62]

From the moment the challenge came, in the form of an ultimatum to the Government on 6 March from the IRAO, O'Higgins acted with the sole purpose of asserting his will over the regime. Events, accidental and otherwise, played into his hands with spectacular ease. The most important development in this regard was Cosgrave's reputed illness. In the middle of the crisis Cosgrave retired to his home in Beechpark where he remained incommunicado: whether Cosgrave's flu was Asiatic or diplomatic has never been resolved. But with Cosgrave's self-imposed exile O'Higgins became Acting President and appointed his former secretary in the Dáil Department of Home Affairs, Patrick McGilligan, as Minister for Industry and Commerce to replace McGrath. The arrival of McGilligan, a contemporary from Clongowes, a UCD lawyer, and like his sponsor also from an Irish parliamentary family decisively tipped the balance of power in the cabinet in O'Higgins' favour. Within the Executive Council O'Higgins now had two firm allies in McGilligan and Desmond FitzGerald the Minister for External Affairs. Patrick Hogan, Minister for Agriculture and perhaps his closest ally, while a member of the Government was not in the Executive Council: a decision which may well have had its origins in curbing O'Higgins' influence in the early days of Cosgrave's leadership. During the course of the crisis, according to Mulcahy, Ernest Blythe, Minister for Finance transferred his allegiance from Cosgrave and realigned himself to the heir apparent.[63]

On the night of 18-19 March, with the IRAO mutineers in the midst of negotiations with the Government, the army under the direction of Adjutant General Gearóid O'Sullivan and with Mulcahy being informed, raided a public house in Parnell Street in Dublin where the leaders of the group were meeting.[64] O'Higgins chose to interpret the raid as evidence of the army authorities once again acting unilaterally without regard to the Government's policy. Mulcahy later made the counter argument that the raid was justified on grounds of national security as intelligence reports indicated that the IRAO were plotting a coup d'état. The following day O'Higgins demanded the resignations of the Army Council: Mulcahy as Minister for Defence and Commander-in-Chief; the Chief-of-Staff, Sean MacMahon; the Adjutant-General, Gearóid O'Sullivan; and the Quartermaster-General, Seán Ó Murthuile. Blythe and MacNeill were dispatched to Cosgrave's house to receive the President's authority as the dismissal of a cabinet minister lay outside the competence of O'Higgins as Acting-President. Mulcahy, on learning over the telephone of the fate of his senior staff officers gave notice of his immediate resignation to O'Higgins without further prompting from Cosgrave.

Compelling the resignations of the Minister for Defence and the entire Army Council within a year of the Civil War's conclusion held considerable risks, not least because the official premise for their dismissal, quite apart from the suspicion that they had reorganised the IRB within the army, was their defiance of executive authority. If Mulcahy and his senior officers had refused to accept O'Higgins' and the Executive Council's authority then there was the distinct risk of yet another mutiny or *coup d'état* as J. J. Lee and Maryann Valiulis have both argued.[65] Indeed Lee has commented in concurrence with Valiulis that O'Higgins' actions would have

> ...been criminally reckless, contrary to the unworthy accusations levelled against him, Mulcahy was as devoted a democrat as O'Higgins himself. It was Mulcahy's restrained response to his dismissal that was crucial to the infant state.[66]

While there is no doubting that the actions of Mulcahy and his senior officers were crucial to a peaceful conclusion, no study of the mutiny episode has ever resolved how or why O'Higgins could so confidently wager the new state's stability against the political inclination of four revolutionary generals three of whom were also senior Republican Brothers.

O'Higgins knew Mulcahy and his staff had not engendered popularity among the officer corps during the process of down-sizing the army after the Civil War from 54,000 to 20,000 troops and support for the generals in the event of them refusing to go could be expected to be less than unanimous.[67] Even if Mulcahy was prepared to resign there were still three other revolutionary generals, all senior republican Brothers including MacMahon, Collins' successor as President, to be taken account of. Here a close evaluation of the temperament of Ó Murthuile, O'Sullivan and MacMahon would have been invaluable. O'Higgins had worked and known them for some time – he had served as O'Sullivan's assistant during his brief sojourn in the army in July-August 1922 – but how exactly they would respond faced with the humiliation of forced resignation by O'Higgins remained a wild card. One possible explanation of O'Higgins' confidence was that he had an insider's knowledge of the IRB. O'Higgins, as a sworn republican brother, would have known that Collins during his tenure as President of the Supreme Council of the IRB, had revised the Brotherhood's constitution making it subservient to the Dáil as the legitimately established Government of Ireland.[68] That revision had been put to the test on 25 November 1921. de Valera had called Mulcahy and his senior officers to the Cabinet to announce his plans for the commissioning of a 'new army' and the restructuring of General Headquarters. The plan was unpopular among the staff officers and there had been much resistance with Eoin O'Duffy even shouting de Valera down. However, and the point was crucial in understanding the culture of the senior officers, much as they disliked and objected to the 'new army' proposal they acepted it as the policy of the civilian Executive.[69]

In 1921 the crucial objection had been the handing over of authority in the army not to the civilian government *per se* but to the Minister for Defence, Cathal Brugha and Collins. O'Higgins knew that by 1924 he had assumed the repugnance which Brugha had suffered from among the senior officers and Brothers in GHQ in 1921. What was more O'Higgins was moving to dismiss not reorganise the senior officers and on what they would hold, with some justification, to be false charges of disobedience and insubordination. O'Higgins had sat in cabinet on 25 November and listened to de Valera explain the 'new army' reforms and he had also witnessed the senior staff officers less than gracious response. O'Higgins could not have been entirely sure that any of the generals would operate within the constitution of the IRB, especially given the humiliation of the *fait accompli* he delivered to them. The Chief-of-Staff Sean MacMahon, did in fact initially refuse to accept the authority of the Executive Council on being ordered to resign, but after initial hesitation he acceded to the Government's decison. The others all resigned their commissions with dignity and full unquestioning deference to the civilian government.

In the course of the crisis O'Higgins did indeed vindicate, at considerable risks, civilian authority over the military institutions of the new state: though that relationship was not fully resolved until power was successfully and peacefully transferred to Fianna Fáil in 1932. But perhaps of equal significance was O'Higgins masterful and breathtakingly confident use of the crisis to advance the interests of his own political constituency within the cabinet. The division within the militarist-republicans wing of the regime played into his hands and he was quick to consolidate every advance which was ceded to him by those he identified as ideological enemies within the regime. As McGrath cancelled out Mulcahy in the cabinet the IRAO cancelled out the IRB in the army and in both instances he was able to replace or ensure the exclusion of not only old revolutionary institutions but their ideological baggage. Within Sinn Féin, and the early treatyite regime, moderate nationalists had for the most part suffered from a slow political advancement. This was in part because of the dominance of radical nationalists, the militarist-republican wing and perhaps most significantly the institutional engineering of the IRB. O'Higgins knew that as long as the old revolutionary order survived in the new regime, advancement of individuals and the state as a whole would be complicated by revolutionary records, past services and degrees of dedication to ideological and institutional values such as the republic and the Brotherhood which had lost their credibility in his view. O'Higgins wrote in May 1924 of McGilligan's appointment

> None of these fellows care a curse about the country or the people in the country. McGilligan, who wasn't "out in 16," has no particular "record" and no particular "Gaelic soul", has done more in two weeks than his predecessor [McGrath] in two years...I have come to the conclusion that men like Hogan and McGilligan...could do more for the country in a year and (even for the realisation of its ideals) than all the Clanns and Brotherhoods could effect in a generation.[70]

The promotion of McGilligan to the cabinet was the most graphic demonstration of a broader policy O'Higgins instituted of promoting individuals from the pre-war elite with which he had been associated at UCD. When in an attempt to rectify these advances in the party in 1925 Cosgrave asked for "Irish-Ireland" nominees for Cumann na nGaedheal's senate panel O'Higgins sponsored JJ Horgan the Cork solicitor and former Redmondite nationalist as well as Arthur Cox and George O'Brien.[71] There was in such a strategy an attempt to leaven the party and regime with moderate nationalists sympathetic to O'Higgins' nationalism. The policy was also, arguably, justified by O'Higgins' desire to see the proper order of Irish society restored with its educated elite doing precisely what it had been educated to do: govern. The revolution in all its shades of intensity had to O'Higgins' mind disagreeably disturbed the proper social order and he for his part in the post-March 1924 regime attempted what might be called the quite restoration of the Irish middle class interest.

O'Higgins found himself in a privileged position because of his raw talent as a politician which Stack, Collins, and de Valera had all identified. But his advancement hinged on the patronage of Collins and the Brotherhood and this connection as well as facilitating elevation also uniquely qualified him, as a moderate, to act against the militarist-republicans and so consolidate his own position within the regime. It was as an insider that he took on the revolutionary generals and used both his experience of them and their own IRB constitution to purge them from the regime. The appointment of O'Duffy as Inspector General of the Defence Forces on 18 March by O'Higgins with senority over the Commander-in-Chief and the Army Council was a masterstroke. In March 1924 O'Duffy was still an Executive member of the Supreme Council of the IRB. However, pandering to O'Duffy's desire for power and status by placing him in command over his colleagues limited the possiblity of a unified response from the senior Brothers and at the same time took the wildest card out of the pack. There was as Lee has noted an element of recklessness in O'Higgins' decision to face down the generals but he carefully chose the ground on which to make his stand.[72] Above all else O'Higgins understood that he had to get a brother to catch a brother.

One accolade however eluded O'Higgins. In the midst of the crisis Cosgrave's wife, Louisa, told Mulcahy's wife Min that O'Higgins wanted Cosgrave to resign.[73] Cosgrave stood alone between his deputy and the ultimate prize of politics – leadership. O'Higgins did not win the chief's throne but much of the power within the new cabinet had nevertheless shifted toward him. Cosgrave, after a miraculous recovery, managed to retrieve the defence portfolio from O'Higgins on 20 March – by which time O'Higgins had ensured that the mutinous officers would not be readmitted to the army – and held it until November when Peter Hughes, a Dundalk publican was appointed minister. O'Higgins could however after March 1924 rely on the support of FitzGerald, McGilligan, and Blythe within a cabinet reduced to six ministers. O'Higgins after March 1924 substantially controlled the cabinet with only Cosgrave and MacNeill maintaining an independent position. Hughes was to prove a ministerial non-entity.[74] Cosgrave returned in March 1924 to a much more peaceful cabinet but he did so in the knowledge that he had failed in the foremost objective of party political leadership: that of keeping his party united.

Those who sympathised with the IRAO mutineers led by McGrath withdrew from the Cumann na nGaedheal party and formed the National Group. The National Group existed as an external pressure group which hoped to extort concessions on both the issues of the mutinous officers' reinstatement in the army and the Government's policy in respect of revolutionary Sinn Fein's agenda. In September Cosgrave made a forlorn attempt to reunite the treatyite coalition by entering negotiations with McGrath mediated by the veteran Irish-American politicians Judge Daniel Cohalan and John Devoy.[75]

The issue of appointing a new Minister of Defence became pivitol in Cosgrave's negotiations with the National Group. The appointment of a minister sympathetic to the National Group and the mutinous officers was to be a prerequisite for the reunification of the party. As a compromise Cosgrave proposed to appoint JJ Egan a deputy from Tullamore as Minister for Defence. Cosgrave's choice of Egan is instructive. He presented Egan as a neutral candidate but in fact Egan was a protégé of O'Higgins.[76] Cosgrave having initially given assurances that a compromise on the officers' reinstatement in the army would be forthcoming was forced to backtrack and disgusted by this McGrath broke off negotiations and resigned from the Dáil with the eight other National Group deputies at the end of October.[77]

O'Higgins in 1924, cut across the complex alliances Collins had constructed in the treatyite regime and which Cosgrave strove to hold together. In this O'Higgins pursued a quiet but effective counter-revolutionary policy. It proved remarkably effective and depended on using revolutionary institutions and their personnel against one another. Similar to his use of O'Duffy in the defence forces O'Higgins nominated the rhetorical extremist and protectionist Minister for Posts and Telegraphs JJ Walsh to suppress the extra-parliamentary party's organisation which was broadly sympathetic to both his nationalist and economic outlooks.[78] In both the cases of O'Duffy and Walsh, personal vanity and promotion overtook any studied consideration of what was happening within the regime and to the revolutionary agenda they professed to sponsor. Mulcahy, contrary to Valiulis' argument that he articulated a policy position antithetical to O'Higgins, willingly co-operated with the usurpation of the party organisation.[79]

The reorientation of the Cumann na nGaedheal regime in 1924 made it better able to survive the collapse of the Boundary Commission in November 1925 through the removal of dissident elements and aggressive nationalists. Eoin MacNeill, the Free State's representative on the Boundary Commission, recorded in his memoir

> ...I had always been on the best of personal terms with O'Higgins but in many ways there had not been much sympathy between us. I knew that long before this he had been saying to people that it was time the "old man got off the tram tracks" and it was at his insistence and upon his motion that my resignation from the Government had been given in.[80]

MacNeill's removal enabled another ally of O'Higgins who shared a similarly conservative view of Irish society and revolution, John Marcus O'Sullivan, Professor of Modern History at UCD, to enter the cabinet as MacNeill's successor as Minister for Education.[81] Like O'Higgins and McGilligan, O'Sullivan came from a provincial upper middle class family and was duly educated at Clongowes, before going on to UCD and on a travelling scholarship to the universities of Bonn and

Heidleberg. Elected to the Dáil in 1923, he was made parliamentary secretary in the Department for Finance in December 1924, and cynically one might observe there he waited patiently for the Boundary Commission to consume MacNeill's political career. When O'Sullivan's appointment was announced in the Dáil it was made by O'Higgins: Cosgrave apparently being indisposed.[82] The appointment of O'Sullivan, somewhat less than an Irish language enthusiast, to the Ministry for Education which up until August 1921 had been the Dáil Ministry of Irish, marked a clear shift away from the revolutionary Sinn Féin's cultural agenda.

The reorientation of the cabinet further secured O'Higgins's position and enabled him to return anew to the issue of partition. He believed himself to have found a solution in Griffith's plans for a dual monarchy settlement which had been Sinn Féin policy until 1917. The proposal was put before the British Government in December 1926, and was met with some interest before being vetoed by the Northern Premier James Craig.[83] Despite this rebuff O'Higgins continued to believe, up until the eve of his death, that only the creation of a Kingdom of Ireland could unite the country and reconcile aspirations for a united Ireland with those of the Ulster Unionists, Britain and the Empire.[84] Such a redirection in politics as dual monarchy demanded a radical reinterpretation, if not a reinvention, of the origins and causes of the Irish revolution. In his address to the Irish Society at Oxford University in October 1924 O'Higgins chose to write out the 1916 rising and instead relocated the genesis of the revolution in the general election of 1918.

> In the general Election [sic] of December 1918 Ireland turned very definitely and emphatically from what was called "constitutional action". She withdrew from Westminster and proceeded to act on the basis that her political centre of gravity lay within herself.[85]

O'Higgins politics had no use for a revolution the origins of which were located in the IRB inspired conspiracy of 1916 in which he took no part and he chose instead to relocate the revolution in a constitutional event which created and legitimised both himself as a revolutionary and the violence which was to follow. This reinterpretation went beyond the elementary needs of creating a revolutionary past which justified a post-revolutionary present. O'Higgins post-treaty refused to reconcile the undemocratic origins of the revolutionary violence with its outcome the new state. In the exchanges with the anti-treatyites which predated the Civil War he claimed that killing without a democratic mandate was murder which had sparked Austin Stack's obvious retort 'Easter Week?'.[86] In what remains a telling passage from his Oxford address O'Higgins argued

> I have ventured to express the opinion that even English historians will come to write of the altered conditions in Ireland in precisely the terms with which Mr.Belloc summarises the French Revolution as "essentially a reversion to the normal – a sudden and violent return to those conditions which are the necessary bases of health in any political community".[87]

O'Higgins' post-revolutionary career can perhaps be best understood as a personal reversion to the normal. He became embroiled in a republican revolution which disintegrated and brought the country to the verge, as he saw it of social collapse. He saw the work of the Government after the Civil War as redeeming the nation from what he understood to be a moral abyss. For the generation and class to which he belonged the republican experiment which led to Civil War negated so much of the incremental progress toward statehood they had been preparing for since the middle of the nineteenth century and which they came to expect as their proprietorial inheritance. The Civil War conformed to the British prejudices which chided so roughly on Irish nationalists' consciousness: that they were incapable of governing themselves. For O'Higgins in particular the creation of a viable state, quite apart from reforming Irish society after the excesses of revolution, was the physical and incontrovertible refutation of that slur. Writing about the Cumann na nGaedheal 1927 manifesto which chartered the achievements of his Government he declared to Hazel Lavery 'It is the vindication of Irish Nationalism.'[88] O'Higgins' reaction to his experience of Civil War forced him to return to his political home of conservative parliamentary nationalism and in so doing he jettisoned much of the ideology of the revolutionary movement he had done so much to bring to power. In his writings of 1922 and after there are unmistakable echoes of earlier fears and forecasts which Redmondite supporters had issued in 1918 as Sinn Féin militant-republicanism had inexorably grown about them. AM 'Serjeant' Sullivan, O'Higgins' own cousin, who had remained in the old parliamentary nationalist fold wrote one such treatise in 1918 – *The road to Irish liberty* – from which O'Higgins subsequently borrowed the structure and the some of the arguments for his 1924 lecture *The Catholic layman in public life*.[89] Sullivan opened in 1918 by offering a Sinn Féiner's description of a republic as being '...a country where people govern themselves, and every man has the right to do whatever he likes.'[90] He continued

In a State in which there was allowed unrestricted exercise of personal desires, the violent and unscrupulous would soon impose their will upon the peaceable and timid; and eventually supreme power would pass into the hands of the one man who had proved himself most crafty in the organisation of violence for his own ends.[91]

Reading Sullivan in the Spring or Summer of 1922 it would have been difficult for O'Higgins to deny the veracity of his argument which he found himself repeating – consciously or subconsciously – in his own propaganda. That Sullivan had predicted not alone the coming of political chaos but the coming of 'The new de Valera' of 1922, only added weight to the old parliamentary nationalist position and further undermined much of what O'Higgins had aligned himself with during the revolutionary years of 1917-21. Whether or not O'Higgins read Sullivan in 1922 is irrelevant. O'Higgins returned to, if he ever really left, the parliamentary tradition in which he had grown up. It was a culture which exemplified parliamentary institutions and remained dubious of the cultural assertions of advanced nationalists. O'Higgins did not revert back to being a Redmondite nationalist but within the new order he sought a compromise with the pre-revolutionary nationalist elite which amounted to an attempt to return to what he saw as the normal. O'Higgins in oblique reference to *The Aeneid of Virgil* reflected in 1921 'As hard as it is to start the revolution, it may be harder to end it, for some of the gifts of the revolution are the gifts of the Danai and contain the germs of death.'[92] Whereas the *Danai* were the Republican Greeks bearing gifts of a wooden horse it was the warning of Laocoon, high-priest of the Trojans that O'Higgins had in mind:

> In a great temper Laocoon came tearing down from the citadel,
> Crying from far:-
>   Citizens, are you all stark mad?
> Do you really believe our foes are gone? Do you imagine
> Any Greek gift is guileless? Is that your idea of Ulysses?
> This thing of wood contains Greek soldiers, or else it is
> A mechanism designed against our walls – to pry into
> Our homes and to bear down on the city; sure some trick
> Is there. No, you must never feel safe with the horse, Trojans.
> Whatever it is, I distrust the Greeks, even when they are
> generous.[93]

So too cried Kevin O'Higgins from the Free State's citadel.

References

1. I wish to acknowledge the generous funding I received from the Faculty of Modern History at Oxford and also the British Academy which made the research for this paper in Ireland possible. I also owe a debt of thanks to James Deegan and Adrian Cosby of Stradbally for showing me the topography and hospitality of county Laois.

2. Terence de Vere White, *Kevin O'Higgins* (Dublin, 1948).

3. Sinead McCoole, *Hazel: a life of Lady Lavery 1880-1935* (Dublin, 1996), chpt.8.

4. Eoghan Harris, 'The man, the myth and the mistress', *The Sunday Tribune Magazine,* 15 Sept. 1996.

5. General Michael J. Costello recalled that during the Civil War there was some surprise in county Laois that Kevin O'Higgins had risen to prominence and not his brother Tom who enjoyed a higher profile in the local volunteers. General Michael J Costello interview with Richard Mulcahy 25 Mar. 1963 (University College Dublin Archive, hereafter UCDA, Mulcahy papers, P7/D/3).

6. Desmond FitzGerald, 'Kevin O'Higgins', *Forum treaty commemorative issue* (Dec. 1946), p. 6.

7. Brian Farrell, *Chairman or chief* (Dublin, 1971), p. 24.

8. JJ Lee, *Ireland: politics and society 1912-85* (Cambridge, 1989), p. 153.

9. In particular the Locke' Distillery Inquiry which implicated and later acquitted de Valera and three Fianna Fáil cabinet ministers in any malpractice associated with the sale of the business. A driving force behind the holding of the inquiry was the deputy for Laois-Offaly, the redoubtable Oliver J Flanagan. Lee, *Ireland,* pp 296-7.

10. For an exposition of the Sullivan family and political genealogy see Serjeant AM Sullivan, *Old Ireland: reminiscences of an Irish K.C.* (London, 1927), pp 12-7.

11. Ibid., p. 12.

12. The prefix 'O' was an affectation the younger members of the family added sometime after the 1918 General Election.

13. *The Nationalist and Leinster Times,* 17 Feb. 1923.

14. J.W.H. Carter, *The Land War and its leaders in Queen's county, 1879-82* (Portlaoise, 1994), p.242

15. James Hogan, 'Kevin O'Higgins: an appreciation', *An t-Oglach* (Oct. 1927), pp 12-3.

16. Eugene McCabe, *Arthur Cox 1891-1965* (Dublin, 1994), pp 53-5.

17. James Meenan, *George O'Brien: a biographical memoir* (Dublin, 1980), p. 33.

18. Literary and Historical Society Minute Book, 20 Feb. 1915, UCDA.

19. *Dáil Éireann treaty debates* (19 Dec. 1921), pp 42-8.

20. Ibid., p. 45.

21. James A Bourke memoir (a), (In the possession of Professor David W. Harkness, Emeritus Professor of Irish History, Institute of Irish Studies, Queen's University Belfast), pp 339-40.

22. Robert Brennan, *Allegiance* (Dublin, 1950), p. 174.

23. Leix and Offaly subscribed through O'Higgins' agency the largest amount of money in Leinster raising £10,030 together. Arthur Mitchell, *Revolutionary Government in Ireland: Dáil Éireann 1919-22* (Dublin, 1995), p. 64.

24. White, *O'Higgins,* p. 36.

25. James. A. Bourke memoir (a), pp 36-7.

26. Seán Ó Murthuile memoir (UCDA, Mulcahy papers P7a/209 (2)), p. 202.

27. *Dáil Éireann Treaty deb.* (3 Jan. 1922), p. 198.

28. Mulcahy later recalled that O'Higgins was difficult with the Cosgraves from the

beginning. William T Cosgrave's brother Philip was a treatyite deputy and temporarily Governor of Mountjoy Jail during 1922-3. Transcript of Conversation between General Richard Mulcahy, Dr Risteárd Mulcahy and Mrs Min Mulcahy, 23 Dec. 1961 (UCDA, Mulcahy papers P7/D/100).

29. Transcript of Conversation between General Richard Mulcahy, Dr Risteárd Mulcahy and Mrs Min Mulcahy, 23 Dec. 1961 (UCDA, Mulcahy papers P7/D/100).

30. White, *O'Higgins,* pp 36-7.

31. For an example of Cosgrave creativity in a crisis see Blythe's account of how Cosgrave persuaded the treatyite-republican wing to accept the oath of allegiance on entering the Dáil on 6 December 1922 in Stephen Collins, *The Cosgrave legacy* (Dublin, 1996), p. 36.

32. John M Regan 'The politics of reaction: the dynamics of treatyite politics', *I.H.S.,* 30, no. 120 (Nov. 1997), pp 544-49.

33. FSL Lyons, *Culture and anarchy in Ireland 1930-1939* (Oxford, 1979), p. 112.

34. Idem.

35. James A Bourke memoir (b), (in the possession of Mr Michael McCormick, London), p. 328.

36. Kevin O'Higgins, *Civil War and the events which led to it* (Dublin, n.d.), p. 28, reprinted from the *Free State,* 18 Mar. 1922

37. Kevin O'Higgins, *Civil War and the events which led to it* (Dublin, n.d.), p. 42, reprinted from the Free State 15 Apr. 1922

38. *King's County Chronicle,* 30 May 1918.

39. Ó Murthuile was secretary of the supreme council of the IRB. Seán Ó Murthuile memoir (UCDA, Mulcahy papers, P7/209), p. 202.

40. Ibid..

41. Ibid..

42. Patrick Buckland, *A history of Northern Ireland* (Dublin, 1981), pp 17-18.

43. Frank Callan, *TM Healy* (Cork, 1996), p. 608.

44. Eoin MacNeill memoir (In the possession of Bridín Tierney, Dublin), p.215.

45. Dick Walsh, *The party: inside Fianna Fáil* (Dublin, 1986), p. 77.

46. De Valera wrote on 5 February 1923 '...I have always tried to think that our opponents are acting from high motives, but there is no doubt there is a bit of the scoundrel in O'Higgins.' De Valera to Joseph McGarrity, 5 Feb. 1923, in Seán Cronin, *The McGarrity papers* (Tralee, 1972), p. 133.

47. Talk between Senator Hayes and Mulcahy about certain aspects of the de Vere White book on Kevin O'Higgins and some previous talk with Doctor Mulcahy. 22 Oct. 1964 (UCDA, Mulcahy papers P7/D/78).

48. O'Higgins to William T.Cosgrave, Confidential Memorandum on the situation in the Free State n.d. 11 Jan. 1923? (UCDA, Mulcahy papers P7b/96/(7-10)).

49. One of the daughters was engaged to be married to a member of the Garda Síochána and former captain in the National Army, Michael O'Higgins who does not appear to have been a relation of the Minister.

50. Copy of letter from O'Higgins to Cosgrave, 17 Aug. 1923 (UCDA, Mulcahy papers, P7a/133).

51. Memorandum to the director of intelligence including an extract from a letter from Maurice Healy solicitor, Cork, to Tim Healy K.C.. (UCDA, O'Malley papers, P17b/169).

52. Tim Healy to Annie Healy, 10 Nov. 1924 (UCDA, Healy papers, P6/A/106).

53. O'Higgins to the Army Inquiry 22 Apr. 1924 (UCDA, Mulcahy papers P7/C/23).

54. Dáil Debates, col. 2287 (17 Nov. 1922).

55. De Valera, quoting O'Higgins speech in a statement to the Dáil on 14 March 1929, refused to use the word rape preferring to misquote the speech he commented '...with others to commit....' I think crime is the word'. Moynihan, *Speeches*, p. 164.

56. Transcript of a conversation between Richard Mulcahy and Michael Costello, 25 Mar. 1963 (UCDA, Mulcahy papers, P7/D/3).

57. Colonel Jephson O'Connell's supplementary statement to the Army Inquiry 9 May 1924 (UCDA, Mulcahy papers, P7/C/15).

58. O'Higgins to every member of the Executive Council, Return of serious crimes, 10 Jan. 1924 (UCDA, Blythe papers, P24/323).

59. Kevin O'Higgins under cross examination by Conor Maguire BL 22 Apr. 1924 at the Army Inquiry (UCDA, Mulcahy papers, P7/C/23).

60. Extract from the Director of Intelligence Tralee 1 Mar. 1924 (Department of Defence Archive, Cathal Brugha Barracks Dublin, M J Costello papers).

61. A military search party arrived at the house but did not enter it on an assurance from McGrath that none of the IRAO leaders were present.

62. Dáil debates, vol. 6 col. 2205-6 (19 Mar. 1924).

63. Note by Mulcahy, 26 Apr. 1965 (UCDA, Mulcahy papers, P7c/2 (28)).

64. Maryann Valiulis, *Portrait of a revolutionary: general Richard Mulcahy and the founding of the Irish Free State* (Dublin, 1992), pp 213-4.

65. Lee, *Ireland*, p. 103; Valiulis, *Portrait*, p. 216.

66. Lee, *Ireland*, p. 103; Valiulis, *Portrait*, p. 216-7.

67. Seán Ó Murthuile's statement to the Army Inquiry 29 Apr. 1924 (UCDA, Mulcahy papers, P7/C/13).

68. See Seán Ó Murthuile memoir (UCDA, Mulcahy papers, P7c/209 (2)), p. 223; J. O'Beirne-Ranelagh, 'The I.R.B. from the Treaty to 1924', *I.H.S.*, 20 (1976), pp. 21-32. Sean Ó Murthuile's statement to the Army Inquiry 29 Apr. 1924 (UCDA, Mulcahy papers, P7/C/13).

69. For Mulcahy's account of the exchange see Valiulis, *Portrait*, p. 107.

70. O'Higgins to Mrs [Collins?] Powell 19 May 1924 (Mulcahy papers, P7/C/8), cited *Valiulis, Portrait*, pp 233-4.

71. O'Higgins to Diamuid O'Hegarty, Secretary to the Executive Council, 6 June 1925 (Blythe papers, P24/229(3)).

72. Lee, *Ireland*, p. 103;.

73. Talk between Senator Hayes and Mulcahy about certain aspects of the de Vere White book on Kevin O'Higgins and some previous talk with Doctor Mulcahy. 22 Oct. 1964 (Mulcahy papers P7/D/78).

74. Confidential note by Maurice Moynihan, 22 Dec. 1948 after a conversation with Major General M.J. Costello formally of army intelligence. (NA, D/T S'5478).

75. Copy of Secretary of IRAO Executive Council's report on negotiations to September 1924 in History of the Irish Republican Army Organisation as revealed in captured documents (MacEoin papers now in UCDA, uncatalogued).

76. Joe McGrath to Judge Daniel Cohalan, 13 Oct. 1924 (American Irish Historical Society, New York, Cohalan papers). For an example of O'Higgins' appreciation of Egan see Kevin O'Higgins to Frank MacDermot 24 June 1927 (NA, MacDermot papers 1065/1/3).

77. Joe McGrath to Judge Daniel Cohalan, 13 Oct. 1924 (American Irish Historical Society, New York, Cohalan papers).

78. Notes on a conversation with Fionán Lynch following meeting of ministers 24 November 1924 by Mulcahy 25 November 1924 (UCDA, Mulcahy papers, P7b/59(40)). For an account of Walsh's jubilant reaction to his new appointment

over the party organisation see Liam de Róiste Journal 27 Jan. 1925 (Cork Archive Institute, U271a Book 52).

79. Maryann Valiulis, 'After the revolution: the formative years of Cumann na nGaedheal', in A. Eyler and R.F.Garratt (eds.), *The uses of the past: essays in Irish culture* (Delaware, 1988), pp 131-2, 140-2; Mulcahy's diary 27 Nov. 1924 (P7/C/99(65-7).

80. Eoin MacNeill Memoir (In the possession of Brídín Tierney, Dublin), p.240.

81. John Marcus O'Sullivan, *Phases of Revolution* (Dublin, n.d., 1924?), passim.

82. Dáil debates, vol. xiv, col 106 (27 Jan. 1926).

83. L.S.Amery to James Craig, 11 Dec. 1926 (University Library Cambridge, Baldwin Papers, 101, pp 212-5); Cabinet: Proposed creation of a kingdom of Ireland note by the Secretary of State for Dominion Affairs 22 Dec. 1926 (Chartwell Trust Papers, Churchill College, Cambridge, 22/105).

84. O'Higgins to Frank MacDermot, 17 June 1927 (NA, MacDermot papers, 1065/1/2).

85. Address by Mr Kevin O'Higgins, Minister for Justice, Irish Free State, to the Irish society at Oxford University, 31 October 1924 (UCDA, MacNeill papers, LA1/F/305), p.4.

86. Cited in RF Foster, *Modern Ireland* (London, 1988), pp 510-1.

87. Address by Mr Kevin O'Higgins, Minister for Justice, Irish Free State, to the Irish society at Oxford University, 31 October 1924 (U.C.D.A., MacNeill papers, LA1/F/305), p. 3.

88. O'Higgins to Hazel Lady Lavery, 10 June 1927 (Gwynn papers in the possession of Sinead McCoole, Dublin).

89. Kevin O'Higgins, *The Catholic layman in public life* (Dublin, 1925). On liberty see Sullivan, pp 4-5 and O'Higgins, pp 4-5. On education and adult suffrage compare Sullivan, pp 11-2 and O'Higgins, pp 9-11.

90. A M Sergeant Sullivan, *The road to Irish liberty* (Dublin, 1918), p. 3.

91. Ibid., p. 4.

92. James Hogan, 'Kevin O'Higgins: an appreciation', An t-Oglach, (Oct. 1927), p. 14.

93. *The Aeneid of Virgil,* Book II, lines 41-9 translation by C. Day Lewis (Oxford, 1979 edn.) p. 160.

Plate 24.1   Kevin O'Higgins.

Plate 24.2   Dr. T.F. O'Higgins,
brother of Kevin.

Chapter 25

POLITICS IN LAOIS-OFFALY 1922-92

MICHAEL GALLAGHER

> 'Laois-Offaly is one of the largest constituencies, one of the most representative of industry, agriculture and employment generally. In that constituency more than any other there is a cross-section of the people of Ireland'.
>
> Liam Hyland TD, *Dáil Debates* 348: 936-7, 29 February 1984

> 'Laois has been described as the political barometer of the country'.
>
> Editorial in *Leinster Express*, 10 February 1973, p. 10

In this chapter we shall examine a number of aspects of politics in Laois-Offaly since independence. We shall ask whether Laois-Offaly has indeed been a 'barometer' of the country, by comparing voting patterns there with the national pattern. We shall examine changing campaigning styles at elections, as documented by the local press. First, we shall look at the political elite of Laois-Offaly, focusing on those candidates who have stood in the constituency, successfully or otherwise, for election to Dáil Éireann.

The Political Elite

From 1922 to 1992 inclusive Laois-Offaly had 25 general elections and three by-elections (in 1926, 1956 and 1984). In total, these 28 contests attracted 108 different candidates, and 33 of these were elected to Dáil Éireann at one or more of these contests.[1] Of these 33, 15 represented Fianna Fáil, 14 Fine Gael[2] and 4 Labour (see list in appendix 1). We shall examine the backgrounds of both TDs and other candidates, exploring the trends over time.[3]

Ten of the 33 TDs have achieved cabinet or junior ministerial office, and six of these became cabinet ministers. The first was Kevin O'Higgins, the subject of another chapter in this volume and the next two were his brother and nephew. Dr T. F. O'Higgins moved to the constituency in 1932, having been returned to the Dáil at a by-election in Dublin in 1929. He became Minister for Defence in the first Inter-Party government in 1948, and Noel Browne, another member of that government, described him as 'probably the most experienced and shrewd politician in the Cabinet', whose advice was respected by the Taoiseach. However, Browne felt that O'Higgins was part of a 'conspiracy' against him on the Mother and Child affair, keeping his colleagues in the Irish Medical Association informed of Browne's difficulties with the scheme both within cabinet and with the bishops.[4] During his first campaign in the constituency it was said of him that 'his trenchant style of speaking and outspoken views are his most striking characteristics' (*Offaly Chronicle* 11 February 1932), and as the leader of the Blueshirts from August 1932 to July 1933 he was a controversial figure.[5] In 1948 he moved to Cork Borough, making way in Laois-Offaly for his son, Tom O'Higgins, who was made Minister for Social Welfare in the second Inter-Party government in 1954. He moved to a Dublin constituency at the 1969 election, and later became Chief Justice after being defeated at presidential elections in 1966 and 1973. All three members of the O'Higgins family lived outside Laois-Offaly, and the first minister actually resident in the constituency was Paddy Lalor, who became Minister for Posts and Telegraphs in 1969 after a rather difficult time as a junior minister,[6] and was later elected a Member of the European Parliament. In 1976 Oliver J. Flanagan was elevated to the cabinet by Liam Cosgrave as Minister for Defence, to general surprise, and in 1992 Brian Cowen was promoted from the backbenches by Albert Reynolds to become Minister for Labour at the age of 32.[7] In addition to these six, four deputies have held junior ministerial rank: William Davin, Ger Connolly, Ber Cowen and Liam Hyland.

The most successful electorally of Laois-Offaly's 33 TDs has been Oliver J. Flanagan, who was elected 14 times and received many more votes than any other candidate during his career (see appendix 1) – over one in ten of all the votes cast at Laois-Offaly elections from 1922 to 1992. Flanagan scraped into the last seat in 1943, but after that he headed the poll at every election until 1977. At his first three campaigns he ran on the label of Monetary Reform groups, who believed that ending the restriction of the money supply by financial institutions would solve all the country's problems. In 1943 Flanagan promised that 'rivers of money would become available' if the Monetary Reform Association came to power (*Offaly Independent* 19 June), and in 1944 he called for 'the destruction of the bankers, the capitalists and the ranchers', though he hastily added that he was not a communist and named some of the religious organisations to which he belonged (*Leinster Express* 10 June). At this time there was an unpleasant anti-semitic streak in his outlook. He stated that the financial policy of all

Irish governments was 'controlled by Jew-Masonic influence, under which the nation and its people would forever find themselves in debt' (*Midland Tribune* 19 June 1943), and in the Dáil a month later he asked why Emergency Orders were directed against only the IRA and not against Jews: 'Until we rout the Jews out of this country it does not matter a hair's breadth what Orders you make'.[8]

He sprang to national prominence in the late 1940s when he alleged that Fianna Fáil ministers were improperly involved in the sale of Locke's Distillery in Kilbeggan, and although he lost the battle, in that the tribunal established to investigate the allegations delivered some scathing judgements on him,[9] he seemed to win the war. He was somehow able to create the impression that he had been vindicated by the tribunal, and he received the highest vote in the country at the 1948 election. Flanagan sat as an independent for the next four years, and in 1952 followed James Dillon, with whom he shared an office in Leinster House and who had become his political mentor, into Fine Gael. He was made a parliamentary secretary in the second Inter-Party government in 1954, and attained this rank again in 1975 in Liam Cosgrave's coalition government, entering the cabinet a year later. By this time Flanagan was seen not as a dangerous radical but as a dyed-in-the-wool conservative on moral issues, where he strongly espoused the view of the Catholic church. While his views were close to Cosgrave's, he was quite out of tune with the thinking of Garret FitzGerald, who became Fine Gael leader in 1977, and spent the rest of his Dáil career on the backbenches.

Although after his 1948 triumph he had declared that his large vote had vindicated his stand on Locke's and shown that 'jobbery and corruption must end' (*Midland Tribune*, 14 February), the accusation of jobbery was one sometimes laid against him. At the very next election, in 1951, he promised that he would secure jobs for as many of his friends as he could, saying that 'he had placed his friends in good jobs in Clonsast and Portarlington, and as warders in prisons, and everywhere he could get in his foot', and claimed that while Fianna Fáil controlled Offaly County Council, he controlled Laois County Council (*Offaly Chronicle*, 30 May 1951). In the 1960s he returned to this theme, declaring that while he knew Fine Gael was opposed to jobbery, 'personally I am a great believer in putting a friend into a good job and a secure position if it can be done' (*Irish Times*, 8 November 1965). Some years later he got involved in a dispute with the then Senator Garret FitzGerald, who advised him to resign from Fine Gael after he had proclaimed his belief in jobbery. Flanagan rather condescendingly offered FitzGerald a 'neophyte's pardon', explaining that when FitzGerald had been in the Dáil for 25 years, he would have a better idea of how to win votes (*Irish Independent*, 8 and 9 February 1968). The memory of this exchange cannot have boosted Flanagan's already slim chances of being appointed to government when FitzGerald became Taoiseach in the 1980s.

After his second victory, he declared presciently that only old age would remove him from Dáil Éireann (*Leinster Express*, 10 June 1944), and 43 years later he retired through illness. His last appearance in Leinster House was a dramatic occasion, as he came from his sick bed to vote in the adjournment debate in December 1986, four months before his death. The scene was recorded in her diary by Gemma Hussey, the Minister for Social Welfare:

> Then, ten minutes before he [the Taoiseach] was to conclude, all heads turned up to the lobby and there was Oliver J. Flanagan, being helped in by Tom O'Donnell and Brendan Griffin on a walking frame. He looked appalling, poor man ... So everyone felt very uneasy indeed, I suppose because we all knew we were in the presence of death, not to put a tooth in it. Anyway, we all filed solemnly past Oliver and shook his hand ... and we all felt rather shook. Tom Fitzpatrick [the Ceann Comhairle] paid a nice tribute to him at the end, to prolonged applause.[10]

Flanagan was a member of Fianna Fáil in the early 1940s, but soon fell out with the party and displayed real animosity towards it – which was fully reciprocated – from his very first election campaign. He was noted from the start for his phenomenal level of constituency work, and in the early years he used to cycle round the constituency to attend his clinics; indeed, he conducted his first campaign on a bicycle, wearing a 'Here comes Oliver' placard on his front and a 'There goes Flanagan' placard on his back. He bombarded ministers with parliamentary questions, on national as well as local subjects. The secret of his electoral success was identified early by one of his Fianna Fáil opponents, who commented that the main cause of his huge vote in 1948 was not his contribution to the Locke tribunal, nor his monetary reform policy, 'about which I would say 99 per cent of his followers know nothing and care less, but rather ... the simple elementary fact that as a public representative in Dáil Éireann and in the County Council of which he is a member, Mr Flanagan is a hard, unsparing and unflagging worker and advocate of his disciples' interests'.[11] To some extent he remained an independent throughout his career: a profile published in 1987 noted that he was 'never a good party man', and had never really tried to build up the constituency party organisation, with which he was indeed increasingly in dispute.[12]

The second most successful Laois-Offaly candidate was Labour's William Davin, returned at every election from 1922 to 1954 inclusive. Davin combined his political career with the role of Dun Laoghaire pier master from 1921 to 1943, and North Wall station controller from 1943 to 1953, but his seat was never in any real danger, and he maintained close connections with the constituency, especially his native Laois. He became a parliamentary secretary in 1954, at the same time as Oliver J. Flanagan, but died two years later. Although highly regarded within the constituency, he made less of an impact within the Labour Party. In 1935 some comments that he made criticising aspects of the trade unions attracted the ire of the party's national executive, which said that if they had been made off the cuff they could be regarded as 'a characteristic piece of febrile irresponsibility', but that since they had been delivered from a script, they were more serious, and it condemned them.[13]

Patrick Boland is the most successful Fianna Fáil TD from the constituency in the period covered, having been returned at each of the 10 elections from June 1927 to 1951 inclusive. Like another long-serving TD of that period, Patrick Gorry, also a farmer, he made little national impact. Most of the other TDs to have been elected several times have been promoted to a ministerial job. Ger Connolly (returned at each election since his first contest in 1969) served for over 7 years as a junior minister; one profile described him as very popular, colourful, and 'as inoffensive as he is unassuming' (*Leinster Express*, 21 November 1992). Tom Enright of Fine Gael sat in the Dáil for 23 years between 1969 and 1992, being perhaps unfortunate never to be offered a ministry despite a solid record of contribution to parliamentary debates. Some of the other TDs for the constituency have also been notable figures. Dr Patrick McCartan, who was returned in 1918, 1921 and 1922, was to run for the presidency in 1945, while Laurence Brady, elected as a Republican TD in 1923, allegedly fired the first shot in 1916 when he shot a donkey near Abbeyleix.[14]

Measuring the parliamentary activity of TDs is difficult, but we can at least quantify the contribution of TDs to Dáil debates and the number of parliamentary questions asked. Table 1 presents figures for the period from 1963 to 1987, and shows that different TDs have had different priorities. In the 1963-69 period the two Fine Gael TDs were the most active parliamentarians, Tom O'Higgins being a particularly frequent speaker in debates and Oliver J. Flanagan an avid tabler of questions. Flanagan's activity fell away after 1973, while Paddy Lalor became more active. Tom Enright contributed steadily on both fronts, as did Brian Cowen after his election in 1984, while Ger Connolly was not a major participant in debates but was an indefatigable asker of

Table 1

Dáil activity of Laois-Offaly TDs, 1963-1987

	17th Dáil (1963-1965)	18th Dáil (1965-1969)	19th Dáil (1969-1973)	20th Dáil (1973-1977)	21st Dáil (1977-1981)	22nd Dáil (1981-1982)	23rd Dáil (1982)	24th Dáil (1982-1987)
Speeches (column inches in Dáil debates)								
Kieran Egan (Fianna Fáil)	1	—	—	—	—	—	—	—
Nicholas Egan (Fianna Fáil)	11	6	—	—	—	—	—	—
Oliver J. Flanagan (Fine Gael)	680	762	675	252	150	44	69	246
Paddy Lalor (Fianna Fáil)	5	195	545	1009	161	—	—	—
Tom O'Higgins (Fine Gael)	347	1080	—	—	—	—	—	—
Henry Byrne (Lab)	—	49	—	—	—	—	—	—
Ger Connolly (Fianna Fáil)	—	—	21	136	107	26	50	275
Ber Cowen (Fianna Fáil)	—	—	28	—	49	0	0	14
Tom Enright (Fine Gael)	—	—	243	187	621	0	20	180
Charles McDonald (Fine Gael)	—	—	—	231	—	—	—	—
Liam Hyland (Fianna Fáil)	—	—	—	—	—	0	17	460
Brian Cowen (Fianna Fáil)	—	—	—	—	—	—	—	158
Parliamentary questions asked								
Kieran Egan (Fianna Fáil)	11	—	—	—	—	—	—	—
Nicholas Egan (Fianna Fáil)	1	9	—	—	—	—	—	—
Oliver J. Flanagan (Fine Gael)	189	561	765	81	146	6	9	69
Paddy Lalor (Fianna Fáil)	15	0	0	283	10	—	—	—
Tom O'Higgins (Fine Gael)	72	51	—	—	—	—	—	—
Henry Byrne (Lab)	—	13	—	—	—	—	—	—
Ger Connolly (Fianna Fáil)	—	—	188	464	192	13	0	686
Ber Cowen (Fianna Fáil)	—	—	116	—	22	14	0	9
Tom Enright (Fine Gael)	—	—	209	46	176	1	43	300
Charles McDonald (Fine Gael)	—	—	—	2	—	—	—	—
Liam Hyland (Fianna Fáil)	—	—	—	—	—	14	7	246
Brian Cowen (Fianna Fáil)	—	—	—	—	—	—	—	298

Note: figures are based on Volumes 203-370 of *Dáil Debates*. Volumes prior to 203 do not separately index speeches and questions, while bound volumes after the period of the 24th Dáil are not available at the time of writing. In the 24th Dáil, Ber Cowen was a TD from 1982 to 1984, and Brian Cowen from 1984 to 1987. Several TDs were cabinet or junior ministers during this period (Paddy Lalor from 1965-1973 and 1977-79, Oliver J. Flanagan from 1975-1977, Ger Connolly from 1979-1981 and in 1982, Ber Cowen in 1982), and ministers do not ask parliamentary questions.

questions, mainly on local issues. The absence of comparable data from other constituencies means that we cannot say whether Laois-Offaly TDs are more active or less active than the average. Of course, such figures should not be used as a measure of how hard TDs work, since contributions can be made in other ways, particularly by constituency work and activity on Dáil committees.

Just how typical have these active participants in the political fray been of the population whose support they sought?

The most striking difference between the political elite and the population is the great under-representation of women in Laois-Offaly politics (see table 2). Remarkably, no woman even stood at a Dáil election in the constituency until Constance Hannify was selected to run for Fine Gael in 1977, and all but four of the 108 Dáil candidates have been men. Neither Fianna Fáil nor Labour has ever picked a female candidate. Only one of the four female candidates, the Progressive Democrats' Cathy Honan, has even managed to save her deposit, and none has been elected. Laois-Offaly is not quite unique in never having elected a woman to the Dáil, but it is one of a diminishing band of constituencies with this unenviable distinction, and this may be related to the general conservatism of the constituency as demonstrated in 'moral issue' referendums (see below). Whether women in Laois-Offaly have not sought party nominations in significant numbers, or have sought them but failed to be selected as candidates, is not known.

Looking at the occupations of Dáil candidates (see table 3), nearly a third have been farmers. Nearly a quarter can be placed in the 'commercial' category (these are mainly small business people such as shopkeepers, publicans and auctioneers), with about a fifth being professionals (mainly teachers, lawyers and doctors). There is no great difference in the profiles of TDs and other candidates. The number of farmers has declined greatly over the years, reflecting both the national pattern and the shrinking size of the labour force employed in agriculture. Of the 57 candidates who first stood for the Dáil up to 1954, 24 (42 per cent) were farmers, compared with only 10 of the 51 candidates (20 per cent) whose electoral debut came after 1954. The main growth has been not in the number of professionals – as is the case at the national level, at least among TDs – but in the number of candidates who can be classified as non-manual employees.

Table 2

Gender of Dáil candidates and TDs

	All candidates		TDs	
	Number	**%**	**Number**	**%**
Male	104	96.3	33	100.0
Female	4	3.7	0	0
Total	108	100.0	33	100.0

Table 3

Occupations of Dáil candidates and TDs

	All candidates		TDs	
	Number	**%**	**Number**	**%**
Manual employee	6	5.6	1	3.0
Non-manual employee	19	17.6	6	18.2
Commercial	25	23.2	10	30.3
Farmer	34	31.5	9	27.3
Professional	22	20.3	7	21.2
Other	2	1.9	0	0
Total	108	100.0	33	100.0

Table 4

Educational background of Dáil candidates and TDs

	All candidates		TDs	
	Number	**%**	**Number**	**%**
First level only	6	5.6	5	15.2
Second level	22	20.4	11	33.3
Third level	17	15.7	8	24.2
Not known	63	58.3	9	27.3
Total	108	100.0	33	100.0

Data on candidates' educational backgrounds is missing in most cases (see table 4), but what information is available shows that most have had at least second-level education, and that TDs have usually had more education than unsuccessful candidates. As would be expected, the proportion of candidates and TDs with at least second-level education is higher for the post-1954 period than for the 1922-54 period.

Examination of the age profiles of TDs and candidates points to the relatively youthful age at which political careers begin. Those candidates who have become TDs first stood for the Dáil in their mid-thirties, and were only 36 when first elected to the Dáil, about a year younger than for TDs across the country.[15] The youngest was Oliver J. Flanagan, a mere 23-year-old when he became a TD, and seven others became TDs in their twenties, with a further 14 in their thirties. Only three (Eugene O'Brien, Eamonn Donnelly and Nicholas Egan) were over 50 when they first became TDs.[16] At any given election, the average age of the candidates has been 43 years.

In the country as a whole, the most common route to the Dáil is through membership of local government, with family connections to a previous TD another useful credential, and this pattern applies in Laois-Offaly as well. In the early years participation in the 1916 rising or the War of Independence was almost essential for an anti-Treatyite to succeed: the first 6 TDs representing the Republicans or Fianna Fáil (John McGuinness, Laurence Brady, Patrick J. Gorry, Patrick Boland, Thomas Tynan and Eamonn Donnelly) all had such a record, and as late as 1954 a new TD (Nicholas Egan) was a veteran of the independence struggle. Matters were different on the pro-Treaty side. Once the 4 pro-Treaty TDs elected in 1921 had retired (Patrick McCartan), moved elsewhere (Kevin O'Higgins), or been defeated at the polls (Joseph Lynch and Francis Bulfin), nearly all of the most visible representatives of the pro-Treatyites were men with no record in the independence struggle – the only exceptions were Dr T. F. O'Higgins and Senator Patrick Doyle – and in some cases (Patrick J. Egan and William Aird) a past association with the Redmondite Irish Parliamentary Party.

Membership of local government helped from the start, and has become more important over the years. Since 1933, in fact, every new TD bar one (Tom O'Higgins) has been a member of either Laois or Offaly County Council before being first elected to the Dáil. Even in the 1920s, before routine patterns of political recruitment had become established, most TDs did have some local government experience. For example, James Dwyer was vice-chairman of Laois County Council when he won the 1926 by-election, Patrick Boland was vice-chairman of Offaly County Council when he was first elected to the Dáil in June 1927, and William Aird was the chairman of Laois County Council when he became a TD in September 1927.

The other main route into the Dáil is through a familial link with a previous TD, and this route has been followed by 5 of the 33 Laois-Offaly TDs. Dr T. F. O'Higgins was the brother of Kevin O'Higgins, and then passed the Fine Gael seat on to his own son in 1948. Charles McDonald, elected in 1973, was related to Oliver J. Flanagan through marriage. More recently, there were two archetypal cases of the handing on of a seat from father to son, when Brian Cowen succeeded his father Ber at the 1984 by-election and Charles Flanagan succeeded Oliver J. at the 1987 election.

The pool of Dáil candidates displays elements of both continuity and circulation. Among those 75 candidates never to have been TDs, more than two-thirds (52 of them) have stood once and only once, with just 5 venturing before the electorate more than three times (see table 5). Nearly 60 per cent of the candidacies of these individuals have resulted in a lost deposit.[17] These candidates have on average received only 2,372 first preferences each time they stood, whereas the 33 to have been TDs have won an average of 6,396 votes at each contest. These 33 individuals have won almost 80 per cent of the votes cast at Laois-Offaly elections between 1922 and 1992, have stood on average at five contests each, and have been elected on average 3.8 times each – much the same as the national average.[18] The period from 1977 to 1992 illustrates especially clearly this picture of a solid core of established politicians maintaining their position at election after election while being challenged by a ambitious pack of would-be TDs whose composition changes constantly as unsuccessful candidates retire from the fray and are replaced by new but rarely more successful aspirants. During this period, which saw seven general elections, 27 candidates stood for election for the first time, yet only four new TDs were elected, and three of these replaced retiring or deceased TDs: Liam Hyland took over Paddy Lalor's seat in 1981; Brian Cowen and Charles Flanagan replaced their fathers in 1984 and 1987, respectively; and in 1992 Pat Gallagher broke the pattern by ousting Fine Gael's Tom Enright. Change in the political participants has been among the challengers, not among the incumbents. Defeat has not been a major occupational hazard for Laois-Offaly TDs: over the 1922-92 period, the careers of only 12 have ended this way, with a further 10 retiring, 3 dying, and 3 moving to other constituencies.

Voting Patterns

In many ways voting patterns in Laois-Offaly have indeed reflected the national trend, as the quotes at the head of this chapter imply, though not to the extent that one could conclude 'As Laois-Offaly goes, so goes the country'. Since 1922, when no anti-Treatyites stood in the constituency, Fianna Fáil has been the strongest party in Laois-Offaly at all but 6 elections (those of June and September 1927, 1954, 1961, 1965 and 1973); Fine Gael received the most votes on the last 5 of those occasions, while Labour won a plurality of the votes in June 1927.

The absence of representatives of the anti-Treaty forces from the

Table 5

Number of times each candidate has stood for Dáil

	All candidates		Candidates who have been TDs		Candidates who have never been TDs	
	Number	%	Number	%	Number	%
1 only	56	51.9	4	12.1	52	69.3
2 or 3	28	25.9	10	30.4	18	24.0
4 or more	24	22.2	19	57.6	5	6.7
Total	108	100.0	33	100.0	75	100.0

1922 election, as a result of the 'Collins-de Valera pact', meant that their support was underestimated in 1923, and there was some surprise when Republican candidates took two of the five seats at the 1923 election, outpolling Cumann na nGaedheal. Cumann na nGaedheal won the by-election in 1926 brought about by the disqualification of one of those Republican TDs, but the next general election, in June 1927, was something of a disaster for the party. Its vote fell, while that of Fianna Fáil rose, and two of its three TDs lost their seats. There was agreement that the party organisation in the constituency, especially in Offaly, had deteriorated. The *Leinster Express* (18 June 1927) concluded that Cumann na nGaedheal had done badly, 'but it could hardly be otherwise, as they really had no organisation at their backs', while the *Offaly Chronicle* (1 September) noted that 'the party's machinery here was not very strong ... [and] the arrangements in the Offaly end were noticeably incomplete'. In Birr, the home base of one of the party's TDs, Francis Bulfin, the machinery was 'practically inoperative' (8 September). In addition, doubts were expressed by the pro-government *Offaly Independent* about the calibre of Cumann na nGaedheal's standard-bearers: 'Some of the candidates put forward, it must be said, were neither popular nor desirable' (18 June 1927). In contrast, Fianna Fáil's preparation for elections was described as 'always second to none' and 'perfect' (*Offaly Chronicle*, 8 September 1927).

In response, Cumann na nGaedheal made a determined effort to improve its appeal at the election that followed in September. A Captain Brophil was sent down from party headquarters in Dublin to beef up the organisation. The unfortunate Bulfin failed to be reselected as a party candidate, and the other defeated TD, Patrick J. Egan, opted for a backroom position. Two new candidates were brought onto the ticket; one of them was William Aird, a high-profile Portlaoise businessman with Redmondite credentials. In addition, two former independent candidates, Michael Cahill and William Cobbe (a Protestant farmer), now rowed in behind the party. These efforts worked. Reports spoke of the energetic party campaign in the constituency, and its vote practically doubled, taking it well ahead of Fianna Fáil, with Aird heading the poll.

However, this new vitality proved short-lived. Aird was to die in 1931, still in his thirties, and by the time of the early 1930s elections the Cumann na nGaedheal organisation seemed to have reverted to its earlier lethargic state. In 1932 the *Offaly Independent* (27 February) contrasted the active concern of Fianna Fáil agents to ensure that all supporters were on the electoral register with Cumann na nGaedheal's 'inattention' to this detail, and the following year it reported that in some districts the Cumann na nGaedheal organisation had become 'quite supine' and characterised by 'inertia' (11 February 1933). While Fianna Fáil had 'an ample supply of cars', 'transport for Cumann na nGaedheal was somewhat limited' (*Offaly Chronicle* 2 February 1933). All this is in line with what is often seen as the traditionally superior nature of the Fianna Fáil organisation compared with its Fine Gael counterpart, which has been described as 'generally debilitated'.[19]

Besides, the Cumann na nGaedheal policy of bringing into its ranks former Redmondites and Unionists – one pursued at national level, and unkindly described by Fianna Fáil as 'the alliance of a dog with its fleas'[20] – had its costs as well as its benefits. A number of TDs left the party during the 1920s, alleging that it was failing to follow in the footsteps of Michael Collins and Arthur Griffith and was becoming too responsive to the agenda of its new friends. In Laois-Offaly, at least one local notable followed the same route: Joseph Bulfin, an Offaly county councillor, defected from Cumann na nGaedheal to Fianna Fáil, explaining that 'he was always a consistent follower of Griffith's policy, but he found that the present Government had wandered away from it' (*Midland Tribune*, 6 February 1932). While Cumann na nGaedheal's opening to former Unionists and Redmondites paid short-term electoral dividends, it has been argued that in the long term its moderate approach made it seem to have 'an ambivalent, reactive and at times even an apparently negative position on the national issue', and as such damaged the party's long-term prospects.[21]

Looking at support for the two main parties in Laois-Offaly and nationally over the 1923-92 period shows that the parties' fortunes locally have generally mirrored national trends, but local factors have clearly also played a part. In Fianna Fáil's case (fig. 25.1), support patterns in Laois-Offaly and in the country as a whole were very similar in the early years, and though in the 1940s Fianna Fáil locally was adversely affected by Oliver J. Flanagan's vote-winning exploits, by 1961 the two lines were back in reasonable synchronicity. Since 1961, though, they follow quite different trajectories; nationally, Fianna Fáil support oscillated until the early 1980s before beginning a sharp decline, while in Laois-Offaly the graph has been steadily upwards. While in 1973 Fianna Fáil was weaker in Laois-Offaly than in Ireland as a whole, by 1992 Laois-Offaly was the party's second strongest of the 41 Dáil constituencies. Somehow Fianna Fáil in Laois-Offaly has been almost immune from the waning support experienced almost everywhere else, and the strength of its organisation and team of candidates in Laois-Offaly must be a major part of the explanation.

Fine Gael's gains and losses in Laois-Offaly have been in the same direction as at national level, though often in more exaggerated form

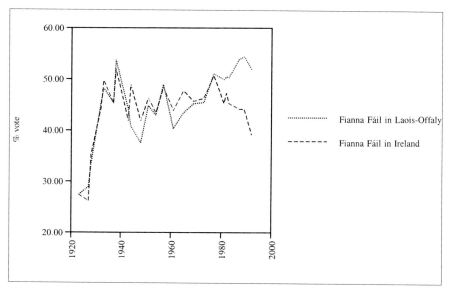

Fig. 25.1   Fianna Fáil strength in Laois-Offaly, and in Ireland, 1923-92.

(fig. 25.2). Fine Gael's fortunes were greatly affected by the Flanagan phenomenon. His arrival on the scene in 1943 clearly drew a lot of support from the party, and its strength in Laois-Offaly lagged well behind its national strength until he joined the party ticket in 1954, transforming Laois-Offaly from one of Fine Gael's weakest areas into its

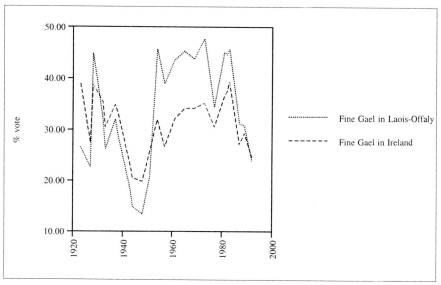

Fig. 25.2   Fine Gael strength in Laois-Offaly, and in Ireland, 1923-92.

fifth strongest constituency. Fine Gael's strength in Laois-Offaly continued to be well above its national level of support, and despite the feeling at both national and local level that Oliver J. was something of a mixed blessing for the party, the precipitate decline in its support in the constituency since his retirement tells its own story. In 1992, Fine Gael's strength in Laois-Offaly fell below its national strength, and it won only one of the five seats, both for the first time since 1951. As for Labour, Laois-Offaly was one of its strongest constituencies up to the 1940s – it averaged over 20 per cent of the votes at each of the first nine general elections – but since then it has struggled. A brief revival in the early 1960s saw Har Byrne elected in 1965, but the story in the 1970s and 1980s was one of a string of lost deposits before Pat Gallagher finally regained a seat for the party in 1992.

Over the period as a whole, all the main parties have fared slightly better on average in Laois-Offaly than in the country generally, with minor parties and independents making relatively little impact. The Laois-Offaly party system, if we can think of it in isolation, has been less fragmented than the Irish party system. In June 1927 the neo-Redmondite National League, which won over 7 per cent of the votes nationally, did not even run a candidate in Laois-Offaly, presumably because the local former supporters of the old Irish Parliamentary Party had by this time been co-opted into Cumann na nGaedheal, while neither the small farmers' Clann na Talmhan, which ran three candidates in the 1943 and 1944 elections, nor Clann na Poblachta, which ran three in 1948, enjoyed any success. Only two individuals have been elected on a label other than Fianna Fáil, Fine Gael or Labour – these were John Finlay of the National Centre Party (which was to merge with Cumann na nGaedheal to form Fine Gael) in 1933, and Oliver J. Flanagan in 1943, 1944, 1948 and 1951 – and both of these subsequently joined and were elected for Fine Gael.

We can examine this more systematically by measuring the degree of correspondence between the parties' support in Laois-Offaly and in Ireland as a whole. Table 6 shows that for both major parties, the two patterns are strongly correlated; put simply, when they do well in Laois-Offaly, they do well across the country, and vice versa. This suggests that these parties' fortunes in Laois-Offaly are determined primarily by national factors, though local ones can certainly make a difference. In Labour's case, the relationship is very weak, indicating the dependence of this smaller party's fortunes, in a single constituency, on the appeal of its leading candidate, which will mean that its local and national fortunes are more likely than those of the major parties to diverge. Turnout patterns in Laois-Offaly and nationally have been practically identical; in both Laois-Offaly and the country as

Table 6

Correlations between parties' support nationally and in Laois-Offaly, at elections 1923-92

	Fianna Fáil support nationally	Fine Gael support nationally	Labour support nationally	Turnout nationally
Fianna Fáil support in Laois-Offaly	0.76**			
Fine Gael support in Laois-Offaly		0.76**		
Labour support in Laois-Offaly			0.14	
Turnout in Laois-Offaly				0.98**

Note: The figures are Pearson's correlation coefficient (r). The higher the figure, the closer the resemblance between the two variables; a value of 1 would indicate complete correspondence. There were 24 elections during this period. ** denotes significant at the .001 level.

a whole, turnout peaked in 1933, at a level of over 80 per cent, and has been dropping steadily since 1977, with turnout in 1992 being at the lowest level since the 1920s.

We can attempt to identify the underlying nature of party competition in Laois-Offaly by looking at the way the various parties' fortunes have waxed and waned in relation to each other. If it is the case that when party A gains, party B loses, we might infer that the two parties are 'fishing in the same pool', i.e. they are in competition for the same bloc of voters. We can assess this by correlating the parties' percentage votes in the constituency over the 24 general elections of the 1923-92 period. The figures, presented in table 7, suggest that Fianna Fáil and Fine Gael are not exactly in head-to-head competition within the constituency. Correlation of the two parties' support records produces a coefficient of +0.19; that is to say, when Fianna Fáil does better, there is a slight tendency for Fine Gael to do better also. Fianna Fáil's main rival seems to be Labour, for when Labour does well, Fianna Fáil generally does badly, and vice versa. Fine Gael's strength is inversely related to support for groups outside the three main parties, and indeed it is true that many such groups and parties – the Farmers' and National Centre parties in the 1920s and 1930s, and the Progressive Democrats in the 1980s and 1990s, not to mention Oliver J. Flanagan in his four elections as an independent – were appealing mainly to social groups that could have been expected otherwise to back Fine Gael. The table also shows that when turnout is higher, Fianna Fáil, and to a lesser extent Fine Gael, tend to fare better. The main difference between the pattern in Laois-Offaly and the national pattern is that at national level Fianna Fáil and Labour support are only weakly related,

Table 7

Correlations between parties' strength in Laois-Offaly, at elections 1923-92

	Fianna Fáil support	Fine Gael support	Labour support	All others' support
Turnout	0.52*	0.31	–0.34	–0.39
Fianna Fáil support	—	0.19	–0.65**	–0.37
Fine Gael support		—	–0.30	–0.85**
Labour support			—	0.03

Note: The figures are Pearson's correlation coefficient (r). The higher the figure, the closer the resemblance between the two variables; a value of 1 would indicate complete correspondence. There were 24 elections during this period. ** denotes significant at the .001 level; * significant at the .01 level.

while Fianna Fáil support is strongly and negatively related to support for groups outside the three main parties. In this respect Laois-Offaly is not exactly a barometer of the country, with the direct link between the fortunes of Labour and Fianna Fáil one distinctive feature of the constituency's politics since 1922.

Table 8 shows that, as would be expected, Fianna Fáil has been the strongest party in Laois-Offaly over the 1922-92 period taken as a whole. Although it has supplied only 35.8 per cent of the candidates, it has received 44.7 per cent of the votes and won 48.0 per cent of the seats. Both Fianna Fáil and Fine Gael have won slightly more of the seats than their share of the votes would justify, but this 'bonus' is not large, and all parties have been reasonably fairly represented in relation to their votes.

Table 8

Party fortunes at elections 1922-92

	% of candidatures	Average number of first preferences received per candidature	% of votes received	% of seats won
Fianna Fáil	35.8	5,889	44.7	48.0
Fine Gael	30.8	5,091	33.2	35.4
Labour	15.4	4,159	13.6	12.6
Progressive Democrats	1.1	4,441	1.0	0
Farmers' parties	2.9	2,849	1.7	0.8
Republican parties	2.9	1,189	0.8	0
Others	11.1	2,141	5.0	3.1
Total	100.0	—	100.0	100.0
Number of cases	279	279	1,317,627	127

Just as it helps a candidate to be a nominee of one of the major parties, especially Fianna Fáil, so, as table 9 shows, does it help to have some elective status before running for the Dáil.[22] Of the 95 candidates who stood when lacking any electoral base, only 10 were elected, and more than half lost their deposits. County councillors and Senators do significantly better than this, and TDs and ministers fare better still. All ministers have been re-elected, while among TDs the great majority have been re-elected and only one (Eugene O'Brien in 1933) has lost his deposit. The number of votes needed to secure election in Ireland is small by international standards, and in fact in Laois-Offaly at general elections a mere 6,000 first preferences have always sufficed. The 5,973 first preferences received by Charles McDonald in November 1982 represent the highest ever polled by an unsuccessful candidate (ironically, this was almost twice as many as McDonald received in 1973, the only time he was elected), and the only other candidates to poll more than 5,500 votes and still be defeated are Liam Hyland (in 1977) and Tom Enright (in 1992), both of whom had long periods in the Dáil to console them. At the other end of the scale, 13 candidates have been elected with fewer than 4,000 first preferences, and two of these received fewer than 3,000, the lowest being the 2,636 votes, only a third of the quota, with which William Davin was re-elected in 1948. In recent times, Laois-Offaly has not been dominated electorally by any one candidate; in 1992, Brian Cowen became the first candidate since 1973 to exceed the quota on the first count at a general election in the constituency.

Throughout the period covered, Offaly has had a slightly larger electorate than Laois – in 1926, Offaly's population was 52,592 compared with 51,540 in Laois, and by the time of the 1991 census the gap had widened to more than 6,000 (58,448 in Offaly, 52,325 in Laois). Given that voters tend to support local candidates, we might expect the normal pattern to be that Offaly-based candidates have

Table 9

Votes won, by elective status of candidate

Elective status	Average number of first preferences received	Number of cases	Number elected	Number losing deposit
Minister	8,211	9	9	0
Outgoing TD	6,467	102	87	1
Senator	4,346	11	3	2
County councillor only	4,296	62	18	15
No elective status	2,842	95	10	52
All candidates	4,723	279	127	70

taken most of the votes and that at most elections three of the constituency's five TDs are Offaly-based and two are Laois-based. Deciding where a candidate is based is straightforward in most cases, but a sizeable minority of candidates have been based outside the constituency. Many of these have strong links with one part of the constituency: for example, William Davin, though resident in Dublin throughout his 34 years as a TD, came from Rathdowney and was an active member of the Laoismen's Society in Dublin, while all three members of the O'Higgins dynasty were also resident in Dublin or Meath while TDs yet had strong roots in Stradbally in County Laois. Indeed, only two TDs have had no real roots in the constituency: Patrick McCartan (elected in 1922) and Eamonn Donnelly (1933), both born in Ulster and resident in Dublin. Of the 33 individuals to have been TDs, 16 were born in Laois, 10 in Offaly and 7 elsewhere (3 in the neighbouring counties of Kildare and Westmeath, and one each in Cork, Dublin, Armagh and Tyrone).

Of the 127 Dáil seats filled in Laois-Offaly over the 1922-92 period (124 at general elections and three in by-elections), 48 have gone to Laois-based candidates, 51 to Offaly-based candidates, and 28 to candidates based outside the county. If we classify the last group according to their original or family base within the constituency, the balance swings sharply in favour of Laois: it has 'won' 74 of the seats, compared with only 51 for Offaly and two won by outsiders. Although roughly the same number of candidates have had their base in each of the two counties, Laois-based candidates have fared over 700 votes better on average, which accounts for their greater electoral success (see table 10). At eight elections (the first in September 1927, the most recent in 1965), resident or expatriate Laoismen have taken four of the five seats at stake. This is partly due to the success of William Davin, who as the leading (and often the only) Labour candidate weighs the record in favour of Laois. If we consider only the two main parties, which at virtually every election have both had at least one candidate from each county, the advantage of Laois is less, though the county has still been the base of 52 per cent of TDs of the two major parties compared with only 46 per cent for Offaly. From 1969, all the TDs have been resident in the constituency, and since then Offaly has had the upper hand, being the base of three of the five candidates at each of the next nine elections except for 1973, when Charles McDonald's narrow defeat of Ber Cowen was a victory not only for Fine Gael over Fianna Fáil but also for Laois over Offaly. Perhaps surprisingly, the main population centres in the two counties have supplied little of the constituency's Dáil representation. Only three TDs have been based in Portlaoise, by some way the largest town in County Laois (two of these,

Table 10

County fortunes at elections 1922-92

	% of candidatures	Average number of first preferences received per candidature	% of votes received	% of seats won
Laois	50.5	5,077	54.3	58.3
Offaly	47.0	4,348	43.2	40.2
Outside the constituency	2.5	4,605	2.4	1.6
Total	100.0	—	100.0	100.0
Number of cases	279	279	1,317,627	127

Laurence Brady and William Aird, were one term TDs in the 1920s, and the third is Charles Flanagan, first elected in 1987). Likewise, only four TDs have been based in Tullamore, the main town in County Offaly: two of these were one term TDs in the 1920s, and there were no more until 1992, by which time Fianna Fáil's Brian Cowen had moved to the town and was joined in Dáil Éireann by Labour's Pat Gallagher.

The assumption that voters back local candidates (the so-called 'friends and neighbours effect') is borne out by evidence from elsewhere in Ireland and indeed from other countries.[23] Do candidates in Laois-Offaly fare best near their own home patch, and do Laois voters vote for Laois-based candidates and Offaly voters for Offaly-based candidates? To answer this question reliably requires information not made publicly available, since election results are published only at constituency level, not at the level of individual polling stations. However, as is well known, the political parties are able to keep 'tallies' of the vote at each polling station by studying the ballot papers as they are checked during the counting process, and these have been made available to the author. The only election where any regional breakdown was published in the local papers was the 1926 by-election, at which Sinn Féin was significantly stronger in Offaly than in Laois (41 per cent compared with 34 per cent), Cumann na nGaedheal was a little stronger there (42 per cent compared with 39 per cent), while Labour was much stronger in Laois (27 per cent compared with 17 per cent in Offaly). This surprised contemporary analysts, who had expected Sinn Féin to head the poll in Offaly and Cumann na nGaedheal to be stronger in Laois, and was attributed to the fact that the Cumann na nGaedheal candidate, James Dwyer, though now living in Laois, had stronger roots in south-west Offaly. By 1992, though, this was reversed: both Fianna Fáil and Fine Gael were slightly stronger in Laois, while Labour was stronger in Offaly.

We can see the friends and neighbours effect illustrated clearly in table 11, which shows how the 14 candidates at the 1992 election fared. In virtually every case, candidates fared better in their own county than in the constituency as a whole, better still in their own local electoral area (there are 5 of these in Laois and 4 in Offaly), and best of all in the ballot boxes from their own home base. Some, such as Brian Cowen and Liam Hyland, virtually swept the board in their home base. Even the independent Edward Delaney, who won a negligible number of votes in all, received one in every six first preferences at his local polling station. The same phenomenon was apparent at the 1994 European Parliament elections, when Fianna Fáil's Liam Hyland, the only candidate from either Laois or Offaly, won a remarkable 62.3 per cent of all the votes cast in Laois.

Table 12 shows the votes won by the candidates in the two counties, and confirms the pattern of candidates faring better in their home county than in the other county. This is especially pronounced for Fianna Fáil, whose four candidates won very few votes outside their own county. Even the constituency-wide poll-topper Brian Cowen received fewer votes in Laois than the combined independents. Both main Fine Gael candidates, in contrast, polled significantly in both counties. The explanation is less likely to be any different orientation of voters of those two parties than the greater efficiency of the Fianna Fáil organisation and its successful management of the vote. There is evidently very little rivalry among the Fianna Fáil candidates across the county boundary – though of course there is plenty within each county – whereas within the Fine Gael camp both the outgoing TDs, Tom Enright and Charles Flanagan, were to some extent roaming the entire constituency in search of support, with seemingly no areas being 'off limits' to anyone and competition being unconstrained. This cross-county voting is not a new development, as Oliver J. Flanagan was widely believed to win a substantial number of votes in Offaly despite his Laois base. In the case of Labour and the Progressive Democrats, the pattern is less stark because they ran only one candidate, so Labour supporters in Laois had to vote for an Offaly-based candidate. Even so, as the table shows, over three-quarters of all Laois votes went to Laois candidates, and an even higher percentage of Offaly votes went to Offaly candidates.

The importance of candidates' geographical base is also evident when votes are transferred. Although most voters rank candidates first and foremost along party lines, locality is a more important factor for some voters, and it is a major secondary consideration for many party-oriented voters. While we will not attempt to quantify this systematically, a few examples illustrate the point. At the 1992 election,

Table 11

The friends and neighbours effect at the 1992 general election in Laois-Offaly

Candidate	Candidate's home base	Whole constituency	Candidate's own county	Candidate's own local electoral area	Candidate's home base
			Candidate's % of votes in:		
Fianna Fáil					
Ger Connolly	Bracknagh	8.0	12.4	30.1	46.4
Brian Cowen	Clara	18.9	34.8	41.3	69.8
Liam Hyland	Ballacolla	15.6	32.2	47.6	67.3
John Moloney	Mountmellick	9.3	17.1	47.8	52.1
Fine Gael					
Molly Buckley	Tullamore	2.2	3.2	5.6	6.8
Tom Enright	Birr	10.7	14.1	29.5	39.2
Charles Flanagan	Mountmellick	10.9	16.8	19.8	21.9
Labour					
Pat Gallagher	Tullamore	13.0	15.8	28.5	43.0
Progressive Democrat					
Cathy Honan	Portarlington	6.6	7.9	17.7	32.6
Sinn Féin					
John Carroll	Birr	1.2	1.9	3.6	3.5
Others					
John Butterfield	Tullamore	2.8	3.3	4.0	2.9
Edward Delaney	Ballyskenagh	0.2	0.4	1.3	16.8
Joe McCormack	Portlaoise	0.5	0.9	2.9	3.2

Source: Local party organisation tally figures.

Note: The home bases of Brian Cowen and Charles Flanagan are taken as their original bases, as shown in the table, even though they have subsequently moved to Tullamore and Portlaoise, respectively.

when on the second count the surplus of Brian Cowen was distributed, 76 per cent of the votes went to the other three Fianna Fáil candidates, showing the importance of party as a factor in voters' ranking of the candidates. The importance of geography is shown by the fact that 72 per cent of them went to other Offaly-based candidates and only 28 per cent to Laois-based candidates. On the 10th count in the same contest, the Laois-based Fianna Fáil candidate John Moloney was eliminated, and his transfers too illustrated the way both factors are important, with party clearly being the stronger force: 57 per cent of his votes went to the Offaly-based Fianna Fáil candidate, 17 per cent to the Laois-based Fine Gael candidate, and only 3 per cent to the Offaly-based Fine Gael candidate.

Table 12

Variations in county voting at the 1992 general election in Laois-Offaly

Candidate	Candidate's county	Votes in Laois	Votes in Offaly	% vote in Laois	% vote in Offaly
Fianna Fáil					
Ger Connolly	Offaly	825	3,448	3.3	12.4
Brian Cowen	Offaly	482	9,662	1.9	34.8
Liam Hyland	Laois	8,143	250	32.2	0.9
John Moloney	Laois	4,311	587	17.1	2.1
Fine Gael					
Molly Buckley	Offaly	231	887	0.9	3.2
Tom Enright	Offaly	1,810	3,926	7.2	14.1
Charles Flanagan	Laois	4,224	1,566	16.8	5.6
Labour					
Pat Gallagher	Offaly	2,510	4,391	10.0	15.8
Progressive Democrat					
Cathy Honan	Laois	1,982	1,537	7.9	5.5
Sinn Féin					
John Carroll	Offaly	190	515	0.8	1.9
Others					
John Butterfield	Offaly	248	912	1.0	3.3
Edward Delaney	Offaly	24	104	0.1	0.4
Joe McCormack	Laois	221	10	0.9	0.0
All Laois-based candidates		18,881	3,950	74.9	14.2
All Offaly-based candidates		6,320	23,845	25.1	85.8
Total		25,201	27,795	100.0	100.0

Source: Local party organisation tally figures.
Note: The actual valid vote was 53,670, nearly 700 more than the total in the table. The difference can be attributed to postal votes and to very minor inaccuracies in the tally.

The suggestion that Laois-Offaly is a barometer for the country as a whole has been reasonably true for contests other than general elections, though with significant exceptions. At most referendums – for example, on adopting the new constitution in 1937, on whether to abolish the PR electoral system in 1968, on European integration in 1972, 1987 and 1992 – the vote in Laois-Offaly has closely mirrored the national vote. Similarly, in most presidential elections, the votes in the constituency have been close to the votes for the country as a whole. Even when presidential candidates have had a close link with the constituency, they have fared little better here than elsewhere: in 1966 and 1973 support for Tom O'Higgins was less than 2 per cent stronger in Laois-Offaly than nationally, and in 1945 the former Laois-Offaly TD Patrick McCartan won only 3 per cent more of the votes in the constituency than nationally. However, on 'moral issue' referendums Laois-Offaly is anything but a barometer of the national mood. It has consistently been one of the most conservative constituencies: in the pro-life referendum of 1983, and the divorce referendums of 1986 and 1995, the more conservative position was supported by about 10 per cent more of the voters than in the country as a whole. For example, in November 1995 the vote against divorce amounted to 59.9 per cent in Laois-Offaly compared with 49.7 per cent across the country, making Laois-Offaly the 10th most conservative among the 41 Dáil constituencies. On 'moral issue' referendums, voters in Laois-Offaly behave much like voters in Connacht-Ulster, and are significantly less likely to support the liberal position than voters in other Leinster constituencies.

Campaigning styles and the local media

Until the advent of local radio in the mid-1980s, the only local media through which campaigns could be fought or reported were provincial newspapers. Four papers have been based in the Laois-Offaly constituency for all or most of our period: the *Leinster Express* (Portlaoise), the *Midland Tribune* (Birr), the *Offaly Chronicle* (Birr), and the *Offaly Independent* (Tullamore). (Some other papers, such as the *Leinster Leader* (Naas) and the *Nationalist and Leinster Times* (Carlow), also carry some coverage of Laois-Offaly politics, but both would have their main circulation outside the constituency.)

The partisan complexion of these papers varied. The *Leinster Express* and the *Offaly Chronicle* took a neutral line in the crucial early years. Neither paper carried an editorial in the 1920s, although both gave particularly generous coverage to Cumann na nGaedheal. The *Offaly Chronicle* introduced editorials for the 1932 general election (though the only advice it gave to its readers was to be sure to vote), but dropped them the following year. The *Leinster Express* did not introduce editorials until 1948, and it too then adopted the anodyne, or prudent, line of simply calling on its readers to vote, in 1961 pleading 'in the name of God and Ireland, come out and vote' (30 September 1961). In 1957 its editorial line could be construed as sympathetic to Fianna Fáil, and in 1969 it criticised both Fianna Fáil and Fine Gael for adopting 'red smear' tactics against Labour, but the first time it explicitly gave advice to its readers was in 1977, when it expressed the hope that the outgoing Fine Gael-Labour government would be replaced by Fianna Fáil, as it indeed it was. By this time, though, the editorial page also carried Mick Mulholland's 'Political Notebook', which was unashamedly pro-Fine Gael.

The other two papers nailed their colours to the mast from the start. The *Offaly Independent* took a strongly pro-Treaty line throughout the 1920s. 'It is essential that at the polls on next Monday the electors vote for the Candidates which have been chosen by Cumann na nGaedheal ... it is above Party; it is above class interest. It stands for the country as a whole', it declared in 1923 (25 August). In 1927 it again sang the praises of the government party, said of Fianna Fáil that 'when it is not dangerous Mr de Valera's party is futile' (4 June), and dismissed the Farmers' Party as 'this group of political futilists' and 'a ranchers' group of reactionaries' (21 May). In the tense political atmosphere of the early 1930s, its rhetoric reached fever pitch. In 1932 it proclaimed that 'Unless they [the people] have lost all sense of proportion, and care very little for their own interests and the interests of their country they will vote for the standard bearers of Cumann na nGaedheal' (13 February), and in 1933 it went even further, thundering: 'Electors, in the name of all that you hold sacred, vote on Tuesday next for the parties of Hope and Happiness, the Cumann na nGaedheal and the Centre (Farmers') Party. May God defend the right' (21 January). By the late 1930s, though, while still supportive of Fine Gael, the editor acknowledged that there was 'little difference' in the programmes of the two main parties (4 June 1938), and by 1948 the paper was prepared to praise Fianna Fáil's record in government as well as that of Cumann na nGaedheal, and took refuge in the 'think carefully before you vote and put the country's interests first' approach.

In contrast, the heart of the *Midland Tribune*, although it expressed support for the Treaty in 1923, was never really with Cumann na nGaedheal, and its advice varied from election to election. During the June 1927 election campaign it advised readers not to back 'reactionary Imperialists, disguised however they might be' (14 May), declared 'absolutely no sympathy' for the Redmondite National League, criticised Fianna Fáil's continued abstention from the Dáil (4 June), and lamented the calibre of candidates across the board: 'most people will agree that many candidates were entirely unsuitable for the responsibilities that they wished to assume. The election speeches were disappointing, and some of them absolutely vulgar' (11 June). At the September 1927 election it expressed the hope that the 'Irish-Ireland elements' of the two main parties would get together, since these had more in common with each other than the better sections of Cumann na nGaedheal had with 'recent recruits to that party' (10 September). In 1932 it criticised both main parties. Unusually for a provincial paper it reserved its warmest words for Labour, advising workers to back it in 1927 (4 June), and in 1932 it suggested that all its readers back Labour. Like the *Offaly Independent*, it saw the 1933 election in very black and white terms, urging voters to return 3 Fianna Fáil TDs and William Davin of Labour, regretting only that 'the combined ex-Unionist, ranching and Imperialist interests' would be strong enough to hold the fifth seat. 'It is now the old question of Ireland versus England. Let Ireland win', it declared (14 January). By 1938, though, it too saw 'very little difference' between the two main parties, and expressed reservations about Fianna Fáil because of a fear that the party might try to abolish the proportional representation electoral system (4 and 11 June).

The local newspapers also convey a good deal of the changing flavour of constituency campaigning. In the early decades the typical report consisted of an account of speeches made by candidates at election meetings, sometimes including details of the heckling that speakers received. The visit of one of the party leaders was a major occasion; for example, when Eamon de Valera visited Tullamore in 1933, he was met outside the town by a torchlight procession and two bands (*Offaly Independent*, 28 January). When he came to Mountmellick in 1954, 'heavy rain fell before and during the meeting, but the large crowd, which included people from all over Laois and Offaly, remained until the meeting ended, at 11.0 pm' (*Leinster Express*, 15 May). A change was noted in the 1956 by-election, when the constituency was swamped by TDs of all parties and ministers. 'Never before in this constituency was there such an emphasis placed on personal canvassing', said the *Leinster Express* (28 April), adding, 'It would appear that the political parties are now more interested in this type of electioneering than in holding public meetings'. In fact, though, door-to-door canvassing had also been employed extensively in the 1926 by-election (*Leinster Express* 30 January), and at the second election of 1927 it was said that Cumann na nGaedheal was cutting back on public meetings in favour of canvassing (*Offaly Chronicle*, 8 and 15 September). By 1961 the *Leinster Express* was looking back nostalgically (8 July) to the days when 'a popular candidate was invariably brought shoulder-high to the platform between lines of lighted torches on the end of long poles; and, as often as not, the nearby hills were lit up with bonfires'. Elections were not without their entertainment aspect. In 1927, the Rathdowney Pipers' Band 'discoursed some appropriate music' at a Labour meeting (*Leinster Express* 7 May), and indeed pipe bands played at many meetings. In 1932 a Labour supporter, dressed as 'Mr Gandhi' went through the streets of Abbeyleix delivering 'a running commentary of a very humorous character on things in general and the election in particular' (*Leinster Express*, 20 February), and in 1933 the government party earned some publicity by sending a donkey through the streets with a poster saying 'Everyone will vote Fianna Fáil but me' (*Offaly*

Independent, 28 January).

The 1950s, 1960s, and 1970s were the heyday of the supplied script, when candidates simply sent in speeches, invariably described as having been delivered to 'a large and enthusiastic audience', although whether the speeches had in fact been written, delivered or even seen by the candidates in question was sometimes debateable. By 1981 the *Leinster Express* commented that even though the two main party leaders, Charles Haughey and Garret FitzGerald, had addressed meetings in the constituency, these had lacked atmosphere. The campaign locally now consisted of 'the respective parties booking advertising space in the newspapers outlining their policies and following this up with an intensive door to door canvass' (6 June). There was a brief revival of outdoor meetings in 1982. In the February campaign Charles Haughey addressed a large meeting in Portlaoise, which 'old stagers' compared with the days of de Valera, and in the November 1982 campaign both parties held final rallies in Portlaoise, which produced some of the fieriest rhetoric ever heard in the constituency. For Fianna Fáil, Albert Reynolds described Garret FitzGerald as 'a cornered rat, a spitting, screaming, scratching cornered rat that would meet its end in the jaws of the cat let out of the bag by … James Prior'. For Fine Gael, Professor John Kelly, addressing a 'cold and small attendance', said that 'many of those in Fianna Fáil were decent but that there was something about them in totality which aims for what is low, ignorant and backward' (*Leinster Express*, 27 November).

By now candidates were complaining of the lack of response to the door-to-door canvass. Ger Connolly said that people did not want canvassers coming round in the evenings, and that there was certainly no point in canvassing at times when popular soap operas were on television (*Leinster Express*, 27 November 1982 and 10 June 1989). A report of the only after-mass meeting held in Edenderry in 1989 suggested that the unfortunate Connolly was in danger of being knocked down by mass-goers who drove away rather than stay and listen to him (*Leinster Express*, 17 June 1989). The after-mass meeting has in fact been in decline for many years, the *Offaly Independent* noting as early as 1954 (15 May) that only a proportion of the congregations bothered to wait to hear the speakers, and that 'the day of the outdoor meeting is gone at least as far as this part of Ireland is concerned'.

An emphasis on door-to-door canvassing creates the need, under the PR-STV electoral system in which candidates of a party are in competition with each other, to decide which candidate gets to canvass where. All candidates like to stake out a personal 'bailiwick' where their rivals (i.e. their running mates) are not welcome, and campaigns can therefore feature allegations of vote-poaching in someone else's territory. In February 1982 Charles McDonald, a defeated Fine Gael candidate, described the party's campaign in the constituency as 'a series of independents running for election without an overall drive' and as 'too personalised', and in November 1982, after another unsuccessful tilt at a seat, he wondered why one of the party's TDs, Tom Enright, had been canvassing so close to his own doorstep, suggesting that Enright 'could have been devoting his time more beneficially in parts of Offaly' (*Leinster Express*, 27 February and 4 December). Such comments bear out the picture that we discussed earlier (see table 12) of more open competition within the Fine Gael than within Fianna Fáil. In Fianna Fáil, competition tends to take place only within each county. After the 1992 election, in which Ger Connolly's vote plunged by nearly 4,000 while that of the other Offaly Fianna Fáil TD Brian Cowen rose by 3,000, Connolly commented that 'the vote management in Offaly didn't work out as well as in former elections' (*Leinster Express*, 5 December). Needless, to say, most such intra-party turf wars never reach the columns of the newspapers.

A constant theme in newspaper reports is the dullness of contemporary campaigns compared with a supposed golden age of excitement, coupled with a desire on the part of politicians to emphasise the harmonious nature of their relationships. At the very first contested Dáil election, in 1922, the *Leinster Express* reported that 'the excitement generally associated with election contests was almost entirely absent', apart from an incident in Donaghmore where armed men forced the presiding officer at the polling booth, a former RUC member, to hand over his responsibilities to his polling clerk (24 June, 17 June). In 1923, when the anti-Treatyites entered the fray, a meeting in Cloghan developed into 'a sort of general melee', but this was exceptional. Generally, election meetings 'were remarkable for the good order, and, above all, the good humour, that prevailed', and indeed, 'very little in the nature of excitement marked the election campaign'. 'The enthusiastic spirit that was evident in the old-time election contests' was missing (*Offaly Independent*, 18 August and 1 September). The anti-Treatyites' spokesman at the after-count speeches said 'how glad he was of the good sentiments and good fellowship that prevailed during the campaign' (*Leinster Express*, 1 September 1923).

The most acrimonious contest in the constituency seems to have been the 1926 by-election, when Cumann na nGaedheal meetings in particular attracted hecklers. At one rally in Abbeyleix there were 'several ugly incidents', and a party organiser challenged a heckler to 'a fistic encounter', but this did not prevent the winning Cumann na nGaedheal candidate referring to the 'good spirit' in which the election had been fought (*Leinster Express*, 20 February and 27 February). The two elections of the early 1930s were tense and sometimes violent affairs across most of the country, but the even temper of politics in Laois-Offaly seemed largely unruffled. In 1932, the Edenderry correspondent of the *Leinster Express* commented (20 February) that 'The numerous agents of all the parties intertwined in the most friendly relations and carried out their duties without the slightest disagreement', and one of the Cumann na nGaedheal candidates, Eugene O'Brien, lent Labour two of his party's cars. Labour's William Davin said that 'no election campaign in which he had been engaged had been fought out in a better spirit' (*Offaly Independent*, 27 February). Even the 1933 campaign produced few sparks, although the *Irish Times* (7 January) reported on a Cumann na nGaedheal meeting in Portarlington when T. F. O'Higgins was heckled and about 40 Blueshirts moved towards the men making the noise. O'Higgins asked the Blueshirts to stand where they were, and warned the hecklers that the Blueshirts 'are the best, and, if it comes to a fight, the toughest element in the country', though no actual fighting seems to have taken place.[24] The 1937 campaign in Tullamore was described as 'the tamest campaign in living memory' (*Midland Tribune*, 3 July), in 1943 the prevailing impression was still of the 'orderliness and good feeling which characterised the election campaign' (*Leinster Express*, 3 July), and in 1948 the *Leinster Express* referred to 'a singularly dull general election' (7 February).

Conclusion

Politics in Laois-Offaly from 1922 to 1992 have in many ways reflected national trends, yet they have also displayed their own distinctive characteristics. There is enough validity in the 'barometer of the nation' metaphor to justify a study of the constituency as a means of gaining insight into the political history of the independent Irish state, yet there is also enough that is specific about Laois-Offaly to justify focusing on the constituency in its own right. As we have seen, the style of election campaigning has changed over the decades, and the composition of the elite has also altered. Yet, in many ways, the main impression is one of continuity, with the structure of competition, and the political alternatives on offer, remaining remarkably stable over this 70-year period. This theme of incremental change within overall stability is one that could also be applied to politics in the Republic of Ireland as a whole from 1922 to 1992.

Appendix 1

TDs for Laois-Offaly elected 1922-1992

TD	First elected	Last elected	Times a candidate	Times elected	Total votes in career
Patrick McCartan (Pro-Treaty SF)	1918	1922	1	1	22,796
Kevin O'Higgins (Pro-Treaty SF)	1918	1922	1	1	6,792
Francis Bulfin (CG)	1921	1923	3	2	14,973
William Davin (Lab)	1922	1954	13	13	88,392
Patrick Egan (CG)	1923	1923	2	1	7,118
John McGuinness (Republicans)	1923	1923	1	1	5,572
Laurence Brady (Republicans)	1923	1923	4	1	15,964
James Dwyer (CG)	1926	Sep 1927	4	3	29,786
John F Gill (Lab)	Jun 1927	Jun 1927	4	1	18,119
Patrick Boland (FF)	Jun 1927	1951	10	10	70,943
Thomas Tynan (FF)	Jun 1927	Jun 1927	2	1	7,080
William Aird (CG)	Sep 1927	Sep 1927	1	1	8,472
Patrick Gorry (FF)	Sep 1927	1948	11	7	48,802
Eugene O'Brien (CG)	1932	1932	2	1	6,453
T F O'Higgins (CG, FG)	1932	1944	6	6	39,721
Eamonn Donnelly (FF)	1933	1933	2	1	12,413
John Finlay (NCP, FG)	1933	1937	3	2	15,833
Daniel Hogan (FF)	1938	1938	6	1	24,850
Oliver J Flanagan (Ind, FG)	1943	Nov 1982	14	14	136,294
Tom O'Higgins (FG)	1948	1965	6	6	33,690
Peadar Maher (FF)	1951	1957	3	3	20,055
Nicholas Egan (FF)	1954	1965	5	4	26,818
Kieran Egan (FF)	1956	1961	4	3	42,106
Paddy Lalor (FF)	1961	1977	5	5	35,501
Henry Byrne (Lab)	1965	1965	3	1	9,586
Tom Enright (FG)	1969	1989	9	8	51,337
Ber Cowen (FF)	1969	Nov 1982	6	5	36,139
Ger Connolly (FF)	1969	1992	9	9	60,080
Charles McDonald (FG)	1973	1973	7	1	28,841
Liam Hyland (FF)	1981	1992	7	6	57,234
Brian Cowen (FF)	1984	1992	4	4	52,410
Charles Flanagan (FG)	1987	1992	3	3	18,335
Pat Gallagher (Lab)	1992	1992	2	1	9,996

Note: The table refers only to these TDs' records in the Laois-Offaly constituency over the period 1922-1992.

References

1. A further 4 of these 108 candidates were elected to the Dáil at another contest. Joseph Lynch, who stood unsuccessfully in 1922, had been elected for Laois-Offaly in 1921; Patrick Belton, who stood in 1923, was later elected to the Dáil from Dublin County; Denis Cullen, who also stood in 1923, was later elected from Dublin North; and Art O'Connor, who stood in the 1926 by-election, had been elected for Kildare constituencies in 1918 and 1921.

2.   Two of these were also elected under other labels: John Finlay in 1933 for the National Centre Party, and Oliver J. Flanagan on four occasions as an independent.

3.   The main sources for information on the backgrounds of TDs and other candidates are Patrick F. Meehan, *The TDs and Senators for Laois and Offaly 1921-1986* (Portlaoise, 1987), and local newspapers, together with national biographical works such as successive editions of W. J. Flynn's *Oireachtas companion* (various editions, 1928 to 1945) and Vincent Browne (ed.), *The Magill book of Irish politics* (Dublin, 1981).

4.   Noel Browne, *Against the Tide* (Dublin, 1986), p. 150.

5.   Maurice Manning, *The Blueshirts* (Dublin, 1987), pp 28, 73.

6.   Teddy Fennelly, 'Paddy Lalor', pp 87-91 in Teddy Fennelly (ed.), *Laois lives* (Portlaoise, 1991), p. 88.

7.   The constituency came close to acquiring another minister in 1938, when the Minister for Education, Thomas Derrig, a Kilkenny TD, surprisingly sought a nomination in Laois-Offaly, but the Laois-Offaly Fianna Fáil convention gave him a mandate to go back to Kilkenny (*Offaly Independent*, 4 June 1938).

8.   Quoted in Joseph T. Carroll, *Ireland in the war years* (Newton Abbot, 1975), p. 137.

9.   J. J. Lee, *Ireland 1912-1985: politics and society* (Cambridge, 1989), pp 296-7.

10.   Gemma Hussey, *At the cutting edge: cabinet diaries 1982-1987* (Dublin, 1990), p. 247.

11.   Letter from David O'Shanahan, NT, in *Offaly Independent*, 14 February 1948.

12.   Profile of Oliver J. Flanagan by John Whelan in *Leinster Express*, 21 February 1987, pp 24-5.

13.   *Irish Times*, 1 July 1935 and 7 July 1935.

14.   Meehan, *TDs and senators*, p. 30. However, another source gives a completely different account of the incident in which the first shot was fired: Jim and Brendan Fleming (eds), *1916 in Laois: an account of the activities of the Laois Volunteers up to and including the 1916 rising* (The Swan, 1996), pp 13-14.

15.   The source for this and other statements about the backgrounds of TDs nationally over the 1922-92 period is Michael Gallagher, 'Long-term patterns in recruitment to the parliamentary elite in the Republic of Ireland', paper presented in the workshop on 'Long-term studies of political recruitment patterns and elite transformation' at the Joint Sessions of the European Consortium for Political Research, Bordeaux, 27 April – 2 May 1995.

16.   According to some sources, Thomas Tynan was 67 or 68 when he became a TD in 1927, but Meehan, *TDs and senators*, p. 32, gives his year of birth as 1879.

17.   Candidates whose vote total fails to reach a fixed threshold (one-third of the quota from 1923 to 1989, one quarter of the quota in 1992) forfeit their deposit, which was £100 at elections from 1923 to 1989 and was raised to £300 in 1992. The quota in a 5-seat constituency such as Laois-Offaly is a sixth of the votes plus one. For a full account of the PR-STV electoral system, see Richard Sinnott, 'The electoral system' in John Coakley and Michael Gallagher (eds), *Politics in the Republic of Ireland*, 2nd ed (Dublin, 1993), pp 67-85.

18.   Seán Donnelly, *Partnership: the story of the 1992 general election* (Rathcoole, 1993), p. 8.

19.   Peter Mair, *The changing Irish party system: organisation, ideology and electoral competition* (London, 1987), pp 119-24.

20.   Warner Moss, *Political parties in the Irish Free State* (New York, 1968), p. 180.

21.   Richard Sinnott, 'Interpretations of the Irish party system' in *European Journal of*

Political Science 12:3 (1984), pp 289-307, at p. 304.

22. This is in line with patterns identified in past research: Michael Marsh, 'Electoral preferences in Irish recruitment: the 1977 election' in *European Journal of Political Research* 9:1 (1981), pp 61-74, at p. 67; Michael Marsh, 'Electoral evaluations of candidates in Irish general elections 1948-82' in *Irish Political Studies* 2 (1987), pp 65-76, at p. 68; Michael Gallagher, 'The election of the 27th Dáil' in Michael Gallagher and Michael Laver (eds), *How Ireland Voted 1992* (Dublin and Limerick, 1993), pp 57-78, at pp 57-8.

23. Paul M. Sacks, 'Bailiwicks, locality and religion: three elements in an Irish Dáil constituency election' in *Economic and Social Review* 1:4 (1970), pp 531-54; P. J. Taylor and R. J. Johnston, *Geography of elections* (London, 1979), pp 274-94.

24. Quoted in Warner Moss, *Political parties in the Irish Free State* (New York, 1968), p. 191n.

William Davin

Oliver J. Flanagan

Patrick J. Lalor

Liam Hyland

Plate 25.1   Laois politicians.

Chapter 26

PORTLAOISE: GENESIS AND DEVELOPMENT

MICHAEL DEIGAN

Introduction

Portlaoise has been the principal town of county Laois since the formation of the Queen's County in 1556, in the reign of Philip and Mary. At first sight, the casual observer could be forgiven for dismissing it as another nondescript collection of uninteresting buildings, with little evidence of any indigenous concern for the care of the physical environment. But the casual observer would be mistaken.

To understand Portlaoise is to uncover a territory rich in social, political and architectural history. The word 'territory' is used advisedly: the O'Connors of Offaly, the O'Carrols of Ely O'Carrol, the Fitzpatricks of Ossory, the Fitzgeralds of Kildare and the McMurragh Kavanaghs have all contributed, with the O'Mores of Leix, to the turbulent history of Portlaoise. The Calendar of State Papers – of Edward VI, Philip and Mary, Elizabeth I and others – refer frequently to Maryborough. The town is woven into accounts of many whose names loom large on a wider stage: Mary Tudor, Elizabeth I, Oliver Cromwell. On closer inspection, the town's form and character read easily into the imprint of that history.

Sir John Bellingham was no stranger to Ireland when he landed in Dalkey on 18 May 1548. As the new lord deputy, he immediately instituted yet another campaign against the O'Mores of Leix, and their allies the O'Connors of Uí Failghe. Ruthless and thorough, the campaign culminated towards the end of July with the killing of many rebels, and the flight to Connaught of the leaders for temporary shelter. Bellingham then set to work to open up passes through forest and bog to provide for the free passage of government troops through Leix and Offaly. He quartered himself in Athy to oversee operations and a decision was made to build a fort in Leix. The construction of Fort Protector in 1548 was primarily for military and political purposes. The hinterland at that time was largely impenetrable because of forests, bogs and eskers. Always ready to rebel, the native Irish were difficult to pin down. They could retreat quickly to areas inaccessible, except at great risk, to pursuing soldiery. Having subdued the natives and exiled their chieftains, Bellingham was anxious to proceed as quickly as possible with the fortification of Leix. Drogheda and Dublin reluctantly provided skilled labour and carts to carry materials for construction of the fort. Although work continued over several years, the fort took shape during that August, and beer was brought from Dublin to celebrate.

In January 1549 there were complaints about lax discipline during the absence of the constable, Sir William Saintloe. St Leger – who had been appointed lord deputy for the second time in July 1550 – received orders early in August to complete the new forts in Leix and Offaly, and to garrison them.[1] He visited the forts and found both in a state of great disorder. During the months of February, March and April 1551, portions of Leix and Offaly were leased by St Leger to certain English gentlemen and soldiers who had been instrumental in suppressing the rebellion. Sir James Crofts, who succeeded St Leger as deputy in May 1551, continued to assign portions of the confiscated lands until his recall in December 1552. One of the conditions of these leases was that the lessee should bear his proportion of all cesses for the safeguarding and victualling of the King's forts, at Dangan and Portlaoise. The fort at Portlaoise – named after Lord Somerset, protector of the boy king Edward VI – was known by the Irish as Campa. Sir Thomas Ratcliffe replaced St Leger as lord deputy in May 1556 and promptly turned to the problems associated with the settlement of Leix. All the country beyond the bog to the west of Fort Protector was reserved for the O'Mores. The eastern area was allocated to the English colonists. A constable, resident at Fort Protector, was to have the same powers locally as the lord deputy had generally. The English were required to build a church in each of twelve stipulated towns within three years and a parson of English birth was to have the tithe. Some local historians think it likely that the old Protestant church beside the courthouse was built at this time.

In June 1557, two important Acts were passed in the parliament of Philip and Mary: (1) an act whereby (a) the crown was declared to be entitled to Leix, Offaly, Slievemargy, Irry and Clanmalire and (b) the same countries made into shires; and (2) an Act for the disposition of Leix and Offaly. In the first Act, which is long and comprehensive, the two shires of Queen's County and King's County (now Laois and Offaly, respectively) were formed. In section two Fort Protector was renamed Maryborough, and in section three the fort in Dangan was renamed Philipstown. The second Act made provisions for the distribution of lands in the two shires. Queen's County came into being on 1 June 1557 and King's County on 29 September 1557. During that summer Ratcliffe – now earl of Sussex – was again engaged in the north. When the O'Connors returned to their old haunts in Offaly, the O'Mores were not slow to do likewise in Leix and a systematic spoliation of the settlers took place under cover of darkness. Many of the settlers met their deaths: Walter Peppard, lessee of a large tract of land in Slievemargy, stated that he lost seventeen men defending his property during this period.

Sussex returned to England early in 1558 and was succeeded by Sir Henry Sidney; but the troubled state of the country led the Queen to reappoint Sussex as lord deputy, and he took up his new duties in Dublin on 1 May 1558. He found Queen's County and King's County completely overrun with Irish. They besieged the fort at Maryborough on 18 May, regarding its capture as inevitable because of their strength in numbers. It happened that Sir Henry Ratcliffe – Sussex's brother and lieutenant of the two shires – was in the fort. He sent out a force of 60 soldiers and 30 kerne under the leadership of Francis Cosby which took the rebels by surprise. Donagh O'Connor and his followers fled in disorder leaving the booty they had collected behind them. Richard Oge, a bastard Geraldine and a man of enormous stature and strength, was killed by Cosby 'with his own hands, which would have been done by no man else'.[2] Mary's death and the accession of Elizabeth I on 17 November 1558 brought no change in government policy. By the end of the year the two countries were so peaceful that Sir Henry Ratcliffe was granted leave of absence until the following Easter. This state of affairs continued throughout the spring as the few O'Connors and O'Mores who had not been pardoned were too weak to cause trouble.

The plantation question again arose. Despite the great expenditure and loss of life in the subjection of the O'Mores and O'Connors and the creation of the two shires under Philip and Mary, there had been no advance in the colonisation of these areas since their leasing by St Leger and Crofts in 1551 and 1552. In February of 1560 Sussex was presented with orders from the Queen which began: 'Our two countries of Leix and Offaly do yet remain unestablished or uninhabited, being planted only with our men of war, whereby they lie in waste without people and our charge is likely to grow daily more intolerable'.[3] Sussex returned in June 1560, as lord lieutenant of Ireland, and immediately turned his attention to the problems in Leix and Offaly. The forts in Maryborough and Philipstown were rebuilt and strengthened, passes were cut and highways opened. A plan of Maryborough as newly reconstructed was drawn up, showing the fort and town with names of residents. This plan or map (see Bradley this volume) was despatched to London for the Queen's appreciation. It is the first visual (as distinct from written) evidence of the built environment of Portlaoise, otherwise Maryborough. It is difficult to do more than speculate about the location of the walls of the town which, according to the map, enclosed an area outside of and surrounding the fort itself.

Figure 26.1 is an unpublished map made available to the author by the Ordnance Survey Office. Dating from 1839, it shows the extent of the perimeter of the fort; the dotted lines indicate the approximate position the demolished 'castle' in the south-west corner would have occupied. The scaled perimeter dimensions of the fort are 416 ft x 340 ft. This tallies reasonably well with a map (fig. 10.1) said to date from 1566 which gives the size of the fort as 120 yards by 100 yards. The size of the square tower is given as 17 yards x 14 yards (Bradley[4] refers to the overall dimensions of the fort as 1120 yards x 1110 yards, which is a misprint). A sketch published in 1791 (fig. 26.2), 'Fort in Maryborough Town', probably represents the remains of the 'castle' as it was then. Bradley speculated concerning the course of the town boundary but concluded that it could only be confirmed only by excavations:

> it is evident ... that archaeology is an important means of learning about Portlaoise's past and of understanding the character and detailed form of the town today. This is more than just an academic pursuit because without an appreciation of the factors which have shaped Portlaoise's present character, steps taken to conserve that character will not be wholly effective, or worse, features basic to its unique identity may be unwittingly destroyed.[5]

In 1566 the state of Ireland was perilous: disorder was rife. On 20 February of that year Francis Cosby was made constable of the castle of Maryborough. On 16 January 1567, Elizabeth wrote to Sidney, lord deputy, approving of his recommendation for the creation of two market towns at Maryborough and Philipstown. The charter of Maryborough was issued by Sidney on 14 March 1570. In December 1578, Tytton informed Burghley that the forts at Maryborough and Philipstown were in a dilapidated condition. On 25 August 1580, Francis Cosby – now general of the Queen's kerne and seneschal of Queen's County – was slain at Glenmalure by Feagh McHugh. It is said that Cosby had foreseen the danger to the crown forces under the recently appointed lord deputy, Grey; but he was not heeded, and advanced boldly to what he knew was certain death. A man of great personal courage and unrivalled experience in Irish warfare, his subjugation of the O'Mores had been ruthless; but as an administrator

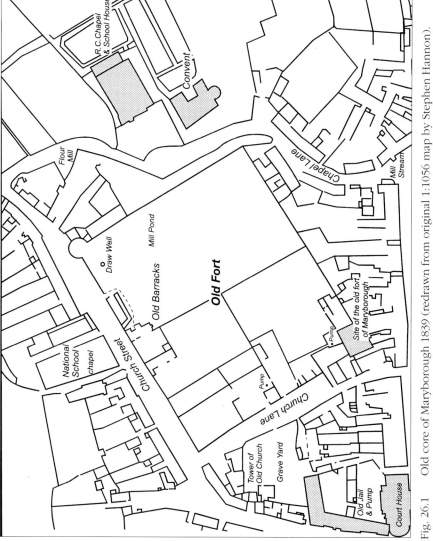

Fig. 26.1   Old core of Maryborough 1839 (redrawn from original 1:1056 map by Stephen Hannon).

Fig. 26.2   Fort in Maryborough (from Grose, *Antiquities,* ii, opposite p. 45).

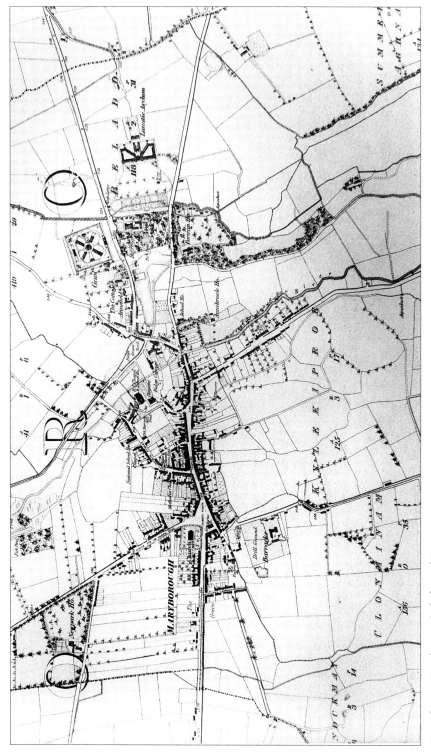

Fig. 26.3   Maryborough 6" first edition.

in Leix he was a failure. News of the rebel victory at Glenmalure spread quickly and the Leix and Offaly natives threw in their lot with Piers Grace and Sir John of Desmond, who were burning and pillaging the towns of Ormond. After razing Abbeyleix to the ground, they proceeded to Maryborough and laid siege to the fort. Having slain some of the defenders they decided to raise the siege, but plundered the town and made off with booty of all kinds.

Hugh O'Neill, earl of Tyrone, was proclaimed a traitor on 28 June 1595, and the Nine Years War began. This was not without effect in Leinster, in October 1595 it was reported to the government that the O'Mores had grown restless, and arrangements were made to strengthen the garrisons in Leix and Offaly. In December 1597 Warham St Leger was in command of the defence of Leix, while Ormond set out for Dundalk to discuss peace terms with O'Neill. On December 5, the rebels, under the protection of the truce, moved into Leix with at least 400 men, under the leadership of Tyrell and Owny McRory O'More. Living off the countryside, they encamped the first day at Slievemargy, and moved to Timahoe the next. St Leger protested at their presence and sent out two companies from Maryborough to watch them. Despite a message from the rebels that they intended no harm, a battle ensued. The two crown companies, numbering 300, were annihilated – only the lieutenant in charge and twenty men escaped. The rebels then proceeded to Maryborough where they burned the town and laid siege to the fort. St Leger wrote, that with the exception of the fort, and where the settlers had castles, the entire country was 'at the pleasure' of the rebels.

In September 1598 the fort at Maryborough had to be relieved from Dublin by Ormond with the loss of some hundreds of soldiers. Again, on 11 January 1599, Ormond with a force of 700 foot and 140 horse, had to break his way through the rebels to victual the fort. Robert, earl of Essex, was appointed lord lieutenant in April 1599 and dispatched with a powerful army to engage O'Neill. However, he was persuaded by the Council to make war on the rebels in Leinster. To this end a force of about 3,000 foot and 300 horse with a heavy train of provisions, some for the fort of Maryborough, set out from Dublin on 9 May. On 16 May Essex, with 500 foot and 200 horse, left the main army at Stradbally and made a short detour to deliver provisions to Maryborough. These were most welcome, as the garrison had been living on horseflesh for twenty days. Essex knighted the fort commander, Rush, on the spot and then proceeded to Ballyknocken to join the main army. The following day the army set out on its journey towards Kilkenny, which required passage through the Pass of Cashel. This has been described by Sir John Harrington, who accompanied the army, as lying between Crosby Duff hill (2.5 miles from Maryborough on the Timahoe road) and Cashel, which is four miles from Maryborough on the Ballyroan road. The royal army was attacked; O'Sullivan estimated that the English lost 500 men, but Essex reported two captains and three or four 'common soldiers' slain. It seems likely that neither side suffered heavy losses, although the location of the battle has thereafter been referred to as the 'Pass of the Plumes' because of the feathers from the helmets of the English which littered the ground. Elizabeth was apparently unimpressed by the tactics adopted by Essex. On 19 July 1599 she informed him that he had many inferiors well suited to carrying out an operation such as the victualling of Maryborough, and that it was high time he moved against Ulster.

By the end of December 1599, the six week truce Essex signed with O'Neill on 15 September had come to an end, and open warfare resumed. After Essex's return to England, Sir Francis Rush, commander of Maryborough, wrote to the lords justices on 7 January 1600 describing the success of a trap he had laid. Rush had arranged for an old English soldier, who was married to a native, to let it be known that he would let the rebels into the fort through a hole which he would open in the vault of the castle. On the night of Friday, 4 January 1600, the rebels entered the vault, where they were surrounded and their retreat cut off. About noon the next day Rush and his 'best men' entered the cellar, killing 34 or 35 and capturing most of the others. Rush states that he lost no men of his own, although for himself, 'I fear I have lost an eye by splinters of shot, and shot in the right hand'. The O'Mores followed up their capture of Ormond in April 1600 with a successful attack on a section of the garrison at Maryborough, in which twenty crown soldiers were killed. Ormond was released on 12 June, but Owny McRory was mortally wounded on 17 August in a skirmish with Mountjoy's forces. This, combined with the terror inflicted by Mountjoy's campaign in Leix, was a serious blow to the O'Mores. The defeat of the Irish at Kinsale in 1601 put an end to all hopes of further resistance by the O'Mores and the O'Connors, and removed forever any hopes they might have had of repossessing their ancestral lands. Following the death of Elizabeth I in 1603, James I (otherwise James VI of Scotland, son of Mary, Queen of Scots) succeeded to the throne. The settlers returned, and by 1610 the transplantation of the O'Mores and their followers – some into Thomond, some into Connaught, most into Kerry – was accomplished. O'Hanlon observed that from 1610 to 1641, 'the annals of the county are uninteresting'.

The Catholic Confederation and the Civil War 1641-52 had some impact on Maryborough and the Queen's County. Roger O'More, grandson of Rory Caoch, is credited with establishing the

Confederation. As leader of the Catholic Party in the Irish House of Commons he made strenuous efforts to bring Catholics and puritans closer. But the puritans turned against the Catholics, and threats of penal laws were heard on all sides. When Roger finally came to the conclusion in 1641 that all hopes for constitutional reform were in vain, he communicated directly with Owen Roe O'Neill. He played a leading part in a plan to seize Dublin castle, but the scheme was thwarted. Soon after the commencement of hostilities in October 1641, Leinster was up in arms. In Leix the O'Mores and their allies attacked and besieged several castles, including the fort at Maryborough, which was reduced to dire straits. In May 1642 the Irish Catholic bishops and noblemen met in Kilkenny, and there established what came to be known as the Confederation of Kilkenny. Owen Roe O'Neill returned to Ireland via Dunkirk, conferring with the Assembly in Kilkenny at the end of that winter. In October 1645 Cardinal Rinuccini arrived in Ireland, and he had discussions with O'Neill in Kilkenny in the Spring of 1646. Towards the end of September 1646, O'Neill took the fort at Maryborough and garrisoned it. When Rinuccini had to leave Kilkenny for fear of being arrested, he came to Maryborough and lived with O'Neill at Kilminchy.

In 1649 the earl of Castlehaven marched on Maryborough, which was held by Captain Phelim O'Neill for Owen Roe. Phelim eventually treated with Castlehaven, and the Irish surrendered the fort on 9 May 1649, but they marched out with their arms and went northwards to join the Ulster general. Early in the Autumn of 1649, Cromwell arrived in Dublin with 5,000 men. He marched to Drogheda and took the town, slaughtering indiscriminately. Marching south, he soon overran the whole country. When he returned to England he left his son-in-law Ireton in command. Ireton's colonel, Hewson, took possession of Maryborough and other places. Although the Irish still had a fair amount of success, the Parliamentary Commissioners and most of the Irish still in arms agreed to terms for a cessation of the war. On 12 May 1652 Maryborough was assigned as the place where Colonel Lewis Moore and his troops should lay down their arms. In that August an Act was passed whereby the Protestant Royalists, as well as the Roman Catholics, forfeited their lands and were transplanted to others. The end of the Cromwellian War signalled the end of the Fort of Maryborough, which, along with Dunamase, was dismantled by Hewson. In 1654, Dr William Petty was appointed to survey the forfeited lands. He was one of the most successful adventurers, having come to Ireland as Cromwell's state apothecary, on a salary believed to be £1 per day. Within a few years he was the owner of 50,000 acres in Kerry, where he laid the foundations of the Landsdowne family and estate. His survey of the Queen's County – as well as giving the acreage and value of the forfeited lands – provides a minute and fairly accurate topographical description of the county.[6]

The history of the Queen's County in the eighteenth century is effectively the history of the Penal Laws. When Anne came to the throne in 1702 it was deemed advisable to conciliate the 'Protestant interest', which viewed with distrust the accession of a daughter of James II. Particular attention was directed to the 'common enemy', and special measures were taken to stay the further growth of popery. Anne reigned until 1714 and was succeeded by George I. During his reign, a map was produced which is of interest. It includes a sketch of the town of Maryborough which suggests that the built-up area now bounded by the Main Street and the southern boundary of the fort was open space (i.e. the area from Fennell's corner to Shaw's corner, including the Regency Hotel and Egan's Restaurant). The map also makes reference to the Common of Maryborough, about which more later. Feehan[7] and Bradley[8] would probably have little difficulty in accepting that this area, along with the present Lower Square, was the original market place. Bradley is also of the opinion that the line of waterfilled ditch shown along the southern wall of the fort in the 1560 map, which was filled in at some time in the interim, may be preserved by the kink in the property line of some Main Street properties on the modern O.S. map. He also writes that Ms. Helen Roe 'informs us that a separate ground rent was paid for this extra stretch of land'. This has been confirmed to the author by Mr. John Bolger, solicitor, whose father resided in what is now John Kennedy's pharmacy, and which backs on to the south wall of the fort. Mr. Bolger Snr.. paid a separate ground rent for the ditch area.

Most of the remarkable happenings in nineteenth century Ireland impacted in some shape or form on the Queen's County and Maryborough. The Act of Union (1800) is referred to later in its implications for the Green, or Commons, of Maryborough. Concerning Catholic Emancipation, O'Hanlon wrote that, 'events ... quickly proved that the hopes and expectations of its supporters were as exaggerated as the fears and alarms of its opponents'.[9] James Fintan Lalor is reputed to have influenced the thinking of John Mitchel and Michael Davitt. Other influences on the region included the Famine, the coming of the railways, the tithe war, Parnell and the Irish Party, land reform, and the abolition of the grand juries, replaced by the county councils under the Act of 1898. The early twentieth century brought further change, with the Great War, the 1916 Rising, and the 'Troubles' of the 1920s. The change of name in 1920 – from Maryborough to Portlaoise, and from Queen's County to county Laois – marks the emergence of native government. Today Portlaoise is a prosperous commercial centre, its growth reflecting its strategic location. Situated at the intersection of a number of national roads, and on the main southern rail links to Dublin, its population is expected to reach 10,000 by the millennium. The last two decades have seen unprecedented expansion in the town's commercial sector, following the construction of James Fintan Lalor Avenue in 1970 and in the development of new housing estates. The rest of this chapter examines how the built environment that is modern Portlaoise emerged out of the town's history.

Evolution of the town

Precise reasons for the original siting of the town remain unclear. For defensive purposes a site closer to the Rock of Dunamase would have made more sense. The presence of a small river, the Blackwater (now the Triogue), must have been an important consideration. The protection offered by the Ridge of Maryborough just a hundred yards away may also have exerted an influence, particularly during the construction phase. The construction of the fort marked the first stage of evolution of the present day Portlaoise. Evidence of what it may have looked like is provided by the map, or plan, drawn up in 1560 and dispatched to London for the Queen's appreciation. Comparison with an unpublished and unfinished map of Maryborough made by the Ordnance Survey in 1839 (figure 26.1) shows that the castle at the southern corner had disappeared by 1839, but the fort's four walls and the circular tower at the northern tip are readily reconciled with the 1560 map.

No trace has ever been recorded, as far as can be ascertained, of the town walls depicted on the earliest map as enclosing an area outside the fort. Another feature depicted on the 1560 map is the sinuous stream, which can be reconciled with the millstream. This survived until recently, and can be seen on any O.S. map. A map produced by Cowley in 1563 depicting Fort Protector in thumbnail sketch form does not suggest the existence of town walls. The arrangement of the houses on the early map does not conform with the street pattern as it is now, nor as it was in 1721. The mill (to the east of the circular tower and close to the millrace) was the site of Odlum's Mill, demolished in 1991 – a continuity that is surely remarkable. The only 'hard' evidence for the existence of buildings outside the fort is The Stonehouse (due east of the Fort) referred to on the 1560 map. This was probably occupied by Anthony Rogers – the name allocated to it – and has a tower on the south gable.

When the Presentation Sisters came to Maryborough in 1824, they took up residence in the remains of the Stonehouse. This building had by then experienced a varied history, having been the constable's house, a gaol, an infirmary and finally the convent. The community extended the building in 1872 and the tower, or what remained of it, was subsumed into the extension. Ms. Dooley, a local historian, writes 'when the Convent was being rebuilt workmen tried to remove the tower, but they found the task so difficult that it was decided to retain and utilise it. Thus it was built up to its present height and the rooms adjoining it were modelled to suit its rotundity'.[10] Ms Dooley says the original walls were about 15 ft. high and the present tower was built on top of these. With the permission of the community, the author examined the basement on 5 December 1991. The original part of the tower has 4 ft. 6 ins. thick walls and an internal diameter of approximately 13 ft. 6 ins. The walls are in extremely good condition and both tower and surrounding spaces are in daily use by the community. Also surviving from the sixteenth century is an underground tunnel which probably connected the fort to the Stonehouse. The following extract is from a collection of papers[11] dated 1901:

> A few years ago when Patsy Lynch was sinking the foundation of the new convent, he lit upon the passage, and, following its course for a few hundred yards, he came upon loads of ridge gravel in heaps ready to be spread over the damp ground, but unused for centuries. Greatly alarmed, he appraised Rev. Dr. Taylor P.P. of the fact; but the doctor, knowing that the grounds were formerly part of the outer defences of the Fort, ordered Patsy to close up the entrance and so it now remains, to be explored when discovered by a more enterprising stonemason.

In 1951 in the course of renovation work at the convent, a tunnel or underground passage was uncovered. The late Major E.A.S. Cosby (a direct descendant of one of the original occupants) was invited to view the 'find', and was accompanied by his wife, Enid Elizabeth. Mrs. Cosby's recollection of the event, as she told the author in November 1991, is of a 'beautifully, built, very big passageway, with an arched roof – to enter you would have to stoop a little. The passage appeared to go west towards the Fort, and in the other direction, towards the rock of Dunamase. It was entered by some of the people present, but for a short distance only, for fear of collapse'. Sister Carmel, who also saw the passage, indicated for the author its width – from her recollection, as about 5 ft. The approximate location of the exposed section of tunnel in indicated on figure 26.4. What may be another tunnel system (although it is more likely to be an underground drain) was discovered in 1974 along the western boundary of the fort, near the old St. Peter's burial ground. Telecom workers, excavating for cable

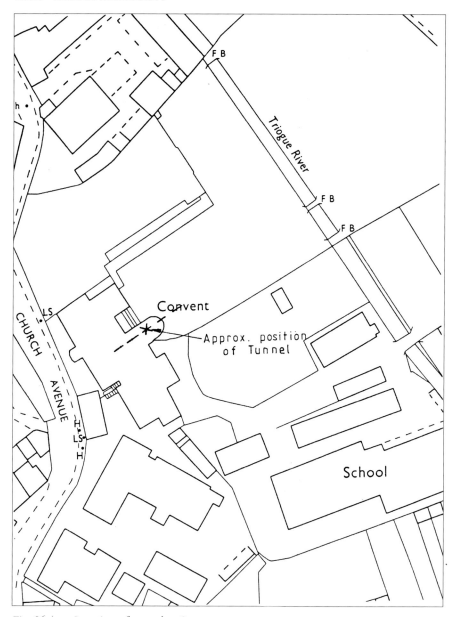

Fig. 26.4   Location of tunnel at Convent.

laying, came upon an underground passage. This was approximately 24 ins. wide by 30 ins. high.

The only other confirmed pre-1700 building still standing is the tower or belfry of what was St. Peter's Church, beside the old gaol. One view is that this may have been built as a Catholic church in the reign of Queen Mary, following the issue of an edict in 1556 that all towns and fortifications were to have a church within three years. There is no record of an incumbent until 1598 when a Rev. David Good is mentioned in respect of a journey to Dublin to seek help for the relief of the fort, which was under siege. It has also been suggested that Cardinal Rinuccini said Mass there in 1648, assisted by Owen Roe O'Neill, when the Confederates held the town. In 1798 John Wesley preached at St. Peter's and described it in glowing terms. However, after the opening of the present church in 1803 it rapidly fell into decay. Some of the old buildings in the vicinity of Pepper's Lane – reputed to have been an access road to the town – may be of sixteenth century vintage. It is likely that parts of other old buildings elsewhere in the town were incorporated into later structures.

Roads

If the first stage in the evolution of the town was the fort, the tunnel and the sixteenth century buildings outside it, the road system may be regarded as the second stage of growth and consolidation. The road pattern was more or less defined by the early eighteenth century. Roads did not exist as such when Fort Protector was commenced in 1548. Leix at that time and for a long time to follow was heavily afforested, making travel very difficult. At the time of the Cowley Map of 1563 the Queen's County had neither towns nor roads. From the time of William and Mary (1689-94) special attention was given to roadmaking by the legislature. In 1734, under George II, an Act was passed to enable the road from Naas to Maryborough to be repaired. The map of the Queen's County by H. Moll, geographer, published in 1727, includes many of the present roads. The Taylor and Skinner maps of 1777 show virtually all of today's road system.

The map of 1721 provides an interesting clue to Maryborough as it may have been at that time. The date may be correct, but the style of presentation suggests this may be a 1721 survey, re-copied later with flamboyant draughtsmanship. It can be inferred that the original market square (Lower Square) was larger than it is now and that the area from Fennell's Corner to Shaws, which backs onto what was the south ditch of the fort, was not built on at that time. Daniel Cahill's Grand Jury Map of 1805 shows how the road system of the Queen's County had consolidated. Of particular interest to Portlaoise is the representation of the old road along the top of the esker (Old Ridge Road); the termination of Church Street at the north-east corner of the fort and the apparent existence of a road, of which no trace remains, running from the present 1914-18 memorial across by the Christian Brothers School and joining the Ridge Road on top of the esker at the south (town) side of the railway bridge.

The built environment

The map prepared by Lieutenant Larcom R. Eng., dated 1832 shows the parish of Maryborough shortly after the building of the new gaol and lunatic asylum. The most reliable early map of Portlaoise is the 6 inch O.S. edition published in 1839 (fig. 26.2). Complementing this is an (unpublished and incomplete) O.S. map of the town from the same year, at a scale of 5 feet to one mile. The 1839 maps are most interesting. The railway has not yet arrived, so there is no Railway Street. The Old Cork Road followed its circuitous path into the Market (Upper) Square. Many notable landmarks are indicated. Some, like the Market House on the Upper Square, are now gone – as indeed is its successor, the Town Hall, burned down in 1945.

Subsequent editions/revisions of the Ordnance Survey maps show the growth of the town in graphic form. Following the original survey in 1839, revisions took place in 1889; 1907; 1959; 1972; 1976 and 1985. The most striking addition to the 1889 revision is the railway, which dates from 1846. Railway Street has appeared, providing access for new development including the Methodist Church. Other major development since 1839 includes The Maltings and the new route of the Cork Road into the Market Square. The layout of the gaol buildings is shown, a practice discontinued in the 1907 and subsequent revisions. The 1907 revision shows very little change over the previous 20 years. The Market House has been replaced by the Town Hall; development has occurred on the entrance of Cork Road to the Market Square and along the Green Road, off the Mountmellick Road; and a row of prison officers houses (since demolished) has been built outside the prison. A town boundary makes its first appearance on this map. The 1959 revision indicates the coming of modern industrialisation and housing. Housing estates have developed at O'Moore Place (off the Cork Road). The large textile factory is shown on Tay Lane, as are the schools and corn store, which were constructed within the walls of the Fort. The Town Hall, burned down in 1945, is of course no longer shown, but Kellyville Park, a speculative estate of 10 private houses, has appeared, along with Kellyville House. But perhaps the most influential imposition on the built environment, though not necessarily the most obvious from the map is the forest of electricity pylons. These followed from the Ardnacrusha Scheme in 1929 and the fact that Portlaoise was chosen as the main transformation station for the new national electricity grid.

In the 1972 revision there are two major additions to the core of the town: (i) the new Catholic church, built in the mid 1960s at the junction of the Stradbally and Dublin Roads, and (ii) the outline of what was to become the present James Fintan Lalor Avenue. This latter development has had an extraordinary impact on the town. It was built as a relief road to cater for the through-traffic which was obliged until then to negotiate the Main Street. In the twenty-five years or so since its construction, the road has facilitated rapid expansion of the town's business and commercial activities. A revision in 1976-7 indicates the 'consolidation' of the James Fintan Lalor project and the opening up of an industrial estate on the former Maryvale lands. Otherwise there is very little change in the core of the town, but extensive building (not shown) was taking place in the suburbs.

The latest O.S. map (actual scale 1:1,00), shows the emergence of roundabouts in the town centre, new commercial building in the car park off James Fintan Lalor Avenue and the new county hall, opened in 1982. Since the making of this map, there has been further development in the core, notably a new free-standing building in the carpark off James Fintan Lalor Avenue; a major shopping centre along the south boundary of the Avenue; a new public library in the carpark with shops below; new offices for the Department of Agriculture; and other developments clustering around James Fintan Lalor Avenue. Estimated expenditure to July 1997 was of the order of £15 m. Recent major road interventions include the by-pass to the south of the town, which started in 1991 and was completed in 1997. A cross link, roughly following the old Mountmellick railway line between Limerick Road and Ballyfin Road, will when completed facilitate further development – in particular, the proposed comprehensive school/college, a new church, and public and private housing. It will also provide a by-pass for traffic with high loads travelling southwest/northeast, which at present has difficulty getting under the low railway bridges on the Limerick and Mountrath roads. The layout and visual character of most Irish towns took form during the eighteenth century. Many of the post-1700 buildings and structures which are part of the urban heritage of Portlaoise are worthy of conservation. The County Council, in the preparation of the current statutory town plan, recognised the importance of conserving the architectural and historical heritage of the town and, accordingly, invoked the available statutory procedure of listing buildings and other items. In addition, the following are of importance in heritage terms: old bridges on the Triogue, including those in convent grounds; old church/chapel at rere of Crokes; convent buildings – 'medieval' tower; cemeteries – Ridge Road, Church Street, Boughlone; Biddy Agahaboes Well (under the railway bridge, Mountrath Road); road on top of Ridge of Maryborough; tunnel system associated with the Fort.

It is worth noting some significant losses – in particular, much of the Fort of Maryborough, the Town Hall, burned down in 1945, the Old Catholic Church and probably the greatest loss to present day Portlaoise

– the Green of Maryborough. This area measured approximately 180 acres and was the property of the Corporation (i.e. the people) of Maryborough. Located along the Mountmellick Road at Coote Street, it was divided between the two borough M.P.s who had lost their seats following the Act of Union in 1800 and the thirteen burgesses then in office. In addition, a further 100 acres of the Green, which had been leased, was reputedly not taken back by the Corporation when the lease lapsed. In all, almost three hundred acres of public property was disposed of by dubious and probably illegal means.

Conclusion

It is a matter of some surprise that any part of Fort Protector survives after almost 450 years. It was built in a hurry, suffered much abuse during its relatively short working life of just 100 years and is now occupied by various private and public interests. Today the fort's heritage value is more readily appreciated and barring accidents any move to damage it further seems unlikely. The conservation issues, in physical terms, are the walls, the rampart tower, the tunnels, the convent and archaeological investigation. The walls and the tower are conspicuous and what survives is in relatively good condition. However, remedial work needs to be carried out without delay, under expert supervision. The existence of a system of tunnels is likely. This should be confirmed and a survey made of its condition and location. Action is needed to protect the system from future damage, either from normal deterioration or external sources. Photographs would have an obvious tourist appeal and would also boost public awareness.

The original Stone House was situated on the site of the convent. The tower in the basement is part of the original building. It has walls approximately 4.5 feet thick and an internal diameter of about 14 feet. It is in remarkably good condition. The tower superstructure as it is today was built on top of the original, probably in the 1872 renovation. The excavation of an area within the fort, and surrounding it, may yield useful information on the early occupants – perhaps by means of a limited 'dig' in the old millrace and/or the perimeter ditch. Any development, however small, in or near the fort, could cause irreversible damage. Property owners within and contiguous to the fort should be made aware of its importance. Any opportunity to acquire ownership of property in this locality should be availed of either by the state or the local authority. A large part of the fort is occupied by the vocational school and the convent national school, and if plans for future educational facilities in the town are to involve their re-location, it would be desirable that the public authorities be afforded an opportunity to acquire the properties.

The possibility of creating a permanent heritage centre on the site, in conjunction with the major development work envisaged at the Old Library building behind the Courthouse will be pursued vigorously and jointly by both public and private interests.

The future

An understanding of the past is essential to understand the present, and to envisage the future. The future of Portlaoise requires thought and consideration to ensure continued prosperity both in Portlaoise town and the county at large. It is the policy of Laois County Council, with the full backing of the public, to maximise the strategic centrality of Portlaoise in terms of industrial and commercial development and locational suitability. The accessibility of the town to the national road network presents an opportunity also for attracting visitors and shoppers from a wide catchment area, as well as capitalising on the extensive volume of passing traffic. Recent developments brought about largely by the designation of certain areas of the town under the urban renewal programme, have resulted in the achievement of a vibrant commercial and service sector and have enabled the Council to pursue its strategy for the creation of an attractive physical environment. A study[12] completed in September 1994 focused on:

(1) an economic strategy for the town centre; (2) broad land-use planning guidelines, including an amenity plan; (3) a detailed study of shop front and street design.

In addition, the following is envisaged by the Council: development of a new pedestrian link via Pepper's Lane; residential/street development at the rear of Meehan House; limited commercial development in refurbished buildings; visual enhancement programme/ upgrading facades and such like; arts/cultural development of property owned by the Council, or capable of being acquired in the Courthouse/Old Library/Fort Protector area; the creation of a pedestrianised area in the town centre with particular reference to landscaping the Market and Lower Squares, including decorative lighting and paving.

In pursuit of the foregoing, the Council has produced an environmental charter[13] and will engage in a continuous review of the designated area proposals and facilitate ongoing discussions with interested parties, such as the Chamber of Commerce and trades organisations and individuals. This pro-active approach will be geared to encourage investment in the further development of the town centre and to ensure that development of the town generally will take place in a balanced way around the core (by extending the residential suburbs to the north).

References

This chapter is based on an unpublished manuscript in Laois County Library on The heritage of Portlaoise by M. Deigan (1991).

1. *Cal. pat. rolls Ire., Henry VII-Eliz.*, p. 220.
2. *Cal. S.P. Ire.*, i, p. 143, no. 30, p. 146, no. 50.
3. *Cal. Carew MSS*, i, p. 292, no. 223.
4. J. Bradley, The urban archaeology of Laois, unpublished manuscript, p. 51. See also Bradley's chapter in this volume.
5. Ibid., pp 55-6.
6. O'Hanlon and O'Leary, *Queen's County*, ii, p. 540.
7. J. Feehan, *Laois: an environmental history*, p. 397.
8. Bradley, Urban archaeology, p. 50.
9. O'Hanlon and O'Leary, *Queen's County*, ii, p. 651.
10. J. Dooley, *Leinster Express*, 9 March 1974.
11. Carey and Matthews, Portlaoise and district, unpublished manuscript in Laois County Library, p. 10.
12. Laois County Council, Portlaoise town centre study (1994).
13. Environmental Working Group, Report to Laois County Council (1994).

Epilogue

TEDDY FENNELLY

> What would we do if all the historians
> were found dead, their voices silent,
> their theories illegible,
> stuffed in their pockets?
>
> When I was twelve the only man
> who knew who built the fence around that field
> was discovered face down in the barley,
> his last words lost on crows.

These lines from a poem by Laois writer, Pat Boran, conjure up for us a world without a history. What would we do if the past was lost forever? What a tragedy that would be!. To really know ourselves and from whence we came we must look into the past. The past is history and without any knowledge of it we would be a poorer people in mind and in spirit and the world would be a poorer place. We are also reminded of the importance of the local historian – his significance at a personal level. He puts our world, our community, our environment in a context to which we can relate at first hand. What a pity so much of the knowledge of local historians go with them to the grave, their last worlds lost on crows!

That is why we must be thankful to those who have bequeathed their acquired knowledge of the past in documentation and in published works to future generations. In Laois we are fortunate that the county's history is recorded in many ancient as well as more recent volumes. The twentieth century has been particularly good to us. Canon O'Hanlon's *History of the Queen's County*, first published in 1907, is a wonderfully detailed, richly woven and scholarly account of Laois in times past, its history, archaeology, geology, folklore and its people. There have been many worthy volumes published on the county in the intervening years not least John Feehan's invaluable, *An environmental history of Laois*, published in 1983. Now, fittingly, as the sands of time run out on the century and the millennium, we have another *magnum opus* on the county, *Laois: History and Society*.

This volume is quite different in style, content and lay-out to Canon O'Hanlon's history but rather than either losing anything in substance by comparison with each other, both gain in their diversity. The books can sit together comfortably on a shelf, complementing each other in combining to provide us with a comprehensive and well vouched account of times past in County Laois.

One of the main sources for researchers of local history is the local newspaper. The *Leinster Express*, founded in 1831, and one of the oldest Irish newspapers still in circulation, has recorded history in the making in Laois each week for the past 168 years. Like life itself, it has had its ups and downs and has seen many changes in policy, style, circulation and ownership. But, happily, it has survived and continues to give a fascinating insight into every aspect of life in the county over all those years.

Although the founder of the *Leinster Express*, Henry W. Talbot, held liberal views and would have wished for his journal to provide a fair and open forum, he was also a businessman and a realist. The reality was that only the more affluent could afford to pay the 5p a copy or the twenty shillings for a yearly subscription he charged for his newspaper. He decided that it was in his own best interest and that of his newspaper to satisfy the tastes of those who called the shots in society and could afford the cover price. The *Leinster Express* adopted the motto – 'The Law, The King, The People' – and remained an organ of the Conservatives for many decades.

Despite Talbot's commercially driven editorial bias his newspaper published speeches and letters of political opponents as well, usually justifying their publication to his Tory readers by appending derisory addenda to such items and castigating the authors in his editorial column. The activities and orations of Daniel O'Connell received particular attention and so too that of his fellow Repealer, 'Honest' Pat Lalor, of Tinnakill, the first Catholic M.P. for Queen's County since the reign of James 11 and father of the agrarian activist and writer, James Fintan Lalor.

In 1887 the *Leinster Express* fell into the ownership of Michael Carey, who continued the conservative tradition but, like Talbot, was a liberal at heart. After the trauma of the Great Famine, the failed Fenian Rising and the Land War, the main thrust of Irish nationalism was now provided by a parliamentary campaign for home rule. Carey opened up the pages of his journal to the nationalist perspective to feed a growing mixed readership. During his time the newspaper expanded with a good dosage of local, national and foreign news and the level of advertising rose sharply. Though busy running his business and keeping in touch with current affairs Mr Carey also took a keen interest in local history and published books on the Queen's County and the Rock of Dunamase.

He was succeeded by his son, Charles Carey, a most affable man distinctive with his white beard, black skullcap and forever in carpet slippers. He was quite passive about business or news and somewhat indifferent about politics. From a public viewpoint he still maintained the conservative line, probably finding it easier to project himself in the manner in which others had come to expect· from a person in his position, rather than having to continually explain and justify his innermost liberal beliefs. He wrote occasional editorials and penned his last one around the time of the Easter Rising in 1916. In it he censured those responsible which earned the wrath of most nationalists who, though not supporting the Rising, empathised with the heroics of the resurgence and recoiled in horror at the executions of Pearse, Connolly and the other leaders. As a *Leinster Express* reporter of a later era recalled, 'by the time I left in 1946 the paper seemed to be gradually living it down'.

The *Leinster Express* has provided a forum for the creative writer from its early decades. The Laois poet, John Keegan, was one such scribe and had his writings first published in its columns. Keegan, the product of a hedge-school, painted with his pen the bleak landscape he saw before him and left an inestimable record of life in his county and further afield in the crime and famine-stricken 1830s and '40s. Among his contributions published in the *Leinster Express* was a six-part series entitled 'Tales of the Rockites' which gave a graphic account of the activities of a secret agrarian society in Laois and adjoining counties. Keegan's works largely remained obscure until their resurrection and reappraisal firstly by Canon O'Hanlon and in more recent times by Tony Delaney, who like Keegan, hails from Shanahoe.

Keegan was a contemporary of James Fintan Lalor and their homes were little more than a stone's throw apart. Coincidentally both died in Dublin in the same year, 1849, and were buried in Glasnevin Cemetery. Keegan was 33 years old when he died in lonely and wretched circumstances during the cholera epidemic of that year and was buried in an unmarked grave. Lalor was 42 and died from a severe attack of an old bronchial complaint. Mourners four deep the length of O'Connell Street followed the hearse. Memorials have been erected to both men in Glasnevin and ceremonies took place there in 1999 to mark the 150th anniversaries of their deaths.

To illustrate the unsettled state of the country in the Lalor/Keegan era and the harshness of punishment meted out to offenders I have selected at random news items from two issues of the *Leinster Express* from the period:

> Thirty-five convicts, under sentence of transportation since last Assizes, left Maryborough, for the hulk at Cove (*sic*) on Monday

711

last under a strong escort of military, accompanied by Mr Ryan, Deputy Governor of the Gaol.

That issue does not record the names, charges or evidence presented but other snippets in the same paper gives an indication of how easy one could get a permanent transfer to faraway places, in both these instances by a certain Judge Jebb.

> Mrs Lucinda Mellafont was tried before Judge Jebb on Monday for forgery of a receipt for £19 – found guilty and sentenced to be transported for life. William Kearney was sentenced at Cork Assizes by Judge Jebb, to transportation for life, for having assaulted a process-server in the discharge of his duty.

Even more gruesome were details of sentences passed and carried out as reported in the issue dated 30 March 1833. Two men and a woman were hanged in Cork, three men all named Murphy, were hanged the same week in Kilkenny, five men were hanged 'at the front of the new Gaol in Tullamore', two men suffered a similar fate in Westmeath, another hanging in Cork was reported and yet another in Clonmel. Nearer home three men were hanged in Maryborough. There is a grisly description of the execution. All in one week of the life of the *Leinster Express.*

By way of contrast let us examine the crime situation one hundred years later. In the issue of the *Leinster Express* of July 23, 1932, in a report on a sitting of Leix Circuit Court we are informed that:

> Mr J.N. McClure, Sheriff for Leix, addressing his Lordship, said that there was no criminal case to go before him, and he, therefore had great pleasure in presenting him with a pair of white gloves. It was a remarkable fact, his Lordship said, that in his judicial capacity with the five counties over which he presided there had been altogether only two criminal cases for disposal, and in these two cases the offenders came from outside the counties in which they were charged. It is remarkable that this freedom from crime has synchronised with the Eucharistic Congress and he could not help thinking that its influence had something to do with these circumstances.

The files of the *Leinster Express* are presently in the process of indexation. The project director is Anne Marie Heskin. The scheme is funded by FÁS and receives support from Laois County Council. This will speed up immensely time spent on research and it will be an invaluable investigative resource for County Laois in the future.

During my school years in the 1950s I can scarcely recall time being put aside for discussing local history or visiting sites of historical importance, of which there were many close at hand. We were still in the early post-war years and the economic situation was far from good. Finding food for the table and the wherewithal to provide for the other necessities of life was the priority with most families. The teachers too were products of the era and stuck rigidly to the curriculum wherein an over abundance of time was wasted on trying to fill our unwilling minds with the strange nuances of old Irish grammar. Irish history had more to do with myths and what little of the genuine article we were taught stopped with the 1916 Rising.

Seán O'Dooley was the exception. Known to one and all as Professor O'Dooley his classes were extra-curricular and though his calls were infrequent and unexpected he was always a welcome visitor. He was a cheerful and revered old world character in his baggy cavalry twill trousers with the legs cut short and tucked in under socks pulled up to the knees. He brightened a dull day in the classroom with vivid accounts of the Seven Septs and the feats of Laois heroes of old. He illustrated for us the locations where battles were fought and treachery prevailed. He penned a series of historical articles for the *Leinster Express* in the 1950s and further features appeared in later decades, provided by his daughter, Johanna O'Dooley.

While there was limited public interest in heritage matters in the 1950s the threat to heritage sites was also minimal. This has changed greatly over the years and ironically at this point in time with interest in heritage matters at an all-time high so too the threat to our ancient heirlooms. Economic advancement and conservation are not always happy bedfellows. The Old Laois Society and later the Laois Heritage Society have acted as guardians of significant sites and antiquities in the county. The Society has attracted a fine and active membership over the years but has suffered somewhat from a lack of premises and funding.

Sport too is very much part of our heritage. Nowhere is the pride on one's county and one's own parish more evident than in the GAA. Despite the relative lack of success there is passion in abundance among fans when Laois teams take the field. Players like Tommy Murphy, Harry Gray and the Delaney clan have given great enjoyment to the fans in times past and the achievements of the minor footballers in recent years have compounded Laois people's inherited pride in their county which, as in other matters and in other times, still battles against enormous odds.

Laois County Council celebrated its centenary in 1999 and one can get a fulsome flavour of life in the county during the past 100 years by following its progress. County Councils replaced the Grand Juries which, in one form or another, had provided a system of Local Government since the Middle Ages. Unlike the Grand Juries, which were. selected and not elected and came for the most part from the ascendancy class, the County Councils were democratically elected and nationalist dominated.

The Local Government (Ireland) Act 1898 which brought the County Councils into being marked, therefore, a radical shift in power at local level and signs of the changing political times were evident at the very first meeting of Laois (Queen's) County Council which was held in the Grand Jury Room in Portlaoise (Maryborough) Courthouse on 22 April 1899. Having elected Patrick A. Meehan M.P., as its first chairman, councillors quickly got into their stride. The first motion, passed unanimously, demanded 'a full and liberal measure of Home Rule as the only solution to the Irish Question for which we shall forever struggle and accede as our indisputable right'. Laois councillors continued to espouse the Home Rule cause until Independence was finally secured in 1922. To give a distinctive identity to the new order of administration in the county, at a meeting of the Council in October 1920 the name Queen's County was changed to the Gaelic name of Laoighis and the county town, Maryborough, was renamed Portlaoighise.

The progress of Laois County Council and its impact on the people and living conditions is fully recorded in a book published in 1999 to mark its centenary entitled, *Laois County Council – The First 100 Years*, which I was pleased to edit.

For my book *Laois Lives* I wrote of Laois as part of the hidden Ireland:

> Its treasures are among Ireland's best kept secrets. It has its majestic and unspoiled mountains, its lovely valleys, its clear-watered winding rivers and its picturesque lakes. It has its forests, its rolling meadows and its far-flung bogs. It has its history-steeped castles, its ancient ruined abbeys and its magnificent big houses which are architectural gems. It has its well preserved round tower, dating from Viking days, and its modern county hall, a prototype for similar buildings of the future. It has its busy towns and its sleepy villages. It has its wide open spaces where the body can wander freely and it has its top security prison from which there is no escape. It has its multi-million high tech industries and its traditional cottage crafts. It has its canal unhurried in its flow and its railway line with its super trains speeding by. But most of all it has its people -somewhat shy and

reserved at first but genuine, warm and friendly and generous to a
fault.

In his Introduction to this volume Pádraig G. Lane reminds us that
Laois has its own unique qualities, its own unique people and its own
unique history. *Laois: History and Society* tells its story from 26 different
aspects written by academics who have researched their subject well.

Fair land of Leix; from Mairgy to Slieve Bloom,
I've trod thy brownest moss, thy green Fraughmore,
Oft grassy vales I've sought where rivers come,
The Barrow deep, Awnbeg, the Gully, Nore;
Much have I wandered steepest footpaths o'er,
Climbed Cullinagh's and Fossey's hearth-strown hills,
Viewing along their sides wild torrents score
Those hollowed courses, traced by gladsome rills,
Dancing through glens or plains their own hoarse music fills.
(From 'The land of Leix' in *The poetical works of Lageniensis (John
Canon O'Hanlon)* (Dublin, 1893), pp 4-5).

General Index

St. Colman of Ougheval,
597-8
St. Lawrence family, 317
St. Leger, Anthony, 216,
218, 220-1, 333, 338,
343, 356
St. Leger, lord deputy,
380-1, 690
St. Leger, Robert, 338
St. Leger, Warham, 696
St. Leger, William, 368,
398-9
St. Leger family, 340
St. Michael's, the English
Church, 278
St. Patrick's Bell, 112
St. Patrick's College,
Carlow, 585-6, 630
St. Patrick's Maynooth, 630
St. Paul's, the French
Church, 278
Stack, Austin, 632, 646,
650
Stanton, Richard, 286
Staunton, Henry, 474
Steele, Richard, 402
Sterne, Laurence, 430
Stokes, (Martyrology), 83
Stokes, Margaret, 97
Stokes, Whitley, 593
Strongbow, earl of Strigoil
and Pembroke, 36, 164-
5, 167, 178, 188, 259,
261
Sullivan, A.M., 650-1
Sullivan, Alexander Martin,
629
Sullivan, Anne, 629
Sullivan, Timothy, 629
Sullivan, Timothy Daniel,
629
Sussex, earl of, 221-4, 226,
228, 234-5, 343-4, 691
Sutcliffe, James, 498
Sutherland, John, 575
Sutton, Richard, 304
Swan, Dr., 523
Sweetman family, 619
Swift, Jonathan, 426
Sydney, Dorcas, 272, 288,
301-2, 304

Sydney, Henry, 288
Sydney, lord deputy, 316
Sydney, Philip, 288

Taillor, Adam, 265
Taylor, Dr., 701
Taylor Map, 703
Teehan, bishop, 468
Tenant League
Association, 610
Tenants' Defence League,
603
Tertiary, 7
The Bruce, 175
Thomond, earl of, 261,
287
Thompson, Edward, 449-
50
Tigernach, 126
Tírechan, 41, 71
Todd, J.H., 588, 593
Tomen, Arthur, 296, 305
Tomrair, 49
Trant, Patrick, 275, 416-8
Treadwell, Victor, 361
Treatyites, 665
Trench, Anthony, 446
Trench, Fredrick, 563, 576
Trench, William, 441
Trench, William Steuart, 4
Trewhiddle style, 109-10
Trinity College, Dublin,
270
Tripartite Life of Patrick,
36, 41
Trois Sermons, 431
Trojans, 651
Troy, archbishop, 468,
471, 476-7
Troy, John, 488
Tuaim Snáma, 47
Tuathal mac Úgaire (rí
Laigean), 52
Turgesius, 126
Tynan, P.J., 612
Tynan, Thomas, 665
Tyrconnell, earl of, 355,
358
Tyrell, captain, 290, 315-8,
404, 696
Tyrone, earl of, 247, 287,

351, 696
Tyrrell, Richard
Tytton, 692

Ua Briain, Muirchertach,
40, 80-1
Ua Conchobuir, Ruaidrí,
81
Ua Conchobuir,
Tairdelbach, 81
Ua Duibh, Flaithnia, 51
Ua Duibh, Lorcán mac
Flaithniadh, 51
Ua Dúnáin, Máel Muire,
80
Ua Mórdha, Cearnach, 53
Ua Mórdha, Cú Chocríche,
80
Ua Mórdha, Fáelán, 80
Ua Mórdha, Laoighseach,
54
Ua Mórdha, Mac-Raith, 51
Ua Mórdha, Mac-Ráith, 80-
1
Ua Néill, Domnall, 53
Uí Anrotháin family, 51
Uí Bairrche family, 51, 67,
71, 80, 163
Uí Bairrche Tíre, 144
Uí Barraiche, 91
Uí Buide family, 50-1, 53,
163-5
Uí Cáellaide family, 164
Uí Cheinnselaig family, 41,
48, 50, 53, 64, 75-6, 78,
80, 91
Uí Chonaill Gabra, 47
Uí Chonchobair Fhailge
family, 38
Uí Chrimthainn Áin family
[See Uí Chrimthannáin
family], 51
Uí Chrimthainn family, 50-
1
Uí Chrimthannáin family,
37, 51-2, 164
Uí Dochlú, 45
Uí Duib family, 51
Uí Dúnlainge, 135
Uí Dúnlainge family, 64,
68, 71, 77

Index of Places